W9-DCI-629

MOON HANDBOOKS®
BIG ISLAND OF HAWAI'I

sunset at Keauhou Bay

ROBERT NILSEN

BIG ISLAND OF HAWAI'I

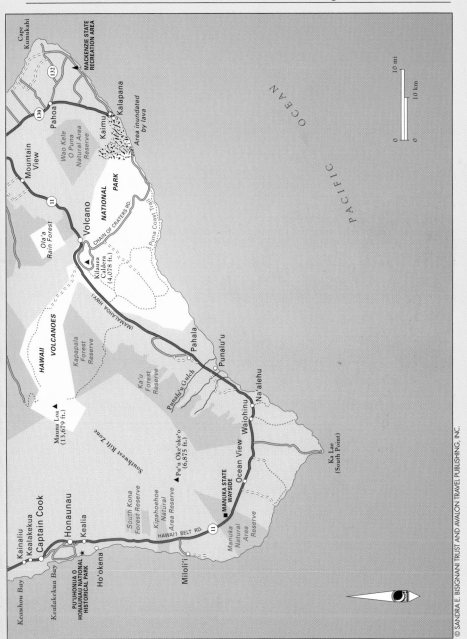

© SANDRA E. BISIGNANI TRUST AND AVALON TRAVEL PUBLISHING, INC.

orchids

MOON HANDBOOKS®

BIG ISLAND OF HAWAI'I

INCLUDING HAWAII VOLCANOES NATIONAL PARK

FIFTH EDITION

ROBERT NILSEN

AVALON
TRAVEL

Moon Handbooks Big Island of Hawai'i
Including Hawaii Volcanoes National Park
Fifth Edition

Robert Nilsen

Text and photographs © Sandra E. Bisignani
Trust, 2003. All rights reserved.
Illustrations © Avalon Travel Publishing, 2003.
All rights reserved.
Maps © Sandra E. Bisignani Trust and Avalon
Travel Publishing, 2003.

Some photos and illustrations are used by permission
and are the property of their original copyright owners.

ISBN: 1-56691-488-4
ISSN: 1531-4138

Editor: Kathryn Ettinger
Series Manager: Kevin McLain
Graphics Coordinator: Susan Snyder
Production Coordinators: Jacob Goolkasian, Justin Marler
Cover Designer: Kari Gim
Interior Designers: Amber Pirker, Alvaro Villanueva, Kelly Pendragon
Map Editor: Naomi Adler Dancis
Cartographers: Mike Morgenfeld, Don Patterson, Naomi Adler Dancis
Indexer: Judy Hunt

Front cover photo: © Laurence Parent

Distributed by Publishers Group West

Printed in the USA by Worzalla

Please send all feedback to:

Moon Handbooks Big Island of Hawai'i

Avalon Travel Publishing
1400 65th Street, Suite 250
Emeryville, CA 94608, USA
atpfeedback@avalonpub.com
www.moon.com

Printing History
1st edition—1990
5th edition—May 2003
5 4 3 2 1

ABOUT THE AUTHOR
Robert Nilsen

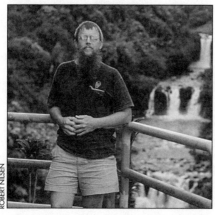

Robert Nilsen was born and raised in Minnesota. His first major excursion from the insular Midwest was a two-year stint in South Korea with the Peace Corps. Following that eye-opening service, he stayed on in Korea independently, teaching and traveling, and soaking up as much of its history and culture as he could. Setting his sights on other lands and cultures, he made a two-year trek through Asia before returning home to the United States, and since then has had the good fortune to return to Asia and the Pacific on numerous occasions. Robert has written *Moon Handbooks South Korea* for Avalon Travel Publishing, and has contributed to *Moon Handbooks Indonesia*.

Since the passing of his good friend J.D. Bisignani, he has shouldered full responsibility for the revision of Moon Handbooks' Hawaii series, which includes *Moon Handbooks Hawaii, Moon Handbooks Kaua'i, Moon Handbooks O'ahu, Moon Handbooks Maui,* and *Moon Handbooks Big Island of Hawai'i.*

It is the many wonderful aspects of the Hawaiian Islands—slack-key guitar, palm-fringed beaches, tropical mountains hikes, the re-emergent culture of the Hawaiian people and their friendly *aloha* spirit—that keep Robert heading back each year.

to Madame Pele and all women of heart

Contents

INTRODUCTION **1**
An Overview
THE LAND **5**
CLIMATE **8**
FLORA AND FAUNA **12**
The Mystery of Migration; Plants, Flowers, and Trees; Birds; The Hakalau Forest
National Wildlife Refuge; Other Hawaiian Animals; Marine Life
HISTORY **22**
The Road from Tahiti; The World Discovers Hawaii; The Unification of Old
Hawaii; Missionaries and Whalers; King Sugar; A Kingdom Passes; Modern
Times
GOVERNMENT **41**
ECONOMY **41**
PEOPLE **44**
The Hawaiians; The Chinese; The Japanese; Caucasians; Filipinos and Others
LANGUAGE **51**
Pidgin; Hawaiian
RELIGION **55**
Hawaiian Beliefs; The Strifes of Maui; Missionaries One and All
ARTS AND MUSIC **59**
Arts of Old Hawaii; Hula and Lei; That Good Old Island Music
FESTIVALS, HOLIDAYS, AND EVENTS **66**

SPECIAL TOPICS

Big Island Temperature and Rainfall 9	*Big Island Ethnicity* 44
Green Flash 10	*Capsule Pidgin* 53
Hurricane Facts 11	*Big Island Museums and Historical Societies* . . 60
Big Island Botanical Gardens 14	*Arts and Culture Information* 65

ON THE ROAD **69**
SPORTS AND RECREATION **69**
Camping; Hiking; Beaches; Scuba; Snorkeling and Snuba; Surfing; Parasailing
and Jetskiing; Kayaking; Ocean Tours; Skiing; Golf; Tennis; Horseback Riding;
Bicycling; Land Tours; Air Tours; Fishing; Hunting
SHOPPING **104**
Shopping Centers; Specialty Shops; Arts to Buy
ACCOMMODATIONS **109**
Hotels; Condominiums; Vacation Rentals; Bed-and-Breakfasts; Hostels; Home
Exchanges

FOOD AND DRINK **116**
Hawaiian Foods; Money-Savers; Food Stores; Fish and Seafood; Munchies and
Island Treats; Tropical Fruits and Nuts; Island Drinks

GETTING THERE **125**
By Air; Domestic Carriers; Foreign Carriers; Tour and Travel Companies

GETTING AROUND **136**
Interisland Carriers; By Ship; Land Transportation; Rental Cars; Rental Agencies;
Alternative Transportation

HEALTH AND SAFETY **145**
Water Safety; Hawaiian Folk Medicine and Cures; Medical Services; Services for
Travelers with Disabilities; Illegal Drugs; Theft and Hassles

WHAT TO TAKE **152**

INFORMATION AND SERVICES **154**
Hawaii Visitors Bureau; Local Resources; Other Information; Money and
Finances

SPECIAL TOPICS

Water Safety Tips *77*	*Big Island Tennis Courts* *92*
Seasickness *87*	*Kukui* *148*
Big Island Golf Courses *90*	

KONA **158**

KAILUA-KONA **159**
Sights; Beaches and Parks; Accommodations; Food; Entertainment; Recreation;
Shopping; Services and Information; Transportation

HOLUALOA **195**

SOUTH KONA **200**
Honalo and Kainaliu; Kealakekua; Captain Cook and Vicinity; Farther South

SPECIAL TOPICS

Ancient Sport of Holua *170*	*Konane* *208*
Kona Coffee *198*	

SOUTH KOHALA **215**

THE COAST **217**
Sights; Beaches and Parks; Luxury Resorts; Vacation Rental Agencies; Food;
Shopping; Recreation; Visitors Information

TOWNS **237**

WAIMEA **241**
History

SIGHTS 244
Sights in Town
PRACTICALITIES 247
Accommodations; Food; Recreation; Shopping; Services and Information

NORTH KOHALA 255
KAWAIHAE COAST 257
NORTH COAST TOWNS 260
Hawi; Kapa'au; Pololu Valley

THE SADDLE ROAD 268
Mauna Kea; Mauna Kea Observatory Complex; Sights Along Route 200; Mauna
Loa

SPECIAL TOPIC
Mauna Kea Observatories' Websites 274

HILO 276
SIGHTS 279
Downtown; Gardens; Beaches
PRACTICALITIES 291
Accommodations; Food; Entertainment; Recreation; Shopping; Services and
Information

SPECIAL TOPICS
Macadamia Nut 286   Shipman House 292

HAMAKUA COAST 308
HONOMU TO HONOKA'A 309
Honomu and Vicinity; Laupahoehoe
HONOKA'A TO KUKUIHAELE 315
Honoka'a and Vicinity; Kukuihaele
WAIPI'O VALLEY 321
History; Recreation; Waimanu Valley

PUNA 328
SOUTHEAST COAST 330
Pahoa and Vicinity; Along the Coast
ALONG THE HAWAI'I BELT ROAD 339
Kea'au; Mountain Towns

VOLCANO VILLAGE 342
  Accommodations; Food; Shopping

SPECIAL TOPIC
Anthurium *340*

HAWAII VOLCANOES NATIONAL PARK **351**
INTRODUCTION 351
KILAUEA CALDERA 357
  Visitors Center Area; Crater Rim Drive
CHAIN OF CRATERS ROAD 363
OTHER PARK AREAS 366
  Ka'u Desert; Small Detours
PRACTICALITIES 369
  Accommodations; Food and Shopping

SPECIAL TOPIC
Volcano Activity *354*

KA'U **372**
TOWNS AND SIGHTS 373
  Pahala; Punalu'u; Na'alehu and Vicinity; South Point; Ocean View

RESOURCES **385**
HAWAIIAN GLOSSARY 386
SUGGESTED READING 391
INTERNET RESOURCES 400
INDEX 403

Keeping Current

In today's world, things change so rapidly that it's difficult for one person to keep up with everything happening in any one place. This is particularly true in Hawaii, where situations are always in flux. Travel books are like automobiles: they require fine tuning and frequent overhauls. You can help us keep this book in shape! If you have any new information, suggestions for improvements, or places that should be included in this book, please let us know. Please also contact us about any inaccuracies or misleading suggestions. We also like hearing from experts in the field, as well as from local hotel and restaurant owners and activity companies.

Robert Nilsen
Moon Handbooks Big Island of Hawai'i
Avalon Travel Publishing
1400 65th Street, Suite 250
Emeryville, CA 94608, USA
atpfeedback@avalonpub.com

Abbreviations

a/c—air conditioning
B&B—bed and breakfast
4WD—four-wheel drive
HVB—Hawaii Visitors Bureau
Hwy.—highway
NWR—National Wildlife Refuge

OHA—Office of Hawaiian Affairs
PADI—Professional Association of
    Dive Instructors
Rte.—Route (highway)
SRA—State Recreation Area
YH—Youth Hostel

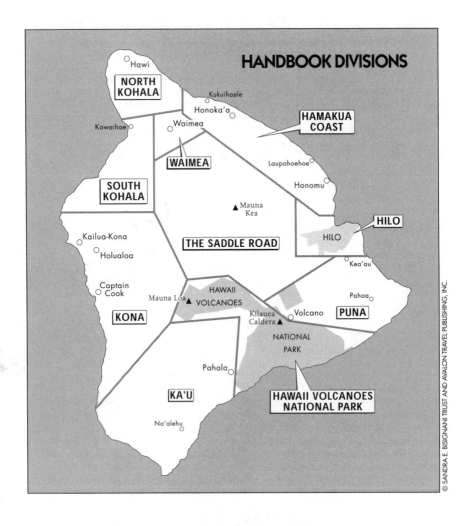

HANDBOOK DIVISIONS

Hawi

NORTH
KOHALA

Kukuihaele

Honoka'a

Kawaihae

Waimea

HAMAKUA
COAST

WAIMEA

Laupahoehoe

Honomu

SOUTH
KOHALA

Mauna
Kea

HILO

Kailua-Kona

Holualoa

THE SADDLE ROAD

HILO

Kea'au

Captain
Cook

Mauna Loa

HAWAII
VOLCANOES

Pahoa

Kilauea
Caldera

Volcano

PUNA

KONA

NATIONAL
PARK

Pahala

KA'U

HAWAII VOLCANOES
NATIONAL PARK

Na'alehu

Maps

Big Island of Hawai'i . . . . ii–iii

INTRODUCTION

Hawaiian Archipelago 2
Mountains of Hawai'i 5
Polynesian Triangle 23
Big Island Land Ownership 42

ON THE ROAD

Big Island Campgrounds 70
Big Island Snorkeling 80
Big Island Golf Courses 89
Pacific Crossroads 126
Hilo International Airport 131
Kona International Airport 132
Interisland Air Routes 137

KONA

Kona 160–161
Kailua-Kona 162
Kailua-Keauhou 167

SOUTH KOHALA

South Kohala 216

WAIMEA

Waimea 242

NORTH KOHALA

North Kohala 256

THE SADDLE ROAD

The Saddle Road 269

HILO

Hilo Vicinity 277
Hilo 278
Downtown Hilo 280

HAMAKUA COAST

Hamakua Coast 309

PUNA

Puna 329
Volcano Village 343

HAWAII VOLCANOES NATIONAL PARK

Hawaii Volcanoes National Park 352

KA'U

Ka'u 374–375

MAP SYMBOLS

═════	Main Road	★	Point of Interest	⌡	Golf Course
════	Other Road	•	Accommodation	☀	Volcanic Cone
=======	Unpaved Road	▾	Restaurant/Bar	▲	Mountain
··········	Trail	▪	Other Location	⋀	Campground
(56)	Highway Shield	✗	Primary Airport		Snorkeling
○	City	✗	Secondary Airport		Water
○	Town or Village	⬥	State/County Park	⟋	Waterfall
		⬛	Gas Station		

Introduction

The island of Hawai'i is grand in so many ways. Its two nicknames, "The Orchid Island" and "The Volcano Island," are both excellent choices: the island produces more of the delicate blooms than anywhere else on earth; and Pele, the fire goddess who makes her mythological home here, regularly sends rivers of lava from the world's largest and most active volcanoes. However, to the people who live here, Hawai'i has had only one real nickname, "The Big Island." Big isn't necessarily better, but when you combine it with beautiful, uncrowded, traditional, and inexpensive, it's hard to beat. More recently and with the growing connection with their cultural roots, some Hawaiians are beginning to refer to the Big Island as Moku O Keawe ("Island of Keawe")

after a well-loved former ruler of the island, Keawe'ikekahiali'iokamoku.

The Big Island was the first to be inhabited by the Polynesian settlers, yet it's geologically the youngest of the Hawaiian Islands at barely a million years old. Like all the islands in the Hawaiian chain, it's a mini-continent whose geographical demarcations are much more apparent because of its size. There are parched deserts, steaming fissures, jet-black sand beaches, raw semi-cooled lava flows, snow-covered mountains, upland pastures, littoral ponds, and lush valleys where countless waterfalls break through the rock faces of thousand-foot-high chasms. There are small working villages that time has passed by, the state's most tropical city, and an arid coast stretching over 90 miles where the sun is guaranteed to shine. You'll find some of the islands' least

Waipi'o Valley

ROBERT NILSEN

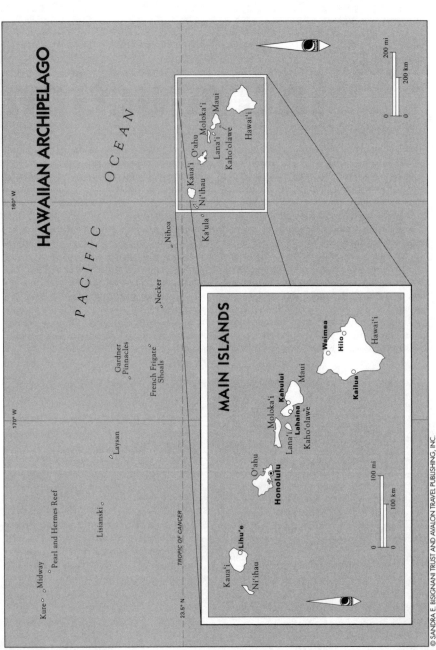

HAWAIIAN ARCHIPELAGO

PACIFIC OCEAN

160° W

170° W

23.5° N

TROPIC OF CANCER

Kure
Midway
Pearl and Hermes Reef

Lisianski

Laysan

Gardner Pinnacles

French Frigate Shoals

Necker

Nihoa

Ka'ula

Kaua'i
Ni'ihau

O'ahu
Moloka'i
Lana'i
Kaho'olawe
Maui

Hawai'i

0   200 mi

0   200 km

MAIN ISLANDS

Kaua'i
Lihu'e
Ni'ihau

O'ahu
Honolulu

Moloka'i
Lana'i
Kahului
Lahaina
Maui
Kaho'olawe

Weimea
Hilo
Kailua
Hawai'i

0   100 mi

0   100 km

© SANDRA E. BISIGNANI TRUST AND AVALON TRAVEL PUBLISHING, INC.

expensive accommodations as well as some of the world's most exclusive resorts.

Historically, the Big Island is loaded with religious upheavals, the births and deaths of great people, vintage missionary homes and churches, reconstructed *heiau,* and even a royal summer palace. Here is the country's largest privately owned ranch, where cowboy life is the norm; America's most famous coffee-producing region; artist communities; and enclaves of the counterculture, where people with alternative lifestyles are still trying to keep the faith of the '60s.

Sportspeople love it here, too. The Big Island is a Mecca for triathletes and offers snow skiing in season, plenty of camping and hiking, the best marlin waters in all the oceans of the world, great horseback riding, and as much water sports activity as anyone would desire.

Direct flights are available to the Big Island, where the fascination of perhaps not "old" Hawaii, but definitely "simple" Hawaii, still lingers.

AN OVERVIEW

Kailua-Kona on the west coast and Hilo on the east side are the two ports of entry to the Big Island. At opposite ends of the island as well as of the cultural spectrum, the two have a friendly rivalry. It doesn't matter at which one you arrive, because a trip to the Big Island without visiting both is unthinkable. Better yet, split your stay between the two, using each as a base while you tour its surrounding areas. The Big Island is the only Hawaiian island big enough that you can't drive around it comfortably in one day, nor should you try. Each of the districts is interesting enough to spend at least one day exploring.

Kona

Kona is dry, sunny, and brilliant, with large expanses of old barren lava flows. When watered, the rich soil blossoms, as in Holualoa and South Kona, renowned for its diminutive **coffee plantations.** Coffee is not the only thing that has blossomed here as **Holualoa** has grown from agricultural community to a small artists' enclave. The town of Captain Cook, named after

the intrepid Pacific explorer, lies just above the very beach where he was slain because of a terrible miscommunication two centuries ago. Ironically, nearby is the restored **Pu'uhonua O Honaunau Heiau,** where mercy and forgiveness were rendered to any *kapu*-breaker or vanquished warrior who made it into the confines of this safe refuge.

Kailua-Kona is the center of Kona. The airport is just north of town, and here lies a major concentration of condos and hotels; the town itself boasts an array of art and designer shops. World-class triathletes come here to train, and charter boats depart in search of billfish and other denizens of the deep. Within Kailua is **Moku'aikaua Church,** a legacy of the very first packet of missionaries to arrive in the islands; and **Hulihe'e Palace,** vacation home of the Kamehameha line of kings. Dominating this entire coastline, **Mt. Hualalai** rises to the east, and northward, the Kona district offers a string of fine beaches.

Kohala

Up the coast in South Kohala is **Hapuna Beach,** one of the best on the island. In 1965, Lawrence Rockefeller opened the Mauna Kea Resort near here. Since then, this resort, along with its sculptured, coast-hugging golf course, has been considered one of the finest in the world. Just south is the Kona Village Resort, whose guests can spend the night in a "simple" grass shack on the beach. Its serenity is broken only by the soothing music of the surf and by the not-so-melodious singing of "Kona nightingales," a pampered herd of wild donkeys that frequents this area. Over the years, other expansive resorts and golf courses have been added here, making this the island's luxury resort area, on a par with any in the state. Upcountry, at the base of the Kohala Mountains, is **Waimea** (Kamuela), center of the enormous **Parker Ranch.** Here in the cool mountains, cattle graze in chest-high grass, and *paniolo* astride their sturdy mounts ride herd in time-honored tradition. Hunters range the slopes of Mauna Kea in search of wild goats and boars, and the Fourth of July is boisterously acknowledged by the wild whoops of cowboys at the world-class Parker Ranch Rodeo.

North Kohala is primarily the hilly peninsular thumb on the northern extremity of the island. Along the coast are beach parks, empty except for an occasional local family picnic. A series of *heiau* dot the coast, and on the northernmost tip a broad plain overlooking a sweeping panorama marks the birthplace of Kamehameha the Great. The main town up here is **Hawi,** holding on after the sugar companies pulled out some years ago. Down the road is Kapa'au, where **Kamehameha's statue** resides in fulfillment of a *kahuna* prophecy. Along this little-traveled road, a handful of artists offer their crafts in small shops. At road's end is the overlook of **Pololu Valley,** where a steep descent takes you to a secluded beach in an area once frequented by some of the most powerful sorcerers in the land.

The Saddle Road

This cross-island road begins just outside of Hilo. It slices across the island through a most astonishing high valley or "saddle" separating the mountains of Mauna Loa and Mauna Kea. Passable, but the bane of car-rental companies, it slides down the western slope of Mauna Kea to meet the Belt Road, from where it's an easy drive to either Waimea or Kona. From the Saddle Road, a spur road heads up to the top of Mauna Kea at 13,796 feet, where a series of astronomical observatories peer into the heavens through the clearest air on earth. Heading south, another road zigzags up the slope of Mauna Loa to a point where a hiking trail continues to the top.

Hilo

Hilo is the oldest port of entry, the most tropical town in Hawai'i, and the only major city on the island's windward coast. The city is one tremendous greenhouse where exotic flowers and tropical plants are a normal part of the landscape, and entire blocks canopied by adjoining banyans are taken for granted. The town, which hosts the yearly Merrie Monarch Festival, boasts Japanese gardens, several tropical gardens, the **Lyman Mission House and Museum,** and a profusion of natural phenomena, including **Rainbow Falls** and **Boiling Pots.** Plenty of rooms are generally available in Hilo, and its variety of restaurants will titillate anyone's taste buds. Both go easy on the pocketbook.

Hamakua Coast

Hamakua refers to the entire northeast coast, where streams, wind, and pounding surf have chiseled the lava into towering cliffs and precipitous valleys known locally by the unromantic name of "gulches." Until recently, all the flatlands here were awash in a green sea of sugarcane; now, no commercial and few private fields remain. A spur road from the forgotten town of Honomu leads to **'Akaka Falls,** whose waters tumble over a 442-foot cliff—the highest sheer drop of water in Hawaii. North along the coastal road is **Honoka'a,** a one-street town of stores, restaurants, and crafts shops. The main road bears left here to the cowboy town of Waimea, but a smaller road inches farther north. It dead-ends at the top of **Waipi'o Valley,** cradled by cliffs on three sides with its mouth wide open to the sea. On its verdant floor, a handful of families live simply by raising taro, a few head of cattle, and horses. Waipi'o was a burial ground of Hawaiian *ali'i,* where *kahuna* traditionally came to commune with spirits. The enchantment of this "power spot" remains.

Puna

Puna lies south of Hilo and makes up the majority of the southeast coast. Here are the greatest lava fields that have spewed from Kilauea, the heart of **Hawaii Volcanoes National Park.** An ancient flow embraced a forest in its fiery grasp, entombing trees that stand like sentinels today in **Lava Tree State Monument. Cape Kumukahi,** a pointed lava flow that reached the ocean in 1868, is officially the easternmost point in Hawaii. Just below it is a string of beaches featuring ebony-black sand. The road skirts the coast before it dead-ends where it has been covered over by lava at the small village of Kaimu. Atop the volcano, miles of hiking trails crisscross the park and one leads to the very summit of Mauna Loa. Kilauea Crater is circled by a rim drive that brings you up close to the sights near the park entrance and where you can lodge or dine at Volcano House, a venerable inn carved into the rim of the crater. From the rim drive, Chain of Craters Road spills off the mountain through a forbidding, yet vibrant, wasteland of old lava flows until it comes to the sea, where this living volcano fumes and throbs.

Ka'u

Ka'u, the southern tip of the island, is primarily a desertlike arid region with pockets of green. On one well-marked trail leading from the main road you'll discover an eerie set of footprints, the remnants of an ill-fated band of warriors who were smothered under the moist ash of a volcanic eruption and whose demise marked the ascendancy of Kamehameha the Great. Like Hamakua, Ka'u was a sugar growing region. Sugar is no more, which has created a tough economic environment, but macadamia nuts, coffee, and other agricultural crops are being raised. Here are some lovely beaches and parks you'll have virtually to yourself. One at Punalu'u has jet-black sand and is known for turtles, while another farther south has a distinctly green color. From the highway, a narrow ribbon of road leads to **Ka Lae** ("South Point"), the most southerly piece of ground in the United States.

The Land

The Big Island is the southernmost and easternmost of the Hawaiian Islands—it is also the largest. This island dwarfs all the others in the Hawaiian chain at 4,028 square miles and growing. It accounts for about 63 percent of the state's total land mass; the other islands could fit within it two times over. With 266 miles of coastline, the island stretches about 95 miles from north to south and 80 miles from east to west. Cape Kumukahi is the easternmost point in the state, and Ka Lae ("South Point") is the southernmost point in the country.

Science and *The Kumulipo* oral history differ sharply on the age of the Big Island. Scientists say that Hawai'i is the youngest of the islands, being a little over one million years old; the chanters claim that it was the first "island-child" of Wakea and Papa. It is, irrefutably, closest to the "hot spot" on the Pacific floor, evidenced by Kilauea's frequent eruptions. The geology, geography, and location of the Hawaiian Islands, and their ongoing drifting and building in the middle of the Pacific, make them among the most fascinating pieces of real estate on earth. The Big Island is the *most* fascinating of them all—it is truly unique.

Separating the Big Island from Maui to the northwest is the 'Alenuihaha Channel, which at about 30 miles wide and over 6,800 feet deep, is the state's second widest and second deepest channel.

The Mountains

The tremendous volcanic peak of **Mauna Kea** ("White Mountain"), located in north-central Hawai'i, has been extinct for over 3,500 years. Its seasonal snowcap earns Mauna Kea its name and reputation as a good skiing area in winter. Over 18,000 feet of mountain below sea level rise

MOUNTAINS OF HAWAI'I

Mauna Kea (13,796 ft.)
Mauna Loa (13,679 ft.)
Hualalai (8,271 ft.)
Kohala (5,480 ft.)
Kilauea (4,078 ft.)
Waimea (2,670 ft.)
Volcano (4,000 ft.)
Kona
Hilo

straight up from the ocean floor—making Mauna Kea actually 31,796 feet tall, a substantial 2,768 feet taller than Mt. Everest; some consider it the tallest mountain in the world. At 13,796 feet above sea level, it is without doubt the tallest peak in the Pacific. Near its top, at 13,020 feet, is **Lake Waiau,** the highest lake in the state and third-highest in the country. Mauna Kea was obviously a sacred mountain to the Hawaiians, and its white dome was a welcome beacon to seafarers. On its slope is the largest adze quarry in Polynesia, from which high-quality basalt was taken to be fashioned into prized tools. The atmosphere atop the mountain, which sits mid-Pacific far from pollutants, is the most rarefied and cleanest on earth. The clarity makes Mauna Kea a natural for astronomical observatories. The complex of telescopes on its summit is internationally staffed and provides data to scientists around the world.

The **Kohala Mountains** to the northwest are the oldest and rise only to 5,480 feet at Kaunu o Kaleihoʻohei peak. This section looks more like the other Hawaiian Islands, with deep gorges and valleys along the coast and a forested interior. As you head east toward Waimea from Kawaihae on Route 19, for every few miles that you travel you pick up about 10 inches of rainfall per year. This becomes obvious as you begin to pass little streams and rivulets running from the mountains.

Mt. Hualalai, at 8,271 feet, is the backdrop to Kailua-Kona. It's home to many of the Big Island's endangered birds and supports many of the region's newest housing developments. Just a few years ago, Mt. Hualalai was thought to be extinct, since the last time it erupted was in 1801. It is now known that within the last 1,000 years, the mountain has erupted about every two or three centuries. In 1929 it suffered an earthquake swarm, which means that a large movement of lava inside the mountain caused tremors. USGS scientists now consider Mt. Hualalai only dormant and very likely to erupt at some point in the future. When it does, a tremendous amount of lava is expected to pour rapidly down its steep sides. From the side of this mountain grows the cone Puʻu Waʻawaʻa.

At 3,967 feet, it's only slightly shorter than the very active Kilauea on the far side of Mauna Loa. Obsidian is found here, and this is one of the few places in Hawaii where this substance has been quarried in large quantities.

Even though **Mauna Loa** ("Long Mountain") measures a respectable 13,679 feet, its height isn't its claim to fame. This active volcano, 60 miles long by 30 wide, comprises 19,000 cubic miles of iron-hard lava, making it the densest and most massive mountain on earth. In 1950, a tremendous lava flow belched from Mauna Loa's summit, reaching an astonishing rate of 6,750,000 cubic yards per hour. Seven lava rivers flowed for 23 days, emitting over 600 million cubic yards of lava that covered 35 square miles. There were no injuries, but the villages of Kaʻapuna and Honokua were partially destroyed along with the Magoo Ranch. Its last eruption, in 1984, was small by comparison yet created fountaining inside the summit crater and a "curtain of fire" along its eastern rift.

The lowest of the island's major peaks, **Kilauea** rises only to 4,078 feet. Its pragmatic name means "The Spewing," and it's the world's most active volcano. In the last hundred years, it has erupted on the average once every 11 months. The Hawaiians believed that the goddess Pele inhabited every volcano in the Hawaiian chain, and that her home is now Halemaʻumaʻu Crater in Kilauea Caldera. Kilauea is the most scientifically watched volcano in the world, with a permanent observatory built right into the crater rim. When it erupts, the flows are so predictable that observers run toward the mountain, not away from it! The flows, however, can burst from fissures far from the center of the crater in areas that don't seem "active." This occurs mainly in the Puna district. In 1959, Kilauea Iki crater came to life after 91 years, and although the flow wasn't as massive as others, it did send blazing fountains of lava 1,900 feet into the air. Kilauea has been very active within the last few years, with eruptions occurring at least once a month and expected to continue. Most activity has been from a vent below Puʻu Oʻo crater. You might be lucky enough to see this phenomenon while visiting.

Island Builders

The Hawaiians worshiped Madame Pele, the fire goddess whose name translates equally well as "Volcano," "Fire Pit," or "Eruption of Lava." When she was angry, she complained by spitting fire, which cooled and formed land. Volcanologists say that the islands are huge mounds of cooled basaltic lava surrounded by billions of polyp skeletons that have formed coral reefs. The Hawaiian Islands are shield volcanoes that erupt gently and form an elongated dome much like a turtle shell. The Big Island is a perfect example of this. Once above sea level, its tremendous weight sealed the fissure below. Eventually the giant tube that carried lava to the surface sunk in on itself and formed a caldera, as evidenced atop Kilauea. More eruptions occur periodically, and they cover the already existing island like frosting on a titanic cake. Wind and water took over and relentlessly sculpted the raw lava into deep crevices and cuts that became valleys. The most dramatic of these scars occur as the numerous gulches and valleys on the east side of the Big Island. Because of less rain and runoff, the west side is smoother, more uniform, and much less etched.

Lava

Lava flows in two distinct types, for which the Hawaiian names have become universal geological terms: **'a'a** and **pahoehoe.** They're easily distinguished in appearance, but chemically they're the same. 'A'a is extremely rough and spiny and will quickly tear up your shoes if you do much hiking over it. Also, if you have the misfortune to fall down, you'll immediately know why they call it 'a'a. Pahoehoe, a billowy, ropelike lava resembling burned pancake batter, can mold itself into fantastic shapes. Examples of both types of lava are frequently encountered on various hikes throughout the Big Island. Other lava oddities that you may spot are peridots (green, gemlike stones called "Pele's Diamonds"); clear, feldsparlike, white cotton candy called "Pele's hair"; and gray lichens known as "Hawaiian snow" covering the older flows. For a full account of recent lava flows and eruptions, see the Hawaii Volcanoes National Park chapter below.

pahoehoe lava

ROBERT NILSEN

Tsunami

"Tsunami" is the Japanese word for "tidal wave." It ranks up there with the worst of them in sparking horror in human beings. But if you were to count up all the people in Hawaii who have been swept away by tidal waves in the last 50 years, the toll wouldn't come close to those killed on bicycles in only a few Mainland cities in just five years. A Hawaiian tsunami is actually a seismic sea wave that has been generated by an earthquake or landslide that could easily have originated thousands of miles away in South America or Alaska. Some waves have been clocked at speeds up to 500 mph. The safest place during a tsunami, besides high ground well away from beach areas, is out on the open ocean, where even an enormous wave is perceived only as a large swell. A tidal wave is only dangerous when it is opposed by land. Hilo has been struck with the two worst tidal waves in modern history. A giant wave smashed the islands on April 1, 1946, and swept away 159 people and over 1,300 homes; Hilo sustained most of these losses. Again, on May 23, 1960, Hilo took the brunt of a wave that rumbled through the business district, killing 61 people.

Earthquakes

These rumblings are also a concern in Hawaii and offer a double threat because they can generate tsunamis. If you ever feel a tremor and are close to a beach, get as far away as fast as possible. The Big Island, because of its active volcanoes, experiences hundreds of technical earthquakes, although 99 percent can only be felt by very delicate equipment. In the last two decades, the Big Island has experienced about one earthquake a year in the range of 5.0–6.0 on the Richter scale, which account for about 60 percent of all quakes of that magnitude in the state. The last major quake on the Big Island occurred in late November 1975, reaching 7.2 on the Richter scale and causing many millions of dollars' worth of damage in the island's southern regions. The only loss of life occurred when a beach collapsed and two people from a large camping party drowned. Like the other islands, the Big Island has an elaborate warning system against natural disasters. You will notice loudspeakers high atop poles along many beaches and coastal areas; these warn of tsunamis, hurricanes, and earthquakes.

The loudspeakers are tested at 11 A.M. on the first working day of each month. All island telephone books contain a civil defense warning and procedures section with which you should acquaint yourself—note the maps showing which areas traditionally have been inundated by tsunamis, and what procedures to follow in case an emergency occurs.

Beaches and Ponds

The Big Island takes the rap for having poor beaches—this isn't true! They are certainly few and far between, but they are spectacular. Hawai'i is big and young, so distances are greater than on other islands, and the wave action hasn't had enough time to grind much new lava and coral into sand. The Kona and Kohala Coast beaches, along with a few nooks and crannies around Hilo, are gorgeous. Puna's beaches are incredible black sand, and the southern part of the island has a string of hidden beaches enjoyed only by those intrepid enough to get to them.

Just north of the Kona Airport is Makalawena, a beautiful white-sand beach. Inland is its associated wetland pond, probably the most important one on the Big Island. Other coastal ponds are located in Kaloko-Honokohau National Historical Park between the Kona Airport and Kailua-Kona, at Kiholo Bay, and at Waikoloa Beach Resort.

Climate

The average temperature around the island varies between 72 and 78°F. Summers raise the temperature to the mid-80s and winters cool off to the low 70s. Both Kona and Hilo seem to maintain a year-round average of about 74°F, and the South Kohala Coast is a few degrees warmer. As usual, it's cooler in the higher elevations, and Waimea sees most days in the mid-60s to low 70s, while Volcano maintains a relatively steady 60°F. Atop Mauna Kea, the temperature rarely climbs above 50°F or dips below 30°F, while the summit of Mauna Loa is about 10 degrees warmer. The lowest recorded temperature on the Big Island (and for the state) was 1°F inside the Mauna Kea summit crater in January 1970, while the highest ever recorded was in April 1931 at Pahala in Ka'u—a scorching (for Hawaii) 100°F.

Altitude drops temperatures about three degrees for every 1,000 feet; if you intend to visit the mountain peaks of Mauna Loa and Mauna Kea (both over 13,000 feet), expect the temperature to be at least 30 degrees cooler than at sea level. On occasion, snows atop Mauna Kea last well into June, with nighttime temperatures at or below freezing.

The Big Island is indeed big—and tall. With its arid desert regions, tropical rainforests, tem-

BIG ISLAND TEMPERATURE AND RAINFALL

Town		Jan.	March	May	June	Sept.	Nov.
Hilo	high	79	79	80	82	82	80
	low	62	62	61	70	70	65
	rain	11	15	7	10	10	15
Kona	high	80	81	81	82	82	81
	low	62	64	65	68	68	63
	rain	4	3	2	0	2	1

Temperature is in degrees Fahrenheit; rainfall is in inches.

perate upland areas, and frigid alpine slopes, the island has 11 of 13 climatic zones.

Precipitation

Weather-wise, the Big Island's climate varies not so much in temperature but precipitation. Hawai'i has some of the wettest and driest coastal areas in the islands. The line separating wet from dry can be dramatic. Waimea, for example, has an actual dry and wet side of town, as if a boundary line split the town in two! Houses on the dry side are at a premium. Kona and Hilo are opposites. The Kona Coast is almost guaranteed to be sunny and bright, receiving as little as 15 inches of rainfall per year but with an average of 28 inches. Both Kona and the Ka'u Desert to the south are in the rain shadow of Mauna Loa, and most rain clouds coming from east to west are pierced by its summit before they ever reach Kona. Hilo is wet, with predictable afternoon and evening showers that make the entire town blossom. Though this reputation keeps many tourists away, the rain's predictability makes it easy to avoid a drenching while exploring the town. Hilo gets an average of 128 inches of rainfall per year, with a record of 153.93 inches set in 1971. It also holds the dubious honor of being the town with the most rainfall recorded by the National Weather Service in a 24-hour period—a drenching 22.3 inches in February 1979.

"So Good" Weather

The ancient Hawaiians had words to describe climatic specifics such as rain, wind, fog, and even snow, but they didn't have a general word for "weather." The reason is that the weather is just about the same throughout the year and depends more on where you are on any given island than on what season it is. The Hawaiians did distinguish between *kau* (drier and warmer summer months of May–Oct. with reliable trade winds from the northeast) and *ho'oilo* (cooler and wetter winter months of Nov.–Apr. with more erratic winds), but this distinction included social, religious, and even navigational factors, far beyond a mere distinction of weather variations.

The Trade Winds

Temperatures in the 50th state are both constant and moderate because of the trade winds, a breeze from the northeast that blows at about 5–15 miles per hour. These breezes are so prevailing that the northeast sides of the islands are always referred to as **windward,** regardless of where the wind happens to blow on any given day. You can count on the trades to be blowing an average of 300 days per year, hardly missing a day during summer, and occurring half the time in winter. While usually calm in the morning, they pick up during the heat of the afternoon, then weaken at night. Just when you need a

GREEN FLASH

Nearly everyone who has visited a tropical island has heard of the "green flash"—but few have seen it. Some consider the green flash a fable, a made-up story by those more intent on fantasy than reality—but the green flash is real. This phenomenon doesn't just happen on tropical islands; it can happen anywhere around the midriff of the earth where an unobstructed view of the horizon is present, but the clear atmosphere of a tropical island environment does seem to add to its frequency. The green flash is a momentary burst of luminescent green color that happens on the horizon the instant the sun sets into the sea. If you've seen the green flash you definitely know; there is no mistaking it. If you think you saw something that might have been green but just weren't sure, you probably didn't see it. Try again another day.

The green flash requires a day where the atmosphere is very clear and unobstructed by clouds, haze, or air pollutants. Follow the sun as it sinks into the sea. Be careful not to look directly at the sun until it's just about out of sight. If the conditions are right, a green color will linger at the spot that the sun sets for a fraction of a second before it too is gone. This "flash" is not like the flash of a camera, but more a change of color from yellow to green—an intense green—that is instantaneous and momentary.

However romantic and magical, this phenomenon does have a scientific explanation. It seems that the green color is produced as a refraction of the sun's rays by the thick atmosphere at the extreme low angle of the horizon. This bending of the sun's light results in the green spectrum of light being the last seen before the light disappears.

Seeing the green flash is an experience. Keep looking, for no matter how many times you've seen it, each time is still full of wonder and joy.

---

cooling breeze, there they are, and when the temperature drops at night, it's as if someone turned down a giant fan.

The trade winds are also a factor in keeping down the humidity. They will suddenly disappear, however, usually in winter, and might not resume for a few weeks. The tropic of Cancer runs through the center of Hawaii, yet the latitude's famed oppressively hot and muggy weather is joyfully absent in the islands. Honolulu, on the same latitude as sweaty Hong Kong and Havana, has an acceptable 60–75 percent daily humidity factor.

Kona Winds

"Kona" means "leeward" in Hawaiian, and when the trades stop blowing, these southerly winds often take over. To anyone from Hawaii, "kona wind" is a euphemism for bad weather, for it brings in hot, sticky air. Luckily, kona winds are most common Oct.–Apr., when they appear roughly half the time. The temperatures drop slightly during the winter so these hot winds are tolerable, and even useful for moderating the thermometer. In the summer they are awful, but luckily—again—they hardly ever blow during this season.

A "kona storm" is another matter. These subtropical low-pressure storms develop west of the Hawaiian Islands, and as they move east they draw winds up from the south. Usual only in winter, they can cause considerable damage to crops and real estate. There is no real pattern to kona storms—some years they come every few weeks while in other years they don't appear at all.

Severe Weather

With all this talk of ideal weather it might seem as if there isn't any bad. Read on. When a storm does hit an island, conditions can be bleak and miserable. The worst storms occur in the fall and winter and often have the warped sense of humor to drop their heaviest rainfalls on areas that are normally quite dry. It's not unusual for a storm to dump more than three inches of rain an hour; this can go as high as 10 inches, making Hawaiian rainfalls some of the heaviest on earth.

Hawaii has also been hit with some walloping hurricanes in the last few decades. There

HURRICANE FACTS

A **tropical depression** is a low-pressure system or cyclone with winds below 39 mph. A **tropical storm** is a cyclone with winds 39–73 mph. A **hurricane** is a cyclone with winds over 74 mph. These winds are often accompanied by torrential rains, destructive waves, high water, and storm surges.

The National Weather Service issues a **Hurricane Watch** if hurricane conditions are expected in the area within 36 hours. A **Hurricane Warning** is issued when a hurricane is expected to strike within 24 hours. The state of Hawaii has an elaborate warning system against natural disasters. You will notice loudspeakers high atop poles along many beaches and coastal areas; these warn of tsunami, hurricanes, and earthquakes. These sirens are tested briefly at the beginning of each month. As the figures below attest, property damage has been great but the loss of life has, thankfully, been minimal.

Major Hurricanes since 1950

Name	Date	Islands Affected	Damages
Hiki	Aug. 1950	Kaua'i	1 death
Nina	Dec. 1957	Kaua'i	—
Dot	Aug. 1959	Kaua'i	$5.5 million
Fico	July 1978	Big Island	—
'Iwa	Nov. 1982	Kaua'i, O'ahu	1 death; $234 million
Estelle	July 1986	Maui, Big Island	$2 million
'Iniki	Sept. 1992	Kaua'i, O'ahu	8 deaths; $1.9 billion

haven't been many, but they've been destructive. The vast majority of hurricanes originate far to the southeast off the Pacific coasts of Mexico and Latin America; some, particularly later in the season, start in the midst of the Pacific Ocean near the equator south of Hawaii. Hurricane season is generally considered June to November. Most pass harmlessly south of Hawaii, but some, swept along by *kona* winds, strike the islands. The most recent and destructive was Hurricane 'Iniki, which battered the islands in 1992, killing eight people and causing nearly $2 billion in damage. It had its greatest effect on Ni'ihau, the Po'ipu Beach area of Kaua'i, and the leeward coast of O'ahu.

Flora and Fauna

THE MYSTERY OF MIGRATION

Anyone who loves a mystery will be intrigued by the speculation about how plants and animals first came to Hawaii. Most people's idea of an island paradise includes swaying palms, dense mysterious jungles ablaze with wildflowers, and luscious fruits just waiting to be plucked. In fact, for millions of years the Hawaiian chain consisted of raw and barren islands where no plants grew and no birds sang. Why? Because they are geological orphans that spontaneously popped up in the middle of the Pacific Ocean. The islands, more than 2,000 miles from any continental landfall, were therefore isolated from the normal ecological spread of plants and animals. Even the most tenacious travelers of the flora and fauna kingdoms would be sorely tried in crossing the mighty Pacific. Those that made it by pure chance found a totally foreign ecosystem. They had to adapt or perish. The survivors evolved quickly, and many plants and birds became so specialized that they were limited not only to specific islands in the chain but to habitats that frequently consisted of a single isolated valley. It was as if after traveling so far, and finding a niche, they never budged again. Luckily, the soil of Hawaii was virgin and rich, the competition from other plants or animals was nonexistent, and the climate was sufficiently varied and nearly perfect for most growing things.

The evolution of plants and animals on the isolated islands was astonishingly rapid. A tremendous change in environment, coupled with a limited gene pool, accelerated natural selection. For example, many plants lost their protective thorns and spines because there were no grazing animals or birds to destroy them. Before settlement, Hawaii had no fruits, vegetables, coconut palms, edible land animals, conifers, mangroves, or banyans. The early Polynesians brought 27 varieties of plants that they needed for food and other purposes. About 90 percent of plants on the Hawaiian Islands today were introduced after Captain Cook first set foot here. Tropical flowers,

wild and vibrant as we know them today, were relatively few. In a land where thousands of orchids now brighten every corner, there were only four native varieties, the least in any of the 50 states. Today, the indigenous plants and animals have the highest rate of extinction anywhere on earth. By the beginning of the 20th century, native plants growing below 1,500 feet in elevation were almost completely extinct or totally replaced by introduced species. The land and its living things have been greatly transformed by humans and their agriculture. This inexorable process began when Hawaii was the domain of its original Polynesian settlers, then greatly accelerated when the land was inundated by Western peoples.

The indigenous plants and birds of the Big Island have suffered the same fate as those of the other Hawaiian Islands; they're among the most endangered species on earth and disappearing at an alarming rate. There are some sanctuaries on the Big Island where native species still live, but they must be vigorously protected. Do your bit to save them; enjoy but do not disturb.

PLANTS, FLOWERS, AND TREES

Hawaii's indigenous and endemic plants, flowers, and trees are both fascinating and beautiful, but, unfortunately, like everything else that was native, they are quickly disappearing. The majority of flora considered exotic by visitors was introduced either by the original Polynesians or by later white settlers. The Polynesians who colonized Hawaii brought foodstuffs, including coconuts, bananas, taro, breadfruit, sweet potatoes, yams, and sugarcane. They also carried along gourds to use as containers, 'awa to make a basic intoxicant, and the ti plant to use for offerings or to string into hula skirts. Non-Hawaiian settlers over the years brought mangoes, papayas, passion fruit, pineapples, and the other tropical fruits and vegetables associated with the islands. Also, most of the flowers, including protea, plumeria, anthuriums, orchids, *heliconia,* ginger, and most hibiscus, have come from every continent on earth. Tropical America, Asia, Java, India, and China have contributed their most beautiful and delicate blooms. Hawai'i is blessed with national and state parks, gardens, undisturbed rainforests, private reserves, and commercial nurseries that offer an exhaustive botanical survey of the island. The following is a sampling of the common native and introduced flora that add dazzling color and exotic tastes to the landscape.

Native Trees

Koa and 'ohi'a are two indigenous trees still seen on the Big Island. Both have been greatly reduced by the foraging of introduced cattle and goats, and through logging and forest fires. The **koa,** a form of acacia, is Hawaii's finest native tree. It can grow to over 70 feet high and has a strong, straight trunk which can measure more than 10 feet in circumference. Koa is a very quick-growing legume that fixes nitrogen in the soil. It is believed that the tree originated in Africa, where it was very damp. It then migrated to Australia, where it was very dry, which caused the elimination of leaves so all that was left were bare stems that could survive in the desert climate. When koa came to the Pacific islands, instead of reverting to the true leaf, its leaf stem just broadened into sickle-shaped, leaflike foliage that produces an inconspicuous, pale-yellow flower. When the tree is young or damaged it will revert to the original feathery, fernlike leaf that evolved in Africa millions of years ago. The

koa does best in well-drained soil in deep forest areas, but scruffy specimens will grow on poorer soil. The Hawaiians used koa as the main log for their dugout canoes, and elaborate ceremonies were performed when a log was cut and dragged to a canoe shed. Koa wood was also preferred for paddles, spears, even surfboards. Today it is still, unfortunately, considered an excellent furniture wood, and although fine specimens can be found in the reserve of Hawaii Volcanoes National Park, loggers elsewhere are harvesting the last of the big trees.

The **'ohi'a** is a survivor and therefore the most abundant of all the native Hawaiian trees. Coming in a variety of shapes and sizes, it grows as miniature trees in wet bogs or as 100-foot giants on cool, dark slopes at higher elevations. This tree is often the first life in new lava flows. The 'ohi'a produces a tuftlike flower—usually red, but occasionally orange, yellow, or white, the latter being very rare and elusive—that resembles a natural pompon. The flower was considered sacred to Pele; it was said that she would cause a rainstorm if 'ohi'a blossoms were picked without the proper prayers. The flowers were fashioned into lei that resembled feather boas. The strong, hard wood was used to make canoes, poi bowls, and especially temple images. 'Ohi'a logs were

koa tree

LOUISE FOOTE

'ohi'a tree

LOUISE FOOTE

also used as railroad ties and shipped to the Mainland from Pahoa. It's believed that the golden spike linking rail lines between the U.S. East and West Coasts was driven into a Puna 'ohi'a log when the two railroads came together in Ogden, Utah.

Ferns

If you travel to Hawaii Volcanoes National Park you will find yourself deep in an amazing, high-altitude tropical rainforest. This unique forest exists because of the 120 inches of annual rainfall, which turns the raw lava into a lush forest. Besides stands of 'ohi'a and koa, you'll be treated to a primordial display of ferns. All new fronds on ferns are called "fiddleheads" because of the way they unfurl and resemble the scrolls of violin heads. Fiddleheads were eaten by Hawaiians during times of famine. The most common ferns are *hapu'u,* a rather large tree fern, and *'ama'uama'u,* a smaller type with a more simple frond. A soft, furry growth around the base of the stalks is called *pulu.* At one time *pulu* was collected for stuffing mattresses, and a factory was located atop Volcanoes. But *pulu* breaks down and forms a very fine dust after a few years, so it never became generally accepted for mattresses.

At high altitudes, young ferns and other plants will often produce new growth that turns bright red as protection against the sun's ultraviolet rays. You'll see it on new foliage before it hardens. Hawaiians called this new growth *liko.* Today, people still make lei from *liko* because it has so many subtle and beautiful colors. 'Ohi'a *liko* is a favorite for lei because it is so striking.

Other Flora

The Hawaiians called the **prickly pear cactus** *panini,* which translates as "very unfriendly," undoubtedly because of the sharp spines covering the flat, thick leaves. The cactus is typical of those found in Mexico and the southwestern United States. It was introduced to Hawaii before 1810 and established itself coincidentally with the cattle brought in at the time; *panini* is very common in North Kohala, especially on the Parker Ranch lands. It is assumed that Don Marin, a Spanish advisor to Kamehameha I, was responsible for importing the plant. Perhaps the early *paniolo* (cowboy) felt lonely without it. The *panini* can grow to heights of 15 feet and is now considered a pest but nonetheless looks as if it belongs. It develops small and delicious pear-shaped fruits. Hikers who decide to

BIG ISLAND BOTANICAL GARDENS

The **Hilo Forestry Arboretum,** located along Kilauea Avenue between Lanikaula and Kawili Streets, is maintained by the Department of Natural Resources, Division of Forestry. Open Mon.–Fri. 8 A.M.–3 P.M.; free for self-guided tour. The site is used for the propagation of rare and endangered plant species, for research, and for experimental pursuits. This arboretum contains examples of most of the trees present in Hawaii, including indigenous and imported specimens.

Nani Mau Gardens, 421 Makalika St., Hilo, 808/959-3500, is open daily 8 A.M.–5 P.M. Admission is $10, $5 per person for an optional tram tour. The 20-acre gardens feature separate areas for hibiscus, anthurium, orchid, gardenia, bromeliad, and other tropical plants. This is the showiest garden on the island, a large, tame, and beautiful display. Plants are labeled.

The **Hilo Tropical Gardens,** 808/969-9873, at 1447 Kalaniana'ole Ave. is the oldest botanical garden on the island, being established in 1948. Open daily except Thurs. and Sun., this garden is small and a bit overgrown in its profusion of plants. Lots of anthuriums and orchids. Entrance is $2 adult for a self-guided tour.

Hawaii Tropical Botanical Gardens, 808/964-5233, open daily 9 A.M.–5 P.M., is a few miles north of Hilo. Admission is $15, children 6–16 $5. Here you are in the middle of a tamed tropical rainforest jungle, walking along one mile of manicured paths among more than 2,000 different species of trees and plants. Admission is adults $15 and children 6–16 $5.

pick the fruit should be careful of small, yellowish bristles that can burrow under the skin and irritate. An attempt is being made to control the cactus in *paniolo* country. *El gusano rojo,* the red worm found in the bottom of Mexican tequila, has been introduced to destroy the plant. It burrows into the cactus and eats the hardwood center, causing the plant to wither and die.

More species of **lobelia** grow in Hawaii than anywhere else in the world. A common garden flower elsewhere, it grows to tree height in Hawaii. You'll see some unique species covered with hair or with spikes. The lobelia flower is tiny and resembles a miniature orchid with curved and pointed ends, like the beak of the native *i'iwi.* This bird feeds on the flower's nectar; it's obvious that both evolved in Hawaii together and exhibit the strange phenomenon of nature mimicking nature.

The Big Island has more species of **gesneriad,** the African violet family, than anywhere else on earth. Many don't have the showy flowers that you normally associate with African violets, but have evolved into strange species with huge, fuzzy leaves.

The *pu'ahanui,* meaning "many flowers," is Hawaii's native hydrangea; it is common in the upland forests of the Big Island.

Tropical Rainforests

When it comes to pure and diverse natural beauty, the United States is one of the finest pieces of real estate on earth. As if purple mountains' majesty and fruited plains weren't enough, it even received a tiny, living emerald of tropical rainforest. A tropical rainforest is where the earth takes a breath and exhales pure sweet oxygen through its vibrant green canopy. Located in the territories of Puerto Rico and the Virgin Islands, and in the state of Hawaii, these forests make up only one-half of 1 percent of the world's total, and they must be preserved. The U.S. Congress passed two bills in 1986 designed to protect the unique biological diversity of its tropical areas, but their destruction has continued unabated. The lowland rainforests of Hawaii, populated mostly by native 'ohi'a, are being razed. Landowners slash, burn, and bulldoze them to create more land for cattle and agriculture and, most distressingly, for wood chips to generate electricity! Introduced wild boars gouge the forest floor, exposing sensitive roots and leaving tiny, fetid ponds where

---

The **World Tropical Botanical Gardens,** 808/963-5427, near Laupahoehoe on the Hamakua Coast, is a garden in the making. While the plan is to cultivate some 30,000 species, arranged in evolutionary groupings, only small sections are open to the public. The impressive three-tier Umauma Waterfall is on the property. Open Mon.–Sat. 9 A.M.–5:30 P.M.; $7 adult and $3 teens.

Amy B. H. Greenwell Ethnobotanical Garden, 808/323-3318, along Rte. 11, between the communities of Kealakekua and Captain Cook. The garden is open Mon.–Fri. 8:30 A.M.–5 P.M. Guided tours are offered on the second Sat. of every month at 10 A.M., but visitors are welcome any time during daylight hours; $4 donation. This 12-acre interpretive ethnobotanical garden has indigenous Hawaiian plants, Polynesian introduced

plants, and Hawaiian medicinal plants. The garden has remnants of the Kona field system, which dates from pre-contact times.

The **Sadie Seymour Botanical Gardens** sits up above the coast in Kailua-Kona. Its plantings are grouped by areas of the world on nearly a dozen terraces. Small but well landscaped, this garden is a quiet retreat in the otherwise dry and hot upper Kona area. **Kealakowa'a Heiau,** an ancient sacred site dedicated to blessing canoes, is on the property. Open daily 9 A.M.–5 P.M. for self-guided tours; admission is free.

Specializing in plants that thrive in the arid zone, **Pua Mau Place,** 808/882-0888, has an appropriate spot in the dry hills just north of Kawaihae. Opened in 2000, it's still young but full of promise. Visit Wed.–Sun. only 10 A.M.–5 P.M.; $8 entrance fee.

mosquito larvae thrive. Feral goats roam the forests like hoofed locusts and strip all vegetation within reach. Rainforests on the higher and steeper slopes of mountains have a better chance as they are harder for humans to reach. One unusual feature of Hawaii's rainforests is that they are "upside down." Most plant and animal species live on the forest floor, rather than in the canopy as in other forests.

Almost half of the birds classified in the United States as endangered live in Hawaii, and almost all of these make their homes in the rainforests. We can only lament the passing of the rainforests that have already fallen to ignorance, but if this ill-fated destruction continues on a global level, we will be lamenting our own passing. We must nurture the rainforests that remain, and with simple enlightenment, let them be.

BIRDS

One of the great tragedies of natural history is the continuing demise of Hawaiian birdlife. Perhaps only 15 original species of birds remain of the more than 70 native families that thrived before the coming of humans. Since the arrival of Captain Cook in 1778, 23 species have become extinct, with 31 more in danger. And what's not known is how many species were wiped out before white explorers arrived. Experts believe that the Hawaiians annihilated about 40 species, including seven species of geese, a rare one-legged owl, ibis, lovebirds, sea eagles, and honeycreepers—all gone before Captain Cook arrived. Hawaii's endangered birds account for 40 percent of the birds officially listed as endangered or threatened by the U.S. Fish and Wildlife Service. In the last 200 years, more than four times as many birds have become extinct in Hawaii as in all of North America. These figures unfortunately suggest that a full 40 percent of Hawaii's endemic birds no longer exist. Almost all of O'ahu's native birds are gone and few indigenous Hawaiian birds can be found on any island below the 3,000-foot level.

Native birds have been reduced in number because of multiple factors. The original Polynesians helped wipe out many species. They altered large areas for farming and used fire to destroy patches of pristine forests. Also, bird feathers were highly prized for making lei, for feather work in capes and helmets, and for the large *kahili* fans that indicated rank among the *ali'i.* Introduced exotic birds and the new diseases they carried are another major reason for reduction of native bird numbers, along with predation by the mongoose and rat—especially upon ground-nesting birds. Bird malaria and bird pox were also devastating to the native species. Mosquitoes, unknown in Hawaii until a ship named the *Wellington* introduced them at Lahaina in 1826 through larvae carried in its water barrels, infected most native birds, causing a rapid reduction in birdlife. Feral pigs rooting deep in the rainforests knock over ferns and small trees, creating fetid pools in which mosquito larvae thrive. However, the most damaging factor by far is the assault upon native forests by agriculture and land developers. The vast majority of Hawaiian birds evolved into specialists. They lived in only one small area and ate a very limited number of plants or insects, which once removed or altered soon killed the birds.

You'll spot birds all over the Big Island, from the coastal areas to the high mountain slopes. Some are found on other islands as well, but the indigenous ones listed below are found only or mainly on the Big Island. Every bird listed is either threatened or endangered.

Hawaii's Own

The *nene,* or Hawaiian goose, deserves special mention because it is Hawaii's state bird and is making a comeback from the edge of extinction. The *nene* is found only on the slopes of Mauna Loa, Hualalai, and Mauna Kea on the Big Island, and in Haleakala Crater on Maui. It was extinct on Maui until a few birds were returned there in 1957, but some experts maintain that the *nene* lived naturally only on the Big Island. *Nene* are raised at the Wildfowl Trust in Slimbridge, England, which placed the first birds at Haleakala; and at the Hawaiian Fish and Game Station at Pohakuloa, along the Saddle Road on Hawai'i. By the 1940s, fewer than 50 birds lived in the wild. Now approximately 125 birds live on Haleakala and 500 on the Big Island. Although the birds can be raised successfully in captivity, their life in the wild is still in question.

The *nene* is believed to be a descendant of the Canadian goose, which it resembles. Geese are migratory birds that form strong kinship ties, mating for life. It's speculated that a migrating goose became disabled, and along with its loyal mate, remained in Hawaii. The *nene* is smaller than its Canadian cousin, has lost a great deal of webbing in its feet, and is perfectly at home away from water, foraging and nesting on rugged and bleak lava flows.

Good places to view *nene* are in Volcanoes National Park at Kipuka Nene, Summit Caldera, Devastation Trail, and Volcanoes Golf Course, at dawn and dusk. The birds gather at the golf course because they love to feed on grasses. The places to view them on the Kona side are Pu'ulani, a housing development north of Kailua-Kona; or Kaloko Mauka, another housing development on the slopes of Mt. Hualalai. At the top of the road up Mt. Hualalai is a trail, also a good place

BOB RACE

The *nene*, the state bird, lives only on Haleakala on Maui and on the slopes of Mauna Loa, Mauna Kea, and Mt. Hualalai.

to see the *nene*. Unfortunately, as the housing developments proliferate and the residents invariably acquire dogs and cats, the *nene* will disappear. The *nene* is a perfect symbol of Hawaii: let it be, and it will live.

The **Hawaiian crow,** or *alala,* is reduced to fewer than 12 birds living on the slopes of Hualalai and Mauna Loa above the 3,000-foot level. It looks like the common raven but has a more melodious voice and, sometimes, dull brown wing feathers. The *alala* breeds in early spring, and the greenish-blue, black-flecked eggs hatch from April to June. It is extremely nervous while nesting, and any disturbance will cause it to abandon its young.

The **Hawaiian hawk** *('io)* primarily lives on the slopes of Mauna Loa and Mauna Kea below 9,000 feet. It travels from there to other parts of the island and can often be seen kiting in the skies over Hawaii Volcanoes National Park, upland from Kailua-Kona, and in remote spots like Waimanu Valley. This noble bird, the royalty of the skies, symbolized the *ali'i.* The *'io* population was once dwindling, and many scientists feared that the bird was headed for extinction. The hawk exists only on the Big Island for reasons that are not entirely clear. The good news is that the *'io* is making a dramatic comeback, also for reasons still unclear. Speculation is that it may be gaining resistance to some diseases, including malaria, or that it may have learned how to prey on the introduced rats, or even that it may be adapting to life in macadamia nut groves and other alternate habitats.

The *'akiapola'au,* a honeycreeper, is a five-inch yellow bird hardly bigger than its name. It lives mainly on the eastern slopes in 'ohi'a and koa forests above 3,500 feet. It has a long, curved upper beak for probing and a smaller lower beak that it uses woodpecker-fashion. The *'akiapola'au* opens its mouth wide, strikes the wood with its lower beak, and then uses the upper beak to scrape out any larvae or insects. Listen for the distinctive rapping sound to spot this melodious singer. The *'akiapola'au* can be seen at the Hakalau National Wildlife Refuge and along the Pu'u O'o Volcano Trail from Volcanoes National Park. It's estimated

M

that only about 1,000 of these birds, one of the rarest of the island's rare winged creatures, are left.

In addition, two other endangered birds of the Big Island are the **koloa maoli,** a duck that resembles the mallard, and the slate gray or white **'alae ke'oke'o** coot.

Marine Birds

Two coastal birds that breed on the high slopes of Hawaii's volcanoes and feed on the coast are the **Hawaiian dark-rumped petrel** (*'ua'u*) and the **Newell's shearwater** (*'a'o*). The *'ua'u* lives on the barren high slopes and craters, where it nests in burrows or under stones. Breeding season lasts from mid-March to mid-October. Only one chick is born and nurtured on regurgitated squid and fish. The *'ua'u* suffers heavily from predation. The *'a'o* prefers the forested slopes of the interior. It breeds Apr.–Nov. and spends its days at sea and nights inland. Feral cats and dogs reduce its numbers considerably. In addition, the *ae'o* Hawaiian black-necked stilt has become endangered.

Forest Birds

The following birds are found in the upland forests of the Big Island. The **'elepaio** is found on other islands but is also spotted in Volcanoes National Park. This long-tailed (often held upright), five-inch brown bird (appearance can vary considerably) can be coaxed to come within touching distance of the observer. Sometimes it will sit on lower branches above your head and scold you. This bird was the special *amakua* (personal spirit) of canoe builders in ancient lore. Fairly common in the rainforest, it is basically a flycatcher.

The **'amakihi** and **'i'iwi** are endemic birds not endangered at the moment. The *'amakihi* is one of the most common native birds; yellowish green, it frequents the high branches of the 'ohi'a, koa, and sandalwood looking for insects, nectar, or fruit. It is less specialized than most other Hawaiian birds, the main reason for its continued existence. The *'i'iwi* is a bright red honeycreeper with a salmon-colored, hooked bill. It's found on Hawaii in the forests above

2,000 feet. It too feeds on a variety of insects and flowers. The *'i'iwi* is known for its harsh voice that sounds like a squeaking hinge, but it is also capable of a melodious song. The *'i'iwi* can be spotted at the top of Kaloko Mauka, a housing development north of Kailua-Kona; at Powerline Road, which goes south off the Saddle Road; and at Pu'u O'o Trail in Volcanoes National Park.

The **'apapane** is abundant on Hawai'i, especially atop Volcanoes, and, being the most common native bird, it's the easiest to see. It's a chubby, red-bodied bird about five inches long with a black bill, legs, wing tips, and tail feathers. It's quick and flitty and has a wide variety of calls and songs, from beautiful warbles to mechanical buzzes. Its feathers were sought by Hawaiians to produce distinctive capes and helmets for the *ali'i*.

The **Hawaiian thrush** (*'oma'o*) is a fairly common bird found above 3,000 feet in the windward forests of Hawai'i. This eight-inch gray bird is a good singer, often seen perching with distinctive drooping wings and a shivering body. The *'oma'o* is probably descended from Townsend's solitaire. The best place to look for it is at the Thurston Lava Tube in Hawaii Volcanoes National Park, where you can see it doing its baby-bird shivering-and-shaking act. A great mimic, it can sound like a cat or even like an old-fashioned radio with stations changing as you turn the dial. Another good place to see the *'oma'o* is along Powerline Road, off the Saddle Road.

The **'akepa** is a four- to five-inch bird. The male is a brilliant orange to red, the female

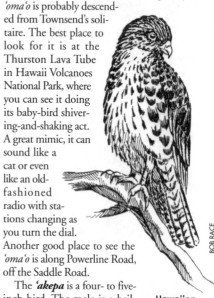

BOB RACE

Hawaiian hawk ('io)

a drab green and yellow. It is found mainly on Hualalai and in windward forests. In ornithological and environmental circles, the *'akepa,* *'akiapola'au,* and **Hawaiian creeper** are lovingly referred to as the Big Three, as they are the rarest of the rare birds of the island and a true joy to spot.

The six-inch, bright yellow *palila* is found only on Hawai'i in the forests of Mauna Kea above 6,000 feet. It depends exclusively upon *mamane* trees for survival, eating its pods, buds, and flowers. *Mamane* seedlings are destroyed by feral sheep. The Department of Land and Natural Resources for some inexplicable reason attempted to introduce sheep on the land that is the main refuge for the *palila,* which greatly endangered the bird's survival. The Sierra Club and Audubon Society immediately sued to prevent this environmental fiasco and won their case in the local courts. The Department of Land and Natural Resources insisted on fighting the decision all the way to the Supreme Court. They lost and reluctantly got rid of the sheep. But instead of letting a bad decision fade away, they compounded their folly by introducing a different type of sheep. They were sued again, lost again, and again fought the decision all the way to the Supreme Court, wasting taxpayers' money every laborious inch of the way. As goes the *mamane,* so goes the *palila.* As goes the *palila,* so goes humanity's attempt to live in harmony with nature.

THE HAKALAU FOREST NATIONAL WILDLIFE REFUGE

The Hakalau Forest National Wildlife Refuge, acquired with the help of the Nature Conservancy but administered solely by the U.S. Fish and Wildlife Service, is a 33,000-acre tract of land north of the Saddle Road that borders the Department of Hawaiian Home Lands land. It's upland forest and former ranch land that drifts down into solid rainforest that is the home of such birds as the endangered *'akiapola'au,* *'akepa,* *'io,* Hawaiian creeper, and *nene,* and the common *i'iwi,* *'oma'o,* *'apapane,* *'amakihi,* *'elepaio,* and *pueo.* The U.S. Fish and Wildlife Ser-

vice is working hard to allow the upper abandoned pastures of this refuge to regenerate with native forests; efforts include fencing, snaring, and hunting to rid the area of feral pigs and cattle, and replanting with koa, 'ohi'a, *opeka,* *pilo,* and other native species while removing introduced and exotic foliage. It's a tremendous task that's mainly being shouldered by the U.S. Fish and Wildlife Service manager Dick Wass and his staff. The refuge is not adequately staffed to accept visits by the general public at all times, but the Maulau Tract, the northernmost section of the refuge, is open for hiking and birding—with prior permission—every weekend. This area is a two-hour drive from Hilo, half of which is over a rugged dirt road traversable only by a 4WD vehicle! Numerous volunteer opportunities are available for various ongoing projects, either in the field or at the greenhouse, for a weekend or weeklong stint. If you *truly* have a dedication to help and aren't afraid to get your hands dirty, contact Dick for a very rewarding experience. To enter the refuge for any reason, contact the office at least three weeks in advance to make arrangements; call 808/933-6915, fax 808/933-6917, write to the Refuge Manager, Hakalau Forest NWR, 32 Kinoole St., Suite 101, Hilo, HI 96720, or email at richard_wass@fws.gov. The refuge is a very beautiful diamond in the rough, encompassing an incredible rainforest.

OTHER HAWAIIAN ANIMALS

Hawaii had only two indigenous mammals, the monk seal or *'ilio holu i ka uaua* (found throughout the islands) and the hoary bat (found primarily on the Big Island); both are threatened and endangered. The remainder of the Big Island's mammals are transplants. But like anything else, including people, that has been in the islands long enough, they take on characteristics that make them "local." There are no native amphibians, reptiles, ants, termites, or cockroaches. All are imported.

The following animals are found primarily on the Big Island. The **Hawaiian hoary bat** (*'ope'ape'a*) is a cousin of the Mainland bat, a strong flier that made it to Hawaii eons ago and developed its own species. Its tail has a whitish coloration, hence its name. Small populations of the bat are found on Maui and Kaua'i, but the greatest numbers of them are on the Big Island, where they have been spotted even on the upper slopes of Mauna Loa and Mauna Kea. The hoary bat has a 13-inch wingspan. Unlike other bats, it is a solitary creature, roosting in trees. It gives birth to twins in early summer and can often be spotted over Hilo and Kealakekua Bays just around sundown.

The **feral dog** *('ilio)* is found on all the islands but especially on the slopes of Mauna Kea, where packs chase feral sheep. Poisoned and shot by local ranchers, their numbers are diminishing. Black dogs, thought to be more tender, are still eaten in some Hawaiian and Filipino communities.

The **feral sheep** is an escaped descendant of animals brought to the islands by Captain Vancouver in the 1790s, and of merinos brought to the island later and raised for their exceptional woolly fleece. It exists only on the Big Island, on the upper slopes of Mauna Loa, Mauna Kea, and Hualalai; by the 1930s, its numbers topped 40,000 head. The fleece is a buff brown, and its two-foot-wide curved horns are often sought as hunting trophies. Feral sheep are responsible for the overgrazing of young *mamane* trees, necessary to the endangered bird *palila*. In 1979, a law was passed to exterminate or remove the sheep from Mauna Kea so that the native *palila* could survive.

The **mouflon sheep** was introduced to Lana'i and Hawai'i to cut down on overgrazing and serve as trophy animals. This Mediterranean sheep can interbreed with feral sheep to produce a hybrid. It lives on the upper slopes of Mauna Loa and Mauna Kea. Unfortunately, its introduction has not been a success. No evidence indicates that the smaller family groups of mouflon cause less damage than the herding feral sheep, and hunters reportedly don't like the meat as much as feral mutton.

The **feral donkey,** better known as the "Kona nightingale," came to Hawaii as a beast of burden. Domesticated donkeys are found on all islands, but a few wild herds still roam the Big Island along the Kona Coast, especially near the exclusive Kona Village Resort at Ka'upulehu.

Feral cattle were introduced by Captain Vancouver, who gave a few domesticated head to Kamehameha; immediately a *kapu* (taboo) against killing them went into effect for 10 years. The lush grasses of Hawaii were perfect and the cattle flourished; by the early 1800s they were out of control and were hunted and exterminated. Finally, Mexican cowboys were brought to Hawaii to teach the locals how to be range hands. From this legacy sprang the Hawaiian *paniolo.*

Most people hardly pay attention to flies, unless one lands on their plate lunch. But geneticists from throughout the world, and especially from the University of Hawaii, make a special pilgrimage to the Volcano area of the Big Island and to Maui just to study the native **Hawaiian drosophila.** This critter is related to the fruit fly and housefly, but there are hundreds of unique native species. The Hawaiian ecosystem is very simple and straightforward, so geneticists can trace the evolutionary changes from species to subspecies through mating behavior. The scientists compare the species between the two islands and chart the differences. Major discoveries in evolutionary genetics have been made through these studies.

MARINE LIFE

The **humpback whale,** known in Hawaii as *kohola,* migrates to Hawaiian waters yearly, arriving in late December and departing by mid-March. While whales can be seen anywhere around the Big Island, some of the best places to view them are along the South Kona Coast, especially at Keauhou, Kealakekua Bay, and Ka Lae ("South Point"), with many sightings off the Puna Coast around Isaac Hale Beach Park, and from the luxury resorts of the South Kohala area.

Hawaii Volcanoes National Park stretches from the top of Mauna Kea all the way down to the sea. It is here, around Apua Point, that three of the last known nesting sites of the very endangered **hawksbill turtle** *(honu 'ea)* are found. This creature has been ravished in the

ROBERT NILSEN

Green sea turtles frequently pull themselves up onto the beach for a rest. Please do not disturb.

Pacific, where it is ruthlessly hunted for its shell, which is made into women's jewelry, especially combs. It is illegal to bring items made from turtle shell into the United States, but the hunt goes on.

While they can be seen more often, **green sea turtles** are also endangered. Periodically, they haul themselves up on a beach to rest and warm up. This is normal and they are OK, even when their mottled green shell begins to turn a bit dusky white. Leave them alone in or out of the water; don't disturb or get too close to them. They'll return to the water when they are good and ready.

Billfish

Although these magnificent game fish live in various South Sea and Hawaiian waters, catching them is easiest in the clear, smooth waters off the Kona Coast. The billfish—swordfish, sailfish, marlin, and a'u—share two distinctive common features: a long, spearlike or swordlike snout, and a prominent dorsal fin. The three main species of billfish caught here are the blue, striped, and black marlin. Of these three, the **blue marlin** is the leading game fish in Kona waters. The blue has tipped the scales at well over 1,000 pounds, but the average fish weighs in at 300–400 pounds. When alive, this fish is a striking cobalt blue, but death brings a color change to slate blue. It feeds on skipjack tuna; throughout the summer, fishing boats look for schools of tuna as a tip-off to blues in the area. The **black marlin** is the largest and most coveted catch for blue-water anglers. This solitary fish is infrequently found in the banks off Kona. Granddaddies can weigh 1,800 pounds, but the average is a mere 200. The **striped marlin** is the most common commercial billfish, a highly prized food served in finer restaurants and often sliced into sashimi. Its coloration is a remarkable royal blue. It leaps spectacularly when caught, giving it a great reputation as a fighter. The striped marlin is smaller than the other marlins, so a 100-pounder is a very good catch.

Coral

Whether you're an avid scuba diver or a novice snorkeler, you'll become aware of Hawai'i's underwater coral gardens and grottoes whenever

INTRODUCTION

you peer at the fantastic seascapes below the waves. Although there is plenty of it, the coral in Hawaii doesn't do as well as in more equatorial areas because the water is too wild and not quite as warm. Coral looks like a plant fashioned from colorful stone, but it's the skeleton of tiny animals, zoophytes, which need algae in order to live. Coral grows best in water that is quite still, where the days are sunny, and where the algae can thrive. Many of Hawaii's reefs have been dying in the last 20 years, and no one seems to know why. Pesticides used in agriculture have been pointed to as a possible cause.

History

THE ROAD FROM TAHITI

Until the 1820s, when New England missionaries began a phonetic rendering of the Hawaiian language, the past was kept vividly alive only by the sonorous voices of special *kahuna* who chanted the sacred *mele*. The chants were beautiful, flowing word pictures that captured the essence of every aspect of life. These *mele* praised the land *(mele 'aina)*, royalty *(mele ali'i)*, and life's tender aspects *(mele aloha)*. Chants were dedicated to friendship, hardship, and favorite children. Entire villages sometimes joined together to compose a *mele;* every word was chosen carefully, and the wise old *kahuna* would decide if the words were lucky or unlucky. Some *mele* were bawdy or funny on the surface but contained secret meanings, often bitingly sarcastic, that ridiculed an inept or cruel leader. The most important chants took listeners back into the dim past before people lived in Hawaii. From these genealogies *(koihonua),* the *ali'i* derived the right to rule, since these chants went back to the gods Wakea and Papa, from whom the *ali'i* were directly descended.

The Kumulipo

The great genealogies, finally compiled in the late 1800s by order of King Kalakaua, were collectively known as *The Kumulipo, A Hawaiian Creation Chant,* basically a Polynesian account of Genesis. Other chants related to the beginning of this world, but *The Kumulipo* sums it all up and is generally considered the best. The chant relates that after the beginning of time, there is a period of darkness. The darkness, however, mysteriously brims with spontaneous life; during this period plants and animals are born, as well as Kumulipo, the man, and Po'ele, the woman. In the eighth chant darkness gives way to light and the gods descend to earth. Wakea is "the sky father" and Papa is "the earth mother," whose union gives birth to the islands of Hawaii. First born is Hawai'i, followed by Maui, then Kaho'olawe. Apparently, Papa becomes bushed after three consecutive births and decides to vacation in Tahiti. While Papa is away recovering from postpartum depression and working on her tan, Wakea gets lonely and takes Ka'ula as his second wife; she bears him the island-child of Lana'i. Not fully cheered up, but getting the hang of it, Wakea takes a third wife, Hina, who promptly bears the island of Moloka'i. Meanwhile, Papa gets wind of these shenanigans, returns from Polynesia, and retaliates by taking up with Lua, a young and virile god. She soon gives birth to the island of O'ahu. Papa and Wakea finally decide that they really are meant for each other and reconcile to conceive Kaua'i, Ni'ihau, Ka'ula, and Nihoa. These two progenitors are the source from which the *ali'i* ultimately traced their lineage, and from which they derived their god-ordained power to rule.

Basically, there are two major genealogical families: the Nanaulu, who became the royal *ali'i* of O'ahu and Kaua'i; and the Ulu, who provided the royalty of Maui and Hawai'i. The best sources of information in English on Hawaiian myth and legend are Martha Beckwith's *Hawaiian Mythology* and the monumental three-volume opus *An Account of the Polynesian Race* compiled by Abraham Fornander from 1878 to 1885. Fornander, after settling in Hawaii, married an *ali'i* from Moloka'i and had an illustrious career as a newspaperman, Maui circuit judge, and finally

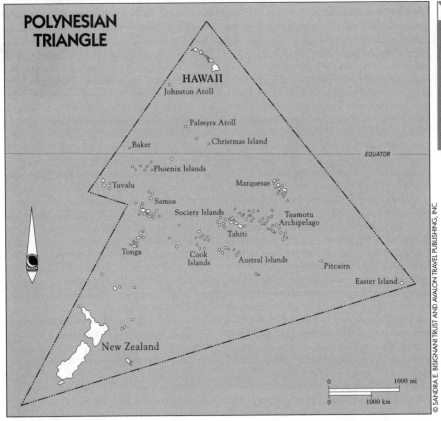

POLYNESIAN TRIANGLE

HAWAII

Johnston Atoll

Palmyra Atoll

Baker

Christmas Island

EQUATOR

Phoenix Islands

Tuvalu

Marquesas

Samoa

Society Islands

Tuamotu Archipelago

Tahiti

Tonga

Cook Islands

Austral Islands

Pitcairn

Easter Island

New Zealand

0   1000 mi

0   1000 km

Supreme Court justice. For years Fornander sent scribes to every corner of the kingdom to listen to the elder *kupuna*. They returned with firsthand accounts, which he dutifully recorded.

The Big Island plays a significant role in Hawaii's history. A long list of "firsts" occurred here. Historians generally believe (backed up by the oral tradition) that the Big Island was the first in the Hawaiian chain to be settled by the Polynesians. The dates now used are A.D. 600–700. Hawai'i is geographically the closest island to Polynesia; Mauna Loa and especially Mauna Kea, with its white summit, present easily spotted landmarks. Psychologically, the Polynesian wayfarers would have been very attracted to Hawai'i as a lost homeland. Compared to

Tahiti and most other South Sea islands (except Fiji), it's huge. It *looked* like the promised land. Some may wonder why the Polynesians chose to live atop an obviously active volcano and not bypass it for a more congenial island. The volcanism of the Big Island is comparatively gentle; the lava flows follow predictable routes and rarely turn killer. The animistic Hawaiians would have been drawn to live where the godly forces of nature were so apparent. The mana (power) would be exceptionally strong, and therefore the *ali'i* would be great. Human sacrifice was introduced to Hawai'i at Waha'ula Heiau in the Puna district in the 13th century, and from there *luakini* (human-sacrifice temples) spread throughout the islands.

The Great Navigators

No one knows exactly when the first Polynesians arrived in Hawaii, but the great "deliberate migrations" from the southern islands seem to have taken place A.D. 500–800, though anthropologists keep pushing the date backward in time as new evidence becomes available. Even before that, however, it's reasonable to assume that the first people to set foot on Hawaiian soil were probably fishermen, or perhaps defeated warriors whose canoes were blown hopelessly northward into unfamiliar waters. They arrived by a combination of extraordinary good luck and an uncanny ability to sail and navigate without instruments, using the sun by day and the moon and rising stars by night. They could feel the water and determine direction by swells, tides, and currents. The movements of fish and cloud formations were also utilized to give direction. Since their arrival was probably an accident, they were unprepared to settle on the fertile but uncultivated lands, having no stock animals, plant cuttings, or women. Forced to return southward, many undoubtedly lost their lives at sea, but a few wild-eyed stragglers must have made it home to tell tales of a paradise to the north where land was plentiful and the sea bounteous. This is affirmed by ancient navigational chants from Tahiti, Moorea, and Bora Bora, which passing from father to son revealed how to follow the stars to the "heavenly homeland in the north." Possibly a few migrations followed, but it's known that for centuries there was no real reason for a mass exodus, so the chants alone remained and eventually became shadowy legend.

From Where They Came

It's generally agreed that the first planned migrations were from the violent cannibal islands that Spanish explorers called the Marquesas, 11 islands in extreme eastern Polynesia. The islands themselves are harsh and inhospitable, breeding a toughness into these people that enabled them to withstand the hardships of long, unsure ocean voyages and years of resettlement. Marquesans were a fiercely independent people whose chiefs could rise from the ranks because of bravery or intelligence. They must have also been a savage-looking lot. Both men and women tattooed themselves in complex blue patterns from head to foot. The warriors carried massive, intricately designed ironwood war clubs and wore carved whale teeth in slits in their earlobes that eventually stretched to the shoulders. They shaved the sides of their heads with sharks' teeth, tied their hair in two topknots that looked like horns, and rubbed their heavily muscled and tattooed bodies with scented coconut oils. Their cults worshiped mummified ancestors; the bodies of warriors of defeated neighboring tribes were consumed. They were masters at building great double-hulled canoes launched from huge canoe sheds. Two hulls were fastened together to form a catamaran, and a hut in the center provided shelter in bad weather. The average voyaging canoe was 60–80 feet long and could comfortably hold an extended family of about 30 people. These small family bands carried all the staples they would need in the new lands.

The New Lands

For five centuries the Marquesans settled and lived peacefully on the new land, as if Hawaii's *aloha* spirit overcame most of their fierceness. The tribes coexisted in relative harmony, especially since there was no competition for land. Cannibalism died out. There was much coming and going between Hawaii and Polynesia as new people came to settle for hundreds of years. Then, it appears that in the 12th century a deliberate exodus of warlike Tahitians arrived and subjugated the settled islanders. They came to conquer. This incursion had a terrific significance on the Hawaiian religious and social system. Oral tradition relates that a Tahitian priest, Pa'ao, found the mana of the Hawaiian chiefs to be low, signifying that their gods were weak. Pa'ao built a *heiau* at Waha'ula on the Big Island, then introduced the warlike god Ku and the rigid *kapu* system through which the new rulers became dominant. Voyages between Tahiti and Hawaii continued for about 100 years, and Tahitian customs, legends, and language became the Hawaiian way of life. Then suddenly, for no recorded or apparent reason, the voyages discontinued and Hawaii returned to total isolation.

COURTESY OF HAWAII STATE ARCHIVES

The islands remained forgotten for almost 500 years until the indomitable English seaman, Capt. James Cook, sighted Oʻahu on January 18, 1778, and stepped ashore at Waimea on Kauaʻi two days later. At that time Hawaii's isolation was so complete that even the Polynesians had forgotten about it. On an earlier voyage, Tupaia, a high priest from Raiatea, had accompanied Captain Cook as he sailed throughout Polynesia. Tupaia demonstrated his vast knowledge of existing archipelagoes throughout the South Pacific by naming over 130 islands and drawing a map that included the Tonga group, the Cook Islands, the Marquesas, and even tiny Pitcairn, a rock in far eastern Polynesia where the mutinous crew of the *Bounty* found solace. In mentioning the Marquesas, Tupaia said, *"he maʻa te kaʻata,"* which means "food is man" or simply "Cannibals!" But remarkably absent from Tupaia's vast knowledge was the existence of Easter Island, New Zealand, and Hawaii.

The next waves of people to Hawaii would be white, and the Hawaiian world would be changed quickly and forever.

THE WORLD DISCOVERS HAWAII

The late 18th century was an extraordinary time in Hawaiian history. Monumental changes seemed to happen all at once. First, Capt. James Cook, a Yorkshire farm boy fulfilling his destiny as the all-time greatest Pacific explorer, found Hawaii for the rest of the world. For better or worse, it could no longer be an isolated Polynesian homeland. For the first time in Hawaiian history, a charismatic leader, Kamehameha, emerged, and after a long civil war he united all the islands into one centralized kingdom. The death of Captain Cook in Hawaii marked the beginning of a long series of tragic misunderstandings between whites and natives. When Kamehameha died, the old religious system of *kapu* came to an end, leaving the Hawaiians in a spiritual vortex. Many takers arrived to fill the void: missionaries after souls, whalers after their prey and a good time, traders and planters

Capt. James Cook

after profits and a home. The islands were opened and devoured like ripe fruit. Powerful nations, including Russia, Great Britain, France, and the United States, yearned to bring this strategic Pacific jewel under their own influence. The 19th century brought the demise of the Hawaiian people as a dominant political force in their own land and with it the end of Hawaii as a sovereign monarchy. An almost bloodless yet bitter military coup followed by a brief Hawaiian Republic ended in annexation by the United States. As the United States became completely entrenched politically and militarily, a new social and economic order was founded on the plantation system. Amazingly rapid population growth occurred with the importation of plantation workers from Asia and Europe, which yielded a unique cosmopolitan blend of races like nowhere else on earth. By the dawning of the 20th century, the face of old Hawaii had been altered forever; the "sacred homeland in the north" was hurled into the modern age. The attack on Pearl Harbor saw a tremendous loss of life and brought Hawaii closer to the United States by a baptism of blood. Finally, on August 21, 1959, after five years as a "territory," Hawaii officially became the 50th state of the United States.

Captain Cook Sights Hawaii

In 1776 Capt. James Cook set sail for the Pacific from Plymouth, England, on his third and final expedition into this still largely unexplored region of the world. On a fruitless quest for the fabled Northwest Passage across the North American continent, he sailed down the coast of Africa, rounded the Cape of Good Hope, crossed the Indian Ocean, and traveled past New Zealand, Tasmania, and the Friendly Islands (where the "friendly" natives hatched an unsuccessful plot to murder him). On January 18, 1778, Captain Cook's 100-foot flagship HMS *Resolution* and its 90-foot companion HMS *Discovery* sighted O'ahu. Two days later, they sighted Kaua'i and went ashore at the village of Waimea. Though anxious to get on with his mission, Cook decided to make a quick sortie to investigate this new land and reprovision his ships. He did, however, take time to remark in his diary about the close resemblance of these newfound people to others he had encountered as far south as New Zealand and marveled at their widespread habitation across the Pacific.

The first trade was some brass medals for a mackerel. Cook also stated that he had never before met natives so astonished by a ship, and that they had an amazing fascination with iron, which they called *ko'i*, Hawaiian for "adze." There is even some conjecture that a Spanish ship under one Captain Gaetano had landed in Hawaii as early as the 16th century, trading a few scraps of iron that the Hawaiians valued even more than the Europeans valued gold.

It was also noted that the Hawaiian women gave themselves freely to the sailors with the apparent good wishes of the island men. This was actually a ploy by the *kahuna* to test if the newcomers were gods or men—gods didn't need women. These sailors proved immediately mortal. Cook, who was also a physician, tried valiantly to keep the 66 men (out of 112) who had measurable cases of venereal disease away from the women. The task proved impossible as women literally swarmed the ships; when Cook returned less than a year later, it was logged that signs of VD were already apparent on some natives' faces.

Cook was impressed with the Hawaiians' swimming ability and with their well-bred manners. They had happy dispositions and sticky fingers, stealing any object made of metal, especially nails. The first item stolen was a butcher's cleaver. An unidentified native grabbed it, plunged overboard, swam to shore, and waved his booty in triumph. The Hawaiians didn't seem to care for beads and were not at all impressed with a mirror. Cook provisioned his ships by trading chisels for hogs, while common sailors gleefully traded nails for sex. Landing parties were sent inland to fill casks with fresh water. On one such excursion a Mr. Williamson, who was eventually drummed out of the Royal Navy for cowardice, unnecessarily shot and killed a native. After a brief stop on Ni'ihau, the ships sailed away, but both groups were indelibly impressed with the memory of each other.

Cook Returns

Almost a year later, when winter weather forced Cook to return from the coast of Alaska, his discovery began to take on far-reaching significance. Cook had named Hawaii the Sandwich Islands, in honor of one of his patrons, John Montague, the Earl of Sandwich. On this return voyage, he spotted Maui on November 26, 1778. After eight weeks of seeking a suitable harbor, the ships bypassed it, but not before the coastline was duly drawn by Lt. William Bligh, one of Cook's finest and most trusted officers. (Bligh would find his own drama almost 10 years later as commander of the infamous HMS *Bounty*.) The *Discovery* and *Resolution* finally found safe anchorage at Kealakekua Bay on the Kona Coast of the Big Island. It is very lucky for history that on board was Mr. Anderson, ship's chronicler, who left a handwritten record of the strange and tragic events that followed. Even more important were the drawings of John Webber, ship's artist, who rendered invaluable impressions in superb drawings and etchings. Other noteworthy men aboard were George Vancouver, who would lead the first British return to Hawaii after Cook's death and introduce many fruits, vegetables, cattle, sheep, and goats; and James Burney, who would become a long-standing leading authority on the Pacific.

By all accounts Cook was a humane and just captain, greatly admired by his men. Unlike the many supremacists of that time, he was known to have a respectful attitude toward any people he discovered, treating them as equals and recognizing the significance of their cultures. Not known as a violent man, he would use his superior weapons against natives only in an absolute case of self-defense. His hardened crew had been at sea facing untold hardship for almost three years; returning to Hawaii was truly like reentering paradise.

A strange series of coincidences sailed with Cook into Kealakekua Bay on January 16, 1779. It was *makahiki* time, a period of rejoicing and festivity dedicated to the fertility god of the earth, Lono. Normal *kapu* days were suspended and willing partners freely enjoyed each other sexually, as well as dancing, feasting, and the islands' version of Olympic games. It was long held in Hawaiian legend that the great god Lono would return to earth. Lono's image was a small wooden figure perched on a tall, mastlike crossbeam; hanging from the crossbeam were long, white sheets of tapa. Who else could Cook be but Lono, and what else could his ships with their masts and white sails be but his sacred floating *heiau*? This explained the Hawaiians' previous fascination with his ships, but to add to the remarkable coincidence, Kealakekua Harbor happened to be considered Lono's private sacred harbor. Natives from throughout the land prostrated themselves and paid homage to the returning god. Cook was taken ashore and brought to Lono's sacred temple, where he was afforded the highest respect. The ships badly needed fresh supplies so the Hawaiians readily gave all they had, stretching their own provisions to the limit. To the sailors' delight, this included full measures of the *aloha* spirit.

The Fatal Misunderstanding

After an uproarious welcome and generous hospitality for over a month, it became obvious that the newcomers were beginning to overstay their welcome. During the interim a seaman named William Watman died, convincing the Hawaiians that the *haole* were indeed mortals,

not gods. Watman was buried at Hikiau Heiau, where a plaque commemorates the event to this day. Incidents of petty theft began to increase dramatically. The lesser chiefs indicated it was time to leave by "rubbing the Englishmen's bellies." Inadvertently many *kapu* were broken by the Englishmen, and once-friendly relations became strained. Finally, the ships sailed away on February 4, 1779.

After plying terrible seas for only a week, *Resolution*'s foremast was badly damaged. Cook sailed back into Kealakekua Bay, dragging the mast ashore on February 13. The natives, now totally hostile, hurled rocks at the sailors. Orders were given to load muskets with ball; firearms had previously only been loaded with shot and a light charge. Confrontations increased when some Hawaiians stole a small boat and Cook's men set after them, capturing the fleeing canoe which held an *ali'i* named Palea. The English treated him roughly; to the Hawaiians' horror, they even smacked him on the head with a paddle. The Hawaiians then furiously attacked the marines, who abandoned the small boat.

Cook Goes Down

Next the Hawaiians stole a small cutter from the *Discovery* that had been moored to a buoy and partially sunk to protect it from the sun. For the first time, Captain Cook became furious. He ordered Captain Clerk of the *Discovery* to sail to the southeast end of the bay and stop any canoe trying to leave Kealakekua. Cook then made a fatal error in judgment. He decided to take nine armed marines ashore in an attempt to convince the venerable King Kalani'opu'u to accompany him back aboard ship, where he would hold him for ransom in exchange for the cutter. The old king agreed, but his wife prevailed upon him not to trust the *haole*. Kalani'opu'u sat down on the beach to think while the tension steadily grew.

Meanwhile, a group of marines fired upon a canoe trying to leave the bay, and a lesser chief, Nookemai, was killed. The crowd around Cook and his men reached an estimated 20,000, and warriors outraged by the killing of the chief armed themselves with clubs and protective straw-mat armor. One bold warrior advanced on Cook and struck him with his *pahoa* (dagger). In retaliation, Cook drew a tiny pistol lightly loaded with shot and fired at the warrior. His bullets spent themselves on the straw armor and fell harmlessly to the ground. The Hawaiians went wild. Lt. Molesworth Phillips, in charge of the nine marines, began a withering fire; Cook himself slew two natives.

Overpowered by sheer numbers, the marines headed for boats standing offshore, while Lieutenant Phillips lay wounded. It is believed that Captain Cook, the greatest seaman ever to enter the Pacific, stood helplessly in knee-deep water instead of making for the boats because he could not swim! Hopelessly surrounded, he was knocked on the head. Countless warriors then passed a knife around and hacked and mutilated his lifeless body. A sad Lieutenant King lamented in his diary, "Thus fell our great and excellent commander."

The Final Chapter

Captain Clerk, now in charge, settled his men and prevailed upon the Hawaiians to return Cook's body. On the morning of February 16 a grisly piece of charred meat was brought aboard: the Hawaiians, according to their custom, had afforded Cook the highest honor by baking his body in an underground oven to remove the flesh from the bones. On February 17 a group of Hawaiians in a canoe taunted the marines by brandishing Cook's hat. The English, strained to the limit and thinking that Cook was being desecrated, finally broke. Foaming with bloodlust, they leveled their cannons and muskets on shore and shot anything that moved. It is believed that Kamehameha the Great was wounded in this flurry, along with four *ali'i,* and 25 *maka'ainana* (commoners) were killed. Finally, on February 21, 1779, the bones of Capt. James Cook's hands, skull, arms, and legs were returned and tearfully buried at sea. A common seaman, one Mr. Zimmerman, summed up the feelings of all who sailed under Cook when he wrote, "… he was our leading star." The English sailed next morning after dropping off their Hawaiian girlfriends who were still aboard.

Captain Clerk, in bad health, carried on with the fruitless search for the Northwest Passage. He died and was buried at the Siberian village of Petropavlovsk. England was at war with upstart colonists in America, so the return of the expedition warranted little fanfare. The *Resolution* was converted into an army transport to fight the pesky Americans; the once proud *Discovery* was reduced to a convict ship ferrying inmates to Botany Bay, Australia. Mrs. Cook, the great captain's steadfast and chaste wife, lived to the age of 93, surviving all her children. She was given a stipend of 200 pounds per year and finished her days surrounded by Cook's mementos, observing the anniversary of his death to the very end by fasting and reading from the Bible.

THE UNIFICATION OF OLD HAWAII

Hawaii was already in a state of political turmoil and civil war when Cook arrived. In the 1780s the islands were roughly divided into three kingdoms: venerable Kalani'opu'u ruled Hawai'i and the Hana district of Maui; wily and ruthless warrior-king Kahekili ruled Maui, Kaho'olawe, Lana'i, and later O'ahu; and Kaeo, Kahekili's brother, ruled Kaua'i. War ravaged the land until

King Kamehameha

COURTESY OF HAWAII STATE ARCHIVES

a remarkable chief, Kamehameha, rose and subjugated all the islands under one rule. Kamehameha initiated a dynasty that would last for about 100 years, until the independent monarchy of Hawaii forever ceased to be. To add a zing to this brewing political stew, Westerners and their technology were beginning to come in ever-increasing numbers. In 1786, Captain Jean-François de La Pérouse and his French exploration party landed in what's now La Perouse Bay near Lahaina, foreshadowing European attention to the islands. In 1786 two American captains, Portlock and Dixon, made landfall in Hawaii. Also, it was known that a fortune could be made on the fur trade between the Pacific Northwest and Canton, China; stopping in Hawaii could make the trip feasible. After this was reported, the fate of Hawaii was sealed.

Hawaii under Kamehameha was ready to enter its "golden age." The social order was medieval, with the *ali'i* as knights owing their military allegiance to the king, and the serflike *maka'ainana* paying tribute and working the lands. The priesthood of *kahuna* filled the posts of advisors, sorcerers, navigators, doctors, and historians. This was Polynesian Hawaii at its apex. But like the uniquely Hawaiian silversword plant, the old culture blossomed, and as soon as it did, began to wither. Ever since, all that was purely Hawaiian has been supplanted by the relentless foreign influences that began bearing down upon it.

Young Kamehameha

The greatest native son of Hawaii, Kamehameha was born under mysterious circumstances in the Kohala district on the Big Island, probably in 1753. He was royal born to Keoua Kupuapaikalaninui, the chief of Kohala, and Kekuiapoiwa, a chieftess from Kona. Accounts vary, but one claims that before his birth, a *kahuna* prophesied that this child would grow to be a "killer of chiefs." Because of this, the local chiefs conspired to murder the infant. When Kekuiapoiwa's time came, she secretly went to the royal birthing stones near Mo'okini Heiau and delivered Kamehameha. She entrusted her baby to a manservant and instructed him to hide the child. He headed for the rugged and remote coast around Kapa'au. Here Kamehameha was raised in the mountains, mostly by men. Always alone, he earned the nickname "the lonely one."

Kamehameha was a man noticed by everyone; there was no doubt he was a force to be reckoned with. He had met Captain Cook when the *Discovery* unsuccessfully tried to land at Hana on Maui. While aboard, he made a lasting impression, distinguishing himself from the multitude of natives swarming the ships by his royal bearing. Lt. James King, in a diary entry, remarked that Kamehameha was a fierce-looking man, almost ugly, but that he was obviously intelligent, observant, and very good-natured. Kamehameha received his early military training from his uncle Kalani'opu'u, the great king of Hawai'i and Hana who fought fierce battles against Alapa'i, the usurper who stole his hereditary lands. After regaining Hawai'i, Kalani'opu'u returned to his Hana district and turned his attention to conquering all of Maui. During this period young Kamehameha distinguished himself as a ferocious warrior and earned the nickname of "the hard-shelled crab," even though old Kahekili, Maui's king, almost annihilated Kalani'opu'u's army at the sand hills of Wailuku.

When the old king neared death, he passed on the kingdom to his son Kiwala'o. He also, however, empowered Kamehameha as the keeper of the family war god Kuka'ilimoku: Ku of the Bloody Red Mouth, Ku the Destroyer. Oddly enough, Kamehameha had been born not 500 yards from Ku's great *heiau* at Kohala, and he had heard the chanting and observed the ceremonies dedicated to this fierce god from his first breath. Soon after Kalani'opu'u died, Kamehameha found himself in a bitter war that he did not seek against his two cousins, Kiwala'o and his brother Keoua, with the island of Hawai'i at stake. The skirmishing lasted nine years until Kamehameha's armies met the two brothers at Moku'ohai in an indecisive battle in which Kiwala'o was killed. The result was a shaky truce with Keoua, a much-embittered enemy. During this fighting, Kahekili of Maui conquered O'ahu, where he built a house of the skulls and bones of his adversaries as a reminder of his omnipotence. He also extended his will to Kaua'i by marrying his half-brother to a high-ranking chieftess of that island. A new factor would resolve this stalemate of power—the coming of the *haole*.

The Olowalu Massacre

In 1790 the American merchant ship *Ella Nora,* commanded by Yankee captain Simon Metcalfe, was looking for a harbor after its long voyage from the Pacific Northwest. Following a day behind was the *Fair American,* a tiny ship sailed by Metcalfe's son Thomas and a crew of five. Simon Metcalfe, perhaps by necessity, was a stern and humorless man who would allow no interference. While his ship was anchored at Olowalu, a beach area about five miles east of Lahaina, some natives slipped close in their canoes and stole a small boat, killing a seaman in the process. Metcalfe decided to trick the Hawaiians by first negotiating a truce and then unleashing full fury upon them. Signaling he was willing to trade, he invited canoes of innocent natives to visit his ship. In the meantime, he ordered that all cannons and muskets be readied with scatter shot. When the canoes were within hailing distance, he ordered his crew to fire at will. Over 100 people were slain; the Hawaiians remembered this killing as "the Day of Spilled Brains." Metcalfe then sailed away to Kealakekua Bay and in an unrelated incident managed to insult Kameiamoku, a ruling chief, who vowed to annihilate the next *haole* ship that he saw.

Fate sent him the *Fair American* and young Thomas Metcalfe. The little ship was entirely overrun by superior forces. In the ensuing battle, the mate, Isaac Davis, so distinguished himself by open acts of bravery that his life alone was spared. Kameiamoku later turned over both Davis and the ship to Kamehameha. Meanwhile, while harbored at Kealakekua, the senior Metcalfe sent John Young to reconnoiter. Kamehameha, having learned of the capture of the *Fair American,* detained Young so he could not report, and Metcalfe, losing patience, marooned his own man and sailed off to Canton. (Metcalfe never learned of the fate of his son Thomas and was later killed with another son while trading with the Native Americans along the Pacific coast of the United States.) Kamehameha quickly realized the sig-

nificance of his two captives and the *Fair American* with its brace of small cannons. He appropriated the ship and made Davis and Young trusted advisors, eventually raising them to the rank of chief. They would all play a significant role in the unification of Hawaii.

Kamehameha the Great

Later in 1790, supported by the savvy of Davis and Young and the cannons from the *Fair American,* which he mounted on carts, Kamehameha invaded Maui, using Hana as his power base. The island's defenders under Kalanikupule, son of Kahekili, who was lingering on Oʻahu, were totally demoralized, then driven back into the death trap of the ʻIao Valley of Maui. There, Kamehameha's forces annihilated them. No mercy was expected and none given, although mostly commoners were slain with no significant *aliʻi* falling to the victors. So many were killed in this sheer-walled, inescapable valley that the battle was called *ka pani wai,* which means "the Damming of the Waters"—literally with dead bodies.

While Kamehameha was fighting on Maui, his old nemesis Keoua was busy running amok back on Hawaiʻi, again pillaging Kamehameha's lands. The great warrior returned home flushed with victory, but in two battles he could not subdue Keoua. Finally, Kamehameha had a prophetic dream in which he was told that Ku would lead him to victory over all the lands of Hawaii if he would build a *heiau* to the war god at Kawaihae. Even before the temple was finished, old Kahekili attempted to invade Waipiʻo, Kamehameha's stronghold. But Kamehameha summoned Davis and Young, and with the *Fair American* and an enormous fleet of war canoes defeated Kahekili at Waimanu. Kahekili had no choice but to accept the indomitable Kamehameha as the king of Maui, although he himself remained the administrative head until his death in 1794.

Now only Keoua remained in the way, and he would be defeated not by war, but by the great mana of Ku. While Keoua's armies were crossing the desert on the southern slopes of Kilauea, the fire goddess Pele trumpeted her disapproval and sent a huge cloud of poisonous gas and mud-ash into the air. It descended upon and instantly killed the middle legions of Keoua's armies and their families. The footprints of this ill-fated army remain to this day outlined in the mud-ash as clearly as if they were deliberately encased in wet cement. Keoua's intuition told him that the victorious mana of the gods had swung to Kamehameha and that his own fate was sealed. Kamehameha sent word that he wanted Keoua to meet with him at Ku's newly dedicated temple in Kawaihae. Both knew that Keoua must die. Riding proudly in his canoe, the old nemesis came gloriously outfitted in the red-and-gold feathered cape and helmet signifying his exalted rank. When he stepped ashore he was felled by Kamehameha's warriors. His body was ceremoniously laid upon the altar along with 11 others who were slaughtered and dedicated to Ku, of the Maggot-Dripping Mouth.

Increasing Contact

By the time Kamehameha had won the Big Island, Hawaii was becoming a regular stopover for numerous ships seeking the lucrative sandalwood trade with China. In February 1791, Capt. George Vancouver, still seeking the Northwest Passage, returned to Kealakekua where he was greeted by a throng of 30,000. The captain at once recognized Kamehameha, who was wearing a Chinese dressing gown that he had received in tribute from another chief who in turn had received it from the hands of Cook himself. The diary of a crew member, Thomas Manby, relates that Kamehameha, missing his front teeth, was more fierce-looking than ever as he approached the ship in an elegant double-hulled canoe propelled by 46 rowers. The king invited all to a great feast prepared for them on the beach. Kamehameha's appetite matched his tremendous size. It was noted that he ate two sizable fish, a king-sized bowl of poi, a small pig, and an entire baked dog. Kamehameha personally entertained the English by putting on a mock battle in which he deftly avoided spears by rolling, tumbling, and catching them in midair, all the while hurling his own spear a great distance. The English reciprocated by firing cannon bursts into the air, creating an impromptu fireworks display. Kame-

hameha requested from Vancouver a full table setting, with which he was provided, but his request for firearms was prudently denied. Captain Vancouver became a trusted advisor of Kamehameha, and told him about the white man's form of worship. He even interceded for Kamehameha with his headstrong queen, Ka'ahumanu, and coaxed her from her hiding place under a rock when she sought refuge at Pu'uhonua O Honaunau. The captain gave gifts of beef cattle, fowl, and breeding stock of sheep and goats. The ship's naturalist, Archibald Menzies, was the first *haole* to climb Mauna Kea; he also introduced a large assortment of fruits and vegetables. The Hawaiians were cheerful and outgoing, and they showed remorse when they indicated that the remainder of Cook's bones had been buried at a temple close to Kealakekua. John Young, by this time firmly entrenched into Hawaiian society, made no request to sail away with Vancouver. During the next two decades of Kamehameha's rule, the French, Russians, English, and Americans discovered the great whaling waters off Hawaii. Their increasing visits shook and finally tumbled the ancient religion and social order of *kapu*.

Finishing Touches

After Keoua was laid to rest, it was only a matter of time until Kamehameha consolidated his power over all of Hawaii. In 1794 the old warrior Kahekili of Maui died and gave O'ahu to his son, Kalanikupule, while Kaua'i and Ni'ihau went to his brother Kaeo. In wars between the two, Kalanikupule was victorious, though he did not possess the grit of his father nor the great mana of Kamehameha. He had previously murdered a Captain Brown, who had anchored in Honolulu, and seized his ship, the *Jackal*. With the aid of this ship, Kalanikupule now determined to attack Kamehameha. However, while en route, the sailors regained control of their ship and cruised to the Big Island to inform and join with Kamehameha. An army of 16,000 was raised and sailed for Maui, where they met only token resistance, destroyed Lahaina, pillaged the countryside, and subjugated Moloka'i in one bloody battle.

The war canoes sailed next for Oʻahu and the final showdown. The great army landed at Waikiki, and though defenders fought bravely, giving up Oʻahu by the inch, they were steadily driven into the surrounding mountains. The beleaguered army made its last stand at Nuʻuanu Pali, a great precipice in the mountains behind present-day Honolulu. Kamehameha's warriors mercilessly drove the enemy into the great abyss. Kalanikupule, who hid in the mountains, was captured after a few months and sacrificed to Ku, the Snatcher of Lands, thereby ending the struggle for power.

Kamehameha put down a revolt on Hawaiʻi in 1796. The king of Kauaʻi, Kaumualiʻi, accepted the inevitable and recognized Kamehameha as supreme ruler without suffering the ravages of a needless war. Kamehameha, for the first time in Hawaiian history, was the undisputed ruler of all the islands of "the heavenly homeland in the north."

Kamehameha's Rule

Kamehameha was as gentle in victory as he was ferocious in battle. Under his rule, which lasted until his death on May 8, 1819, Hawaii enjoyed a peace unlike any the warring islands had ever known. The king moved his royal court to Lahaina, where in 1803 he built the "Brick Palace," the first permanent building of Hawaii. The benevolent tyrant also enacted the "Law of the Splintered Paddle." This law, which protected the weak from the exploitation of the strong, had its origins in an incident of many years before. A brave defender of a small overwhelmed village had broken a paddle over Kamehameha's head and taught the chief—literally in one stroke—about the nobility of the commoner.

However, just as Old Hawaii reached its golden age, its demise was at hand. The relentless waves of *haole* both innocently and determinedly battered the old ways into the ground. With the foreign ships came prosperity and fanciful new goods after which the *aliʻi* lusted. The *makaʻainana* were worked mercilessly to provide sandalwood for the China trade. This was the first "boom" economy to hit the islands,

but it set the standard of exploitation that would follow. Kamehameha built an observation tower in Lahaina to watch for ships, many of which were his own returning laden with riches from the world at large. In the last years of his life Kamehameha returned to his beloved Kona Coast, where he enjoyed the excellent fishing renowned to this day. He had taken Hawaii from the darkness of warfare into the light of peace. He died true to the religious and moral *kapu* of his youth, the only ones he had ever known, and with him died a unique way of life. Two loyal retainers buried his bones after the baked flesh had been ceremoniously stripped away. A secret burial cave was chosen so that no one could desecrate the remains of the great chief, thereby absorbing his mana. The tomb's whereabouts remains unknown, and disturbing the dead remains one of the strictest *kapu* to this day. The Lonely One's kingdom would pass to his son, Liholiho, but true power would be in the hands of his beloved but feisty wife Kaʻahumanu. As Kamehameha's spirit drifted from this earth, two forces sailing around Cape Horn would forever change Hawaii: the missionaries and the whalers.

MISSIONARIES AND WHALERS

The year 1819 was of the utmost significance in Hawaiian history. It marked the death of Kamehameha, the overthrow of the ancient *kapu* system, the arrival of the first "whaler" in Lahaina, and the departure of Calvinist missionaries from New England determined to convert the heathen islands. Great changes began to rattle the old order to its foundations. With the *kapu* system and all of the ancient gods abandoned (except for the fire goddess Pele of Kilauea), a great void was left in the souls of the Hawaiians. In the coming decades Hawaii, also coveted by Russia, France, and England, was finally consumed by America. The islands had the first American school, printing press, and newspaper *(The Polynesian)* west of the Mississippi. Lahaina, in its heyday, became the world's greatest whaling port, accommodating over 500 ships during its peak years.

The Royal Family

Maui's Hana district provided Hawaii with one of its greatest queens, Ka'ahumanu, born in 1768 in a cave within walking distance of Hana Harbor. At the age of 17 she became the third of Kamehameha's 21 wives and eventually the love of his life. At first she proved totally independent and unmanageable and was known to openly defy her king by taking numerous lovers. Kamehameha placed a *kapu* on her body and even had her attended by horribly deformed hunchbacks in an effort to curb her carnal appetites, but she continued to flout his authority. Young Ka'ahumanu had no love for her great, lumbering, unattractive husband, but in time (even Captain Vancouver was pressed into service as a marriage counselor) she learned to love him dearly. She in turn became his favorite wife, although she remained childless throughout her life. Kamehameha's first wife was the supremely royal Keopuolani, who so outranked even him that the king himself had to approach her naked and crawling on his belly. Keopuolani produced the royal children Liholiho and Kauikeaouli, who became King Kamehameha II and III, respectively. Just before Kamehameha I died in 1819 he appointed Liholiho his successor, but he also had the wisdom to make Ka'ahumanu the *kuhina nui,* or queen regent. Initially, Liholiho was weak and became a drunkard. Later he became a good ruler, but he was always supported by his royal mother Keopuolani and by the ever-formidable Ka'ahumanu.

Kapu Is Pau

Ka'ahumanu was greatly loved and respected by the people. On public occasions, she donned Kamehameha's royal cloak and spear and, so attired and infused with the king's mana, she demonstrated that she was the real leader of Hawaii. For six months after Kamehameha's death, Ka'ahumanu counseled Liholiho on what he must do. The wise *kuhina nui* knew that the old ways were *pau* (finished) and that Hawaii could not hope to function in a rapidly changing world under the *kapu* system. In November 1819, Ka'ahumanu and Keopuolani prevailed upon Liholiho to break two of the oldest and most sacred *kapu* by eating with women and by allowing women to eat previously forbidden

COURTESY OF HAWAII STATE ARCHIVES

the great Queen Ka'ahumanu, by ship's artist Louis Choris from the Otto Von Kotzebue expedition, circa 1816 foods such as bananas and certain fish. Heavily fortified with strong drink and attended by other high-ranking chiefs and a handful of foreigners, Ka'ahumanu and Liholiho ate together in public. This feast became known as *Ai Noa* ("Free Eating"). As the first morsels passed Ka'ahumanu's lips, the ancient gods of Hawaii tumbled. Throughout the land, revered *heiau* were burned and abandoned and the idols knocked to the ground. Now the people had nothing but their weakened inner selves to rely on. Nothing and no one could answer their prayers; their spiritual lives were empty and in shambles.

Missionaries

Into this spiritual vortex sailed the brig *Thaddeus* on April 4, 1820. It had set sail from Boston on October 23, 1819, lured to the Big Island by Henry Opukaha'ia, a local boy born at Napo'opo'o in 1792. Coming ashore at Kailua-Kona, the Reverends Bingham and Thurston were granted a one-year trial missionary period by King Liholiho. They established themselves on the Big Island and O'ahu and from there began the transformation of Hawaii. The missionaries were people of God, but also practical-minded Yankees. They brought education, enterprise, and most importantly, unlike the transient seafarers, a commitment to stay and build. By 1824, the new faith had such a foothold that Chieftess Keopuolani climbed to the fire pit atop Kilauea and defied Pele. This was even more striking than the previous breaking of the food *kapu*, because the strength of Pele could actually be seen. Keopuolani ate forbidden *'ohelo* berries and cried out, "Jehovah is my God." Over the next decades the governing of Hawaii slipped away from the Big Island and moved to the new port cities of Lahaina on Maui and, later, Honolulu.

Rapid Conversions

The year 1824 also marked the death of Keopuolani, who was given a Christian burial. She had set the standard by accepting Christianity, and a number of the *ali'i* had followed the queen's lead. Liholiho had sailed off to England, where he and his wife contracted measles and died. Their bodies were returned by the British in 1825, on the HMS *Blonde* captained by Lord Byron, cousin of *the* Lord Byron. During these years, Ka'ahumanu allied herself with Reverend Richards, pastor of the first mission in the islands, and together they wrote Hawaii's first code of laws based upon the Ten Commandments. Foremost was the condemnation of murder, theft, brawling, and the desecration of the Sabbath by work or play. The early missionaries had the best of intentions, but like all zealots they were blinded by the single-mindedness that was also their greatest ally. They weren't surgically selective in their destruction of native beliefs. *Anything* native was felt to be inferior, and they set about wiping out all traces of the old ways. In their rampage they reduced the Hawaiian culture to ashes, plucking self-will and determination from the hearts of a once-proud people. More so than the whalers, they terminated the Hawaiian way of life.

The Early Seamen

A good portion of the common seamen of the early 19th century came from the dregs of the Western world. Many a whoremongering drunkard had awoken from a stupor and found himself on the pitching deck of a ship, discovering to his dismay that he had been "pressed into naval service." For the most part these sailors were a filthy, uneducated, lawless rabble. Their present situation was dim, their future hopeless, and they would live to be 30 if they were lucky and didn't die from scurvy or a thousand other miserable fates. They snatched brief pleasure in every port and jumped ship at every opportunity, especially in an easy berth like Lahaina. They displayed the worst elements of Western culture, which the Hawaiians naively mimicked. In exchange for *aloha* they gave drunkenness, sloth, and insidious death by disease. By the 1850s the population of native Hawaiians tumbled from the estimated 300,000 reported by Captain Cook in 1778 to barely 60,000. Common conditions such as colds, flu, venereal disease, and sometimes smallpox and cholera decimated the Hawaiians, who had no natural immunities to these foreign ailments. By the time the missionaries arrived, *hapa haole* children were common in Lahaina streets.

The earliest merchant ships to the islands were owned or skippered by lawless opportunists who had come seeking sandalwood after first filling their holds with furs from the Pacific Northwest. Aided by *ali'i* hungry for manufactured goods and Western finery, they raped Hawaiian forests of this fragrant wood so coveted in China. Next, droves of sailors came in search of whales. The whalers, decent men at home, left their morals back in the Atlantic and lived by the slogan "no conscience east of the Cape." The delights of Hawaii were just too tempting for most.

Two Worlds Tragically Collide

The 1820s were a time of confusion and soul-searching for the Hawaiians. When Kamehameha II died the kingdom passed to Kauikeaouli (Kamehameha III), who made his lifelong residence in Lahaina. The young king was only nine years old when the title passed to him, but his power was secure because Ka'ahumanu was still a vibrant *kuhina nui*. The young prince, more so than any other, was raised in the cultural confusion of the times. His childhood was spent during the very cusp of the change from old ways to new, and he was often pulled in two directions by vastly differing beliefs. Since he was royal born, he was bound by age-old Hawaiian tradition to mate and produce an heir with the highest-ranking *ali'i* in the kingdom. This mate happened to be his younger sister, the Princess Nahi'ena'ena. To the old Hawaiian advisors, this arrangement was perfectly acceptable and encouraged. To the increasingly influential missionaries, incest was an unimaginable abomination in the eyes of God. The problem was compounded by the fact that Kamehameha III and Nahi'ena'ena were drawn to each other and were deeply in love. The young king could not stand the mental pressure imposed by conflicting worlds. He became a teenage alcoholic too royal to be restrained by anyone in the kingdom, and his bouts of drunkenness and womanizing were both legendary and scandalous.

Meanwhile, Nahi'ena'ena was even more pressured because she was a favorite of the missionaries, baptized into the church at age 12. She

too vacillated between the old and the new. At times she was a pious Christian, at others she drank all night and took numerous lovers. As the prince and princess grew into their late teens, they became even more attached to each other and hardly made an attempt to keep their relationship from the missionaries. Whenever possible, they lived together in a grass house built for the princess by her father.

In 1832, the great Ka'ahumanu died, leaving the king on his own. In 1833, at the age of 18, Kamehameha III announced that the "regency" was over and that all the lands in Hawaii were his personally, and that he alone was the ultimate law. Almost immediately, however, he decreed that his half-sister Kina'u would be "premier," signifying that he would leave the actual running of the kingdom in her hands. Kamehameha III fell into total drunken confusion, until one night he attempted suicide. After this episode he seemed to straighten up a bit and mostly kept a low profile. In 1836, Princess Nahi'ena'ena was convinced by the missionaries to take a husband. She married Leleiohoku, a chief from the Big Island, but continued to sleep with her brother. It is uncertain who fathered the child, but Nahi'ena'ena gave birth to a baby boy in September 1836. The young prince survived for only a few hours, and Nahi'ena'ena never recovered from the physical ordeal. She died in December 1836 and was laid to rest in the mausoleum next to her mother, Keopuolani, on the royal island in Mokuhina Pond in Lahaina. After the death of his sister, Kamehameha III became a sober and righteous ruler. Often seen paying his respects at the royal mausoleum, he ruled longer than any other king, until his death in 1854.

The Missionaries Prevail

In 1823, the first mission was established in Lahaina, Maui, under the pastorate of Reverend Richards and his wife. Within a few years, many of the notable *ali'i* had been, at least in appearance, converted to Christianity. By 1828 the cornerstones for Waine'e Church, the first stone church on the island, were laid just behind the palace of Kamehameha III. The struggle between missionaries and whalers centered on public drunkenness and the servicing of sailors by native women. The normally God-fearing whalers had signed on for perilous duty that lasted up to three years, and when they anchored in Lahaina they demanded their pleasure. The missionaries were instrumental in placing a curfew on sailors and prohibiting native women from boarding ships, which had become customary. These measures certainly did not stop the liaisons between sailor and *wahine,* but they did impose a modicum of social sanction and tolled the end of the wide-open days. The sailors were outraged; in 1825 the crew from the *Daniel* attacked the home of the meddler, Reverend Richards. A year later a similar incident occurred. In 1827, confined and lonely sailors from the whaler *John Palmer* fired their cannons at Reverend Richards' newly built home.

Slowly the tensions eased, and by 1836 many sailors were regulars at the Seamen's Chapel adjacent to the Baldwin home. Unfortunately, even the missionaries couldn't stop the pesky mosquito from entering the islands through the port of Lahaina. The mosquitoes arrived from Mexico in 1826 aboard the merchant ship *Wellington.* They were inadvertently carried as larvae in the water barrels and democratically pestered everyone in the islands from that day forward, regardless of race, religion, or creed.

Foreign Influence

By the 1840s Honolulu was becoming the center of commerce in the islands; when Kamehameha III moved the royal court there from Lahaina, the ascendant fate of the new capital was guaranteed. In 1843, Lord Paulet, commander of the warship *Carysfort,* forced Kamehameha III to sign a treaty ceding Hawaii to the British. London, however, repudiated this act, and Hawaii's independence was restored within a few months when Queen Victoria sent Admiral Thomas as her personal agent of good intentions. The king memorialized the turn of events by a speech in which he uttered the phrase, *"Ua mau ke e'a o ka 'aina i ka pono"*

("The life of the land is preserved in righteousness"), now Hawaii's motto. The French used similar bullying tactics to force an unfavorable treaty on the Hawaiians in 1839; as part of these heavy-handed negotiations they exacted a payment of $20,000 and the right of Catholics to enjoy religious freedom in the islands. In 1842 the United States recognized and guaranteed Hawaii's independence without a formal treaty, and by 1860 over 80 percent of the islands' trade was with the United States.

The Great Mahele

In 1840, Kamehameha III ended his autocratic rule and instituted a constitutional monarchy. This brought about the Hawaiian Bill of Rights, but the most far-reaching change was the transition to private ownership of land. Formerly, all land belonged to the ruling chief, who gave wedge-shaped parcels called *ahupua'a* to lesser chiefs to be worked for him. The commoners did all the real labor, their produce heavily taxed by the *ali'i*. The fortunes of war, the death of a chief, or the mere whim of a superior could force a commoner off the land. The Hawaiians, however, could not think in terms of "owning" land. No one could *possess* land; one could only *use* land; its ownership was a strange, foreign concept. (As a result, naive Hawaiians gave up their lands for a song to unscrupulous traders, which remains a basic and unrectified problem to this day.) In 1847 Kamehameha III and his advisors separated the lands of Hawaii into three groupings: crown land (belonging to the king), government land (belonging to the chiefs), and the people's land (the largest parcels). In 1848, 245 *ali'i* entered their land claims in the *Mahele Book,* assuring them ownership. In 1850 the commoners were given title in fee simple to the lands they cultivated and lived on as tenants, not including house lots in towns. Commoners without land could buy small *kuleana* (farms) from the government at 50 cents per acre. In 1850, foreigners were also allowed to purchase land in fee simple, and the ownership of Hawaii from that day forward slipped steadily from the hands of its indigenous people.

KING SUGAR

It's hard to say just where the sugar industry began in Hawaii. The Koloa Sugar Plantation on the southern coast of Kaua'i successfully refined sugar in 1835. Others tried, and one success was at Hana, Maui, in 1849. A whaler named George Wilfong hauled four blubber pots ashore and set them up on a rocky hill in the middle of 60 acres he had planted in sugar. A team of oxen turned "crushing rollers" and the cane juice flowed down an open trough into the pots, under which an attending native kept a roaring fire burning. Wilfong's methods of refining were crude but the resulting high-quality sugar turned a neat profit in Lahaina. The main problem was labor. The Hawaiians, who made excellent whalers, were basically indentured workers. They became extremely disillusioned with their contracts, which could last up to 10 years. Most of their wages were eaten up by manufactured commodities sold at the company store, and it didn't take long for them to realize that they were little more than slaves. At every opportunity they either left the area or just refused to work.

Imported Labor

The **Masters and Servants Act of 1850,** which allowed importation of laborers under the contract system, ostensibly guaranteed an endless supply of cheap labor for the plantations. Chinese laborers were imported but were too enterprising to remain in the fields for a meager $3 per month. They left as soon as opportunity permitted and went into business as small merchants and retailers. In the meantime, Wilfong had sold out, releasing most of the Hawaiians previously held under contract, and his plantation fell into disuse. In 1860 two Danish brothers, August and Oscar Unna, bought land at Hana to raise sugar. They solved the labor problem by importing Japanese laborers, who were extremely hardworking and easily managed. The workday lasted 10 hours, six days a week, for a salary of $20 per month plus housing and medical care. Plantation life was very structured, with stringent rules governing even bedtimes and lights out. A worker was fined for being late or for smoking on the job. The workers had great difficulty functioning under these circumstances, and improvements in benefits and housing were slowly gained.

Sugar Grows

The demand for "Sandwich Island Sugar" grew as California became populated during the gold rush, and increased dramatically when the American Civil War demanded a constant supply. The only sugar plantations on the Mainland were small plots confined to the Confederate states, whose products would hardly be bought by the Union and whose fields, later in the war, were destroyed. By the 1870s it was clear to the planters, still mainly New Englanders, that the United States was their market; they tried often to gain closer ties and favorable tariffs. The Americans also planted rumors that the British were interested in annexing Hawaii; this put pressure on the U.S. Congress to pass the long-desired **Reciprocity Act,** which would exempt sugar from import duty. It finally passed in 1875, in exchange for U.S. long-range rights to the strategic naval port of Pearl Harbor, among other concessions. These agreements gave increased political power to a small group of American planters whose outlooks were similar to those of the post–Civil War South, where a few powerful whites were the virtual masters of a multitude of dark-skinned laborers. Sugar was now big business and the Hana district alone exported almost 3,000 tons per year. All of Hawaii would have to reckon with the "sugar barons."

Changing Society

The sugar plantation system changed life in Hawaii physically, spiritually, politically, and economically. Now boatloads of workers came not only from Japan but from Portugal, Germany, and even Russia. The white-skinned workers were most often the field foremen *(luna)*. With the immigrants came new religions, new animals and plants, unique cuisines, and a plantation language known as pidgin, or better yet, *da' kine*. Many Asians and, to a lesser extent, the other groups—including the white plantation owners—intermarried with Hawaiians. A new class of people properly termed "cosmopolitan" but more familiarly and aptly known as "locals" was emerging. These were the people of multiple race backgrounds who couldn't exactly say *what* they were but it was clear to all just *who* they were. The plantation owners became the new "chiefs" of Hawaii who could carve up the land and dispense favors. The Hawaiian monarchy was soon eliminated.

A KINGDOM PASSES
The Beginning of the End

Like the Hawaiian people themselves, the Kamehameha dynasty in the mid-1800s was dying from within. King Kamehameha IV (Alexander Liholiho) ruled 1854–1863; his only child died in 1862. He was succeeded by his older brother Kamehameha V (Lot Kamehameha), who ruled until 1872. With his passing, the Kamehameha line ended. William Lunalilo, elected king in 1873 by popular vote, was of royal, but not Kamehameha, lineage. He died after only a year

Queen Lili'uokalani

in office, and, being a bachelor, left no heirs. He was succeeded by David Kalakaua, known far and wide as the "Merrie Monarch," who made a world tour and was well received wherever he went. He built 'Iolani Palace in Honolulu. He was personally in favor of closer ties with the United States and helped push through the Reciprocity Act. Kalakaua died in 1891 and was replaced by his sister Lydia Lili'uokalani, last of the Hawaiian monarchs.

The Revolution

When Lili'uokalani took office in 1891, the native population was at a low of 40,000, and she felt that the United States had too much influence over her homeland. She was known to personally favor the English over Americans. She attempted to replace the liberal constitution of 1887 (adopted by her pro-American brother) with an autocratic mandate in which she would have had much more political and economic control of the islands. When the McKinley Tariff of 1890 brought a decline in sugar profits, she made no attempt to improve the situation. Thus, the planters saw her as a political obstacle to their economic growth; most of Hawaii's American planters and merchants were in favor of a rebellion. She would have to go! A central spokesperson and firebrand was Lorrin Thurston, a Honolulu publisher who, with a central core of about 30 men, challenged the Hawaiian monarchy. Although Lili'uokalani rallied some support and had a small military potential in her personal guard, the coup was ridiculously easy—it took only one casualty. Captain John Good shot a Hawaiian policeman in the arm and that did it. Naturally, the conspirators could not have succeeded without some solid assurances from a secret contingent in the U.S. Congress as well as outgoing president Benjamin Harrison, who favored Hawaii's annexation. Marines from the *Boston* went ashore to "protect American lives," and on January 17, 1893, the Hawaiian monarchy came to an end.

The provisional government was headed by Sanford B. Dole, who became president of the Hawaiian Republic. Lili'uokalani surrendered not

History 39

INTRODUCTION

to the conspirators but to U.S. ambassador John Stevens. She believed that the U.S. government, which had assured her of Hawaiian independence, would be outraged by the overthrow and would come to her aid. Incoming president Grover Cleveland *was* outraged, and Hawaii wasn't immediately annexed as expected. When queried about what she would do with the conspirators if she were reinstated, Lili'uokalani said that they would be hung as traitors. The racist press of the times, which portrayed the Hawaiians as half-civilized, bloodthirsty heathens, publicized this widely. Since the conspirators were the leading citizens of the land, the queen's words proved untimely. In January 1895 a small, ill-fated counterrevolution headed by Lili'uokalani failed, and she was placed under house arrest in 'Iolani Palace. Officials of the republic insisted that she use her married name (Mrs. John Dominis) to sign the documents forcing her to abdicate her throne. She was also forced to swear allegiance to the new republic. Lili'uokalani went on to write *Hawaii's Story* and the lyric ballad "Aloha O'e." She never forgave the conspirators and remained "queen" to the Hawaiians until her death in 1917.

Annexation

The overwhelming majority of Hawaiians opposed annexation and desired to restore the monarchy. But they were prevented from voting by the new republic because they couldn't meet the imposed property and income qualifications—a transparent ruse by the planters to control the election. Most *haole* were racist and believed that the "common people" could not be entrusted with the vote because they were childish and incapable of ruling themselves. The fact that the Hawaiians had existed quite well for 1,000 years before the white man even reached Hawaii was never considered. The Philippine theater of the Spanish-American War also prompted annexation. One of the strongest proponents was Alfred Mahon, a brilliant naval strategist who, with support from Theodore Roosevelt, argued that the U.S. military must have Hawaii in order to be a viable force in the Pacific. In addition, Japan, victorious in its recent war with China, protested the American intention to annex, and in so doing prompted even moderates to support annexation for fear that the Japanese themselves coveted the prize. On July 7, 1898, President McKinley signed the annexation agreement, and this "tropical" fruit" was finally put into America's basket.

MODERN TIMES

Hawaii entered the 20th century totally transformed from what it had been. The old Hawaiian language, religion, culture, and leadership were all gone; Western dress, values, education, and recreation were the norm. Native Hawaiians were now unseen citizens who lived in dwindling numbers in remote areas. The plantations, new centers of social order, had a strong Asian flavor; more than 75 percent of their workforce was Asian. There was a small white middle class, an all-powerful white elite, and a single political party ruled by that elite. Education, however, was always highly prized, and by the turn of the 20th century all racial groups were encouraged to attend school. By 1900, almost 90 percent of Hawaiians were literate (far above the national norm), and schooling was mandatory for all children ages six to 15. Intermarriage was accepted, and there was a mixing of the races like nowhere else on earth. The military became increasingly important to Hawaii. It brought in money and jobs, dominating the island economy. The Japanese attack on Pearl Harbor, which began U.S. involvement in World War II, bound Hawaii to America forever. Once the islands had been baptized by blood, the average Mainlander felt that Hawaii was American soil. A movement among Hawaiians to become part of the Union began to grow. They wanted a real voice in Washington, not merely a voteless delegate as provided under their territory status. Hawaii became the 50th state in 1959, and the jumbo-jet revolution of the 1960s made it easily accessible to growing numbers of tourists from all over the world.

Military History

A few military strategists realized the importance of Hawaii early in the 19th century, but most didn't recognize the advantages until the Spanish-American War. It was clearly an unsinkable ship in the middle of the Pacific from which the United States could launch military operations. Troops were stationed at Camp McKinley, at the foot of Diamond Head, the main military compound until it became obsolete in 1907. Pearl Harbor was first surveyed in 1872 by General Schofield. Later, a military base named in his honor, Schofield Barracks, was a main military post in central Oʻahu. It first housed the U.S. Fifth Cavalry in 1909 and was heavily bombed by the Japanese at the outset of World War II. Pearl Harbor, first dredged in 1908, was officially opened on December 11, 1911. The first warship to enter was the cruiser *California*. Ever since, the military has been a mainstay of island economy. Unfortunately, there has been long-standing bad blood between locals and military personnel. Each group has tended to look down upon the other.

Pearl Harbor Attack

On the morning of December 7, 1941, the Japanese carrier *Akagi,* flying the battle flag of the famed Admiral Togo of the Russo-Japanese War, received and broadcast over its PA system island music from Honolulu station KGMB. Deep in the bowels of the ship a radio man listened for a much different message, coming thousands of miles from the Japanese mainland. When the ironically poetic message "east wind rain" was received, the attack was launched. At the end of the day, 2,325 U.S. servicemen and 57 civilians were dead; 188 planes were destroyed; 18 major warships were sunk or heavily damaged; and the United States was in the war. Japanese casualties were ludicrously light. The ignited conflict would rage for four years until Japan, through the bombings at Nagasaki and Hiroshima, was vaporized into total submission. At the end of hostilities, Hawaii would never again be considered separate from America.

Statehood

A number of economic and political reasons explain why the ruling elite of Hawaii desired statehood, but put simply, the vast majority of people who lived there, especially after World War II, considered themselves Americans. The first serious mention of making "The Sandwich Islands" a state was in the 1850s under President Franklin Pierce, but it wasn't taken seriously until the monarchy was overthrown in the 1890s. For the next 50 years statehood proposals were made repeatedly to Congress, but there was stiff opposition, especially from the southern states. With Hawaii a territory, an import quota system beneficial to Mainland producers could be enacted on produce, especially sugar. Also, there was prejudice against creating a state in a place where the majority of the populace was not white.

During World War II, Hawaii was placed under martial law, but no serious attempt to intern the Japanese population was made, as in California. There were simply too many Japanese, and many went on to gain the respect of the American people with their outstanding fighting record during the war. Hawaii's own 100th Battalion became the famous 442nd Regimental Combat Team, which gained notoriety by saving the Lost Texas Battalion during the Battle of the Bulge and went on to be *the* most decorated battalion in all of World War II. When these GIs returned home, no one was going to tell them that they were not loyal Americans. Many of these AJAs (Americans of Japanese Ancestry) took advantage of the GI Bill and received higher educations. They were from the common people, not the elite, and they rallied grassroots support for statehood. When the vote finally occurred, approximately 132,900 voted in favor of statehood, with only 7,800 votes against. Congress passed the Hawaii State Bill on March 12, 1959, and on August 21, 1959, President Eisenhower announced that Hawaii was officially the 50th state.

Government

The major difference between the government of the state of Hawaii and those of other states is that it's "streamlined," and in theory more efficient. There are only two levels of government: the state and the county. With no town or city governments to deal with, considerable bureaucracy is eliminated. Hawaii, in anticipation of becoming a state, drafted a constitution in 1950 and was ready to go when statehood came. Politics and government are taken seriously in the Aloha State, which consistently turns in the best national voting record per capita. For example, in the first state elections, 173,000 of 180,000 registered voters voted—a whopping 94 percent of the electorate. In the election to ratify statehood, hardly a ballot went uncast, with 95 percent of the voters opting for statehood. The bill carried in every island of Hawaii except Ni'ihau, where most of the people (total population 250 or so) were of relatively pure Hawaiian blood. After Hawaii officially became a state on August 21, 1959, Honolulu became the state capital.

Breaking a 40-year Democratic hold on power in the state and becoming the first female to hold the position, former Maui mayor and Republican Linda Lingle was elected as governor in 2002.

County of Hawai'i

The current mayor of the county of Hawai'i is Harry Kim, Democrat. The mayor is assisted by an elected county council consisting of nine members, one from each council district around the island. Hilo is the county seat.

Of the 25 State Senatorial Districts, Hawai'i County is represented by three. The First District takes in the whole northern section of the island: the Hamakua Coast, Mauna Kea, North and South Kohala, and part of North Kona. The Second District is mainly Hilo and its outlying area. The Third comprises Puna, Ka'u, South Kona, and most of North Kona. Hawai'i County has six of 51 seats in the State House of Representatives. For Internet information on Hawai'i County see www.hawaii-county.com.

Economy

Hawaii's mid-Pacific location makes it perfect for two prime sources of income: tourism and the military. Tourists come in anticipation of endless golden days on soothing beaches, while the military is provided with the strategic position of an unsinkable battleship. Each economic sector nets Hawaii about $4 billion annually, money that should keep flowing smoothly and even increase in the foreseeable future. These revenues remain mostly aloof from the normal ups and downs of the Mainland U.S. economy. Also contributing to the state revenue are manufacturing, construction, and agriculture (mainly sugar and pineapples). As long as the sun shines and the balance of global power requires a military presence, the economic stability of Hawaii is guaranteed.

Tourism

The first hotel in Hawai'i was the **Volcano**

House, which overlooked Kilauea Crater and was built in 1866. Today, over 3,000 island residents are directly employed by the hotel industry, and many more indirectly serve the tourists. Of the slightly more than 9,500 hotel and condo rooms, the greatest concentration is in Kona. Kona hotels have the lowest occupancy rate in the state, rarely rising above 60 percent. The occupancy rates for Kohala and Hilo are only slightly higher. Hawai'i receives about 1.1 million tourists annually, about 21,000 on any given day. Of the major islands, it ranks third in number of annual visitors, following O'ahu and Maui.

Hilo and the east side traditionally were where tourists went when they visited the Big Island. By and large, that's where the people were and that's where the facilities were built. Few people ventured out beyond this enclave, and traveling was not so easy. There was a hotel in Kailua, but

BIG ISLAND LAND OWNERSHIP

Hawai'i
2,578,073 Acres

STATE

FEDERAL

HAWAIIAN HOMELANDS

SMALL PRIVATE

LARGE PRIVATE

fewer people lived there and the infrastructure was not as sophisticated. In the mid-'60s, luxury resorts started to be built on the sunny Kohala and Kona Coasts, and condominiums followed soon after. Tourists loved the sun and began to flock to the west side. Slowly it built up, then rapidly, and now the Kona-Kohala Coast has far eclipsed the Hilo side as the preferred vacation spot on this island, with nearly three times as many visitors as the wet side.

Agriculture

The Big Island's economy is the state's most agriculturally based. Over 5,000 farmhands, horticultural workers, and *paniolo* work the land to produce about one-third of the state's vegetables and melons, over 75 percent of the total fruit production, 95 percent of the papaya, 75 percent of the bananas, 95 percent of the avocados, and 50 percent of the guavas. Much of the state's taro is also produced on the Big Island, principally in the Waipi'o Valley and along the

Hamakua Coast, and ginger production has become a major economic factor with more than six million pounds grown annually. The Big Island also produces some 50 million pounds of macadamia nuts yearly, about 90 percent of the total amount grown in the state. While that's still a respectable number, it's less than half the world's total. Hawai'i used to have the only commercial coffee plantations in the country, but now coffee is grown on all the major Hawaiian islands. Due to the increased interest in gourmet Kona coffee, the coffee industry's share in the economy of the island is increasing, and the Big Island grows about three million pounds of coffee every year. More than 350 horticultural farms produce the largest number of orchids and anthuriums in the state, leaving the Big Island awash in color and fragrance. Other exotic flowers and foliage are also a growing concern. In the hills, entrepreneurs raise *pakalolo* (marijuana), which has become the state's most productive although illicit cash crop.

Hawai'i used to be the state's largest sugar grower, with over 150,000 acres in cane. These commercial fields produced four million tons of refined sugar, 40 percent of the state's output. The majority of sugar land was along the Hamakua Coast, long known for its abundant water supply. At one time, the cane was even transported to the mills by water flumes. Other large pockets of cane fields were found on the southern part of the island in Ka'u and Puna, as well as at the northern tip in North Kohala. With the closing of the last mill in 1996, sugar is no longer grown commercially on the island. Still, small entrepreneurial farms grow it on greatly reduced acreage. The big cane trucks have ceased to roll, and the few remaining smokestacks stand in silent testimony to a bygone era.

The upland Kona district is a splendid area for raising coffee; it gives the beans a beautiful tan. Lying in Mauna Loa's rain shadow, the district gets dewy mornings followed by sunshine and an afternoon cloud shadow. Kona coffee has long been accepted as gourmet quality and is sold in the better restaurants throughout Hawaii and in fine coffee shops around the world. It's a dark, full-bodied coffee with a rich aroma. Approximately 650 small farms produce nearly $15 million a year in coffee revenue. Few, however, make it a full-time business. The production of Kona coffee makes up only about one-tenth of 1 percent of the coffee grown around the world. The rare bean is often blended with other varietals. When sold unblended it is quite expensive.

Hawai'i's cattle ranches produce over five million pounds of beef per year, 50 percent of the state's total. More than 450 independent ranches are located on the island, with total acreage of over 650,000 acres, but they are dwarfed both in size and production by the massive Parker Ranch, which alone has 225,000 acres and is about two-thirds the size of O'ahu. While beef is the largest player in the livestock market, pork, dairy products, eggs, poultry, sheep, goats, and bees also are components, and together constitute perhaps half of the island's livestock revenues.

Military

On average, about 60 military personnel are stationed on the Big Island at any one time, with about the same number of dependents. Most of these people are attached to the enormous Pohakuloa Military Reserve in the center of the island; a lesser number are at a few minor installations around Hilo, Kailua, and at Kilauea Volcano.

Land Ownership

Hawai'i County comprises over 2.5 million acres. Of this total, the state controls about 800,000 acres, mostly forest preserves and undeveloped land; the federal government has large acreage in the Hawaii Volcanoes National Park, Pohakuloa Military Training Area, and Hakalau Forest National Wildlife Refuge. Large landowners control most of the rest except for about 116,000 acres of Hawaiian Homelands. The major large landowners are the Bishop Estate, Parker Ranch, and the Samuel Damon Estate.

M

People

Nowhere else on earth can you find such a kaleidoscopic mixture of people as in Hawaii. Every major race is accounted for, and over 50 ethnic groups are represented throughout the islands, making Hawaii the most racially integrated state in the country. Its population of 1.2 million includes some 80,000 permanently stationed military personnel and their dependents. Until the year 2000, when California's white population fell below 50 percent, Hawaii was the only U.S. state where whites were not the majority. About 56 percent of Hawaiian residents were born there, 26 percent were born on the U.S. Mainland, and 18 percent are foreign-born.

The population has grown steadily in recent times, but it fluctuated wildly in times past. In 1876, it reached its lowest ebb, with only 55,000 permanent residents. This was the era of large sugar plantations; their constant demand for labor was the primary cause for importing various peoples from around the world and led to Hawaii's racial mix. World War II saw the population swell from 400,000 to 900,000. Most of the 500,000 military personnel left at war's end, but many returned to settle after getting a taste of island living.

Hawai'i Population Figures

With 149,000, the Big Island has the second-largest island population in Hawaii, just over 12 percent of the state's total. However, it has the least population density of the main islands, with about 37 people per square mile; two-thirds urban, one-third rural. The Hilo area has the largest population with 47,000 residents, followed by North and South Kona with about 37,000, Puna at 31,000, South Kohala at 13,000, and the Hamakua Coast, North Kohala, and Ka'u each between 6,000 and 8,000. Within the last dozen years, the areas of Puna and South Kohala have experienced the greatest increases in population. There is no ethnic majority on the Big Island; population numbers include 32 percent Caucasian, 28 percent mixed, 27 percent Asian, 11 percent Hawaiian, and 2 percent other.

BIG ISLAND ETHNICITY

Caucasian:	32 percent
Mixed:	28 percent
Asian:	27 percent
Hawaiian:	11 percent
Other:	2 percent

THE HAWAIIANS

The study of the native Hawaiians is ultimately a study in tragedy because it ends in their near demise as a viable people. When Captain Cook first sighted Hawaii in 1778, there were an estimated 300,000 natives living in relative harmony with their ecological surroundings; within 100 years a scant 50,000 demoralized and dejected Hawaiians existed almost as wards of the state. Today, although more than 240,000 people claim varying degrees of Hawaiian blood, experts say that fewer than 1,000 are pure Hawaiian, and this is stretching it.

It's easy to see why people of Hawaiian lineage can be bitter over what they have lost, being strangers in their own land now, much like Native Americans. The overwhelming majority of "Hawaiians" are of mixed heritage, and the wisest take the best from all worlds. From the Hawaiian side comes simplicity, love of the land, and acceptance of people. It is the Hawaiian legacy of *aloha* that remains immortal and adds that special elusive quality that *is* Hawaii.

Polynesian Roots

The Polynesians' original stock is muddled and remains an anthropological mystery, but it's believed that they were nomadic wanderers who migrated from both the Indian subcontinent and Southeast Asia through Indonesia, where they learned to sail and navigate on protected waterways. As they migrated they honed their sailing skills until they could take on the Pacific, and as they moved, they absorbed people from other cultures and races until they had coalesced into what we now know as Polynesians.

Abraham Fornander, still considered a major authority on the subject, wrote in his 1885 *Account of the Polynesian Race* that he believed the Polynesians started as a white (Aryan) race that was heavily influenced by contact with the Cushite, Chaldeo-Arabian civilization. He estimated their arrival in Hawaii at A.D. 600, based on Hawaiian genealogical chants. Modern science seems to bear this date out, although it remains skeptical about his other surmises. According to others, the intrepid Polynesians who actually settled Hawaii are believed to have come from the Marquesas Islands, 1,000 miles southeast of Hawaii. The Marquesans were cannibals and known for their tenacity and strength, attributes that would serve them well.

The Caste System

Hawaiian society was divided into rankings by a strict caste system determined by birth, and from which there was no chance of escaping. The highest rank was the *ali'i*, the chiefs and royalty. The impeccable genealogies of the *ali'i* were traced back to the gods themselves, and the chants *(mo'o ali'i)* were memorized and sung by professionals (called *ku'auhau*) who were themselves *ali'i*. Rank passed from both father and mother, and custom dictated that the first mating of an *ali'i* be with a person of equal status.

A *kahuna* was a highly skilled person whose advice was sought before any major project was undertaken, such as building a house, hollowing a canoe log, or even offering a prayer. The *mo'o kahuna* were the priests of Ku and Lono, and they were in charge of praying and following rituals. They were very powerful *ali'i* and kept strict secrets and laws concerning their various functions.

Besides this priesthood of *kahuna*, there were other *kahuna* who were not *ali'i* but commoners. The two most important were the healers *(kahuna lapa'au)* and the black magicians *(kahuna 'ana'ana)*, who could pray a person to death. The *kahuna lapa'au* had a marvelous pharmacopoeia of herbs and spices that could cure over 230 diseases common to the Hawaiians. The *kahuna 'ana'ana* could be hired to cast a love spell over a person or

cause his or her untimely death. They seldom had to send out a reminder for payment!

The common people were called the *maka'ainana*, "the people of land"—farmers, artisans, and fishermen. The land they lived on was owned by the *ali'i*, but they were not bound to it. If the local *ali'i* was cruel or unfair, the *maka'ainana* had the right to leave and reside on another's lands. The *maka'ainana* mostly loved their local *ali'i* much like a child loves a parent, and the feeling was reciprocal. *Maka'ainana* who lived close to the *ali'i* and could be counted on as warriors in times of trouble were called *kanaka no lua kaua*, "a man for the heat of battle." They were treated with greater favor than those who lived in the backcountry, *kanaka no hi'i kua*, whose lesser standing opened them up to discrimination and cruelty. All *maka'ainana* formed extended families called *'ohana* who usually lived on the same section of land, called *ahupua'a*. Those farmers who lived inland would barter their produce with the fishermen who lived on the shore, and thus all shared equally in the bounty of land and sea.

A special group called *kauwa* was a landless, untouchable caste confined to living on reservations. Their origins were obviously Polynesian, but they appeared to be descendants of castaways who had survived and become perhaps the aboriginals of Hawaii before the main migrations. It was *kapu* for anyone to go onto *kauwa* lands, and doing so meant instant death. If a human sacrifice was needed, the *kahuna* would simply summon a *kauwa*, who had no recourse but to mutely comply. To this day, to call someone *kauwa*, which now supposedly means only servant, is still considered a fight-provoking insult.

Kapu and Day-to-Day Life

Occasionally there were horrible wars, but mostly the people lived quiet and ordered lives based on a strict caste society and the *kapu* system. Famine was known but only on a regional level, and the population was kept in check by birth control, crude abortions, and the distasteful practice of infanticide, especially of baby girls. The Hawaiians were absolutely loving and nurturing parents under most circumstances and would even take in a *hanai* (adopted child or oldster), a lovely practice that lingers to this day.

A strict division of labor existed among men and women. Men were the only ones permitted to have anything to do with taro: this foodstuff was so sacred that there were a greater number of *kapu* concerning taro than concerning man himself. Men pounded poi and served it to the women. Men also were the fishermen and the builders of houses, canoes, irrigation ditches, and walls. Women tended to other gardens and shoreline fishing and were responsible for making tapa cloth. The entire family lived in the common house called the *hale noa.*

Certain things were *kapu* between the sexes. Primarily, women could not enter the *mua* (man's eating house), nor could they eat with men. Certain foods, such as pork, coconut, red fish, and bananas, were forbidden to women, and it was *kapu* for a man to have intercourse before going fishing, engaging in battle, or attending a religious ceremony. Young boys lived with the women until they underwent a circumcision rite called *pule ipu.* After this was performed, they were required to keep the *kapu* of men. A true Hawaiian settlement required a minimum of five huts: the men's eating hut; women's menstruation hut; women's eating hut; communal sleeping hut; and prayer hut. Without these five separate structures, Hawaiian "society" could not happen, since the *i'a kapu* (forbidden eating between men and women) could not be observed.

Ali'i could also declare a *kapu* and often did so. Certain lands or fishing areas were temporarily made *kapu* so that they could revitalize. Even today, it is *kapu* for anyone to remove all the *'opihi* (a type of limpet) from a rock. The great King Kamehameha I even placed a *kapu* on the body of his notoriously unfaithful child bride, Ka'ahumanu. It didn't work! The greatest *kapu* (*kapu moe*) was afforded to the highest ranking *ali'i:* anyone coming into their presence had to prostrate themselves. Lesser ranking *ali'i* were afforded the *kapu noho:* lessers had to sit or kneel in their presence. Commoners could not let their shadows fall upon an *ali'i* or enter an *ali'i's* house except through a special door. Breaking a *kapu* meant immediate death.

The Causes of Decline

Less than 100 years after Captain Cook's arrival, King Kalakaua found himself with only 48,000 Hawaiian subjects. Wherever the king went, he would beseech his people, *"Ho'oulu lahui,"* "Increase the race," but it was already too late. It was as if nature herself had turned her back on these once-proud people. Many of their marriages were barren, and in 1874, when only 1,400 children were born, a full 75 percent died in infancy. The Hawaiians could do nothing but watch as their race faded from existence.

The ecological system of Hawaii has always been exceptionally fragile and this included its people. When the first whites arrived they found a great people who were large, strong, and virile. But when it came to fighting off the most minor diseases, the Hawaiians proved as delicate as hothouse flowers. To exacerbate the situation, the Hawaiians were totally uninhibited toward sexual intercourse between willing partners, and they engaged in it openly and with abandon. Unfortunately, the sailors who arrived were full of syphilis and gonorrhea. The Hawaiian women brought these diseases home and, given the nature of Hawaiian society at the time, the diseases spread like wildfire. By the time the missionaries came in 1820 and helped to halt the unbridled fornication, they estimated the native population at only 140,000—less than half of what it had been—only 40 years after initial contact! In the next 50 years measles, mumps, influenza, and tuberculosis further ravaged the people. Furthermore, Hawaiian men were excellent sailors, and it's estimated that during the whaling years at least 25 percent of all able-bodied Hawaiian men sailed away, never to return.

But the coup de grace that really ended the Hawaiian race as such was that racial newcomers to the islands were attracted to the Hawaiians and the Hawaiians were in turn attracted to them. With so many interracial marriages, the Hawaiians literally bred themselves out of existence. By 1910, there were still twice as many full-blooded Hawaiians as mixed-bloods, but by 1940 mixed-blooded Hawaiians were the fastest-growing group, and full-blooded the fastest declining.

Hawaiians Today

Many of the Hawaiians who moved to the cities became more and more disenfranchised. Their folk society stressed openness and a giving nature but downplayed the individual and the ownership of private property. These cultural traits made them easy targets for users and schemers until they finally became either apathetic or angry. Most surveys reveal that although Hawaiians number only 13 percent of the population, they account for almost 50 percent of the financially destitute families and also about half of all arrests and illegitimate births. Ni'ihau, a privately owned island, is home to about 160 pure-blooded Hawaiians, representing the largest concentration of them, per capita, in the islands. The Robinson family, which owns the island, restricts visitors to invited guests only.

The second-largest concentration is on Moloka'i, where 2,700 Hawaiians, living mostly on 40-acre *kuleana* of Hawaiian Home Lands, make up 40 percent of that island's population. The majority of mixed-blooded Hawaiians, 240,000 or so, live on O'ahu, where they are particularly strong in the hotel and entertainment fields. People of Hawaiian extraction are still a delight to meet, and anyone so lucky as to be befriended by one long regards this friendship as the highlight of his or her travels. The Hawaiians have always given their *aloha* freely to all the peoples of the world, and it is we who must acknowledge this precious gift.

THE CHINESE

Next to Yankees from New England, the Chinese are the oldest migrant group in Hawaii, and their influence has far outshone their meager numbers. They brought to Hawaii, along with their individuality, Confucianism, Taoism, and Buddhism, although many have long since become Christians. The Chinese population, at 56,000, makes up only 5 percent of the state's total, and the vast majority reside on O'ahu. As an ethnic group they account for the least amount of crime, the highest per capita income, and a disproportionate number of professionals.

The First Chinese

No one knows his name, but an unknown Chinese immigrant is credited with being the first person in Hawaii to refine sugar. This Asian wanderer tried his hand at crude refining on Lana'i in 1802. Fifty years later the sugar plantations desperately needed workers, and the first Chinese brought to Hawaii under the newly passed Masters and Servants Act were 195 coolies from Amoy, who arrived in 1852. These conscripts were contracted for three to five years and given $3 per month plus room and board. This was for 12 hours a day, six days a week, and even in 1852 these wages were the pits. The Chinese almost always left the plantations the minute their contracts expired. They went into business for themselves and promptly monopolized the restaurant and small-shop trades.

The Chinese Niche

Although many people in Hawaii considered all Chinese ethnically the same, they were actually quite different. The majority came from Guangdong Province in southern China. They were two distinct ethnic groups: the Punti made up 75 percent of the immigrants, and the Hakka made up the remainder. In China, they remained separate from each other, never mixing; in Hawaii, they mixed out of necessity. For one thing, hardly any Chinese women came over at first, and the ones who followed were at a premium and gladly accepted as wives, regardless of ethnic background. The Chinese were also one of the first groups who willingly intermarried with the Hawaiians, from whom they gained a reputation for being exceptionally caring spouses.

The Chinese accepted the social order and kept a low profile. For example, during the turbulent labor movements of the 1930s and 1940s in Hawaii, the Chinese community produced not one labor leader, radical intellectual, or left-wing politician. When Hawaii became a state, one of the two senators elected was Hiram Fong, a racially mixed Chinese. Since statehood, the Chinese community has carried on business as usual as they continue to rise both economically and socially.

THE JAPANESE

Most scholars believe that (inevitably) a few Japanese castaways floated to Hawaii long before Captain Cook arrived, and they might have introduced the iron with which the islanders seemed to be familiar before white explorers arrived. The first official arrivals from Japan were ambassadors sent by the Japanese shogun to negotiate in Washington; they stopped en route at Honolulu in March 1860. But it was as plantation workers that the Japanese were brought en masse to the islands. A small group arrived in 1868, and mass migration started in 1885.

In 1886, because of famine, the Japanese government allowed farmers mainly from southern Honshu, Kyushu, and Okinawa to emigrate. Among these were members of Japan's little-talked-about untouchable caste, called *eta* or *burakumin* in Japan and *chorinbo* in Hawaii. They gratefully seized this opportunity to better their lot, an impossibility in Japan. The first Japanese migrants were almost all men. Between 1897 and 1908 migration was steady, with about 70 percent of the immigrants being men. Afterwards, migration slowed because of a "gentlemen's agreement," a euphemism for racism against the "yellow peril." By 1900 there were over 60,000 Japanese in the islands, constituting the largest ethnic group.

AJAs, Americans of Japanese Ancestry

Parents of most Japanese children born before World War II were *issei* (first generation), who considered themselves apart from other Americans and clung to the notion of "we Japanese." Their children, the *nisei,* or second generation, were a different matter altogether. In one generation they had become Americans, and they put into practice the high Japanese virtues of obligation, duty, and loyalty to the homeland; that homeland was now unquestionably America. After Pearl Harbor was bombed, the FBI kept close tabs on the Japanese community, and the menace of the "enemy within" prompted the decision to place Hawaii under martial law for the duration of the war. It has since been noted that not a single charge of espionage or sabotage was ever reported against the Japanese community in Hawaii during the war.

AJAs as GIs

Although Japanese had formed a battalion during World War I, they were insulted by being considered unacceptable American soldiers in World War II. Some Japanese Americans volunteered to serve in labor battalions, and because of their flawless work and loyalty, it was decided to put out a call for a few hundred volunteers to form a combat unit. Over 10,000 signed up! AJAs formed two distinguished units in World War II: the 100th Infantry Battalion and later the 442nd Regimental Combat Team. They landed in Italy at Salerno and even fought from Guadalcanal to Okinawa. They distinguished themselves by becoming *the* most decorated unit in American military history.

The AJAs Return

Many returning AJAs took advantage of the GI Bill and received college educations. The "Big Five" corporations for the first time accepted former AJA officers as executives, and the old order was changed. Many Japanese became involved with Hawaiian politics, and the first elected to Congress was Daniel Inouye, who had lost an arm fighting in World War II. Hawaii's past governor, George Ariyoshi, elected in 1974, was the country's first Japanese American to reach such a high office. Most Japanese, even as they climb the economic ladder, tend to remain Democrats.

Today, one out of every two political offices in Hawaii is held by a Japanese American. In one of those weird quirks of fate, it is now the Hawaiian Japanese who are accused by other ethnic groups of engaging in unfair political practices—nepotism and reverse discrimination. Many of these accusations against AJAs are undoubtedly motivated by jealousy, but the AJAs' record in social fairness issues is not without blemish; true to their custom of family loyalty, they do stick together.

There are now 290,000 people in Hawaii of Japanese ancestry (and another 100,000 of mixed Japanese blood), nearly one-quarter of the state's population. They are the least likely of any ethnic group in Hawaii to marry outside of their group—especially the men—and they enjoy a higher-than-average standard of living.

CAUCASIANS

White people have a distinction separating them from all other ethnic groups in Hawaii: they are lumped together as one. You can be anything from a Protestant Norwegian dockworker to a Greek Orthodox shipping tycoon, but if your skin is white, in Hawaii you're a *haole*. What's more, you could have arrived at Waikiki from Missoula, Montana, in the last 24 hours, or your *kama'aina* family can go back five generations, but again, if you're white, you're a *haole*.

The word *haole* has a floating connotation that depends upon the spirit in which it's used. It can mean everything from a derisive "honky" or "cracker" to nothing more than "white person." The exact Hawaiian meaning is clouded, but some say it meant "a man of no background," because white men couldn't chant a genealogical *koihonua* telling the Hawaiians who they were. The word eventually evolved to mean "foreign white man" and, today, simply "white person."

White History

Next to Hawaiians themselves, white people have the oldest stake in Hawaii. They've been there as settlers in earnest since the missionaries of the 1820s and were established long before any other migrant group. From the 19th century until statehood, old *haole* families owned and controlled mostly everything, and although they were generally benevolent, philanthropic, and paternalistic, they were also racist. They were established *kama'aina* families, many of whom made up the boards of the Big Five corporations or owned huge plantations and formed an elite social circle that was closed to the outside. Many managed to find mates from among close family acquaintances.

Their paternalism, which they accepted with grave responsibility, at first only extended to the Hawaiians, who saw them as replacing their own *ali'i*. Asians were considered primarily instru-

ments of production. These supremacist attitudes tended to drag on in Hawaii until quite recent times and are today responsible for the sometimes sour relations between white and non-white people in the islands. Today, all white people are resented to a certain degree because of these past acts, even though they personally were in no way involved.

White Plantation Workers

In the 1880s the white landowners looked around and felt surrounded and outnumbered by Asians, so they tried to import white people for plantation work. None of their schemes seemed to work out. Europeans were accustomed to a much higher wage scale and better living conditions than were provided on the plantations. Although only workers and not considered the equals of the ruling elite, they still were expected to act like a special class. They were treated preferentially, which meant higher wages for the same jobs performed by Asians. Some of the imported workers included: 600 Scandinavians in 1881; 1,400 Germans in 1881–1885; 400 Poles in 1897–1898; and 2,400 Russians in 1909–1912. Many proved troublesome, like the Poles and Russians, who staged strikes after only months on the job. Many quickly moved to the Mainland. A contingency of Scots, who first came as mule skinners, did become successful plantation managers and supervisors. The Germans and Scandinavians were well received and climbed the social ladder rapidly, becoming professionals and skilled workers.

The Depression years, not as economically bad in Hawaii as in the continental United States, brought many Mainland whites seeking opportunity, mostly from the South and the West. These new people tended to be even more racist toward brown-skinned people and Asians than the *kama'aina haole*, and they made matters worse. They also competed more intensely for jobs. The racial tension generated during this period came to a head in 1932 with the infamous Massie Rape Case, in which five local men were accused on circumstantial evidence of raping the wife of a naval officer. The five were finally acquitted, but Thomas Massie and his mother-in-law, with the assistance of several others, killed one of the boys. Found guilty at their trial, these whites served just one hour for the murder.

The Portuguese

The last time anyone looked, Portugal was still attached to the European continent, but for some anomalous reason the Portuguese weren't considered *haole* in Hawaii for the longest time. About 12,000 arrived between 1878 and 1887, and another 6,000 came between 1906 and 1913. Accompanied during this period by 8,000 Spanish, they were considered one and the same. Most of the Portuguese were illiterate peasants from Madeira and the Azores, and the Spanish hailed from Andalusia. They were very well received, and because they were white but not *haole,* they made a perfect "buffer" ethnic group. Committed to staying in Hawaii, they rose to be skilled workers—the *"luna* class" on the plantations. However, they de-emphasized education and became very racist toward Asians, regarding them as a threat to their job security.

By 1920, the 27,000 Portuguese made up 11 percent of the population. After that they tended to blend with the other ethnic groups and weren't counted separately. Portuguese men tended to marry within their ethnic group, but a good portion of Portuguese women married other white men and became closer to the *haole* group, while another large portion chose Hawaiian mates and grew further away. Although they didn't originate pidgin English (see "Language," below), the unique melodious quality of their native tongue did give pidgin that certain lilt it has today. Also, the ukulele was closely patterned after the *cavaquinho,* a Portuguese stringed folk instrument.

The White Population

Today Caucasians make up the largest racial group in the islands at about 25 percent of the population. With mixed white blood, that number jumps to nearly 40 percent. They are spread evenly throughout Kaua'i, O'ahu, Maui, and the Big Island, with much smaller percentages on

Moloka'i and Lana'i. On the Big Island, there are concentrations in Hilo, North Kona, South Kohala, and Waimea. In terms of pure numbers, the white population is the fastest growing in the islands because most people settling in Hawaii are white Americans predominantly from the West Coast.

FILIPINOS AND OTHERS

The Filipinos who came to Hawaii brought high hopes of amassing personal fortunes and returning home as rich heroes; for most it was a dream that never came true. Filipinos had been American nationals ever since the Spanish-American War of 1898 and as such weren't subject to immigration laws that curtailed the importation of other Asian workers at the turn of the 20th century. The first to arrive were 15 families in 1906, but a large number came in 1924 as strikebreakers. The majority were illiterate peasants called Ilocanos from the northern Philippines; about 10 percent were Visayans from the central cities. The Visayans were not as hardworking or thrifty but were much more sophisticated. From the first, Filipinos were looked down upon by all the other immigrant groups and were considered particularly uncouth by the Japanese. The value they placed on education was the least of any group, and even by 1930 only about half could speak rudimentary English, the majority remaining illiterate. They were billeted in the worst housing, performed the most menial jobs, and were the last hired and first fired.

One big difference between Filipinos and other groups was that the men brought no Filipino women to marry, so they clung to the idea of returning home. In 1930 there were 30,000 men and only 360 women. This hopeless situation led to a great deal of prostitution and homosexuality; many of these terribly lonely bachelors would feast and drink on weekends and engage in their gruesome but exciting pastime of cockfighting on Sundays. When some did manage to find wives, their mates were inevitably part Hawaiian. Filipino workers continued to be imported, although sporadically, until 1946, so even today there are a few old Filipino bachelors who never managed to get home, and the Sunday cockfights remain a way of life.

The Filipinos constitute 14 percent of Hawaii's population, some 170,000 individuals, with almost 75 percent living on O'ahu. Some 275,000 are of mixed Filipino blood. Many visitors to Hawaii mistake Filipinos for Hawaiians because of their dark skin, and this is a minor irritant to both groups. Some streetwise Filipinos even claim to be Hawaiians, because being Hawaiian is "in" and goes over well with the tourists, especially the young women tourists. For the most part, these people are hardworking, dependable laborers who do tough work for little recognition. They remain low on the social totem pole and have not yet organized politically to stand up for their rights.

Other Groups

About 10 percent of Hawaii's population is made up of a conglomerate of other ethnic groups. Of these, one of the largest and fastest growing is Korean, with 25,000 people. About 8,000 Koreans came to Hawaii from 1903 until 1905, when their government halted emigration. During the same period about 6,000 Puerto Ricans arrived, and today about 30,000 consider themselves a Puerto Rican mix. There were also two attempts made in the 1800s to import other Polynesians to strengthen the dying Hawaiian race, but they were failures. In 1869 only 126 central Polynesian natives could be lured to Hawaii, and from 1878 to 1885 2,500 Gilbert Islanders arrived. Both groups became immediately disenchanted with Hawaii. They pined away for their own islands and departed for home as soon as possible.

Today, however, 16,000 Samoans have settled in Hawaii, and with more on the way they are one of the fastest-growing minorities in the state. For unexplainable reasons, Samoans and native Hawaiians get along extremely poorly and have the worst racial tensions and animosity of any groups. The Samoans ostensibly should represent the archetypal Polynesians that the Hawaiians are seeking, but it doesn't work that way. Samoans are criticized by Hawaiians for their hot tempers, lingering feuds, and petty jealousies. They're clannish and are often the butt of "dumb" jokes. This racism seems especially ridiculous, but that's the way it is.

Just to add a bit more exotic spice to the stew, there are about 22,000 blacks, 3,500 Native Americans, 4,000 Tongans, 7,000 other Pacific Islanders, and 8,000 Vietnamese refugees living on the islands.

Language

Hawaii is part of America and people speak English there, but that's not the whole story. If you turn on the TV to catch the evening news, you'll hear "Walter Cronkite" English, unless of course you happen to tune in to a Japanese-language broadcast designed for tourists from that country. You can easily pick up a Chinese-language newspaper or groove to the music on a Filipino radio station, but let's not confuse the issue. All your needs and requests at airports, car-rental agencies, restaurants, hotels, or wherever you happen to travel will be completely understood, as well as answered, in English. However, when you happen to overhear islanders speaking, what they're saying will sound somewhat familiar but you won't be able to pick up all the words, and the beat and melody of the language will be noticeably different.

Hawaii—like New England, the Deep South, and the Midwest—has its own unmistakable linguistic regionalism. All the ethnic peoples who make up Hawaii have enriched the English spoken there with words, expressions, and subtle shades of meaning that are commonly used and understood throughout the islands. The greatest influence on English has come from the Hawaiian language itself, and words such as "aloha," "hula," "lu'au," and "mahalo" are familiarly used and understood by most Americans.

Other migrant peoples, especially the Chinese, Japanese, and Portuguese, influenced the local dialect to such an extent that the simplified plantation lingo they spoke has become known as "pidgin." A fun and enriching part of the "island experience" is picking up a few words of Hawaiian and pidgin. English is the official language of the state, business, education, and perhaps even the mind; but pidgin is the language of the people, the emotions, and life, while Hawaiian remains the language of the heart and the soul.

Note: Many Hawaiian words are commonly used in English, appear in English dictionaries, and therefore would ordinarily be subject to the rules of English grammar. The Hawaiian language, however, does not pluralize nouns by adding an "s"; the singular and plural are differentiated in context. For purposes of this book, and to highlight the Hawaiian culture, the Hawaiian style of pluralization will be followed for common Hawaiian words. The following are some examples of plural Hawaiian nouns treated this way in this book: *haole* (not *haoles*), *kahuna*, lei, lu'au, and *nene*.

PIDGIN

The dictionary definition of pidgin is a simplified language with a rudimentary grammar used as a means of communication between people speaking different languages. Hawaiian pidgin is a little more complicated than that. It had its roots during the plantation days of the 19th century when white owners and *luna* (foremen) had to communicate with recently arrived Chinese, Japanese, and Portuguese laborers. It evolved as a simple language of the here and now, primarily concerned with the necessary functions of working, eating, and sleeping. It has an economical noun-verb-object structure (although not necessarily in that order).

Hawaiian words make up most of pidgin's non-English vocabulary. It includes a good smattering of Chinese, Japanese, and Samoan; the distinctive rising inflection is provided by the melodious Mediterranean lilt of the Portuguese. Pidgin is not a stagnant language. It's kept alive by hip new words introduced by people who are "so radical," and especially by slang words introduced by teenagers. It's a colorful English, like "jive" or "ghettoese" spoken by American blacks, and is as regionally unique as the speech of Cajuns in rural Louisiana bayous. *Maka'ainana* of all socioethnic backgrounds can at least understand pidgin. Most islanders are proud of it, while some consider it a low-class jargon. The Hawaiian House of Representatives has given pidgin an official sanction, and most people feel that it adds a real local style and should be preserved.

Pidgin Lives

Pidgin is first learned at school, where all students, regardless of background, are exposed to it. The pidgin spoken by young people today is "fo' real" different from that of their parents. It's no longer only plantation talk but has moved to the streets and picked up some sophistication. At one time there was an academic movement to exterminate it, but that idea died away with the same thinking that insisted on making left-handed people write with their right hand. It is strange, however, that pidgin has become the unofficial language of Hawaii's grassroots movement, when it actually began as a white owners' language that was used to supplant Hawaiian and all the languages brought to the islands.

Although hip young *haole* use pidgin all the time, it has gained the connotation of being the language of the nonwhite locals and is part of the "us against them" way of thinking. All local people, *haole* or not, do consider pidgin their own island language and don't really like it when it's used by *malihini* (newcomers). If you're in the islands long enough, you don't have to bother learning pidgin; it'll learn you. There's a book sold all over the islands called *Pidgin to da Max,* written by (you guessed it) a *haole* from Nebraska named Doug Simonson. You might not be able to understand what's being said by locals speaking pidgin (that's usually the idea), but you should be able to *feel* what's being meant.

CAPSULE PIDGIN

The following are a few commonly used words and expressions that should give you an idea of pidgin. It really can't be written properly, merely approximated, but for now, *"Study da' kine an' bimbye it be mo' bettah, brah! OK? Lesgo."*

an' den—and then? big deal; so what's next?

auntie—respected elderly woman

bad ass—very good

bimbye—after a while; bye and bye. "Bimbye, you learn pidgin."

blalah—brother, but actually only refers to a large, heavy-set, good-natured Hawaiian man

brah—all the bros in Hawaii are brahs; brother; pal. Used to call someone's attention. One of the most common words even among people who are not acquainted. After a fill-up at a gas station, a person would say "Tanks, brah."

chicken skin—goose bumps

cockaroach—steal; rip off. If you really want to find out what *cockaroach* means, just leave your camera on your beach blanket when you take a little dip.

da' kine—a catchall word of many meanings that epitomizes the essence of pidgin. *Da' kine* is a euphemism for pidgin and is substituted whenever the speaker is at a loss for a word or just wants to generalize. It can mean: you know? watchamacallit; of that type.

geev um—give it to them; give them hell; go for it. Can be used as an encouragement. If a surfer is riding a great wave, the people on the beach might yell, "Geev um, brah!"

grinds—food

hana ho—again. Especially after a concert the audience shouts "hana ho" (one more!).

hele on—let's get going

howzit?—as in "howzit, brah?" what's happening? how's it going? The most common greeting, used in place of the more formal "How do you do?"

huhu—angry! "You put the make on the wrong da' kine wahine, brah, and you in da' kine

trouble if you get one big Hawaiian blalah plenty huhu."

lesgo—let's go! do it!

li'dis an' li'dat—like this or that; a catch-all grouping especially if you want to avoid details; like, ya' know?

lolo buggah—stupid or crazy guy (person). Words to a tropical island song go, "I want to find the lolo who stole my pakalolo."

mo' bettah—better, real good! great idea. An island sentiment used to be, "mo' bettah you *come* Hawaii." Now it has subtly changed to, "mo' bettah you *visit* Hawaii."

ono—number one! delicious; great; groovy. "Hawaii is ono, brah!"

pakalolo—literally "crazy smoke"; marijuana; grass; reefer

pakiki head—stubborn; bull-headed

pau—a Hawaiian word meaning finished; done; over and done with. *Pau hana* means end of work or quitting time. Once used by plantation workers, now used by everyone.

seestah—sister, female

shaka—hand wave where only the thumb and baby finger stick out, meaning thank you, all right!

sleepah—slippers, flip-flops, zori

stink face—(or stink eye) basically frowning at someone; using facial expression to show displeasure. Hard looks. What you'll get if you give local people a hard time.

swell head—burned up; angry

talk story—spinning yarns; shooting the breeze; throwing the bull; a rap session. If you're lucky enough to be around to hear *kupuna* (elders) "talk story," you can hear some fantastic tales in the tradition of old Hawaii.

tanks, brah—thanks, thank you

to da max—all the way

waddascoops—what's the scoop? what's up? what's happening?

HAWAIIAN

The Hawaiian language sways like a palm tree in a gentle wind. Its words are as melodious as a love song. Linguists say that you can learn a lot about people through their language; when you hear Hawaiian you think of gentleness and love, and it's hard to imagine the ferocious side so evident in Hawaii's past. With its many Polynesian root words easily traced to Indonesian and Malay, Hawaiian is obviously from this same stock. The Hawaiian spoken today is very different from old Hawaiian. Its greatest metamorphosis occurred when the missionaries began to write it down in the 1820s, but in the last couple of decades there has been a movement to reestablish the Hawaiian language. Not only are courses in it offered at the University of Hawaii, there is a successful elementary immersion school program in the state, some books are being printed in it, and more and more musicians are performing in it. Many scholars have put forth translations of Hawaiian, but there are endless, volatile disagreements in the academic sector about the real meanings of Hawaiian words. Hawaiian is no longer spoken as a language except on Ni'ihau, and the closest tourists will come to it are in placenames, street names, and words that have become part of common usage, such as "aloha" and "mahalo." A few old Hawaiians still speak it at home, and sermons are delivered in Hawaiian at some local churches. Kawaiaha'o Church in downtown Honolulu is the most famous of these, but each island has its own.

Wiki Wiki Hawaiian

Thanks to the missionaries, the Hawaiian language is rendered phonetically using only 12 letters. They are the five vowels, a-e-i-o-u, sounded as they are in Italian; and seven consonants, h-k-l-m-n-p-w, sounded exactly as they are in English. Sometimes "w" is pronounced as "v," but this only occurs in the middle of a word and always follows a vowel. A consonant is always followed by a vowel, forming two-letter syllables, but vowels are often found in pairs or even triplets. A slight oddity about Hawaiian is

the glottal stop called 'okina. This is an abrupt break in sound in the middle of a word such as "oh-oh" in English and is denoted with a reversed apostrophe ('). A good example is ali'i; or even better, the O'ahu town of Ha'iku, which actually means "Abrupt Break."

Pronunciation Key

For those unfamiliar with the sounds of Italian or other Romance languages, the vowels are sounded as follows:

A—in stressed syllables, pronounced as in "ah" (that feels good!). For example, Haleakala is pronounced "hah-lay-AH-kah-lah." Unstressed syllables are pronounced "uh" as in "again" or "above." For example, Kamehameha would be "kah-MAY-hah-MAY-hah."

E—short "e" is "eh," as in "pen" or "dent" (thus hale is "HAH-leh"). Long "e" sounds like "ay" as in "sway" or "day." For example, the Hawaiian goose (nene) is a "nay nay," not a "knee knee."

I—pronounced "ee" as in "see" or "we" (thus pali is pronounced "PAH-lee").

O—pronounced as in "no" or "oh," such as "KOH-uh" (koa) or "OH-noh" (ono).

U—pronounced "oo" as in "do" or "stew"; for example, "KAH-poo" (kapu) or "POO-nah" (Puna).

Diphthongs

There are also eight vowel pairs known as "diphthongs" (ae-ai-ao-au-ei-eu-oi-ou). These are the sounds made by gliding from one vowel to another within a syllable. The stress is placed on the first vowel. In English, examples would be soil and bail. Common examples in Hawaiian are lei and heiau.

Stress

The best way to learn which syllables are stressed in Hawaiian is by listening closely. It becomes obvious after a while. There are also some vowel sounds that are held longer than others; these can occur at the beginning of a word, such as the first "a" in 'aina, or in the middle of a word, like the first "a" in lanai. Again, it's a matter of tuning your ear and paying attention. When written, these stressed vowels, called kahako, occur with a macron, or short line, over them. Stressed vowels with marks are not written as such in this book. No one is going to give you a hard time if you mispronounce a word. It's good, however, to pay close attention to the pronunciation of street names and place-names because many Hawaiian words sound alike—a misplaced vowel here or there could be the difference between getting where you want to go and getting lost.

Religion

The Lord saw fit to keep His island paradise secret from humans for a few million years, but once we finally arrived we were awfully thankful. Hawaii sometimes seems like a floating tabernacle; everywhere you look there's a church, temple, shrine, or *heiau*. The islands are either a very holy place, or there's a powerful lot of sinning going on that would require so many houses of prayer. Actually, it's just America's "right to worship" concept fully employed in microcosm. All the peoples who came to Hawaii brought their own forms of devotion. The Polynesian Hawaiians praised the primordial creators, Wakea and Papa, from whom their pantheon of animistically inspired gods sprang. Obviously to a modern world these old gods would never do. Unfortunately for the old gods, there were too many of them, and belief in them was looked upon as superstition, the folly of semicivilized pagans. So the famous missionaries of the 1820s brought Congregational Christianity and the "true path" to heaven.

Inconveniently, the Catholics, Mormons, Reformed Mormons, Adventists, Episcopalians, Unitarians, Christian Scientists, Lutherans, Baptists, Jehovah's Witnesses, Salvation Army, and every other major and minor denomination of Christianity that followed in their wake brought their own brands of enlightenment and never quite agreed with each other. Chinese and Japanese immigrants established the major sects of Buddhism, Confucianism, Taoism, and Shintoism. Allah is praised, the Torah is chanted in Jewish synagogues, and nirvana is available at a variety of Hindu temples. If the spirit moves you, a Hare Krishna devotee will be glad to point you in the right direction and give you a "free" flower for only a dollar or two. If the world is still too much with you, you might find peace at a Church of Scientology, or meditate at a Kundalini yoga institute, or perhaps find relief at a local assembly of Baha'i. Anyway, rejoice, because in Hawaii you'll not only find paradise, you may even find salvation.

HAWAIIAN BELIEFS

The Polynesian Hawaiians worshiped nature. They saw its forces manifested in a multiplicity of forms to which they ascribed godlike powers, and they based daily life on this animistic philosophy. Handpicked and specially trained storytellers chanted the exploits of the gods. These ancient tales, kept alive in a special oral tradition called *mo'olelo,* were recited only by day. Entranced listeners encircled the chanter; in respect for the gods and in fear of their wrath, they were forbidden to move once the tale was begun. This was serious business during which a person's life could be at stake. It was not like the telling of *ka'ao,* which were simple fictions, tall tales, and yarns of ancient heroes related for amusement and to pass the long nights. Any object, animate or inanimate, could be a god. All could be infused with mana, especially a dead body or respected ancestor.

'Ohana had personal family gods called *'aumakua* on whom they called in times of danger or strife. There were children of gods called *kupua* who were thought to live among humans and were distinguished either for their beauty and strength or for their ugliness and terror. It was told that processions of dead *ali'i,* called "Marchers of the Night," wandered through the land of the living, and unless you were properly protected it could mean death if they looked upon you. There were simple ghosts known as *akua lapu* who merely frightened people. Forests, waterfalls, trees, springs, and a thousand forms of nature were the manifestations of *akua li'i,* "little spirits" who could be invoked at any time for help or protection. It made no difference who or what you were in old Hawaii; the gods were ever-present and took a direct and active role in your life.

Behind all of these beliefs was an innate sense of natural balance and order. It could be interpreted as positive-negative, yin-yang, plus-minus, life-death, light-dark, whatever, but the main idea was that everything had its opposite. The time of darkness when only the gods lived was *po.* When the great gods descended to the earth and created light, this was *ao* and humanity was born. All of these *mo'olelo* are part of *The Kumulipo,* the great chant that records the Hawaiian version of creation. From the time the gods descended and touched the earth at Ku Moku on Lana'i, the genealogies were kept. Unlike the Bible, these included the noble families of female as well as male *ali'i.*

Heiau

A *heiau* is a Hawaiian temple. The basic *heiau* was a masterfully built and fitted rectangular stone wall that varied in size from about as big as a basketball court to as big as a football field. Once the restraining outer walls were built, the interior was backfilled with smaller stones and the top dressing was expertly laid and then rolled, perhaps with a log, to form a pavementlike surface. All that remains of Hawaii's many *heiau* are the stone platforms or walls. The buildings upon them, made from perishable wood, leaves, and grass, have long since disappeared.

Some *heiau* were dreaded temples where human sacrifices were made. Tradition says that this barbaric custom began at Waha'ula Heiau on the Big Island in the 12th century and was introduced by a ferocious Tahitian priest named Pa'ao. Other *heiau,* such as Pu'uhonua o Honaunau, also on the Big Island, were temples of refuge where the weak, widowed, orphaned, and vanquished could find safety and sanctuary.

Idols

The Hawaiian people worshiped gods who took the form of idols fashioned from wood,

feathers, or stone. The eyes were made from shells and until these were inlaid, the idol was dormant. The hair used was often human hair, and the arms and legs were usually flexed. The mouth was either gaping or formed a wide figure-eight lying on its side, and more likely than not was lined with glistening dog teeth. Small figures made of woven basketry were expertly covered with feathers. Red and yellow feathers were favorites taken from specific birds by men whose only work was to roam the forests in search of them.

Ghosts

The Hawaiians had countless superstitions and ghost legends, but two of the more interesting involve astral travel of the soul and the "Marchers of the Night." The soul, *'uhane,* was considered by Hawaiians to be totally free and independent of its body, *kino.* The soul could separate, leaving the body asleep or very drowsy. This disembodied soul *(hihi'o)* could visit people and was considered quite different from a *lapu* or ordinary spirit of a dead person. A *kahuna* could immediately recognize if a person's *'uhane* had left the body, and a special wreath was placed upon the head to protect the person and to facilitate reentry.

If confronted by an apparition, you could test to see if it was indeed dead or still alive by placing leaves of an *'ape* plant upon the ground. If the leaves tore when they were walked upon, the spirit was merely human, but if they remained intact it was a ghost. Or you could sneak up and startle the vision, and if it disappeared it was a ghost. Also, if no reflection of the face appeared when it drank water from an offered calabash, it was a ghost. Unfortunately, there were no instructions to follow once you had determined that you indeed had a ghost on your hands. Maybe it was better not to know! Some people would sprinkle salt and water around their houses, but this kept away evil spirits, not ghosts.

There are also many stories of *kahuna* restoring a soul to a dead body. First they had to catch it and keep it in a gourd. They then placed beautiful tapa and fragrant flowers and herbs about the body to make it more enticing. Slowly, they would coax the soul out of the gourd until it reentered the body through the big toe.

Death Marchers

One inexplicable phenomenon that many people attest to is *ka huaka'i o ka po,* "Marchers of the Night." This march of the dead is fatal if you gaze upon it, unless one of the marchers happens to be a friendly ancestor who will protect you. The peak time for "the march" is 7:30 P.M.–2 A.M. The marchers can be dead *ali'i* and warriors, the gods themselves, or the lesser *'aumakua.* When the *'aumakua* march there is usually chanting and music. *Ali'i* marches are more somber. The entire procession, lit by torches, often stops at the house of a relative and might even carry him or her away. When the gods themselves march, there is often thunder, lightning, and heavy seas. The sky is lit with torches, and they walk six abreast, three gods and three goddesses. If you get in the way of a march, remove your clothing and prostrate yourself. If the marching gods or *'aumakua* happen to be ones to which you prayed, you might be spared. If it's a march of the *ali'i,* you might make it if you lie face upward and feign death. If you *do* see a death march, the last thing that you'll worry about is lying naked on the ground looking ridiculous.

THE STRIFES OF MAUI

Of all the heroes and mythological figures of Polynesia, Maui is the best known. His "strifes" are like the great Greek epics, and they make excellent tales of daring that elders loved to relate to youngsters around the evening fire. Maui was abandoned by his mother, Hina of Fire, when he was an infant. She wrapped him in her hair and cast him upon the sea where she expected him to die, but he lived and returned home to become her favorite. She knew then that he was a born hero and had strength far beyond that of ordinary mortals. His first exploit was to lift the sky. In those days the sky hung so low that humans had to crawl around on all fours. A seductive young woman approached Maui and asked him to use his great strength to lift the sky. In fine heroic fashion, the big boy agreed, if the beautiful woman would euphemistically "give him a drink from her gourd." He then obliged her by lifting the sky, and he might even have made the earth move for her once or twice.

More Land

The territory of humankind was small at that time. Maui decided that more land was needed, so he conspired to "fish up islands." He descended into the land of the dead and petitioned an ancestress to fashion him a hook from her jawbone. She obliged and created the mythical hook, *Manai ikalani.* Maui then secured a sacred *'alae* bird, which he intended to use for bait, and bid his brothers to paddle him far out to sea. When he arrived at the deepest spot, he lowered *Manai ikalani,* baited with the sacred bird, and his sister, Hina of the Sea, placed it into the mouth of "Old One Tooth," who held the land fast to the bottom of the waters. Maui then exhorted his brothers to row but warned them not to look back. They strained at the oars with all their might and slowly a great land mass arose. One brother, overcome by curiosity, looked back, and when he did so, the land shattered into all of the islands of Polynesia.

Further Exploits

Maui still desired to serve humanity. People were without fire, the secret of which was held by the sacred *'alae* birds, who learned it from Maui's far distant mother. Hina of Fire gave Maui her burning fingernails, but he oafishly kept dropping them into streams until all had fizzled out and he had totally irritated his generous progenitor. She pursued him, trying to burn him to a cinder; Maui chanted for rain to put out her scorching fires. When she saw that they were being quenched, she hid her fire in the barks of special trees and informed the mud hens where they could be found, but first made them promise never to tell humans. Maui knew of this and captured a mud hen, threatening to wring its scrawny, traitorous neck unless it gave up the secret. The bird tried trickery and told Maui first to rub together the stems of sugarcane, then banana, and even taro. None worked, and Maui's determined rubbing is why these plants have hollow roots today.

Finally, with Maui's hands tightening around the mud hen's gizzard, the bird confessed that fire could be found in the *hau* tree and also the sandalwood, which Maui named *'ili aha* ("fire bark") in its honor. He then rubbed all the feathers off the mud hen's head for being so deceitful, which is why their crowns are featherless today.

The Sun Is Snared

Maui's greatest deed, however, was in snaring the sun and exacting a promise that it would go slower across the heavens. The people complained that there were not enough daylight hours to fish or farm. Maui's mother could not dry her tapa cloth because the sun rose and set so quickly. She asked her son to help. Maui went to his blind grandmother, who lived on the slopes of Haleakala and was responsible for cooking the sun's bananas, which he ate every day in passing. She told him to personally weave 16 strong ropes with nooses from his sister's hair. Some say these came from her head, but other versions insist that it was no doubt Hina's pubic hair that had the power to hold the sun god. Maui positioned himself with the rope, and as each of the 16 rays of the sun came across Haleakala, he snared them until the sun was defenseless and had to bargain for his life. Maui agreed to free him if he promised to go more slowly. From that time forward the sun agreed to move slowly and Haleakala ("The House of the Sun") became his home.

MISSIONARIES ONE AND ALL

In Hawaii, when you say "missionaries," it's taken for granted you're referring to the small and determined band of Congregationalists who arrived aboard the brig *Thaddeus* in 1820, and the follow-up groups, called "companies" or "packets," that reinforced them. They were sent from Boston by the American Board of Commissioners for Foreign Missions (ABCFM), which learned of the supposed sad and godless plight of the Hawaiian people through returning sailors and especially through the few Hawaiians who had come to America to study.

The person most instrumental in bringing the missionaries to Hawaii was a young man named Opukaha'ia. He was an orphan befriended by a ship's captain and taken to New England, where he studied theology. Obsessed with the desire to return home and save his people from certain damnation, Opukaha'ia wrote accounts of life in Hawaii that were published and widely read. These accounts were directly responsible for the formation of the Pioneer Company to the Sandwich Islands Missions in 1819. Unfortunately, Opukaha'ia died in New England from typhus the year before they left.

"Civilizing" Hawaii

The first missionaries had the straightforward task of bringing the Hawaiians out of paganism and into Christianity and civilization. They met with terrible hostility—not from the natives, but from the sea captains and traders who were very happy with the open debauchery and wanton whoremongering that was status quo in the Hawaii of 1820. Many direct confrontations between these two factions even included the cannonading of missionaries' homes by American sea captains who were denied the customary visits of island women, thanks to meddlesome "do-gooders." The most memorable of these incidents involved "Mad Jack" Percival, the captain of the USS *Dolphin,* who bombed a church in Lahaina to show his rancor. In actuality, the truth of the situation was much closer to the sentiments of James Jarves, who wrote, "The missionary was a far more useful and agreeable man than his Catholicism would indicate; and the trader was not so bad a man as the missionary would make him out to be." The missionaries' primary aim might have been conversion, but the most fortuitous by-product was education, which raised the consciousness of every Hawaiian, regardless of religious affiliation. In 40 short years Hawaii was considered a civilized nation well on its way into the modern world, and the American Board of Missions officially ended its support in 1863.

Non-Christians

By the turn of the 20th century, both Shintoism and Buddhism, brought by the Japanese and Chinese, were firmly established in Hawaii. The first official Buddhist temple was Hongpa Hongwanji, established on Oʻahu in 1889. All the denominations of Buddhism account for 17 percent of the island's religious total, and there are about 50,000 Shintoists. The Hindu religion has perhaps 2,000 adherents, and about the same number of Jewish people live throughout Hawaii with only one synagogue, Temple Emanu-El, on Oʻahu. The largest number of people in Hawaii (300,000) remain unaffiliated, and about 10,000 people are in new religious movements and lesser-known faiths such as Baha'i and Unitarianism.

Arts and Music

Referring to Hawaii as "paradise" is about as hackneyed as you can get, but when you specify "artists' paradise" it's the absolute truth. Something about the place evokes art (or at least personal expression) from most people. The islands are like a magnet: they not only draw artists to them, but they draw art *from* the artists.

The inspiration comes from the astounding natural surroundings. The land is so beautiful yet so raw; the ocean's power and rhythm are primal and ever-present; the riotous colors of flowers and fruit leap from the deep-green jungle background. Crystal water beads and pale mists turn the mountains into mystic temples, while rainbows ride the crests of waves. The stunning variety of faces begging to be rendered suggests that all the world sent delegations to the islands. And in most cases it did! Inspiration is everywhere, as is art, good or bad.

Sometimes the artwork is overpowering in itself and in its sheer volume. Though geared to the tourist's market of cheap souvenirs, there is hardly a shop in Hawaii that doesn't sell some item that falls into the general category of "art." You can find everything from carved monkey-face coconut shells to true masterpieces. The Polynesian Hawaiians were master craftspeople, and their legacy still lives in a wide variety of wood carvings, basketry, and weavings. The hula is art in swaying motion, and the true form is studied rigorously and taken very seriously. There is hardly a resort area that doesn't offer the "bump and grind" tourist hula, but even these revues are accompanied by proficient local musicians. Nightclubs offer "slack-key" balladeers, and island music performed on ukuleles and on Hawaii's own steel guitars spills from many lounges.

Vibrant fabrics that catch the spirit of the islands are rendered into muʻumuʻu and aloha shirts at countless local factories. They're almost a mandatory purchase! Pottery, heavily influenced by the Japanese, is a well-developed craft at numerous kilns. Local artisans fashion delicate jewelry from coral and olivine, while some ply the whaler's legacy of etching on ivory, called scrimshaw. There are fine traditions of quilting, flower art in lei, and street artists working in every medium from airbrush to glass.

ARTS OF OLD HAWAII

Since everything in old Hawaii had to be fashioned by hand, almost every object was either a genuine work of art or the product of a highly refined craft. With the "civilizing" of the natives, most of the "old ways" disappeared, including the old arts and crafts. Most authentic Hawaiian art exists only in museums, but with the resurgence of Hawaiian roots, many old arts are being revitalized, and a few artists are becoming proficient in them.

Magnificent Canoes

The most respected artisans in old Hawaii were the canoe makers. With little more than a stone adze and a pump drill, they built canoes that could carry 200 people and last for generations—sleek, well proportioned, and infinitely seaworthy. The main hull was usually a gigantic koa log, and the gunwale planks were minutely drilled and sewn to the sides with sennit rope. Apprenticeships lasted for years, and a young man knew that he had graduated when one day he was nonchalantly asked to sit down and eat with the master builders. Small family-sized canoes with

BIG ISLAND MUSEUMS AND HISTORICAL SOCIETIES

Pacific Tsunami Museum, 130 Kamehameha Ave., 808/935-0926, open Mon.–Sat. 9 A.M.–4 P.M., is housed in the art-deco-style First Hawaiian Bank building near the bay front in Hilo. It's dedicated to those who lost their lives in the destructive tidal waves that hit and virtually destroyed the city in 1946 and 1960. Visual displays, video film, and computer links all add to the educational focus of this organization, but the most moving aspect are the photographs of the last two terribly destructive tsunami to hit the city. Admission for adults is $5.

Lyman Mission House and Museum, 276 Haili St. in Hilo, 808/935-5021, open Mon.–Sat. 9 A.M.–4:30 P.M., was first opened in 1932. The main building is a New England–style structure from 1839, the oldest wood frame house on the island. It contains furniture and household goods from Rev. and Mrs. Lyman and other missionary families on the island. In a modern annex are a collection of Hawaiian artifacts and items of daily use in the Island Heritage Gallery and a very fine collection of rocks and minerals in the Earth Her-itage Gallery. Admission is $5 adults, $2.50 children 6–18.

Hulihe'e Palace, a Victorian-style building in downtown Kailua-Kona, 808/329-1877, open Mon.–Fri. 9 A.M.–4 P.M., Sat. and Sun. 10 A.M.–4 P.M., is one of three royal palaces in the state. Used by the Hawaiian monarchs until 1916, it now contains countless items owned and used by the royal families. It's a treasure house and well worth a look. Adult admission is $5, $4 senior, $1 student. Guided or self-guided tours.

Parker Ranch Historic Homes are located a few miles outside Waimea, 808/885-5433, open daily 10 A.M.–5 P.M.; $8.50 admission adults. Pu'opelu, the ranch home of the Parker family, is a structure to be appreciated in and of itself, but it also houses artwork of world-prominent European artists, Chinese glass art, and antique furniture collected by Richard Smart, the last of the Parker line. Reconstructed on the grounds is Mana House, the original Parker ranch home from 1847, also open for viewing.

outriggers were used for fishing and perhaps carried a spear rack; large oceangoing double-hulled canoes were used for migration and warfare. On these, the giant logs had been adzed to about two inches thick. A mainsail woven from pandanus was mounted on a central platform, and the boat was steered by two long paddles. The hull was dyed with plant juices and charcoal, and the entire village helped launch the canoe in a ceremony called "drinking the sea."

Carving and Weaving

Wood was a primary material used by Hawaiian craftsmen. They almost exclusively used koa because of its density, strength, and natural luster. It was turned into canoes, wood ware, calabashes, and furniture used by the *ali'i*. Temple idols were another major product of wood carving. Various stone artifacts were also turned out, including poi pounders, mirrors, fish sinkers, and small idols.

Hawaiians became the best basket makers and mat weavers in all of Polynesia. *Ulana* (woven mats) were made from *lau hala* (pandanus) leaves. Once split, the spine was removed and the leaves stored in large rolls. When needed they were soaked, pounded, and then fashioned into various floor coverings and sleeping mats. Intricate geometrical patterns were woven in, and the edges were rolled and well fashioned. Coconut palms were not used to make mats in old Hawaii, but a wide variety of basketry was made from the aerial root *'ie'ie*. The shapes varied according to use. Some baskets were tall and narrow, some were cones, others were flat like trays, while many were woven around gourds and calabashes.

A strong tradition of weaving and carving has survived in Hawaii, and the time-tested material of *lau hala* is still the best, although much is now made from coconut fronds. You can purchase anything from beach mats to a woven hat,

Kamuela Museum, located west of downtown Waimea, 808/885-4724, open daily 8 A.M.–5 P.M., is a wonderfully eclectic private collection of Hawaiiana, upcountry *paniolo* life, Asian artifacts, and photos of the Parker family. This museum has many items that you might expect to find in a much larger big-city museum. Admission is $5, $2 for children under 12.

Parker Ranch Museum in the visitor center at the Parker Ranch Shopping Center, 808/885-7655, is open daily 9 A.M.–5 P.M. (tickets sold until 4 P.M.); adult admission is $6. This is an exhibit of Parker family history and a brief history of ranching and *paniolo* life on the Big Island. Many display items plus a video are offered.

Kona Historical Society Museum, just south of the town of Kealakekua, 808/323-3222, is open Mon.–Fri. 9 A.M.–3 P.M.; $2 admission. Housed in a native stone and lime mortar general store from 1875, this museum has a small collection of glassware and photographs. An archive of Kona-area historical items is housed in the basement and is open by appointment only.

Onizuka Space Center, 808/329-3441, is located at the Kona International Airport. Its hours are 8:30 A.M.–4:30 P.M. daily except Thanksgiving, Christmas, and New Year's Day; $3 admission. This center is a memorial to Hawaii's first astronaut and a space education facility for adults and children. It includes interactive and static exhibits, models, audiovisual displays, and lots of reading material.

The **Laupahoehoe Train Museum,** 36-2377 Mamalahoa Hwy., near the Laupahoehoe Lookout, 808/962-6300, is a small but wonderful view into the life and times of trains and life along the train line of the Hamakua Coast. The museum is open Mon.–Fri. 9 A.M.–4:30 P.M., weekends 10 A.M.–2 P.M. Entrance is $3 adult, $2 for children and seniors.

The **Thomas A. Jaggar Museum** is a state-of-the-art venture with multimedia displays depicting the geology and volcanology of the Kilauea Caldera and entire volcano zone in Hawaii Volcanoes National Park. Open daily 8:30 A.M.–5 P.M., admission free.

and all share the desirable qualities of strength, lightness, and ventilation.

Feather Work

This highly refined art was practiced on the islands of Tahiti, New Zealand, and Hawaii, but the fashioning of feather helmets and idols was unique to Hawaii. Favorite colors were red and yellow, which came only in a very limited supply from a small number of birds such as the *'o'o, 'i'iwi, mamo,* and *'apapane.* Professional bird hunters in old Hawaii paid their taxes to *ali'i* in prized feathers. The feathers were fastened to a woven net of *olona* cord and made into helmets, idols, and beautiful flowing capes and cloaks. These resplendent garments were made and worn only by men, especially during battle when a fine cloak became a great trophy of war. Feather work was also employed in the making of *kahili* and lei, which were highly prized by the noble *ali'i* women.

Tapa Cloth

Tapa, cloth made from tree bark, was common throughout Polynesia and was a woman's art. A few trees such as the *wauke* and *mamaki* produced the best cloth, but a variety of other types of bark could be utilized. First the raw bark was pounded into a feltlike pulp and beaten together to form strips (the beaters had distinctive patterns that also helped make the cloth supple). The strips were decorated by stamping (a form of block printing) and dyed with natural colors from plants and sea animals in shades of gray, purple, pink, and red. They were even painted with natural brushes made from pandanus fruit, with an overall gray color made from charcoal. The tapa cloth was sewn together to make bed coverings, and fragrant flowers and herbs were either sewn or pounded in to produce a permanent fragrance. Tapa cloth is still available today, but the

Hawaiian methods have been lost, and most comes from other areas of Polynesia.

HULA AND LEI

Hula

The hula is more than an ethnic dance; it is the soul of Hawaii expressed in motion. It began as a form of worship during religious ceremonies and was only danced by highly trained men. It gradually evolved into a form of entertainment, but in no regard was it sexual. The hula was the opera, theater, and lecture hall of the islands all rolled into one. It was history portrayed in the performing arts. In the beginning an androgynous deity named Laka descended to earth and taught men how to dance the hula. In time the male aspect of Laka departed for the heavens, but the female aspect remained. The female Laka set up her own special hula *heiau* at Ha'ena Point on the Na Pali Coast of Kaua'i, where it still exists. As time went on women were allowed to learn the hula. Scholars surmise that men became too busy wresting a living from the land to maintain the art form.

Men did retain a type of hula for themselves called *lua*. This was a form of martial art employed in hand-to-hand combat that evolved into a ritualized warfare dance called *hula ku'i*. During the 19th century, the hula almost vanished because the missionaries considered it vile and heathen. King Kalakaua is generally regarded as saving it during the 1800s, when he formed his own troupe and encouraged the dancers to learn the old hula. Many of the original dances were forgotten, but some were retained and are performed to this day. Although professional dancers were highly trained, everyone took part in the hula. *Ali'i,* commoners, young, and old all danced.

Today, hula *halau* (schools) are active on every island, teaching hula and keeping the old ways and culture alive. (Ancient hula is called *hula kahiko* and modern renditions are known as *hula auana.*) Performers still spend years perfecting their techniques. They show off their accomplishments during the fierce competition of the Merrie Monarch Festival in Hilo every April.

The winning *halau* is praised and recognized throughout the islands.

Hawaiian hula was never performed in grass skirts; tapa or ti-leaf skirts were worn. Grass skirts came to Hawaii from the Gilbert Islands, and if you see grass and cellophane skirts in a "hula revue," it's not traditional. Almost every major resort offering entertainment or a lu'au also offers a revue. Most times, young island beauties accompanied by local musicians put on a floor show for the tourists. It'll be fun, but it won't be traditional. A hula dancer has to learn how to control every part of her/his body, including facial expressions, which help to set the mood. The hands are extremely important and provide instant background scenery. For example, if the hands are thrust outward in an aggressive manner, this can mean a battle; if they sway gently overhead, they refer to the gods or to creation; they can easily become rain, clouds, sun, sea, or moon. Watch the hands to get the gist of the story, but as one wise guy said, "You watch the parts you like, and I'll watch the parts I like!" The motion of swaying hips can denote a long walk, a canoe ride, or sexual intercourse. Foot motion can portray a battle, a walk, or any kind of conveyance. The overall effect is multidirectional synchronized movement. The correct chanting of the *mele* is an integral part of the performance. These story chants, accompanied by musical instruments, make the hula very much like opera; it is especially similar in the way the tale unfolds.

Lei Making

Any flower or blossom can be strung into a lei, but the most common are carnations or the lovely smelling plumeria. Lei, like babies, are all beautiful, but special lei are highly prized by those who know what to look for. Of the different stringing styles, the most common is *kui*—stringing the flower through the middle or side. Most "airport-quality" lei are of this type. The *humuhumu* style, reserved for making flat lei, is made by sewing flowers and ferns to a ti, banana, or sometimes *hala* leaf. A *humuhumu* lei makes an excellent hatband. *Wili* is the winding together of greenery, ferns, and flowers into short, bouquet-type lengths. The most tradi-

HAWAIIAN LEI

crown

lau hala

fern

'ilima

plumeria

DIANA LASICH HARPER

tional form is *hili,* which requires no stringing at all but involves braiding fragrant ferns and leaves such as maile. If flowers are interwoven, the *hili* becomes the *haku* style, the most difficult and most beautiful type of lei.

The Lei of the Land

Every major island is symbolized by its own lei made from a distinctive flower, shell, or fern. Each island has its own official color as well, though it doesn't necessarily correspond to the color of the island's lei. The island of Hawai'i's lei is made from the red (or rare creamy white or orange) 'ohi'a lehua blossom. The lehua tree grows from sea level to 9,000 feet and produces an abundance of tufted flowers.

THAT GOOD OLD ISLAND MUSIC

The missionaries usually take a beating when it's recounted how much Hawaiian culture they destroyed while "civilizing" the natives. However,

they seem to have done one thing right. They introduced the Hawaiians to the diatonic musical scale and immediately opened a door to latent and superbly harmonious talent. Before the missionaries, the Hawaiians knew little about melody. Though sonorous, their *mele* were repetitive chants in which the emphasis was placed on historical accuracy and not on "making music." The Hawaiians, in short, didn't *sing.* But within a few years of the missionaries' arrival, they were belting out good old Christian hymns, and one of their favorite pastimes became group and individual singing.

Early in the 1800s, Spanish vaqueros from California were imported to teach the Hawaiians how to be cowboys. With them came guitars and moody ballads. The Hawaiian *paniolos* (cowboys) quickly learned how to punch cows and croon away the long lonely nights on the range. Immigrants who came along a little later in the 19th century, especially from Portugal, helped create a Hawaiian-style music. Their biggest influence was a small, four-stringed instrument called a *braga* or *cavaquinho*. One owned by Augusto Dias was the prototype of a homegrown Hawaiian instrument that became known as the ukulele. "Jumping flea," the translation of ukulele, is an appropriate name devised by the Hawaiians when they saw how nimble the fingers were as they "jumped" over the strings.

King Kalakaua (The Merrie Monarch) and Queen Lili'uokalani were both patrons of the arts who furthered the Hawaiian musical identity at the turn of the 20th century. Kalakaua revived the hula and was also a gifted lyricist and balladeer. He wrote the words to "Hawaii Pono," which became the anthem of the nation of Hawaii and later the state anthem. Lili'uokalani wrote the hauntingly beautiful "Aloha O'e," which is often pointed to as the "spirit of Hawaii" in music. Detractors say that its melody is extremely close to the old Christian hymn, "Rock Beside the Sea," but the lyrics are so beautiful and perfectly fitted that this doesn't matter.

Just prior to Kalakaua's reign, a Prussian bandmaster, Capt. Henri Berger, was invited to head the fledgling Royal Hawaiian Band, which he turned into a very respectable orchestra lauded by many visitors to the islands. Berger was open-minded and learned to love Hawaiian music. He collaborated with Kalakaua and other island musicians to incorporate their music into a Western format. He headed the band for 43 years, until 1915, and was instrumental in making music a serious pursuit of talented Hawaiians.

Popular Hawaiian Music

Hawaiian music has a unique twang, a special feeling that says the same thing to everyone who hears it: "Relax, sit back in the moonlight, watch the swaying palms as the surf sings a lullaby." This special sound is epitomized by the bouncy ukulele, the falsettos of Hawaiian crooners, and the smooth ring of the "steel" or "Hawaiian" guitar. The steel guitar is a variation originated by Joseph Kekuku in the 1890s. Stories abound of how Joseph Kekuku devised this instrument; the most popular versions say that Joe dropped his comb or pocketknife on his guitar strings and liked what he heard. Driven by the faint

rhythm of an inner sound, he went to the machine shop at the Kamehameha Schools and turned out a steel bar for sliding over the strings. To complete the sound he changed the catgut strings to steel and raised them so they wouldn't hit the frets. Voilà!—Hawaiian music as the world knows it today.

The first melodious strains of **slack-key guitar** (*ki ho'alu*) can be traced back to the time of Kamehameha III and the vaqueros from California. The Spanish had their way of tuning the guitar and played difficult and aggressive music that did not sit well with Hawaiians, who were much more gentle and casual in their manners.

Hawaiians soon became adept at making their own music. At first, one person played the melody, but it lacked fullness. There was no body to the sound. So, as one *paniolo* fooled with the melody, another soon learned to play bass, which added depth. But, players were often alone, and by experimenting they learned that they could get the right hand going with the melody, and at the same time play the bass note with the thumb to improve the sound. Singers also learned that they could "open tune" the guitar to match their rich voices.

Hawaiians believed knowledge was sacred, and what is sacred should be treated with utmost respect—which meant keeping it secret, except from sincere apprentices. Guitar playing became a personal art form whose secrets were closely guarded, handed down only to family members, and only to those who showed ability and determination. When old-time slack-key guitar players were done strumming, they loosened all the strings so no one could figure out how they had had their guitars tuned. If they were playing, and some interested folks came by who weren't part of the family, the Hawaiians stopped what they were doing, put their guitars down, and put their feet across the strings to wait for the folks to go away. As time went on, more and more Hawaiians began to play slack-key, and a common repertoire emerged.

Accomplished musicians could easily figure out the simple songs, once they had figured out how the family had tuned the guitar. One of the most popular tunings was the "open G." Old Hawaiian folks called it the "taro patch tune." Different songs came out, and if you were in the family and were interested in the guitar, your elders took the time to sit down and teach you. The way they taught was straightforward—and a test of your sincerity at the same time. The old master would start to play. He just wanted you to listen and get a feel for the music—nothing more than that. You brought your guitar and *listened*. When you felt it, you played it, and the knowledge was transferred. Today, only a handful of slack-key guitar players know how to play the classic tunes classically. The best-known and perhaps greatest slack-key player was Gabby Pahinui, with The Sons of Hawaii. He has passed away but left many recordings behind. A slack-key master still singing and playing is Raymond Kane. None of his students are from his own family, and most are *haole* musicians trying to preserve the classical method of playing.

Hawaiian music received its biggest boost from a remarkable radio program known as "Hawaii Calls." This program sent out its music from the Banyan Court of Waikiki's Moana Hotel from 1935 until 1975. At its peak in the mid-1950s, it was syndicated on over 700 radio stations throughout the world. Ironically, Japanese pilots heading for Pearl Harbor tuned in island music as a signal beam. Some internationally famous classic tunes came out of the '40s and '50s. Jack Pitman composed "Beyond the Reef" in 1948; over 300 artists have recorded it and it has sold well over 12 million records. Other million-sellers include: "Sweet Leilani," "Lovely Hula Hands," "The Cross-eyed Mayor of Kaunakakai," and "The Hawaiian Wedding Song."

By the 1960s, Hawaiian music began to die. Just too corny and light for those turbulent years, it belonged to the older generation and the good times that followed World War II. One man was instrumental in keeping Hawaiian music alive during this period. Don Ho, with his "Tiny Bubbles," became the token Hawaiian musician of the 1960s and early 1970s. He's persevered long enough to become a legend in his own time, and his Polynesian Extravaganza at the

ARTS AND CULTURE INFORMATION

East Hawai'i Cultural Council, Box 1312, Hilo, HI 96721, 808/961-5711, publishes *Art Centering,* a monthly newsletter of what's happening artistically and culturally on the Big Island. The publication includes a good monthly calendar of events with listings from exhibit openings to movies. Associated groups are the East Hawai'i Cultural Center, Big Island Dance Council, Hawai'i Concert Society, Hilo Community Players, and Bunka No Izumi.

Volcano Art Center, 808/967-8222, promotes visual and performing arts at Volcano and offers community art classes and workshops. The Art Center publishes the *Volcano Gazette,* a monthly newsletter detailing events it sponsors.

Hilton Hawaiian Village packed visitors in until the early 1990s. He's now at the Waikiki Beachcomber and still doing a marvelous show. Al Harrington, "The South Pacific Man," until his retirement had another Honolulu "big revue" that drew large crowds. Of this type of entertainment, perhaps the most Hawaiian was Danny Kaleikini, the Ambassador of Aloha, who entertained his audience with dances, Hawaiian anecdotes, and tunes on the traditional Hawaiian nose flute.

The Beat Goes On

Beginning in the mid-'70s, islanders began to assert their cultural identity. One of the unifying factors was the coming of age of "Hawaiian" music. It graduated from the "little grass shack" novelty tune and began to include sophisticated jazz, rock, and contemporary rhythms. Accomplished musicians whose roots were in traditional island music began to highlight their tunes with this distinctive sound. The best embellish their arrangements with ukuleles, steel guitars, and traditional percussion and melodic instruments. Some excellent modern recording artists have become island institutions. The local people say that you know the Hawaiian harmonies are good if they give you "chicken skin."

Each year special music awards, **Na Hoku Hanohano,** or Hoku for short, are given to distinguished island musicians. The following are some of the Hoku winners considered by their contemporaries to be among the best in Hawaii: Barney Isaacs and George Kuo, Na Leo Pilimihana, Robi Kahakalau, Kealii Reichel, Darren Benitez, Sonny Kamahele, Ledward Kaapana, Hapa, Israel Kamakawiwioʻole, Amy Hanaialiʻi, and Pure Heart. Some, unfortunately, are no longer among the living, but their recorded music can still be appreciated.

Past Hoku winners who have become renowned performers include the Brothers Cazimero, who are blessed with beautiful harmonic voices; Krush, highly regarded for their contemporary sounds; The Peter Moon Band, fantastic performers with a strong traditional sound; Kapono and Cecilio; and The Beamer Brothers. Others include Loyal Garner, Del Beazley, Bryan Kessler & Me No Hoa Aloha, George Kahumoku, Jr., Olomana, Genoa Keawe, and Irmagard Aluli.

For those with access to the Internet, you can check out the Hawaiian music scene at one of the following sites: Hawaiian Music Island, www.mele.com; Nahenahenet, www.nahenahe.net; and Hawaiian Music Guide, www.hawaii-music.com. While not the only sites on the Web, they are a good place to start. For listening to Hawaiian music on the Web, try http://kkcr.org or www.hotspots.hawaii.com/IRH.

Festivals, Holidays, and Events

In addition to all the American national holidays, Hawaii celebrates its own festivals, pageants, ethnic fairs, and a multitude of specialized exhibits. They occur throughout the year—some particular to only one island or locality, others, such as Aloha Festivals and Lei Day, celebrated on all the islands. At festival time, everyone is welcome. Many happenings are annual events while others are onetime affairs. Check local newspapers and the free island magazines for exact dates. Island-specific information is also available on the Web; check the calendar listing at www.bigisland.org for events on Hawaiʻi.

For additional events of all sorts throughout the state, visit the calendar of events listing on the HVB website at http://calendar.go-hawaii.com, or visit the State Foundation of Culture and the Arts calendar, which features arts and cultural events, activities, and programs at www.state.hi.us/sfca/culturecalendar.

January
During **The Volcano Wilderness Marathon and Rim Runs,** the truly energetic run 26 miles through the desolate Kaʻu Desert, while a 10-mile race around the Caldera Crater Rim and a five-mile run down into and out of the Kilauea Caldera features over 1,000 participants.

February
The **Waimea Cherry Blossom Festival** showcases ethnic presentations, Japanese cultural events, a parade, and a tea ceremony.

March
The month rumbles in with the **Kona Stampede** at Honaunau Arena, Honaunau, Kona. *Paniolo* provide plenty of action during the full range of rodeo events.

The end of March is dedicated to Prince Kuhio, a member of the royal family and Hawaii's first delegate to the U.S. Congress. **Prince Kuhio Day** is a state holiday honoring the prince, held on March 26, his birthday.

April
Wesak, or **Buddha Day,** is on the Sunday closest to April 8 and celebrates the birthday of Gautama Buddha. Ornate offerings of tropical flowers are placed at temple altars throughout Hawaii.

The **Merrie Monarch Festival** in Hilo sways with the best hula dancers that the islands' hula *halau* have to offer. Gentle but stiff competition features hula in both its ancient *(kahiko)* and modern *(auana)* forms. The festival runs for a week on a variable schedule from year to year. It's immensely popular with islanders, so hotels, cars, and flights are booked solid. This is the state's most prestigious hula competition. For information call the HVB at 808/935-9168.

May

May 1 is May Day to the communist world, but in Hawaii red is only one of the colors when everyone dons a lei for **Lei Day.** Festivities abound throughout Hawaii.

Honoka'a Annual Western Week End at Honoka'a is a fun-filled weekend with a Western theme. It includes a cookout, parade, rodeo, and dance.

The annual **Spring Arts Festival** held at the Wailoa Center in Hilo is a juried art show featuring mixed media artwork by Big Island artists.

The **Annual Keauhou-Kona Triathlon** at Keauhou Bay is open to athletes unable to enter the Ironman and to anyone in good health. Each of its three events is half as long as in the Ironman, and it allows relay-team racing for each grueling segment.

June

King Kamehameha Day, June 11, is a state holiday honoring Kamehameha the Great, a Big Island native son, with festivities on all islands. Check local papers for times and particulars. Hilo is hospitable with a *ho'olaule'a* (large, festive party), parades, art demonstrations, entertainment, and contests.

Hilo flashes its brilliant colors with the **Annual Hilo Orchid Society Show** at the Hilo Civic Auditorium, and the **Annual Big Island Bonsai Show,** Wailoa Center, Hilo. Both are sometimes scheduled for April or July.

Bon Odori, also called O Bon Festival, the Japanese festival of departed souls, features dances and candle lighting ceremonies held at numerous Buddhist temples throughout the island. These festivities change yearly and can be held anytime from late June to early August.

July

Every year on the weekend closest to July 1, the weeklong **Pu'uhonua O Honaunau National Historical Park Annual Cultural Festival** is held at the national park south of Kealakekua

Bay. This free event features traditional Hawaiian arts and crafts, music, dance, and food, and everyone is welcome.

The week of the **Fourth of July** offers the all-American sport of rodeo along with parades. Don't miss the **Parker Ranch 4th of July Horse Races and Rodeo** in Waimea. The epitome of rodeo by Hawaii's top cowboys is set at the Parker Ranch, the largest privately owned ranch in all of America—including Texas, pardner!

The **Kilauea Volcano Wilderness Runs** is held over rough lava, in and out of volcanic craters, and through 'ohi'a and fern forests within the Hawaii Volcanoes National Park.

With well-known headliners and newcomers alike, the annual **Big Island Slack-Key Guitar Festival** is held in Hilo, sponsored by the East Hawai'i Cultural Center.

Held in Kona, the **Na Pua 'O Ke Kai** billfish tournament is a daylong fishing event for women.

August

The **Pro-Am Billfish Tournament,** held in the waters off Kona, precedes and is a qualifying meet for the more famous annual **Hawaiian International Billfish Tournament,** held about one week later. A world-renowned tournament and the Big Daddy of them all, the HIBT has been held every year since 1959. Contact organizers at 808/329-6155 for information on either event, or see www.konabillfish.com.

August 17 is **Admission Day,** a state holiday recognizing the day that Hawaii became a state.

On the weekend closest to Admission Day, a royal procession, traditional hula, lei workshops, games, and crafts are on the schedule at the **Hawaiian Cultural Festival** at Pu'ukohola Heiau in Kawaihae.

The **International Festival of the Pacific** features a "Pageant of Nations" in Hilo. Folk dances, complete with authentic costumes from throughout Asia and the Pacific, add a rare excitement to the festivities. Other events include a parade, hula, and food from the Pacific.

Kailua-Kona hosts the annual **Queen Lili'uokalani Outrigger Canoe Race** every Labor Day weekend. Single-hull, double-hull, and one-person events are held over a two-day period. Run between Kailua and Honaunau, this 18-mile race is the longest in the state, with over 2,500 paddlers in competition.

September

In early September don't miss the **Parker Ranch Round-Up Rodeo** at ranch rodeo arena in Waimea.

The **Hawai'i County Fair** at Hilo is an old-time fair held on the grounds of Hilo Civic Auditorium.

Aloha Festivals celebrate Hawaii's own "intangible quality," *aloha*. This two-month series of several dozen individual festivals includes parades, lu'au, athletic competitions, historical pageants, balls, and various entertainment. The spirit of *aloha* is infectious and all are welcome. Check local papers and tourist literature for happenings near you or visit www.alohafestivals.com.

October

When they really "wanna have fun," super-athletes come to the **Ironman Triathlon World Championship** at Kailua-Kona. A 2.4-mile open-ocean swim, followed by a 112-mile bike ride, and topped off with a full 26.2-mile marathon is their idea of a good day. Call the Ironman Office at 808/329-0063 or go to www.ironmanlive.com.

Lasting two weekends, the **Hamakua Music Festival** features island musicians and those of national fame. While jazz is always scheduled, classical and Hawaiian music are also sometimes performed. For information, call 808/775-3378 or visit www.hamakuamusicfestival.com.

November

Taste the best coffee commercially grown in the United States at the annual **Kona Coffee Cultural Festival** in Kailua-Kona. This festival is the longest-running foods festival in the state and celebrates a product that's been growing in the region for about 175 years. Parades, arts and crafts, ethnic foods, and entertainment are part of the festivities. See www.konacoffeefest.com for information.

Celebrating another of the island's agricultural products, the **Taro Festival** is held yearly in Honoka'a.

November 11, **Veterans Day,** is a national holiday celebrated by parades.

The **Hawaii International Film Festival** showcases new and engaging films, mainly from Asian and Pacific Rim countries. On the Big Island, these films show at various theaters around the island. Call 808/528-3456 or 800/752-8193 for information about what's playing and where, or check out www.hiff.org.

December

The people of Hilo celebrate a New England Christmas in memory of the missionaries with **A Christmas Tradition,** held at the Lyman House Memorial Museum, Hilo, 808/935-5021. To get a jump on it, the **Annual Waimea Christmas Parade** is held in Waimea toward the beginning of the month.

On **New Year's Eve** hold onto your hat, because they do it up big in Hawaii. The merriment and alcohol flow all over the islands. Firecrackers are illegal, but they go off everywhere. Beware of hangovers and "amateur" drunken drivers.

On the Road

You'll have no problem having fun on the Big Island. Everybody goes outside to play. You can camp and hike, drive golf balls over lagoons, smack tennis balls at private and public courts, ski, snorkel, windsurf, gallop a horse, bag a wild turkey, spy a rare bird, or latch onto a marlin that'll tail-walk across a windowpane sea. Choose your sport and have a ball.

CAMPING

The Big Island has the best camping in the state, with more facilities and less competition for campsites than on the other islands. Nearly three dozen parks fringe the coastline and sit deep in the interior; almost half offer camping. The others boast a combination of rugged hikes, easy strolls, self-guided nature walks, swimming, historical sites, and natural phenomena. The ones with campgrounds are state-, county-, and nationally operated, ranging from remote walk-in sites to housekeeping cabins. All require camping permits—inexpensive for the county and state parks, free for the national parks. Camping permits can be obtained by walk-in application to the appropriate office or by writing ahead. Although there is usually no problem obtaining campsites, when writing, request reservations well in advance, allowing a minimum of one month for letters to go back and forth.

General Camping Information

Most campgrounds have pavilions, fireplaces, toilets (sometimes pit), and running water, but usually no individual electrical hookups. Pavilions often have electric lights, but sometimes campers appropriate the bulbs, so it's wise to carry your own. Drinking water is available, but at times brackish water is used for flushing toilets and

ROBERT NILSEN

lava-covered road

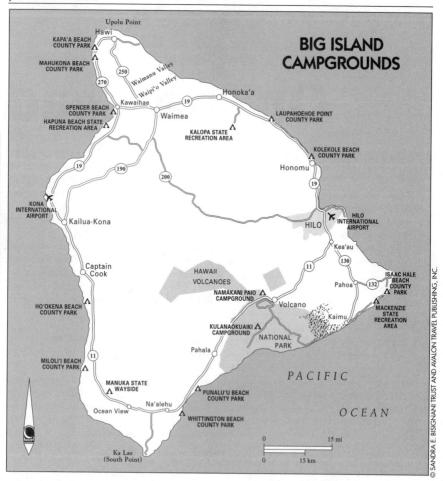

BIG ISLAND CAMPGROUNDS

© SANDRA E. BISIGNANI TRUST AND AVALON TRAVEL PUBLISHING, INC.

for showers, so read all signs regarding water. Backcountry shelters have catchment water, but never hike without an adequate supply of your own. Cooking fires are allowed in established fire pits, but no wood is provided. Charcoal is a good idea, or bottled fuel for those hiking. When camping in the mountains, be prepared for cold and rainy weather. Women, especially, should never hike or camp alone, and everyone should exercise precaution against theft, though it's not as prevalent as on the other islands.

County Parks

The county-maintained parks are open to the public for day use, and permits are only required for overnight tent and RV camping. For information write: Department of Parks and Recreation, County of Hawaii, 101 Pauahi St., Suite 6, Hilo, HI 96720, 808/961-8311. You can obtain a permit by mail or pick it up in person, Mon.–Fri. 7:45 A.M.–4 P.M. If you'll be arriving after hours or on a weekend, have the permits mailed to you. Branch offices (all with reduced hours) are located at Hale Halawai in Kailua-

Kona, 808/327-3565; in Waimea Community Center in Waimea, 808/887-3014; in Yano Hall in Captain Cook, 808/323-3060; in Naʻalehu, 808/939-2510; and in Pahala, 808/928-3102. Fees are adults, $5 per day; children 13–17, $2 per day; youngsters under 12, $1 per day. Pavilions for exclusive use are $25 per day with kitchen, $10 without. Camping is limited to one week at any one site June–Aug. and to two weeks at any one site for the rest of the year. County parks that allow camping are as follows. Puna: Isaac Hale; Hamakua: Kolekole and Laupahoehoe; North Kohala: Kapaʻa and Mahukona; South Kohala: Spencer; South Kona: Hoʻokena and Miloliʻi; and Kaʻu: Punaluʻu and Whittington.

State Parks

Day use of state parks is free, with no permit required, but you will need one for tent camping and for cabins. Five consecutive nights is the limit for either camping or cabins at any one site. If you want a permit, at least one week's notice is required regardless of availability. You can pick up your permit at the state parks office Mon.–Fri. 8 A.M.–3:30 P.M., but again it saves time if you do it all by mail. Write: Department of Land and Natural Resources, Division of State Parks, P.O. Box 936 (75 Aupuni St. #204), Hilo, HI 96721, 808/974-6200.

Camping is permitted only at Kalopa and MacKenzie State Recreation Areas and Manuka State Wayside, where there is a $5 fee per campsite per night. Forest cabins are located at Kalopa SRA, and A-frame cabins are at Hapuna Beach SRA. The four-person A-frames are a flat $20 per night. The group housekeeping cabins at Kalopa SRA are $55 for up to eight people. When writing for permits, specify exactly which facility you require, for how long, and for how many people. Located along the Saddle Road near Pohakuloa Military Camp, Mauna Kea State Park is now closed to overnight use but day use is still permitted.

Hawaii Volcanoes National Park

For overnight backcountry camping in Hawaii Volcanoes National Park, permits are required but available free through the park Visitors Cen-

ter. Your stay is limited to seven days per campground per year. There are a half dozen walk-in primitive campsites and two trail cabins in the park; you can't reserve them and should expect to share them with other hikers. Applications for camping and hiking are taken only one day in advance. No open fires are permitted. At primitive campsites along the coast, there are three-sided, open shelters that offer a partial covering against the elements. Camping is also available at both Namakani Paio and Kulanaokuaiki drive-in campgrounds, but there are no shower facilities. There is no charge for tent camping at these two campsites and no reservations are required. For information on camping and hiking in the park, write Hawaii Volcanoes National Park, P.O. Box 52, Hawaii National Park, HI 96718, or stop by the Visitors Center, 808/985-6000, open daily 7:45 A.M.–5 P.M.

A-frame cabins are provided at Namakani Paio Campground, and arrangements are made through Volcano House, Hawaii Volcanoes National Park, HI 96718, 808/967-7321, 800/325-3535. It's first-come, first-served. A cooking pavilion has fireplaces, but no wood or drinking water is provided. The 10 small cabins available at this campground can be reserved through Volcano House. Each sleeps up to four people and costs $40 single or double, and $8 each for a third or fourth person. Linens, soap, towels, and a blanket are provided, but you would be wise to bring an extra sleeping bag as it can get cold. Each cabin contains one double bed and two single bunk beds and an electric light, but no electrical outlets. There is a picnic table and barbecue grill for each cabin, but you'll need to bring your own charcoal and cooking utensils. Check in at Volcano House after 3 P.M. and check out by noon.

Other Camping Areas

Camping is allowed by permit at three campsites on Kamehameha Schools Bishop Estate land in Waipiʻo Valley. For specific information and to obtain a free permit, contact Bishop Estate's Kona office, 808/332-5300, 78-6831 Aliʻi Drive, Suite 232, Kailua-Kona, HI 96740, at least two weeks in advance of your intended trip.

You will receive an application, which you must sign and return. There are no toilets in the valley, so you must bring your own "Port-A-Potty" with you and take it out when you leave!

Camping is also permitted farther north along the coast in Waimanu Valley. Apply for a free camping permit from the Division of Forestry and Wildlife, P.O. Box 4849, Hilo, HI 96720, 808/974-4221, no more than one month in advance. Nine campsites are available, each with a fireplace, and three composting toilets are shared among the campers. Camping is limited to six nights.

HIKING

Hiking on the Big Island

Hiking on the Big Island is stupendous. There's something for everyone, from civilized walks to the breathtaking 'Akaka Falls to huff-puff treks to the summit of Mauna Loa. The largest number of trails, and the most outstanding according to many, are laced across Volcanoes National Park.

After all, this is the world's most active volcano. You can hike across the crater floor, spurred on by the knowledge that it can shake to life at any moment. Or dip down off the mountain and amble the lonely trails in the Ka'u Desert or remnants of the King's Coastal Trail in Puna. The most important thing to do, before heading out in Volcanoes, is to stop at park headquarters and inquire about trail conditions. Make absolutely sure to register, giving the rangers your hiking itinerary. In the event of an eruption, they will be able to locate you and send a helicopter if necessary. Follow this advice—your life may depend upon it! Everyone can enjoy vistas on Devastation Trail or Sulfur Bank or at the Thurston Lava Tube without any danger whatsoever. In the north you'll find Waipi'o, Waimanu, and Pololu Valleys. All offer secluded hiking and camping where you can play Robinson Crusoe on your own beach and gather a variety of island fruits from once-cultivated trees gone wild. The State Division of Forestry and Wildlife also maintains a number of trails in various locations around

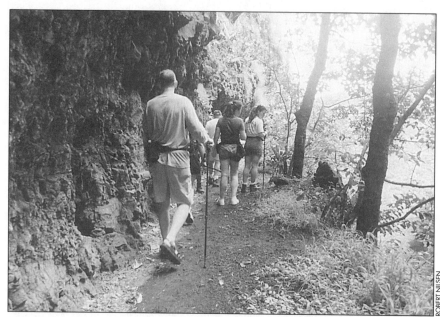

The trail to Kapoloa Falls cuts across the steep side walls of Pololu Valley.

the island that cater to all levels of hikers. Check with them for details and maps.

Hiking Tips

Hike with someone—share the experience. If possible, don't hike or camp alone, especially if you're a woman. Don't leave your valuables in your tent, and always carry your money, papers, and camera with you. At the least, let someone know where you are going and when you plan to be back; supply an itinerary and your expected route, then stick to it. Buy and use a trail map, and stay on designated trails—this not only preserves Hawai'i's fragile environment, it also keeps you out of dangerous areas. Occasionally, trails will be closed for maintenance, so stay off these routes. Many trails are well maintained, but trailhead markers are sometimes missing. Look for mileage markers along many park and forest reserve trails to gauge your progress. They are usually white metal stakes set about a foot off the ground with numbers indicating the distance from a trailhead. The trails themselves can be muddy, which can make them treacherously slippery.

Wear comfortable clothing. Shorts and a T-shirt will suffice on many trails, but long pants and long-sleeved shirts are better where it's rainy and overgrown. Bring a windbreaker or rain gear—it can rain and blow at any time. Wear sturdy walking or hiking shoes that you don't mind getting wet and muddy—it's almost guaranteed on some trails. Sturdy shoes will be imperative on trails over lava. Some very wet spots and stream crossings may be better done in tabi or other water shoes. Your clothes may become permanently stained with mud—a wonderful memento of your trip. Officials and others often ask hikers to pick clinging seeds off their clothes when coming out at the trailhead and to wash off boots so as not to unintentionally transport seeds to non-native areas.

Always bring food because you cannot, in most cases, forage from the land. Carry plenty of drinking water, at least two quarts per day. Heat can cause your body to lose water and salt. If you become woozy or weak, rest, take salt, and drink water as you need it. Remember, it takes much more water to restore a dehydrated per-

son than to stay hydrated as you go; take small, frequent sips. No matter how clean it looks, water in most streams is biologically polluted and will give you bad stomach problems if you drink it without purifying it first; either boil it or treat it with tablets. For your part, please don't use the streams as a toilet.

Wear sunscreen, as the sun can be intense and UV rays penetrate the clouds. Bring and use mosquito repellent—even in paradise pesky bugs abound. Carry a dedicated trash bag and pack out all your garbage.

Many trails are used by hunters of wild boar, deer, or game birds. If you hike in hunting areas during hunting season, wear brightly colored or reflective clothing. Often, forest reserve trails have check-in stations at trailheads. Hikers and hunters must sign a logbook, especially if they intend to camp. The comments by previous hikers are worth reading for up-to-the-minute information on trail conditions.

Many roads leading to the trailheads are marked for 4WD vehicles only. Heed the warnings, especially during rainy weather, when roads are very slick and swollen streams can swallow your rental car. Remember that going in may be fine, but a sudden storm can leave you stranded. Be mindful of flash floods; small creeks can turn into raging torrents with upland rains. Never camp in a dry creekbed.

Twilight is short in the islands, and night sets in rapidly. In June, sunrise is around 6 A.M. and sunset 7 P.M.; in December, these occur at 7 A.M. and 6 P.M. If you become lost, find an open spot and stay put; at night, stay as dry as you can. If you must continue, walk on ridges and avoid the gulches, which have more obstacles and make it harder for rescuers to spot you. Do not light a fire. Some forest areas can be very dry and fire could spread easily. Fog is only encountered at the 1,500- to 5,000-foot level, but be careful of disorientation.

Generally, stay within your limits, be careful, and enjoy yourself.

Hiking and Camping Equipment

Like everything else you take to the Big Island, your camping and hiking equipment should be lightweight and durable. Camping equipment size and weight should not cause a problem with baggage requirements on airlines: if they do, it's a tip-off that you're hauling too much. One odd luggage consideration you might make is a small Styrofoam cooler packed with equipment. Exchange the gear for food items when you get to Hawai'i; if you intend to car camp successfully and keep food prices down, you'll definitely need a cooler. You can also buy one on arrival for only a few dollars.

Consider a frame backpack or a convertible pack that turns into a soft-side suitcase, plus a day pack. You'll need a lightweight **tent,** preferably with a rainfly and a sewn-in waterproof floor. This will save you from getting wet and miserable and will keep out mosquitoes, cockroaches, ants, and the few stinging insects on Hawai'i. Atop Mauna Loa, where you can expect cold and wind, a tent is a must; in fact you won't be allowed to camp without one. **Sleeping bags** are a good idea, although you can get along at sea level with only a blanket. Down-filled or high-quality synthetic bags are necessary for Mauna Kea, Mauna Loa, or any high-altitude camping—you'll freeze without one.

Camp stoves are needed because there's very little available wood, it's often wet in the deep forest, and open fires are often prohibited. If you'll be car camping, take along a multi-burner stove; for hiking, a backpacker's stove will be necessary. The grills found at some (not all) campgrounds are popular with many families that go often to the beach parks for an open-air dinner. You can buy a very inexpensive charcoal grill at many variety stores throughout Hawai'i. It's a great idea to take along a **lantern.** This will give car campers added safety. Definitely take a **flashlight,** replacement batteries, and a few small **candles.** A complete **first-aid kit** can mean the difference between life and death and is worth the extra bulk. Hikers, especially those leaving the coastal areas, should take rain gear, plastic ground cloth, utility knife, compass, safety whistle, mess kit, water purification tablets, biodegradable "Camp Suds" or similar soap, a canteen, nylon cord, sewing kit (dental floss works as thread), and waterproof matches (buy matches in Hawaii as it is illegal to take flammable materials on an airplane). In a film

container, pack a few nails, safety pins, fishhooks, line, and bendable wire. Nothing else does what these do and they're all handy for a million and one uses. If you find a staff or hiking stick at the beginning of a trail, consider using it—others obviously found it useful—but leave it at the trailhead for others to use when you return.

Rental Equipment and Sales

A number of stores sell and a few stores rent **camping equipment,** but their supplies are limited. Try **Hilo Surplus Store,** 148 Mamo Ave., downtown Hilo, 808/935-6398; **Pacific Rent-All,** 1080 Kilauea Ave., Hilo, 808/935-2974; and **Kona Rent All,** 808/329-1644. Although what they carry is not necessarily of the backpacker variety, **Kmart** in Kailua and **Wal-Mart** in both Kailua and Hilo have camping supplies. Check **Hawaii Forest and Trail** retail shop in Kailua-Kona, 808/331-8505, for a quality but limited selection of hiking gear, books, and maps.

Guided Hikes

If you're not familiar with good bird-watching spots on Hawai'i, contact Rob or Cindy Pacheco at **Hawaii Forest and Trail,** 74-5035B Queen Ka'ahumanu Hwy., Kailua-Kona, HI 96740, 808/331-8505, 800/464-1993, fax 808/331-8704, info@hawaii-forest.com, www.hawaii-forest.com. This well-established naturalist company uses powerful 4WD vans to get you to where the less common birds are found. Its three exclusive bird-watching tours take you to the rainforests of the Pu'u O'o Ranch, the Hakalau National Wildlife Refuge on the eastern slope of Mauna Kea, and the forests on the leeward slope of Mauna Kea. Other tours include the Valley Waterfall Adventure to the spectacular Pololu Valley of North Kohala, a mule ride along the rim of the Pololu Valley, a tour to Hawaii Volcanoes National Park, and the Mauna Kea Summit and Stars adventure. All tours are kept to a maximum of 10 people, are guided by knowledgeable naturalists, include food and beverage, provide all necessary equipment, and include pickup and drop-off from specified locations on the Kona side. The trip to Pololu Waterfall and the mule ride, both half-day affairs, are $95 adult or $85 for children ages 8–12. The rest are full-day tours that run $145 adult and $105 child. Children are welcome on all trips except for the Mauna Kea Summit adventure, which has an age limit of 16. Any of these tours will certainly be a highlight of your vacation.

A well-established and reputable hiking company that will help you stretch your legs in the great outdoors yet have minimal impact on the land is **Hawaiian Walkways,** 808/775-0372, 800/457-7759, hiwalk@aloha.net, www.hawaiianwalkways.com. Run by Hugh Montgomery and his wife Kaulana, this company will teach you about the land you walk through and help you appreciate its diversity and sanctity. Hikes are easy to moderate and generally last three to five hours. Four basic hikes take you to the rim of Waipi'o Valley for a peek into the Valley of Kings, into Hawaii Volcanoes National Park to discover the secrets of Kilauea volcano, up on the mist-shrouded slopes of Mt. Hualalai, and to the many *kipuka* along the Saddle Road. Custom hikes can also be arranged. The Waipi'o rim hike is offered daily, while the others can be arranged and customized to the guests' needs. Both the Waipi'o Waterfall Adventure and the Kona Cloud Forest Botanical Walk run $85 per person. The Kilauea Volcano Discovery and Saddle Road Exploration are $175 for the first person, $100 for each additional adult, and $50 for children. A small day pack, walking stick, rain gear, lunch, and drinks are provided, as is expert commentary by the knowledgeable owner/guides. A hike with Hawaiian Walkways is not only good physical exercise, it's an excellent introduction to the natural world of the Big Island. Two thumbs up.

For a more educational, "guided geologic adventure" on one of the earth's most changeable pieces of real estate, try **Hawaii Volcano GeoVentures,** P.O. Box 816, Volcano, HI 96785, tel./fax 808/985-9901, geoventures@aloha.net, http://planet-hawaii.com/hea/volcano. With a focus on the Kilauea volcano area and guided by a geologist/educator, these trips take you nose to nose with the wonders of the living earth.

Island Outfitters offers a more out-of-the-way adventure with helicopter flights from the Kohala resorts to remote Honokane Nui Valley

on the Hamakua Coast and then a naturalist-led hike within the valley. The 3.5-hour tour runs $380 per person and the 6.5-hour tour is $680. Contact Island Outfitters at P.O. Box 4441, Hilo, HI 96720, 808/966-7933, 800/840-9974, fax 808/966-6931, islehike@aloha.com, www.islandoutfittershawaii.com.

With eight- and 10-day hiking and multi-sport tours to the Big Island and/or Maui and Kaua'i, **Hawaiian Adventure Tours** offers a different sort of opportunity for those who want more of a long-term catered excursion. These two tours run $1,750–2,000 per person with a minimum of three or four, include all arrangements and most costs within the islands, and are run roughly on a monthly basis. For information and reservations, contact the company at P.O. Box 1269, Kapa'au, HI 96755, 808/889-0227, 800/659-3544, advtours@aloha.net, www.hawaiiadventuretours.com.

The **Kona Hiking Club,** 808/325-0012, is a fairly loosely organized group of individuals that offers no-cost hikes on the first Saturday of the month. Meet at 8 A.M. at the parking lot behind the Sibu Restaurant in Kailua-Kona and bring your own lunch. Hikes run to various destinations, some to private land that cannot be accessed any other way.

Helpful Departments and Organizations

The Department of Land and Natural Resources, Division of Forestry and Wildlife, 1151 Punchbowl St., Honolulu, HI 96813, 808/548-2861, is helpful in providing trail maps, accessibility information, hunting and fishing regulations, and general forest rules. Its "Hawai'i Recreation Map" is excellent and free. On the Big Island, contact the DLNR, Division of Forestry and Wildlife, P.O. Box 4849, Hilo, HI 96720, 808/974-4221. This office has trail descriptions for those trails under its jurisdiction and select maps for some of those trails. The DLNR **State Parks Division,** P.O. Box 936, Hilo, HI 96721, 808/974-6200, puts out a brochure on camping, permits, general rules, and recreational opportunities. The following organizations can provide general information on wildlife, conservation, and organized hiking trips, although they are not based on Hawai'i: **Hawaiian Audubon Society,** 850 Richards St., Suite 505, Honolulu, HI 96813-4709, www .hawaii-audubon.50megs.com; and **Sierra Club, Hawaii Chapter,** P.O. Box 2577, Honolulu, HI 96803, 808/538-6616, www.hi.sierraclub.org.

Hiking and Camping Books

Two helpful camping books are *Hawaii: A Camping Guide,* by George Cagala, and Richard McMahon's *Camping Hawai'i.*

For a well-written and detailed hiking guide, complete with maps, check out *Hawaii Trails* by Kathy Morey, *Hiking Hawaii, The Big Island* by Robert Smith, or *Hawaiian Hiking Trails* by Craig Chisholm.

Topographical Maps and Nautical Charts

For detailed topographical maps, write **U.S. Geological Survey,** Information Services, P.O. Box 25286, Denver, CO 80225, call 703/648-4888, 800/USA-MAPS, or visit www.usgs.gov. **Basically Books** in downtown Hilo at 160 Kamehameha Ave., 808/961-0144, has a great selection of all types of maps, including topographical maps for hikers, NOAA nautical and aeronautical charts, and Defense Mapping Agency charts of the Pacific. On the Kona side, try **Big Island Marine, Inc.,** 73-4840 Kanalani St., #A-1, Kailua-Kona, HI 96740, 808/329-3719; or **Kona Marine,** in the Honokohau Small Boat Harbor, 808/329-1012, for nautical charts. The **Hawaii Forest and Trail** retail store, 808/331-8505, in Kailua across from the entrance to Honokohau Marina, carries USGS maps. Also useful, but not for hiking, are the University of Hawai'i Press reference maps of each island. For nautical charts, write **National Ocean Service,** Riverdale, MD 20737-1199, 301/436-6990, 800/638-8972.

BEACHES

Being the youngest island, Hawai'i has far fewer beaches than any of the other major Hawaiian islands, and all but a handful of these shoreline retreats are small affairs often with volcanic rock intrusions. All beaches are open to the public. Most are accessed through beach parks, but some access is over private property. All hotels and condominiums must by law offer pathway access to beaches they front, and each has some parking set aside for public use.

Generally speaking, beaches and shorelines on the north and west coasts of the island have high surf conditions and strong ocean currents during winter months—use extreme caution—and those on the south and east experience some high surf during the summer months. A few county beaches have lifeguards. For lifeguard hours and locations, call the Department of Parks and Recreation at 808/961-8694. At some beaches, flags will warn you of ocean conditions. A yellow flag means use caution. A half-yellow, half-red sign signifies caution because of strong winds. A red flag indicates hazardous water conditions—beach closed, no swimming. In addition, yellow and black signs are sometimes posted at certain beaches to indicate other warnings: dangerous shore break, high surf spot, strong currents, presence of jellyfish, or beach closed.

Before you head to the beach, take a drive to the local shop for a cheap woven beach mat. Whalers General Store, ABC markets, other sundries shops, Longs Drugs, Wal-Mart, Kmart, and the like have them for $1–1.50. Hotel sundries shops sometimes also carry the exact same thing for about a dollar more. Sometimes condos, B&Bs, and vacation rental homes will have them for guests to use, but don't necessarily count on it.

East Side Beaches

The east side has few accessible beaches. The best are in the Hilo area. Hilo Waterfront beach is a nice long crescent of gray/white sand, but few use this beach for swimming. Locals head out east of downtown to **Onekahakaha Beach, Leleiwi Beach,** and **Richardson's Beach,** which are all small pockets of white sand bound by rugged lava shoreline. The only other beaches of note along this coast are the long, black-sand **Waipi'o Beach** in Waipi'o Valley and the smaller **Waimanu Beach** in a valley farther north. The use of either of these two valley beaches is discouraged unless the water is glassy smooth.

South Side Beaches

Black sand typifies the beaches along the south coast. The best, near Kalapana and Kaimu, have been overrun by lava flows in the past 15 years, although new ones are being created. Beaches that still draw swimmers in Puna are **Isaac Hale Beach** (also called Pohoiki), and the half-hidden **Kehena Beach.** In Ka'u, the best and easiest to get to is black sand **Punalu'u Beach.** Near the windswept South Point is **Green Sand Beach,** an oddity for sure, but it's better to look at than to swim at, unless it's totally calm.

West Side Beaches

Miloli'i and **Ho'okena** are two local and fairly isolated beaches in South Kona. They're both fine for a day out, but you have to make an effort to get to either. North Kona has more and much more easily accessible beaches. **Kahalu'u Beach** is the first of these, and while the swimming is fine, the snorkeling is better. **Disappearing Sands Beach** (also called White Sand Beach) is also good when the sand is there and is a popular spot for boogie boarders. Perhaps the most gentle for kids and an all-around good place to have your first dip into the Kona waters is **Kailua Bay Beach** in front of the King Kamehameha's Kona Beach Hotel. There are pockets of sandy beach at the Old Kona Airport State Recreation Area, but better beaches are found farther north at Kaloko-Honokohau National Historical Park and Kona Coast State Park.

The best beaches on the island dot the Kohala Coast. An almost perfect crescent, white sand beach fronts the Kona Village Resort. The sandy bottom, clear water, and palm-fringed shore will certainly let you know that you're floating in paradise. Longer and straighter is the ever-popular **'Anaeho'omalu Beach,** which fronts the Outrigger Waikoloa Beach Resort. Not only is the swimming good here, but you can indulge in a wide variety of water sports. Diminutive beaches hug the coast at the Mauna Lani Resort, but the island's best beaches are just a few miles away. **Hapuna Beach** and **Kauna'oa Beach**

WATER SAFETY TIPS

Observe the water before you enter. Note where others are swimming or snorkeling and go there. Don't turn your back on the water. Dive under incoming waves before they reach you. Come in *before* you get tired.

When the wind comes up, get out. Stay out of water during periods of high surf. High surf often creates riptides that can pull you out to sea. If caught in a riptide, don't panic. Swim parallel to the shore until you are out of the strong pull. Be aware of ocean currents, especially those within reefs that can cause riptides when the water washes out a channel.

If you are using water equipment, make sure it all works properly. Wear a T-shirt when snorkeling; it could save you from a major sunburn.

Stay off of coral. Standing on coral damages it, as does breaking it with your hands.

Leave the fish and turtles alone. Green sea turtles are an endangered species, and a fine of up to $10,000 can be levied on those who knowingly disturb them. Have a great time looking, but give them space.

in front of the Mauna Kea Hotel are the crown jewels of Big Island beaches: white sand, gentle slope, and long and narrow sand strip. Swimming is great, and snorkeling is also noteworthy. Both are fronted by first-class luxury hotels, and Hapuna Beach also has public facilities.

SCUBA

If you think that Hawaii is beautiful above the sea, wait until you explore below. Warm tropical waters that average 75–80°F year-round and coral growth make it a fascinating haven for reef fish and aquatic plantlife. You'll discover that Hawaiian waters are remarkably clear, with excellent visibility. Fish in every fathomable color parade by. Lavender clusters of coral, red and gold coral trees, and over 1,500 different types of shells carpet the ocean floor. In some spots the fish are so accustomed to humans that they'll nibble at your fingers. In other spots, lurking moray eels add the special zest of danger. Sharks and barracuda pose less danger than scraping your knee on the coral or being driven against the rocks by a heavy swell. There are enormous but harmless sea bass and a profusion of sea turtles. All this awaits you below the surface of Hawaii's waters.

Hawai'i has particularly generous underwater vistas open to anyone donning a mask and fins. Snorkel and dive sites, varying in difficulty and challenge, are accessible from the island. Sites can be totally hospitable, good for families and first-time snorkelers who want an exciting but safe frolic; or they can be accessible only to the experienced diver.

Those in the know consider the deep diving along the steep drop-offs of Hawai'i's geologically young coastline some of the best in the state. The ocean surrounding the Big Island has not had a chance to turn the relatively new lava to sand, which makes the visibility absolutely perfect, even to depths of 150 feet or more. There's also 60–70 miles of coral belt around the Big Island, which adds up to a magnificent diving experience. Only advanced divers should attempt deep-water dives, but beginners and snorkelers will have many visual thrills inside the protected bays and coves. While most people head to the west (Kona) side, there is very good diving on the east side as well. As always, weather conditions will dictate how the water and underwater conditions will be, so always inquire about sites and conditions with one of the dive shops before you head for the water.

If you're a scuba diver you'll have to show your C Card before local shops will rent you gear, fill your tanks, or take you on a charter dive. Plenty of outstanding scuba instructors will give you lessons toward certification, and they're especially reasonable because of the stiff competition. Prices vary, but you can take a three- to five-day semiprivate certification course including all equipment for about $350–500. Divers unaccustomed to Hawaiian waters should not dive alone regardless of their experience. Most opt for dive tours to special dive grounds guaranteed to please. These vary also, but an accompanied single-tank dive where no boat is involved goes for about $50, expect to spend $80–100

for a two-tank boat dive, and most introductory dives will be about $130. Special charter dives, night dives, and photography dives are also offered. Most companies pick you up at your hotel, take you to the site, and return you home. Basic equipment costs $25–35 for the day, and most times you'll only need the top of a wet suit.

The alternative to boat dives is shore diving. *Shore Diving in Kona* is a great book listing sites, equipment, regulations, and suggestions for successful and safe dives. If your budget is limited and you're an experienced shore diver, it's a way to have a great outing at a reasonable price.

Scuba Shops and Tour Companies

There are about two dozen companies on the Big Island, mostly on the Kona side, that offer scuba instruction and escorted dives and rent scuba equipment.

One of the best outfits to dive with on the Big Island is **Dive Makai** in Kona, 808/329-2025, www.divemakai.com, operated by Tom Shockley and Lisa Choquette. These very experienced divers have run this service for years and have many dedicated customers. Both Tom and Lisa are conservationists who help preserve the fragile reef. They've worked very hard with the Diver's Council to protect dive sites from fish collectors and to protect the reef from destruction by anchors. Their motto, "We care," is not a trite saying, as they continue to preserve the reef for you and your children.

Another excellent diving outfit is **Jack's Diving Locker,** 75-5819 Ali'i Dr. in the Coconut Grove Marketplace, 808/329-7585, 800/345-4807, www.jacksdivinglocker.com, a responsible outfit that does a good job of watching out for its customers and taking care of the reef. Owners Teri and Jeff Leicher, along with their crew, run diving and snorkeling excursions along the Kona Coast from Kealakekua Bay to Keahole Point, which takes in over 50 dive sites (most of which have permanent moorings to protect the reef from damage by anchoring). Jack's also specializes in snorkel sales and rentals, scuba equipment rentals, and certification classes. Dives run the gamut from a one tank beach dive at $50 to a multiday, multidive arrangement for $265.

Big Island Divers, 75-5467 Kaiwi St., 808/329-6068, 800/488-6068, www.bigislanddivers.com, departing from Honokohau Harbor on a custom-built 35-foot dive boat, offers a very inexpensive scuba certification course that's given on four consecutive Saturdays or Wednesdays, so you must intend to stay on the Big Island for that length of time. The normal four-day course costs about $499. Big Island Divers offers a two-tank, two-location dive for $89, as well as introductory and night dives.

Kohala Divers along Route 270 in the Kawaihae Shopping Center, 808/882-7774, www.kohaladivers.com, open daily 8 A.M.–5 P.M., offers scuba certification, snorkel equipment rentals for $10, and scuba equipment rentals for $15. The company leads two-tank dives for $99, a night dive for $125, an introductory dive for $145, and will take snorkelers along for $45 if there's room on the boat. It's a bit far to go from Kailua-Kona but great if you're staying at one of the Kohala resorts or in Waimea. A full-service dive shop, this company is the farthest north along the Kohala Coast.

Nearby in Kawaihae is **Mauna Kea Divers,** 808/882-1544, www.maunakeadivers.com, who have somewhat cheaper prices and will model a tour for you if you have special needs or desires.

Kona Coast Divers, 74-5614 Palani Rd., Kona, 808/329-8802, 800/562-3483, www.konacoastdivers.com, is owned and operated by longtime Kona Coast diver Jim Robertson. This outfit is efficient and to the point. There are many dive options, including a two-tank boat dive, $80; night dive, $99; a manta ray dive, $65; and an introductory dive, $135. Full underwater gear is sold and rented.

Sandwich Isle Divers, 808/329-9188, www.sandwichisledivers.com, is owned and operated by Steve and Larry, longtime Kona Coast divers who know all the spots. They have a custom, six-passenger dive boat, great for small, personalized trips for avid divers. They offer competitive rates for instruction and day and night dives: certified diver with all gear for $95, introductory dive at $120, and a night dive for $75. Their office is in the Kona Marketplace.

A twist on the usual snorkel adventure is offered by **Torpedo Tours Hawaii,** 808/938-0405, www.torpedotours.com, which does shore and boat dives as well as certification. Small groups are important here. To provide a little extra power, this company provides "torpedo" scooters, battery powered motors that pull you through the water at two mph, for some dives: $55–90 from shore or $129 for a torpedo dive from a boat.

Eco-Adventures at the King Kamehameha's Kona Beach Hotel in Kailua, 808/329-7116, 800/949-3483, offers daily morning, afternoon, and night boat charters as well as beach dives and open water certification. Eco-Adventures is conveniently located and offers good value for your money.

If you only want a shore dive, try **Ocean Eco Tours,** 808/324-7873, www.oceanecotours.com. This company says it specializes in beginners, and certification courses are taught.

Honu Sports, 808/938-9795, near the Royal Kona Resort in Kailua, offers several shore and boat dives for $89–99 and an introductory boat dive for $139. The use of a propulsion torpedo scooter is an added $40.

For those still dancing to the primordial tune of residual DNA from our one-celled, ocean-dwelling ancestors, *Kona Aggressor II* is a "live-aboard" dive boat, 808/329-8182, 800/344-5662, www.aggressor.com or www.pac-aggressor.com, departing Kona every Saturday for six days of diving along the Kona Coast toward South Point. Passengers dive up to five times per day and night, as the *Aggressor* completely fulfills its motto of "Eat, Sleep, and Dive." This is the Cadillac of dive cruises, and everything on board is taken care of. Rates run $1,995 per person.

The **Nautilus Dive Center,** 382 Kamehameha Ave., Hilo, 808/935-6939, www.downtownhilo.com/nautilus, open Mon.–Sat. 9 A.M.–4 P.M., is one of the longest-established dive companies on the Hilo side. This full-service dive center offers instruction, rentals, and guided dives at lower prices than on the more frequented Kona side. But don't be fooled, the Hilo side has some very good diving. Two popular spots are Leleiwi Beach and Richardson's Beach.

Two other shops in Hilo that offer a variety of boat and shore dives, as well as a multitude of other water activities, are **Aquatic Perceptions,** 808/933-1228; and **Planet Ocean Watersports,** 200 Kanoelehua Ave., 808/935-7277.

SNORKELING AND SNUBA
Snorkeling

Scuba diving requires expensive special equipment, skills, and athletic ability. Snorkeling, in comparison, is much simpler and enjoyable to anyone who can swim. In about 15 minutes you can be taught the fundamentals of snorkeling—you really don't need formal instructions. Other snorkelers or dive-shop attendants can tell you enough to get you started. Because you can breathe without lifting your head, you get great propulsion from the fins and hardly ever need to use your arms. You can go for much greater distances and spend longer periods in the water than if you were swimming. Experienced snorkelers make an art of this sport and you, too, can see and do amazing things with a mask, snorkel,

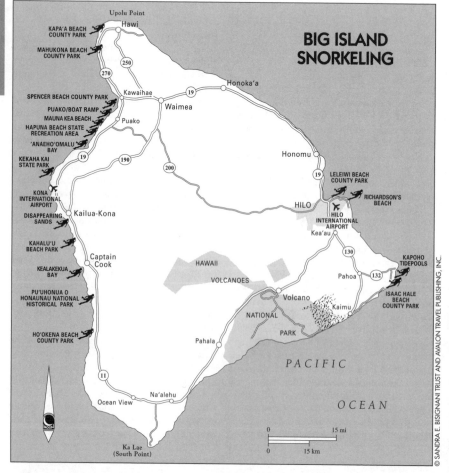

BIG ISLAND SNORKELING

© SANDRA E. BISIGNANI TRUST AND AVALON TRAVEL PUBLISHING, INC.

and flippers. Don't, however, get a false sense of invincibility and exceed your limitations.

Miles of coral reef ring the island, and it's mostly close to shore so you don't have to swim too far out to see coral communities. Some of the most popular snorkeling sites are listed below. Kona: Kekaha Kai State Park, Pawai Bay, Disappearing Sands Beach, Kahaluʻu Beach Park, Kealakekua Bay by the Captain Cook monument (often said to be the best on the island), at Puʻuhonua O Honaunau in Honaunau Bay. Kohala: ʻAnaehoʻomalu Beach, Hapuna Beach, Mauna Kea Beach, Puako coastal area, Spencer Beach County Park, Mahukona Beach County Park, Kapaʻa Beach County Park. Hilo: Leleiwi Beach County Park, Richardson's Beach. Puna: Kapoho tidepools, Isaac Hale Beach Park.

Snorkel Rental

Larger hotels and some condos often have snorkel equipment for guests, but if it isn't free, it will almost always cost more than if you rent it from a dive shop. Many activity booths and virtually all dive shops rent snorkel gear at competitive rates. Depending upon the quality of gear, snorkel gear rental runs about $3–9 an hour or $9–30 a day. Many of the places that rent snorkel gear will also rent boogie boards, usually at about $5–8 a day.

Good old **Snorkel Bob's,** in the parking lot in front of Huggo's Restaurant in Kailua-Kona, 808/329-0770, www.snorkelbob.com, offers some of the best deals for snorkel rental in Hawaii (free snorkeling maps and advice). This gear can be taken interisland and turned in at any Snorkel Bob's location. Depending on the type, snorkel gear will cost $2.50–9 a day or $9–35 a week.

At the beach in front of the King Kamehameha's Kona Beach Hotel, the **Kona Beach Shack** not only rents snorkel gear at $7 a day, they also rent kayaks, paddleboats, boogie boards, and other beach and water equipment. Open daily 9 A.M.–5 P.M.

The 1940 Pontiac woody wagon out front points you to **Kahaluʻu Bay Surf and Sea,** 808/322-4338, located just down the road and across the street from Kahaluʻu Bay and beach

park. This shop can set you up with snorkel gear, surfboards, kayaks, and other water equipment at a fair price.

One of the cheapest for weeklong rentals, **Miller's Snorkeling,** 808/326-1771, at the Kona Bali Kai condo, south of Kailua-Kona along Aliʻi Drive, rents complete snorkel gear for $7 per day or $15 per week and has other beach gear and accessories.

In Hilo, look for snorkel gear at **Nautilus Dive Center,** 382 Kamehameha Ave. at the edge of the downtown strip, 808/935-6939, where snorkel gear runs $5 a day.

Snorkel Boats

Snorkel cruises can be booked through the various activity centers along the Kona and Kohala Coasts and at your hotel travel desk. Snorkeling, scuba, and snuba excursions are also provided by the following: **Fair Wind,** 808/322-2788, 800/677-9461 off-island, www.fair-wind.com, a well-established company with the 60-foot catamaran *Fair Wind II,* has a great reputation and is sure to please. Its boat leaves daily from magnificent Keauhou Bay and stops at Kealakekua Bay in front of the Captain Cook monument. This boat has a diving platform and water slide, sunning deck, and easy access steps into the water. All equipment is on board, and scuba and snuba are options for an additional fee. The 4.5-hour morning cruise runs $89 for adults, $50 for children 4–12; the 3.5-hour afternoon tour is $55 and $35, respectively. A continental breakfast and lunch or snacks and beverages are served.

Departing from the Kailua pier and sailing north to Pawai Bay, **Body Glove Cruises,** 808/326-7122, 800/551-8911, www.bodyglovehawaii.com, is a full-fledged snorkel and scuba company offering a bar and lunch aboard their boat. Costs for the morning and afternoon snorkel sails on the *Body Glove* run $84 adult/$46 child and $52 adult/$32 child, respectively. In season, whale-watching trips may take the place of the afternoon snorkel sail.

Kamanu Charters, 808/329-2021, 800/348-3091, www.kamanu.com, Kona's original snorkel sail, in business over 30 years, provides a full day of fun with beer and snacks included in the price.

ON THE ROAD

REEF FISH

blue-spotted cowfish

Hawaiian lionfish

saddleback wrasse

manta ray

Potter's angelfish

bluestripe butterflyfish

mottled moray

manini

moorish idol

trumpetfish

lagoon *humu*

red-lipped parrotfish

threadfin butterflyfish

Achilles tang

uhu

They pilot a true sailing catamaran and take fewer passengers—a maximum of 24. Sails leave from the Honokohau Marina for Pawai Bay at 9 A.M. and 1:30 P.M., $65 adults and $45 kids 12 and under. Kamanu Charters is a good choice for a fun-filled sail and snorkel experience.

Leaving from Kailua pier on a morning snorkel tour is **Dream Cruises,** 808/326-6000, www.dream-cruises.com. On board are snorkel gear, a water slide, and a water trampoline. This ship provides a fun-filled adventure on its four-hour cruise for $75 adult and $40 children under 17.

At Waikoloa Beach Resort 'Anaeho'omalu Bay, there are two companies offering snorkel services, plus a wide range of other beach and water activities. **Ocean Sports and Activities,** 808/886-6666, 888/742-5234, www.hawaiioceansports .com, and **Red Sail Sports,** 808/886-2878, 877/733-7245, www.redsail.com, both run morning snorkel tours from the beach on sleek catamarans for about $65. Red Sail also has sailings from Hapuna Beach. At the Four Seasons Resort, **Hualalai Water Sports,** 808/325-8222, also offers various sail and/or snorkel options from $55 to $90. Other luxury resorts also operate their own boats.

Inflatable Zodiac rafts also offer daily snorkel tours down the Kona Coast to Kealakekua Bay (see "Zodiac," below).

Snuba

Part scuba, part snorkeling, snuba is a fairly recent underwater concept that is perfect for an introductory underwater adventure. Tethered to a flotation raft bearing a scuba tank, the only apparatus you wear is a regulator, weight belt, mask, and flippers. Your descent is limited to 20 feet, but the fun isn't. For those who feel timid about scuba diving or who just want a new, fun-filled adventure, snuba might be the answer.

Snuba Big Island, Inc., 808/326-7446, can set you up for this new adventure. Dives take place four times every day at the beach in front of King Kamehameha's Kona Beach Hotel or at one of the Kohala Coast beaches. The basic snuba experience costs about $59 per person, and you must be at least eight years old. Alternatively, you can snuba (and snorkel) at Kealakekua Bay on the twice-daily sail with the Fair Wind sailing boat for the cost of their sail plus $49 per person.

SURFING

Surfing off the Big Island is rather uninspiring compared to that off the other islands. Overall, the reefs are treacherous and the surf is lazy. Some surfers bob around off Hilo Bay, and sometimes in Kealakekua Bay on the Kona side. Puna also attracts a few surfers off Pohoiki Beach, and during the right conditions, others make the trip down to the beach in Waipi'o Valley. One spot that seems to have a good deal of interest for local surfers is Honoli'i Beach, a few miles north of Hilo. Generally, the north and west shores boast better swells during the winter, the east and south shores in summer. If you're thinking about buying or renting a surfboard, try **Orchid Land Surfshop,** 262 Kamehameha Ave. in downtown Hilo, 808/935-1533, www.surfolhawaii.com; or **Honolua Surf Co.,** at the Kona Inn Shopping Village in Kailua-Kona, 808/329-1001, for starters. Be sure to ask there about what's happening with the water when you're on-island. For surf lessons, try **Ocean Eco Tours** in Kona, 808/324-7873; **Hawaii Lifeguard Surf Instructors** on the Kona side, 808/324-0442; or **Kahalu'u Bay Beach Rentals,** 808/322-4338, near Kahalu'u Beach Park in Keauhou.

Windsurfing

The Big Island seems nearly bereft of good windsurfing locations. By all accounts, 'Anaeho'omalu Bay at Waikoloa Beach Resort on the Kohala Coast is the best place to sail. For instruction and rental equipment, check with **Ocean Sports and Activities,** 808/886-6666, 888/742-5234, at the Outrigger Waikoloa Resort, which rents boards at $20 an hour and gives 60 minutes of instruction for $45.

PARASAILING AND JETSKIING

UFO Parasailing, 808/325-5836, 800/359-4836, offers boat platform takeoff and landing that's safe and easy for young and old alike. A

"400 feet for seven minutes" atmospheric ride runs $47 and the "800 feet for 10 minutes" stratospheric ride is $57. For those tempted to leave orbit, they'll let out 1,200 feet of rope for $67. Reduced rates are available for early birds, and boat ride-alongs are $18. You, too, can dangle from a parachute and put your life in the hands of these fun-filled Kona guys who will streak you through the air. The boat leaves from the Kailua pier; check in at the office across the street from the pier. Parasailing on the Big Island is done year-round.

If you want speed but know that staying on the water is more your style, try **Aloha Jet Ski Rentals,** 808/329-2745. To take a powerful Kawasaki for a spin around the bay any day except Monday, you must be 18 years old to drive and at least 12 to ride. Rates run $45 for a half hour, $65 an hour, and $10 for a second person. No experience necessary.

KAYAKING

Ocean kayaking has gained much popularity in Hawai'i in the last several years. Although the entire coastline would offer adventure for the expert kayaker, most people try sections of the coast near Kealakekua Bay or Puako and east out of Hilo that offer excellent shoreline variation and great snorkeling. While you can rent kayaks and go where you want, there are a few companies that offer guided trips to exceptional places. Open-cockpit rental kayaks generally run about $25 for a single or $45–50 for a tandem per day and come with all necessary gear and sometimes a car rack. Occasionally, companies will rent by the hour or week. Tours vary, but run about $65–80 for a half day.

In Captain Cook, **Adventures in Paradise,** 808/323-3005, 866/824-2337, www.bigislandkayak.com, is the company to see. Contact Geoff Hand for kayak rentals or tours. Rentals run $25 per person, and tours are $79 per person and usually run near Honaunau Bay or at Kealakekua Bay. Geoff knows the water and will make your tour an experience. As he allows time for snorkeling, he'll point out the many reef fish and other sea creatures that inhabit this coastline.

Also near Kealakekua Bay are **Aloha Kayak Co.** in Honalo, 808/322-2868, www.alohakayak.com; **Kona Boy's Kayaks** between Honalo and Kealakekua, 808/328-1234; and **Kealakekua Bay Kayak** in the town of Kealakekua, 808/323-3329, www.konakayak.com.

In Kailua, try **Ocean Safaris,** 808/326-4699, www.oceansafariskayaks.com, for half-day guided tours in the Keauhou area for $59 or an early bird tour of Kailua Bay for $30. Otherwise, try **Honu Sports,** 808/938-9795, www.honusports.com.

For kayak rentals in the Hilo area, contact **Aquatic Perceptions,** 808/935-9997. Kayak rental starts at $15 for four hours single and goes up from there; tours start at $25 per person. **Planet Ocean Watersports,** 808/935-7277, at 100 Kamehameha Ave. also rents kayaks and offers kayak tours.

In Waimea, **C&S Outfitters,** 808/885-5005, rents kayaks at $25 for a half day, $30 per day, and $120 a week, and this includes a roof rack. From here, recommended paddle areas are Puako in the summer and Kealakekua in the winter.

A twist on the kayak business is offered by **Flum'in da Ditch,** 808/889-6922, 877/449-6922, www.flumindaditch.com, located near the big banyan tree in Hawi. On an outing with this company, you'll float about three scenic miles of the Kohala irrigation flume, over small ravines, and through tunnels in the remote, private lands of North Kohala. Guided by experts and utilizing specially designed five-person inflatable kayaks, you'll not only experience the beauty of the surrounding rainforest and rugged scenery but you'll also absorb a lesson in the history and culture of this area. No experience required. Bring an extra set of dry clothes. Tours go daily at 8:30 A.M. and 12:30 P.M. and run $85 for adults and $65 for children ages 5–18.

OCEAN TOURS

Whether it's skimming across the ocean surface on a trim sloop, diving by submarine to view coral fields, or watching whales breach and play, there are many and various ocean tours to excite visitors to the Big Island. Virtually all of

ON THE ROAD

these tours stay on the Kona side of the island. Some of the more popular options follow.

Zodiac Tours

Captain Zodiac, 808/329-3199, 800/422-7824, www.captainzodiac.com, will take you on a fantastic ocean odyssey beginning at Honokohau Small Boat Harbor just north of Kailua-Kona, from where you'll skirt the coast south all the way to Kealakekua Bay. A Zodiac is a very tough, motorized rubber raft, sometimes with a rigid fiberglass bottom. It looks like a big, horseshoe-shaped inner tube that bends itself and undulates with the waves like a floating water bed. These seaworthy craft, powered by twin Mercury 280s, have five separate air chambers for unsinkable safety. Skippers take you and up to 15 others for a thrilling ride down the Kona Coast, pausing along the way to whisk you into sea caves, grottoes, and caverns, and if it's the right time of year you have the added benefit of seeing whales. The Kona Coast is also marked with ancient ruins and the remains of villages, which the captains point out, and about which they relate historical anecdotes as you pass by. You stop at Kealakekua Bay, where you can swim and snorkel in this underwater conservation park. Round-trips departing at 8 A.M., and again at 1 P.M., take about four hours and cost $78 adults, $63 children 4–12. Captain Zodiac also provides a light tropical lunch of fresh exotic fruit, taro chips, fruit juice, iced tea, and sodas. All you need are a bathing suit, sun hat, towel, suntan lotion, camera, and sense of adventure.

Fair Wind, 808/332-2788, 800/677-9461, www.fair-wind.com, does similar tours on its 28-foot, rigid-bottom Zodiac raft with inboard diesel, the *Orca,* but these tours leave from Kailua pier. Leaving at 8:30 A.M., morning tours run four hours with snorkel stops at Kealakekua Bay and one other location; $73 adult, $60 children 6–12. Three-hour afternoon tours start at 1 P.M. and make just one stop at Kealakekua Bay; $55 adult, $45 children.

Sea Quest, 808/325-7238, www.seaquesthawaii.com, runs a similar inflatable raft snorkel tour to Kealakekua Bay from Keauhou Bay with numerous stops along the way to explore sea caves

and other coastline features. Morning and afternoon departures are available and cost $75 and $56, respectively. These smaller rafts take only up to six guests.

Using a smaller inflatable raft for more intimate groups, **Dolphin Discoveries,** 808/322-8000, www.dolphindiscoveries.com, also offers raft and snorkel trips to Kealakekua Bay from Keauhou Bay boat ramp. Morning and afternoon trips are given daily. The four-hour morning tour runs $74 adult and $59 kids 5–15; the three-hour afternoon tour is $55 per person. These folks are very focused on the study and research of dolphins, whales, and other sea animals, so your trip will be educational. Part of your fee goes to support marine conservation programs.

Sailing Tours

Sailing is a year-round adventure, and boats take advantage of the steady breezes and fine weather along the Kona Coast. In season (Nov.–Apr.), sailing companies offer fascinating whale-watching adventures as part of the bargain.

One of the only true monohull charter sailing ships on the island, the *Honu,* is put in the water by **Honu Sail Charters,** 808/896-4668, www.sailkona.com, which runs half-day, full-day, and sunset sailing tours on their sleek sailboat from Honokohau Marina. Half-day tours, including snorkeling and snacks, run $80, full-day tours run $120, while the sunset tour with *pu pu* is $60; maximum of six guests.

The *Maile,* berthed at Kawaihae Harbor, P.O. Box 44335, Kamuela, HI 96743, 808/326-5174, 800/726-SAIL, is a 50-foot Gulfstar sloop available for luxury sailing charters and shorter-term whale-watching, snorkeling, and fishing expeditions. Skippered by Ralph Blancato, a U.S. Coast Guard–certified Master, the sloop offers competitive prices on half- or full-day charters, sunset sails, and long-term rental. Offering more than just a sailing trip, Blancato teaches his guests about marinelife, reef ecology, and island environment. Aside from her commercial use, the *Maile* also functions as the research boat for both the Ocean Mammal Institute and the Oceanic Society.

SEASICKNESS

Many people are affected by motion sickness, particularly on sailing vessels. If you tend to get queasy, try one of the following to prevent symptoms. Although there are others, oral medications widely available through pharmacies are Dramamine, Bonine, and Triptone. Running about $4 a box, Dramamine and Bonine may cause drowsiness in some people, Triptone seems not to. Although these medications are usually taken just before boarding a ship, they might work better if a half dose is taken the night before and another half dose is taken the morning of your ride. In all cases, however, take medication as prescribed by the manufacturer.

An alternative to medication is Seabands, elastic bands worn around the wrists that put gentle pressure on the inside of the wrist by way of a small plastic button. They are available at pharmacies and at most scuba shops for about $10 and can be reused until the elastic wears out. Follow directions for best results.

Without medication or pressure bands, you can still work to counter the effects of motion sickness. The night before, try not to eat too much, particularly greasy food, and don't drink alcohol to excess. If your stomach begins to feel upset, try a few soda crackers. If you begin to feel dizzy, focus on the horizon or a mountaintop—something stationary—and try to direct your thoughts to something other than your dizziness or queasiness. With children (and perhaps adults as well), talking about what animal figures they can see in the clouds or how many houses they can spot along the shoreline may be enough to distract them until they begin feeling better.

Dinner Cruises

Captain Beans' Polynesian Cruise, 808/329-2955, is a Kona institution that will take you aboard its glass-bottom bargelike boat daily at 5:15 P.M. from Kailua pier. During the very tame cruise you'll spot fish, listen to island music, and enjoy a sunset dinner. The cost is $52 (slightly more for those staying in the Kohala resorts), and this includes dinner, beverages, and transportation. This cruise is only open to those age 21 and older. Captain Beans' is the bus tour version of a water cruise.

The smaller trimaran *Kona Dream* runs more personal dinner cruises off the Kona Coast nightly 5:30–7:30 P.M. Dinner, beverages, and soft island music are all included for $50 adults and $33 children 4–12. A nice sunset is thrown in for free.

Glass-Bottom Boat Tours

Marian of the **Kailua Bay Charter Company,** 808/324-1749, does glass-bottom boat tours from the Kailua pier, daily on the hour 10 A.M.–2 P.M. Taking only 44 passengers, this cruise runs $25 adults or $10 for kids ages 5–12. Sunset cruises are also available. **Aloha Adven-**

ture Cruise, 808/331-2992, runs a two-hour dolphin watch/glass-bottom boat tour daily at 9:30 A.M. and noon from the Kailua pier. Monday, Wednesday, and Friday evenings, the crew turns its attention above water and runs a sunset cruise departing at 5:15 P.M. All cruises are aboard the *Coral Sea,* run $49, and feature island music, *pu pu,* two cocktails, and, of course, the fine sunset. **Ocean Sports and Activities** at 'Anaeho'omalu Bay at Waikoloa Resort offer half-hour glass-bottom boat trips for $15 and a similar tour is offered at Kona Village Resort.

Whale-Watching Cruises

Three-hour whale-watching tours on the 40-foot boat *Lady Ann* are offered by **Captain Dan McSweeney's Whale Watching Adventures,** 808/322-0028, 888/942-5376, www.ilovewhales.com. While many are interested in looking only for the humpback whales, Dan, a marine biologist and whale researcher, takes visitors year-round so they can also learn about different kinds of whales and other ocean mammals that inhabit this coast. This is an educational trip, the best the island has to offer. If you want to see whales and learn about these beautiful mammals in the process, go with Dan. The *Lady Ann* leaves from the Honokohau Marina every day from mid-December through mid-April, and Tuesday, Thursday, and Saturday the rest of the year. Tours run $54.50 adults and $34.50 children.

From December through May, most of the Zodiac, snorkel, scuba, catamaran, and sailing boats also run whale-watching tours in addition to or in place of their other activities.

Submarine Tours

Atlantis Submarine, 808/329-6626, 800/548-6262, allows everyone to live out the fantasy of Captain Nemo on a silent cruise under the waves off Kailua-Kona. After checking in at the office at the King Square Shopping Center, you board a launch at Kailua pier that takes you on a 10-minute cruise to the waiting submarine tethered offshore. You're given all of your safety tips on the way there. The underwater portion lasts about a half hour. As you descend to 120 feet, notice that everything white, including teeth, turns pink because the ultraviolet rays are filtered out. The only colors you can see clearly beneath the waves are blues and greens because water is 800 times denser than air and filters out the reds and oranges. Everyone gets an excellent seat with a viewing port; there's not a bad seat in this 48-passenger submarine, so you don't have to rush to get on. Don't worry about being claustrophobic, either—the sub is amazingly airy and bright, with aircraft-quality air blowers above the seats. Cruises run at 8:30 A.M., 10 A.M., 11:30 A.M., and 1:30 P.M., although the times may change according to the season, and cost $84 for adults and $42 for children. Atlantis joins with other island tour operators to offer discounted prices when you combine a submarine trip with a lu'au, a whale watch or snorkel cruise, or a helicopter ride.

SKIING

Bored with sun and surf? Strap the "boards" to your feet and hit the slopes of Mauna Kea for one of the most unique ski adventures in the world. Numerous popular runs have been named by those who ski the mountain often. There are no lifts, and you'll need a 4WD to get to the top and someone willing to pick you up again "down slope." You can rent 4WDs from a number of car-rental agencies, but if that seems like too much hassle, contact **Ski Guides Hawaii,** P.O. Box 1954, Kamuela, HI 96743, 808/885-4188, www.skihawaii.com. Here you can rent skis, and they'll provide the "lifts" to the top. Skis, boots, and poles (or snowboards and shoes) rent for $50 a day; the popular full-day ski/snowboard tour with equipment, ride and driver, ski guide, and lunch goes for $250 per person (minimum three). Other ski packages and cross-country ski tours are available and priced on request. For additional information, check out the Ski Association of Hawaii at www.hawaiisnowskiclub.com.

You can expect snow Dec.–May, but you can't count on it. It's most probable during February and March, and occasionally it stays as late as June or July. Generally speaking, your chances for skiable snow are better the few days after a moisture-laden front has moved across the island, blanketing the top with a white covering. More snow comes in La Niña years and less during El Niño. A few points of note: The top of Mauna Kea is over 13,500 feet, so nearly everyone suffers from some sort of altitude sickness. This is exacerbated by heavy physical exercise, so you should be in top physical condition if you plan to ski. There is nothing under the snow except unforgiving lava rock, so ski with caution. Also, there are no services above the 9,000-foot level on the mountain, so bring food and lots of water, and enough gas to get you there and back again.

GOLF

The Big Island has some of the most beautiful golf links in Hawaii. The Kohala-area courses taken together are considered by some to be the crown jewel of the state's golf options. Robert Trent Jones Sr. and Jr. have both built exceptional courses here. Dad built the Mauna Kea Beach Hotel course, while the kid built his at the Waikoloa Beach Resort. The Mauna Kea course bedevils many as the ultimate challenge. Other big name golf course architects (and players) such as Jack Nicklaus, Arnold Palmer, and Tom Weiskopf have added their talents here as well. Sometimes the Kohala golf courses are used for tournament play, like the Senior Skins Tournament at the Francis H. I'i Brown South Course. If the Kohala courses are too rich for your blood, there are a few in the Kailua area that are less expensive, or you can play a round in Hilo for $20 and hit nine holes in Honoka'a for $15. How about golfing at Volcano Golf Course, where if you miss a short putt, you can blame it on an earthquake?

Most golf courses offer lessons. Many have driving ranges, some that are lighted. All except for two have pro shops and clubhouses with a restaurant or snack shop. Greens fees listed in the chart are for non-Hawaii residents. Most courses offer reduced *kama'aina* rates and discount rates for play that starts later in the day. Be sure to ask about these rates as they often afford substantial savings. Guests of resorts affiliated with a golf course also get reduced greens fees.

Deciding at the last minute to golf? Want a discount rate? Willing to golf where it may not

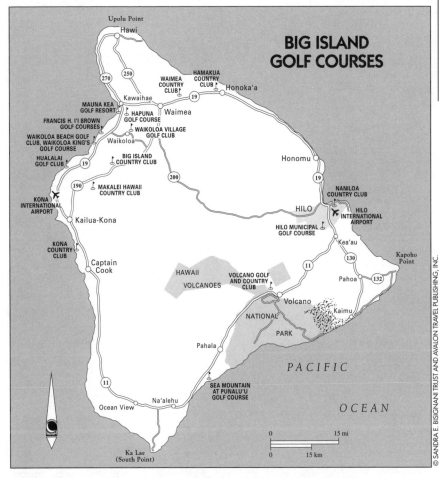

BIG ISLAND GOLF COURSES

Course	Par	Yards	Fees	Cart	Clubs
Big Island Country Club 71-1420 Mamalahoa Hwy. Kailua-Kona, HI 96740 808/325-5044	72	6,510	$85	incl.	$30
Frances H. I'i Brown Golf Courses					
South Course	72	6,938	$185	incl.	$37.50
North Course 68-1310 Mauna Lani Dr. Kohala Coast, HI 96743 808/885-6655	72	6,913	$185	incl.	$37.50
Hamakua Country Club P.O. Box 344 Honoka'a, HI 96727 808/775-7244	33	2,496 (9 holes)	$15	none	none
Hapuna Golf Course 62-100 Kauna'oa Dr. Kohala Coast, HI 96743 808/880-3000	72	6,534	$145	incl.	$40
Hilo Municipal Golf Course 340 Haihai St. Hilo, HI 96720 808/959-7711	71	6,325	$20–25	$14.50	$15
Hualalai Golf Club (resort guests only) 100 Ka'upulehu Dr. Kailua-Kona, HI 96745 808/325-8480	72	6,632	$165	incl.	$60
Kona Country Club					
Mountain Course	72	6,673	$95	incl.	$30
Ocean Course 78-7000 Ali'i Dr. Kailua-Kona, HI 96740 808/322-2595	72	6,806	$115	incl.	$30
Makalei Hawaii Country Club 72-3890 Hawaii Belt Rd. Kailua-Kona, HI 96740 808/325-6625	72	7,041	$110	incl.	$25

ON THE ROAD

Course	Par	Yards	Fees	Cart	Clubs
Mauna Kea Golf Course 62-100 Mauna Kea Beach Dr. Kohala Coast, HI 96743 808/882-5400	72	6,737	$195	incl.	$40
Naniloa Country Club 120 Banyan Dr. Hilo, HI 96720 808/935-3000	35	2,740 (9 holes)	$25–30 (18 holes)	$7.50 (9 holes)	$10
Sea Mountain at **Punaluʻu Golf Course** P.O. Box 190 Pahala, HI 96777 808/928-6222	72	6,416	$32–35	incl.	$25
Volcano Golf and Country Club Piʻi Mauna Dr. Hawaii Volcanoes Nat'l Park, HI 96718 808/967-7331	72	6,547	$62.50	incl.	$16
Waikoloa Beach Golf Club 1020 Keana Pl. Waikoloa, HI 96738 808/885-6060	70	6,566	$150	incl.	$35
Waikoloa King's Golf Course 600 Waikoloa Beach Dr. Waikoloa, HI 96738 808/886-7888	72	6,594	$150	incl.	$35
Waikoloa Village Golf Club 68-1792 Melia St. Waikoloa, HI 96738 808/883-9621	72	6,814	$80	$20	$35
Waimea Country Club P.O. Box 2155 Kamuela, HI 96743 808/885-8053	72	6,661	$65	incl.	$25

ON THE ROAD

BIG ISLAND TENNIS COURTS

County Courts

Under jurisdiction of the County Department of Parks and Recreation, 25 Aupuni St., Hilo, HI 96720, 808/961-8740. No fee for use, and no reservations are necessary but might be appropriate on weekends.

Town	Location	No. of Courts	Lighted
Hilo	Ainaole Park	1	No
Hilo	Hakalau Park	2	No
Hilo	Hoʻolulu Park	8	Yes
Hilo	Lincoln Park	4	Yes
Hilo	Lokahi Park	2	Yes
Hilo	Malama Park	2	No
Hilo	Mohouli Park	2	No
Hilo	Panaʻewa Park	2	No
Honokaʻa	Papaʻaloa Park	2	Yes
Honokaʻa	Honokaʻa Park	2	No
Puna	Kurtistown Park	1	No
Puna	Shipman Park	2	No
Kaʻu	Kaʻu High School	2	No
Kaʻu	Naʻalehu Park	2	No
Captain Cook	Greenwell Park	1	Yes
Keauhou	Higashihara Park	1	No
Kona	Old Kona Airport	4	Yes
Kona	Kailua Playground	1	Yes
Waimea	Waimea Park	2	Yes
Kapaʻau	Kamehameha Park	2	Yes

necessarily be your first choice? Try **Stand-by Golf,** 808/322-2665, 888/645-2665, where you can arrange tee times for great savings. Call one day in advance or in the morning on the day you want to play.

For printed information on golf in Hawaii, pick up a copy of *Guide to Golf: Hawaiian Islands* or *Fins and Fairways* magazines, or the newspaper-format *Hawaiʻi Golf News and Travel.*

Some tipping on golf courses is the norm. A $1 tip to the bag drop attendant is custom-ary, $2 if a bag boy takes your bags from the car, and a couple bucks extra if he cleans your clubs for you.

TENNIS

Many tennis courts dot the Big Island, and plenty of them are free. County courts are under the control of the Department of Parks and Recreation, which maintains a combination of lighted and unlit courts around the island. Usually cement, these county courts can be reserved by

Hotel and Private Courts Open to the Public

Town	Location	Fee	No. of Courts	Lighted
Pahala	Sea Mountain Resort 808/928-6200	None	4	No
Keauhou	Keauhou Beach Resort 808/322-6112	$5/hr	6	Yes
Kailua-Kona	Royal Kona Resort 808/334-1093	$10/day	6	Yes
Kailua-Kona	King Kamehameha's Kona Beach Hotel 808/334-9889	$5/hr	4	Yes
Waikoloa	Waikoloa Village 808/883-9704	none	2	Yes
Waimea	Hawaii Prep Academy 808/881-4037	$20	4	Yes
Kohala	Outrigger Waikoloa Beach Resort 808/886-6666	$10/hr	6	No
Kohala	Hilton Waikoloa Village Resort 808/881-2222	$30/hr	8	No
Kohala	Mauna Lani Tennis Garden 808/885-1485	$20/hr	10	No
Kohala	Mauna Kea Beach Resort 808/882-5420	$25/day	13	No
Kohala	The Orchid at Mauna Lani Tennis Pavilion 808/887-7532	$30/day	10	No

calling the number listed in the accompanying chart. No fees are charged for these public courts, but play is on a first-come, first-served basis. Court rules apply, and only soft-sole shoes are allowed. Please care for equipment and stick to time limits, especially if there are other players waiting to play. Some private and hotel courts are open to the public for a fee, while others restrict play to guests only. Most private courts have a plexipave or similar surface. Although each facility differs, private clubs usually have pro shops, offer equipment rental, and arrange clinics and lessons. Court play is regulated according to accepted rules, and proper attire is required, including proper shoes.

HORSEBACK RIDING

One of the most exciting and intimate ways to discover Hawai'i is from atop a well-trained horse. All horseback tours are guided. Most guides are extremely knowledgeable about the area's unique flora and fauna and are able to "talk story" about the ancient tales and legends pertaining to the ride site. For your safety and comfort, make sure to wear long pants (jeans are best) and closed-toe shoes. Also, don't forget about the tropical sun—bring a hat and sunblock as well. Most riding stables take riders eight years old or older, and some have a weight limit—usually around 220 pounds. Snacks and drinks are provided on most rides over a couple of hours. Horseback riding is not allowed on beaches in Hawaii.

Waipi'o Na'alapa Stables, 808/775-0419, offers one of the most unique rides on Hawai'i, with stables in the valley. The owner and her family have lived in Waipi'o Valley for over 25 years and know its history, geology, and legends intimately. There is pickup service from Kukuihaele "up top" for the 9:30 A.M. and 1 P.M. rides; $75 per person for 2.5 hours. If you have time, don't miss this wonderful adventure!

Waipi'o On Horseback, 808/775-7291, also offers horseback riding through fabulous Waipi'o Valley. These 2.5-hour, morning and afternoon sightseeing rides, $75 for adults and $55 for kids, are good for all riding levels.

For a ride up on Waipi'o's rim, looking down into Hawai'i's largest and most spectacular valley, try **Waipi'o Ridge Stables,** 808/775-1007, www.topofwaipio.com/horse.htm. This outfit offers a 2.5-hour rim ride to valley vistas, through former sugarcane land for $75. The 5.5-hour ride adds a side trip to a waterfall where you stop for lunch and a swim. It runs $145. Rides leave at 8:45 A.M. and 12:45 P.M. from Waipi'o Valley Artworks in Kukuihaele.

Enjoyable rides are also offered by the **Mauna Kea Resort Stables** (for nonguests also), 808/882-4288, located in Waimea—turn between K. M. Seeds and Ace Hardware and follow the signs. The Parker Ranch lends the resort a *paniolo* to guide you over the quarter-million acres of open range on the slopes of Mauna Kea, morning or afternoon. The stable is open Mon.–Sat. 9 A.M.–3 P.M. Rates are $40 per person for a one-hour ride and $70 for the two-hour ride; special trail rides available on request. Eight years old is the minimum age for riders; 210 pounds is the maximum weight.

Paniolo Riding Adventures, 808/889-5354, offers horseback riding on a working ranch in the Kohala Mountains north of Waimea. With

your comfort in mind, they offer chaps, rain slickers, cowboy hats, and fleece saddle covers to keep you happy where the sun don't shine. Prices vary according to the ride, from novice to cowpoke, but a typical 2.5-hour open range ride will run about $89. After your guide matches you with an appropriate steed, you head out onto the 11,000 acre range. Aside from the horseback rides, the ranch also offers mountain biking, hiking, and archery.

Kohala Na'alapa Stables, 808/889-0022, offers open-range rides onto the historic Kahua Ranch, high in the Kohala Mountains. Rides are offered daily at 9 A.M. and 1:30 P.M.; 2.5-hour rides are priced $75, 1.5-hour rides $55.

Using horses from its own working ranch in Waimea, **Dahana Ranch,** 808/885-0057, gives riders free-range rides on its own property. Rides leave five times a day; 1.5-hour rides are $55, 2.5-hour rides are $100 and include a barbecue lunch. Experienced or not, no problem; riders age three and up, and up to 300 pounds are okay. For those with lots of experience, a two-hour advanced rider only ride also runs $100. Good upcountry range landscape.

Kings' Trail Rides O'Kona, 808/323-2388, has an office along Route 11, at mile marker 111, high above the Kona Coast between Kealakekua and Captain Cook. The wranglers will lead you (four to six people maximum) on a custom trail ride down to Captain Cook's monument on the shores of Kealakekua Bay. This four-hour trip, departing at 9 A.M. (two hours of actual riding), includes snorkeling in the bay, along with a delicious picnic lunch. The price is $95. No riders over 230 pounds or under age seven, please.

Rain Forest Trailrides, 808/322-7126, takes you on horseback across the face of the Hualalai Mountains. Open daily 9 A.M.–5 P.M., it offers rides several rides each day from about $35 an hour.

Kapapala Ranch, 808/968-6585, offers excursions on its working ranch in Ka'u just outside the town of Pahala. Rides run $75 for the two-hour experience. The ranch will also arrange overnight camping trips on the property that can be done by horse, hiking, pack mules, or 4WD vehicle.

Not a horse ride per se, a Kohala Mule Trail Adventure is offered by **Hawaii Forest and Trail,** 808/331-8505. These three-hour rides leave daily at 8:30 A.M. and 12:30 P.M. from near the Pololu Lookout and head uphill for a look into this old and historic valley. Rates are $95 adults and $85 for kids 8–12.

Wagon Rides

Waipio Valley Wagon Tours, 808/775-9518, is a mule-drawn tour of the magnificent Waipi'o Valley. The 1.5-hour tours leave four times daily at 9:30 and 11:30 A.M., and 1:30 and 3:30 P.M. The cost is $40 for adults or $20 for children under 12 and includes transportation down into the valley.

BICYCLING

Pedaling around the Big Island can be both fascinating and frustrating. If you circle the island, it's nearly 300 miles around on its shortest route. Most pick an area and bike there. Generally, roads are well paved, but the shoulders are often torn up. With all the triathletes coming to Hawaii, and all the fabulous, little-trafficked roads, you'd think the island would be great for biking! It is, but you are better off bringing your own bike than renting. If you do rent, instead of a delicate road bike, you'll do better with a cruiser for pedaling around town or along the beach or a mountain bike that can handle the sometimes poor road conditions as well as open up the possibilities of off-road biking. Even experienced mountain bikers should be careful on the often extremely muddy and rutted trails.

Wear a helmet, bring sunglasses, use bike gloves, and wear appropriate bike shoes. If possible, have a bike pump, extra tube, and repair kit with you. Bring plenty of water and snacks. Take a map, but get information from a bike shop for the kind of riding that you want to do before you head out.

For those who desire off-street trails to paved roads, pick up a copy of the Big Island Mountain Bike Association's off-road, public-access trail guide at either HVB office or at most bike shops on the island. This guide is also available on the

Web at www.interpac.net/~mtbike. In addition to an introduction to the organization and safety tips, each trail is briefly described and accompanied by a rudimentary map, directions to the start of the trail, and any additional information that's necessary to complete the ride. The type of ride, length in distance, ride time, elevation change, and level of expertise needed is also listed. Trails vary from flat shoreline jaunts to rugged mountain workouts, for riders from beginners to advanced. Check it out before you ride; this information comes from experienced island riders. For additional information contact BIMBA at P.O. Box 6819, Hilo, HI 96720-8934, or call 808/961-4452.

For general information on biking in Hawaii, contact **Hawaii Bicycling League,** P.O. Box 4403, Honolulu, HI 96812-4403. This nonprofit organization promotes biking as recreation, sport, and transportation; encourages safe biking practices; conducts biking education; and advocates for biking issues. It publishes a monthly newsletter, *Spoke-n-Words,* filled with news of the organization's business, its bicycle safety program for kids, and rides that are open to the public, as well as current bicycle issues and sponsored bicycle competitions throughout the state. If you are a bicycle rider living in the islands or simply want a subscription to the newsletter, write for membership information.

For mountain biking and trail information on all the major islands, pick up a copy of *Mountain Biking the Hawaiian Islands* by John Alford, Ohana Publishing, Honolulu, HI 96824.

Getting your bike to Hawai'i from one of the neighbor islands is no problem. All of the interisland carriers will fly it for you for about $20 one-way on the same flight as you take—just check it in as baggage. Bikes must be packed in a box or hard case, supplied by the owner. Handlebars must be turned sideways and the pedals removed or turned in. Bikes go on a space-available basis only—usually not a problem, except, perhaps, during bicycle competitions. In addition, a release of liability for damage must be signed before the airline will accept the bike. If you plan ahead, you can send your bike the previous day by air freight.

Getting your bike to Hawaii from the Mainland will depend upon which airline you take. Some will accept bicycles as baggage traveling with you (approximate additional charge of $50)—they may or may not have to be broken down and boxed in a bicycle box—while others will only take them as air freight, in which case the rates are exorbitant. Check with the airlines well before you plan to go or explore the possibility of shipping it by sea through a freight company.

Bicycle Shops and Rentals

For rentals, try the following. **Hawaiian Pedals,** in the Kona Inn Shopping Plaza, 808/329-2294, rents mountain bikes and hybrids at $15 for five hours or $20 for 24 hours, with discounted rates for longer needs. Bike racks and baby seats are also for rent. Open daily.

The **Bike Works,** 74-5599 Lehua St., Ste. F-3, next to Gold's Gym in the Old Kona Industrial Area, 808/326-2453, sells, services, and rents mountain and road bikes and bike gear. This Kailua-Kona full-service shop is perhaps the best on the island. Daily rates run $20–30; five-hour and multiday rates can also be arranged. Closed on Sunday, so Saturday rentals are for two days.

B&L Bike and Sports, 808/329-3309, handles lots of rental road and mountain bikes, as well as sales and repair. Bikes generally run $30 a day to $150 a week. The official Ironman Triathlon bike shop, B&L is located across from the Hilo Hattie shop in Kailua-Kona.

Dave's Bike and Triathlon Shop, 808/329-4522, is located in the Kona Square Shopping Center just across Ali'i Drive from the water. Dave's rents road, mountain, hybrid, and suspension bikes from $15 a day to $60 a week. All rentals include helmet, water bottles, map, bicycle lock, and road advice. Dave is a font of information, one of the best bicycle men on the island.

When in Hilo, check out **Hilo Bike Hub,** 318 E. Kawila, 808/961-4452, for sales and service of all kinds of high-quality bikes and accessories. This shop and its owner are heavy into the mountain biking scene, including the Big Island Mountain Biking Association, and have in-

formation about all the island races. Crossbreed mountain bikes rent for $25 a day, front suspension bikes are $20, and full suspension bikes run $45. Closed Sunday, so Saturday rentals are for two days.

Also in Hilo is **Mid Pacific Wheels,** 1133C Manono St., 808/935-6211, where you can get a more standard bike for $15 a day; and **Aquatic Perceptions,** 808/933-1228, where you can rent a mountain bike or cross for about $30 a day or a recumbent tandem for a bit more.

In Waimea, try **C & S Outfitters,** 808/885-5005, for wheels that will get you up to the high country. Rental rates are $25–35 for five hours, $30 for 24 hours, or $130 for a week; helmet, pump, and patch kit are included. Bike carriers and trailers can also be arranged.

Bicycle Tours

Mauna Kea Mountain Bikes runs four different group tours for beginners to advanced riders. The beginner tour runs for 21 miles down Highway 250 over the shoulder of the Kohala Mountains to Hawi. This is a morning tour for a minimum of four riders; transportation back from Hawi is included. An intermediate ride on back roads around Waimea lets you get a feel for upcountry range country and farmland. The technical rainforest ride is a challenge, not long but lots of ups and downs through muddy single-track trails. The real crowning ride, however, is the ride down Mauna Kea from the summit to the Saddle Road. On this one you have to be in very good shape and be focused. Rides vary from two to four hours and rates range from $50 to $120. For details, call 808/883-0130 or 888/682-8687.

Aquatic Perceptions of Hilo, 808/935-9997, www.multi-sport-hawaii.com, a multisport activity company, offers a bicycle "Jungle Coastal Tour" of Puna. Starting in Pahoa, the group mounts mountain bikes and heads down the leisurely country roads to the south coast. From there, it's along the sometimes-canopied, sometimes-steamy coastal road as far as the new black sand beach and lava fields of Kaimu. The return to Hilo is by van. Four other bike tours are also offered, ranging from a ride around Kilauea

Caldera to one along the North Kohala Coast. These rides are designed for an average rider, run four to eight hours, and cost $70–135.

Kona Coast Cycling Tours in Kona, 808/327-1133, 877/592-2453, www.cyclekona.com, offers a number of different tours to various parts of the island. The Kohala Mountain Downhill, Coffee Country Ride, and Old Mamalahoa Highway Ride all run 6–8 hours and cost $95 per person. The North Kohala Adventure is a bit longer and runs $145. Custom rides and support can also be arranged.

Paniolo Adventures, 808/889-5354, does off-road mountain biking on their ranch outside Waimea for $85 per person for an average ride. While beginner and moderate rides are given, technical rides can be accommodated for advanced riders. All equipment, drinks, and snacks provided.

Three Mainland-based companies also do multiday bicycle touring. **Backroads,** 801 Cedar St., Berkeley, CA 94710, 510/527-1555, 800/462-2848, fax 510/527-1444, goactive @backroads.com, www.backroads.com, goes easy on the environment with its bicycle and multisport trips to the Big Island. The six-day circle-island bike tour concentrates on the Kona Coast, Volcano, and North Kohala. It's offered Oct.–Apr. and costs $2,298. Backroads also does a six-day multisport trip that takes you into the major scenic areas of the island; it runs $2,398, available Oct.–Apr. All on-island arrangements are included.

Bicycle Adventures, P.O. Box 11219, Olympia, WA 98508, 800/443-6060, office @bicycleadventures.com, www.bicycleadventures.com, also organizes road trips around the Big Island, mostly on less-used roads that take in many of the best sights that the island offers. The eight-day trip circles the island from Hilo, with departures monthly Oct.–June. Rides average 45 miles a day with overnights planned mostly at inns and small hotels. These all-inclusive tours cover everything you'll need while on the island and the cost is $2,354 plus $144 bike rental.

Getaway Adventures also offers similar six- and eight-day round-island rides Nov.–Apr. that include swimming, kayaking, and snorkeling.

These trips start in Hilo and head around the bottom of the island. Rates are $1,699 and $1,999, respectively, with a bike rental fee of $130. For additional information and reservations, contact the company at 1117 Lincoln Ave., Calistoga, CA 94515, 800/499-2453, www.getawayadventures.com.

LAND TOURS
Bus and Shuttle Tours
Most tour companies run vans, but some larger companies also use buses. Though cheaper, tours on full-sized coaches are generally less personalized. Wherever a bus can go, so can your rental car—but on a tour you can relax and enjoy the scenery without worrying about driving. Also, tour drivers are very experienced with the area and know many stories and legends with which they annotate and enrich your trip. Tours generally run $40–70 per person and either circle the island or have Kilauea volcano as their main feature. Narrated and fairly tame bus tours are operated by **Roberts Hawaii,** 808/329-1688 (Kona), 808/966-5483 (Hilo), 800/831-5541, www.robertshawaii.com; and by **Polynesian Adventure Tours,** 808/329-8008, 800/622-3011, www.polyad.com. **Jack's Tours,** 808/961-6666, 808/329-2555, also runs various group bus tours to major sights on the island. **Dieter's Creative Hawaiian Isle Tours,** 888/290-1000, www.dieters-hawaii.com, does guided minibus tours of Hilo and the volcano areas in German (other languages on request). Dieter's German-language tours are also offered on Maui and O'ahu.

Adventure Van Tours
Waipio Valley Shuttle, 808/775-7121, offers a 90-minute tour down to Waipi'o Valley ($40 adults, $20 children under 11). The air-conditioned 4WD vans leave from Waipi'o Valley Artworks in Kukuihaele Mon.–Sat. twice in the morning and twice in the afternoon. This is the easiest way into the valley and the guys know what they're doing as they've been at it since 1970.

For a trip to the rim for a look down into Waipi'o Valley, contact **Waipi'o Rim Backroad**

ON THE ROAD

Adventures, 808/775-1122, 877/757-1414, www.topofwaipio.com/4x4.htm. This three-hour tour, $85 adult or $40 for kids 12 and under, takes in former sugarcane land, backcountry roads, and unparalleled vistas overlooking the valley. A short hike is included that brings you to a small waterfall and pool. On this adventure, you ride in comfort and lunch is provided.

Mauna Kea Summit Adventures, 808/322-2366, 888/322-2366, www.maunakea.com, owned and operated by Pat Wright, has been taking visitors on high-adventure trips around the Big Island for the last 20 years. Your comfort and safety as you roam the Big Island are ensured as you ride in sturdy turbo diesel Ford vans with 4WD, air-conditioning, sound system, first aid kit, and oxygen! The premier tour is an eight-hour journey to the top of Mauna Kea. Pat or one of his drivers not only fills your trip with stories, anecdotes, and fascinating facts during the ride, they top off the safari by setting up an eight-inch telescope not far from the Onizuka Center so you can get a personal view of the heavens through the rarefied atmosphere atop the great mountain. Mauna Kea Summit Adventures will pick you up at your hotel in Kailua-Kona at about 4 P.M. If you're staying on the Hilo side, he will meet you at a predetermined spot along the Saddle Road. The price is $150, with hot savory drinks, soup and sandwiches, and good warm parkas included. Special trips for photography, hiking, astronomy, and shore fishing can also be tailored to your needs.

Hawaii Forest and Trail, 808/331-8505, 800/464-1993, www.hawaii-forest.com, offers much the same summit and stargazing tour from the Kona side at $145 per person.

Arnott's Lodge and Hiking Adventures, 98 Apapane Rd., Hilo, HI 96720, 808/967-7097, www.arnottslodge.com/activity.html, offers a variety of hiking adventures to its guests and nonguests alike who are looking for more than an ordinary group tour. While the tours offered do change periodically, several have remained popular. They include a hike to the lava flow at Hawaii Volcanoes National Park, a waterfall and valleys hike, and the sunset and stargazing trek to the top of Mauna Kea. These are full eight-hour trips—some longer—and the cost is $48 for those staying at Arnott's Lodge in Hilo and $75 for others. Each trip takes only as many as the van will carry and goes only when the weather is cooperative. Some restrictions on age and physical condition apply, so be sure to check with the staff at Arnott's Lodge, or check out the website for the current list of adventures.

ATV Tours

ATV Outfitters Hawaii, 808/889-6000, www.outfittershawaii.com, runs breezy four-wheel motorcycle tours across former Kohala sugar plantation land to rainforest and coastal sights at the northern tip of the island. The 1.5-hour ride is $90 and the five-hour ride costs $250. You'll ride over back roads and fields, through lush gullies to waterfalls, come to the edge of ocean cliffs, or dip down to a pebble beach. These fully equipped machines let you get to places that you wouldn't be able to otherwise. Safe and reliable, the four-wheelers are easy to operate even for those who have had no experience on a motorcycle. Helmets, gloves, and goggles are supplied and instruction is given. To ride, you must be at least 16 years old and 90–300 pounds. Wear long pants and closed-toe shoes.

AIR TOURS

Helicopter Tours

Air tours are a great way to see the Big Island, but they are expensive, especially when the volcano is putting on a mighty display. Expect to spend a minimum of $100 for a front-row seat to watch the amazing light show from the air. Some discounts may be offered seasonally and for booking over the Internet. Kilauea volcano erupting is like winning the lottery for these small companies, and many will charge whatever the market will bear. To get the best view of the volcanic activity, schedule your flight for the morning, no later than 2 P.M. Later, clouds and fog can set in to obstruct your view. While the volcano is the premier focus of these tour companies, some also offer tours up the Hamakua Coast for a view of the sea cliffs, deep valleys, waterfalls, and the

North Kohala Mountains, and most do a modified round-island tour that takes in the volcano, east and west coastlines, and Hamakua valleys and waterfalls. Helicopter flights from the Hilo Commuter Terminal are very competitively priced, with savings on volcano tours over the companies operating out of the Kona Commuter Terminal; however, there are more flights out of Kona as there are more tourists on that side. Additionally, flights by Blue Hawaiian Helicopters also leave out of the Waikoloa Heliport, located across the highway from the entrance to Waikoloa Resort at the intersection of Queen Kaʻahumanu Highway and Waikoloa Road.

Everyone has an opinion as to which company offers the best ride, the best narration, or the best service. All the helicopter companies on Hawaiʻi are safe and reputable—nearly all pilots have been trained by the military—and most fly five-seat A-Stars, with a few four-passenger Bell JetRangers and Hughes 500s still in use. Most have two-way microphones so you can communicate with the pilot. Each gives a preflight briefing to go over safety regulations and other details. Remember that the seating arrangement in a helicopter is critical to safety. The preflight crew is expertly trained to arrange the chopper so that it is balanced, and with different people of various sizes flying every day, their job is very much like a chess game. This means that the seating goes strictly according to weight. If you are not assigned the seat of your choice, for safety's sake, please do not complain. Think instead that you are part of a team whose goal is not only enjoyment but also to come back safe and sound. It's very difficult not to have a fascinating flight, no matter where you sit.

Almost all riders want to take photographs of their helicopter tour. Who wouldn't? Here are a few things to consider. Most of the newer helicopters are air-conditioned, which means that the windows don't open, so you might experience glare or some distortion. If you need absolutely clear shots, choose a chopper where the windows open or go with the one that flies with its doors off. Also, if you are the only one taking pictures on a tour and you're seated in the middle of the rear seat, you won't be happy. Again, ask for a ride in a smaller rig where everyone gets a window seat.

Flying out of the Hilo Airport in a four-passenger Bell JetRanger III helicopter is **Tropical Helicopters,** 808/961-6810, www.tropicalhelicopters.com. Tropical is a small company that gives personal attention to passengers. Its popular 40-minute volcano flight runs $99. An expanded 50-minute flight runs the same basic route but gives you additional flight over waterfalls in the Hilo area for $138. The ultimate "Feel the Heat" flight, $158, takes you for an up-close look at the volcano activity—with the doors off!

Safari Helicopters, 808/969-1259, 800/326-3356, info@safariair.com, www.safariair.com, also flies only from Hilo. Flights from Hilo run 45 minutes and 60 minutes, $149–199, and concentrate on the volcano and nearby waterfalls. Safari uses new air-conditioned A-Star craft. This is a reputable company with a good reputation, and pilots give you a memorable flight. Safari also flies on Kauaʻi.

With its spotless safety record and large operation, **Blue Hawaiian Helicopters,** 808/961-5600 (Hilo), 808/886-1768 (Waikoloa), or 800/745-2583, www.bluehawaiian.com, operates several A-Star helicopters from the Waikoloa Heliport on the Kona side and additional A-Stars from the Hilo Airport. Volcano flights from Hilo go for $165 and last about 50 minutes. From Waikoloa, a two-hour circle-island flight costs $340 and a shorter Kohala Mountain and valley tour goes for $175. Blue Hawaiian also offers flights on Maui.

Flying out of Kona, **Sunshine Helicopters,** 808/882-1233, 800/622-3144, www.sunshinehelicopters.com, runs a 45-minute Kohala Mountain and Hamakua Valley tour at $160, a 45-minute volcano flight for $175, and a two-hour circle-island flight for $390. Sunshine offers packages with Atlantis Submarine and Body Glove snorkel trips for reduced rates on activities. Sunshine also operates helicopter flights on Maui.

Leaving from the Hilo Airport, **Paradise Helicopters,** 808/969-7392, is close to the volcano and offers tours there for $145.

Fixed-Wing Air Tours

For fixed-wing air tours, try one of the following. **Big Island Air,** 808/329-4868, 800/303-8868, offers small-plane flights from Kona Airport, two-person minimum. A volcano tour in an eight-passenger Cessna costs $135 per person, and a round-island/volcano flight is $185. Every seat is a window seat, and the wings in the new plane are set above the windows. The plane can be chartered for $550 an hour from Kona or $660 an hour from Hilo.

For smaller planes, also with wings above the windows, try **Island Hopper,** 808/969-2000, which offers flights from both the Hilo and Kona Airports. Volcano and waterfall tours, $69–79, go from Hilo, but the longer flights from Kona are $149 for a volcano tour and $189 for a circle-island tour.

With similar flights and prices is **Mokulele Flight Service,** 808/326-7070, 866/260-7070, www.mokulele.com. Circle-island tours, $203, go from Kona, while the volcano tours, $75, run from Hilo.

Ballooning

Dawn hot air balloon rides over the Parker Ranch in Waimea are offered by **Paradise Balloons,** 808/877-6455, 866/887-6455, www.paradiseballoons.com. Takeoff and landing (hopefully) are from near Pu'opelu just outside of town. The tour begins around 6:30 A.M. and offers you an unparalleled view of the ranch and western side of the Big Island. Flights cost $240 adults or $190 for children 5–12; reservations are necessary. Dress warmly as it can be quite cold that early and that high.

FISHING

Hawaii has some of the most exciting and productive "blue waters" in all the world. Here you can find a sportfishing fleet made up of skippers and crews who are experienced professional anglers. You can also fish from jetties, piers, rocks, or the shore. If rod and reel don't strike your fancy, try the old-fashioned throw net, or take along a spear when you go snorkeling or scuba diving. There's nighttime torch fishing that requires special skills and equipment, and freshwater fishing in public areas. Streams and irrigation ditches yield introduced trout, bass, and catfish. While you're at it, you might want to try crabbing for

The Kona Coast of Hawai'i offers fishing enthusiasts a great opportunity for a chance at catching one of the big "blues."

Kona and Samoan crabs, or working low-tide areas after sundown hunting octopus, a tantalizing island delicacy.

Deep-Sea Fishing

Hawaii is positioned well. Within eight miles there are waters to depths of 18,000 feet. Most game-fishing boats work the waters on the calmer Kona side of the island. Some skippers, carrying anglers who are accustomed to the sea, will also work the much rougher windward coasts and island channels where the fish bite just as well. Trolling is the preferred method of deep-sea fishing; this is done usually in waters of 1,000–2,000 fathoms (a fathom is six feet). The skipper will either "area fish," which means running in a crisscross pattern over a known productive area, or "ledge fish," which involves trolling over submerged ledges where game fish are known to feed. The most advanced marine technology, available on many boats, sends sonar beeps searching for fish. On deck, the crew and anglers scan the horizon in the age-old Hawaiian tradition—searching for clusters of seabirds feeding on bait fish pursued to the surface by the huge and aggressive game fish. "Still fishing" or "bottom fishing" with hand-lines yields some tremendous fish.

The Game Fish

The most thrilling game fish in Hawaiian waters is marlin, generically known as "billfish" or *a'u* to the locals. The king of them is the blue marlin, with record catches of well over 1,000 pounds. The mightiest caught in the waters off this island was a huge 1,649 pounds—reeled in in 1984. There are also striped marlin and sailfish, which often go over 200 pounds. The best times for marlin are during spring, summer, and fall. The fishing tapers off in January and picks up again by late February. "Blues" can be caught year-round, but, oddly enough, when they stop biting it seems as though the striped marlin pick up. Second to the marlin are tuna. *'Ahi* (yellowfin tuna) are caught in Hawaiian waters at depths of 100–1,000 fathoms. They can weigh 300 pounds, but 25–100 pounds is common. There are also *aku* (skipjack tuna) and the delicious *ono*, which average 20–40 pounds.

Mahimahi is another strong, fighting, deep-water game fish abundant in Hawaii. These delicious fish can weigh up to 70 pounds. Shore fishing and bait casting yield *papio,* a jack tuna. *Akule,* a scad (locally called *halalu*), is a smallish schooling fish that comes close to shore and is great to catch on light tackle. *Ulua* are shore fish and can be found in tidepools. They're excellent eating, average two to three pounds, and are taken at night or with spears.

'O'io are bonefish that come close to shore to spawn. They're caught by bait casting and bottom fishing with cut bait. They're bony, but they're a favorite for fish cakes and *poki. Awa* is a schooling fish that loves brackish water. It can grow up to three feet long and is a good fighter; a favorite for throw-netters, it's even raised commercially in fishponds. Besides these there are plenty of goatfish, mullet, mackerel, snapper, sharks, and even salmon.

Fishing Charters

The fishing around the Big Island's Kona Coast ranges from excellent to outstanding! It's legendary for marlin fishing, but there are other fish in the sea. A large fleet of charter boats with skilled captains and tested crews is ready, willing, and competent to take you out. Most boats are berthed at Honokohau Small Boat Harbor just north of Kailua-Kona. The best time of year for big blues is July–Sept.; August is the optimum month. Rough seas can keep boats in for a few days during December and early January, but by February all are generally out.

You can hire a boat for a private or share charter, staying out for a full day or half day. Boat size varies, but four anglers per midsize boat is average. No matter the size, most boats will take no more than six anglers. The range of rates are private, full day $375–800, half day $250–500; share, full day $150–175, half day $85–115. Full days are eight hours, half days four, with three-quarter days and overnighters available. No licenses are required and all gear is provided. Bring your own lunch, beverages, and camera.

To charter a boat contact the individual captains directly, check at your hotel activities desk, or book through one of the following agencies.

Charter Services Hawaii, operated by Ed Barry, 808/334-1881, 800/567-2650, fishing@aloha .net, www.konazone.com, offers more than 50 boats in all sizes and price ranges. Ed also offers complete packages including room, car, and boat, along with a cash prize of $1 million if you book through his agency and top the world record. If you're after a company that's knowledgeable about getting you onto a boat and that will bring you to waters where you'll have the opportunity to catch one of the twirling and gigantic "big blues," this is the place to come.

Located on the dock at Honokohau Harbor, **The Charter Desk,** 808/329-5735, 888/566-2487, charter@aloha.net, www.charterdesk.com, represents some 50 boats in the harbor. This is another well-respected and competent company that works hard at matching clients to boats.

The **Kona Charter Skippers Association,** 808/329-3600, 800/762-7546, konafish@hawaii .rr.com, www.konabiggamefishing.com, is another agency that tries to match you and your desires with the right boat and captain.

Most of the island's 80 charter boats are berthed at Honokohau Harbor off Route 19, about midway between downtown Kailua and Kona Airport. Fish are weighed in daily 11 A.M.–1 P.M. and 3–5 P.M. Big fish are hardly ever weighed in at Kailua pier in front of the King Kamehameha's Kona Beach Hotel as they used to be for the tourists. Honokohau Harbor has far eclipsed Kailua pier, which is now tamed and primarily for swimmers, triathletes, and body-boarders. A few boats also leave from Keauhou Bay and Kawaihae Harbor on the west side, and some use the river mouth in Hilo.

An excellent publication listing some boats and general deep-sea fishing information is *Fins and Fairways,* P.O. Box 9014, Kailua-Kona, HI 96745, 808/325-6171, www.fishkona.com. This tabloid, published by Capt. Tom Armstrong and available free at newsstands and in hotel and condo lobbies, is filled with descriptions of boats, phone numbers, captains' names, maps, and photos of recent catches. For general fishing information and a listing of tournaments throughout the islands, pick up a copy of the *Hawaii Fishing News* at a newsstand or supermarket.

You can also contact **The Hawaiian International Billfish Association,** P.O. Box 4800, Kailua-Kona, HI 96740, 808/329-6155, www.konabillfish.com, for details on upcoming tournaments and "what's biting and when."

Of course, the bar at the Harbor House Restaurant at the Honokohau Marina might be just as easy a place to get quick, reliable, and up-to-the-minute information on how the fish are biting as well as which boats seem to be having the best luck.

Coastal Fish

You don't have to hire a boat to catch fish! The coastline is productive too. *Ulua* are caught all along the coast south of Hilo, and at South Point and Kealakekua Point. *Papio* and *halalu* are caught in bays all around the island, while *manini* and *'ama'ama* hit from Kawaihae to Puako. Hilo Bay is easily accessible to anyone, and the fishing is very exciting, especially at the mouth of the Wailuku River. Catch limits for 21 species of marine fish and eight crustaceans and shellfish are regulated, so check state guidelines.

Freshwater Fish

Hawaii has only one native freshwater game fish, the *'o'opu.* This goby is an oddball with fused ventral fins. It grows to 12 inches long and is found on all the islands. Introduced species include largemouth and smallmouth bass, bluegill, catfish, *tucunare,* oscar, carp, and tilapia. The *tucunare* is a tough, fighting, good-tasting game fish introduced from South America, similar to the oscar and from the same region. Both have been compared to bass but are of a different family.

The tilapia is from Africa and has become common in Hawaii's irrigation ditches. The snakehead is an eel-like fish that inhabits the reservoirs and is a great fighter. The channel catfish can grow to over 20 pounds; it bites best after sundown. Or go for carp—with its broad tail and tremendous strength, it's the poor man's game fish. All of these species are best caught with light spinning tackle or with a bamboo pole and trusty old worm. A catch limit is in effect for eight species of freshwater fish.

Fishing Rules

All game fish may be taken year-round except trout, *'ama'ama, moi,* and certain crustaceans (check specific regulations). Licensed fishing is limited to the **Waiakea Public Fishing Area,** a state-operated facility in downtown Hilo. This 26-acre pond offers a variety of saltwater and brackish-water species. A license is needed for freshwater fishing only. A **Freshwater Game Fishing License** is good for one year, July 1–June 30. Licenses cost $25 for nonresidents; $10 for seven-day tourist use; $20 for 30-day tourist use; $5 for residents over age 15 and active duty military personnel, their spouses, and dependents under age 15; and $3 for children ages 9–15; licenses are free to senior citizens over age 65 and children under age nine when accompanied by an adult with a license. You can pick up a license at sporting goods stores or at the Division of Aquatic Resources, 75 Aupuni St., Hilo, HI 96720, 808/974-6201. Be sure to ask for the *Hawaii Fishing Regulations* and *Freshwater Fishing in Hawaii* booklets. Fishing is usually allowed in most State Forest Reserve Areas. Owners' permission must be obtained to fish on private property.

HUNTING

Most people don't think of Hawaii as a place for hunting, but actually it's quite good. Seven species of introduced game animals and 15 species of game birds are regularly hunted. Not all species of game animals are open on all islands, but every island offers hunting. Huge unpopulated expanses of grassland, forest, and scrubby mountainside are very good for hunting. The Big Island's game includes wild pig, sheep, and goats, plus a variety of pheasant, quail, dove, francolin, partridge, sandgrouse, and wild turkey. Public game lands are located throughout the island; a license is required to take birds and game.

Information

Hunting rules and regulations are always subject to change. Also, environmental considerations often change bag limits and seasons. Make sure to check with the State Division of Forestry and Wildlife for the most current information.

Request the *Rules Regulating Game Bird Hunting, Rules Regulating Game Mammal Hunting,* and *Hunting in Hawaii* brochures. Direct inquiries to: Department of Land and Natural Resources, Division of Forestry and Wildlife Office, 19 East Kawili Ave., Hilo, HI 96720, 808/974-4221.

General Hunting Rules

Hunting licenses are mandatory in order to hunt on public, private, or military land anywhere in Hawaii. They're good for one year beginning July 1 and cost $20 for residents and military personnel, $105 for nonresidents, free to senior citizens. Licenses are available from sporting goods stores and from the various offices of the Division of Forestry and Wildlife. This government organization also sets and enforces the rules, so contact it with any questions. Generally, hunting hours are from a half hour before sunrise to a half hour after sunset. Checking stations are maintained, where hunters must check in before and after hunting.

Rifles must have a muzzle velocity greater than 1,200-foot-pounds. Shotguns larger than .20 gauge are allowed, and muzzle loaders must have a .45 caliber bore or larger. Bows must have a minimum draw of 40 pounds for straight bows, 35 pounds for a recurve bow, and 30 pounds for compounds. Arrows must be broadheads. The use of hunting dogs is permitted only for certain species of birds and game, and when dogs are permitted, only smaller caliber rifles and shotguns, and spears and knives, may be used—no big bore guns or shotguns. Hunters must wear orange safety cloth on front and back no smaller than a 12-inch square. Certain big-game species are hunted only by lottery selection; contact the Division of Forestry and Wildlife two months in advance. Guide service is not mandatory but is advised if you're unfamiliar with hunting in Hawaii. You can hunt on private land only with permission, and you must possess a valid hunting license. Guns and ammunition brought into Hawaii must be registered with the chief of police of the corresponding county within 48 hours of arrival. Also, firearms must be unloaded and in a locked case as checked luggage to be transported by plane to the state.

Game Animals

All game animals on Hawaii have been introduced. Some have adapted admirably and are
becoming well entrenched, while the existence of
others is still precarious. **Feral pigs** are escaped
domestic pigs that have gone wild and are found
on all islands except Lana'i. The stock is a mixture
of original Polynesian pigs and subsequently introduced species. Feral pigs are hunted with dogs
and usually killed with a spear or long knife—pig
hunting is not recommended for the timid or
tenderhearted. These beasts' four-inch tusks and
fighting spirit make them tough and dangerous.
Feral goats come in a variety of colors. Found on
all islands except Lana'i, they have been known to
cause erosion and are viewed as a pest in some
areas, especially on Haleakala. Openly hunted
on all islands, goat meat is considered delicious
when properly prepared. **Mouflon sheep** are native to Corsica and Sardinia. They do well on
Lana'i and on the windswept slopes of Mauna
Loa and Mauna Kea, where they're hunted at

various times by public lottery. **Feral sheep** haunt
the slopes of Mauna Kea and Mauna Loa at
7,000–12,000 feet. They travel in flocks and destroy vegetation. It takes determination and a
good set of lungs to bag one, especially with a
bow and arrow.

Game Birds

A number of game birds are found on most of the
islands. Bag limits and hunting seasons vary, so
check with the Division of Forestry and Wildlife
for details. **Ring-necked pheasant** is one of the
best game birds; it is found on all the islands.
The **Kalij pheasant** from Nepal is found only on
the Big Island, where the **green pheasant** is also
prevalent. **Francolins**—gray, black, and Erck-
el's—are similar to partridges. They are hunted on
all islands with dogs, and taste great when roasted. There are also **chukar** from Tibet; a number of **quail,** including the Japanese and
California varieties; **doves;** and the **wild Rio
Grande turkeys.**

Shopping

The following is an overview of the main shopping areas and their locations around the island.
Hawai'i has plenty of stores, from large malls to
small boutique shops, art galleries, bookstores,
and gift shops. Almost every town has at least a
gas station and market, and the bigger towns
have supermarkets, health food stores, and local
markets. Greater detail is available in the individual travel chapters.

SHOPPING CENTERS

General shopping centers are found in Hilo,
Kailua-Kona, and Waimea. Like most shopping
malls, these have a variety of stores whose offerings
include apparel, jewelry, dry goods, sporting goods,
food, photography supplies, and outdoor rentals.

Hilo Malls

The main shopping center in Hilo is the **Prince
Kuhio Plaza** at 111 E. Pua'inako. This is Hilo's
newest and the island's largest full-service, diver-

sified shopping mall. Across the street is **Waiakea Center** with a Borders Books and Music, a
natural foods store, and Wal-Mart. **Pua'inako
Town Center** is located up the road at 2100 Kanoelehua Avenue and has lots of food outlets.
An older and much eclipsed shopping center is
Kaiko'o Mall at 777 Kilauea Avenue near the
center of town. Smaller but still vibrant with its
many local shops is the **Hilo Shopping Center,**
located about a half mile up Kilauea Avenue.

Kona Malls

Two commodities you're guaranteed in Kailua-
Kona are plenty of sunshine and plenty of shopping. **Kona Inn Shopping Village** is located in
central Kailua and has more than 40 shops selling
everything from fabrics to fruits. Between the
King Kamehameha's Kona Beach Hotel Mall
and the new **Coconut Grove Marketplace** along
Ali'i Drive, there are at least half a dozen small
shopping plazas that cater to tourists. Heading inland from the pier along Palani Road are generally

newer and larger shopping centers, more local shops where the local people buy. Going up the way, they are the **King Kamehameha Mall, North Kona Shopping Center, Kopiko Plaza, Lanihau Center,** and the **Kona Coast Shopping Center,** each with a fine diversity of shops. Along Queen Kaʻahumanu Highway you'll find the large, new **Crossroads Center** and the **Makalapua Center.** At the south end, **Keauhou Shopping Center** is conveniently located at the corner of Aliʻi Drive and Kamehameha III Road, with everything from a post office to a supermarket.

Waimea Malls

After the diversity of shopping malls in Kailua and Hilo, it's like a breath of fresh air to have fewer choices. In Waimea, try the newly renovated **Parker Ranch Shopping Center,** which has several dozen shops, including a grocery, general merchandise stores, and restaurants. Almost across the street is the **Waimea Center,** Waimea's newest mall. The smaller **Parker Square Shopping Mall** has a clutch of fine boutiques and shops.

SPECIALTY SHOPS

Fine Art Galleries

While Hilo is not the hotbed of art galleries, one shop in which to stop for a look is **Dreams of Paradise** in the S. Hata Building along Kamehameha Avenue. This shop displays a wide variety of art from painting to fabric, and many of the artists live on the island.

While heading up the Hamakua Coast, visit the **Woodshop Gallery** along Honomu's main street, where large wood furniture, small wood boxes, painting, pottery, glass, and all sorts of arts and crafts deserve a look. In Honokaʻa, the **Bamboo Gallery** is a spacious showroom where you will find an eclectic mix of wood, fiber, canvas, and glass art, all displayed in a sparse Oriental style. At the end of the road in Kukuihaele is **Waipiʻo Valley Artworks,** showcasing exclusive artwork of distinguished island artists.

If you are after an exquisite piece of art, a unique memento, or an inexpensive but distinctive souvenir, make sure to visit the **Volcano Art Center** in Hawaii Volcanoes National Park. This is a real treasure and an exquisite showcase for island artists.

In the village of Kainaliu in South Kona, look for **The Blue Ginger Gallery,** displaying the owners' art as well as artists' works from all over the island. Nearly across the street is the **Lavender Moon Gallery** with more exquisite art.

Holualoa is an artists' community. In town you'll find a converted and brightly painted coffee mill that's home to the **Kona Arts Center,** a community art cooperative since 1965. Also in town are half a dozen small but outstanding galleries, including **Studio 7, Holualoa Gallery,** and **Ululani.**

Down in Kailua-Kona you'll find **Rift Zone Gallery** in the Coconut Grove Marketplace, which carries a broad spectrum of art styles and media, mostly by local artists. The ubiquitous **Wyland Galleries** has a shop at Waterfront Row. While featuring paintings by Wyland himself, it does showcase a handful of other big-name island artists.

Many of the luxury resorts along the Kohala Coast have an art gallery in their clutch of shops. One standout among the bunch is the **Amaury St. Giles Modern Art Gallery** at the Hapuna Beach Resort. It's worth a look for the eclectic modern pieces collected there.

Along the north shore in Kapaʻau across from the Kamehameha statue is **Ackerman Gallery,** where you'll find the work of artist Gary Ackerman along with displays of local pottery, carvings, and one-of-a-kind jewelry.

Gift Shops

Kimura's Lauhala Shop in Holualoa has been selling and producing its famous *lau hala* hats ever since local weavers began bartering their creations for groceries in 1915.

For a genuine gift item, search the shelves of the **Huliheʻe Palace Gift Shop.** Not only will you find something to take home as a remembrance, you'll be supporting this wonderful institution. **Alapaki's** at Keauhou Shopping Center sells traditional island arts and crafts, some of the tourist variety and some genuine. You can always find a good deal at **The Little Grass Shack** in Kealakekua, an institution in the area. It may look like a tourist trap, but don't let that stop you from going in and finding some authentic souvenirs.

Hilo has a good number of antiques and collectibles shops, and you'll find more along the main drag in tiny Honoka'a up the Hamakua Coast.

Searchers for the New Age and metaphysicians of all stripes will find a book, tape, aroma, incense, or reading to fit their needs at **The Rainbow Path** in Captain Cook.

As on every island, **Hilo Hattie's** is the place to stop for right-price, if not the most exceptional, gifts and clothing. Hilo Hattie's has one shop in Hilo and a second in Kailua.

Bookstores

Two aspects of a quality vacation are knowing what you're doing and thoroughly relaxing while doing it. Nothing helps you do this better than a good book. The following bookstores offer full selections.

In Hilo, **Basically Books,** downtown at 160 Kamehameha Ave., has a good selection of Hawaiiana, out-of-print books, and the island's best selection of maps and charts. It also features a very good selection of travel books. At the Prince Kuhio Plaza are the **Book Gallery** and **Waldenbooks,** both full-selection bookstores. Newest to town and the largest on the east side of the island is **Borders Books and Music** at the Waiakea Shopping Center.

Kailua-Kona also has a huge **Borders Books and Music** up above town on Henry Street. In town at the Kona Plaza Shopping Arcade is the **Middle Earth Bookshoppe,** smaller but more personal with a great selection of books and maps.

The **Kohala Book Shop** in Kapa'au purportedly is the largest used bookstore in the Pacific and does book searches.

Other shops with a wide selection of Hawaiiana are the gift shops at the **Lyman Museum** and **Hulihe'e Palace.** Numerous gift shops throughout the island and hotel sundries shops also carry books on Hawaiian subjects. Books on health,

cooking, natural foods, and nutrition can be found at **Abundant Life Natural Foods** and **Island Naturals** in Hilo, **Kona Natural Foods** in Kailua, and **Healthway II** in Waimea.

For books on diving, snorkeling, reef fish, and marine topics, check dive shops and water sport activity shops. Some outdoor adventure shops carry books on camping, hiking, and natural history, like the Hawaii Forest and Trail shop near the marina in Kailua.

Film and Film Developing

Photographic film—print, slide, color, black and white—is available on Hawai'i, but color print film is the most widely available. Camera shops carry a variety, but film can also be found at gift shops, sundries stores, most activity outlets, and general merchandise stores throughout the island.

Longs Drugs, Wal-Mart, and **Kmart** all sell and develop film at reasonable prices. For greater selection of film types and full-service options, try **Zac's** or **Hawaiian Camera Supply** in Kailua-Kona.

ARTS TO BUY

Wild Hawaiian shirts or bright mu'umu'u, especially when worn on the Mainland, have the magical effect of making wearers "feel" like they're in Hawaii, while at the same time eliciting spontaneous smiles from passers-by. Maybe it's the colors, or perhaps it's just the "vibe" that signifies "party time" or "hang loose," but nothing says Hawaii like alohawear. There are more than a dozen fabric houses in Hawaii turning out distinctive patterns, and many dozens of factories creating their own personalized designs. These factories often have attached retail outlets, but in any case you can find hundreds of shops selling alohawear. Aloha shirts were the brilliant idea of a Chinese merchant in Honolulu, who used to hand-tailor them and sell them to the tourists who arrived by ship in the glory days before World War II. They were an instant success. Mu'umu'u or "Mother Hubbards" were the idea of missionaries, who were appalled by Hawaiian women running about au naturel and insisted on covering their new Christian converts from head to foot. Now the roles are reversed, and it's Mainlanders who come to Hawaii and immediately strip down to as little clothing as possible.

Alohawear

At one time alohawear was exclusively made of cotton or from manmade, natural fiber–based rayon, and these materials are still the best for any tropical clothing. Beware, however: polyester has slowly crept into the market! No material could possibly be worse for the island climate, so when buying your alohawear make sure to check the label for material content. On the bright side, silk also is used and makes a good material but is a bit heavy for some. Mu'umu'u now come in various styles and can be worn for the entire spectrum of social occasions in Hawaii. Aloha shirts are basically cut the same as always, but the patterns have undergone changes, and apart from the original flowers and ferns, modern shirts might depict an island scene in the manner of a silk-screen painting. A basic good-quality mu'umu'u or aloha shirt is guaranteed to be worth its price in good times and happy smiles. The connoisseur might want to purchase *The Hawaiian Shirt, Its Art and History* by R. Thomas Steele. It's illustrated with more than 150 shirts that are now considered works of art by collectors the world over.

Scrimshaw

The art of etching and carving on bone and ivory has become an island tradition handed down from the times of the great whaling ships. Examples of this Danish sailor's art date all the way back to the 15th century, but, like jazz, it was really popularized and raised to an art form by Americans—whalers on decade-long voyages from "back east" plying vast oceans in search of great whales. Frederick Merek, who sailed aboard the whaling ship *Susan,* was the best of the breed; however, most sailors only carved on the teeth of great whales to pass the time and have something to trade for whiskey, women, and song in remote ports of call. When sailors, most of whom were illiterate, sent scrimshaw back to family

J.D. BISIGNANI

woven palm-frond baskets and hats

and friends, it was considered more like a post-card than artwork. After the late 1800s, scrimshaw faded from popular view and became a lost art form until it was revived, mostly in Lahaina, during the 1960s. Today, scrimshaw can be found throughout Hawaii, but the center remains the old whaling capital of Lahaina, Maui.

Wood Carvings

One surviving Hawaiian art is wood carving. Old Hawaiians used koa almost exclusively because of its density, strength, and natural luster, but koa is becoming increasingly scarce—though many pieces are still available. Costly milo and monkeypod are also excellent woods for carving and have largely replaced koa. You can buy tikis, bowls, and furniture at numerous shops. Countless inexpensive carved items are sold at variety stores, such as hula dancers or salad servers, but most of these are imported from Asia or the Philippines.

Weaving

The minute you arrive in Hawaii, you should shell out $2 for a woven beach mat. This is a necessity, not a frivolous purchase, but it definitely won't have been made in Hawaii. What is made in Hawaii is *lau hala*. This is traditional Hawaiian weaving from the leaves *(lau)* of the pandanus *(hala)* tree. These leaves vary greatly in length, with the largest over six feet, and they have a thorny spine that must be removed before they can be worked. The color ranges from light tan to dark brown. The leaves are cut into strips one-eighth inch to one inch wide and are then employed in weaving. Any variety of items can be made or at least covered in *lau hala*. It makes great purses, mats, baskets, and table place mats.

Woven into a hat, *lau hala* is absolutely superb but should not be confused with a palm-frond hat. A *lau hala* hat is amazingly supple and even when squashed will pop back into shape. A good one is expensive and with proper care will last for years. All *lau hala* should be given a light application of mineral oil on a monthly basis, especially if it's exposed to the sun. For flat items, iron over a damp cloth and

keep purses and baskets stuffed with paper when not in use. Palm fronds also are widely used in weaving. They, too, are a great natural raw material, but not as good as *lau hala*. Almost any woven item, such as a beach bag woven from palm, makes a good authentic yet inexpensive gift or souvenir.

Quilts

Along with the gospel and the will to educate, the early missionaries brought skills and machines to sew. Aside from wanting to cover the naked bodies of their new converts, many taught the Hawaiians how to quilt together small pieces of material into designs for the bed. Quilting styles and patterns varied over the years and generally shifted from designs familiar to New Englanders to those more pleasing to Hawaiian eyes, and a number of standard patterns include leaves, fruits, and flowers of the islands. Most Hawaiian-design quilts seen for sale in the islands today are now made in the Philippines under the direction of Hawaiian designers. Because of labor costs, they are far less expensive than any quilt that is actually made in Hawaii. Generally speaking, quilts 24 inches square run about $75, those 48 inches square about $180–250, and those for queen- and king-size beds from $1,200–1,500. When available, quilts made in Hawaii can be several times as expensive.

Gift Items

Jewelry is always an appreciated gift, especially if it's distinctive, and Hawaii has some of the most original. The sea provides the basic raw materials of pink, gold, and black corals that are as beautiful and fascinating as gemstones. Harvesting coral is very dangerous work. The Lahaina beds off Maui have one of the best black coral lodes in the islands, but unlike reef coral, these trees grow at depths bordering the outer limits of a scuba diver's capabilities. Only the best can dive 180 feet after the black coral, and about one diver per year dies in pursuit of it. Conservationists have placed great pressure on the harvesters of these deep corals, and the state of Hawaii has placed strict limits and guidelines on the firms and divers involved.

Puka shells (with small, naturally occurring holes) and *'opihi* shells are also made into jewelry. Many times these items are very inexpensive, yet they are authentic and are great purchases for the price.

Hawaii also produces some unique food items appreciated by most people. Jars of macadamia nuts and butters are great gifts, as are bags of rich, gourmet-quality Kona coffee. Guava, pineapple, passion fruit, and mango are often gift-boxed into assortments of jams, jellies, and spicy chutneys. And for that special person in your life, you can bring home island fragrances in bars of soap and bottles of perfumes and colognes in the exotic scents of gardenia, plumeria, and even ginger. All of the above items are reasonably priced, lightweight, and easy to carry.

Accommodations

Finding suitable accommodations on the Big Island is never a problem. The 9,500-plus rooms available at the island's 170 properties have the lowest annual occupancy rate of any in the islands at only 60 percent. Except for the height of the high seasons and during the Merrie Monarch Festival in Hilo, you can count on finding a room at a bargain. The highest concentration of rooms is strung along Ali'i Drive in Kailua-Kona—over 5,000 in condos, apartment hotels, and standard hotels. Hilo has almost 2,000 rooms; many of its hotels have "gone condo," and you can get some great deals. The rest are scattered around the island in small villages from Na'alehu in the south to Hawi in the north, where you can almost count on being the only off-island guest. You can comfortably stay in the cowboy town of Waimea, or perch above Kilauea crater at one of the oldest hotel sites in the islands. There are bed-and-breakfasts, and the camping is superb, with a campsite almost guaranteed at any time.

The Big Island has a tremendous range of accommodations. A concentration of the state's greatest luxury resorts within minutes of each other is on the Kohala Coast. All are superb, with hideaway "grass shacks," exquisite art collections as an integral part of the grounds, picture-perfect gardens, world-ranked golf courses, and perfect crescent beaches. Kona has fine reasonably priced hotels like the King Kamehameha's Kona Beach Hotel and Royal Kona Resort in downtown Kailua, and the Keauhou Beach Resort just south toward Keauhou. Interspersed among the big hotels are smaller hotels and condominiums with homey atmospheres and great rates. Hilo offers the best accommodations bargains. The first-class Hilo Hawaiian Hotel is priced like a midrange hotel on the other islands, and then there are gems like the Dolphin Bay Hotel that give you so much for your money it's embarrassing. And for a real treat, head to Hawaii Volcanoes National Park and stay at one of the bed-and-breakfasts tucked away there, or at Volcano House, where raw nature has thrilled kings, queens, and luminaries like humorist Mark Twain for over a century. If you want to get away from everybody else, it's no problem, and you don't have to be rich to do it. Pass-through towns like Captain Cook and Waimea have accommodations at very reasonable prices. Or try a self-growth or yoga retreat in Puna at Kalani Oceanside Resort or Yoga Oasis, or a meditation retreat at the Wood Valley Buddhist Temple above Pahala.

HOTELS

Hotels come in all shapes and sizes, from 10-room, family-run affairs to high-rise giants. The neighbor islands have learned an aesthetic lesson from Waikiki, however, and build low-rise resorts that don't obstruct the view and blend more readily with the surroundings. Every year more hotels are built and older ones renovated. Whatever accommodations you want, you'll generally find them on the Big Island.

Types of Hotel Rooms

Most readily available and least expensive is a bedroom with bath—the latter sometimes shared in the most inexpensive older hotels. Some hotels can also offer you a studio (a large sitting room that converts to a bedroom), a suite (a bedroom with sitting room), or an apartment with full kitchen plus at least one bedroom. Kitchenettes are often available and contain refrigerators, sinks, and stoves, usually in a small corner nook or fitted together as one space-saving unit. Kitchenettes cost a bit more but save you a bundle by allowing you to prepare some of your own meals. To get that vacation feeling while keeping costs down, eat breakfast in, pack a lunch for the day, and go out to dinner. If you rent a room with a kitchenette, make sure all the appliances work as soon as you arrive. If they don't, notify the front desk immediately, and if the hotel will not rectify the situation, ask to be moved or ask for a reduced rate. Hawaii has cockroaches, so put all food away.

Check-in is usually 3 P.M. or 4 P.M., although if your room is ready, you can sometimes get in early. Call to ask. Checkout is most often 11 A.M. or noon. Some of the more expensive hotels and resorts offer express checkout, and a TV video checkout system is offered by others.

Amenities

All hotels have some of them, and some hotels have all of them. Air-conditioning is available in most, but under normal circumstances you won't need it. Balmy trade winds provide plenty of breezes, which flow through louvered windows and doors in many hotels. Ceiling fans are better. TVs are most often included, but not always, as are entertainment centers with stereos and CD players; pay-per-view movies are almost always an option. In-room phones are usually provided, but a service charge of up to $.85 per call is almost always tacked on, even for local calls. A few hotels have purposefully created an environment without phones, TVs, or entertainment centers so that you can get plugged into your surroundings and stay disconnected from other distractions. Swimming pools are very com-

mon, even though the hotel may sit right on the beach. There is almost always a restaurant of some sort—usually several—a coffee shop or two, a bar, a cocktail lounge, and sometimes a sundries shop, clothing store, or art gallery. While most rooms stock complimentary coffee and tea, goodies from the honor bar will be charged to your bill.

Some hotels also offer tennis courts or golf courses either on the premises or affiliated with the hotel; usually an activity or concierge desk can book you into a variety of daily outings. Plenty of hotels offer Laundromats on the premises, and the better places also have pick-up and delivery laundry services. Hotel towels can be used at the pool and beach. Many hotels have installed clotheslines that pull out over the bathtub and are to be used for drying wet clothes. Dry your swimsuits there, as hotels don't want you to drape your wet suit over the balcony outside. Bellhops get about $1 per bag or $5 a load on a rolling cart, and maid service is free, though maids are customarily tipped $1–2 per time—a bit more if kitchenettes are involved or if you've been a piggy. Self-parking is (usually) free, and often valet parking is provided at a nominal fee or for a tip. Where parking is very limited, it will often be in garage structures, and a fee of about $10 a night will be levied.

Most places have in-room safes for securing your valuables, but many charge $1.50–2 for the privilege. Most hotels offer a children's program with supervised activities, excursions, and food during weekday daytime hours—sometimes seasonally—most often for children 5–12 years of age, which ranges from free to $50 a kid. Hotels can often arrange special services like baby-sitters (in house or with a local licensed caregiver), all kinds of lessons, and special entertainment activities. A few even have bicycles and snorkeling equipment to lend. They'll receive and send mail for you, cash your traveler's checks, and take messages. For your convenience, each room should be equipped with a directory of hotel services and information, and some hotels also include information about area sights, restaurants, and activities.

Hotel Rates: Add 11.4 Percent Tax

Every year Hawaiian hotels welcome in the New Year by hiking their rates by about 10 percent. Hawaii, because of its gigantic tourist flow and tough competition, offers hotel rooms at universally lower rates than most developed resort areas around the world; even with the 11.4 percent tax (7.25 percent accommodations tax, plus 4.16 percent general excise tax), there are still many reasonable rates to be had. The basic **daily rate** is geared toward double occupancy; singles are hit in the pocketbook. Single rates, when offered, are cheaper than doubles, but not usually by much. Many hotels will charge for a double and then add an additional charge ($10 to $75) for extra persons up to a certain number. Plenty of hotels offer the **family plan,** which allows children, usually 17 and under, to stay in their parents' room free if they use the existing beds. If another bed or crib is required, there is an additional charge. Some hotels—not always the budget ones—let you cram in as many as can sleep on the floor with no additional charge. Only a limited number of hotels offer the **American plan,** where breakfast and dinner are included with the night's lodging. **Discounts** of various sorts are offered, but these vary by hotel. Some of the typical discounts are AAA, AARP, car and room, room and breakfast, fifth-night free, and *kama'aina* (state resident) rates. **Business/corporate rates** are usually offered to anyone who can at least produce a business card. **Weekly and monthly** rates will save you approximately 10 percent off the daily rate. In all cases, make sure to ask about other-than-published rates because this information won't necessarily be volunteered. In addition to regular hotel charges and taxes, some luxury hotels and resorts now charge a "resort fee" that is used to offset a variety of amenities and parking costs that would otherwise be charged for individually.

While some hotels have a single basic rate throughout the year, most have a tiered pricing policy based on times of the year. This often translates as regular- and value-season rates (which may be referred to differently at different hotels), while some also include holiday rates. Some hotels have a **minimum stay** policy, usu-

ally three days, but this can increase to 7–10 days during the Christmas and New Year holidays. While the difference between "high season" and "low season" is less distinct than it used to be, Hawaii's **peak season** still runs from just before Christmas until after Easter and then again throughout the summer, when rooms are at a premium. Value-season rates, when rooms are easier to come by, are often about 10 percent below the regular rate.

In Hawaiian hotels you always pay more for a good view. Terms vary slightly, but usually "oceanfront" means your room faces the ocean and your view is mostly unimpeded. "Ocean view" is more vague. It could be a decent view, or it could require standing on the dresser and craning your neck to catch a tiny slice of the sea sandwiched between two skyscrapers. "Garden view" means just that, and "mountain view" may mean that you have a view of a mountain or simply that you have a view away from the ocean. Rooms are designated and priced upward with garden view or mountain view being the least expensive, then ocean view and oceanfront rooms. Suites are invariably larger and more expensive, and these usually get the best locations and views.

Note: Prices listed are based on a standard published rate, double occupancy, without taxes or other charges added, unless otherwise noted.

Payment, Deposits, and Reservations

The vast majority of Hawaiian hotels accept foreign and domestic traveler's checks, personal checks preapproved by the management, cash, and most major credit cards. Reservations are always the best policy, and they're easily made through travel agents or by contacting the hotel directly. In all cases, bring documentation of your confirmed reservations with you in case of a mix-up.

Deposits are not always required to make reservations, but they do secure them. Some hotels require the first night's payment (or several) in advance. Reservations without a deposit can be legally released if the room is not claimed by 6 P.M. Whether by phone call, email, fax, or letter, include your dates of stay and type of room in your request for a reservation, and make sure that the hotel sends you a copy of the confirmation. All hotels and resorts have **cancellation requirements** for refunding deposits. The time limit on these can be as little as 24 hours before arrival or as much as 30 days. Some hotels require full **advance payment** for your entire stay, especially during peak season or during times of crowded special events, such as the Merrie Monarch Festival in Hilo. Be aware of the time required for a cancellation notice *before* making your reservation deposit—especially when dealing with advance payment. If you have confirmed reservations, especially with a deposit, and there is no room for you, or one that doesn't meet prearranged requirements, you should be given the option of accepting alternate accommodations. You are owed the difference in room rates if there is any. If there is no room whatsoever, the hotel is required to find you one at a comparable hotel and to refund your deposit in full.

CONDOMINIUMS

The main qualitative difference between a condo and a hotel is in amenities. At a condo, you're more on your own. You're temporarily renting an apartment, so there won't be any bellhops and rarely a bar, restaurant, or lounge on the premises, though many times you'll find a sundries store. The main lobby, instead of having that grand-entrance feel of many hotels, is more like an apartment-house entrance, although there might be a front desk. Condos can be studios (one big room), but mostly they are one- or multiple-bedroom affairs with a complete kitchen. Reasonable housekeeping items should be provided: linens, furniture, and a fully equipped kitchen. Most have TVs and phones, but remember that the furnishings provided are up to the owner. You can find brand-new furnishings that are top of the line, right down to "garage sale" bargains. Inquire about the furnishings when you make your reservations. Maid service might be included on a limited basis (for example, once weekly), or you might have to pay extra for it.

Condos usually require a minimum stay, although some will rent on a daily basis, like hotels.

Minimum stays when applicable are often three days, but seven is also commonplace, and during peak season, two weeks isn't unheard of. Swimming pools are common, and depending on the "theme" of the condo, you can find saunas, weight rooms, hot tubs, and tennis courts. A nominal fee, often $10–15, is usually charged for more than two people. Generally speaking, studios can sleep two, a one-bedroom place will sleep four, two-bedroom units will sleep six, and three-bedroom units will sleep eight. Most have a sleeper couch in the sitting room that folds out into a bed. You can find clean, decent condos for as little as $450 per week, all the way up to exclusive apartments for well over $2,000. Most fall into the $700–1,000 per week range. The method of paying for and reserving a condo is just about the same as for a hotel. However, requirements for deposits, final payments, and cancellation charges are much stiffer than in hotels. Make absolutely sure you fully understand all of these requirements when you make your reservations.

The real advantage of condos is for families, friends who want to share accommodations, and especially travelers on long-term stays, for which you will always get a special rate. The kitchen facilities save a great deal on dining costs, and it's common to find units with their own mini-washers and dryers. To sweeten the deal, many condo companies offer coupons that can save you money on food, gifts, and activities at local establishments. Parking space is ample for guests, and as at hotels, plenty of stay/drive deals are offered. Like hotels, condos usually charge $.60–$1 for local, credit card, or collect calls. Some have in-room safes, but there will be a daily charge of $1.50–1.75 for their use. Pay-per-view, in-room movie service is usually available for $8.95–16.95 per movie. Many now also have a lost key fee, which may be as steep as $75, so don't lose it! If you can't produce it, you pay for it.

Hotel/Condominium Information

One of the best sources of hotel/condo information is the **Hawaii Visitors Bureau** and its island branches. While planning your trip, either visit one nearby or write to the bureau in

Hawaii. (Addresses are given in the "Information and Services" section later in this chapter.) Request a copy of the current Accommodation/Dining/Entertainment Guide. This handy booklet lists all the hotel/condo members of the HVB, with addresses, phone numbers, facilities, and rates. General tips are also given.

Condo Booking and Reservations

The following is a partial list of companies with a number of properties on the Big Island. Vacation rental agencies listed below can also offer this service for condominiums.

Aston Hotels and Resorts, 2250 Kuhio Ave., Honolulu, HI 96815, 808/931-1400, 800/321-2558 in Hawaii, 800/922-7886 Mainland, 800/445-6633 Canada, http://aston-hotels.com.

Outrigger Hotels and Resorts, 2375 Kuhio Ave., Honolulu, HI 96815, 800/688-7444, www.outrigger.com.

Marc Resorts Hawaii, 2155 Kalakaua Ave., Honolulu, HI 96815, 808/926-5900, 800/535-0085, marc@aloha.net, www.marcresorts.com.

Go Condo Hawaii, 800/452-3463, www.gocondohawaii.com.

Hawaii Condo Exchange, 800/442-0404, http://hawaiicondoexchange.com.

VACATION RENTALS

Vacation rentals are homes or cottages that are rented to visitors, usually for a week or longer. Sometimes shorter rentals can be arranged. These rentals come with all the amenities of condo units, but they are usually free-standing homes. Meals are not part of the deal, so that is your responsibility. There are numerous vacation rentals throughout the island, and many of these advertise by word of mouth, in magazine ads, and with websites. Perhaps the best way to locate a vacation rental, at least the first time you visit the island, is through a rental/real estate agent. This can be handled either on Hawai'i, or by phone, fax, email, or through the mail. Everything from simple beach homes to luxurious hideaways are put into the hands of rental agents. The agents have descriptions of the properties and terms of

the rental contracts, and many will furnish photographs. Be aware that some places levy out-cleaning fees in addition to the rental rate. When contacting an agency, be as specific as possible about your needs, length of stay, desired location, and how much you're willing to spend. If handled through the mail, the process may take some time; write several months in advance. Be aware that during high season, rentals are at a premium; if you're slow to inquire there may be slim pickin's.

The following is a list of major vacation rental agencies on the west side of Hawai'i.

Hawaii Vacation Rentals, 7 Puako Beach Dr., Kamuela, HI 96743, 808/882-7000, fax 808/882-7607, seaside@aloha.net, www.bigisland-vacation.com, handles properties almost exclusively in Puako.

South Kohala Management, P.O. Box 384900, Waikoloa, HI 96738, 808/883-8500, 800/822-4252, fax 808/883-9818, info@southkohala.com, www.southkohala.com, handles premium properties only at the luxury resorts in Kohala.

MacArthur & Company, 65-1148 Mamalahoa Hwy., Kamuela, HI 96743, 808/885-8885, 877/885-8285, info@letsgohawaii.com, www.letsgohawaii.com, manages numerous rental homes mostly in the Kohala resort area, Puako, and Waimea.

Aldridge Associates, 808/883-8300, has vacation rentals in Waikoloa.

Century 21 All Islands, 75-5689 Ali'i Drive, Kailua-Kona, HI 96740, 808/326-2121, 800/546-5662, fax 808/329-6768, www.islandsrentals.com/BigIsland/Aloha-C21.html, handles mostly economy to midrange condo units in Kailua and Keauhou.

Property Network, 75-5799 Ali'i Dr., Kailua-Kona, HI 96740, 808/329-7977, 800/358-7977, fax 808/329-1200, vacation@hawaii-kona.com, www.hawaii-kona.com; handles the full range of condos along the Kona Coast.

West Hawaii Property Services, 78-6831 Ali'i Dr., Ste. 234A, Kailua-Kona, HI 96740, 808/322-6696, 800/799-5662, fax 808/324-0609, whps@ilhawaii.com, www.konarentals.com, has a good range of places from economy to deluxe.

Keauhou Property Management, 76-6225 Kuakini Hwy., Ste. C105, Kailua-Kona, HI 96740, 808/326-9075, 800/745-5662, fax 808/326-2055.

Sunquest Vacations, 77-6435 Kuakini Hwy., Kailua-Kona, HI 96740, 808/329-6488, 800/367-5168 Mainland, 800/800-5662 Canada, fax 808/329-5480, www.sunquest-hawaii.com.

Knutson and Associates, 75-6082 Ali'i Dr., Ste. 8, Kailua-Kona, HI 96740, 808/329-6311, 800/800-6202, fax 808/326-2178, www.konahawaiirentals.com, manages midrange condo units and a few vacation homes mostly in the central Kona area.

A smaller company with about half condo units and half homes is **C. J. Kimberly Realtors,** 75-5875 Kahakai Rd., Kailua-Kona, HI 96740, 808/329-4321, 888/780-7000, fax 808/329-5533, cjkimberly@aloha.net, www.cjkimberlyrealtors.com.

Action Team Realty, 75-5660 Kopiko St., Ste. B4, Kailua-Kona, HI 96740, 808/329-8626, 800/335-3347, www.konacondo.com, handles many condo units in about a dozen and a half properties, as well as a number of individual homes, in Kona.

BED-AND-BREAKFASTS

Bed-and-breakfast (B&B) inns are hardly a new idea. The Bible talks of the hospitable hosts who opened the gates of their homes and invited the wayfarer in to spend the night. B&Bs have a long tradition in Europe and were commonplace in revolutionary America. Nowadays, lodging in private homes called bed-and-breakfasts is becoming increasingly fashionable throughout the United States, and Hawaii is no exception with about 100,000 B&B guests yearly.

Points to Consider

The primary feature of bed-and-breakfasts is that every one is privately owned and therefore uniquely different from every other. The range of B&Bs is as wide as the living standards in the United States. You'll find everything from a semi-mansion in the most fashionable residential area to a little grass shack offered by a down-home fisherman and his family. This means that it's particularly important for the guest to choose a host family with whom his or her lifestyle is compatible.

Unlike at a hotel or a condo, you'll be staying *with* a host (usually a family), although your room will be private, with private baths and separate entrances quite common. You can make arrangements directly or you might want to go through an agency (listed below), which acts as a go-between, matching host and guest. It is best to call these agencies, but you can also write. Agencies have a description of each B&B they rent for, its general location, the fees charged, and a good idea of the lifestyle of the host family. What the agency will want to know from you is where you want to stay, what type of place you're looking for, your price range you're willing to pay, arrival and departure dates, and other items that will help them match you with a place. (Are you single? Do you have children? Are you a smoker? etc.) You, of course, can do all the legwork yourself, but these people know their territory and guarantee their work. If you find that a situation is incompatible, they will find another that works. They also inspect each B&B and make sure that all have a license and insurance to operate. Most can also arrange discount rental car and interisland airfares for you.

Since B&Bs are run by individual families, the times that they will accept guests can vary according to what's happening in their lives. This makes it imperative to write well in advance: three months is good; earlier is too long and too many things can change. Four weeks is about the minimum time needed to make all necessary arrangements. Expect a minimum stay requirement (three days is common). B&Bs are not long-term housing, although it's hoped that guest and host will develop a friendship and that future stays can be as long as both desire.

As with condos, B&Bs have different requirements for making and holding reservations and for payment. Most will hold a room with a credit card deposit or check covering a certain percentage of the total expected bill. Be aware, however, that some B&Bs do not accept credit cards or personal checks, so you must pay in cash, traveler's checks, or money orders. Always inquire about the method of payment when making your initial inquiries.

B&B Agencies

Operating strictly for establishments on the Big Island is **Hawaii Island B&B Association,** a local organization that monitors its members for quality standards. For information about HIBBA, write P.O. Box 1890, Honoka'a, HI 96727, contact hibba@stayhawaii.com, or see www.stayhawaii.com. Its brochure lists member accommodations with addresses, telephone and fax numbers, email and website addresses, rates, and descriptions.

A top-notch B&B agency with over 200 homes is **Bed and Breakfast Hawaii,** operated by Evelyn Warner and Al Davis. They've been running this service since 1978, and their reputation is excellent. Bed and Breakfast Hawaii, P.O. Box 449, Kapa'a, HI 96746, 808/822-7771, 800/733-1632, reservations@bandb-hawaii.com, http://bandb-hawaii.com.

One of the most experienced agencies, **Bed And Breakfast Honolulu (Statewide),** 3242 Kaohinanai Dr., Honolulu, HI 96817, 808/595-7533, 800/288-4666, fax 808/595-2030, rainbow@hawaiibnb.com, www.hawaiibnb.com, owned and operated by Mary Lee and Gene Bridges, began in 1982. Since then, they've become masters at finding visitors the perfect accommodations to match their desires, needs, and pocketbooks. Their repertoire of guest homes includes more than 400 rooms, half on O'ahu and the other half scattered around the state.

All Island Bed and Breakfast, 823 Kainui Dr., Kailua, HI 96734, 808/263-2342, 800/542-0344, fax 808/263-0308, cac@aloha.net, can match your needs up with about 700 homes throughout the state.

Hawaii's Best Bed and Breakfast, P.O. Box 520, Kamuela, HI 96743, 808/885-4550, 800/262-9912, fax 808/885-0559, bestbnb@aloha.net, http://bestbnb.com, has listings all over the state and is known for excellent service.

Since 1982, **Go Native Hawaii** has helped people find the right place to stay on the five

major islands. Call 808/935-4178 or 800/662-8483, email reservations@gonativehi.com, or go to www.gonativehi.com.

HOSTELS

The Big Island has several very reasonably priced hostels operating at this time. Perhaps the truest hostel experience on the Big Island is at **Holo Holo In** in Volcano, P.O. Box 784, Volcano Village, HI 96785, 808/967-7950, fax 808/967-8025, holoholo@interpac.net, www.enable.org/holoholo. Located at 19-4036 Kalani Honua Rd., the Holo Holo In is set up with a kitchen, dorms, private rooms, baths, a sauna, and a laundry, and is closed during the day. Rates are $17 per person for the dorm ($15 for AYH members), or $40 per couple for a private room. Please bring your own sheets, or there will be a nominal extra charge.

Arnott's Lodge, 98 Apapane Rd., Hilo, HI 96720, 808/969-7097, fax 808/961-9638, info@arnottslodge.com, www.arnottslodge.com, offers a dormitory bunk for $17, and semiprivate rooms with a shared bath, kitchen, and living room for $37–57. Tenting space is also available on the lawn. Arnott's also offers inexpensive hiking excursions.

Patey's Place, 5-195 Ala Ona Ona St., Kailua-Kona, HI 96740, 808/326-7018, fax 808/326-7640, www.hawaiian-hostels.com, will set you up in a bunk for $19.50, a semiprivate room for $27.50, and a private room for $35–46.

The **Hotel Honoka'a Club,** P.O. Box 247, Honoka'a, HI 96727, 808/775-0678, 800/808-0678, honokaac@gte.net, http://home1.gte.net/honokaac, has three private hostel rooms for $35 and two communal rooms for $15 in its basement level. All rooms share bathrooms and kitchen facilities.

In Mt. View is **Pineapple Park B&B Hostel,** P.O. Box 639, Kurtistown, HI 96760, 808/968-8170, 877/965-2266, park@aloha.net, www.pineapple-park.com. A bed in the bunk room here runs $20, while other types of rooms run $55 and up. Pineapple Park has another hostel in the town of Captain Cook, tel./fax 808/323-2224, 877/865-2266, where dorms are $20 and other rooms run $40–65. This one has the same Web address, but the email is ppark@aloha.net.

Down on the south end of the Kona Coast is the quiet **Kaimana Guest House and Hostel,** P.O. Box 946, Captain Cook, HI 96704, 808/328-2207, kaimanavacations@msn.com, www.kaimanavacations.com. Hostel beds run $20, a private single room is $30, and a private double room costs $40.

HOME EXCHANGES

One other method of staying in Hawaii, open to homeowners, is to offer the use of your home in exchange for the use of a home in Hawaii. This is done by listing your home with an agency that facilitates the exchange and publishes a descriptive directory. To list your home and to find out what is available, contact one of the following agencies:

Homelink USA, P.O. Box 47747, Tampa, FL 33647, 813/975-9825, 800/638-3841, fax 813/910-8144, usa@homelink.org, www.homelink.org.

Intervac U.S., 30 Corte San Fernando, Tiburon, CA 94920, 800/756-4663, fax 415/435-7440, info@intervacus.com, www.intervacus.com.

Food and Drink

Hawaii is a gastronome's Shangri-la, a sumptuous smorgasbord in every sense of the word. The varied ethnic groups that have come to Hawaii in the last 200 years have all brought their own special enthusiasm and culture—and lucky for all, they didn't forget their cook pots, hearty appetites, and exotic taste buds.

The Polynesians who first arrived found a fertile but desolate land. Immediately they set about growing taro, coconuts, and bananas, and raising chickens, pigs, fish, and dogs, though the latter was reserved for nobility. Harvests were bountiful, and the islanders thanked the gods with the traditional feast called the lu'au. Most foods were baked in the underground oven *imu.* Participants were encouraged to feast while relaxing on straw mats and enjoying the hula and various entertainments. The lu'au is as popular as ever and is a treat that's guaranteed to delight anyone with a sense of eating adventure.

The missionaries and sailors came next, and their ships' holds carried barrels of ingredients for puddings, pies, dumplings, gravies, and roasts—the sustaining "American foods" of New England farms. The mid-1800s saw the arrival of boatloads of Chinese and Japanese peasants, who wasted no time making rice instead of bread the staple of the islands. The Chinese added their exotic spices, cooking complex Sichuan dishes as well as workers' basics like chop suey. The Japanese introduced shoyu (soy sauce), sashimi, boxed lunches *(bento),* delicate tempura, and rich, filling noodle soups. The Portuguese brought their luscious Mediterranean dishes of tomatoes, peppers, and plump, spicy sausages; nutritious bean soups; and mouthwatering sweet treats like *malasadas* (holeless donuts) and *pao dolce* (sweet bread). Koreans carried crocks of zesty kimchi and quickly fired up grills for *pulgogi,* marinated beef cooked over a fire. Filipinos served up their delicious adobo stews of fish, meat, or chicken in a rich sauce of vinegar and garlic.

Recently, Thai and Vietnamese restaurants have been offering their irresistible dishes next door to restaurants serving fiery burritos from Mexico or elegant marsala cream sauces from France. The ocean breezes of Hawaii not only cool the skin but waft with them some of the most delectable aromas on earth, making the taste buds tingle and the spirit soar.

HAWAIIAN FOODS

Hawaiian cuisine, the oldest in the islands, consists of wholesome, well-prepared, and delicious foods. All you have to do on arrival is notice the size of some of the local boys (and women) to know immediately that food to them is indeed a happy and serious business. An oft-heard island joke is that "local men don't eat until they're full; they eat until they're tired." Many Hawaiian dishes have become standard fare at a variety of restaurants, eaten at one time or another by anyone who spends time in the islands. Hawaiian food in general is called *kaukau;* cooked food is *kapahaki,* and something broiled is called *ka'ola.* Any of these prefixes on a menu will let you know that Hawaiian food is served. Usually inexpensive, it will definitely fill you and keep you going.

Traditional Favorites

In old Hawaii, although the sea meant life, many more people were involved in cultivating beautifully tended garden plots of taro, sugarcane, breadfruit, and various sweet potatoes *('uala)* than with fishing. They husbanded pigs and barkless dogs *('ilio),* and prized *moa* (chicken) for their feathers and meat but found eating the eggs repulsive. Their only farming implement was the *'o'o,* a sharpened hardwood digging stick. The Hawaiians were the best farmers of Polynesia, and the first thing they planted was taro, a tuberous root that was created by the gods at the same time as humans. This main staple of the old Hawaiians was made into poi. Every lu'au will have poi, a glutinous purple paste. It comes in liquid consistencies referred to as one-, two-, or three-finger poi. The fewer fingers you need to eat it, the thicker it is. Poi is one of the most nutritious carbohydrates known, but people tend to find it bland and tasteless until they are used to it. Some of the best poi, fermented for a day or so, has an acidic bite. Poi is made to be eaten *with* something, but locals who love it pop it in their mouths and smack their lips. Those unaccustomed to it will suffer constipation if they eat too much.

While poi fell out of favor during the middle of the 20th century, it is once again becoming popular, and several sizable factories are now producing poi for sale. You can find plastic containers of this food refrigerated in many supermarkets and local food stores. In addition, deep-fried slices of taro root, plain or spiced, are now packaged and sold like potato chips.

A favorite dessert is *haupia,* a custard made from coconut. *Limu* is a generic term for edible seaweed, which many people still gather from the shoreline and eat as a salad, or mix with ground *kukui* nuts and salt as a relish. A favorite Hawaiian snack is *'opihi,* small shellfish (limpets) that cling to rocks. Those who gather them always leave some on the rocks for the future. Cut from the shell and eaten raw by all peoples of Hawaii, *'opihi* sell for $150 per gallon in Honolulu—a testament to their popularity. A general term that has come to mean "hors d'oeuvres" in Hawaii is *pu pu.* Originally the name of a small shellfish, it is now used for any finger food. A traditional liquor made from ti root is *'okolehao.* It literally means "iron bottom," reminiscent of the iron blubber pots used to ferment it.

Pacific Rim (a.k.a. "Hawaiian Regional") Cuisine

At one time the "tourist food" in Hawaii was woeful. Of course, there has always been a handful of fine restaurants, but for the most part the food lacked soul, with even the fine hotels opting to offer second-rate renditions of food more appropriate to large Mainland cities. Surrounded by some of the most fertile and pristine waters in the Pacific, you could hardly find a restaurant offering fresh fish, and it was an ill-conceived boast that even the fruits and vegetables lying limp on your table were "imported." Beginning with a handful of extremely creative and visionary chefs in the early 1980s, who took the chance of perhaps offending the perceived simple palates of visitors, a delightfully delicious new cuisine was born. Based upon the finest traditions of continental cuisine—including, to a high degree, its sauces, pastas, and presentations—the culinary magic of Pacific Rim boldly combines the pungent spices of Asia, the fantastic fresh vegetables, fruits, and fish of Hawaii, and, at times, the earthy cooking methods of the American Southwest. The result is a cuisine of fantastic tastes, subtle yet robust and satiating but health-conscious—the perfect marriage of fresh foods prepared in a fresh way. Now restaurants on every island proudly display menus labeled "Pacific Rim." As always, some are better than others, but the general result is that "tourist food" has been vastly improved and everyone benefits. Many of these exemplary chefs left lucrative and prestigious positions at Hawaii's five-diamond hotels and opened signature restaurants of their own, making this fine food much more available and affordable.

In 1998, a new and younger group called Hawaiian Island Chefs came together to further enhance the variety and offering of innovative foods made with island-grown produce and the bounty of the sea. In addition, this group has as one of its goals to influence culinary programs in the state in order to help carry on this fine tradition. With the incredible mix of peoples and cultures in Hawaii, the possibilities are endless, and this new group of chefs intends to shepherd the experience along.

Lu'au

The lu'au is an island institution. For a fixed price, you get to gorge yourself on a tremendous variety of island foods, sample a few island drinks, and have a night of entertainment as well. Generally, lu'au run from about 5 or 5:30 P.M. to 8:30 or 9 P.M. Food is usually served buffet-style, and while all have pretty much the same format, the type of food and entertainment differ somewhat.

To have fun at a lu'au you have to get into the swing of things. Entertainment is provided by local performers in what is usually called a "Polynesian Revue." This includes the tourist's hula, the fast version with swaying hips and dramatic lighting, a few wandering troubadours singing Hawaiian standards, and someone swinging swords or flaming torches. Some also offer an *imu* ceremony where the pig is taken from the covered oven. All the Hawaiian standards like poi, *haupia, lomi* salmon, *laulau* (a package of meat, fish, and veggies wrapped in ti leaves), and *kalua* (*imu*-baked) pig are usually served. If these don't suit your appetite, various Asian dishes, plus chicken, fish, and roast beef are most often also on the table. If you leave a lu'au hungry, it's your own fault!

The lu'au master starts the *imu* on the morning of the gathering; stop by and watch. He lays the hot stones and banana stalks so well that the underground oven maintains a perfect 400°F. In one glance, the lu'au master can gauge the weight and fat content of a succulent porker and decide just how long it should be cooked. The water in the leaves covering the pig steams and roasts the meat so that it falls off the bone. Local wisdom has it that "all you can't eat in the *imu* are the hot stones."

Lu'au range in price, about $55–79 for adults and about half that for children, including entertainment. This is the tourist variety—a lot of fun, but definitely a show. The least expensive, most authentic, and best lu'au are often put on by local churches or community groups. If you ask locals "Which is the best?" you won't get two to agree. It's literally a matter of taste. Following is a list of the lu'au presently available on the Big Island. These dinner/show festivities are only presented at major tourist hotels in Kailua-Kona and Kohala. For full descriptions, see the listings in the appropriate travel chapters.

Tihati's Drums of Polynesia Lu'au at the Royal Kona Resort, 808/331-1526. Monday, Wednesday, and Friday. Lots of fun but not too traditional.

Island Breeze Lu'au at the beach in front of King Kamehameha's Kona Beach Hotel, 808/326-4969, is held every Sunday, Tuesday, Wednesday, Thursday, and Friday evening on the grounds of King Kamehameha's last residence.

The **Friday Night Lu'au** at Kona Village Resort, 808/325-5555, is the longest-running lu'au on the island and always offers a sumptuous meal. Highly recommended.

The **Royal Lu'au** at the Outrigger Waikoloa Beach, 808/886-6789, is offered on Sunday and Wednesday. 'Anaeho'omalu Bay makes a nice backdrop for this lu'au and the performance is rousing. Gets good mention from locals.

The **Old Hawaii *Aha'aina* Lu'au** at the Mauna Kea Beach Hotel, 808/822-5810, is held on Tuesday. Perhaps the most traditional of the bunch, performance is by *Kumu Hula* Nani Lim and company. It gets high marks on the food and a fine seaside setting.

Every Friday, **Legends of the Pacific** is performed at Hilton Waikoloa Village, 808/885-1234.

MONEY-SAVERS

Only one thing is better than a great meal: a great meal at a reasonable price. The following are island institutions and favorites that will help you eat well and keep prices down.

Kaukau Wagons

These are lunch wagons, but instead of slick, stainless-steel jobs, most are old delivery trucks converted into portable kitchens. Some say they're a remnant of World War II, when workers had to be fed on the job; others say that the meals they serve were inspired by the Japanese *bento,* a boxed lunch. You'll see these wagons parked along beaches, in city parking lots, or on busy streets. Usually a line of local people will be placing their orders, especially at lunchtime—a tip-off that the wagon serves delicious, nutritious island dishes at reasonable prices. They might have a few tables, but basically they serve food to go. Most of their filling meals are about $3.50, and they specialize in the "plate lunch."

Plate Lunch

One of the best island standards, these lunches give you a sampling of authentic island food that can include teriyaki chicken, mahimahi, *laulau,* and *lomi* salmon, among others. They're on paper or Styrofoam plates, are packed to go, and usually cost less than $3.50. Standard with a plate lunch is "two-scoop rice" and a generous dollop of macaroni or other salad. Full meals, they're great for keeping down food costs and for instant picnics. Available everywhere, from *kaukau* wagons to restaurants.

Bento

Bento are the Japanese rendition of the box lunch. Aesthetically arranged, they are full meals. They are often sold in supermarkets and in some local eateries with take-out counters.

Saimin

Special "saimin shops" as well as restaurants serve this hearty, Japanese-inspired noodle soup. Saimin is a word unique to Hawaii. In Japan, these soups would be called *ramin* or *soba,* and it's as if the two were combined into "saimin." A large bowl of noodles in broth, stirred with meat, chicken, fish, shrimp, or vegetables, costs only a few dollars and is big enough for an evening meal. The best place to eat saimin is in a local hole-in-the-wall shop run by a family.

Early-Bird Specials

Even some of the island's best restaurants in the fanciest hotels offer "early-bird specials"—meals from the regular menu offered to diners who come in before the usual dinner hour, which is approximately 6 P.M. You pay as little as half the normal price and can dine in luxury on some of the best foods. The specials are often advertised in free tourist magazines, which might also include coupons for two-for-one meals or limited dinners at much lower prices.

Buffets

Buffets are also quite common in Hawaii, and like lu'au are all-you-can-eat affairs. Offered at a variety of restaurants and hotels, they usually cost $12 and up, but will run $25–35 in the better hotels. The food ranges considerably from passable to quite good. At lunchtime, they're priced lower than at dinner, and breakfast buffets are cheaper yet. Buffets are always advertised in free tourist literature, which often include discount coupons.

FOOD STORES
Supermarkets

Groceries and picnic supplies can be purchased in almost every town on the island. Many of the markets in the smaller towns also sell a limited selection of dry goods and gifts. The general rule is the smaller the market, the higher the prices. The largest and cheapest stores with the biggest selections are found in Hilo and Kailua-Kona.

The island's major supermarkets, **KTA Super Store, Sack 'n Save,** and **Safeway,** each have at least one branch store in both Hilo and Kailua-Kona. **KTA Super Store** also has a supermarket in Waimea, while **Sure Save** has a location in Kea'au. Waikoloa Village is serviced by the large and modern **Waikoloa Village Market.**

ON THE ROAD

These smaller markets should meet your needs as you travel around the Big Island. Along the eastern Hamakua Coast you'll find **T. Kaneshiro Store** and **K. K. Super-Mart** in Honoka'a. On the Kohala peninsula look for **M. Nakahara** and **K. Takata** stores for general supplies in Hawi. The only place along the South Kohala Coast for supplies is **Puako General Store** in the tiny village of Puako, while south of Kailua-Kona you'll find **Kimura's Market** in Kainaliu, **Kamigaki Market** in Kealakekua, and **Shimizu Market** in Honaunau. South of Hilo in Pahoa is **Pahoa Cash and Carry.** In Volcano village try **Kilauea General Store** and **Volcano Store** just before entering Hawaii Volcanoes National Park. The Ka'u district has **Island Market** in Na'alehu, which bills itself as the southernmost market in the United States, **Wong Yuen Store** in Wai'ohinu, and the **Ocean View Market** and **Kahuku Market** in Ocean View.

Health Food Stores

Abundant Life Natural Foods in downtown Hilo at 292 Kamehameha Ave. has been doing business since 1977. Open daily, the store stocks a full selection of fresh fruit and vegetables, bulk and packaged foods, vitamins, minerals, and supplements, and it has a food counter for ready-made and made-to-order wholesome eats. In a newer and larger store in the Waiakea Center is **Island Naturals.** This market and deli offers about the same services and products. While heading south from Hilo to Volcanoes, stop along Route 11 at **Kea'au Natural Foods** or in Pahoa at **Pahoa Natural Groceries.**

On the Kona side, try the full-service **Kona Natural Foods** in the new Crossroads Center. Its sister store, **Healthways II,** is located in Waimea. South of Kailua in Kainaliu, look for the small but well-stocked **Evie's Natural Foods.** Aside from bulk and packaged foods, fresh produce, and supplements, each store does fresh food preparation on the premises and has prepared foods in a cooler case.

Farmers' and Fish Markets

On Wednesdays and Saturdays 7 A.M.–3 P.M., check out the **Hilo Farmers' Market** at Kamehameha Avenue and Mamo Street, fronting the bay in the center of the downtown area. This is a lively affair with an incredible variety of goods for sale. At the Cooper Center in Volcano, you'll find produce, flowers, and baked goods at the **Volcano Farmers' Market** every Sunday 8–10 A.M. In Pahoa, **Caretakers of Our Land Farmers' Market** pulls out their wares on Saturday 7:30 A.M.–noon at the Sacred Heart Catholic Church. On Sunday 9 A.M.–1 P.M., head back down the highway near mile marker 8 to find food, flowers, clothing, and a whole variety of other items.

For locally grown produce on the west side of the island try the **Kona Farmers' Market** every Wednesday, Friday, Saturday, and Sunday 7 A.M.–3 P.M. at the parking lot along Ali'i Drive across from Hale Halawai. The **Waimea Farmers' Market,** held every Saturday 7 A.M.–noon, is where local farmers come to sell their produce, much of which is organic, at the Hawaiian Homes Hall about two miles east of town. Also on Saturday at about the same time is the **Parker School Farmers' Market,** held at the school grounds.

In addition to these organized markets, you will find individual roadside stands set up here and there around the island that also sell fruit, vegetables, flowers, and other such items.

FISH AND SEAFOOD

Anyone who loves fresh fish and seafood has come to the right place. Island restaurants specialize in seafood, and it's available everywhere. Pound for pound, seafood is one of the best dining bargains on the Big Island. You'll find it served in every kind of restaurant, and often the fresh catch-of-the-day is proudly displayed on ice in a glass case. The following is a sampling of the best.

Mahimahi

This excellent eating fish is one of the most common, most popular, and least expensive on Hawai'i. It's referred to as "dolphin" but is definitely a fish, not a mammal. Mahimahi can weigh 10–65 pounds; the flesh is light and moist. This fish is broadest at the head. When caught it's a dark olive color, but after a while the skin turns iridescent shades of blue, green, and yellow. It can be served as a main course or as a patty in a fish sandwich.

A'u

This true island delicacy is a broadbill swordfish or marlin. It's expensive even in Hawaii because the damn thing's so hard to catch. The meat is moist and white—truly superb. If it's offered on the menu, order it. It'll cost a bit more, but you won't be disappointed.

Ono

Ono means "delicious" in Hawaiian, so that should tip you off to the taste of this wahoo, or king mackerel. *Ono* is regarded as one of the finest eating fishes in the ocean, and its flaky white meat lives up to its name.

Manini

These five-inch fish are some of the most abundant in Hawaii and live in about 10 feet of water. They school and won't bite a hook but are easily taken with spear or net. Not often on menus, they're favorites with local people, who know best.

Ulua

This member of the crevalle jack family weighs 15–100 pounds. Its flesh is white and has a steak-like texture. It's delicious and often found on menus.

Uku

This gray snapper is a favorite with local people. The meat is light and firm and grills well.

'Ahi

A yellowfin tuna with distinctive pinkish meat, *'ahi* is a great favorite cooked or served raw in sushi bars.

Moi

This is the Hawaiian word for "king." The fish has large eyes and a sharklike head. Considered one of the finest eating fishes in Hawaii, it's best during the autumn months.

Seafood Potpourri

Other island seafood found on menus includes *'opihi,* a small shellfish (limpet) that clings to rocks and is considered one of the best island delicacies, eaten raw; *'alo'alo,* similar to tiny lobsters; crawfish, plentiful in taro fields and irrigation ditches; *'ahipalaka,* albacore tuna; octopi and squids (calamari); and sharks of various types.

'A'ama are the ubiquitous little black crabs that you'll spot on rocks and around pier areas. They're everywhere. For fun, local fishermen will try to catch them with poles, but the more efficient way is to throw a fish head into a plastic bucket and wait for the crabs to crawl in and trap themselves. The *'a'ama* are about as big as two fingers and make delicious eating.

Limu is edible seaweed that has been gathered as a garnish since precontact times and is frequently found on traditional island menus. There's no other seaweed except *limu* in Hawaii. Because of this, the heavy, fishy-ocean smell that people associate with the sea but which is actually that of seaweed is absent in Hawaii.

Poki is a seafood salad made with a variety of fish, seafood, seaweed, onions, and other seasonings that is often found in deli sections of supermarkets.

Sushi

A finger-size block of sticky rice, topped with a slice of (usually) raw fish or other sea creature. A delicacy in Japan and appreciated in Hawaii as a fine food.

MUNCHIES AND ISLAND TREATS

Certain finger foods, fast foods, and island treats are unique to Hawaii. Some are meals in themselves, others are snacks. Here are some of the best and most popular.

Pu Pu

Pronounced as in "Winnie the Pooh Pooh," these are little finger foods and hors d'oeuvres. They can be anything from crackers to cracked crab. Often, they're given free at lounges and bars and can even include chicken drumettes, fish kabobs, and tempura. At a good display of them you can have a free meal.

Crackseed

A sweet of Chinese origin, crackseed can be any number of preserved and seasoned fruits and seeds. Favorites include coconut, watermelon, pumpkin seeds, mango, plum, and papaya. Distinctive in taste, crackseed takes some getting used to but makes a great trail snack. It is available in all island markets. Also look for dried fish (cuttlefish) on racks, usually near the crackseed. Nutritious and delicious, it makes a great snack.

Shave Ice

This real island institution makes the Mainland "snow cone" melt into insignificance. Special machines literally shave ice to a fluffy consistency. It's mounded into a paper cone and your choice from dozens of exotic island syrups is generously poured over it. Get a straw and spoon and just slurp away.

Taro Chips

These are like potato chips but made from the taro root. If you can find them fresh, buy a bunch, as they are mostly available packaged.

Malasadas and *Pao Dolce*

Two sweets from the Portuguese, *malasadas* are holeless donuts and *pao dolce* is sweet bread. Sold in island bakeries, they're great for breakfast or as treats.

Lomi Lomi Salmon

This salad of salmon, tomatoes, and onions with garnish and seasonings often accompanies "plate lunches" and is featured at buffets and lu'au.

TROPICAL FRUITS AND NUTS

Some of the most memorable taste treats from the islands require no cooking at all: the luscious tropical and exotic fruits and vegetables sold in markets and roadside stands or just found hanging on trees, waiting to be picked. Make sure to experience as many as possible. The general rule

in Hawaii is that you are allowed to pick fruit on public lands, but the amount should be limited to personal consumption. The following is a sampling of some of Hawaii's best produce.

Bananas

No tropical island is complete without them. There are more than 70 species in Hawaii, with hundreds of variations. Some are for peeling and eating, while others are cooked. A "hand" of bananas is great for munching, backpacking, or picnicking. Available everywhere— and cheap.

DIANA LASICH HARPER

common banana

Avocados

Brought from South America, avocados were originally cultivated by the Aztecs. They have a buttery consistency and nutty flavor. Hundreds of varieties in all shapes and colors are available fresh year-round. They have the highest fat content of any fruit next to the olive.

Coconuts

What tropical paradise would be complete without coconuts? Indeed, these were some of the first plants brought by the Polynesians. The coconut was very important to the Hawaiians and every part was used. A tree was planted when a child was born as a prayer for a good food supply throughout life. The trunks were used for building homes and *heiau* and carved into drums to accompany hula. The husks became bowls, utensils, and even jewelry. *'Aha,* sennit rope braided from the husk fiber, was renowned as the most saltwater-resistant natural rope ever made.

Truly tropical fruits, coconuts know no season. Drinking nuts are large and green, and when shaken you can hear the milk inside. You get about a quart of fluid from each. It takes skill to open one, but a machete can handle anything.

coconut palm

DIANA LASICH HARPER

Mangoes

This is one of the most delicious fruits known to humans. Mangoes grow wild all over the islands; the ones on the leeward sides of the islands ripen Apr.–June, while the ones on the windward sides can last until October. They're found in the wild on trees up to 60 feet tall. The only problem is how to stop eating them once you start!

Papayas

This truly tropical fruit has no real season but is mostly available in the summer. Papayas grow on branchless trees and are ready to pick as soon as any yellow appears. Of the many varieties, the "solo papaya," meant to be eaten by one person, is the best. Split them in half, scrape out the seeds and have at them with a spoon.

Passion Fruit

Known by their island name of *liliko'i*, passion fruit make excellent juice and pies. The small yellow fruit (similar to lemons but smooth-skinned) is mostly available in summer and fall. Many grow wild on vines, waiting to be picked. Slice off the stem end, scoop the seedy pulp out with your tongue, and you'll know why they're called "passion fruit."

Guavas

These small, round, yellow fruits are abundant in the wild, where they ripen from early summer to late fall. They're considered a pest—so pick all you want. A good source of vitamin C, they're great for juice, jellies, and desserts.

Macadamia Nuts

The king of nuts was brought from Australia in 1892. Now it's the state's fourth-largest agricultural product, producing 40 percent of the world's output. Some 90 percent of the state's harvest comes from the Big Island. These nuts are creamy in color, crispy in texture, round in shape and about the size of a marble, slightly sweet, and available plain, roasted, candied, or buttered.

Cut the stem end flat so that it will stand, then bore a hole into the pointed end and put in a straw or hollow bamboo. Coconut water is slightly acidic and helps balance alkaline foods. Spoon meat is a custardlike gel on the inside of drinking nuts. Sprouted coconut meat is also an excellent food. Split open a sprouted nut, and inside is the yellow fruit, like a moist sponge cake. "Millionaire's salad" is made from the heart of a coconut palm. At one time an entire tree was cut down to get to the heart, which is just inside the trunk below the fronds and is like an artichoke heart except that it's about the size of a watermelon. In a downed tree, the heart stays good for about two weeks.

breadfruit

DIANA LASICH HARPER

Breadfruit

This island staple provides a great deal of carbohydrates, but many people find the baked, boiled, or fried fruit bland. It grows all over the islands and is really thousands of little fruits growing together to form a ball that can be as big as a watermelon.

ON THE ROAD

Litchis

Called nuts but really small fruit with thin red shells, litchis have sweet, juicy white flesh that tastes somewhat like a green grape that surrounds a hard inner seed. **Rambutan** are similar in flesh but have a soft, spiky, and somewhat thicker red covering.

Potpourri

Along with the above, you'll find pineapples (including the white, sweet, and less acidic Sugarloaf variety), oranges, limes, kumquats, thimbleberries, and blackberries in Hawaii, as well as carambolas (star fruit), wild cherry tomatoes, and tamarinds.

ISLAND DRINKS

To complement the fine dining in the islands, bartenders have been busy creating their own tasty concoctions. The full range of beers, wines, and standard drinks is served in Hawaii, but for a real treat you should try mixed drinks inspired by the islands. Most look very innocent because they come in pineapples, coconut shells, or tall frosted glasses. They're often garnished with little umbrellas or sparklers, and most have enough fruit in them to give you your vitamins for the day. Rum is used as the basis of many of them; it's been an island favorite since it was introduced by the whalers of the 19th century. Many hotel and restaurant bars concoct their own blends and give them enticing names. At fancy hotels expect to pay $6–7 for a drink; at other locations, about $5–6. Here are some of the most famous: Mai Tai, a mixture of light and dark rum, orange curaçao, orange and almond flavoring, and lemon juice; Chi Chi, a simple concoction of vodka, pineapple juice, and coconut syrup—a real sleeper because it tastes like a milk shake; Blue Hawaii, vodka and blue curaçao; Planter's Punch, light rum, grenadine, bitters, and lemon juice—a great thirst quencher; and Singapore Sling, a sparkling mixture of gin and brandy with cherry and lemon juice.

Drinking Laws

There are no state-run liquor stores; all kinds of spirits, wines, and beers are available in markets and shops, generally open during normal business hours, seven days a week. The drinking age is 21, and no towns are "dry." Legal hours for serving drinks depend on the type of establishment. Hours generally are as follows: hotels, 6 A.M.–4 A.M.; discos and nightclubs where there is dancing, 10 A.M.–4 A.M.; bars and lounges where there is no dancing, 6 A.M.–2 A.M. Most restaurants serve alcohol, and in many that don't, you can bring your own.

Local Brews

Khalsa and Cameron Healy, a father-and-son team known to their friends and family as "Pops" and "Spoon," are the owners and hands-on brewmasters at **Kona Brewing Company,** 75-5629 Kuakini Hwy., in the North Kona Shopping Center in Kailua-Kona, 808/334-1133, a small, spotless, state-of-the-art brewery producing about 600 barrels per month. Free brewery tours and tastings are given weekdays at 10:30 A.M. and 3 P.M., and the brewpub serves simple meals for lunch and dinner. At this stage, the company produces nine varieties on the island plus additional seasonal beers with its bottled beers brewed in California according to its specifications for commercial distribution. Three of its classics are Longboard Lager, a mild-hop, cold-aged beer; Pacific Golden Ale, a classic malty ale, light and perfect for sipping at the beach; and Fire Rock Pale Ale, a darker, hoppy beer, perfect with a meal. You can find beer from the Kona Brewing Co. at many bars and fine restaurants throughout Hawaii. For additional information, see www.konabrewingco.com. In March, Kona hosts the **Kona International Brewers' Festival,** another great endeavor started by the dynamic dad and son duo in 1995.

The Big Island's second brewery is **Mehana Brewing Company,** 275 E. Kawili St. in Hilo, 808/934-8211. In business since 1996, this microbrewery makes five varieties of light beer with no preservatives that are brewed for the tropical climate and distributed in stores and select restaurants in the islands. The tasting room is open during regular business hours.

Coffee

Kona coffee at one time held the distinction of being the only coffee grown in the United States. It has grown for about 175 years in the upland district of Kona and is a rich, aromatic, truly fine coffee. If it's offered on the menu, have a cup. Recently, coffee from Maui, Moloka'i, O'ahu, and Kaua'i has entered the market.

Getting There

With the number of visitors each year approaching eight million—and another several hundred thousand just passing through—the state of Hawaii is one of the easiest places in the world to get to . . . by plane. About half a dozen large North American airlines (plus additional charter airlines) fly to and from the islands. About the same number of foreign carriers, mostly from Asia and Oceania, also touch down there on a daily basis. Hawaii is one of the most hotly contested air markets in the world. The competition among carriers is fierce, and this makes for sweet deals and a wide choice of flights for the money-wise traveler. It also makes for pricing chaos. It's almost impossible to find airline prices that hold true for more than a month—if that long. Familiarize yourself with the alternatives at your disposal so that you can make an informed travel selection.

Almost all travelers to the Big Island arrive by air. A few lucky ones come by private yacht. The cruise ship *Norwegian Star* docks at Hilo every week and additional cruise ships stop less frequently at both Hilo and Kona. For the rest, the island's two major airports are at Hilo and Kona, with a few commercial flights going to Kamuela. While a few airlines offer flights directly to the Big Island, most routings will still take you through Honolulu.

Airlines usually adjust their flight schedules about every three months to account for seasonal differences in travel and route changes. Before planning a trip to and around the islands, be sure to contact the airlines directly, view their Internet sites, or go through your travel agent for the most current information on routes and flying times.

When to Go

The prime tourist season starts two weeks before Christmas and lasts until Easter. It picks up again with summer vacation in early June and ends once more in late August. Everything is usually much more heavily booked and prices are inflated. Hotel, airline, and car reservations are a must at this time of year. You can generally save 10–50 percent and a lot of hassle if you travel in the "off-season"—September to early December, and mid-April (after Easter) until early June. Recently, the drop in numbers of tourists during the off-season has not been nearly as substantial as in years past, indicating the increasing popularity of the island at all times of the year, but you'll still find the prices better and the beaches, trails, campgrounds, and even restaurants less crowded. The local people will be happier to see you, too.

BY AIR

There are two categories of airlines that you can take to Hawaii: **domestic,** meaning American-owned, and **foreign**-owned. An American law, penned at the turn of the 20th century to protect American shipping, says that *only* an American carrier can transport you between two American cities. In the airline industry, this law is still very much in effect. It means, for example, that if you want a round-trip flight between San Francisco and Honolulu, you *must* fly on a domestic carrier. If, however, you are flying from San Francisco to Tokyo, you are at liberty to fly a foreign airline, and you may even have a stopover in Hawaii, but you must continue to Tokyo or some other foreign city and cannot fly back to San Francisco on the foreign airline. Travel agents know this, but if you're planning your own trip be aware of this fact.

Flights to Hawaii

Depending on where you are coming from, you may have to fly from your home to a "gateway

PACIFIC CROSSROADS

ASIA

JAPAN

Tokyo
Hong Kong
Manila
PHILIPPINES

AUSTRALIA

Sydney

NEW ZEALAND

Auckland

Tahiti

NORTH AMERICA

Anchorage

Seattle
San Francisco
Los Angeles

SOUTH AMERICA

HAWAII

TROPIC OF CANCER

EQUATOR

TROPIC OF CAPRICORN

3847 mi.
5543 mi.
5293 mi.
2780 mi.
2678 mi.
2397 mi.
2557 mi.
2741 mi.
4393 mi.
5070 mi.

2500 mi
2500 km

© SANDRA E. BISIGNANI TRUST AND AVALON TRAVEL PUBLISHING, INC.

city," from where flights go to Hawaii, either direct or nonstop. On direct flights you fly from point A to point B without changing planes; it doesn't mean that you don't land in between. Direct flights do land, usually once to board and deplane passengers, but you sit cozily on the plane along with your luggage and off you go again. Nonstop is just that; you board and when the doors open again you're at your destination. All flights from the West Coast gateway cities are nonstop, God willing—because there is only the Pacific in between!

Flights to the Big Island

Most island flights in the past landed at Hilo International Airport. With the Kona Coast gaining popularity, domestic flights from the Mainland have shifted to that side of the island, and the only direct international connection to the Big Island lands there as well. United Airlines operates nonstop flights to the Big Island from the Mainland—daily flights from San Francisco and Los Angeles to Kona International Airport. In past peak seasons, United has run a flight to Hilo International Airport, but it's an on-and-off affair depending on the number of travelers. Aloha Airlines flies from Oakland, California, to Kona, and Japan Airlines offers daily flights from Tokyo.

All other major domestic and foreign carriers fly you to Honolulu and have arrangements with either Hawaiian Airlines or Aloha Airlines for getting you to the Big Island. This sometimes involves a plane change, but your baggage can be booked straight through. If you fly from the Mainland with Hawaiian or Aloha, you have the added convenience of dealing with just one airline. Several charter airlines also fly to the Big Island nonstop from the Mainland.

Travel Agents

At one time people went to a travel agent the same way they went to a barber or beautician, loyally sticking with one. Most agents are reputable professionals who know what they're doing. They should be members of the American Society of Travel Agents (ASTA) and licensed by the Air Traffic Conference (ATC). Most have the inside track on the best deals,

and they'll save you countless hours calling 800 numbers and listening to elevator music while on hold or checking with umpteen Internet ticket sellers. Unless you require them to make very special arrangements, their services are usually free or nearly so—they are paid a commission by the airlines and hotels they book for you. In recent years these commissions have been greatly reduced, in some cases abandoned altogether, causing some to start charging a small fee for their services.

If you've done business with a travel agent in the past and were satisfied with the services and prices, by all means stick with him or her. If no such positive rapport exists, then shop around. Ask friends or relatives for recommendations; if you can't get any endorsements go to the *Yellow Pages*. Call two or three travel agents to compare prices. Make sure to give all of them the same information and be as precise as possible. Tell them where and when you want to go, how long you want to stay, which class you want to travel, and any special requirements. Write down their information. It's amazing how confusing travel plans can be when you have to keep track of flight numbers, times, prices, and all the preparation information. When you compare, don't look only for the cheapest price. Check for convenience in flights, amenities of hotels, and any other fringe benefits that might be included. Then make your choice of agent and, if he or she is willing to give you individualized service, stick with that agent from then on.

Agents become accustomed to offering the same deals to many clients because they're familiar with the arrangements and because the deals have worked well in the past. Sometimes these are indeed the best, but if they don't suit you, don't be railroaded into accepting them. Any good agent will work with you. After all, it's your trip and your money.

Consolidators are companies that buy blocks of seats on certain flights and then turn around and sell them. Their buying price must be very cheap because their prices are some of the best that you can find. They often list their toll-free phone numbers in local phone directories and just as often run ads in large city newspapers—

often in the Sunday travel section. With the proliferation of the Internet, the number of online travel companies has also mushroomed, and many of these companies offer great deals. As with consolidators, online travel companies come and go, so use a company that has previously worked with you or someone you know. Again, the range in prices can be substantial, so check around with different companies before you send your money.

Package Tours

For the independent traveler, practical package deals that include only flight, car, and lodging are okay. Agents put these together all the time and they just might be the best, but if they don't suit you, make arrangements separately. A package *tour* is totally different. On these you get your hand held by an escort, eat where they want you to eat, go where they want you to go, and watch Hawaii slide by your bus window. For some people, especially groups, this might be the way to do it, but everyone else should avoid the package tour. You'll see Hawaii best on your own, and if you want a tour you can arrange one there, which is often cheaper. Once arrangements have been made with your travel agent, make sure to take all receipts and letters of confirmation (hotel, car) with you to Hawaii. They probably won't be needed, but if they are, nothing will work better in getting results.

Mainland and International Fares

There are many categories of airfares, but only three apply to the average traveler: first class, coach, and excursion (APEX). Traveling **first class** seats you in the front of the plane, gives you free drinks, a wider choice of meals, a wider seat with more legroom, and access to VIP lounges, if they exist. There are no restrictions, no penalties for cancellations or rebooking of return flights, and no advance booking or minimum-stay requirements.

Coach, the way most people fly, is totally adequate. You sit in the plane's main compartment behind first class. Your seats are comfortable but they're narrower and you don't have as much legroom. Drinks cost you a few dollars and you

have a limited choice of meals, but that's about it. Coach offers many of the same benefits as first class and costs about 30 percent less. You can buy tickets up until takeoff, you have no restrictions on minimum or maximum stays, you receive liberal stopover privileges, and you can cash in your return ticket or change your return date with no penalties.

Excursion or advance payment excursion (APEX) fares are the cheapest. You are accommodated on the plane exactly the same as if you were flying coach. There are, however, some restrictions. You must book and pay for your ticket in advance (7–14 days is usual, sometimes up to 30 days). You must book your return flight at the same time, and under most circumstances you can't change either without paying a stiff penalty. Also, your stopovers are severely limited and you will have a minimum/maximum stay period. Only a limited number of seats on any one plane are set aside for APEX fares, so book as early as you can. Also, if you must change travel plans, you can go to the airport and get on as a standby passenger using a discounted ticket, even if the airline doesn't have an official standby policy. There's always the risk that you won't get on, but you do have a chance, as well as priority over an actual standby customer.

Standby is exactly what its name implies: You go to the airport and wait around to see if any flights going to Hawaii have an empty seat. You can save some money, but you cannot have a firm itinerary or limited time. Since Hawaii is such a popular destination, standbys can wait days before catching a plane.

Charters

Charter flights were at one time only for groups or organizations that had memberships in travel clubs. Now they're open to the general public. A charter flight is an entire plane or a block of seats purchased at a quantity discount by a charter company and then resold to customers. Because they are bought at wholesale prices, charter fares can be the cheapest available. As in package deals, only take a charter flight if it is a "fly only" or perhaps includes a car. Most importantly, make sure that the charter company is reputable. It should belong to the same organizations (ASTA and ATC) as most travel agents. If not, check the company out at the local chamber of commerce.

More restrictions apply to charters than to any other flights. You must pay in advance. If you cancel after a designated time, you can be penalized severely or lose your money entirely. You cannot change departure or return dates and times. However, up to 10 days before departure the charter company is legally able to cancel, raise the price by 10 percent, or change time and dates. They must return your money if cancellation occurs or if changed arrangements are unacceptable to you. Mostly they are on the up-and-up and flights go smoothly, but there are horror stories. Be careful. Be wise. Investigate!

Tips

Flights from California take about five hours, and a bit longer from the Northwest or Pacific Canada; you gain two hours over Pacific Standard Time when you land in Hawaii (three hours during daylight saving time). From the East Coast it takes about 11 hours and you gain five hours over Eastern Standard Time. Flights from Japan take about seven hours, and there is a five-hour difference between the time zones. Travel time between Sydney, Australia, or Auckland, New Zealand, and Hawaii is about nine hours. They are ahead of Hawaii time by 20 and 22 hours, respectively. Try to fly Monday–Thursday, when flights are cheaper and easier to book. Pay for your ticket as soon as your plans are firm. If prices go up, there will be no charge added, but merely booking doesn't guarantee the lowest price. Make sure that airlines, hotels, and car agencies get your phone number too—not only your travel agent's—in case any problems with availability arise (travel agents are sometimes closed on weekends). It's not necessary, but it's a good idea to call and reconfirm flights 24–72 hours in advance.

First-row (bulkhead) seats are good for people who need more legroom, but bad for watching the movie. Airlines will give you special meals (vegetarian, kosher, low calorie, low salt), often at no extra charge, but you must notify them

in advance. If you're "bumped" from an overbooked flight, you're entitled to a comparable flight to your destination within one hour. If more than an hour elapses, you get denied-boarding compensation, which goes up proportionately with the amount of time you're held up. Sometimes this is cash or a voucher for another flight to be used in the future. You don't have to accept what an airline offers on the spot, if you feel they aren't being fair.

Traveling with Children

Fares for children ages 2–12 are often 30–50 percent less than adult fares, although the exact amount will depend on the season and flight; children under two not occupying a seat travel free. If you're traveling with an infant or active toddler, book your flight well in advance and request the bulkhead seat or first row in any section and a bassinet if available. Many carriers have fold-down cribs with restraints for the child's safety and comfort. Toddlers appreciate the extra space provided by the front-row seats. Be sure to reconfirm, and arrive early to ensure this special seating. On long flights you'll be glad that you took these extra pains.

Although most airlines have coloring books, puppets, etc., to keep your child busy, it's always a good idea to bring your own. These can make the difference between a pleasant flight and a harried ordeal. Also, remember to bring baby food, diapers, and other necessities, as airlines may not be equipped with exactly what you need. Make all inquiries ahead of time so you're not caught unprepared.

Baggage

You are allowed two free pieces of luggage—one large, the other smaller—and a carry-on bag. The two checked pieces can weigh up to 70 pounds each; an extra charge is levied for extra weight. The larger bag can have an overall dimension (height plus width plus length) of 62 inches; the smaller, 55 inches. Your carry-on must fit under your seat or in the overhead storage compartment. Purses and camera bags are not counted as carry-ons and may be taken aboard. Surfboards and bicycles are about $50 extra from the Mainland but this may vary by airline; enclosed golf bags can be sent as checked luggage at no extra charge. Although they make great mementos, remove all previous baggage tags from your luggage; they can confuse handlers. Attach a sturdy holder with your name and address on the handle, or use a stick-on label on the bag itself. Put your name and address inside the bag, and the address where you'll be staying in Hawaii if possible. Carry your cosmetics, identification, money, prescriptions, tickets, reservations, a change of underwear, camera equipment and film, and perhaps a change of shirt or blouse in your carry-on.

Visas

Entering Hawaii is like entering anywhere else in the United States. Foreign nationals must have a current passport and most must have a proper visa, an ongoing or return air ticket, and sufficient funds for the proposed stay in Hawaii. A visa application can be made at any U.S. embassy or consular office outside the United States and must include a properly filled out application form, two photos 1.5 inches square, and a non-refundable fee of $65. Canadians do not need a visa or passport but must have proper identification such as a passport, driver's license, or birth certificate. Visitors from 28 countries do not need a visa to enter the United States for 90 days or less. As this list is amended periodically, be sure to check in your country of origin to determine whether you need a visa for U.S. entry.

Agricultural Inspection

Everyone visiting Hawaii must fill out a "Plant and Animals Inspection Form" and present it to the appropriate official upon arrival in the state. Anyone carrying any of the listed items must have these items inspected by an agricultural inspection agent at the airport. For information on just what is prohibited, contact any U.S. Customs Office or check with an embassy or consulate in foreign countries.

Remember that before you leave Hawaii for the Mainland, all of your bags are again subject to an agricultural inspection, a usually painless procedure taking only a minute or two. To facili-

tate your departure, leave all bags unlocked until after inspection. There are no restrictions on beach sand from below the high water line, coconuts, prepackaged sugarcane, dried flower arrangements, fresh flower lei, pineapples, certified pest-free plants and cuttings, seashells, seed lei, and wood roses. However, avocado, litchi, and papaya must be treated before departure. Some other restricted items are berries, fresh gardenias, roses, jade plants, live insects, snails, cotton, plants in soil, soil itself, and sugarcane. Raw sugarcane is okay, however, if it is cut between the nodes, has the outer covering peeled off, and is split into fourths.

Foreign countries may have different agricultural inspection requirements for flights from Hawaii (or other points in the United States) to those countries. Be sure to check with the proper foreign authorities for specifics.

Pets and Quarantine

Hawaii has a very rigid pet quarantine policy designed to keep rabies and other Mainland diseases from reaching the state. All domestic pets are subject to a **120-day quarantine** (a 30-day quarantine is allowed if certain pre-arrival and post-arrival requirements are met—inquire), and this includes substantial fees for boarding. Unless you are contemplating a move to Hawaii, it is not feasible to take pets. For complete information, contact the Department of Agriculture, Animal Quarantine Division, 99-951 Halawa Valley St., 'Aiea, HI 96701, 808/483-7151.

Big Island Airports

The largest airport on the Big Island is **Hilo International Airport,** which services Hilo and the eastern half of the island. Formerly known as Gen. Lyman Field, it was named after Gen. Albert Kuali'i Brickwood Lyman, the first ethnic Hawaiian to become a Brigadier General (1942) in the U.S. Army. This airport is remarkably close to downtown Hilo. It's a modern facility with full amenities, and its runways can handle jumbo jets. Interisland flights from here connect directly to Kona, Kahului, and Honolulu, from where you can get to any other airport in the state. The two-story terminal has an information center, a restaurant, a number of vendors, restrooms, and telephones. There is no bank, money exchange, or post office. As you look at the terminal building, the departure lounge is in the center beyond the check-in counters and agricultural inspection station. Arrivals are on the right and the arrival area has baggage claim, restrooms, public telephones, and a small tourist information booth that's usually open when flights are arriving. To the left of the departure area are a number of helicopter tour company counters. Major car-rental agencies have booths to the front of the terminal across the traffic lanes. There is no public transportation to or from the airport; a taxi for the three-mile ride to town costs about $8–12. Public parking is in a large lot behind the car rental booths. Parking fees run $1 for the first half hour, $1 for each additional hour, and a maximum of $7 per day. Along the airport road, a short way in toward town, is the old commuter terminal building where one more helicopter company has its office and where you check in for their tours.

Kona International Airport is nine miles north of Kailua-Kona and handles the air traffic for Kona, Kohala, and the west side of the island. The Kona Airport is surrounded by fields of black lava. This airport handles a growing amount of air traffic from other island cities and all the Mainland and international flights, eclipsing Hilo as the island's major air transportation hub. Interisland flights arrive from Hilo, Honolulu, and Kahului; Mainland and international flights arrive from San Francisco, Los Angeles, Oakland, and Tokyo. During winter, charter flights also fly in from Vancouver. The terminal is a series of open-sided, nonconnected, Polynesian-style buildings. There are no jetways; everyone boards and deplanes by stairway onto the tarmac. Departures leave near the center of this cluster, where you also find the agricultural inspection station; arrivals come to either end. Most Hawaiian, American, and Japan Airlines departures are from the left-hand side; Aloha and United Airlines use mostly the right-hand side. Here too are lockers, telephones, restrooms,

KONA INTERNATIONAL AIRPORT

RUNWAY

TERMINALS

PARKING

To Kohala Resorts

ONIZUKA
SPACE CENTER

RENTAL
CAR
BOOTHS

TERMINALS

PARKING

RENTAL CAR
BASEYARDS

19

SCALE NOT AVAILABLE

COMMUTER TERMINAL

To Kailua-Kona, 7 miles

© SANDRA E. BISIGNANI TRUST AND AVALON TRAVEL PUBLISHING, INC.

land, with no facilities whatsoever and no scheduled flights. Both airports are serviced on request by small charter airlines.

DOMESTIC CARRIERS

The following are the major domestic carriers to and from Hawaii. The planes used are primarily wide-body D10, L10, and 747s, with a smaller 737, 767, and the like flown now and again. A list of the "gateway cities" from which they fly direct and nonstop flights is given, but "connecting cities" are not. The majority of flights, by all carriers, land at Honolulu International Airport, with the remainder of flights going directly to Kaua'i, Maui, and Hawai'i. Only the established companies are listed. Entrepreneurial small airlines pop up now and again and specialize in dirt-cheap fares. There is a hectic frenzy to buy their tickets and business is great for a while, but then the established companies lower their fares and the gamblers fold.

visitor information booths near both baggage claim areas, various food vendors, lei stands, and other shops. Car-rental agencies have booths across the circle road. The public parking lot is open 5:30 A.M.–9 P.M.; it costs $1 for the first half hour, $1 each hour after that, and $7 maximum for 24 hours. There is no public transportation to the airport. A private cab to your hotel in Kailua-Kona will be $12 or more. The commuter terminal just down the road is for helicopter and fixed-wing tourist flight check-in.

Waimea-Kohala Airport is just outside Waimea (Kamuela). There are few amenities and no public transportation into town. Only a few weekly commuter flights are scheduled between Waimea and Honolulu. **Upolu Airport** is a lonely strip on the extreme northern tip of the is-

Hawaiian Airlines

Hawaiian Airlines operates daily direct flights from Los Angeles, San Francisco, Sacramento, and Ontario, California; Las Vegas; Phoenix (via Los Angeles); Seattle; and Portland to Honolulu, with daily flights between Maui and Los Angeles, San Francisco, and Seattle. Scheduled flights to the South Pacific run between Honolulu and Pago Pago, Samoa on Monday, Wednesday, and Friday, and on Saturday to Papeete, Tahiti. Hawaiian Airlines has expanded its service to the West Coast over the past few years, so there may very well be additional destinations and service in the future. Hawaiian Airlines offers special discount deals with Dollar rental cars and select major island hotels. Contact Hawaiian Airlines at 800/882-8811 in Hawaii, 800/367-5320 Mainland and Canada, www.hawaiianair.com.

Aloha Airlines

Aloha Airlines flies daily between Honolulu and Oakland, Burbank, and Orange County, California; Las Vegas via both Oakland and Orange County; and Vancouver, Canada. From Honolulu, there are connecting flights to all islands. Aloha also flies daily between Maui and Oakland and Orange County; Phoenix via Orange County; Las Vegas via Oakland; and Vancouver. Four days a week, there are flights from Kona direct to Oakland. In addition, Aloha Airlines operates flights on Monday and Wednesday to the Marshall Islands in Micronesia, with stops at Johnston Atoll and Kwajalein, and a Sunday charter flight to Christmas Island. The Aloha flight to Midway Island seems to be an on-again, off-again thing, so if you are interested in visiting that very remote island, check with the airlines to see if that flight is currently in operation. Like Hawaiian, Aloha Airlines has been expanding its West Coast operation, so greater variety will undoubtedly be in store in the future. For information, call 800/554-4833 in Hawaii, 800/367-5250 Mainland and Canada, www .alohaairlines.com.

United Airlines

Since its first island flight in 1947, United has become top dog in flights to Hawaii. United's Mainland routes connect more than 100 cities to Hawaii. The main gateway cities of San Francisco and Los Angeles have direct daily flights to Honolulu, with additional flights from Denver on the weekends; flights from all other cities connect through these three cities. United also offers direct flights to Maui, Kona, and Kaua'i from San Francisco and Los Angeles. Continuing through Honolulu, United flights go to Tokyo (Narita), where connections can be made for other Asian cities. United offers a number of packages, including flight and hotel on O'ahu, and flight, hotel, and car on the neighbor islands. United partners with Aloha Airlines and deals with Hertz rental cars. United is the "big

guy" and intends to stay that way—its packages are hard to beat. Call 800/241-6522 or visit www.united.com.

American Airlines

American offers daily flights to Honolulu from Los Angeles, San Francisco, Dallas/Fort Worth, and Chicago. It also flies daily from Los Angeles and Dallas/Fort Worth nonstop to Maui, and to Kona and Kaua'i from Los Angeles. American does not fly to points in Asia or other Pacific destinations from Hawaii. American partners with Hawaiian Airlines. Call 800/433-7300 or visit www.aa.com.

Continental Airlines

Flights from all Mainland cities to Honolulu connect via Los Angeles, Newark, and Houston. Also available are direct flights from Honolulu to Guam, from where flights run to numerous other Asian and Pacific cities and islands. Continental partners with Hawaiian Airlines. Call 800/525-0280, 800/231-0856 for international information, or visit www.continental.com.

Northwest Airlines

Northwest flies into Honolulu from Los Angeles, Seattle, San Francisco (via Seattle), Minneapolis, and Detroit (via Minneapolis or Seattle). There are onward nonstop flights to Narita and Osaka in Japan, from where all other Asian destinations are connected. Call 800/225-2525 or visit www.nwa.com.

Delta Air Lines

In 1985, Delta entered the Hawaiian market; when it bought out Western Airlines its share became even bigger. Delta has nonstop flights to Honolulu from Dallas/Fort Worth, Los Angeles, San Francisco, Salt Lake City, and Atlanta, and a nonstop flight to Maui from Los Angeles. Call 800/221-1212 or visit www.delta.com.

FOREIGN CARRIERS

The following carriers operate throughout Asia and Oceania but have no U.S. flying rights. This means that in order for you to vacation in

Hawaii using one of these carriers, your flight must originate or terminate in a foreign city. You can have a stopover in Honolulu with a connecting flight to a neighbor island. For example, if you've purchased a flight on Japan Air Lines from San Francisco to Tokyo, you can stop in Hawaii, but you must then carry on to Tokyo. Failure to do so will result in a stiff fine, and the balance of your ticket will not be refunded.

Air Canada

Nonstop flights from Canada to Honolulu originate in Vancouver and Toronto, and from Vancouver to Maui. In Hawaii, you can use either Hawaiian Airlines or Aloha Airlines to get to other island destinations. Call 888/247-2262 or visit www.aircanada.ca.

Air New Zealand

Flights link New Zealand, Australia, and numerous South Pacific islands to Honolulu, with continuing flights to Mainland cities. All flights run via Auckland, New Zealand. Call 800/262-1234 or visit www.airnz.com.

Japan Air Lines

The Japanese are the second-largest group, after Americans, to visit Hawaii. JAL flights to Honolulu originate in Tokyo (Narita), Nagoya, and Osaka (Kansai). In addition, there are flights between Tokyo (Narita) and Kona on the Big Island. JAL flights continue beyond Hawaii to San Francisco and Los Angeles. Call 800/525-3663 or visit www.jal.co.jp.

Qantas

Daily flights connect Sydney and Melbourne, Australia, with Honolulu; all other flights feed through these cities. Call 800/227-4500 or visit www.qantas.com.au.

China Airlines

Routes to Honolulu with China Airlines are only from Taipei, and all go through Tokyo. Connections are available in Taipei to most Asian capitals. Call 800/227-5118 or visit www.china-airlines.com.

Korean Air

Korean Air offers some of the least expensive flights to Asia. All flights are direct between Honolulu and Seoul, with connections there to many Asian cities. Call 800/438-5000 or visit www.koreanair.com.

Air Pacific

Air Pacific offers once-weekly nonstop flights between Nadi, Fiji, and Honolulu. Contact 808/227-4446 or see www.airpacific.com.

Polynesian Airlines

If flying to Samoa, use Polynesian Airlines for weekly flights directly from Honolulu to Apia. Call 808/842-7659 or see www.polynesianairlines.co.nz.

Philippine Airlines

Twice-weekly, nonstop flights between Honolulu and Manila are handled through Philippine Airlines. Call 808/435-7725 or visit www.philippineair.com.

Other Airlines

Aside from the above airlines, large volume charter operators book flights to the various islands with such carriers as **Canada 3000, American Trans Air, Ryan International,** and **Skyservice USA.**

TOUR AND TRAVEL COMPANIES

Many tour companies advertise packages to Hawaii in large city newspapers every week. They offer very reasonable airfares, car rentals, and accommodations. The following companies offer great deals and have excellent reputations. This list is by no means exhaustive.

Pleasant Hawaiian Holidays

A California-based company specializing in Hawaii, Pleasant Hawaiian Holidays makes arrangements for flights, accommodations, and transportation only. For flights, it primarily uses American Trans Air, but also uses select commercial airlines and regularly scheduled flights. Aside from the air connection, Pleasant Hawaiian offers a choice of accommodation levels from budget to luxury, a fly/drive option if you have your own accommodation, and numerous perks, like a flower greeting lei, first morning orientation, service desks at hotels, and coupons and gift certificates. Pleasant Hawaiian is easy to work with and stands behind its services. A deposit is required after booking and there is a time frame for full payment that depends upon when you make your reservation. Fees are assessed for making changes after booking, so be sure to apprise yourself of all financial particulars. Most major travel agents work with Pleasant Hawaiian but you can also contact them directly at 2404 Townsgate Rd., Westlake Village, CA 91361, 800/742-9244, www.pleasantholidays.com.

SunTrips

This California-based tour company runs flights to Hawaii from Los Angeles and San Francisco. It offers flight, accommodation, and/or car rental packages that match any for affordability. Your price will depend upon your choice of accommodations and type of car. Using both charter and commercial air carriers, SunTrips does not offer assigned seating until you get to the airport. They recommend you get there two hours in advance, and they ain't kidding! This is the price you pay for getting such inexpensive air travel. Remember that everyone on your incoming flight makes a beeline for the rental car's shuttle van after landing and securing their baggage. If you have a traveling companion, work together to beat the rush by leaving your companion to fetch the baggage while you head directly for the van as soon as you arrive. Pick your car up, then return for your partner and the bags. Even if you're alone, you could zip over to the car-rental center and then return for your bags without having them sit very long on the carousel. SunTrip financial regulations are similar to those at Pleasant Hawaiian; be sure to inquire. Contact SunTrips, 2350 Paragon Dr., San Jose, CA 95131, 800/786-8747, or at www.suntrips.com.

Council Travel Services

These full-service, budget-travel specialists are a subsidiary of the nonprofit Council on International Educational Exchange, and the official U.S. representative to the International Student Travel Conference. They'll custom-design trips and programs for everyone from senior citizens to college students. Bona fide students have extra advantages, however, including eligibility for the International Student Identification Card (ISIC), which often gets you discount fares and waived entrance fees to tourist attractions. Groups and business travelers are also welcome. For full information, call 800/226-8624, or write to Council Travel Services at one of these offices: 530 Bush St., San Francisco, CA 94108, 415/421-3473; or 205 E. 42nd St., New York, NY 10017, 212/822-2700. For additional retail locations and information, see www.counciltravel.com.

STA Travel

STA Travel is a full-service travel agency specializing in student travel, regardless of age. Those under 26 do not have to be full-time students to get special fares. Older independent travelers can avail themselves of services, although they are ineligible for student fares. STA works hard to get you discounted or budget rates. Many tickets issued by STA are flexible, allowing changes with no penalty, and are open-ended for travel up to one year. STA has some 300 offices around the world. For information, call 800/781-4040 or visit www.statravel.com. STA also maintains Travel Help, a service available at all offices designed to solve all types of problems that may arise while traveling. STA is a well-established travel agency with an excellent and well-deserved reputation.

Ocean Voyages

This unique company offers seven- and 10-day itineraries aboard a variety of yachts in the Hawaiian Islands. The yachts, equipped to carry 2–10 passengers, ensure individualized sail training. The vessels sail throughout the islands, exploring hidden bays and coves, and berth at different ports as they go. This opportunity is for anyone who wishes to see the islands in a timeless fashion, thrilling to sights experienced by the first Polynesian settlers and Western explorers. For rates and information, contact Ocean Voyages, 415/332-4681.

Ecotours to Hawaii

Sierra Club Trips offers Hawaii trips for nature lovers who are interested in an outdoor experience. Various trips include birding on the Big Island, and kayak and camping trips on Kaua'i. All trips are led by experienced guides and are open to Sierra Club members only ($35 per year to join). For information, contact the Sierra Club Outing Department, 85 2nd St., 2nd Fl., San Francisco, CA 94105, 415/977-5522, www .sierraclub.org/outings.

Educational Trips

Not a tour per se, but an educational opportunity, **Elderhostel Hawaii** offers short-term programs on five of the Hawaiian Islands. Different programs focus on history, culture, cuisine, and the environment in association with one of the colleges or universities in the islands. Most programs use hotels for accommodations. For information, contact Elderhostel, 11 Avenue de Lafayette, Boston, MA 02111-1746, 877/426-8056, www.elderhostel.org.

Getting Around

The first thing to remember when traveling on the Big Island is that it *is* big, twice as large as the other Hawaiian Islands put together and over four times larger than the state of Rhode Island. A complete range of vehicles is available for getting around—everything from sedans to 4WD off-road vehicles to mopeds. Hawai'i, like O'ahu, has passable public transportation but it is not frequent. Choose the conveyance that fits your style, and you should have no trouble touring the Big Island.

INTERISLAND CARRIERS

Getting to and from the Big Island via the other islands is easy and convenient. The only effective way for most visitors to travel between the Hawaiian Islands is by air. Luckily, Hawaii has excellent air transportation that boasts one of the industry's safest flight records. All interisland flights have a no-smoking regulation. Items restricted on flights from the Mainland and from overseas are also restricted on flights within the state. Baggage allowances are the same as anywhere, except that due to space constraints, carry-on luggage on the smaller prop planes may be limited in number and size. The longest direct interisland flight in the state, 214 miles, is from Honolulu to Hilo and takes about 45 minutes.

Hawaiian and Aloha have competitive prices, with interisland flights at about $80 each way, with substantial savings for state residents. With both airlines, you can save per ticket by purchasing a booklet of six **flight coupons** that run $408. These are only available in-state at any ticket office or airport counter and are transferable. Just book a flight as normal and present the filled-in voucher to board the plane. Perfect for families or groups of friends. Hawaiian Airlines coupons are good for six months, Aloha Airlines coupons for one year. Hawaiian also offers a 10-coupon booklet that can be mailed to Mainland visitors that is $732—allow two weeks.

Additionally, each airline offers passes that are good for unlimited travel anywhere that the airline flies, but they are nontransferable and may only be used on consecutive days. You may purchase these passes in-state or before you arrive in Hawaii. Hawaiian Airlines has the "Hawaiian Island Pass": five days at $310, seven days at $320, 10 days at $419, and 14 days at $479. Fares for children ages 2–11 are about 10 percent less. Aloha Airlines offers one "7-day Island Pass" with up to four flights per day for $336 with the same conditions.

Note: Although every effort has been made for up-to-date accuracy, remember that schedules are constantly changing. The following should be used only as a point of reference.

Please call the airlines listed below for their current schedules.

Hawaiian Airlines

Contact Hawaiian Airlines on the Big Island at 808/935-0858 in Hilo or 808/326-1214 in Kona, 800/882-8811 in Hawaii, 800/367-5320 Mainland and Canada, www.hawaiianair.com. The majority of flights to the Big Island with Hawaiian Airlines run between Honolulu and Kona; 14 flights (about 40 minutes) are spread throughout the day from approximately 5:15 A.M. to 8 P.M. One of these flights stops at Kahului, Maui. A similar schedule applies to Hilo. All other Hawaiian Airlines flights originating in Hilo or Kona go through Kahului or Honolulu. Hawaiian Airlines partners with American Airlines, Continental Airlines, and Northwest Airlines.

Aloha Airlines

Aloha Airlines, 808/935-5771 on the Big Island, 800/367-5250 Mainland and Canada, www.alo-haair.com, also services the Big Island with flights from the neighboring islands. Its 15 daily Honolulu–Kona runs start at 5:10 A.M., with the last at 6:50 P.M.; one dozen Honolulu-to-Hilo flights depart throughout the day, 5:10 A.M.–6:30 P.M. Connecting through Honolulu, there are 10 daily flights to Lihu'e, Kaua'i, from Kona and Hilo. Aloha also flies once a day from both Kona and Hilo to Kahului, Maui, and once a day between Hilo to Kona. Aloha Airlines partners with United Airlines.

Island Air

A subsidiary of Aloha Airlines, **Island Air,** 800/652-6541 in Hawaii, 800/323-3345 nationwide, www.alohaair.com, no longer flies to the Big Island.

Pacific Wings

This carrier is a local and reputable commercial airline that seems to fill the gaps that the bigger airlines often miss. On the Big Island, it only services the Waimea Airport on regularly scheduled flights. Daily flights depart Honolulu and arrive in Waimea at 5:55 P.M. These flights deplane and depart at 6:10 P.M. for Kahului, Maui, where they arrive at 6:50 P.M. Every day except Sunday, a plane leaves Waimea at 8 A.M. direct for Honolulu, arrival at 9:10 A.M. On Sunday, the flight leaves at 3:10 P.M. and arrives in Honolulu at 4:20 P.M. Pacific Wings also does "flightseeing" tours from its base on Maui and is available for charters. For other information and flight schedules, contact the airline at Kahului Airport Commuter Terminal, Kahului, HI 96732, 808/873-0877, www.pacificwings.com.

BY SHIP

In 2001, American Hawaii Cruises stopped all service within the Hawaiian Islands. For years, this company had operated seven-day cruises to four of the islands, and hopefully will resume operation at some time in the future.

Since December 2001, Norwegian Cruise Lines (a subsidiary of Star Cruises PLC of Malaysia) has run a weekly seven-day round-trip cruise with their luxury liner *Norwegian Star*. This ship leaves Honolulu Sunday evening and cruises to Hilo for its first stop. Leaving there, it spends a day at sea before arriving at Fanning Island in the Republic of Kiribati. One day of sailing back returns the ship to Kahului, then to Nawiliwili Harbor on Kaua'i, and then back to port in Honolulu. This trip can also be started on Maui. For information and pricing, contact Norwegian Cruise Lines, 7665 Corporate Center Dr., Miami, FL 33126, 800/327-7030, www.ncl.com.

LAND TRANSPORTATION

The most common way to get around Hawai'i is by rental car. The abundance of agencies keeps prices competitive. As always, reserve during peak season, but in the off-season you may take your chances by shopping around to score a good deal at the last minute. Hawai'i also has limited public bus service, expensive taxis, and reasonable bicycle, motorcycle, and moped rentals. Hitchhiking, while illegal on the Big Island, is still used by some to get around.

Highway Overview

Getting around the Big Island is fairly easy. There is one main highway called the Hawai'i Belt Road (also called Mamalahoa Highway) that cir-

Cruise ships make frequent stops at both Hilo and Kona.

ROBERT NILSEN

cles the island, one cross-island highway called the Saddle Road, and a few other highways and secondary roadways. The Hawai'i Belt Road is known by different numbers in various sections around the island, and this may lead to some confusion. Connecting Kailua-Kona and Hilo around the south end, the number is Highway 11. Major roads that lead off of it are Napo'opo'o Road, which runs down to Kealakekua Bay; Ke Ala O Keawe Road to Pu'uhonua O Honaunau National Historical Park; South Point Road, which drops down to the southernmost tip of the island; Chain of Craters Road, which leads through Hawaii Volcanoes National Park to the lava-covered littoral Puna Coast; and Kea'au-Pahoa Road (Highway 130) from Kea'au to the hinterland of Puna. In Puna, Kapoho-Pahoa Road (Highway 132) and Kapoho-Kalapana Beach Road (Highway 137) make a circle with Highway 130 from Pahoa, down along the shore, and back again.

Going north from Kailua-Kona, the Hawai'i Belt Road (Highway 190), which starts off for the first few miles as Palani Road, cuts across the upper slopes of the volcanoes to Waimea. Slicing through coffee country, as part of the Belt Road, is Highway 180. From Honalo, Route 11 heads down toward Kailua, first as Kuakini Highway, which itself makes a tangent into town, and then continues as Queen Ka'ahumanu Highway. Heading north from Kailua, Queen Ka'ahumanu Highway becomes Route 19. In Kawaihae, it turns uphill to Waimea, becoming Kawaihae Road. In Waimea, Highways 19 and 190 merge, and Highway 19 becomes the designation as the Hawai'i Belt Road continues along and down the Hamakua Coast back to Hilo. Connecting Highway 19 and Highway 190 through the town of Waikoloa is Waikoloa Road. In Honoka'a, Highway 240 leaves the Belt Road and runs north to the edge of Waipi'o Valley. North Kohala is cut by two roads. Akoni Pule Highway (Highway 270) runs along the coast up and around the tip as far as the Pololu Valley. Connecting this road and the town of Waimea is the Kohala Mountain Road (Highway 250). Off-limits to most rental cars, the Saddle Road (Highway 200) rises to about 6,500 feet between the tall peaks of Mauna Loa and Mauna Kea, making a shortcut between Hilo and Waimea or the Kohala Coast. From along the Saddle Road, 4WD roads lead up to the observatories atop Mauna Kea and nearly to the top of Mauna Loa.

RENTAL CARS

Rental car options in Hawaii are as numerous as anywhere in the United States, from a subcompact to a full-size luxury land yacht. The most numerous seem to be compact cars and midsize sedans, but convertibles and 4WD jeeps are very popular, and some vans and SUVs are also available. Automatics far outnumber standard-shift cars, and some companies don't even carry standard-shift vehicles. What's best for you must meet your needs—and your pocketbook. If your vacation will mostly be spent at the hotel, seeing a few sights, and going out to dinner, get yourself a comfortable midsize or luxury car. If you get a big fatso luxury car, it'll be great for puttin' on the ritz at the resort areas, but you'll feel like a hippopotamus in the backcountry. Are you young and/or adventurous—on a honeymoon perhaps? Try a sporty model. There's nothing like cruising along the coast in a convertible with the top down. Got kids? Be sure to rent a car with four doors or a van. Want to get off the main highway? A compact with standard shift or a jeep might be best for you. Main roads on the Big Island are broad and well paved, but the back roads, where much of the fun is, can be narrow, twisty affairs. You'll appreciate the downshifting ability of standard transmissions on curves and steep inclines, if you can get it. Most cars now come with cloth seats. If yours doesn't, sitting on a towel will help—no one likes a hot and sticky vinyl or leather seat. Air-conditioning is standard on all but the cheapest rentals, but it hardly seems necessary in this environment. Automatic window and door locks are common but will not come on all rentals. While you'll want to be paying attention to the scenes around you, a radio is great for getting in touch with local Hawaiian tunes and for weather and surf reports. Most companies have child seats available for rent on a daily basis, $5 a day or

$40–50 maximum, and many can install right- or left-hand controls for handicapped drivers; most agencies require 48–72 hours advance notice to install hand controls.

Tips and Cautions

Most car companies charge you a fee if you rent the car in Hilo and drop it off in Kona, and vice versa. The agencies are prejudiced against the Saddle Road and the spur road leading to South Point, both of which offer some of the *most* spectacular scenery on the island. The prejudice is unfounded because both roads are paved, generally well maintained, and no problem if you take your time. Staff claim the insurance will not cover you if you have a mishap on these roads. A good automobile policy at home will cover you in a rental car, but definitely check this before you take off. The road to the top of Mauna Kea is a 4WD only road. Heed the signs, not so much for going up, but for needed braking power coming down. Don't even hint of these intentions to the car-rental agencies, or they won't rent you a car. Avis and Harper allow you to drive the Saddle Road, and Harper rents 4WDs for the Mauna Kea road.

No way whatsoever should you attempt to drive down to Waipi'o Valley in a regular car! The grade is unbelievably steep, and only a 4WD can make it. Put simply, you have a good chance of being killed if you try it in a car.

Gas stations are farther apart than on the other islands, and sometimes they close very early. As a rule, fill up whenever the gauge reads half full.

Both Hilo International Airport and Kona International Airport have a gauntlet of car-rental booths and courtesy phones outside the terminals.

Requirements

Car rental agencies impose a variety of requirements on the renter, but the most important clauses are common. Before renting, check that you fulfill the requirements. Generally, you must be 21 years old—a few agencies will rent to 18-year-olds while some require you to be 25 for certain vehicles. You must possess a valid driver's license—licenses from most countries are accepted, but if you are not American, get an International Driver's License to be safe. You should also have a major credit card in your name. This is the easiest way to rent a car. Some companies will take a deposit, but it will be very stiff. It could easily be $50 per day on top of your rental fees and sometimes much more. In addition, they may require a credit check on the spot, complete with phone calls to your employer and bank. If you damage the car, charges will be deducted from your deposit, and the car company itself determines the extent of the damages. Some companies *will not* rent you a car without a major credit card in your name, no matter how much of a deposit you are willing to leave; this is even true for Hawaiian residents who want to rent a car on other islands.

When to Rent

On this one, you'll have to make up your own mind, because it's a "bet" that you can either win or lose. But it's always good to know the odds before you plop down your money. You can reserve your car in advance when you book your air ticket, or play the field when you get there. If you book in advance, you'll obviously have a car waiting for you, but the deal that you made is the deal that you'll get—it may or may not be the best available. On the other hand, if you wait, you can often take advantage of on-the-spot deals. However, you're betting that cars are available. You might be totally disappointed and not be able to rent a car at all, or you might make a honey of a deal.

If you're arriving during the peak seasons of Christmas, Easter, or summer vacation, absolutely *book your car in advance*. Rental companies have their numbers down pretty well and seem to have plenty of cars, but all may be accounted for during these periods. Even if you can find a junker from a fly-by-night company, they'll price-gouge you mercilessly. If you're going off-peak, you stand a very good chance of getting the car you want at a price you like. It's generally best to book ahead; car companies have toll-free numbers. At least call them for an opinion of your chances of getting a car upon your intended arrival.

Rates

The super-cheap rates on eye-catcher brochures refer to subcompacts. The price goes up with the size of the car. As with options on a new car, the more luxury you get, the more you pay. All major car rental companies in Hawaii use a flat rate option. The flat rate is best, providing a fixed daily rate and unlimited mileage. Some of the smaller local companies may have a mileage rate option. Mileage rate costs less per day, but you are charged for every mile driven. Mileage rates are best if you drive less than 30 miles per day—but even on an island that isn't much!

Rental rates vary by company, as do the names they use to categorize their vehicles. The following rates are fairly representative for most categories: subcompact, $45 a day, $225 a week; compact, $55/260; midsize, $65/300; full size, $75/350; luxury, $110/575; convertible and Jeep, $100/500; van, $110/575. Substantial discounts, often 10–15 percent, are offered for weekday, weekly, and monthly rentals. It's sometimes cheaper to rent a car for the week even if you're only going to use it for five days. If you'll be on more than one island, check to see if weekly and monthly rates can be split between neighboring islands. Most of the car companies, local and national, offer special rates and deals, like AAA discounts. These deals fluctuate too rapidly to give any hard-and-fast information. They are common, however, so make sure to inquire. Don't expect that rental companies will let you know about any deals they have. Also, peak periods have "blackouts," during which normally good deals no longer apply.

These rates aren't your only charges, however. On top of the actual rental fee, you must pay an airport access fee, airport concession fee, state tax, and a road tax surcharge—in total, an additional 25–30 percent.

Warning: If you keep your car beyond your contract, you'll be charged the highest daily rate unless you notify the rental agency beforehand. *Don't keep your car longer than the contract specifies without notifying the company.* Companies are quick to send out their repossession specialists. You might find yourself in a situation with your car gone, a warrant for your arrest, and an extra charge on your bill. A simple courtesy call notifying the company of your intentions saves a lot of headaches and hassle.

Insurance

Before signing your car-rental agreement, you'll be offered various "insurance" coverage options. Although these also vary somewhat by company, they fall into general categories: loss/damage option runs about $15 a day; uninsured motorist protection, $7 a day; and liability protection, $13 a day. In addition, some also offer personal effects protection for $5 a day in case your property gets stolen. Since insurance is already built into the contract (don't expect the rental agency to point this out), what you're really buying is a waiver on the deductible ($500–1,000) in case you crack up the car. If you have insurance at home, you will almost always have coverage on a rental car—including your normal deductible—although not all policies are the same, so check with your agent. Also, if you haven't bought the agency's waiver and you do have a mishap, the rental agency may put a claim against your credit card on the spot for the amount of the deductible, even if you can prove that your insurance will cover the charge. They'll tell *you* to collect from your insurance company because they don't want to be left holding the bag on an across-the-waters claim. If you have a good policy with a small deductible, it's not worth paying the extra money for the waiver, but if your own policy is inadequate, buy the insurance. Also, most major credit cards offer complimentary car-rental insurance as an incentive for using their cards to rent the car. Simply call your credit card company to see if this service is included.

Driving Tips

Wear your seat belt—it's the law! Police keep an eye out for miscreants and often ticket those who do not use their restraints. Protect your small children as you would at home with car seats. Either bring one from home or rent one from a car rental company. Rental prices and availability vary, but all the agencies can make arrangements if you give them enough notice.

The mile markers on back roads are great for pinpointing sights and beaches. The lower number on these signs is the highway number, so you can always make sure that you're on the right road.

In most cases, you'll only get one key for your rental car. Don't lock it inside. If you do, call AAA (or other auto emergency service that you may have) and ask for assistance. Failing that, a local locksmith can open your car for a fee or the rental car agency can send out a second key by taxi, but both of these options can get quite pricey.

Gas prices in Hawaii are above the national average, sometimes by as much as 30–40 cents a gallon. Prices may be a few cents per gallon more expensive in communities that are more distant from the main population centers.

There are few differences between driving in Hawaii and on the Mainland. Just remember that many people on the roads are tourists and can be confused about where they're going. Since many drivers are from somewhere else, there's hardly a "regular style" of driving in the islands. A farmer from Iowa accustomed to poking along on back roads can be sandwiched between a frenetic New Yorker who's trying to drive over his roof and a super-polite but horribly confused Japanese tourist who normally drives on the left.

In Hawaii, drivers don't generally honk their horns except to say hello or signal an emergency. It's considered rude, and honking to hurry someone might earn you a knuckle sandwich. Hawaiian drivers reflect the climate: they're relaxed and polite. Often on smaller roads, they'll brake to let you turn left when they're coming at you. They may assume you'll do the same, so be ready, after a perfunctory turn signal from another driver, for him or her to turn across your lane. The more rural the area, the more apt this is to happen. Don't expect it in the large cities.

It may seem like common sense, but remember to slow down when you enter the little towns strung along the circle-island route. It's easy to bomb along on the highway and flash through these towns, missing some of Hawaii's best scenery. Also, rural children expect *you* to be watchful and may assume that you are going to stop for them when they dart out into the crosswalks.

Respect Do Not Enter and Private Property signs—*Kapu* means the same thing.

Most insurance companies warn you that their cars are not supposed to be driven off paved roads—read your policy. This seems absolutely ridiculous for 4WD vehicles, but may be true nonetheless. When a road is signed for 4WD only, assume that's the case for a good reason. Also, most rental companies prohibit you from taking their rental vehicles across the Saddle Road.

Speed limits change periodically along the highways of Hawai'i, particularly when they pass through small towns. Police routinely check the speed of traffic by use of radar equipment. Be aware of this so you don't go home with more than a suntan. Unlike on the other islands, there are long stretches of open road on the Big Island. On some of these, you may become mesmerized by the road and unconsciously increase your speed. Pay attention.

There are a few emergency call boxes along the highways of the Big Island that are connected directly to an emergency response network. These telephones are to be used strictly for emergency calls when you have car trouble. They are in yellow boxes on tall poles topped by small solar panels.

BYO Car

If you want to bring your own car, write for information to: Director of Finance, Division of Licenses, 1455 S. Beretania St., Honolulu, HI 96814. However, unless you'll be in Hawaii for a bare minimum of six months and will spend all your time on one island, don't even think about it. It's an expensive proposition and takes time and plenty of arrangements. To ship a car from the U.S. West Coast to Hawaii, the cost is about $825 to Honolulu, and an additional $50 to any other island. To save on rental costs, it would be better to buy and sell a car there, or to lease for an extended period. For information about motor vehicle registration on the Big Island, contact the County Motor Vehicle Registration office: 808/961-8351 in Hilo or 808/327-3543 in Kona. For driver licensing, contact the Police Department: 808/961-2222 in Hilo or 808/327-3580 in Kona.

RENTAL AGENCIES

The following are major firms represented at both the Hilo and Kona Airports. Kona numbers begin with a "3" while Hilo numbers start with a "9."

Dollar, 808/961-6059, 808/329-2744, 800/ 800-4000, www.dollarcar.com, has an excellent reputation and very competitive prices. Dollar rents mostly Chrysler vehicles: sedans, Jeeps, and convertibles. Great weekly rates, and all major credit cards accepted.

Alamo, 808/961-3343, 808/329-8896, 800/ 327-9633, www.goalamo.com, has good weekly rates and mostly GM cars.

National, 808/935-0891, 808/329-1674, 800/227-7368, www.nationalcar.com, features GM and Nissan cars and accepts all major credit cards. National sometimes rents without a credit card if you leave a $100 per day deposit— less if you take full insurance coverage.

Avis, 808/935-1290, 808/327-3000, 800/321-3712, www.avis.com, features late-model GM cars as well as most imports and convertibles.

Budget, 800/527-0700, www.budget.com, offers competitive rates on a variety of late-model Ford and Lincoln-Mercury cars and specialty vehicles.

Hertz, 808/935-2896, 808/329-3566, 800/ 654-3011, www.hertz.com, is competitively priced with many fly/drive deals. Hertz features Ford vehicles.

Thrifty, 808/961-6698, 808/329-1339, 800/367-2277, www.thrifty.com, handles mostly Chrysler vehicles.

Some years ago, local companies abounded, but today only one has survived with any significance. At **Harper,** in Hilo at 808/969-1478, Kona at 808/329-6688, or 800/852-9993, you can rent a car, truck, seven- to 15-passenger van, RV, or 4WD for driving up to Mauna Kea. Good competitive rates.

Travelers with Disabilities

Accessible Vans of Hawaii, 296 Alamaha St., Ste. C, Kahului, Maui, HI 96732, 808/ 871-7785, 800/303-3750 in Hawaii, fax 808/871-7536, carol@accessiblevanshawaii.com, www.accessiblevanshawaii.com, is a private company, owned and operated by Dave McKown, who has traveled the world with his paraplegic brother. Dave knows firsthand the obstacles faced by people with disabilities, and his disabled associate does as well. Accessible Vans of Hawaii provides a full-service travel agency, booking rooms, flights, and activities for the physically disabled. Wheelchair lift–equipped minivans and full-size vans are rented on O'ahu, Maui, Kaua'i, and the Big Island for $115 a day, $599 a week, or $2,250 a month, plus tax. This company also sells new and used vans set up for disabled owners, mobility products, and travel accessories. Dave and his associate are good sources of information for any traveler with disabilities.

Motorcycles and Mopeds

DJ's Rentals, 808/329-1700, 800/993-4647, http://harleys.com, open daily 7:30 A.M.–6 P.M., is located directly across from King Kamehameha's Hotel in Kailua-Kona in an outdoor booth. DJ's rents mopeds, scooters, and motorcycles. Rental costs are one-person mopeds, $15 half day, $25 daily, and $125 a week; two-person scooters (capable of attaining highway speeds), $25 half day, $45 daily, and $225 a week. Big Twin Harleys run $145 daily or $90 half day, and others rent for about 20 percent less. A half day is 7:30 A.M.–noon or noon–6 P.M.

Motor Home RVs

If you don't want to stop at a hotel every night, why not take your hotel with you? **Island RV,** 73-4820 Kuakini Hwy., Kailua-Kona, HI 96740, 808/334-0464, 800/406-4555, lets you do just that when you rent a motor home RV; you can go at your own pace and stop where you want. The RVs sleep up to six and come with all the necessary cooking and sleeping gear. The rental rate runs about $250 a day or $1,500 a week, but the weekly rate includes airport pickup, itinerary planning, park registration fees, and the last night in a Kona hotel.

Harper car rental company also rents RVs, 808/969-1478 in Hilo, 808/329-6688 in Kona, or 800/852-9993.

ALTERNATIVE TRANSPORTATION

Hele-On Bus

The county of Hawai'i maintains the Mass Transit Agency, known throughout the island as the **Hele-On Bus.** For information, schedules, and fares contact the Mass Transit Agency at 25 Aupuni St., Hilo, HI 96720, 808/961-8744, open Mon.–Fri. 7:45 A.M.–4:30 P.M. The main bus terminal is in downtown Hilo at Mo'oheau Park, just at the corner of Kamehameha Avenue and Mamo Street. Recently, it's been completely rebuilt and modernized. Like bus terminals everywhere, it has a local franchise of derelicts and down-and-outers, but they leave you alone. The Hele-On Bus system now has a mostly modern fleet of large buses that are clean and comfortable. The Hele-On operates Mon.–Fri. approximately 6 A.M.–6 P.M., depending on the run, except for the route to Kona and Kohala, which also operates Saturdays, and the route from North Kohala to the Kohala resorts, which operates daily. There are a number of intra-Hilo routes with additional intercity routes to points around the periphery of the island, but these all operate on a very limited schedule, sometimes only once a day. If you're in a hurry then definitely forget about taking the bus, but if you want to meet the people of Hawai'i, there's no better way. The base fare is $.75, which increases whenever you go into another zone. Transfers are given free if you must change buses, but these must be used within an hour. A number of discount fares (monthly, round-trip, multiple-ticket, disabled, senior citizen, student) are available. Have exact change for the fare when you board. You can also be charged an extra $1 for a large backpack or suitcase. Don't worry about that—the Hele-On is one of the best bargains in the country. Large items like surfboards, boogie boards, and bicycles are not allowed.

There are four basic intercity routes connecting to Hilo. One—the longest bus route—goes from Kealia, south of Captain Cook, all the way to Hilo on the east coast via Kailua-Kona, Waikoloa, Waimea, Honoka'a, and Laupahoehoe. Operating Mon.–Sat., this journey covers 110 miles in just over four hours and costs $6 for the entire distance, the most expensive fare in the system. Additional intra-Kona buses run just between Kealia and Kailua on weekdays. You can take the southern route from the Ocean View post office through Ka'u, Na'alehu, and Hawaii Volcanoes National Park to Hilo. This trip takes just 2.5 hours and costs $5.25. A third route to Hilo runs from Pahoa through Kea'au, while the fourth starts in Waimea then proceeds down the coast through Honoka'a and Honomu to Hilo. In the Kohala district, a daily bus runs every weekday morning from Kapa'au through Hawi to the various Kohala resorts and returns in the late afternoon.

Shuttle Services

Kona and Kohala are serviced by a three-part shuttle system that together is called the **Kona Coast Express,** 808/329-1688 or 800/831-5541. The Kona Town Trolley runs from Keauhou pier at its southern end to King Kamehameha's Kona Beach Hotel, stopping at a number of condos along this stretch as well as at Keauhou Shopping Center, Hilo Hattie's, and the Kona Inn Shopping Village. The Kohala Coast-Waikoloa Resort Express Bus makes stops at all the Kohala resorts and at the King's Shopping Center. The Kona Coast Express Bus connects passengers between these southern and northern sections of the system. Transfer stations are located at the King's Shopping Center in Waikoloa and the King Kamehameha's Kona Beach Hotel in Kailua. An all-day pass on either the Kona Town Trolley or the Kohala Coast-Waikoloa Resort Express Bus is $5 per person. A $15 all-day pass lets you transfer from one section to the other and use the entire system. Tickets are available from the driver. The Kona Town Trolley runs 8:45 A.M.–10:15 P.M., the Kohala Coast-Waikoloa Resort Express Bus runs 6:15 A.M.–11 P.M., and the connecting Kona Coast Express Bus runs 8 A.M.–10:15 P.M.; each runs at approximately 90-minute intervals.

Kailua-Kona also has the **Ali'i Shuttle,** 808/775-7121, which cruises Ali'i Drive but makes different stops than the Kona Town Trolley. This white bus runs about every 90 minutes,

8:40 A.M.–7:40 P.M. At the north end it stops at the Lanihau Center, King Kamehameha's Hotel, Kona Inn Shopping Village, Hulihe'e Palace, and Royal Kona Resort. On the way south, pickups are at Magic Sands Beach and Kahalu'u Beach Park. On the south end it stops at Keauhou Shopping Center, and Kona Country Club. Rides are $2 each way, $5 for a day pass, $20 for a weekly pass, or $40 for a monthly pass.

Taxis

Both the Hilo and Kona Airports always have taxis waiting for fares. Fares are regulated. From Hilo's airport to downtown costs about $12, to the Banyan Drive hotels about $8. From the Kona Airport to hotels and condos along Ali'i Drive in Kailua fares run $19–32, north to Waikoloa Beach Resort they run about $40, and are approximately $60 as far north as the Mauna Kea Resort. Obviously, a taxi is no way to get around if you're trying to save money. Most taxi companies, both in Kona and Hilo, also run sightseeing services for fixed prices. In **Kona** try Kona Airport Taxi, 808/329-7779; Paradise Taxi, 808/329-1234; Laura's Taxi, 808/326-5466; or C&C Taxi, 808/329-6388. In **Hilo** try Hilo Harry's Taxi, 808/935-7091; A-1 Bob's Taxi, 808/959-4800; and Percy's Taxi, 808/969-7060.

An alternative in the Kona area is **Speedy Shuttle,** 808/329-5433. Operating 7 A.M.–10 P.M. daily, Speedy Shuttle runs multi-seat vans, so its prices are cheaper per person the more people you have riding. It also would be appropriate if you have lots of luggage. Sample rates from the Kona Airport are $17 to downtown Kailua-Kona, $24 to the south end of Kailua and the Keauhou area, and $30 for a ride up to Waikoloa Beach Resort. Speedy Shuttle has a courtesy phone at the airport for your convenience. Reservations a day ahead are not necessary but may be helpful to get a ride at the time you want.

Hitchhiking

The old thumb works on the Big Island about as well as anywhere else. Though hitchhiking is technically illegal, the police seem to have much more important things to pay attention to than going after those just trying to get down the road. Stay off the roadway, be low-key, but make your intentions known. Some people hitchhike rather than take the Hele-On Bus not so much to save money but to save time! It's a good idea to check the bus schedule (and routes), and set out about 30 minutes before the scheduled departure. If you don't have good luck hitching a ride, just wait for the bus to come along and hail it. It'll stop.

Health and Safety

In a survey published some years ago by *Science Digest,* Hawaii was cited as the healthiest state in the United States in which to live. Indeed, Hawaiian citizens live longer than residents anywhere else in America: men to 76 years and women to 82. Lifestyle, heredity, and diet help with these figures, but Hawaii is still an oasis in the middle of the ocean, and germs just have a tougher time getting there. There are no cases of malaria, cholera, or yellow fever. Because of a strict quarantine law, rabies is also nonexistent. On the other hand, tooth decay, perhaps because of a wide use of sugar and the enzymes present in certain tropical fruits, is 30 percent above the national average. With the perfect weather, a multitude of fresh-air activities,

soothing negative ionization from the sea, and a generally relaxed and carefree lifestyle, everyone feels better there. Hawaii is just what the doctor ordered: a beautiful, natural health spa. That's one of its main drawing cards. The food and water are perfectly safe, and the air quality is the best in the country.

Handling the Sun

Don't become a victim of your own exuberance. People can't wait to strip down and lie on the sand like beached whales, but the tropical sun will burn you to a cinder if you're silly. The burning rays come through more easily in Hawaii because of the sun's angle, and you don't feel them as much because there's always a cool breeze. The worst part of the day is 11 A.M.–3 P.M. The Big Island lies between 19 and 20 degrees north latitude, not even close to the equator, but it's still over 1,000 miles south of sunny Southern California beaches. You'll just have to force yourself to go slowly. Don't worry; you'll be able to flaunt your best souvenir, your golden Hawaiian tan, to your green-with-envy friends when you get home. It's better than showing them a boiled lobster body with peeling skin! If your skin is snowflake white, 15 minutes per side on the first day is plenty. Increase by 15-minute intervals every day, which will allow you a full hour per side by the fourth day. Have faith; this is enough to give you a deep golden, uniform tan. If you lie out on the beach or are simply out in the sun during the day, use sunblock lotion that has greater strength than you use at home—most people recommend SPF 25 or higher—and reapply every couple of hours. If you do burn, try taking aspirin as quickly as you can. No one knows exactly what it does, but it seems to provide some relief. Alternatively, apply a cold compress or aloe juice, but be careful with aloe because it may stain clothing.

Whether out on the beach, hiking in the mountains, or just strolling around town, be very aware of dehydration. The sun and wind tend to sap your energy and your store of liquid. Bottled water in various sizes is readily available in all parts of Hawaii. Be sure to carry some with you or stop at a store or restaurant for a fill-'er-up.

Don't forget about your head and eyes. Use your sunglasses and wear a brimmed hat. Some people lay a towel over their neck and shoulders when hiking and others will stick a scarf under their hat and let it drape down over their shoulders to provide some protection.

Haole Rot

A peculiar condition caused by the sun is referred to locally as *haole* rot. It's called this because it supposedly affects only white people, but you'll notice some dark-skinned people with the same condition. Basically, the skin becomes mottled with white spots that refuse to

tan. You get a blotchy effect, mostly on the shoulders and back. Dermatologists have a fancy name for it, and they'll give you a fancy prescription with a very fancy price tag to cure it. It's common knowledge throughout the islands that Selsun Blue shampoo has an ingredient that stops the white mottling effect. Just wash your hair with it and then make sure to rub the lather over the affected areas, and it should clear up.

Bugs

Everyone, in varying degrees, has an aversion to vermin and creepy crawlers. Hawaii isn't infested with a wide variety, but it does have its share. Mosquitoes were unknown in the islands until their larvae stowed away in the water barrels of the *Wellington* in 1826 and were introduced at Lahaina. They bred in the tropical climate and rapidly spread to all the islands. They are a particular nuisance in the rainforests. Be prepared and bring a natural repellent like citronella oil, available in most health stores on the islands, or a commercial product available in groceries and drugstores. Campers will be happy to have mosquito coils to burn at night as well.

Cockroaches are very democratic insects. They hassle all strata of society equally. They breed well in Hawaii, and most hotels are at war with them, trying desperately to keep them from being spotted by guests. One comforting thought is that in Hawaii they aren't a sign of filth or dirty housekeeping. They love the climate like everyone else, and it's a real problem keeping them under control.

Beware the Slipper Dog

Every neighborhood has one, and they always strike in the middle of the night. Because of the custom of no shoes inside, a pile of slippers invariably graces the entrance to most homes, somewhat like a free-form sculpture or cosmic artificial plant. In the morning, a slipper or multiple slippers—but never two from the same pair—is missing. Instantly resignation and recognition set in. Slipper Dog! So, if you see a local person, or even a tourist, walking down the street a bit lopsided wearing one pink size-9 slipper, and one black size-12 slipper, you will be observing at close hand a victim of the Slipper Dog.

WATER SAFETY

Hawaii has one very sad claim to fame: More people drown here than anywhere else in the world. Moreover, there are dozens of injuries every year from scuba and snorkeling accidents, including broken necks and backs. These statistics shouldn't keep you out of the sea, because it is indeed beautiful—benevolent in most cases—and a major reason to go to Hawaii. But if you're foolish, the sea will bounce you like a basketball and suck you away for good. The best remedy is to avoid situations you can't handle. Don't let anyone dare you into a situation that makes you uncomfortable. "Macho men" who know nothing about the power of the sea will be tumbled into Cabbage Patch Kids dolls in short order. Ask lifeguards or beach attendants about conditions, and follow their advice. If local people refuse to go in, there's a good reason. Even experts get in trouble in Hawaiian waters. Some beaches are as gentle as lambs and you would have to tie an anchor around your neck to drown there. Others, especially on the north coasts during the winter months, are frothing giants.

While beachcombing, and especially when walking out on rocks, never turn your back to the sea. Be aware of undertows (the waves drawing back into the sea). They can knock you off your feet. Before entering the water, study it for rocks, breakers, reefs, and riptides. Riptides are powerful currents, like rivers in the sea, that can drag you out. Mostly they peter out not too far from shore, and you can often see their choppy waters on the surface. If caught in a "rip," don't fight to swim directly against it; you'll lose and only exhaust yourself. Swim diagonally across it, while going along with it, and try to stay parallel to the shore. Don't waste all your lung power yelling, and rest by floating.

When bodysurfing, never ride straight in; come to shore at a 45-degree angle. Remember, waves come in sets. Little ones can be followed by giants, so watch the action awhile instead of plunging right in. Standard procedure is to duck under a breaking wave. You can survive even thunderous oceans using this technique. Don't try to swim through a heavy froth and never turn your back and let it smash you. Don't swim alone if possible, and obey all warning signs. Hawaiians want to entertain you, and they don't put up signs just to waste money. The last rule is, "If in doubt, stay out."

Yikes!

Sharks live in all the oceans of the world. Most mind their own business and stay away from shore. Hawaiian sharks are well fed—on fish—and don't usually bother with unsavory humans. If you encounter a shark, don't panic! Never thrash around because this will trigger its attack instinct. If it comes close, scream loudly.

Portuguese man-of-wars put out long, floating tentacles that sting if they touch you. It seems that many floating jellyfish are blown into shore by winds on the eighth, ninth, and 10th days after the full moon. Don't wash the sting off with freshwater, as this will only aggravate it. Hot saltwater will take away the sting, as will alcohol (the drinking or the rubbing kind), aftershave lotion, and meat tenderizer (MSG), which can be found in any supermarket or Chinese restaurant.

Coral can give you a nasty cut, and it's known for causing infections because it's a living organism. Wash the cut immediately and apply an antiseptic. Keep it clean and covered, and watch for infection.

Poisonous sea urchins, such as the lacquer-black *wana,* can be beautiful creatures. They are found in shallow tidepools and will hurt you if you step on them. Their spines will break off, enter your foot, and burn like blazes. There are cures. Vinegar and wine poured on the wound will stop the burning. If those are not available, the Hawaiian solution is urine. It might seem ignominious to have someone pee on your foot, but it'll put the fire out. The spines will disintegrate in a few days, and there are generally no long-term effects.

Hawaiian reefs also have their share of moray eels. These creatures are ferocious in appearance but will never initiate an attack. You'll have to poke around in their holes while snorkeling or scuba diving to get them to attack. Sometimes this is inadvertent on the diver's part, so be careful where you stick your hand while underwater.

Present in streams, ponds, and muddy soil, **Leptospirosis** is a *freshwater*-borne bacteria, deposited by the urine of infected animals. From two to 20 days after the bacteria enter the body, there is a *sudden* onset of fever accompanied by chills, sweats, headache, and sometimes vomiting and diarrhea. Preventive measures include: staying out of freshwater sources where cattle and other animals wade and drink; not swimming in freshwater if you have an open cut; and not drinking stream water.

HAWAIIAN FOLK MEDICINE AND CURES

Hawaiian folk medicine is well developed, and its cures for common ailments have been used effectively for centuries. Hawaiian *kahuna* were highly regarded for their medicinal skills, and Hawaiians were by far some of the healthiest people in the world until the coming of the Europeans. Many folk remedies and cures are used to this day and, what's more, they work. Many of the common plants and fruits that you'll encounter provide some of the best remedies. When roots and seeds and special exotic plants are used, the preparation of the medicine is as painstaking as in a modern pharmacy. These prescriptions are exact and take an expert to prepare. They should never be prepared or administered by an amateur.

Common Curative Plants

Arrowroot, a treatment for diarrhea, is also a powerful narcotic used in rituals and medicines. Kava *(Piper methysticum)*, also called 'awa, is chewed and the juice is spat into a container for fermenting. Used as a medicine for urinary tract infections, rheumatism, and asthma, it also induces sleep and cures headaches. A poultice for wounds is made from the skins of ripe bananas. Peelings have a powerful antibiotic

KUKUI

Reaching heights of 80 feet, the *kukui* (candlenut) was a veritable department store to the Hawaiians, who made use of almost every part of this utilitarian giant. Its nuts, bark, or flowers were ground into potions and salves to be taken as a general tonic, applied to ulcers and cuts as an effective antibiotic, or administered internally as a cure for constipation or asthma attacks. The bark was mixed with water and the resulting juice was used as a dye in tattooing, tapa-cloth making, and canoe painting, and as a preservative for fishnets. The oily nuts were burned in stone holders as a light source, and they were ground and eaten as a condiment called *'inamona*. Polished nuts took on a beautiful sheen and were strung as lei. Lastly, the wood itself was hollowed into canoes and used as fishnet floats.

LOUISE FOOTE

quality and contain vitamins A, B, and C, phosphorus, calcium, and iron. The nectar from the plant was fed to babies as a vitamin juice. Breadfruit sap is used for healing cuts and as a moisturizing lotion. Coconut is used to make moisturizing oil, and the juice was chewed, spat into the hand, and used as a shampoo. Guava is a source of vitamins A, B, and C. Hibiscus has been used as a laxative. *Kukui* nut oil makes a gargle for sore throats and a laxative, plus the flowers are used to cure diarrhea. *Noni,* an unappetizing hand grenade–shaped fruit that you wouldn't want to eat unless you had to, reduces tumors, diabetes, and high blood pressure, and the juice is good for diarrhea. Sugarcane sweetens many concoctions, and the juice of toasted cane was a tonic for sick babies. Sweet potato is used as a tonic during pregnancy and juiced as a gargle for phlegm. Tamarind is a natural laxative and contains the most acid and sugar of any fruit on earth. Taro has been used for lung infections and thrush, and as a suppository. Yams are good for coughs, vomiting, constipation, and appendicitis.

MEDICAL SERVICES

Hospitals

On the east side, 24-hour medical help is available from **Hilo Medical Center,** 808/974-4700. While in Ka'u, seek help from the **Ka'u Hospital** in Pahala, 808/928-8331. On the west side, try **Kona Community Hospital** in Kealakekua, 808/322-9311. **The North Hawaii Community Hospital** in Kamuela, 808/885-4444, services the northern part of the island.

Medical Clinics

For minor emergencies and urgent care in Kona, try **Hualalai Urgent Care,** 808/327-4357, and **Kaiser Permanente,** 808/334-4400. In Hilo, try **Kaiser Permanente,** 808/934-4000, or **Hilo Medical Associates,** 808/934-2000. In Waimea, use the **Lucy Henrigues Medical Center,** 808/885-7351, and in Honoka'a, see the **Hamakua Health Center,** 808/775-7204.

Pharmacies

Longs Drugs, KTA Super Store, and **Kmart** all have pharmacies.

Others that should meet your needs are: **Village Pharmacy,** 808/885-4418, in Waimea; **Hilo Pharmacy,** 808/961-9267, along the bay front; **Kealakekua Pharmacy,** 808/322-1639, in Kealakekua; **Waikoloa Pharmacy,** 808/883-8484, in Waikoloa; and **Kamehameha Pharmacy,** 808/889-6161, in Kapa'au.

SERVICES FOR TRAVELERS WITH DISABILITIES

A person with a disability can have a wonderful time in Hawaii; all that's needed is a little planning. The following general advice should help your planning.

Commission on Persons with Disabilities

This commission was designed with the express purpose of aiding handicapped people. It is a source of invaluable information and distributes self-help booklets, which are published jointly by the Disability and Communication Access Board and the Hawaii Centers for Independent Living. Any person with disabilities heading to Hawaii should write first or visit these offices on arrival. For the *Aloha Guide To Accessibility* (Part I is free; $3–5 charge for Parts II and III), write or visit Hawaii Centers for Independent Living, 414 Kuwili St., #102, Honolulu, HI 96817, 808/522-5400. On Hawai'i, write either Center for Independent Living—East Hawai'i, 400 Hualani St., #16D, Hilo, HI 96720, 808/935-3777; or Center for Independent Living—West Hawai'i, 81-6627 Mamalahoa Hwy., Ste. B5, Kealakekua, HI 96750, 808/323-2221.

General Information

The key for a smooth trip is to make as many arrangements ahead of time as possible. Tell the transportation companies and hotels you'll be dealing with the nature of your handicap in advance so that they can make arrangements to accommodate you. Bring your medical records and notify medical establishments of your arrival if you'll be needing their services. Travel with a friend or make arrangements for an aide on arrival. Bring your own wheelchair if possible and let airlines know if it is battery-powered; boarding interisland flights often requires steps. Airlines can board you early on special lifts, but they must know that you're coming. Many hotels and restaurants accommodate persons with disabilities, but always call ahead just to make sure.

Hawai'i Services

At Hilo Airport, all passengers arrive or leave via a jetway on the second level, and there are escalators, stairs, and some elevators between levels. Baggage claim, bathrooms, and telephones are accessible. Parking is convenient in designated areas. The Kona Airport is all one level. Boarding and deplaning is possible for the handicapped by lift. There are no jetways. Bathrooms and telephones are accessible, and there is specially designated handicapped parking.

For specially equipped rental vans, contact **Accessible Vans of Hawaii,** 800/303-3750. All rental car agencies can install hand controls on their cars if given enough notice—usually 48–72 hours. Your own state handicap placard will be honored here. Medical help, nurses, and companions can be arranged through the **Center for Independent Living,** 808/935-3777 in Hilo or 808/323-2221 in Kona. Doctors are referred by **Hilo Medical Center,** 808/974-4700, and the **Kona Community Hospital,** 808/322-9311. Medical equipment rentals are available in Hilo from **Apria Healthcare,** 808/969-1221, **Rainbow Medical Supply,** 808/935-9393, and **Shiigi Drug,** 808/935-0001; and in Kona from **Big Island Medical Supply,** 808/323-3313.

ILLEGAL DRUGS

The use and availability of illegal, controlled, and recreational drugs are about the same in Hawaii as throughout the rest of America. Cocaine is available on the streets of the main cities, especially Honolulu. Although most dealers are small-time, the drug is brought in by organized crime. Cocaine trafficking fans out from Honolulu.

Another drug menace infesting Hawaii is "ice." Ice is smokable methamphetamine that wires a user for up to 24 hours. The high lasts longer and is cheaper than the one obtained with cocaine or its derivative, "crack." Users quickly become dependent, despondent, and violent because ice robs them of sleep as well as their dignity. Its use is particularly prevalent among late-night workers. Many of the violent deaths in Honolulu have been linked to the growing use of ice.

However, the main drug available and most commonly used in Hawaii is marijuana, which is locally called *pakalolo*. There are also three varieties of psychoactive mushrooms that contain the hallucinogen psilocybin. They grow wild but are considered illegal controlled substances.

Pakalolo Growing

In the 1960s and 1970s, mostly *haole* hippies from the Mainland began growing pot in the more remote sections of the islands, such as Puna on Hawai'i and around Hana on Maui. They discovered what legitimate planters had known for centuries: plant a broomstick in Hawaii, treat it right, and it'll grow. *Pakalolo,* after all, is only a weed, and it grows in Hawaii like wildfire. The locals quickly got into the act when they realized that they, too, could grow a "money tree." As a matter of fact, they began resenting the *haole* usurpers, and a quiet and sometimes dangerous feud has been going on ever since. Much is made of the viciousness of the backcountry "growers" of Hawaii, as in other areas of the states. There are tales of booby traps and armed patrols guarding plants in the hills, but mostly it's a cat-and-mouse game between the authorities and the growers. If you, as a tourist, are tramping about in the forest and happen upon someone's "patch," don't touch anything. Just back off and you'll be okay. Pot is one of the largest monetary turnovers of any crop in the islands, and as such, is now considered a major source of agricultural revenue, albeit illicit and underground. There are all kinds of local names and varieties of pot in Hawaii. Dealers will sometimes approach you. Their normal technique is to stroll by and in a barely audible whisper offer, "Buds?"

THEFT AND HASSLES

Theft and minor assaults can be a problem, but they're usually not violent or vicious as in some Mainland cities. Mostly, it's a local with a chip on his shoulder and few prospects who will ransack your car or make off with your camera. A big Hawaiian or local guy will be obliged to flatten your nose if you look for trouble, but mostly it will be sneak thieves out to make a fast buck.

From the minute you sit behind the wheel of your rental car, you'll be warned not to leave valuables unattended and to lock up your car tighter than a drum. Signs warning about theft at most major tourist attractions help to fuel your paranoia. Many hotel and condo rooms offer safes so you can lock your valuables away and relax while getting sunburned. Stories abound about purse snatchings and surly locals itching to give you a hard time. Well, they're all true to a degree, but Hawaii's reputation is much worse than the reality. In Hawaii you'll have to observe two golden rules: if you look for trouble, you'll find it; and a fool and his camera are soon parted.

Theft

The majority of theft in Hawaii is of the "sneak thief" variety. If you leave your hotel door unlocked, a camera sitting on the seat of your rental car, or valuables on your beach towel, you'll be inviting a very obliging thief to pad away with your stuff. You have to learn to take precautions, but they won't be anything like those employed in rougher areas of the world—just normal American precautions.

If you must walk alone at night, stay on the main streets in well-lit areas. Always lock your hotel door and windows and place valuable jewelry in the hotel safe. When you leave your hotel for the beach, there is absolutely no reason to carry all your traveler's checks and credit cards or a big wad of money. Just take what you'll need for drinks and lunch. If you're uptight about leaving money in your beach bag, stick it in your bathing suit. American money is just as negotiable when damp. Don't leave your camera on the beach unattended. Ask a person nearby to watch your things for you while you go for a dip. Most people won't mind at all, and you can repay the favor.

While sightseeing in your shiny new rental car, which immediately brands you as a tourist, again, don't take more than what you'll need for the day. Many people lock valuables away in the trunk, but remember that most good car thieves can "jimmy" it as quickly as you can open it with your key. If you must, for some reason, leave your camera or valuables in your car, lock them in the trunk, stash them under a seat back that's been reclined, or consider putting them under the hood. Thieves usually don't look there, and on most modern cars you can only pop the hood with a lever inside the car. It's not fail-safe, but it's worth a try.

Campers face special problems because their entire scene is open to thievery. Most campgrounds don't have any real security, but who, after all, wants to fence an old tent or a used sleeping bag? Many tents have zippers that can be secured with a small padlock. If you want to go hiking and are afraid to leave your gear in the campground, take a large green garbage bag with you. Transport your gear down the trail and then walk off through some thick brush. Put your gear in the garbage bag and bury it under leaves and other light camouflage. That's about as safe as you can be. You can also use a variation on this technique instead of leaving your valuables in your rental car.

Hassles

Another self-perpetuating myth about Hawaii is that "the natives are restless." An undeniable animosity exists between locals (especially those with some Hawaiian blood) and *haole*. Fortunately, this prejudice is directed mostly at the group and not at the individual. The locals are resentful of the *haole* who came, took their land, and relegated them to second-class citizenship. They realize that this is not the average tourist and can tell what you are at a glance. Tourists usually are treated with understanding and are given a type of immunity. Besides, Hawaiians are still among the most friendly, giving, and understanding people on earth.

Haole who live in Hawaii might tell you stories of their children having trouble at school. They could even mention an unhappy situation at some schools called "beat-up-a-*haole*" day, and you might hear that if you're a *haole* it's not a matter of "if" you'll be beaten up, but "when." Truthfully, most of this depends upon your attitude and your sensitivity. The locals feel infringed upon, so don't fuel these feelings. If you're at a beach park and there is a group of local people in one area, don't crowd them. If you go into a local bar and you're the only one of your ethnic group in sight, you shouldn't have to be told to leave. Much of the hassle involves drinking. Booze brings out the worst prejudice on all sides. If you're invited to a beach party, and the local guys start getting drunk, make this your exit call. Don't wait until it's too late.

Most trouble seems to be directed toward white men. White women are mostly immune from being beaten up, but they have to beware of the violence of sexual abuse and rape. Although plenty of local women marry white men, it's not a good idea to try to pick up a local woman. If you're known in the area and have been properly introduced, that's another story. Women out for the night in bars or discos can be approached if they're not in the company of local guys. Maintain your own dignity and self-respect by treating others with dignity and respect. Most times you'll reap what you sow.

What to Take

It's a snap to pack for a visit to the Big Island. Everything is on your side. The weather is moderate and uniform on the whole, and the style of dress is delightfully casual. The rule of thumb is to pack light: few items, and clothing light in both color and weight. What you'll need will depend largely on your itinerary and your desires. Are you drawn to the nightlife, the outdoors, or both? If you forget something at home, it won't be a disaster. You can buy everything you'll need in Hawaii. As a matter of fact, Hawaiian clothing, such as mu'umu'u and aloha shirts, is one of the best purchases you can make, both in comfort and style. It's quite feasible to bring only one or two changes of clothing with the express purpose of outfitting yourself while there. Prices on bathing suits, bikinis, and summer wear in general are quite reasonable.

Matters of Taste

A grand conspiracy in Hawaii adhered to by everyone—tourist, traveler, and resident—is to "hang loose" and dress casually. Best of all, alohawear is just about all you'll need for comfort and virtually every occasion. The classic mu'umu'u is large and billowy, and aloha shirts are made to be worn outside the pants. The best of both are made of cool cotton. Rayon isn't too bad, but polyester is hot, sticky, and not authentic. Not all mu'umu'u are of the "tent persuasion." Some are very fashionable and form-fitted with peekaboo slits up the side, down the front, or around the back. *Holomu* are mu'umu'u fitted at the waist with a flowing skirt to the ankles. They are not only elegant, but perfect for "stepping out."

Basic Necessities

As previously mentioned, you really have to consider only two "modes" of dressing in Hawaii: beachwear and casual clothing. The following list is designed for the midrange traveler carrying one suitcase or a backpack. Remember that there are Laundromats and that you'll be spending a considerable amount of time in your bathing suit. Consider the following: one or two pairs of light cotton slacks for going out and about, and one pair of jeans for hiking and riding horses; two or three casual sundresses; three or four pairs of shorts for beachwear and sightseeing; four to five short-sleeved shirts or blouses and one long-sleeved; three or four colored and printed T-shirts that can be worn for anything from hiking to strolling; a beach cover-up; a brimmed hat for rain and sun—the crushable floppy type is great for purse or day pack, or pick up a straw or woven hat here for about $10; two or three pairs of socks are sufficient, nylons you won't need; two bathing suits; plastic bags to hold wet bathing suits and laundry; five to six pairs of underwear; towels (optional, because hotels provide them, even for the beach); a first-aid kit, pocket-size is sufficient; suntan lotion and insect repellent; and a day pack or large beach purse. And don't forget your windbreaker, perhaps a shawl for the evening, and an all-purpose jogging suit. A few classy restaurants in the finest hotels require men to wear a sport coat for dinner. If you don't have one, most hotels can supply you with one for the evening.

In the Cold and Rain

Two occasions for which you'll have to consider dressing warmly are visits to mountaintops and boat rides where wind and ocean sprays are factors. You can conquer both with a jogging suit or sweat suit and a featherweight, water-resistant windbreaker. If you intend to visit Mauna Kea or Mauna Loa, it'll be downright chilly. Your jogging suit with a hooded windbreaker/raincoat will do the trick for all occasions. If you're going to camp or hike, you should add another layer, a woolen sweater being one of the best. Wool is the only natural fiber that retains most of its warmth-giving properties even if it gets wet. Several varieties of "fleece" synthetics currently on the market also have this ability. If your hands get cold, put a pair of socks over them. Tropical rain showers can happen at any time so you might consider a fold-up umbrella, but the sun quickly breaks through and the warming winds blow. Nighttime winter temperatures may drop into the lower 60s or upper 50s, so be sure to have a sweater and long pants along.

Shoes

Dressing your feet is hardly a problem. You'll most often wear zori (rubber thongs) for going to and from the beach, leather sandals for strolling and dining, and jogging shoes for hiking and sightseeing. Tevas and other types of outdoor strap sandals are good for general sightseeing and beach and water wear. A few discos require leather shoes, but it's hardly worth bringing them just for that. If you plan on heavy-duty hiking, you'll definitely want your hiking boots. Lava, especially 'a'a, is murderous on shoes. Most back-country trails are rugged and muddy, and you'll need those good old lug soles for traction. If you plan moderate hikes, jogging shoes should do.

Specialty Items

The following is a list of specialty items that you might consider bringing along. They're not necessities but most will definitely come in handy. A pair of binoculars really enhances sightseeing—great for viewing birds and sweeping panoramas, and almost a necessity if you're going whale-watching. A folding, Teflon-bottomed travel iron makes up for cotton's one major shortcoming, wrinkles. Most accommodations offer irons, but you can't always count on it. Nylon twine and miniature clothespins are handy for drying garments, especially bathing suits. Commercial and hotel Laundromats abound, but many times you'll get by with hand-washing a few items in the sink. A radio/tape recorder provides news, weather, and entertainment, and it can be used to record impressions, island music, and a running commentary for your slide show. Although the wind can be relied upon to dry wet hair, it leaves a bit to be desired in the styling department, so consider bringing a hair dryer. As with the iron, most accommodations have these, but not all. Flippers, mask, and snorkel can easily be bought or rented in Hawaii but don't weigh much or take up much space in your luggage either.

ON THE ROAD

Information and Services

HAWAII VISITORS BUREAU

The HVB is a top-notch organization providing help and information to all of Hawaii's visitors. Anyone contemplating a trip to Hawaii should visit or write the HVB and inquire about any specific information that might be required, or visit its website, www.gohawaii.com. The HVB's advice and excellent brochures on virtually every facet of living, visiting, or simply enjoying Hawaii are free. The material offered is too voluminous to list, but for basics, request individual island brochures, maps, vacation planners (also on the Web at www.hshawaii.com), and an all-island members directory of accommodations, restaurants, entertainment, and transportation. Allow two to three weeks for requests to be answered.

HVB Offices Statewide

Statewide offices include **HVB Administrative Office,** Waikiki Business Plaza, 2270 Kalakaua Ave., Ste. 801, Honolulu, HI 96815, 808/923-1811; **Visitor Information Office,** Royal Hawaiian Shopping Center, 2201 Kalakaua Ave., Ste. 401A, Honolulu, HI 96815, 808/923-1811; **O'ahu Visitors Bureau,** 733 Bishop St., Ste. 1872, Honolulu, HI 96813, 808/524-0722, 877/525-6242, www.visit-oahu.com; **Big Island HVB, Hilo Branch,** 250 Keawe St., Hilo, HI 96720, 808/961-5797, 800/648-2441, www.big-island.org; **Big Island HVB, Kona Branch,** 250 Waikoloa Beach Dr., Ste. B15, Waikoloa, HI 96738, 808/886-1655; **Kaua'i HVB,** 4334 Rice St., Ste. 101, Lihu'e, HI 96766, 808/245-3971, 800/262-1400, www.kauaivisitorsbureau.org; and **Maui HVB,** 1727 Wili Pa Loop, Wailuku, HI 96793, 808/244-3530, 800/525-6284, www.visitmaui.com.

Two other helpful organizations are the **Moloka'i Visitors Association,** P.O. Box 960, Kaunakakai, HI 96748, 808/553-3876, 800/800-6367; and **Destination Lana'i,** P.O. Box 700, Lana'i City, HI 96763, 808/565-7600, 800/947-4774, www.visit-lanai.net.

Additional online information pertaining to the island of Hawai'i can be found at the official County of Hawai'i website, www.hawaii-county.com.

North American Offices

West Coast: 180 Montgomery St., Ste. 2360, San Francisco, CA 94104, 415/248-3800; 1172 S. Main St., #369, Salinas, CA 93901, 831/455-1839; 4150 Mission Blvd., Ste. 200A, San Diego, CA 92109, 858/270-2390.

Midwest: 625 N. Michigan Ave., Ste. 1737, Chicago, IL 60611, 312/654-4542.

East Coast: 1100 N. Glebe Rd., #760, Arlington, VA 22201, 703/525-7770.

Canada: c/o Comprehensive Travel, 1260 Hornby St., #104, Vancouver, B.C., Canada V6Z 1W2, 604/669-6691.

European Offices

United Kingdom: P.O. Box 208, Sunbury on Thames, Middlesex, England, TW16 5RJ, tel. 208/941-4009.

Germany: Noble Kommunikation GmbH, Luisenstrasse 7, 63262 Neu-Isenburg, Germany, tel. 180/223-040.

South American Office

Uruguay: c/o Yamandu Rodriguez 1390, 11500 Montevideo, Uruguay, tel. 2/606-0277.

Asian/Pacific Offices

Japan: Kokusai Bldg., 2F, 3-1-1, Marunouchi, Chiyoda-ku, Tokyo 100, Japan, tel. 3/3201-0430; Sumitomo Nakanoshima Bldg., 2F, 3-2-18, Nakanoshima, Kita-gu, Osaka 530, Japan, tel. 6/6443-8015.

Korea: c/o Travel Press, Seoul Center Bldg., 12th Fl., 91-1, Sokong-dong, Chung-gu, Seoul 100-070, Korea, tel. 2/777-0033.

China: A606, COFCO Bldg., 8 Jianguomen Nei Dajie, Beijing, China 100005, tel. 10/6527-7530; Shanghai Centre, 1376 Nanjing Rd. West, Room 527, Shanghai, China 200040, tel. 21/6279-8099.

Taiwan: Wish (Wei Yuan) Company, 9F-1, #21, Lane 22, Hsein Yen Road, Wen Shan Area, Taipei 117, Taiwan, tel. 2/2934-8323.

Hong Kong: Pacific Leisure Group, c/o Pacam Limited, 10F, Tung Ming Bldg., Room 1003, 40 Des Voeux Rd. Central, Hong Kong SAR, China, tel. 2524-1361.

New Zealand: c/o Walshes World, 14 Shortland St., Level 6, Auckland, New Zealand, tel. 9/379-3708.

Australia: c/o The Sales Team, Ste. 602A, Level 6, 97-103 Pacific Hwy., North Sydney, NSW 2060, Australia, tel. 2/9955-2619.

Other Tourism-Related Information Sources

The **visitor information booths** at the two island airports, 808/934-5838 in Hilo or 808/329-3423 in Kona, are good sources of information available on arrival.

LOCAL RESOURCES
Emergencies
For **police, fire, and ambulance** anywhere on the Big Island, dial **911.**

For **nonemergency police** assistance and information: 808/935-3311.

Civil Defense: In case of natural disaster such as hurricanes or tsunamis on the Big Island, call 808/935-0031.

Coast Guard Search and Rescue: 800/552-6458.

Sexual Assault Crisis Line: 808/935-0677.

Weather, Marine, and Volcano Reports, and Time of Day
For recorded information on **local island weather,** call 808/961-5582; for the **marine report,** call 808/935-9883; and for **volcano activity,** call 808/985-6000. For time of day, dial 808/961-0212.

Consumer Protection
If you encounter problems with accommodations, bad service, or downright rip-offs, try the following: the Chamber of Commerce in Hilo, 808/935-7178, or in the Kona/Kohala area,

808/329-1758; the Office of Consumer Protection, 808/933-0910; or the Better Business Bureau of Hawaii on O'ahu, 877/222-6551.

Post Office
Normal business hours are Mon.–Fri. 8 A.M.–4:30 P.M., Sat. 9 A.M.–1 P.M. The central post office on Hawai'i is in Hilo, and there are 25 branch post offices in towns around the island.

Laundromats
There are perhaps a dozen self-service Laundromats on the Big Island. Most are open about 7 or 7:30 A.M. and close in the early evening. They usually request that the last load of laundry be put in no later than an hour before closing, to allow for drying time. Washers usually take $1 or $1.25—in quarters—for a wash cycle. Dryers take one quarter for a 10-minute spin, and usually require 40–50 minutes to dry a full load. Newer and better-run self-service laundries provide soap dispensers with one-wash boxes of soap at $.50 a box, change machines, and folding tables—not all have these services. A few also offer wash, dry, and fold service for a fee.

Luxury hotels usually do not have self-service laundry facilities on the premises but provide laundering and dry-cleaning service for a fee. Condos most often do have washers and dryers, sometimes in the units but more often on each floor of a building or in a detached structure; rental homes almost always provide washers and dryers. Some B&Bs also provide this service while others do not—ask when you make your reservation, if it's important. Some sort of laundry facility can be found at hostels.

Reading Material
Libraries are located in towns and schools all over the island. The main branch is at 300 Waianuenue Ave., Hilo, 808/933-8888. This location can provide information regarding all libraries. In Kailua-Kona, the library is at 75-140 Hualalai Rd., 808/327-4327. Branch libraries are located in all major towns. Check with each individual branch for times and services. Library cards are available free for Hawaii state residents and military personnel stationed

in Hawaii, $25 for nonresidents that's valid for five years, and $10 for three months for visitors. Free Internet access is available to library card holders.

Free **tourist literature** and the narrow-format, magazine-style *This Week Big Island, Spotlight's Big Island Gold,* and *Big Island Beach and Activity Guide,* are available at the airport, many hotels, and most restaurants and shopping centers around the island. They come out monthly or quarterly and contain money-saving coupons, information on local events and activities, shopping and restaurants, and island maps. The small-format magazine-style *Coffee Times* focuses on cultural and historical topics, while the newspaper-format *Hawai'i Island Journal* concentrates on issues of the day and has a very good island calendar of events section. With a focus on activities and fun things to do, *101 Things to Do on Hawaii the Big Island* is a great resource and also has money-saving coupons. Publications with local orientation are *Kohala Mountain News, Kona Times, Hamakua Times* and *The Waimea Gazette. Big Island Drive Guide* is available from the car rental agencies and contains tips, coupons, and good maps. The Hawaii AAA *Tourbook* is also very useful. Other publications of interest are the in-flight magazines of Aloha and Hawaiian Airlines.

Daily island newspapers include *Hawaii Tribune-Herald,* a Hilo publication (www.hilo-hawaiitribune.com), and *West Hawaii Today,* published in Kona (www.westhawaiitoday.com), both owned by the same parent company and both costing $.50 daily and $1 on Sunday. Providing an alternative and progressive view on island issues is the *Ka'u Landing,* a monthly out of Ocean View (www.kau-landing.com).

Hawaii's two main English-language dailies are the *Honolulu Star Bulletin* (www.starbulletin.com) and the *Honolulu Advertiser* (www.honoluluadvertiser.com), $.75 daily or $2 on Sunday. *USA Today* and other papers with nationwide distribution can also be picked up at newsstands and some bookshops. The Japanese-English *Hawaii Hochi* and the Chinese *United Chinese Press* are also available, as is the twice-monthly English-language *Hawaii Filipino Chronicle.* All are available on the Big Island.

Island Radio Stations

More than a dozen radio stations broadcast on the Big Island. Most broadcast only on either the Hilo or Kona side, while a few send signals to both sides. Among the most popular are:

KIPA 620 AM: Rainbow Radio: easy listening contemporary

KPUA 670 AM: news and sports

KHPR 90.7 FM Hawaii Public Radio

KAOE 92.7 FM rock and roll

KWXX 94.7 FM: island music, light contemporary rock, Jawaiian (Hawaiian reggae)

KBIG 97.9 and 106.1 FM: contemporary adult

KAPA 99.1 and 100.3 FM: Hawaiian and island tunes

OTHER INFORMATION
Telephone

The telephone system on the main islands is modern and comparable to any system on the Mainland. Any phone call to a number on that island is a local call; it's long distance when dialing to another island. As they do everywhere else in the United States, long-distance rates go down at 5 P.M. and again at 11 P.M. until 8 A.M. the next morning. Rates are cheapest from Friday at 5 P.M. until Monday at 8 A.M. Local calls from public telephones cost $.30 or $.35. Public telephones are found at hotels, street booths, restaurants, most public buildings, and some beach parks. It is common to have a phone in most hotel rooms and condominiums, though a service charge is usually collected, even on local calls. Emergency calls are always free. You can "direct dial" from Hawaii to the Mainland and more than 160 foreign countries. Undersea cables and satellite communications ensure top-quality phone service. Toll-free calls are preceded by 800, 888, 877, or 866; there is no charge to the calling party. Many are listed in the text. For directory assistance: local, 411; interisland, 555-1212; Mainland, 1-(area code) 555-1212; toll free, 800/555-1212. The area code for all the islands of Hawaii is 808.

Time Zones

There is no daylight saving time in Hawaii. When daylight saving time is not observed on the

Mainland, Hawaii is two hours behind the West Coast, four hours behind the Midwest, five hours behind the East Coast, and 11 hours behind Germany. Hawaii, being just east of the international date line, is almost a full day behind most Asian and Oceanic cities. Hours behind these countries and cities are: Japan, 19 hours; Singapore, 18 hours; Sydney, 20 hours; New Zealand, 22 hours; Fiji, 22 hours.

Electricity

The same electrical current is in use in Hawaii as on the U.S. Mainland and is uniform throughout the islands. The system functions on 110 volts, 60 cycles of alternating current (AC). Appliances from Japan will work, but there is some danger of burnout, while those requiring the normal European voltage of 220 will not work.

Distance, Weights, and Measures

Hawaii, like all of the United States, employs the "English method" of measuring weights and distances. Basically, dry weights are in ounces and pounds; liquid measures are in ounces, quarts, and gallons; and distances are measured in inches, feet, yards, and miles. The metric system is known but is not in general use.

Island Facts

Hawai'i has three fitting nicknames: the Big Island, the Volcano Island, and the Orchid Island. It's the youngest, most southerly, and largest (4,028 square miles) island in the Hawaiian chain. Its color is red, the island flower is the red 'ohi'a lehua, and the island lei is fashioned from the lehua blossom.

MONEY AND FINANCES

Currency

U.S. currency is among the drabbest in the world. It's all the same size and color; those unfamiliar with it should spend some time getting acquainted so that they don't make costly mistakes. U.S. coins in use are $.01, $.05, $.10, $.25, $.50, and $1 (uncommon); paper currency is $1, $2 (uncommon), $5, $10, $20, $50, and $100. Bills larger than $100 are not in common usage. Since 1996, new designs have been issued for the $100, $50, $20, $10, and $5 bills. Both the old and new bills are accepted as valid currency.

Banks

Full-service bank hours are generally Mon.–Thurs. 8:30 A.M.–4 P.M. and Fri. until 6 P.M. There are no weekend hours, and weekday hours will be a bit longer at counters in grocery stores and other outlets. All main towns on Hawai'i have one or more banks: Hilo, Kailua-Kona, Waimea, Kealakekua, Honoka'a, Pahoa, Waikoloa, Pahala, and Hawi. Virtually all branch banks have ATMs for 24-hour service, and these can be found at some shopping centers and other venues around the island. ATMs work only when the Hawaiian bank you choose to use is on an affiliate network with your home bank. Banks sell and cash traveler's checks, give cash advances on credit cards, and exchange and sell foreign currency (sometimes with a fee). Major banks on the Big Island are American Savings Bank, Bank of Hawaii, First Hawaiian Bank, and Central Pacific Bank.

Traveler's Checks

Traveler's checks are accepted throughout Hawaii at hotels, restaurants, car-rental agencies, and in most stores and shops. However, to be readily acceptable they should be in U.S. currency. Some larger hotels that frequently have Japanese and Canadian guests will accept their currency. Banks accept foreign-currency traveler's checks, but it'll mean an extra trip and inconvenience. It's best to get most of your traveler's checks in $20–50 denominations; anything larger will be hard to cash in smaller shops and boutiques, though not in hotels.

Credit Cards

More and more business is transacted in Hawaii using credit cards. Almost every form of accommodation, shop, restaurant, and amusement accepts them. For renting a car they're almost a must. With "credit card insurance" readily available, they're as safe as traveler's checks and sometimes even more convenient. Write down the numbers of your cards in case they're stolen. Don't rely on them completely, because there are some establishments that won't accept them.

Kona

Kona is long and lean and takes its suntanned body for granted. This district *is* the west coast of the Big Island and lies in the rain shadows of Mauna Loa and Mauna Kea. You can come here expecting brilliant sunny days and glorious sunsets, and you won't be disappointed; this reliable sunshine has earned Kona the nickname "The Gold Coast." Offshore, the fishing grounds are legendary, especially for marlin that lure game-fishing enthusiasts from around the world. There are actually two Konas, north and south, and both enjoy an upland interior of forests, ranches, and homesteads while most of the coastline is low, broad, and flat. If you've been fantasizing about swaying palms and tropical jungles dripping with

wild orchids, you might be in for "Kona shock," especially if you fly directly into the Kona Airport. Around the airport the land is raw black lava that can appear as forbidding as the tailings from an old mining operation. Don't despair. Once in town, trees form a cool canopy and flowers add color at every turn.

The entire Kona district is old and historic. This was the land of Lono, god of fertility and patron of the Makahiki Festival. It was also the spot where the first missionary packet landed and changed Hawaii forever, and it's been a resort since the 19th century. In and around **Kailua** are restored *heiau,* a landmark lava church, and a royal summer palace where the monarchs of Hawaii came to relax. The coastline is rife with historical sites: lesser *heiau,* petroglyph fields, fishponds, and

Structures at Pu'uhonua O Honaunau have been constructed in a style and method of long ago.

ROBERT NILSEN

a curious sporting slide dating from the days of the *makahiki*. Below the town of Captain Cook is **Kealakekua Bay,** the first and main *haole* anchorage in the islands until the development of Honolulu Harbor. This bay's historical significance is overwhelming, alternately being a place of life, death, and hope from where the spirit of Hawaii was changed for all time. Here on the southern coast is a Hawaiian "temple of refuge," restored and made into a National Historical Park. The majority of Kona's sights are strung along Route 11. Except for Kailua-Kona, where a walking tour is perfect, you need a rental car to visit the sights; the Big Island's Hele-On Bus runs too infrequently to be feasible. If you're walking, pick up a copy of the pamphlet *Walking Tour of Historic Kailua Village,* put out by the Kona Historical Society.

Kailua-Kona is the heart of North Kona, by far the most developed area in the district. Its **Ali'i Drive** is lined with shops, hotels, and condos, and by and large, the shoreline vista peeks out between them. To show just how fertile lava can be when tended, miles of multihued bougainvillea and poinsettias line Ali'i Drive like a lei. Above Kailua is the former coffee town and now artists'

community of **Holualoa.** This upcountry village sits on the lower slope of **Mount Hualalai** (8,271 feet), and it's here that local people still earn a living growing vegetables and taro on small truck farms high in the mountain coolness. But it has been—and still is—coffee that is the most famous agricultural product of the upcountry region and its dominant economic force. Just a few miles north of Kailua, the land turns dry, and huge swaths of black lava interspersed with arid scrubland become characteristic of the terrain from here through South Kohala to Kawaihae.

South Kona begins near the town of **Captain Cook.** Southward continues a region of diminutive coffee plantations where bushes grow to the shoulder of the road and the air is heady with the rich aroma of roasting coffee. South Kona is rural and far less populated. It's a rugged region, and the road stays high above the coastline. Farther south, rough but passable roads branch from the main highway and tumble toward hidden beaches and tiny fishing villages where time just slips away. From north to south, Kona is awash in brilliant sunshine, and the rumble of surf and the plaintive cry of seabirds create the music of peace.

Kailua-Kona

SIGHTS

Ahu'ena Heiau

Directly seaward of King Kamehameha's Kona Beach Hotel, at the north end of "downtown" Kailua, is the restored Ahu'ena Heiau. Built on an artificial island in Kamakahonu (Eye of the Turtle) Beach, it's in a very important historical area. Kamehameha I, the great conqueror, came here to spend the last years of his life, settling down to a peaceful existence after many years of war and strife. The king, like all Hawaiians, reaffirmed his love of the *'aina* and tended his own royal taro patch on the slopes of Mt. Hualalai. After he died, his bones were prepared according to ancient ritual on a stone platform within the temple, then taken to a secret burial place, which is believed to be just north of town somewhere near

Wawahiwa'a Point. It was Kamehameha who initiated the first rebuilding of Ahu'ena Heiau, a temple of peace and prosperity dedicated to Lono, god of fertility. The rituals held here were a far cry from the bloody human sacrifices dedicated to the god of war, Kuka'ilimoku, that were held at Pu'ukohola Heiau, which Kamehameha had built a few leagues north and a few decades earlier. At Ahu'ena, Kamehameha gathered the sage *kahuna* of the land to discourse in the Hale Mana (main prayer house) on topics concerning wise government and statesmanship. It was here that Liholiho, Kamehameha's son and heir, was educated, and it was here that as a grown man he sat down with the great queens, Keopuolani and Ka'ahumanu, and broke the ancient *kapu* of eating with women, thereby destroying the old order.

KONA

To Waimea

To Kawaihae

190

BIG ISLAND
COUNTRY CLUB

(MAMALAHOA HWY)

KA'AHUMANU HWY

Pu'uanahulu

Pu'u Wa'awa'a
(3,967 ft)

Pu'u Papa
(3,950 ft)

Hainoa
(4,083 ft)

Pu'u Iki
(3,417 ft)

Potato
Hill

Hualalai
(8,271 ft)

North

Kona

approximate
range of
Kona coffee
production

DAI FUKUJI BUDDHIST TEMPLE

PU'U WA'AWA'A
RANCH

MAKALEI
HAWAII
COUNTRY
CLUB

QUEEN K HWY

BELT RD.

HAWAII

Hu'ehu'e
Ranch

Hinaka
Crater

KALOKO DR.

Honokohau
(Palani Junction)

Pu'u La'la'au
(6,526 ft)

SEE "KAILUA-KONA" MAP

SEE "KAILUA-KEAUHOU" MAP

Holualoa

Holualoa

180

11

Kahalu'u

Honalo

Kainaliu

Kealakekua

GREENWELL
ETHNOBOTANICAL

KONA HOSPITAL

KEALAKEKUA

Kahalu'u Bay

Keikiwaha Point

Keauhou Bay

KONA COUNTRY CLUB

LANAKILA CONGREGATIONAL CHURCH

ST. PAUL'S CATHOLIC CHURCH

WHITE SANDS BEACH COUNTY PARK

Holualoa Bay

Kailua Bay

KONA INDUSTRIAL AREA

OLD KONA AIRPORT
STATE RECREATION AREA

HONOKOHAU MARINA

Kailua
Kona

KALOKO
INDUSTRIAL
PARK

Kaloa

KALOKO-HONOKOHAU
NATIONAL HISTORIC PARK

Kaloko Fishpond

KAMEHAMEHA
PRESUMED BURIAL SITE

Wawaloli Beach

Pine Trees

NELHA FACILITY

Keahole Point

KONA
INTERNATIONAL
AIRPORT

ONIZUKA
SPACE CENTER

19

KEKAHA KAI
STATE PARK

Makolea Point

Mahai'ula Bay

Mahai'ula Point

Kawili Point

Makalawena Beach

Nawaikulua Point

HUALALAI
GOLF CLUB

FOUR SEASONS RESORT

KONA VILLAGE
RESORT

Kua Bay

Wauakauhi Bay

Kiholo Pond

Kiholo Bay

Kiholo Point

Waikoloa Beach

KONA

PACIFIC

KONA

KONA

N

CAPTAIN COOK MONUMENT

KAHIKOLU CONGREGATIONAL CHURCH

Honaunau

Napo'opo'o

ST. BENEDICT'S PAINTED CHURCH

approximate range of Kona coffee production

South Kona

Keokea

Kealia

Ke'ei

KEALAKEKUA BAY STATE UNDERWATER PARK
HIKIAU HEIAU STATE MONUMENT
NAPO'OPO'O BEACH COUNTY PARK

Kealakekua Bay

160

HONAUNAU RODEO

PU'U HONAUNAU NATIONAL HISTORIC PARK (CITY OF REFUGE)

Ho'okena

Loa Point

Kapulo Bay

HO'OKENA BEACH COUNTY PARK

Leperanoa Rock

Ka'u Loa Point

KIPAHOEHOE NATURAL AREA RESERVE

MACADAMIA NUT FARM

Ho'opuloa

Ho'opuloa

MANUKA STATE WAYSIDE

Hawaiian Ocean View Estates

11

To Na'alehu and Volcanoes

Kipahoehoe Bay

Miloli'i

Arched Rock

MANUKA NATURAL AREA RESERVE

MILOLI'I BEACH COUNTY PARK

Miloli'i Bay

HOLUA (SLIDE)

Honomalino Bay

Moku O Kaha'ilani Rock

Pu'u Hinahina Bay

COAST

OCEAN

10 mi

10 km

© SANDRA E. BISIGNANI TRUST AND AVALON TRAVEL PUBLISHING, INC.

KONA

KAILUA-KONA

To Captain Cook and Volcano

To Captain Cook and Holualoa

To Captain Cook and Volcano

To Keauhou

KONA REEF

KONA BILLFISHER

TRES HOMBRES

HALE KONA KAI

PARKING

SNORKEL BOB'S

ROYAL KONA RESORT

COCONUT GROVE MARKETPLACE

PARKING

HUGO'S RESTAURANT

ALI'I SUNSET PLAZA

KONA ISLANDER INN

WATERFRONT ROW

ST. MICHAEL'S CATHOLIC CHURCH

UNCLE BILLY'S KONA BAY HOTEL

HALE HALAWAI COUNTY PARK

Kailua Bay

LIBRARY

PARKING

MORMON CHURCH

BANK OF HAWAII

KONA INN SHOPPING VILLAGE

VERNA'S DRIVE-IN

KONA MARKET PLACE

MIDDLE EARTH BOOKSHOPPE

PATEY'S PLACE

MOKU'AIKAUA CHURCH

HULIHE'E PALACE

Kailua

seawall

BASIL'S

PARKING

KONA BANYAN COURT

AKI'S CAFE

KAILUA PIER

BORDERS BOOKS AND MUSIC

HENRY ST.

KONA RANCH HOUSE

KONA SEASIDE

OCEAN VIEW INN

KONA SQUARE

seawall

Kamakahonu Beach

LANIHAU CENTER

KOPIKO PLAZA

B&L BIKE AND SPORTS

QUINN'S INN

WAL-MART

CROSSROADS CENTER

KONA SEASIDE MALL

HILO HATTIE

HAWAIIAN CAMERA

KING KAMEHAMEHA MALL

KING KAMEHAMEHA'S KONA BEACH HOTEL

AHU'ENA HEIAU

FIRE STATION

POST OFFICE

BANK

BANK

PALANI RD.

QUEEN

NORTH KONA SHOPPING CENTER

KONA BREWING COMPANY

KONA COAST SHOPPING CENTER

To Waimea

To Airport and Kawaihae

KA'AHUMANU HWY.

ALOHA

KONA DR.

HUALALAI RD.

KALANI ST.

ALA ONAONA

KUAKINI

ALI'I DR.

0.1 mi

0.1 km

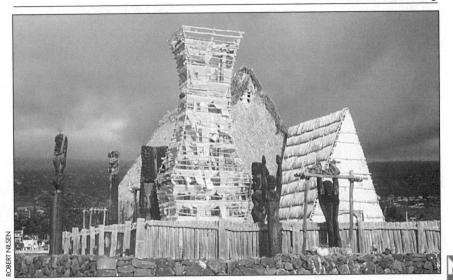

ROBERT NILSEN

Ahu'ena Heiau

The tallest structure on the temple grounds is the *'anu'u* (oracle tower), where the chief priest, in deep trance, received messages from the gods. Throughout the grounds are superbly carved *kia akua* (temple image posts) in the distinctive Kona style, considered some of the finest of all Polynesian art forms. The spiritual focus of the *heiau* was humanity's higher nature, and the tallest figure, crowned with an image of the golden plover, was that of Koleamoku, a god of healing. Another interesting structure is a small thatched hut of sugarcane leaves, Hale Nana Mahina, which means "house from which to watch the farmland." Kamehameha would come here to meditate while a guard kept watch from a nearby shelter. The commanding view from the doorway affords a sweeping panorama from the sea to the king's plantations on the slopes of Mt. Hualalai. Though the temple grounds, reconstructed under the auspices of the Bishop Museum, are impressive, they are only one-third their original size. The *heiau* itself is closed to visitors but you can get a good look at it from the shore. Free tours offered by King Kamehameha's Kona Beach Hotel take you down to the *heiau* and include a tour of its own hotel grounds as well. The hotel portion of the tour includes a walk through the lobby, where various artifacts and artworks are displayed, and features an extremely informative botanical tour that highlights the medicinal herbs of old Hawaii. The hotel tours begin at 1:30 P.M. weekdays; call 808/329-2911. Don't miss this excellent educational opportunity, well worth the time and effort!

Kailua Pier

While in the heart of downtown, make sure to visit the Kailua Pier, which is set directly in front of Ahu'ena Heiau. Tour boats and the occasional fishing boat use this facility, so there is some activity on and off all day. Shuttle boats also use this pier to ferry passengers from cruise ships to town for land excursions. While it varies throughout the year, more of these large ships make Kailua a port of call during the late spring and autumn months than the rest of the year, but an interisland cruise ship makes a regular stop here once a week.

Moku'aikaua Church

Kailua is one of those towns that would love to contemplate its own navel if it could only find it. It doesn't really have a center, but if you had to pick one, it would be the 112-foot steeple of Moku'aikaua Church. This highest structure in town has been a landmark for travelers and seafarers ever since the church was completed in January 1837. Established in 1820, the church claims to be the oldest house of Christian worship in Hawaii. The site was given by King Liholiho to the first Congregationalist missionaries, who arrived on the brig *Thaddeus* in the spring of that year. Taking the place of two previous grass structures, the construction of this building was undertaken in 1835 by the Hawaiian congregation under the direction of Rev. Asa Thurston. Much thought was given to the orientation of the structure, designed so the prevailing winds blow through the entire length of the church to keep it cool and comfortable. The walls of the church are fashioned from massive, rough-hewn lava stone, mortared with plaster made from crushed and burned coral that was bound with *kukui* nut oil. The huge cornerstones are believed to have been salvaged from a *heiau* built in the 15th century by King Umi that had occupied this spot. The masonry is crude but effective—still sound after more than 165 years.

Inside, the church is extremely soothing, expressing a feeling of strength and simplicity. The resolute beams are native 'ohi'a, pegged together and closely resembling the fine beamwork used in barns throughout 19th-century New England. The pews, railings, pulpit, and trim are all fashioned from koa, a rich brown, lustrous wood that begs to be stroked. Although the church is still used as a house of worship, it also has the air of a museum, housing paintings of historical personages instrumental in Hawaii's Christian past. The crowning touch is an excellent model of the brig *Thaddeus,* painstakingly built by the men of the Pacific Fleet Command in 1934 and presented to the church in 1975. The church is open daily from sunrise to sunset, and volunteer hostesses may be around to answer your questions from late morning to mid-afternoon.

Moku'aikaua Church

ROBERT NILSEN

ROBERT NILSEN

Hulihe'e Palace—holiday home of Hawaiian royalty

Hulihe'e Palace

Go from the spiritual to the temporal by walking across the street from Moku'aikaua Church and entering Hulihe'e Palace. This two-story Victorian structure commissioned by Hawaii's second governor, John Kuakini, dates from 1838. A favorite summer getaway for all the Hawaiian monarchs who followed, especially King Kalakaua, it was used as such until 1914. At first glance, the outside is unimpressive, but the more you look the more you realize how simple and grand it is. The architectural lines are those of an English country manor, and indeed Great Britain was held in high esteem by the Hawaiian royalty. Inside, the palace is bright and airy. Most of the massive furniture is made from koa. Many pieces were constructed by foreigners, including the German Wilhelm Fisher. The most magnificent pieces include a huge formal dining table, 70 inches in diameter, fashioned from one solid koa log. Upstairs is a tremendous four-poster bed that belonged to Queen Kapi'olani, and two magnificent cabinets that were built

by a Chinese convict serving a life sentence for smuggling opium. King Kalakaua heard of his talents and commissioned him to build the cabinets. They proved to be so wonderfully crafted that after they were completed the king pardoned the craftsman.

Prince Kuhio, who inherited the palace from his uncle, King Kalakaua, was the first Hawaiian delegate to Congress. He decided to auction off all the furniture and artifacts to raise money, supposedly for the benefit of the Hawaiian people. Providentially, the night before the auction each piece was painstakingly numbered by the royal ladies of the palace, and the name of the person bidding for the piece was dutifully recorded. In the years that followed, the **Daughters of Hawai'i,** who now operate the palace as a museum, tracked down the owners and convinced many to return the items for display. Most of the pieces are privately owned, and because each is unique, the owners wish no duplicates to be made. It is for this reason, coupled with the fact that flashbulbs can fade the wood, that a strict *no* *photography* policy is enforced. The palace was opened as a museum in 1928!

Historical artifacts are displayed in a downstairs room. Delicate and priceless heirlooms on display include a tiger-claw necklace that belonged to Kapi'olani. You'll also see a portrait gallery of Hawaiian monarchs. Personal and mundane items are on exhibit as well—there's an old report card showing a 68 in philosophy for King Kalakaua—and lining the stairs is a collection of spears reputedly belonging to the great Kamehameha himself.

Hulihe'e Palace, 808/329-1877, is on the *makai* side of Ali'i Dr., open Mon.–Fri. 9 A.M.–4 P.M., Sat. and Sun. 10 A.M.–4 P.M. You can look around on your own or ask the staff for a tour, which usually lasts 45 minutes. Admission is $5 adults, $4 seniors, $1 students. A hostess knowledgeable in Hawaiiana is usually on duty to answer questions.

The **Palace Gift Shop,** small but with quality items, is on the grounds next door to the palace. Open daily except Sunday. It offers a fine selection of koa sculptures of fish, sharks, and even a turtle, along with Hawaiiana books and postcards. Just outside is a saltwater pond with tropical fish.

Historical Walking Tour

The Kona Historical Society offers a leisurely one- to 1.5-hour guided walking tour of the Ahu'ena Heiau, Moku'aikaua Church, Hulihe'e Palace, and other nearby sights Mon.–Fri. at 9 and 11 A.M., for $15 per person. Advance reservations are necessary. You can tour each of these sites on your own, but you can learn so much more from a knowledgeable guide. Make reservations at 808/323-3222, and wear comfortable shoes and a hat.

Up Above Town

At the intersection of Kuakini and Queen Ka'ahumanu Highways, on the grounds of the Kona Outdoor Circle Education Center, is a landscaped sliver of land called the **Sadie Seymour Botanical Gardens.** Grouped and planted on nearly a dozen terraces are typical plants that grow in Hawaii that are originally from

royal crest on the front of Hulihe'e Palace

ROBERT NILSEN

other areas of the world. Small but well landscaped, this garden is a quiet retreat in the otherwise dry and hot upper Kona area. Open daily 9 A.M.–5 P.M. for self-guided tours, there is no admission but donations are accepted.

Adjacent to the botanical gardens is **Kealakowaʻa Heiau,** an ancient sacred site dedicated to blessing canoes. This blessing was done after the rough shape had been cut in the upland forest but before the final work was completed at the beach. Consisting of four separate platforms, this *heiau* was reputedly built around 1600 by King Umi. There is currently no admittance to the *heiau* as the area is being preserved, but it is easily seen when looking over the surrounding stone wall.

Along Aliʻi Drive

Aliʻi Drive heads south from Kailua, passing the majority of Konaʼs accommodations on its way to **Keauhou.** On the mountain side of the road, a continuous flow of flowers drapes the shoulder like a femme fataleʼs seductive boa, while seaside the coastline slips along, rugged and bright, making Aliʻi Drive a soothing sight.

At your first stop, near White Sands Beach, look for the historic **Hale Halawai O Holualoa Congregational Church** built in 1855 by Rev. John D. Paris. Services are still held every Sunday at 9 A.M. The base of the church is mostly original lava rock topped with a new roof. The cemetery area is peaceful and quiet and offers a perfect meditative perch from which to scan the coast below. Back on the road, look for signs to Kahaluʻu Beach Park; pull in and park here.

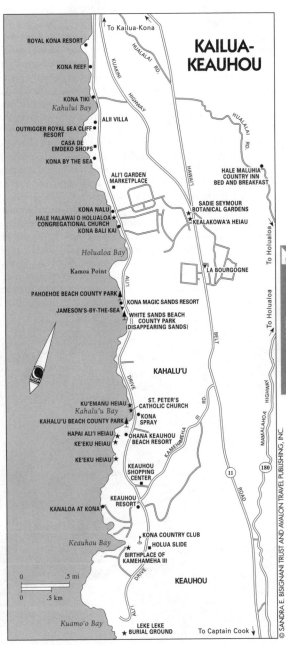

On the rocky northern shore of this bay is **St. Peter's Catholic Church.** Its diminutive size, capped by a blue tin roof that winks at you from amidst the lava like a bright morning glory in an ebony vase, has earned it the nickname Little Blue Church. Built in 1889 on the site of an old, partially reclaimed *heiau,* the church is a favorite spot for snapshots. Inside, simplicity reigns with bare wood walls and a plain crucifix. The only splash of color is a bouquet of fresh flowers on the altar. To the right of the church as you face it are the remains of **Ku'emanu Heiau,** a temple where chiefs would pray for good surfing conditions. Their prayers must have worked, as surfers today still gracefully ride the waves offshore within sight of this rock platform. On the grounds of the Ohana Keauhou Beach Resort, a 10-minute walk south along the coast, are the remains of **Kapuanoni Heiau** and **Hapai Ali'i Heiau.** Just beyond that, at water's edge and fronting the abandoned Kona Lagoons hotel property, is the **Ke'eku Heiau.** All are unrestored historical sites that still show signs of being used, and all offer vantage points from which to view the coast.

Near the end of the road is **Keauhou Bay.** Here you'll find a cluster of historical sites, and the small boat harbor and boat ramp. Look for a monument marking the birthplace of Kamehameha III in 1814. Local people come to fish from the pier around 5 P.M. for *halalu,* a tough little fish to catch. Along the shoreline are a number of partially developed *heiau* sites. A small home stuck on a point of land on the edge of the bay is where John Wayne married his wife Pilar in 1954, and it marks the site of the first modern house built on the bay. Opposite the harbor, at the end of King Kamehameha III Road is Keauhou Park and beach access, an area of lawn, pavilion, sand volleyball court, and restrooms.

At the very end of the Ali'i Drive, past the Kona Country Club golf course, is the **Leke Leke Burial Grounds.** Laid to rest here are troops that fought under the leadership of Kekuaokalani, keeper of the war god Ku after the death of King Kamehameha I, in an attempt

St. Peter's Catholic Church

J.D. BISIGNANI

ROBERT NILSEN

Ku'emanu Heiau overlooks a time-honored surfing spot.

KONA

to sustain the traditional religious and social order of the Hawaiian people. More than 300 died here at Kuano'o Bay, using firepower obtained from the foreigners. This battle was the violent end to the old ways and symbolized the shaky introduction of the Western overlay on Hawaiian society.

North of Town

Honokohau Harbor, three miles north of Kailua-Kona, is a huge small-boat harbor and deep-sea fishing facility that has eclipsed the old Kailua Pier. This is the premier fishing harbor on the island, is used by other water-sport activity companies and sailboats, and is frantic with energy during the various "billfish tournaments" held throughout the year. The harbor area is full of fishing-oriented shops, including Kona Marine for nautical charts, and is also home to the Harbor House Restaurant, where you can hear a yarn from Kona's old salts. Primarily, this is where you come to see huge fish caught that day and talk to the skippers of the deep-sea fish-

ing boats that go after them. When you pull into the marina, you'll see a road that goes off to the left. Head that way toward the tan building, to where the pier and the weigh-station are located. The huge fish will be hoisted, measured, and photographed while the skippers and their crews clean and prepare the boats for the next day's outing. **Weigh in** is every day 11 A.M.– 1 P.M. and 3–6 P.M., basically when the boats return from their half-day and full-day trips; call 808/334-1881 for information. If you are fascinated by deep-sea fishing, this is your chance to pick a likely boat and to get acquainted with the crew.

The future is now at the amazing Ocean Technology facilities located just south of the airport between mile markers 95 and 94, where you'll find a turnoff heading toward the sea. This is the **Natural Energy Laboratory of Hawaii Authority (NELHA),** www.nelha.org. Incredible things are being done here. For example, cold water from 2,000 feet below the surface of the ocean is placed in a turbine with warm surface

ANCIENT SPORT OF *HOLUA*

In principle, *holua* was similar to snow sledding, and mostly a "chiefly" sport of the *ali'i*. Sleds were long two-runner affairs, perhaps six inches wide and eight feet long or longer, stabilized by cross bracing and grab bars on which the person would lie. These sleds were launched down a slope that was up to one mile in length and ended at or near the ocean. Only a few of these slopes remain, largely fallen into disrepair or taken apart to make way for modern constructions. Most prominent on the Big Island, the largest known sledding course was Kaneaka in Keauhou, the remains of which lie on the Kona Country Club *makai* golf course. Look for it across the road from the club house. These slopes were constructed of volcanic rock and filled in with small pebbles to make a flat top. It is believed that this flat top was then covered with layers of large leaves (maybe banana or *ti*) or thatching to provide a slippery surface for sledding. Once on the runway, there was no stopping until the sled got to the bottom—or went over the side. The danger associated with this sport must have been an important component of its thrill. With no steering mechanism, the chance of disaster seems large. *Holua* seems to have slowly died out through the 1800s, perhaps, as some have suggested, after the Makahiki Festival—which may have been its principle forum—ceased to be a central component of the Hawaiian cultural tradition. No one in living memory is purported to have actually seen the sport in action. Only recently has there been much attention turned to its understanding. Few examples of a *holua* sled have survived—the best is displayed at the Bishop Museum in Honolulu—and few accounts relate anything about the sport. Aside from a few brave, modern souls who have tried short sections of slope for the thrill, this sport has not yet been brought back by the resurgence of ancient Hawaiian culture. Perhaps its time is still to come.

water, a process that generates electricity and also provides desalinated water. In addition, the cold water is used for raising very un-Hawaiian things such as alpine strawberries, lobsters, abalone, sea cucumbers, commercial black pearls, and Japanese flounder, as well as for raising *limu,* a local edible seaweed, oysters, clams, and shrimp. Others use its alternative energy source to make fish jerky, to grow shiitake mushrooms, and even to raise tropical fish that will become living bouquets of color in fish tanks around the world. Cyanotech, a leading manufacturer of marine products for worldwide nutrition and pharmaceutical markets, uses the facilities to make spirulina, available in health food stores, as well as numerous other products and ingredients. Tours are offered Wed. and Thurs. at 10 A.M.; call 808/329-7341 for reservations. Tours run about one hour in length; donations are accepted. If you choose to take a tour, don't be overwhelmed by the size of the complex; the products are brought to a central area for your viewing. A short self-guided tour will introduce you to the basics of what is done here. Behind this facility is the Ho'ona Historic Preserve, an area of home sites and graves from a late-19th-century Hawaiian community. Cutting across the NELHA area up near the highway is a section of the old King's Trail. The NELHA access road is open 6 A.M.–8 P.M.

Dedicated to Hawaii's own Col. Ellison S. Onizuka and to the men and women who tragically perished aboard the spacecraft *Challenger* on January 28, 1986, the **Onizuka Space Center** is located at Kona International Airport, P.O. Box 833, Kailua-Kona, HI 96745, 808/329-3441, www.planet-hawaii.com/astronautonizuka. Hours are daily 8:30 A.M.–4:30 P.M. except Thanksgiving, Christmas, and New Year's Day; admission is $3 adults, $1 children. From this tragedy, a living memorial and space education facility was erected. Inside the modern, well-appointed building children and adults alike can marvel at human exploration of space by viewing exhibits like a "moon rock," a scale model of a space shuttle and space station, an interactive staffed maneuvering unit, a real space suit, and a theater showing educational videos throughout the day. There

Kamakahonu Beach on Kailua Bay is gentle enough for the kids.

is a gift shop with plenty of fascinating reading material concerning the international effort to explore the heavens. Stop in before flying out.

BEACHES AND PARKS

If Kona is short on anything, it is beaches. The ones that it has are adequate and quite striking in their own way, but they tend to be small, few, and far between. People expecting a huge expanse of white sand will be disappointed. These beaches do exist on the Big Island's west coast, but they are north of Kailua-Kona in the Kohala district. Kona does, however, have beaches alive with marinelife, providing excellent and safe snorkeling and top-notch tidepool exploration opportunities.

The following are the main beaches in and around Kailua-Kona. For descriptions of South Kona beaches see below.

Kamakahonu Beach

You couldn't be more centrally located than at "Eye of the Turtle" Beach. Find it in downtown

Kailua-Kona next to Kailua Pier, in front of King Kamehameha's Kona Beach Hotel. Local people refer to it as "Kids' Beach" because it is so gentle and safe, perfect for a refreshing dip. Big kids come here to play too, when every year world-class athletes churn the gentle waters into a fury at the start of the Ironman Triathlon. Rent snorkel gear, kayaks, and other water gear for reasonable prices from the Beach Shack, located in front of the hotel, or from other shops nearby. Restrooms and telephones are located at the inland end of the pier.

Ali'i Drive Beaches

White Sands Beach County Park (a.k.a. **Magic Sands** or **Disappearing Sands**) is an excellent spot for a dip—if the sand is there. Every year, usually in winter, the sands are stripped away by heavy seas and currents, exposing rough coral and making the area too rugged for the average swimmer. People still come during those months because it's a good vantage point for observing migrating humpback whales. The sands always come back, and, when they do, the beach is terrific for all kinds of water sports, including body-surfing and snorkeling. White Sands is known locally as a great boogie-boarding and bodysurfing spot. The best board surfing is just north of the beach in a break the locals call "Banyans." White Sands' amenities include drinking water, showers, and restrooms, making the beach a favorite spot with local people and tourists.

Just before White Sands park is the small and narrow **Pahoehoe Beach County Park.** With its seawall, lawn, palm trees, and walkways, its a good place to suntan on the grass or picnic in the shade, but the rocky shoreline is not a place to swim.

Kahalu'u Beach Park on Kahalu'u Bay has always been a productive fishing area. Even today, fishermen come to "throw net." You'll occasionally see large family parties surrounding their favorite fish with a huge *hukilau* net, then sharing their bounty among all participants. Because of this age-old tradition, the area has not been designated a marine conservation district. Kahalu'u became a beach park in 1966. This ensured that the people of Kona would always have access to this favorite spot, which quickly became surrounded by commercial development. Ohana Keauhou Beach Resort occupies the land just to the south. Amenities at the park include picnic tables, showers, restrooms, a lifeguard, and even a basketball court. Often a *kaukau* wagon and snorkel rental truck are also there for those who didn't prepare well enough. The swimming is very good, but the real attraction is snorkeling. The waters are very gentle, and Kahalu'u is a perfect place for families or beginning snorkelers, as the water is generally only six to eight feet deep. However, stay *within* the bay because a powerful and dangerous rip current lurks outside. The shoreline waters are alive with tropical fish: angelfish, parrotfish, unicorn fish, the works. Unfortunately, Kahalu'u is often crowded, but it is still worth a visit. The reef offshore makes great waves and this bay has been a great surfing spot for centuries.

Old Kona Airport State Recreation Area

In 1970 the old Kona Airport closed and the state of Hawaii turned it into a beach park. Take Kuakini Highway north from downtown until it ends. Often used on weekends by families for picnics and other gatherings, facilities include showers, restrooms, and a picnic area near the water, plus athletic fields, a gymnasium and aquatic center, and a children's playground near the entrance. Parking is unlimited along the old runway, where you can also walk, bike, in-line skate, or jog. The park gate closes at 8 P.M. The white-sand beach is sandwiched between the black lava at water's edge and the runway. You can enter the water at some shallow inlets, but the bottom is often rocky (be sure to wear water shoes) and the waters can be treacherous during high surf. The safest spot is a little sandy cove at the southern end of the beach. Swimming is generally not good here, but sunbathing is great. Tidepooling is good when the water is low. Snorkeling is fine at the northern end of the beach, and offshore a break at "Shark Rocks" makes the old airport popular with Kona surfers. The waters in front of the park are a 217-acre marinelife conservation district protected from motorized boat usage but open to scuba divers and snorkelers.

Kaloko-Honokohau National Historical Park

All types of people come to **Honokohau Beach,** including fishermen, surfers, and snorkelers, but it was primarily known as a clothing-optional beach. That status drastically changed when the area officially became part of Kaloko-Honokohau National Historical Park. At the Honokohau Small Boat Harbor, stay to the right and park at the end of the access road in a dirt parking lot near the Kona Sailing Club. Follow the well-worn path into the vegetation on the far side of the berm, and keep walking for a few minutes to the beach.

This area, more toward Kaloko just up the coast, was heavily populated during old Hawaiian days, and plenty of archaeological sites—mostly fishponds, ruins of houses, *heiau*, a small *holua* slide, and a few petroglyphs—are found along the shoreline. Most of these sites are protected; if you come to an archaeological area, obey all posted signs and approach with great care and respect.

Remember, it is imperative that you do not touch, disturb, or remove any historical artifacts. The coarse, gray-sand beach offers safe swimming in somewhat shallow water. There are no facilities except bathrooms at each entrance.

Nudity is officially illegal within the park. Camping and open fires, also illegal, are citable offenses under federal regulations. Near the north end of the beach and over the dunes is "Queen's Bath" (called "Anchialine Bath" by the park service). Because it is under consideration as a historical site, swimming in the pond is prohibited. **Kaloko Beach,** about a 10-minute hike north of Queen's Bath, has great snorkeling in only 10–20 feet of water. Here, you can explore a series of sea arches. The entire area is a favorite with green sea turtles, which make their presence known mainly in the evenings. Two large fishponds in the park have been rehabilitated to a more natural environment and are home to several endangered waterbirds that include the *ae'o* (stilt) and the *alae ke'oke'o* (Hawaiian coot).

Dedicated in 1978, the 1,160-acre Kaloko-Honokohau National Historical Park can be entered either from Honokohau Small Boat Harbor or via Kaloko Gate, just off Hwy. 19 across from the Kaloko Industrial Park, and a mile-long hike. The gate is open daily 8 A.M.–3:30 P.M. For information, call the park office at 808/329-6881.

North Kona Beaches

The next beach you come to heading north is the famous **Pine Trees** surfing beach, located near the NELHA facility just south of the airport. Where the long access road turns abruptly to the right, look for a well-worn dirt road leading to the left away from NELHA, and follow it to Pine Trees. Although famous with surfers and the site of many competitions, Pine Trees (none of which are in evidence) is not a good swimming beach. There are a few one-towel coves along the rocky shoreline where you can gain access to the water, but mostly it's a place from which to observe the action. You can also follow the road toward the NELHA facility a short way to **Wawaloli Beach,** a large, sandy, public beach, fronted by rock and coral. Here are a few volleyball nets, a restroom, and some picnic tables.

Kekaha Kai State Park

Recently opened and well marked, the Kekaha Kai (Kona Coast) State Park stretches north, encompassing several sandy secluded beaches in its 1,642-acre domain. The first is about two miles north of the airport between mile markers 91 and 90; open 9 A.M.–7 P.M., except Wed. Follow the rugged but passable dirt road for about 1.5 miles to one of the closest beaches to Kailua-Kona. The semi-improved area has toilets and picnic tables built around palm trees. The land rises before getting to the coarse, salt-and-pepper sand beach. The swimming is usually safe here except in winter and some come to snorkel, but always be careful.

Before you get to the official parking area, notice a walking path off to the right. It is a 10-minute walk to Mahai'ula Bay and its magnificent **Mahai'ula Beach.** This crescent of tan sand stretches for about 200 yards, with shade trees coming down almost to the water's edge. Completely unimproved and fairly secluded, it's a great beach to "get away from it all" for the day. Back from the water here are the remains of an abandoned red beach house that once belonged to the Magoon family, longtime island residents and major stockholders in Hawaiian Airlines. These buildings have appeared as a movie set over the years. Walk north from Mahai'ula Beach along an arrow-straight path across a hot stretch of rough lava for about 15 minutes to the smaller and more secluded white-sand **Makalawena Beach.** Local boys love to bodysurf here in winter. Alternatively, drive two miles farther north, between mile markers 89 and 88, look for the Pu'u Ku'ili cinder cone, whose vegetation has been given a crew cut by the trade winds. Turn here on a very rugged, 4WD-only dirt road that takes you down to Makalawena. En route to this totally secluded area, you'll pass over rough lava and coral and eventually come to a gate, where you park. Proceed on foot, and you'll have your choice of three wonderful beaches; all are frequented by green sea turtles. At the north end of these beaches is a small brackish but mostly freshwater pond, the domain of *nanini* fish and a harmless brine shrimp. If you do not have 4WD, you can still enjoy this area, but it means a hike of

KONA

about 30 minutes. Be sure to bring water, especially if you intend to spend the day.

A few minutes farther north by car, just past the cinder cone, you'll find another rugged lava and coral road. If you have 4WD you can go to the end of the road and then walk to the beach, but you can also walk for about 15 minutes from the turnout near the highway. The well-worn path leads you to **Kua Bay,** a famous swimming and boogie-boarding beach. Kua Bay can also be reached in about 30 minutes by a path over coral and lava from Kukio Beach, which is next to the Four Seasons Resort.

ACCOMMODATIONS

Almost all of Kona's accommodations lie along the six miles of Ali'i Drive from Kailua-Kona to Keauhou. Most hotels/condos fall in the moderate to expensive range. A few inexpensive hotels are scattered here and there along Ali'i Drive, and back up in the hills are a "sleeper" or two, cheap but decent. The following list should provide you with a good cross section.

It's sad but true: except for the limited beach parks at Ho'okena and Miloli'i, south of Kailua-Kona, there is *no official camping* in all of the Kona district. Campers wishing to enjoy the coast must go north to the Kohala district to find a campground, or south to Ka'u. Some unofficial camping does exist in Kona, but as always, this generates certain insecurities. Bivouacking for a night or two in any of the unofficial camp spots should be hassle-free. Good luck!

Hostel

Patey's Place, 75-195 Ala Ona Ona St., Kailua-Kona, HI 96740, 808/326-7018, fax 808/326-7640, www.hawaiian-hostels.com, is a reasonably priced and friendly hostel. Upon arrival, it will appear as though a section of the living sea was taken from the coast and moved whole into a residential area of Kona. You will be cohabiting with whales, mermaids, and dolphins, all rendered by airbrush *air*tist Paul Fullbrook, an Aussie artist who was undoubtedly a green sea turtle in his past life. Rates are bunk room $19.50, semi-

private $27.50, private room $35 single, and big room $46. No meals are provided. A $10 key and linen deposit is returned on departure. Patey's also provides transportation to and from the airport for $10. There are body boards, fishing gear, snorkel gear, and bike rentals at reasonable fees; lockers; safe deposit box; inexpensive email access; and free and invaluable information. All rooms are clean, lockable, and cooled by cross ventilation and ceiling fans. The hostel is also outfitted with four full bathrooms, three kitchens, a 2nd-floor sunset deck, laundry facilities, gas barbecues, and an activities desk. You shouldn't expect, nor will you find, the standards of a five-star resort, but Patey's is an excellent choice for the adventurer, budget traveler, or anyone who enjoys a dynamic international crowd.

$50–150

For a reasonable and homey hotel, try the **Kona Tiki Hotel,** 75-5968 Ali'i Dr., Kailua-Kona, HI 96740, 808/329-1425, fax 808/327-9402, one of the first accommodations south of "downtown." At more than 50 years old, this is one of the oldest vacation hotels along the coast, and although of an old style without the luxury, the place is kept up. Sandwiched between the ocean and the road, it's a bit noisy during the day but quiets down at night except for the lullaby of the rolling surf. The Kona Tiki features refrigerators in all rooms, some kitchenettes, a complimentary continental breakfast daily, and a small guest pool. The 15 refurbished rooms are clean, with ceiling fans but no phones or televisions, and all units face the ocean so everyone gets a view. Prices are $59–65 for a standard room with queen or queen and twin bed, and $70 for a kitchenette; extra person $8, three-day minimum, no credit cards.

Kona Seaside Hotel is a basic but well-cared-for downtown hotel at 75-5646 Palani Rd., Kailua-Kona, HI 96740, 808/329-2455, 800/560-5558, fax 808/329-6157, www.konaseasidehotel.com. Part of the island-owned Sand and Seaside Hotel chain, most rooms here have a/c, cross ventilation, and lanai, and there's self-service laundry on the premises. A sundeck and central courtyard surround one swimming pool; a second pool is located near the front entrance. Prices range from $98 standard to $120 deluxe, with AAA and AARP discounts and room and car packages available. The Kona Seaside operates two adjacent restaurants, one that serves a self-service continental breakfast, and the second that serves lunch and dinner. The Seaside Shopping Center is located next door.

Uncle Billy's Kona Bay Hotel, at 75-5744 Ali'i Dr., Kailua-Kona, HI 96740, 808/329-1393, 800/367-5102, resv@unclebilly.com, www.unclebilly.com, is a locally owned hotel in the center of town, run by Uncle Billy and his Kona family. Its best feature is the friendly and warm staff. The hotel is a remaining wing of the old Kona Inn, the rest of which was torn down to accommodate the shopping center across the road. The semicircular hotel is built around a central courtyard and garden containing Kimo's Family Buffet, a bar, and a swimming pool. Uncle Billy's is a bit of a throwback to Kona's earlier days, still it's comfortable, clean, and convenient, but not plush. The rooms are a combination of moderate and superior with a/c, TV, and mini-fridge. Rates begin at $84–94, and $94 with kitchenette; many discounts and package rates are available.

$150–250

King Kamehameha's Kona Beach Hotel in downtown Kailua-Kona at 75-5660 Palani Rd., Kailua-Kona, HI 96740, 808/329-2911, 800/367-6060, reservations@hthcorp.com, www.konabeachhotel.com, is one of the only Kona hotels that has its own beach and is located on a spot favored by Hawaiian royalty; Kamehameha the Great spent the last days of his life here and it's adjacent to the restored Ahu'ena Heiau. The walls of the lobby are lined with historical artifacts; portraits of the Kamehameha royal family beginning with the great chief Kamehameha are displayed in the reception area; two *kahili* stand nearby as signs of royalty; and a feather cape and hat also adorn one wall. Other displays make up this mini-museum, and it's worth a look even if you are not staying here. Pick up a brochure about these artifacts at the front desk. In addition, weekly events are put on to introduce guests to aspects of Hawaiian art and culture. Rooms each

feature a lanai with a sweeping panorama of the bay or Mt. Hualalai. Prices for the 460 rooms are $135–200 for standard to oceanfront rooms and up to $550 for a three-bedroom suite, additional person $30, and children under 18 stay free when sharing their parents' room. The hotel features the Kona Beach Restaurants, Billfish Bar, Island Breeze lu'au, tennis courts, a plethora of shops, a freshwater pool, and a beach, as well as an activities desk, guided historical tours, Internet access for guests, and self-service laundry. The King Kamehameha's Kona Beach Hotel is an older property, but its well run by a proud staff, well maintained to keep a high standard, and good value for your money.

The **Royal Kona Resort,** 75-5852 Ali'i Dr., Kailua-Kona, HI 96740, 808/329-3111, 800/919-8333, www.royalkona.com, has figuratively and literally become a Kona landmark. The hotel, built like rising steps with the floor below larger than the one above, commands a magnificent view from its perch atop a beautiful promontory of black lava that anchors the south end of downtown Kailua. All 450 rooms are spacious, and each includes a lanai. Standard rates run from $160 for a garden view to $180 for an ocean view and $240 for an oceanfront room, with the oceanfront corner king rooms costing $260. Many packages are available. On the property, you can dine for breakfast or dinner in the Tropics Cafe Restaurant, which has a lovely sun-soaked veranda with a sweeping view of the surrounding coastline. The Windjammer, an open-air lounge next door, features entertainment several evenings each week. The hotel pool has an upper kiddies' pool and a lower, re-tiled main pool adjacent to the rolling surf, and an ocean-fed beach lagoon is sheltered from the force of the waves by huge black lava boulders. Between the main building and the beach tower is the small coconut grove. Here, the *imu* is fired up every Monday, Wednesday, and Friday evening, creating delectable morsels for the famous Kona sunset lu'au that comes complete with island entertainment that fills the grounds with music and laughter. The tennis courts, attended by a professional staff, are lit for nighttime play. Other

KONA

full-service amenities include a self-serve laundry, free parking, exercise spa classes, baby-sitters, and no charge for children under 17 years of age sharing a room with their parents. The Royal Kona Resort keeps alive the tradition of quality service at a quality hotel.

The **Ohana Keauhou Beach Resort,** 78-6740 Ali'i Dr., Kailua-Kona, HI 96740, 808/322-3441, 800/462-6262, is built on a historic site that includes the remains of two *heiau,* a reconstruction of King Kamehameha III's summer cottage, two freshwater springs, and several fishponds. Kahalu'u Beach Park is adjacent with its white-sand beach, and the entire area is known for fantastic tidepools. This famous Kona hotel underwent an extensive renovation in 1999 and the result is a wonderful feeling of old-fashioned Hawaii. To set the mood, paintings by Hawaii's Herb Kane hang on the walls and reflect the heritage of the two dugout canoes in the lobby. Throughout the hotel, soothing greens and sand-beige colors coordinate with the period-style furniture to make this a restful retreat.

Rates range from $199 for a garden view up to $299 for deluxe oceanfront room, with suites at $600; rates are lower during value season and many special discounts are available all year. Each of the 311 rooms has a/c, TV, phone, private lanai, and small refrigerator. The hotel has the Kama'aina Terrace restaurant that's open for breakfast and dinner; the Kalanikai lunch café near the water, which serves wraps, sandwiches, and other light fare; and a lobby lounge where you'll hear free music most nights. The resort also has a swimming pool, activities desk, the Lamont's sundries store, Kailua Artists Gallery, Kolona salon and day spa, and a fitness center. In keeping with the new outlook, the hotel is offering daily activities and presentations in Hawaiian dance, music, arts and crafts, and a torch lighting ceremony. A free cultural tour is offered daily that takes you around to the historical sites on the hotel grounds. For the tennis player, Island Slice Tennis is on the property. Although not the largest, the Keauhou Beach Hotel is the finest hotel property in the Kailua area.

Kanaloa at Kona is one of the premier condominiums in the Kailua-Keauhou area.

Condominiums

Economy: A few reasonably priced and attractive condominium apartments include the following. **Kona Islander Inn** hotel-style condominium apartments, 75-5776 Kuakini Hwy., Kailua-Kona, HI 96740, 808/329-3181, are well appointed for a reasonable price. Conveniently located within walking distance of downtown Kailua-Kona, they're tucked into a tight but well-landscaped garden next door to St. Michael's and Kealoakamalamalama Churches. The style is "turn-of-the-20th-century plantation" shaded by tall palms. All rental units have phone, off-road parking, a/c, TV, and refrigerators. Rates are $70–80. Reservations for this and the following two condos can also be made through Hawaii Resorts Management, 800/622-5348, www.konahawaii.com, which manages units in more than a dozen other mostly economical to moderate condos along this coast.

Kona Billfisher, 808/329-9277, offers apartment-style condos with full kitchens, pool, barbecues, limited maid service, and gazebo. One-bedroom units cost $85 daily for up to four persons, two-bedroom units $110 for up to six guests. Weekly and monthly rates and discounts are available; minimum three days.

Kona Magic Sands Resort, 808/329-9393, couldn't get closer to the water. It sits on oceanside lava directly adjacent to White Sands Beach. Here, you can lounge poolside and eat at Jameson's Restaurant without leaving the property. The studios have full kitchens, color TV, and phones. Rates run $125 during high season or $95 during low season; three nights minimum.

Set next to the Royal Kona Resort is the small and quiet **Hale Kona Kai,** 75-5870 Kahakai Rd., Kailua-Kona, HI 96740, tel./fax 808/329-2155, 800/421-3996. These one-bedroom, oceanfront apartments are fully equipped condo units with lanai, and a swimming pool and laundry facilities are on the premises. Room rates are $125–135 a night, three-night minimum, $10 for each additional person over two.

On a narrow property that slides down to the sea, the contemporary-style **Alii Villa,** 808/329-1288, look as if they came out of the 1960s with their straight lines and architectural concrete blocks. Set amidst plentiful vegetation, with a swimming pool and two barbecue grills in the middle of the property, these condos run in the $75–145 range during high season.

Small in comparison, **Kona Seaspray** rents condo units in its two-building complex at 78-6665 Ali'i Dr., with an exceptional setting across from Kahalu'u Bay and St. Peter's Church. Spacious, well-kept, with all amenities, and a small pool on property, these units start at $700 a week. Kona Seaspray is popular so call well in advance; 808/322-2403, fax 808/322-0105, seaspraykona@aol.com, www.konaseaspray.com.

Set kitty-corner to the Keauhou Shopping Center and just a short walk from the Kona Country Club Golf Course is the **Keauhou Resort,** 78-7039 Kamehameha III Rd., Kailua-Kona, HI 96740, 808/322-9122, 800/367-5286, fax 808/322-9410, keauhouresort@konanet.net, a town house complex of low-rise units in a garden of bougainvillea and other tropical plants. One- and two-bedroom units have electric kitchens, washers and dryers, telephones, and color TV, and there are two pools on the property. Reasonable rates run $85 a day for a one-bedroom garden unit to $117 for a two-bedroom ocean-view unit; five night minimum stay.

Moderate: Just outside the central Kailua area, at the start of "condo row," is **Kona Reef,** a Castle Resort property at 75-5999 Ali'i Dr., Kailua-Kona, HI 96740, 808/329-2959. Finely appointed units look out over the central garden and pool to the sea beyond. Each unit is set up with full kitchen, washer and dryer, and all you need for an easy stay. One-, two-, and three-bedroom suites run $190–230 high season, slightly less during low season, and can sleep four to eight people. For reservations, contact the condo direct or call Castle Resorts at 800/272-5275 in Hawaii, 800/367-5004 nationwide, www.castleresorts.com.

Only steps from the stone church Hale Halawai O Holualoa is **Kona Nalu.** A small property with a few more than a dozen units, it's not only quiet but relatively central on this Kona strip. Expect rates in the $215–235 range for two-bedroom oceanfront units. Contact Sunquest Vacations, 800/357-5168, for information and reservations.

A Marc Resort property, **Kona Bali Kai,** 76-6246 Ali'i Dr., Kailua-Kona, HI 96740, 808/329-9381, 800/535-0085, fax 808/326-6056, is a very decent, comfortable place with a swimming pool, activities desk, concierge, and sundries shop on property. The studio, one-, and two-bedroom units have a fully equipped kitchen, TV and VCR, and phone for local calls. All apartments are individually owned so the decor differs, but most have muted colors and a tropical feel. Rates run $169–299. While some units are directly on the ocean, others are on the mountain side of Ali'i Drive, so they may or may not have an ocean view. This is a good choice for being close to town but not in the center of the hubbub.

Expensive: The **Outrigger Royal Sea Cliff Resort,** 75-6040 Ali'i Dr., Kailua-Kona, HI 96740, 808/329-8021, 800/688-7444, winner of the AAA Three-Diamond Award, offers classy condo apartments. The alabaster contemporary building features rooms fronting a central garden courtyard, and the stark white color inside and out provide a Mediterranean feel. The unobstructed views of the black lava coast from most rooms are glorious, and a perfect day-ending activity is sunsets enjoyed on your private lanai. Amenities include free tennis, daily maid service, cable color TV, freshwater and seawater swimming pools, jet spa and sauna, and activities desk. Units here are spacious and regular season rates start with a studio at $233 and move to one bedrooms $263–310, two bedrooms $298–363, with a few oceanfront villas at $803. The "family plan" allows children under 18 to stay at no charge when using existing beds; otherwise there's a $20 daily extra person charge.

Kona by the Sea, 75-6106 Ali'i Dr., Kailua-Kona, HI 96740, 808/327-2300, 800/321-2558 in Hawaii, 800/922-7866 Mainland and Canada, is a beautifully situated condominium with extraordinary coastal views. Like many of Kona's properties, it has no beach, but there is a pool on the premises and an activities desk. From the balcony of your suite overlooking a central courtyard, you can watch the aqua-blue surf crash onto the black lava rocks below. Each spacious one- or two-bedroom unit has two bathrooms,

tiled lanai, modern full kitchen, living room with fold-out couch, dining room, color cable TV, and central air. Like its near neighbor, this property is also a AAA Three-Diamond Award winner. Regular season prices are $300–335 for one-bedroom units and $370–390 for two-bedroom units.

Outrigger's **Kanaloa at Kona,** 78-261 Manukai St., Kailua-Kona, HI 96740, 808/322-9625, 800/688-7444, is situated in a quiet upscale residential area away from traffic at the southern end of Kailua-Kona in Keauhou. This is one of those special places where you feel you get more than you pay for. The one- and two-bedroom units are enormous. Bigger isn't always better, but in this case it is. Each individually owned and decorated unit comes equipped with a complete and modern kitchen, two baths, a lanai with comfortable outdoor furniture, a wet bar for entertaining, and a washer and dryer. Rates for the tastefully furnished units range from $250 for one-bedroom, fairway-view villas to $360 for two-bedroom units with loft on the ocean; the rooms can accommodate four and six people, respectively, at no extra charge. Two nights minimum. Many package rates and discounts are available. A security officer is on duty at all hours, and on the grounds you'll find three swimming pools and whirlpool spas, two lighted tennis courts for guest use only, gas barbecue grills, an activities desk with free morning coffee, and even a fine-dining restaurant and cocktail lounge overlooking the black rocky shore. The complex itself consists of some three dozen low-rise units that lie between the Kona Country Club and the water, and the grounds are finely landscaped. This is a place that feels like vacation. If you would like to escape the hustle and bustle but stay near the action, the Kanaloa at Kona is the place. It's a winner.

Vacation Rental Agencies

With the multitude of condos and rental houses along this coast, there are plenty of agencies to do the looking for you. It's often better the first time around to let one of the agencies find one to fit your needs and then look for something else for next time while you're on the island. Try one of the following for condominium units or rental homes.

Sunquest Vacations, 77-6435 Kuakini Hwy., Kailua-Kona, HI 96740, 808/329-6488, 800/ 367-5168 in the U.S., 800/800-5662 in Canada, fax 808/329-5480, www.sunquest-hawaii.com, manages over 200 units in some 30 condo properties in the Kona area, with nearly two dozen homes. By and large, these units are midrange. They also arrange car rentals, tours, and activities. This company is one of the "big boys" and has a well-deserved reputation.

Century 21 All Islands, 75-5689 Ali'i Dr., Kailua-Kona, HI 96740, 808/326-2121, 800/ 546-5662, fax 808/329-6768, www.islandsrentals .com/BigIsland/Aloha-C21.html, handles mostly economy to midrange condo units in Kailua and Keauhou.

Property Network, 75-5799 Ali'i Dr., Kailua-Kona, HI 96740, 808/329-7977, 800/358-7977, fax 808/329-1200, vacation@hawaii-kona.com, www.hawaii-kona.com, handles the full range of condos along the Kona Coast in about two dozen different properties plus a handful of homes; economy to midrange.

For mostly upper-end condo units in the Keauhou area, try **Keauhou Property Management Company,** 76-6225 Kuakini Hwy., Ste. C-105, Kailua-Kona, HI 96740, 808/326-9075, 800/745-5662, fax 808/326-2055.

Knutson and Associates, 75-6082 Ali'i Dr., Ste. 8, Kailua-Kona, HI 96740, 808/329-6311, 800/800-6202, fax 808/326-2178, www.kona-hawaiirentals.com, manages midrange condo units and a few vacation homes mostly in the central Kona area.

With roughly 150 properties, of which about two dozen are homes, **West Hawaii Property Services, Inc.,** 78-6831 Ali'i Dr., Ste. 234A, Kailua-Kona, HI 96740, 808/322-6696, 800/ 799-5662, fax 808/324-0609, whps@ilhawaii .com, www.konarentals.com, has a good range of places from economy to deluxe.

A smaller company with about half condo units and half homes is **C. J. Kimberly Realtors,** 75-5875 Kahakai Rd., Kailua-Kona, HI 96740; 808/329-4321, 888/780-7000, fax

808/329-5533, cjkimberly@aloha.net, www .cjkimberlyrealtors.com.

Action Team Realty, 75-5660 Kopiko St., Ste. B4, Kailua-Kona, HI 96740, 808/329-8626, 800/335-3347, www.konacondo.com, handles many condo units in about a dozen and a half properties, as well as a number of individual homes, in Kona.

FOOD
Inexpensive

"So, for the budget traveler," you've been asking yourself, "which is the best restaurant in town, with the most food at the lowest prices, with that down-home atmosphere?" **The Ocean View Inn,** 808/329-9998, is it! The gigantic menu of Chinese, American, Japanese, and Hawaiian food is like a mini-directory. Lunch and dinner range $8–12, and a huge breakfast goes for about $5. It's open daily except Mon., 6:30 A.M.–2:45 P.M. and 5:15–9 P.M., with the bar open daily 6:30 A.M.–9 P.M. Located across from the seawall near King Kamehameha's Kona Beach Hotel, it's always crowded with local people, a sure sign that the food is good.

The **Royal Jade Garden,** in the Lanihau Center, 808/326-7288, open daily 10:30 A.M.– 9:30 P.M., is a Chinese restaurant where you get an amazing amount of well-prepared food for a moderate price. Run-of-the-mill chow mein, noodle soup, and meat dishes of chicken, duck, pork, or beef cost $6–9. More expensive items include lobster with black bean sauce and a variety of fresh fish and seafood. In the Royal Jade there's no decor, but if you are hungry and on a tight budget, this is one of the best values in town.

Aki's Cafe, 808/329-0090, located across from the seawall, is a moderately priced Japanese/ American restaurant offering breakfast, lunch, and dinner. Breakfast can be three-egg omelettes, an eggs Benedict scramble, pancakes, or a Japanese breakfast with eggs, miso soup, rice, and your choice of meat. Lunch can be California-roll sushi, fried noodles to which you can add chicken or shrimp, or curry with rice. The dinner menu offers marinated New York steak, chicken

KONA

teriyaki, garlic pasta, and its well-known fish and chips. Aki's is a centrally located, simple restaurant that adds a nice touch to ordinary food.

King Yee Lau, 808/329-7100, located in the Ali'i Sunset Plaza across from the seawall and open Mon.–Sat. 11 A.M.–2 P.M., nightly 5–9 P.M., offers an all-you-can-eat lunch buffet and the usual Chinese dishes like pressed crispy duck, beef with ginger sauce, and shrimp with seasoned vegetables, most priced under $9. Many vegetarian selections are offered.

Kimo's Family Buffet, located in the heart of Kailua in the courtyard of Uncle Billy's Kona Bay Hotel, 808/329-1393, serves very reasonably priced breakfast and dinner buffets. The breakfast buffet runs $5.95, dinner buffet $10.95, and a Sunday brunch $6.95. These prices can't be beat, but don't expect a lavish layout or a gourmet production.

Part of a small chain on the island, **Verna's Drive-In** on Kuakini Hwy. is where many local people go for inexpensive fast food like plate lunches, sandwiches, omelettes, burgers, and drinks. Open all day. Totally local.

In a freestanding booth in the Lanihau Center, **Chili by Max,** open Tues.–Sat. 10 A.M.–4 P.M., is famous for its award-winning oven-baked chili, made with beef or sautéed tofu. Also on the bill of fare are kosher hot dogs, chili dogs, chili nachos, baked potatoes, chicken breast sandwiches, tacos, and ice cream.

In the Kopiko Plaza, along Palani Rd. and just down from the Lanihau Center, you'll find several places to eat, including Hama Yu and Kona Mix Plate. **Kona Mix Plate,** 808/329-8104, open Mon.–Sat. 10 A.M.–8 P.M., is a no-frills counter restaurant serving standard Japanese, Korean, and American breakfasts, sandwiches, and plates like teriyaki beef, *kalbi* ribs, and shrimp platters for about $8, with a few items up to $15. While not special, the food is acceptable and inexpensive, and there always seems to be a line at lunch—a good sign. Stop by **Hama Yu Japanese Restaurant,** 808/331-8888, daily except Sun. for lunch and dinner. Lunch meals might be noodles, *donburi,* or tempura, while dinner is usually a bit fuller with items like teriyaki and *kobayashi* for $16–25 or sushi and sashimi

for $25–35. Hama Yu has a sister restaurant up the coast at the King's Shops in Waikoloa.

Although the Kona industrial area doesn't sound inviting, it is a great place to find inexpensive food, along with stores where the *people* shop. To get to the industrial area, head for the airport, and about one minute north of the junction of Rte. 19 (the airport road) and Palani Rd., make a left on Kaiwi St. Or follow Kuakini Rd., a major intersection off Palani Rd. just a minute from the seawall, to Kaiwi St. The triangle formed by Kaiwi and Kuakini is primarily the old industrial area. Behind the Kailua Candy Company in this area is the **Orchid Thai Cuisine** restaurant, 808/327-9437. Located in a small strip-mall setting, the ambience is plain pedestrian but the food is better than average. Open Mon.–Fri. 11 A.M.–9 P.M., you'll find all your usual favorite Thai dishes like chicken *satay;* papaya salad; *pad thai* noodles; red, green, and yellow curries; plus a host of other items. Most main dishes run $7.50–8.50; takeout is available on all orders.

If you're hungry for a quick bite while up at the Crossroads Shopping Center, stop in **Manna Korean Barbecue** for inexpensive Korean/American/Hawaiian foods where most items are under $7.

Harbor House, at the Honokohau Small Boat Harbor, 808/326-4166, open daily 10:30 A.M.–8:30 P.M., features one of Kona's longest bars. Harbor House is more or less an open-air pavilion, but it is actually quite picturesque as it overlooks the harbor. If you are interested in a charter fishing boat, this is the best place to come to spin a yarn with the local skippers who congregate here daily in the late afternoon. Over the bar hangs a gigantic 1,556-pound marlin, almost as big as the Budweiser sign. Strategically placed TVs make it a good sports bar, and the jukebox has a great selection of oldies and contemporary tunes. You can not only quaff a variety of draft beers here, you can order off the bill of fare for grilled bacon cheeseburgers with fries, shrimp and chips, crab-salad sandwiches, clam chowder, and the like. Harbor House is one of the truly *colorful* places in Kailua-Kona, and one of the best places to relax and have a hassle-free brew. It's also a place where the fish stories you tell might easily become exaggerated with the number of beers you drink.

Bakeries, Delis, and Coffee

You can't get "hotter" than **Lava Java,** 808/327-2161, one of Kona's popular coffeehouse/restaurants, open daily 6 A.M.–10 P.M. in the Ali'i Sunset Plaza across from the seawall. Here, local people and tourists alike come to kick back, read the papers, and actually engage in the lost art of conversation. Sandwiches, soups, and salads are major menu items. Try the turkey and ham for $7.95, a garden burger for $6.95, Polish dog for $3.75, Greek wrap for $5.95, chicken salad for $6.95, or chips and salsa for $4.95. Lava Java has a counter offering muffins, cookies, root-beer floats, Kona coolers made with tropical fruit sorbet, Italian sodas, ice cream, and bulk 100 percent Kona coffee by the pound. Reasonable Internet access is available.

Down the road next to Huggo's is **Java on the Rock,** an early morning coffee bar serving freshly brewed Kona coffee, espresso, and a variety of fresh-baked pastries. Takeout is an option, but perhaps it would be better to sit along the waterfront and savor your drink while you enjoy the harbor scene. A friendly place with lots of "Aloha." Open daily 6–11 A.M. except major holidays. For something a bit more substantial at the same great location, try lunch or the late lunch menu from 2:30–4:30 P.M.

Buns in the Sun bakery and deli, 808/326-2774, at the back of the Lanihau Center, is open daily from 5 A.M. but closes by mid-afternoon. Buns not only sells fresh-brewed gourmet coffee, pastries, and bread, it also makes American-standard and Hawaiian-style breakfasts, unique lunch sandwiches, tasty wraps, and more. If you're out and about, this is a good stop.

The **French Bakery,** 808/326-2688, open weekdays 5:30 A.M.–3 P.M., Sat. 5:30 A.M.–2 P.M. in the Old Kona Industrial Area, is a budget gourmet deli/restaurant where the food is great and the prices are low. Not only does it have the full range of pastries, breads, and other goodies you would expect, it has wonderful and inexpensive sandwiches and coffee.

Nearby is **Pot Belli Deli,** 808/329-9454, open weekdays 7 A.M.–4 P.M.. The refrigerated deli case holds such things as chicken, ham, or tuna salad sandwiches, spinach pie, and bagels with cream cheese. The shelves hold all the condiments and extras you need for a terrific picnic lunch. You can get your order to go or eat at one of the few booths inside.

If you're looking for pastries and sandwiches while at the Keauhou Shopping Center, head for **Daylight Donuts and Deli,** 808/324-1833; open from 6 A.M.

Moderate

Cafe Sibu, in the Kona Banyan Court, 808/329-1112, open daily 11:30 A.M.–2 P.M. for lunch and 5–9 P.M. for dinner, is an Indonesian restaurant serving savory marinated meats and vegetables spiced with zesty sauces and flame grilled. The restaurant, across from the seawall under the big banyan tree, has only a few outside tables and makes a light attempt at decor with a few antique Indonesian masks. If you're hungry, go for the *gado gado* for $11.50, an Indonesian salad layered with spices and peanut sauce that can be dinner for one or an appetizer salad for two or three. *Saté,* curry, and stir-fry dishes can be made with chicken, beef, pork, shrimp, or vegetables for $10.25–14.25, or try the truly authentic *ayam panggang pedis,* a grilled and marinated spicy chicken. Although slightly more expensive, the combination plates are good deals, as they let you try a number of items. Lunch prices are a couple bucks cheaper. Cafe Sibu definitely serves some of the tastiest and most interesting, moderately priced food in Kailua-Kona.

Look for a bright *akachochin,* a red paper lantern, marking the entrance to **Bistro Yokohama** in the Ali'i Sunset Plaza, 808/329-9661, open Mon.–Fri. 11:30 A.M.–1:30 P.M. and Mon.–Sat. 5:30–9 P.M. for dinner. Inside is simplicity: Japanese kites, light wood furniture, and a few glowing lanterns. The classic lunches include *soba* sukiyaki, *teishoku, donburi,* or a fixed-plate lunch, such as *donkatsu* pork cutlets, that includes an appetizer, salad, rice, and miso soup. Some traditional dinner entrées are cooked right at your table, like sukiyaki or *shabu shabu,* thin

KONA

slices of beef and assorted vegetables boiled in stock, and most dinners are in the $20 range. Although in a shopping plaza, both the atmosphere and cuisine are genuine.

A few steps away is **Thai Rin Thai Restaurant,** 808/329-2929. Open Mon.–Sat. for lunch and dinner and Sun. for dinner only, this restaurant offers lunch for under $8 and dinners for around $10, with chef's specials like crab stir-fry and deep-fried fish for $13–21. Located in the heart of the strip, this is a convenient choice.

The **Kona Ranch House,** 808/329-7061, located at the corner of Kuakini Hwy. and Ololi Rd., is a delightful restaurant with something for everyone. It has two rooms: the family-oriented Paniolo Room, where hearty appetites are filled family-style; and the elegant Plantation Lanai, where both your palate and sense of beauty are satiated. This cheery restaurant is well regarded in town and epitomizes plantation dining. The Kona Ranch House is the type of establishment where you get more than you pay for. The menu is mostly standard American fare with a heavy dollop of fish and seafood. It's a popular place, you may need reservations for breakfast on the weekends. Open 6:30 A.M.–2 P.M. for breakfast and lunch, and Sun. for brunch. Reservations are taken for dinner, served 4:30–9 P.M. Meats are a large part of the extensive menu—some are from the Parker Ranch—and most dinner entrées run $14–20.

Basil's Pizzeria and Restaurant in downtown Kailua-Kona, 808/326-7836, open daily 11 A.M.–10 P.M., is a place that makes its own pizza dough. Individual gourmet pizzas are $5.95–10.95, depending upon your choice of toppings; New York–style pizza, 14-inch and 16-inch, is $10.95–17.95. Besides pizza, Basil's offers soup of the day for $3.50, Italian antipasto at $7.95, angel hair primavera for $10.95, shrimp marinara for $14.95, eggplant parmigiana at $10.95, and an assortment of other fine Italian foods. A nightly "fresh catch special" is priced around $15, or you can order any number of sandwiches for under $7. Pizza by the slice is available 11 A.M.–5 P.M. only, and you can do takeout. If you don't care to come down, Basil's offers free delivery of any menu item in the Kailua area. So go ahead, recline on your condo lanai and call Basil's, and they'll be over *molto rapido.*

Cassandra's Greek Taverna, 808/334-1066, open daily 7 A.M.–10 P.M., on the 2nd floor directly across from the Kona pier, is decorated in a predominant blue and white motif reminiscent of the Greek Isles. Breakfast runs 7–11 A.M., and lunch is served 11 A.M.–4 P.M., with most items under $9. Dinner expands the lunch menu and includes such offerings as traditional appetizers like dolmades (grape leaves stuffed with meat and rice) and *keftedes* (pan-fried Greek meatballs), and savory entrées like a gyro plate, Greek-style baby-back pork ribs, shrimp *posidonian,* or souvlaki made with chicken, beef, or lamb. Prices are usually $14–25, a platter for two runs $45; full bar. This is the place to come to for eastern Mediterranean food. Earthy, vibrant Greek music to stir the soul wafts through the air, and belly dancing is performed for guests on Friday and Saturday evenings.

Quinn's, across from King Kamehameha's Kona Beach Hotel, 808/329-3822, is Kona's socially eclectic bar and grill where everyone from local bikers to pink-roasted tourists and tournament anglers are welcomed. It's also a roost for night owls who come here to munch and have a beer or mixed drink when everything else in town is closed. The inside bar is cozy, friendly, and sports-oriented. Quinn's is open daily for lunch 11 A.M.–5 P.M. and for dinner 5–11 P.M. For lunch, a gigantic mound of shrimp and crab salad is wonderful. The fresh catch-of-the-day sandwiches with salad or charbroiled burgers are a deal. Fill up for under $10. Dinner entrées are juicy filet mignon, chicken stir-fry, and fresh catch sautéed or broiled. Main entrées are $19–23 and all include soup or dinner salad, vegetable, rice, and Quinn's home-fried potatoes. For the less hearty eater, reasonably priced specialties include tenderloin tips sautéed in brandy with onions, shrimp and chips, and fish and chips, all for less than $10.50.

Cool down with a frosty margarita and watch life go by as you perch on a stool at the upstairs location of **Pancho and Lefty's,** 808/326-2171, near the summer palace. Happy hour, running 3–6 P.M., offers 12-ounce drafts for $1 and big, potent 16-ounce margaritas for $2.75. Open daily 11 A.M.–10 P.M. for food, menu selections begin with appetizers such as buffalo wings, skinny dippers (potatoes covered with bacon and cheese, guacamole and sour cream, or refried beans and cheese), and nachos. Full dinners include taco salad, seafood salad with crisp greens, enchiladas, or fajitas—steak, chicken, or seafood (fresh catch). Specials are enchilada rancheros, *carne asada,* seafood Vera Cruz, or a tamale dinner. Most everything is in the $10–17 range, with a few items for two over $20. Pancho and Lefty's is a good-time place with satisfying food that's easy on the budget.

When you enter the Kaloko Industrial Park, just past mile marker 97 and about three miles north from Kailua-Kona, the setting makes you think you're after plumbing supplies. That's here too, but you'll also find terrific food prepared by one of Hawaii's greatest chefs at **Sam Choy's Kaloko Restaurant,** 808/326-1545, open daily 6 A.M.–2 P.M. and Sun. from 7 A.M. To get there, turn right onto Hinalani St., go up one block and take a right onto Kanalani St., and a left two blocks down onto Kauhola St. Look for Sam's in a nondescript gray building halfway up the hill on the right. The atmosphere is pleasant enough, but those who have dined on Sam's sumptuous creations come for the food! Breakfasts like the ultimate stew omelette (a three-egg omelette filled with Sam's beef stew) for $7.50, steak and eggs for $10.95, or any one of the various "loco moco" will keep you going most of the day. The lunch menu includes fresh island fish prepared *poke* style and then flash-fried for $7.50, saimin at $3, and Kaloko noodle mania for $7.50. While not the cheapest in town, the portions are large and the flavors perfect.

Up in the Crossroads Shopping Center on Henry St. is a wonderful gourmet restaurant that serves meals at moderate prices. This is Amy Ota's **Oodles of Noodles,** 808/329-9222. Don't be put off by the shopping center location—the food is great and the rich colorful decor, low light, and dark tile floor are conducive to a fine meal. Oodles serves a fusion of East and West, with such items as Japanese *udon,* Thai rice noodles, and Italian pasta, that leads to unique and surprising flavors. Almost everything has noodles of some sort in it, including the appetizers, soups, and salads, and with many items you can create your own combinations. Some menu selections include crisp Thai calamari in noodle nest, red miso *ramen* with shiitake mushrooms and tofu, Asian risotto, Peking duck with herbs and spices, and *aglio olio* linguini with shellfish, and there are always featured specials. Most lunch entrées cost under $12, dinners from $14–24, while the appetizers, soups, and salads run $7–15. Food here is a treat for the taste buds, and the variety of noodle dishes is outstanding. Amy's restaurant is an excellent choice.

With a menu that's at least twice as long as you might expect to find, **Bangkok House** Thai restaurant, 808/329-7764, serves plentiful food in a pleasing setting in the King Kamehameha Mall. Your choices include standard Thai fare, with soups, curries, rice, noodles, and vegetarian dishes, plus many surprises. Most entrées run $8–10, with specials up to $15. The lunch menu is a few bucks cheaper.

Overlooking the Royal Kona Resort tennis courts is **Tres Hombres,** 808/329-2173, a Mexican restaurant with a strong island influence. *Taquitos,* tostadas, burritos, *chili rellenos,* fajitas, and all the usual offerings are on the menu, as are steak, fish, and seafood items. Lunch and dinner have roughly the same menu, with few items more than $17. Before dinner, stop at the bar for a cool one and watch the sunset. Open Sun.–Thurs. 11:30 A.M.–9 P.M. and Fri. and Sat. until 10 P.M. This is a good choice for Mexican. For a more local Mexican restaurant, try **Reuben's,** 808/329-4686, down on Kuakini Hwy.

Bubba Gump's, adjacent to Waterfront Row, is one of the newest of the midrange restaurants along Ali'i Dr. It's a fun, family restaurant that, of course, does shrimp and seafood.

Moving back a generation brings you to the **Hard Rock Cafe,** 808/329-8866, upstairs in the Coconut Grove Marketplace, where the 1970s and 1980s is the theme. Music accompanies your meal and memorabilia covers the walls. The Hard Rock has standard American fare with many burger and sandwich choices, plus items like hickory barbecued chicken, smoked pork chops, and fresh catch of the day, mostly under $10. Of course, there is a bar to serve drinks and a counter that sells Hard Rock merchandise. Open daily 11 A.M.–11 P.M., 11:30 P.M. on Fri. and Sat.

Upstairs in another of the Coconut Grove Shopping Center buildings is **Lulu's,** 808/331-2633, a breezy, open-air place with food as pleasing as the setting. *Pu pu,* sandwiches, burger, and sides are mostly under $10, and the signature ribs and pork chops go for $13.95. After dinner, move to the long bar for a good-time brew.

Downstairs from Lulu's is **Durty Jake's,** 808/329-7366. Open all day, food here is easy, and dinner specials are barbecue chicken and Cajun fish and shrimp. A long list of *pu pu* are on the menu for those who don't care for a full meal. As it's on the sidewalk level, Durty Jake's has plenty of walk-by traffic, runs happy hour 4–6 P.M. daily, and offers live music Tues.–Sat. nights.

Up above the sand volleyball court at the rear of Coconut Grove Marketplace is the **Outback Steakhouse,** 808/326-2555. An eatery from down under, this is an easygoing place—appropriate for Hawaii—that's open for dinner daily 4:30–10 P.M., with happy hour until 7 P.M. Start your meal with bloomin' onions, kookaburra wings (buffalo chicken wings), or Brisbane caesar salad. Ranging $12–22, main entrées include Ayers Rock steak, ribs on the barbie, Alice Springs chicken, or Walhalla pasta. A theme restaurant with an adventurous clientele, Outback Steakhouse is worth a try.

South of town in the Keauhou Shopping Center is the breezy, easygoing **Drysdale's Too** restaurant, 808/322-0070, where you can get burgers, sandwiches, hot dogs, gyros, and any number of meat and meatless dishes, plus soups, salads, tropical drinks, and beer. A friendly, comfortable place, it's somehow familiar, and you'll be happy that it won't cost an arm and a leg. Burgers and sandwiches run $6–10, while most entrées are less than $15.

Expensive

At **Huggo's Restaurant,** on Ali'i Dr. next door to the Royal Kona Resort, 808/329-1493, it's difficult to concentrate on the food because the setting is so spectacular. If you were any closer to the sea, you'd be in it, and of course the sunsets are great. Because it is built on a pier, you can actually feel the floor rock. Huggo's is open Mon.–Fri. 11:30 A.M.–2:30 P.M. for full lunch service, 2:30–4:30 P.M. for late-lunch sandwiches only served at the bar, and 5:30–10 P.M. for dinner, with entertainment most nights. Lunch is reasonable, with tasties like Huggo's club, a pizza with your choice of toppings for around $10, or a classic Huggo's burger. The dinner menu is superb and starts with fresh sashimi and seafood chowder made from clams and fresh fish and seasoned with sherry, cream sauce, and butter. The best entrées come from the sea just outside the door and are priced daily at around $26. Also worth trying is shrimp scampi, Australian lobster tail, and chicken with ginger orange sauce. Huggo's has been in business for more than 30 years and is consistently outstanding. Enjoy free *pu pu* Mon.–Fri. 4–6 P.M. while sipping a cocktail as the red Kona sun dips into the azure sea.

The Kona Inn Restaurant at the Kona Inn Shopping Village, 808/329-4455, open daily for lunch and dinner, is a lovely but lonely carryover from the venerable old Kona Inn. On entering, notice the marlin over the doorway and a huge piece of hung glass through which the sunset sometimes forms prismatic rainbows. The bar and dining area are richly appointed in native koa and made more elegant with a mixture of turn-of-the-20th-century wooden chairs, polished hardwood floors, and sturdy open-beamed ceilings. If you want to enjoy the view, try a cocktail and some of the *pu pu* served until closing. Lunch is reasonable at the café grill, serving mostly light foods, sandwiches, burgers, soups, and salads. Dinner is served 5:30–9:30 P.M., reservations recommended. The menu is heavy on fish and meat but offers a few Asian stir-fry dishes and pastas. Expect dinner entrées to run $15–25. The Kona Inn Restaurant epitomizes Kona beachside dining, and the view is simply superb.

Michaelangelo's, in Waterfront Row, 808/329-4436, is run by Mike Medeiros— a true *Mediterraneo* if there ever was one. It is open for lunch daily 11 A.M.–4 P.M. and for dinner until 10 P.M., with happy hour 11 A.M.– 5 P.M. Every night of the year from 10 P.M. until 2 A.M., the restaurant converts into a disco, so there's music and dancing for late-night revelers. Savory selections include antipasto for $9.95–15.95, soup of the day for $5.95, and specialty salads that could make a meal. The lunch menu is a simplified and slightly less expensive version of the evening menu. The dinner menu, with most entrées in the $16–25 range, includes spaghetti marinara, chicken parmesan, lava-fire calamari, or cioppino. A children's menu helps keep costs down for families. The large oceanfront room is appointed with open-beamed ceilings joined by distinctive copper couplings, with Casablanca fans.

Also in Waterfront Row, **Beachcomber's,** 808/329-2451, open daily for lunch 11 A.M.– 2 P.M. and dinner 5–9 P.M., has a good reputation for service, value, and well-prepared food. Primarily, it is a steak and seafood house with most dinner entrées costing $20–28, with lobster or combination plates with lobster much pricier. Several options are prime rib, rack of lamb, spiced yellowfin *'ahi,* and Australian cold-water lobster tail. The Sunday brunch menu is a variation of the daily lunch fare. The location is very pleasant, away from the street noise and with a good view of the sea.

The **Kona Beach Restaurant,** at King Kamehameha's Kona Beach Hotel, 808/329-2911, is open daily for breakfast and dinner and is especially known for its Sunday champagne brunch served 9 A.M.–1 P.M., $25.95 for adults. The long tables are laden with fruit, vegetables, pasta salad, peel-and-eat shrimp, omelettes, waffles, hot entrées from fresh catch to sashimi, and desserts so sinful you'll be glad that someone's on their knees praying at Sunday services. Friday and Saturday nights are very special because of the Prime Rib & Seafood Buffet at $24.95, which brings hungry people from around the island. Other nights also have their special buffets: Monday is Hawaiian for $13.95, Tuesday features crab and tempura at $19.95, Wednesday brings Chinese delicacies for $15.95, and Thursday is an Italian buffet priced at $15.95. Dinner is served 5:30–8 P.M., until 9 P.M. on Fri. and Sat. Served 6–10 A.M., the breakfast buffet for $11.95 is a deal, and there are children's prices for all meals. The Kona Beach Restaurant is sure to please. The restaurant itself is tasteful, but the best feature is an unobstructed view of the hotel's beach, especially fine at sunset.

If you're staying out near Keauhou, rather than driving into town, reserve a seat at the casually elegant **Kama'aina Terrace Restaurant,** 808/322-3441, at the Ohana Keauhou Beach Resort. Open to the ocean breezes, from your table you can look out across the grass lawn to the rocky shoreline. While the restaurant is open for breakfast, it is perhaps best in the evening. Appetizers, soups, and salads run $7–12. For an entrée, choose from such items as chili-crusted *'ahi,* oven-roasted chicken, marinated rib-eye steak, or a lamb chop, all in the $18–25 range.

Also out in Keauhou, located at the Outrigger Kanaloa at Kona condominium, is **Edward's at Kanaloa,** 808/322-1434. Edward's provides outdoor seating under a covered arbor at the oceanside, nearly on the rocks. This is a perfect spot for a sunset dinner: small, intimate, and romantic. The staff is attentive, there is an extensive wine list, and a bar can set you up with any drink that you wish. While American-style breakfasts and light lunches are served, the restaurant is best known for dinner. Start your evening meal with a stuffed mussel appetizer and move on to a chilled gazpacho soup. All in the $20–24 range, the short menu has medallions of pork with prunes, rack of lamb, tenderloin of beef *gaufrettes,* grilled chicken breast, and local fresh fish. Choosing dessert is a difficult task, as your choices include praline chocolate mousse cake, crème brûlée, roasted Kea'au banana tiramisu, and the like. An excellent choice for a night out, reservations are required and a guest pass to the property is necessary.

Fine Dining

Oui oui, Monsieur, but of course we have zee restaurant *français.* It is **La Bourgogne,** 808/329-6711, open Mon.–Sat. 6–10 P.M., located at the corner of Nalani St., about three miles south of downtown Kailua-Kona along Rte. 11. For those who just can't live without escargot or real French onion soup, you've been saved. How much will it set you back? Plenty, *mon petit!* Cold and hot appetizers include *pâté du chef* for $8.95, and escargots de Bourgogne for $7.95, while scrumptious French onion soup for $6.95 or homemade lobster bisque for $7.50 will follow. For salads, order greens with local goat cheese or greens with mango and lobster. Titillating seafood and poultry entrées, $25–32, feature fresh catch of the day; lobster braised with shallots, tomato, brandy, and cream; and roast duck breast with raspberries and pine nuts. Meat courses, $26–32, include delectable roast rack of lamb with creamy mustard sauce, tenderloin of venison with sherry and pomegranate sauce, and osso bucco veal shank in red wine. Top off your gourmet meal with fresh, made-in-house desserts like crème brûlée or a lemon tartlet. This restaurant, small and slightly out of the way, is definitely worth a visit for those who enjoy exceptional food—a memorable gastronomic experience. Definitely call for reservations, perhaps a couple of days in advance.

Jameson's-by-the-Sea, 77-6452 Ali'i Dr., 808/329-3195, is open for lunch weekdays 11 A.M.–2:30 P.M. and dinner every evening 5:30–9:30 P.M. Jameson's makes a good attempt at elegance with high-backed wicker chairs, crystal everywhere, white linen table settings, and a back-lit fish tank in the entry. The sea foams white and crashes on the shore just outside the restaurant's open windows. The quality of the food is very good, just shy of gourmet. People come here for fish, and they are never disappointed. The lunch menu lists appetizers like sashimi, salmon pâté, and fried calamari, and a variety of sandwiches. The dinner menu offers the same appetizers but adds a seafood platter with sashimi, shrimp, and fresh oysters. The dinner entrées range from fresh catches like *opakapaka, ono,* and mahimahi to fried shrimp and scallops with oyster sauce and Chinese pea pods. Other full meals include filet mignon with béarnaise sauce, baked stuffed shrimp, sesame chicken, and shrimp curry with mango chutney, mostly

under $27. For dessert, save room for the assortment of homemade chiffon pies.

Brewery

The **Kona Brewing Company** has been creating quality beer since the mid-1990s. It produces nearly a dozen varieties from a light lager to a dark porter, perhaps the best known of which are Pacific Golden Ale, Fire Rock Pale Ale, and Longboard Lager, with additional seasonal brews. Bar beer is brewed on the premises at a rate of about 150 barrels a week, but retail bottled beer is brewed in California according to Kona Brewing Company's recipe. Free brewery tours and tastings are given weekdays at 10:30 A.M. and 3 P.M., but if you miss the tour, stop by the brewery and café anyway to try a beer or two. The café serves mostly pizza, salads, and sandwiches, nothing elegant, but a good complement to the brew. A seat at the bar gets you up close to all the action there, or you may choose a booth inside or a table out on the lanai where you can watch the sun go down as easily as the beer in your tall, cool glass. The kitchen is open until 10 P.M., the bar later. Periodic live music is performed, mostly on Sundays. Located behind Zac's Business Center in the North Kona Shopping Center, Kona Brewpub is open for lunch and dinner daily.

ENTERTAINMENT

The most memorable evening experience for most is free: watching the sunset from Kailua Pier and taking a leisurely stroll along Ali'i Drive. Otherwise, Kona nights come alive mainly in the restaurants and dining rooms of the big hotels and fancier restaurants. The two lu'au have "Polynesian Revues" of one sort or another, which are generally good, clean, sexy fun, but of course these shows are limited only to the lu'au guests. For those who have "dancin' feet" or wish to spend the evening listening to live music, there's a small but varied selection from which to choose.

Huggo's Restaurant, with its romantic waterfront setting along Ali'i Dr., and the attached Huggo's on the Rocks, feature music 8:30 P.M.–

12:30 A.M. The entertainment changes nightly: karaoke, smooth Jawaiian, other mellow contemporary sounds, or a touch of rock or jazz now and again.

For other music over the dinner hour and beyond, try **Durty Jake's** at the Coconut Grove Marketplace or the **Kona Brewpub**, which has live music, particularly on Sunday.

The **Aston Keauhou Beach Resort** soothes you with easy listening, Hawaiian style, at the veranda bar, nightly except Sunday and Monday.

At the Royal Kona Resort's open-air **Windjammer Lounge,** sip a flavorful tropical concoction while watching the sun melt into the Pacific. Entertainment is offered several evenings a week, featuring hula at sundown.

In downtown Kailua-Kona, the **Billfish Bar** at King Kamehameha's Kona Beach Hotel has live entertainment Friday and Saturday 6–9 P.M., featuring mellow Hawaiian music.

Kimo's Family Buffet at the Kona Bay Hotel offers a free hula show 6–8 P.M. Tues.–Sun. during dinner. As the entertainment is performed outdoors near the pool, passersby are also treated to lovely strains of Hawaiian music and swaying hips.

From 6–7 P.M. on Friday, stop by for a free Polynesian show at the Keauhou Shopping Center.

After all the other bars and restaurants have closed, head to **Michaelangelo's** for disco dancing every night 10 P.M.–2 A.M. at Waterfront Row.

For a quiet beer, sports talk, or just hanging out with the local people, try the bars at **Quinn's** or **Ocean View Inn,** both in downtown Kailua-Kona.

Makalapua Stadium Cinemas, 808/327-0444, located up by the Kmart, or the **Keauhou 7 Cinemas,** 808/324-7200, at the Keauhou Shopping Center, both show first-run movies. Tickets run $7.50 for adults. Call for times and current showings.

Lu'au

Tihati's Drums of Polynesia Lu'au, at the Royal Kona Resort, 808/329-3111, held every Monday, Wednesday, and Friday, offers an evening of entertainment and feasting, Hawaiian style. The lu'au begins at 5:15 P.M. and is followed by an open bar, lavish buffet, and thrilling entertainment for three fun-filled hours. Many supposedly authentic lu'au play-act with the *imu*-baked pig, but here it is carved and served to the guests. Prices are $55 adults, $25 children ages 6–12, free for children under age five. For the show only, which starts at 7 P.M., the rates are $28 adult and $18 children 6–12. Reservations are strongly recommended.

King Kamehameha's Kona Beach Hotel, 808/326-4969, sways with Hawaiian chants during its famous **Island Breeze Lu'au** held every Sunday, Tuesday, Wednesday, Thursday, and Friday on the beach and grounds of King Kamehameha's last residence, Ahu'ena. The pig is placed into the *imu* every morning at 10:15 A.M. and the festivities begin in the evening with a lei greeting at 5:30 P.M., followed by a crafts demonstration, torch-lighting, and an *imu* ceremony at 6 P.M. Cocktails flow 6–8 P.M.; the 22-course lu'au dinner is served 6:30–8:30 P.M., with the Polynesian show starting at 7:30 P.M. Prices are $55 adults, $21 children 6–12, free for children five and under. Limited cocktail and show seating runs $30 adult and $14.50 children. Reservations are required. Call 808/326-4969 or stop by the lu'au desk in the lobby of the hotel; www.islandbreezeluau.com.

RECREATION

Snorkeling and More

For snorkeling equipment rental, try **Snorkel Bob's,** 808/329-0770, www.snorkelbob.com, located across from Huggo's; it has some of the best prices, equipment, and services on the island. Gear, which includes mask, snorkel tube, and fins, is rented for a 24-hour day or by the week. The snorkel set runs $2.50–9 a day or $9–35 a week, depending on the quality. Rental boogie boards are also available, and Bob and his crew can arrange tours as well.

The **Kona Beach Shack,** 808/329-7494, at the King Kamehameha's Kona Beach Hotel, not only rents snorkel gear at $7 a day, they also rent kayaks, paddleboats, boogie boards, and other beach and water equipment. The Beach Shack also can arrange guided kayak and snorkel tours, outrigger canoe rides, snuba, an underwater tour that involves wearing a diver's helmet, and most activities that take place from the Kailua Pier. Open daily 9 A.M.–5 P.M.

Miller's Snorkeling, 808/326-1771, at the Kona Bali Kai condo, rents complete snorkeling gear for $7 per day or $15 per week. It also rents boogie boards and beach accessories and is open daily 8 A.M.–5 P.M.

Next to Snorkel Bob's in a small freestanding building is **Honu Sports,** 808/938-9795. Honu Sports does snorkel, scuba, and kayak rental and tours.

Others in town that rent scuba equipment and/or offer guided tours are **Jack's Diving Locker,** 808/329-7585, **Kona Coast Divers,** 808/329-8802, **Sandwich Isle Divers,** 808/329-9188, and **Big Island Divers,** 800/329-6068. Most dive shops also rent snorkel gear.

Bicycling
Dave's Bike and Triathlon Shop, 808/329-4522, owned and pedaled by triathlete Dave Bending, is located just a long stride or two from the beginning of the Ironman Triathlon across from King Kamehameha's Kona Beach Hotel in the Kona Square Shopping Center. Dave rents mountain bikes, hybrids, full-suspension bikes, and a few road bikes from $15 a day to $60 a week. Prices include helmet, water bottles, map, bicycle lock, and, most importantly, road advice. Dave knows his stuff, so pay heed! If you want to do more than just pedal along the beach, come see Dave.

Hawaiian Pedals, at the Kona Inn Shopping Village, 808/329-2294, rents basic mountain bikes and hybrids. A sister store, the **Bike Works,** 808/326-2453, 74-5599 Lehua St., Ste. F-3, up in the industrial area, rents suspension mountain bikes and road bikes. Rates for 24 hours are $20 for mountain and hybrids, $25 for road and front-suspension bikes, and $30 for full-suspension mountain bikes. Five-hour and multi-day rates can also be arranged. Hawaiian Pedals is open daily; the Bike Works is closed on Sunday, so if you rent a bike there on Saturday you must rent it for two days.

Boats anchored in Kailua Bay take guests for ocean recreation.

ROBERT NILSEN

B&L Bike and Sports, 808/329-3309, offers bike sales, repair, and as many rental bikes as any other shop in town. Located just across the street from Hilo Hattie's, B&L rents road and mountain bikes for $30 a day or $150 a week.

Submarine Tour

One company in Kailua offers a once-in-a-lifetime, below-the-surface-of-the-water experience to view undersea life at the fish eye level. **Atlantis Submarine,** 808/329-6626, 800/548-6262, allows everyone to live out the fantasy of Captain Nemo on a silent cruise under the waves. This underwater dive lasts about a half hour and descends to 120 feet, where everything seems to turn to blues and greens. You cruise in air-conditioned comfort and have great viewing out the two-foot-diameter windows. Cruises run four times a day 8:30 A.M.–1:30 P.M.; the price is $84 adults and $42 children. Find the office across the street from the pier.

Sunset Dinner Cruise

Captain Beans' Polynesian Cruise departs Kailua Pier daily at 5:15 P.M. and returns at about 8 P.M. If you are after a pleasant but not adventurous sunset cruise, take this one, but keep in mind that this is the bus tour equivalent of a boat ride. On board, you are entertained while the bar dispenses liberal drinks and the deck groans with an all-you-can-eat buffet. The best part—after the sunset—is that you get a terrific panorama of the Kona Coast from the sea. You can't help having a good time on this cruise, and if the boat sinks with all that food and booze in your belly, you're a goner—but what a way to go! Minimum age is 21 years, $52 includes tax, tip, and transportation from area hotels. Reservations suggested; call 808/329-2955.

Tennis

The Royal Kona Resort has four latexite courts, three of which are lighted for night play, that are open to resort guests and nonguests alike. Court fees are a reasonable $10 per day. Avid tennis players should check the weekly rates. Instruction can be arranged and racquets rented for $3–8.

Call the pro shop at 808/334-1093 to reserve court time, particularly for night play.

Island Slice Tennis, 808/322-6112, at the Keauhou Beach Hotel, offers reserved tennis play on six lighted courts for $5 for the first hour and $10 after that. Round robins are held at various times throughout the week and instruction runs $40 an hour.

Golf

The **Kona Country Club** is a lovely golf course near the end of Ali'i Drive that has 18-hole ocean and mountain courses, with grand views over this eminently rocky coast. Greens fees run $95 for the mountains course and $115 for the ocean course, $75 and $85, respectively, after noon. The pro shop is open daily and the adjacent Vista Restaurant at the clubhouse serves breakfast and lunch. Call 808/322-2595 for tee times.

If the local golf courses are just too expensive or if you're just not sure enough about your game, spend some time first at the **Swing Zone** miniature golf course and practice at the Menehune Country Club 18-hole grass putting course that's shaped like the Big Island itself. One round runs $6 and includes a putter and balls, no players under age 12; golf rules apply. This course has no lights so it's daytime play only. Also at the Swing Zone is a full-size driving range that's lit at night; a pail of 60 balls costs $6. If these two aren't enough to wear you out, try the batting cage, also lit, where $1 buys 10 pitches. Open daily until 9 P.M., the Swing Zone is located across the street from the Old Airport Beach Park; 808/329-6909.

SHOPPING

The Kailua-Kona area has an abundance of two commodities near and dear to a tourist's heart: sunshine and shopping malls. Below is a selection of Kona-area shopping centers and malls, including a general idea of what they contain.

Shopping Along Ali'i Drive

King Kamehameha's Kona Beach Hotel Mall, fully air-conditioned, features a cluster of specialty shops which include an ABC Store, selling wine, liquor, and beer along with suntan lotions, gift items, magazines, novels, and T-shirts; Jewel Palace, sparkling with watches and fine jewelry fashioned from gold and silver; Silver Reef, featuring Hawaiian-motif jewelry, glassware, Japanese dolls, and porcelainware; and a host of other gift, craft, and apparel shops. The most intriguing of the bunch is the Made on the Big Island store, with its large sampling of local crafts and gifts.

Kitty-corner to King Kamehameha's Hotel is the **Kona Seaside Mall,** where most shops open daily 9 A.M.–6 P.M. Here you'll find Neptune's Garden, creating rainbows with its display of stained glass art fashioned into lamps, creative hangings, and vases, plus a few paintings. For clothing, try Tropical Tees for casual wear, Sandal Stop, Eel Skin Liquidators, and Bubi's Sportswear Center of Kona. Other shops are the Kona Coast Sunglass Company, Goldfish Jewelry, and DJ's Rentals for motorcycles and scooters.

The **Kona Square Shopping Center,** next to the Seaside Mall, features Mermaid's By The Sea, a distinctive ladies' and children's clothing boutique bright with alohawear, pareu, sundresses and evening dresses, and a ceiling hung with cherubic angels if you're not sharing your Hawaii vacation with one of your own. Directly across from Mermaid's is Island Silversmiths, Kona's oldest modern-day shop, in business since 1973, so you know it's doing something right. This tiny mall also has Dave's Bike and Triathlon Shop, UFO Parasail, and Maui Divers Jewelry.

Just down the way, the **Kona Banyan Court** has a dozen shops with a medley of goods and services. Unison is a surfing shop with T-shirts, sandals, hats, and boogie boards. The most impressive shop in the complex is Big Island Jewelers, owned and operated by brothers Flint and Gale Carpenter, master goldsmiths. The shop motto, "Have your jewelry made by a Carpenter," applies to custom-made jewelry fashioned to their or your personal design. Big Island Jewelers, in business since 1983 and open daily, does repairs and also carries a full line of pearls and loose stones that you can have mounted into any setting you wish. Cafe Sibu is located in the rear.

Kitty-corner from Hulihe'e Palace is **Kona Marketplace,** which offers a variety of shops in several adjacent buildings selling everything from diamonds to bathing suits. The restaurant Poncho and Lefty's has a prominent spot on the 2nd floor of one of the buildings. Here too is Kona Jewelers, specializing in fine jewelry and ceramics; Serendipity for fashions; the jam-packed Aloha From Kona specializes in baubles, bangles, postcards, handbags, and purses; and the Kona Flea Market stuck to the rear of the mall sells inexpensive travel bags, shells, beach mats, suntan lotion, and all the junk that you could want. For art, look at Kim Taylor Reece Gallery, Rapozo Gallery, or Aloha Art. Sandwich Isle Divers can set you up for a dive along this exciting coast. In the alley behind Poncho and Lefty's is the Middle Earth Bookshoppe, one of the best on the island.

One of the largest malls in Kailua is the **Kona Inn Shopping Village.** It spreads south from Hulihe'e Palace in a long meandering series of buildings, taking the place of what was the old Kona Inn Hotel. This shopping village boasts more than 40 shops selling fabrics, fashions, art, gems and jewelry, food, bicycles, souvenirs, and gifts. One shop in this mall is Hula Heaven, which specializes in vintage Hawaiian shirts and modern reproductions, plus some Hawaiiana collectibles. Prices for these fashionable shirts range from $50 for the "look-alikes" to $1,000 for the rarest of the classics. Because many of the items on display date from the 1940s and 1950s, the shop is like a trip back in time. Other stores include Kona Jewelry Factory, featuring island-inspired jewelry; Pacific Fine Art has an array of paintings and graphics from around the country; Surf N' Sandals for an amazing collection of coverings for your feet and head; Fare Tahiti Fabrics for incidental travel bags, pareu, and fabrics; Island Salsa featuring one-of-a-kind designer T-shirts, alohawear for the entire family, ladies' evening wear, swimwear, and dinner clothes; Golden Orchid Originals, a women's resort wear and casual wear shop; Kona Inn Jewelry, for worldwide treasures—one of the oldest and best-known shops for a square deal in Kona; Flamingo's for contemporary island clothing and evening wear mainly for women, Honolua Surf Co. and Sgt. Leisure for tropical wear, and an ABC Store for sundries.

Waterfront Row is a shopping and food complex in the center of downtown Kailua-Kona. Built of rough-cut lumber, it's done in period architecture reminiscent of an outdoor promenade in a Boston shipyard at the turn of the 20th century. Here, Crazy Shirts sells unique island creations that are wearable memories of your trip to the island, Bad Ass Coffee Company dispenses black brew by the cup or by the pound, and Wyland Galleries of Hawaii displays island-inspired paintings and sculpture. Restaurants include Beachcomber's for steaks and seafood and Michaelangelo's for fine Italian cuisine.

The smaller **Ali'i Sunset Plaza** has Japanese and Thai restaurants, the Lava Java coffee shop, and other shops that include the Kipuka Smoke Shop for cigars and accessories, Mana Beads and Jewelry, and Kilauea Clothing Company for vintage prints and alohawear.

Newest to the Kailua strip, located just down from the Royal Kona Resort, is **Coconut Grove Marketplace.** This shopping plaza, with its sand volleyball court, has about a dozen shops that include Rift Zone Gallery for a great collection of artwork. You can find coverings for your eyes at Sunglass Hut, fine clothing and alohawear at Malia Kane and Tropics, jewelry from Pia Moana Pearls, and Jack's Diving Locker can set you up on a scuba tour. Hungry? You'll find Hard Rock Cafe, Lulu's Restaurant, Durty Jack's, and Outback Steakhouse here.

Shopping Along Palani Road

There are several malls on both sides of Palani Road, which heads away from the water, starting at the King Kamehameha Hotel. They include the following.

Backing up against King Kamehameha's Kona Beach Hotel is the small **King Kamehameha Mall,** where you will find, among other shops, the Kona Wine Market, with the town's largest selection of wines, Bangkok House Restaurant, and a couple of small shops for flowers, lei, and gift baskets.

Up from the King Kamehameha Mall is the **North Kona Shopping Center,** where Video Showplace, Body Glove cruises, Zac's Business Center, Kona Brewing Company and Brewpub, and Hele Mai laundry are located.

In the **Kona Sports Center** is B&L Bike and Sports shop. The official Ironman store, it has one of the largest selections of sporting equipment in town. Across the road is the Kona location of **Hilo Hattie's,** 808/329-7200, open 9:30 A.M.–5:30 P.M., where you can find family fashions, gifts, souvenirs, music, and packaged island foods. Hilo Hattie's offers free transportation to and from hotels in the area. Just around the corner is the **Kopiko Plaza,** a small mall with a smattering of inexpensive restaurants.

The **Lanihau Center,** along Palani Road between Kuakini Hwy. and Queen Ka'ahumanu Hwy., offers Longs Drugs for sundries and photo supplies; an assortment of restaurants including Buns in the Sun, Chili by Max, and Royal Jade Garden. Here as well are a Sack 'n Save supermarket, three banks, and the Kailua-Kona post office.

Across Palani Road, **Kona Coast Shopping Center** features a KTA Super Store for groceries and sundries, Starbucks Coffee, a couple of inexpensive eateries, a handful of fashion shops, and a Blockbuster Video where you can rent a movie for the evening. Blockbuster is open 10 A.M.–midnight weekend, until 11 P.M. on weekdays.

Along Queen Ka'ahumanu Highway

At the corner of Queen Ka'ahumanu Hwy. and Henry Street is the new **Crossroads Center.** The two big stores here are Wal-Mart and Safeway, but other places of note are the fine restaurant Oodles of Noodles, Kona Natural Foods, and a Bank of Hawaii branch office. Across Henry Street in its own building is a huge Borders Books and Music store for the town's largest selection of books, CDs, and maps.

The new **Makalapua Center** above the old Kona Industrial Area has a huge Kmart which is open 6 A.M.–midnight daily for all general shopping needs, including clothing, household goods, and camping and athletic supplies. Macy's also has a big store here for family fashions, and the multiplex **Makalapua 7 Cinemas** has a screen to explore your every fantasy.

For those with a membership, Costco is located at the back of the Kaloko Industrial Park, north of Kailua-Kona on the way to the airport.

Keauhou Shopping Center

If, god forbid, you haven't found what you need in Kailua, or if you suddenly need a "shopping fix," the Keauhou Shopping Center is at the corner of Ali'i Drive and Kamehameha III Road in Keauhou. Look for flags waving in the breeze high on the hill marking the entrance. This mall houses over 40 shops and is one of the newest in the area. You can find all your food and prescription needs at KTA Super Store, the largest in the area, and mail your postcards at a branch post office. Head to Longs Drugs for everything from foot care products to photo developing, and Ace Hardware for nuts and bolts. For food, Drysdale's Too is an indoor/outdoor bar and grill where you can relax over a cold beer or choose from an extensive sandwich menu; you could also have a pizza at Rocky's Pizza, a taste of Asia at Royal Thai Cafe, a morning pick-me-up at Daylight Donuts and Deli, or a jolt at Bad Ass Coffee. Other shops include the Showcase Gallery, for glassware, paintings, ceramics, and local crafts; Borderlines and Paradise Found Boutique for apparel; and Alapaki's Hawaiian Gifts for a fine sampling of island gifts and souvenirs from black coral jewelry to koa bowls, and a replica of a Hawaiian double-hulled canoe made of coconut and cloth with traditional crab-claw sails to *tutu* dolls bedecked in colorful mu'umu'u. Alapaki's represents some one hundred artist and craftspeople from all the major islands.

Art and Specialty Shops

The **Palace Gift Shop** is located on the grounds of Hulihe'e Palace. Open daily except Sunday, it has quality Hawaiian craft items nice enough for gifts or memorabilia and a good collection of postcards and books on Hawaiiana.

One of the few art galleries in Kailua is the **Rift Zone Gallery,** 808/331-1100, located in the Coconut Grove Marketplace. This gallery displays the whole spectrum of artwork, almost exclusively from Big Island artists, including ceramics by Robert Joiner, bronze sculpture, paintings, wood art, furniture, and art glass. If you're looking to purchase art made in Hawaii, this is an excellent place to start.

Two other shops to look at for island art are **Wyland Galleries** at Waterfront Row, 808/334-0037, and **Kailua Village Artists Galleries,** 808/329-6653, a co-op gallery of Big Island artists at the Ohana Keauhou Beach Resort.

Hawaii Forest and Trail is a tour company that leads wonderful bird-watching, hiking, and mule ride eco-adventures around the island. It now has a retail store just up from the entrance to Honokohau Harbor that carries a small selection of hiking and outdoor supplies, adventure clothing, first-aid supplies, books, and USGS maps. While you're here, look into the company's tours. They are excellent.

Kailua Candy Company, 808/329-2522, www.kailua-candy.com, is located in the old Kona Industrial area on the corner of Kuakini Hwy. and Kiawi Streets. It was recognized as one of the "top 10 chocolate shops in the United States" in the February 1993 issue of *Bon Appetit* magazine. All the chocolates are made of the finest ingredients available, and all would try the willpower of Gandhi, but the specialty is the macadamia nut *honu,* Hawaiian for turtle. Shipping of all boxed candy is available at the cost of postage plus a handling fee. Open Mon.–Sat. 8 A.M.–6 P.M., until 4 P.M. on Sunday, have a peek through the plate glass windows into the kitchen to watch the work being done on weekdays and nibble samples of the products any day.

The **Banyan Tree Bazaar** (not really the name, but no one has bothered to give it one yet) is along Ali'i Drive across from the seawall. Look for local merchants selling locally made necklaces, earrings, and bracelets. Others sell various artworks, along with an array of inexpensive but neat tourist junk.

Food Markets

KTA Super Stores, open daily 6 A.M.–midnight, are generally the cheapest markets in town and are located at the Kona Coast Shopping Center along

Palani Rd. and at the Keauhou Shopping Center, at the extreme south end of Ali'i Drive at its junction with Kamehameha III Road. They're well stocked with sundries; an excellent selection of Asian foods, fresh veggies, fish, and fruit; and a smattering of health food. The market also contains a full-service pharmacy.

You'll also find a **Sack 'n Save** supermarket in the Lanihau Center, open 5 A.M.–midnight; and a **Safeway** in the newer Crossroads Center up on Henry Street.

Kona Wine Market, in the small King Kamehameha Mall, 75-5626 Kuakini Hwy., 808/329-9400, open Mon.–Sat. 9 A.M.–8 P.M., Sunday 10 A.M.–6 P.M., is the best wine shop on the Kona Coast. It features an impressive international selection of wine and varietals and a large cooler holds a fine selection of beer, both domestic and imported. Store shelves also hold wonderful gourmet munchies like Indian chutney, Sicilian olives, mustards, dressings, marinades, smoked salmon, hearty cheeses, and even pasta imported from Italy. Cigar smokers will also appreciate the humidor filled with fine cigars from around the world.

Kona Reef Liquor and Deli is south of town center at the Casa De Emdeko condominium. It's well stocked with liquor, drink, and packaged groceries, but at convenience-store prices, and the deli does simple food items. Open until 10 P.M., 8 P.M. on Sundays.

Outdoor Markets

You'll find the **Kona Farmers' Market,** held every Wednesday, Friday, Saturday, and Sunday 7 A.M.–3 P.M. at the parking lot across from Hale Halawai County Park and Uncle Billy's Kona Hotel. A great place for locally grown fruits and vegetables, flowers, coffee, and crafts, this market has many booths that sell non-food items.

About two miles south of the pier on the *mauka* side of Ali'i Drive is the outdoor **Ali'i Gardens Marketplace,** open 9 A.M.–5 P.M. Wed.–Sunday. Vendors sell local produce, flowers, crafts, and some clothing and jewelry.

Health Food Stores

Kona keeps you healthy with **Kona Natural Foods** in the Crossroads Shopping Center on Henry Street, 808/329-2296, open Mon.–Sat. 9 A.M.–9 P.M., Sunday until 7 P.M. Besides a good assortment of health foods, there are cosmetics, books, and dietary and athletic supplements. Vegetarians will like the ready-to-eat and inexpensive sandwiches, salads, soups, smoothies, and juices. Shelves are lined with teas, organic vitamins and herbs, and packaged foods. A cooler is filled with organic juices, cheeses, and soy milk. A refrigerator holds organic produce, while bins are filled with bulk grains. Overall a good store, there seems to be a greater emphasis on nutrition than natural organic foods.

A **General Nutrition Center,** located in the Lanihau Center and open daily from 10 A.M., is stocked with vitamins, food supplements, and minerals.

Bookstores

In Kailua-Kona be sure to venture into **Middle Earth Bookshoppe,** 808/329-2123, tucked back in behind Kona Marketplace next to St. Michael's Church along Ali'i Drive. Open Mon.–Sat. 9 A.M.–9 P.M., Sunday to 6 P.M., this jam-packed bookstore has shelves laden with fiction, nonfiction, paperbacks, hardbacks, travel books, Hawaiiana, and lots of good maps. A great place to browse, much more intimate than the big chain stores.

In the North Kona Shopping Center, around back behind Zac's, is **Bargain Books,** 808/326-7790. Open daily, this shop has shelves stacked full of used books at half the cost of new books. If you're looking for a cheap read or just like browsing, have a look here.

The largest bookstore in town, however, is **Borders Books and Music,** 808/331-1668, at the corner of Queen Ka'ahumanu Hwy. and Henry Street. As at all Borders, you have a huge selection of paperbacks and hardcover books in all genres, a great Hawaiiana section, and a wide selection of maps, postcards, magazines, newspapers, and CDs. Special readings and musical events are held throughout the month, and Cafe Espresso is there for you when you get thirsty.

Photo Needs

Zac's Business Center, 808/329-0006, in the North Kona Shopping Center, is open

Mon.–Fri. 8 A.M.–7 P.M., Saturday 9 A.M.–6 P.M., and Sunday 10 A.M.–4 P.M. Although Zac's offers excellent photo lab services and sells a variety of film, this is much more than a photo store. Other services available are copies, fax, wrapping and shipping, printing, computer rental, and Internet connection.

Longs Drugs' photo departments at both the Lanihau Center and Keauhou Shopping Center have excellent prices on film and camera supplies. Both **Kmart** and **Wal-Mart** have one-hour photo finishing departments.

Located above the Kona Divers shop on Palani Road, **Hawaiian Camera Supply,** 808/326-7355, offers sales, service, and repair of cameras and sells a limited selection of film.

SERVICES AND INFORMATION
Emergencies and Health
The **Kona Community Hospital,** 808/322-9311, is located in Kealakekua, about 10 miles south of central Kailua-Kona with 24-hour emergency care.

For minor emergencies and urgent care, try **Hualalai Urgent Care,** at the Crossroads Medical Center on Henry Street, 808/327-4357; or **Kaiser Permanente,** 75-184 Hualalai Rd., 808/334-4400.

Longs Drugs in Kailua and Keauhou, **KTA Super Stores** in Keauhou, and **Kmart** at the Makalapua Center all have pharmacies.

Information
Numerous activity information gazebos are located at the various malls in town, usually open until early evening, that can handle your questions about everything from dining to diving.

The **Kailua-Kona Public Library,** 808/327-4327, is at 75-140 Hualalai Rd., up from Hale Halawai Park. Open Tues. 10 A.M.–8 P.M., Wed. and Thurs. 9 A.M.–6 P.M., Fri. 11 A.M.–5 P.M., and Sat. 9 A.M.–5 P.M.; closed Sunday and Monday.

Services
The First Hawaiian Bank, Bank of Hawaii, and the American Savings Bank all have branches

and ATM machines at or next to the Lanihau Center on Palani Road. Bank of Hawaii also maintains ATM machines at KTA Super Stores and the Safeway supermarket.

The Kailua-Kona **post office** is at 74-5577 Palani Rd., at the Lanihau Center.

Zac's Business Center, 808/329-0006, is a full-service business, computer, shipping, printing, and photo developing shop at the North Kona Shopping Center. Internet access runs $8 an hour or $2.75 for 15 minutes.

Mailboxes, The Business Center, 808/329-0038, in the Crossroads Shopping Center also does packing, shipping, copies, and offers Internet access.

There are other Internet cafés in town, such as Lava Java, which generally charge $2–3 for 15 minutes or $7–8 an hour.

For a self-serve Laundromat, try **Hele Mai Laundromat** at the rear of the North Kona Shopping Center, open 6 A.M.–8:45 P.M.; **Tyke's Laundromat** at 74-5483 Kiawe St. in the old Kona Industrial Area, open 6:30 A.M.–9:30 P.M. daily; or the **Kona Wash Tub** along Alapa Street, which is open daily 8 A.M.–8 P.M. All have drop-off service.

TRANSPORTATION
If you want to concentrate on the scenery and not the driving, take the **Ali'i Shuttle,** 808/775-7121. Painted white, the bus runs daily every 90 minutes (more or less) along Ali'i Drive 8:40 A.M.–7:40 P.M. and charges $2 each direction ($5 for a day pass, $20 weekly). The terminal points are Lanihau Shopping Center on the north end and Keauhou Shopping Center on the south end, with pickups at major hotels and beaches along the way. You can hail the bus and it will stop if possible.

Taxis will also do the trick for getting around town but can be quite expensive when going long distances. An alternative that works particularly well with groups is **Speedy Shuttle,** 808/329-5433, operating 7 A.M.–10 P.M. daily. Speedy Shuttle mainly services Kailua, Keauhou, and Kohala resort areas but will go farther for a price. It has a courtesy phone at the airport for your convenience in getting into town. Rates for single travelers from the airport to downtown Kailua run about $17 or $24 as far south as the Keauhou Beach Hotel. Going north, rates are about $30 to the Waikoloa Beach Resort or $38 to the Mauna Lani Resort area. Rates for groups are higher but the price per person drops dramatically.

Holualoa

Holualoa (The Sledding Course) is an undisturbed mountain community perched high above the Kailua-Kona Coast with many of the island's most famous artists creating art in galleries that line up paintbrush to easel along its vintage main street. Prior to its transformation to an art community, Holualoa had another history. In days past, general stores, hotels, restaurants, bars, and pool halls lined its streets. Before Hawaii found its potential for tourism and started to develop its coastal areas, rural Hawaii was primarily agricultural, and the farms, and consequently most of the people, were located on the mountainsides. Large agricultural areas sustained working communities, and Holualoa was one such population center. While agriculture is still a big part of the local economy, it has been bolstered by tourism and the arts. Get there by taking the spur Rte. 182, known as **Hualalai Road,** off Rte. 11 (Queen Ka'ahumanu Hwy.) from Kailua-Kona, or by taking Rte. 180 (Mamalahoa Hwy.) from Honalo in the south or from Palani Junction in the north (where Rte. 190 and Rte. 180 meet). Nine-mile-long Rte. 180, a narrow mountain road that parallels Rte. 11, gives you an expansive view of the coastline below. Climbing Hualalai Road also affords glorious views of the coast. Notice the immediate contrast of the lush foliage against the scant vegetation of the lowland area. On the mountainside, bathed in tropical mists, are tall forest trees interspersed with banana, papaya, and mango trees. Flowering trees pulsating in the green canopy explode in vibrant reds, yellows, oranges, and purples. This is coffee country, so you'll see acres of coffee trees at numerous plantations and several coffee stands along Rte. 180, with more along Rte. 11 farther to the south. If you want to get away from the Kona heat and dryness, head up to the well-watered coolness of Holualoa at 1,400 feet in elevation. When leaving Holualoa for points south, stay on Rte. 180, the Mamalahoa Hwy., a gorgeous road with great views from the heights. Going north, take Rte. 180 until it meets Rte. 190, which leads around the western flank of Mt. Hualalai and very gradually uphill to Waimea. For the coast, Kaiminani Drive cuts down through the residential area of Kalaoa just north of Kailua-Kona, or, farther north, take Waikoloa Road to the South Kohala coastal region.

For the past one hundred years or so, a string of small dry goods and general merchandise stores dotted what are now Routes 180 and, south of Honalo, 11. Many of these stores were built by new immigrants to cater to the then-growing number of coffee workers and small-time farmers. Along this 20-mile stretch were some 90 stores. Most are now gone, some have been converted to other uses, but a few still function as they always have. Some are still operated by the original family, but most have different names, different owners, or different uses. Some of the best known are Komo Store, Kimura Lauhala Shop, Ushijima Store, Oshima Store, Kamigaki Market, and Fujihara Store. As you drive this road, stop in to get a sense of what these stores were like and consider what impact they had on the economy of the area. To help you along, pick up a copy of the *Guide to Kona Heritage Stores* put out by the Kona Historical Society.

Galleries and Shops

After you wind your way up Hualalai Road through this verdant jungle area, you suddenly enter the village and are greeted by the **Kimura Lauhala Shop,** 808/324-0053, open weekdays 9 A.M.–5 P.M., Saturday until 4 P.M., closed Sunday. The shop, still tended by the Kimura family, has been in existence since 1915. In the beginning,

Kimura's was a general store, but it always sold *lau hala* and became famous for its hats, which local people would make to barter for groceries. Famous on, and later off, the island, only *Konaside* hats have a distinctive pull-string that makes the hat larger or smaller. The older generation Kimuras, and most of the friends who helped manufacture the hats, are getting on in age and can no longer keep up with the demand. Many hatmakers have passed away, and few young people are interested in keeping the art alive. Kimura's still has handmade hats, but the stock is dwindling. All *lau hala* weavings are done in Kona, while some of the other gift items are brought in. Choose from authentic baskets, floor mats, handbags, slippers, and of course an assortment of the classic sun hats. Also for an authentic souvenir, look for a round basket with a strap, the original Kona coffee basket.

After Kimura's follow the road for a minute or so to enter the actual village, where the library, post office, and a cross atop a white steeple welcome you to town. The tiny village, complete with its own elementary school, is well kept, with an obvious double helping of pride put into this artists' community by its citizens. In the center of town is **Paul's Place,** a well-stocked country store, open weekdays 7 A.M.–8 P.M., weekends 8 A.M.–8 P.M.

Along the main road is a converted coffee mill, gaily painted and decorated, and currently the home of the nonprofit **Kona Arts Center,** open Tues.–Sat. 10 A.M.–4 P.M., which began as a labor of love by husband and wife artist team Robert and Carol Rogers. Uncle Bob, as he was affectionately known, passed away, but Aunt Carol is still creating art at the center. Both had an extensive background in art teaching. They moved from San Francisco to Holualoa in 1965 and began offering community workshop classes. Workshops and exhibitions continue, and there is always some class or other going on. Much of the work is displayed in the small gallery at the entrance, where you may find everything from hobby crafts to serious renderings, including paintings, basketry, pottery, sculptures, and even tie-dyed shirts. The center is very friendly and welcomes guests with a cup of Kona coffee. Stop by to view the art or observe a class in progress. For those who desire to put hand to piece, $35 gets you a month's membership, and you can attend workshops any or all days; a different project is done every day. The building is rickety and old, and the floor incredibly uneven, but it's obviously filled with good vibrations and love.

Next to Kona Arts Center is **Cinderella's,** 808/322-2474, an antiques and collectibles shop open Tues.–Sat. noon–5 P.M. Here you find furniture, art, knickknacks, jewelry, and much from estate sales.

At the upper end of town is the **Shelly Maudsley White Gallery,** 808/322-5220, open Monday, Tuesday, Thursday, and Friday, or other days by appointment. The gallery displays the works of accomplished watercolorist Shelly Maudsley White. Tropical flora and fauna is the theme, and the hibiscus, exotic birds, plumeria-scented forests, and hilarious yet pointed marine works confirm her philosophy that "there is more happening on this earth than what meets the eye." Also shown are meticulous and artistic fine woodwork by a local furniture maker.

A premier shop in town, **Studio 7,** 808/324-1335, open Tues.–Sat. 11 A.M.–5 P.M., is owned and operated by Hiroki and Setsuko Morinoue, who both studied at the Kona Art Center. The shop showcases Setsuko and Hiroki's work, along with that of about two dozen other Big Island artists. Hiroki works in many media but primarily does large watercolors or woodblock prints. Setsuko, Hiroki's wife, is a ceramicist and displays her work with about six other potters. Check out the "neoclassical" silk-screen prints, free-form bowls, and wooden bracelets. Strolling from room to room in Studio 7 is like following a magic walkway where the art is displayed simply but elegantly, a legacy of the owners' very Japanese sense of style.

"He's a potter, I'm a painter," is the understatement uttered by Mary Lovein, the female half of the artistic husband and wife team of Mary and Matthew Lovein. They produce and display their lovely and inspired artwork at **Holualoa Gallery,** 808/322-8484, www.lovein.com, open Tues.–Sat. 10 A.M.–5 P.M. Mary uses acrylics and airbrush to create large, bold, and bright seascapes and landscapes of Hawaii. Matthew specializes in *raku:* magnificent works of waist-high vases, classic Japanese-style ceramics glazed in deep rose, iridescent greens, crinkled gray, and deep periwinkle blue. Mary and Matthew collaborate on some of the larger pieces. Matt creates the vessel and, while it is still greenware, Mary paints its underglaze. Other artists featured in the shop are Cecilia Faith Black, who does delicate jewelry; Patricia Van Asperen-Hume, who creates fused glassworks; Frances Dennis, who hand-paints romantic Hawaiian imagery on porcelain, and multi-media artist Charles Corda who creates metal sculpture and acrylic images. Also displayed are works in ceramic, glass, wood, and carved Plexiglas; most of the inspiring works are done in a contemporary or modernist style.

The flora and fauna of Hawaii come alive in **Ululani,** 808/322-7733, www.ululani.com, open Tues.–Sat. 10 A.M.–4 P.M. The bright and airy studio, once the home of "grease monkeys," showcases original paintings, many of the flora, fauna, and scenery of the islands, by the shop's owners. Also displayed is artwork by Herb Kane, world renowned for his dream-reality paintings of Hawaii and its people. Aside from the paintings, you'll find prints, posters, and cards created from original works, T-shirts, pottery, and jewelry.

Nearly across the street is **Hawaii Color Fine Art** gallery, 808/324-1590, which features impressionist paintings mostly by owners Darrell and Pat Hill.

Using Hawaiian woods, David Reisland shows his skill at working and turning wood to create innovative designs. See the result at the **David Reisland Fine Woodworking** gallery, 808/325-6863, on the main street of town.

Holualoa's original post office, toward the south end of the community, houses both **Hale O Kula** goldsmith gallery, 808/324-1688, and **Capell Gallery,** 808/937-8893. Sam, the goldsmith, doesn't need much room, so he has the back. He works mostly in gold, silver, and precious stones; he also creates bronze sculptures and ceramics… very, very small sculptures. Doing mostly commission work, his shop is only open by appointment, but he does display a few other island jewelers' works outside his door. The Capell Gallery up front treats you to original works by the owner—*plein air* oil paintings of tropical scenes, some of contemporary style, and multiple-block, wood block prints.

A side road, easily spotted along Holualoa's main street, leads you up to **Koyasan Daishiji Shingon,** a Japanese Buddhist mission with distinctive red-orange buildings and a stone-lantern lined entrance that was 100 years old in 2002. The mission is basic, simple, and unpretentious, combining Japanese Buddhism with a Hawaiian air. The roof has the distinctive shape of a temple, but unlike those found in Japan, which are fashioned from wood, this is corrugated iron. Getting to the temple takes only a few minutes, and coming back down the road rewards you with an inspiring vista of Kona and the sea.

Note: Keep in mind that it is customary for most of the galleries to be *closed on Monday.*

Coffee Plantation

Holualoa and the mountainside south of here is prime coffee growing area. Literally hundreds of small farms produce beans to be turned into America's most favorite drink. The farms in this region produce about one third of the state's total coffee production, and there are several mills along the strip that process the beans. Everyone knows Kona coffee and those who drink this black brew hold it in high esteem for its fine character. Every year in November, the Kona Coffee Cultural Festival is held to celebrate coffee, the importance this agricultural crop has had on the region for some 175 years, and the people of the area who make it possible.

One mile south of Kimura's is the **Holualoa Kona Coffee Company** plantation and mill, 77-6261 Mamalahoa Hwy., Holualoa, HI 96725, 808/322-9937, 800/334-0348, www.konalea.com. This mill is open to visitors weekdays 7:30 A.M.–4 P.M. for a free tour of the milling and roasting process and coffee tasting. If you haven't ever been introduced to how coffee gets from tree to cup, this would be a good opportunity to discover how it's done. Although a small operation, this mill handles coffee beans from dozens of area farmers. A retail shop on site sells estate coffee; it can also be ordered by mail.

KONA COFFEE

A coffee belt runs like a band through Kona. Generally speaking, it's a swath of mountainside 800–1,400 feet in elevation, about two miles inland from the coast, from one to two miles wide, and perhaps 25 miles long. In this warm upland region, watered by cool morning mists and rains, warmed by the afternoon sun, and cooled by evening breezes, coffee trees have an ideal climate in which to grow. Within this band, about 2,500 acres are planted in coffee, producing about 2.5 million pounds of the beans, which amounts to about one-third of the state's production. Most coffee estates here are small, in the 3–20 acre range, and there are about 600 individual growers. Kona has been known for decades as a region that produces exceptional coffee. Until a few short years ago, it was the only area in the state (and country) that grew coffee. Now, farms on each of the main Hawaiian Islands also produce the bean.

Arabica coffee trees are grown in Kona. Trees will produce beans at a young age and keep producing until at least 80 years old if properly tended. Newly formed, coffee "cherries" are green. Most contain two beans, but a small portion have single, more or less round beans called peaberries. When the cherries ripen they turn red. Kona coffee beans are picked by hand, a tough and tedious job, but one that produces quality fruits. Harvest generally takes place for the five

months from September through January, with the lower elevation fields starting earlier and the higher elevation fields ending later. After picking, the beans are brought to the mill to be processed. The first step is wet milling, where the outer covering is removed and the slimy inner liquid released. The beans are then rinsed and dried to a specific moisture content, and the silver skin-like covering is taken off. Beans are then separated according to their shape and size by a shaker, graded by quality and substance, bagged, and weighed before they are certified for bulk shipping. Roasting is another matter. Most roasting is done either the traditional way in a drum roaster or by a newer hot air method. Various roasts include light, medium, dark, and the result is determined primarily by the temperature while the length of roasting time is less of a factor. After waiting a few hours for carbon dioxide to off-gas, roasted coffee is packaged. Roughly seven pounds of hand picked coffee cherries are required to make one pound of roasted coffee.

About a dozen Kona coffee plantations are open for year-round visitation of their property and mills. A few are listed in the text; others have signs along the road you will see as you drive through this region. To help you on your way, pick up a copy of the *Kona Coffee Country Driving Tour* brochure, put out by the Kona Coffee Cultural Festival.

ROBERT NILSEN

In this upland area, other coffee producers that have retail shops are UCC Hawaii, www.ucc-hawaii.com, Ferrari, and Blue Sky, www.konablueskycoffee.com. The Ferrari shop is located in Holualoa, UCC Hawaii has a stand a couple of miles north of the village, and Blue Sky is situated along Hualalai Rd. just below Mamalahoa Highway. Blue Sky also offers tours of its mill weekdays and Saturdays.

Accommodations

The shocking pink **Kona Hotel,** along Holualoa's main street, 808/324-1155, primarily rents its 11 units to local people who spend the workweek in Kailua-Kona's seaside resorts and then go home on weekends. They are more than happy, however, to rent to any visitor passing through and are a particular favorite with Europeans. The Inaba family opened the hotel in 1926, and it is still owned and operated by Goro Inaba and his wife Yayoko, who will greet you at the front desk upon arrival. A clean room with bare wooden floors, a bed and dresser, no phone or television in the room, and shared baths down the hall goes for $20 single, $26 double, and $30 with twin beds. Call ahead for reservations. No meals are served, but Mrs. Inaba will make coffee in the morning if you wish. The hotel is simple, clean, and safe, and while not stupendous, the view from the back rooms is more than worth the price.

A wooden jewel box nestled in velvet greenery waits to be opened as it rests on the edge of Holualoa high above the wide, rippling, cerulean Pacific. **The Holualoa Inn Bed and Breakfast,** at 76-5932 Mamalahoa Hwy., P.O. Box 222, Holualoa, HI 96725, 808/324-1121 or 800/392-1812, fax 808/322-2472, inn@aloha.net, www.konaweb.com/HINN, was the retirement home of Thurston Twigg-Smith, CEO of the *Honolulu Advertiser* and member of an old *kama'aina* family. Mr. Twigg-Smith built the original home in 1978, but tragically, it burned to the ground. Undaunted, he rebuilt, exactly duplicating the original. After living here a few years Mr. Twigg-Smith decided it was too quiet and peaceful and went back to live in Honolulu. In 1987 it was converted into a B&B. The home

is a marvel of taste and charm—light, airy, and open. Follow the serpentine drive from Holualoa's main road into the midst of vibrant foliage daubed with red hibiscus, manicured thickets of ripening coffee, sun-yellow papaya, and wind-swirled palms. The home at the end of the drive pleasantly shocks the senses. Top to bottom, it is the natural burnished red of cedar and eucalyptus. Here the Hawaiian tradition of removing your shoes upon entering a home is made a pleasure. The eucalyptus floors, softly polished, cool, and smooth, massage your feet; the roof rides above the walls so the air circulates easily. The front lanai is pure relaxation, and stained glass puncturing the walls here and there creates swirls of rainbow light. Throughout the home are original artworks done by the Twigg-Smith family. A pool table holds king's court in the commodious games room, as doors open to a casual yet elegant sitting room where breakfast is served. A back staircase leads to a gazebo, floored with tile and brazenly open to the elements, while the back lanai is encircled by a roof made of copper. From here, Kailua-Kona glows with the imaginative mistiness of an impressionist painting, and, closer by, 40 acres are dotted with coffee trees and cattle raised by the family. Just below is the inn's swimming pool, tiled in blue with a torch ginger motif, and off to the side the hot tub. The six island-theme rooms run $175–225 and all differ in size and decor, discounts for stays longer than seven days, and breakfast is served to all guests. Some years back, Mr. Twigg-Smith was offered $7 million for the home. Much to our benefit, he declined. This is a gem.

Above Kailua on the road to Holualoa, surrounded by lush tropical foliage that permeates the air with a sweet perfume, perches **Hale Maluhia Country Inn Bed and Breakfast,** 76-770 Hualalai Rd., Kailua-Kona, HI 96740, 808/329-1123 or 800/559-6627, fax 808/326-5487, kona@hawaii-inns.com, www.hawaii-inns.com/hi/kna/hmh, a hideaway lovingly tended by hosts Ken and Sue Smith. Built and furnished in rustic Hawaiian style with a Victorian twist, this Christian B&B offers accommodations in the main house or the separate Banyan Cottage. The interiors of the central house and cottage feature

KONA

open-beamed ceilings, plenty of natural wood trim, koa cabinets, and full kitchens. On the property are an outdoor stone-and-tile Japanese *ofuro* (spa) with massage jets, and a massage table where your cares and aches will float away on the evening breeze. Two relaxing common areas are outfitted with board games, a pool table, a large library, and surround sound color TV/VCR (with a large video library), while five lanai present the natural drama of a Michelangelo sunset nightly; all are wheelchair friendly. Ken spoils you every morning with a sumptuous home-cooked breakfast buffet laden with tropical fruits and juices, fresh bread and pastries, savory breakfast meats, herbal teas, and robust Kona coffee. All rooms are decorated with Hawaiian and provincial antique furniture and feature private baths. Rates are $90–125 for a guest room in the main house, and $150 for

the Banyan Cottage; discounts are offered for longer stays. Hale Maluhia (House of Peace) is all that its name implies.

Food

The enticing aroma of rich coffee has been wafting on the breeze in this mountain community ever since the **Holuakoa Cafe** opened its doors in 1992. Just up the hill from the Kona Hotel, the cafe, 808/322-2233, open Mon.–Fri. 6:30 A.M.–3 P.M., and weekends 8 A.M.–3 P.M., serves wonderful coffee, juices, and herbal teas, salads, sandwiches, and smoothies. The cafe also serves as a revolving art gallery for local artists and displays a few boutique, souvenir, and craft items. You can sit inside at a table or enjoy your coffee and pastry alfresco on the veranda, from where the two-block metropolis of Holualoa sprawls at your feet.

South Kona

Kailua-Kona's Ali'i Drive eventually dead-ends in Keauhou. Before it does, King Kamehameha III Road turns up the mountainside and joins Rte. 11, which in its central section is called the Kuakini Highway. This road, heading south, quickly passes the towns of **Honalo, Kainaliu, Kealakekua, and Captain Cook,** and farther on whisks through the smaller communities of **Honaunau, Keokea,** and **Kealia.** These mountainside communities lie along a 10-mile strip of Rte. 11, and if it weren't for the road signs, it would be difficult for the itinerant traveler to know where one village ends and the next begins. You'll have ample opportunity to stop along the way for gas, food, or sightseeing. These towns have some terrific restaurants, fine bed-and-breakfast accommodations, specialty shops, and unique boutiques. If you are up for some off-the-beaten-track sightseeing, you won't be disappointed. At Captain Cook, you can dip down to the coast and visit Kealakekua Bay, or continue south to **Pu'uhonua O Honaunau,** a reconstructed temple of refuge, the best in the state. Farther south still, little-traveled side roads take you to the sleepy seaside villages of

Ho'okena and **Miloli'i,** where an older, slower lifestyle is still the norm.

HONALO AND KAINALIU

This dot on the map is at the junction of Routes 11 and 180. Not much changes here, and the town is primarily known for the red and white **Dai Fukuji Soto Buddhist Mission** temple at the beginning of town. This temple is open during the day for those who care for a look. Inside are two ornate altars; feel free to take photos but please remember to remove your shoes. A short distance down a side road is the older **St. Paul's Catholic Church** (1864). Also up the way, and again on the ocean side of the highway, is **Lanakila Congregational Church,** erected in 1867.

Kainaliu is larger and more of a town, with a choice of shopping, restaurants, and a theater. It's just a mile or less up the road from Honalo, and it seems as if these two communities mesh into one.

Food

Teshima's Restaurant in Honalo is open daily 6:30 A.M.–1:45 P.M. and 5–9 P.M. Here, in un-

Dai Fukuji Soto Buddhist Mission in Honalo

pretentious surroundings, you can enjoy a full American, Hawaiian, or Japanese lunch for about $7 and dinner for $10–15. A lunch specialty is the bento box lunch for $6.75 that includes rice balls, luncheon meat, fried fish, teriyaki beef, kamaboku (fish cake), and Japanese roll. Evening meals include fresh catch, tempura, donburi, udon noodles, and a teishoku full meal. Since 1940, Teshima's has been a mom-and-pop (and kids) family restaurant. If you're interested in a good square meal, you can't go wrong here.

Aloha Angel Café, 808/322-3383, open daily 8 A.M.–3 P.M. for breakfast and lunch, is part of the lobby of the Aloha Theater in Kainaliu. The enormous yet economical breakfasts feature locally grown eggs, homemade muffins, and potatoes. Lunchtime sandwiches, around $8, are super-stuffed with varied morsels, from tofu and avocado to turkey breast. There are also a variety of soups, salads, and wraps. For a snack choose from an assortment of homemade baked goods that you can enjoy with an espresso or cappuccino. Order at the counter and then sit on the lanai that overlooks a bucolic scene. There is table service for dinner, served 5–9 P.M. daily inside the newer dining room to the side. The dinner menu changes periodically, but may include items like taro-crusted fresh *ahi,* Cajun spice chicken, filet mignon, and scampi with basil pesto, all of which run $14–22. This is an excellent place for food any time of the day.

At the south end of town, in the Mango Court, is **Evie's Natural Foods,** 808/322-0739, open weekdays 8 A.M.–7 P.M., weekends 9 A.M.–5 P.M. This full-range health food store serves freshly made, organic and wholesome sandwiches, soups, and other delicious foods at its deli. It also has "grab 'n go" items in a cooler. Evie's stocks plenty of coffee, herbs, vitamins and minerals, some fresh produce, packaged natural foods, and an assortment of bulk grains.

The **Standard Bakery** in town has breads, baked goods and wonderful hot *malasadas* to take for the road.

Entertainment

The **Aloha Theater** in Kainaliu hosts productions of the semi-professional local repertory company, Kona Association of the Performing Arts, which puts on about six plays per year that run for about three weeks each. Check the local newspaper, HVB office, or look for posters here and there around town. The theater periodically hosts other types of stage performances, live music, dance, and art films and is a venue for the Hawaii International Film Festival in November. Show times and ticket prices differ for all performances in this completely refurbished and well-appointed theater (built 1929–32), so call the box office for details at 808/322-2323.

Shopping

There is not much in the way of shopping in Honalu except for a gas station and kayak rental shop. You'll have much better luck in Kainaliu.

The **Blue Ginger Gallery,** 808/322-3898, open Mon.–Sat. 9 A.M.–5 P.M., showcases the art of owners Jill and David Bever, as well as over 100 artists' works from all over the island. David creates art pieces in stained glass, fused glass, and wood. Jill paints on silk, creating fantasy works in strong primary colors. Using her creations as base art, she then designs one-of-a-kind clothing items that can be worn as living art pieces. The small but well-appointed shop brims with paintings, ceramics, sculptures, woodwork, fiber art, and jewelry. As a compliment to the local artwork, about one half the gallery holds imported Asian art and craft items, including Polynesian masks, carved elephants, Buddha heads, and batiks from Indonesia. The Blue Ginger Gallery is a perfect place to find a memorable souvenir of Hawaii.

A wonderful assemblage of paintings, line drawings, and other forms of art are on display at **Lavender Moon Gallery,** 808/324-7708. Along with the works of owners Patricia and Dux Missler, you'll find the captivating pencil sketches of Kathy Long, the contemporary paintings of Megan Long, her daughter, and the renderings of Hawaiian children by Mary Koski, her mother.

In the Basque Building across from Kimura's are the Eternal Wave and Capstone galleries. The **Eternal Wave Gallery,** 808/322-3203, displays pottery, prints, candles, woodwork, and more by mostly local artists. An intriguing col-

lection, it has perhaps more common quality pieces than the works in other galleries in town. Next door is **Capstone Gallery,** 808/322-3377, which displays local and mainland painters of a contemporary style, including those of owner Eric Tore.

Paradise Found, 808/332-2111, has "clothing for the adventurous." This shop is an eclectic mix of women's and men's clothing, alohawear, accessories, and some furniture and art objects. All are new but some are reproduction pieces of masterful older designs.

For those looking for antiques and collectibles, have a peek at **Creative Costumes,** 808/322-9600, in the Vintage Eye Plaza building. Not only does this shop have clothing and accessories, it handles a wide variety of other old treasures.

Surfin' Ass Coffee Company, 808/324-7733, open daily 7 A.M.–9 P.M., is a coffee and espresso bar where they roast their own beans on the premises in a Royal No. 4 Roaster manufactured in 1910, probably the last operational roaster of its type left in the state. After watching the roasting, take your cup of coffee and a homemade pastry to the rear of the shop, where you'll find an indoor stone grotto area away from the noise of the street. This was the original Bad Ass coffee shop. From here, the revolution spread.

Big Island Crafts & Gifts, 808/322-0642, open daily 10 A.M.–6 P.M., has a very surprising interior, filled as it is with authentic jewelry, shells, and beadwork. Many of the items are purchased from local people and include hula instruments, *lau hala* weavings, Ni'ihau shellwork, Hawaiian fishhook pendants, *kukui* nut lei, and even an assortment of Hawaiian food products like mustard and salad dressings. Hanging on the walls are carvings of tikis, dolphins, turtles, and owls, the *'aumakua* of ancient Hawaii. For the children, there are Hawaiian dolls, and children of all ages will love a replica of a sea-going canoe with the distinctive crab claw sail. For those who can't live without another T-shirt, you'll find them, as well as artificial flower lei. Look for this down-home craft shop across from Surfin' Ass Coffee Company.

Oshima Dry Goods is well stocked with drugs, fishing supplies, magazines, a huge collection of fabric, and some wines and spirits. Also in town is **Kimura Market,** a general grocery store with some sundries, and **H. Kimura Store** for bolts of fabric. Oshima's and H. Kimura's are two of the stores along this road that still function pretty much the same as they have for decades.

As you are leaving the built-up area of Kainaliu, look for the **Island Books** "Used Books Bought and Sold" sign. Open daily 9 A.M.–7 P.M. (usually), this shop stocks a general mix of titles, but history, geography, Hawaiiana, and a good selection of used travel books are the specialty. Here's a great place to purchase some casual reading material and save money at the same time; 808/322-2006.

At the south end of town in the Mango Court is a shop selling hemp products: clothing, oils, and other items. All material is imported due to the U.S. prohibition on the production of hemp fiber. Stop in to have a look at the items for sale and to learn about this, one of mother nature's most versatile and useful natural gifts.

KEALAKEKUA

Kealakekua is one of the old established towns along the road, but it has a newer look with more modern buildings and small subdivisions. In town are a post office and library, a small shopping center, gas station, several eateries, a few gift shops, and an antiques store. Just south of town on the road up to the schools is **Christ Church Episcopal,** established in 1867 as the first Episcopal church in the islands. Newer is the Kona Hongwanji Mission.

As coffee farms do in other areas of Kona, the **Greenwell Farm Coffee Mill** grows and roasts its own estate coffee. Located downhill from the Kona Historical Society Museum, the mill runs tours of its orchard and processing facility Mon.–Sat. 8 A.M.–4 P.M., and its retail stand is only happy to sell half-pound, one-pound, and five-pound packages of its best roast.

Kona Historical Society Museum

The main building of the Kona Historical Society

ROBERT NILSEN

coffee mill and drying shed of the D. Uchida Coffee Farm, a typical small operation from the second quarter of the 20th century

Museum was originally a general store built around 1875 by local landowner and businessman H. N. Greenwell using native stone and lime mortar made from burnt coral. Now on both the Hawaii and National Registers of Historic Places, the building served many uses, including the warehousing and packaging of sweet oranges raised by Greenwell, purported to be the largest, sweetest, and juiciest in the world. The museum, 808/323-3222, open weekdays 9 A.M.–3 P.M. with a $2 donation for admission, is located one-quarter mile south of Kealakekua. The main artifact is the building itself, but inside, you will find a few antiques like a surrey and glassware, and the usual photographic exhibits with themes like coffee growing and ranching—part of the legacy of Kona. The basement of the building houses archives filled with birth and death records of local people, photographs both personal and official, home movies, books, and maps, most of which were donated by the families of Kona. The archives are open to the public by appointment only. To the rear is the Kona Historical Society office.

The **Kona Historical Society,** P.O. Box 398, Captain Cook, HI 96704, www.konahistorical.org, is a non-profit organization whose main purpose is the preservation of Kona's history and the dissemination of historical information. Sometimes the society sponsors lectures and films, which are listed in the local newspapers. They also offer 4WD tours of the Kona area ($55) three times per year, usually in March, July, and November, and a historical boat tour in late January ($20) that takes you from Kailua-Kona south along the coast. There is no fixed schedule, but if you are in the area during those times of year, it would be well worth the trouble to contact the museum to find out if these excellent tours are being offered. A Captain Cook lecture tour at Kealakekua Bay and an archaeological tour of Keauhou can also be arranged by appointment only, with a minimum of three people. However, walking tours of the historical district of Kailua ($15) are regularly scheduled Mon.–Fri. at 9 A.M. and 11 A.M.: 24-hour advance reservation, please. The tours usually last about 1.5

hours at a leisurely pace. Wear a hat and comfortable walking shoes.

Another excellent tour is the walking tour conducted at the historic **D. Uchida Coffee Farm,** now listed on the National Register of Historic Places, but begun by Japanese immigrants in the early years of the 1900s. The Living History Farm guided tour ($15), offered weekdays on the hour from 9 A.M.–1 P.M., takes you to a working farm with original authentic buildings, machinery, and live animals, and explains how the farm and its workers fit into the multiethnic Kona community. With groups of 12 or more, costumed interpreters will perform chores typical of such a farm from that era, so the tour is a representation of what daily life was like when the farm operated from 1925 to 1945. Look for it at mile marker 110. For any of these fine historical society tours, make reservations by calling 808/323-2005.

Although not up and running yet, future plans of the historical society call for the reconstruction of a ranching homestead and the establishment of a living history museum there.

Amy B. H. Greenwell Ethnobotanical Garden

You can not only smell the flowers but feel the history of the region at the Amy B. H. Greenwell Ethnobotanical Garden, along Rte. 11 south of Kealakekua at mile marker 110, 808/323-3318, www.bishopmuseum.org/greenwell. The garden is open Mon.–Fri. 8:30 A.M.–5 P.M., with guided tours on the second Saturday of every month at 10 A.M.; suggested donation, $4. Greenwell died in 1974 and left her lands to the Bishop Museum, which then opened a 12-acre interpretive ethnobotanical garden, planting it with indigenous Hawaiian plants, Polynesian introduced plants, and Hawaiian medicinal plants. At the beginning of the walking path through the lower section of the garden, take a fact sheet that describes the garden, complete with self-guided tour map. Represented here are four zones: coastal, agricultural, lowland dry forest, and upland wet forest. Within these sections are plants typical of the zone. The garden contains remnants of the Kona field system, dating from precontact times when a broad network of stone ridges delineated intensive agriculture fields that were spread over some 30 square miles and sustained a large population.

Food

The **Korner Pocket Bar and Grill,** 808/322-2994, serving lunch and dinner weekdays 11 A.M.–10 P.M., is a family-oriented restaurant and friendly pool bar where you can get excellent food and drink at very reasonable prices. The Korner Pocket sits below the highway in the small shopping center on Haleki'i Street. Grill selections are a poolroom burger, fresh catch, or scrumptious bistro burger of grilled beef on crusty sourdough topped with fresh mushrooms sautéed in wine garlic sauce. Dinners are tempting items like fresh catch for $14, top sirloin for $10, and baby back ribs for $12, its encore entrée. The complete bar is well stocked with wines and spirits, or you can wash down your sandwich with an assortment of draft beers. The Pocket rocks with live music on weekends and hosts a pool tournament on Tuesdays. The Korner Pocket looks as ordinary as a Ford station wagon, both inside and out, but the food is surprisingly good.

At the crest of the hill is the tiny **Kona Mountain Cafe,** 808/323-2700, open daily from 6:30 A.M.. Kona Mountain Cafe is a coffee shop with some tasty and nutritious sandwiches, pastries, and other eats. A full range of drinks, smoothies, ice cream, are also on the menu. A good stop for a longer trip down the highway, there is a fine view off the back lanai, and Internet access for a minimal charge.

Near the south end of town is the **Peacock House** Chinese restaurant, 808/323-2366. Open Mon.–Sat. for lunch and dinner and Sunday for dinner only, this is a reasonably priced local eatery with a typically long list of menu selections. No MSG upon request.

On your way out of town going south, stop by **Chris's Bakery** and pick up a snack for the road. A variety of pastries are available here, but Chris's is best known for *malasadas,* made fresh daily. Don't come by too late, however. While open daily at 6 A.M., they close up shop at 1 P.M.

Shopping

The Grass Shack, a.k.a. The Little Grass Shack, 808/323-2877, open Mon.–Sat. 9 A.M.–5 P.M., sometimes Sunday noon–5 P.M., is an institution in Kealakekua, owned and operated by *kama'aina* Lish Jens. It looks like a tourist trap, but don't let that stop you from going in and finding some authentic souvenirs, most of which come from the area or from Ms. Jens's many years of traveling and collecting. The items *not* from Hawaii are clearly marked with a big sign that says, Sorry These Items Were Not Made In Hawaii. But the price is right. There are plenty of trinkets and souvenir items, as well as a fine assortment of artistic pieces, especially wooden bowls, hula items, exquisite Ni'ihau shellwork, and Hawaiian masks. A shop specialty is items made from curly koa. Each piece is signed with the craftsperson's name and the type of wood used. Others are made from Norfolk pine and *milo.* A showcase holds jewelry and tapa cloth imported from Fiji, and a rack holds tapes of classic Hawaiian musicians from the '40s and '50s. The shop is famous for its distinctive *lau hala* hats, the best hat for the tropics.

The full-service **Kamigaki Market** is open most days 7 A.M.–9 P.M. and from 8:30 A.M. on Sunday.

Horseback Riding

Kings' Trail Rides O'Kona, 808/323-2388, www.konacowboy.com, is located along the highway at mile marker 111. Rides from here go down a jeep and hiking trail to Kealakekua Bay and the Captain Cook monument. With morning departures, the four-hour trip includes two hours of riding followed by snorkeling in the bay and a picnic lunch. The price is $95 per person, limited to six riders. The ride office doubles as a retail shop and is open daily 7:30 A.M.–5 P.M. There you can purchase koa boxes, plantation coffee, Tropical Temptation chocolates like chocolate-covered coffee beans, along with cowboy items like spurs, western belts, and a full assortment of tack.

Kayaking

Just before Kealakekua is **Kona Boys** kayak rental

and tour outfit, 808/328-1234. Rental kayaks run $25 single or $45.50 double and a guided tour of Kealakekua Bay for $125 per person. If you're just after rental snorkel gear, they have it for $5–7.50 a day.

CAPTAIN COOK AND VICINITY

Captain Cook is the last of the big towns along this highway. You can get gas, food, and lodging here, shop for some arts and crafts, and wash your clothes. Captain Cook is the gateway to the sights on the coast. In town is the Greenwell County Park with its numerous athletic fields, and next door is the county administration sub-office. Beyond this, the smaller towns are each but a few houses that create wide spots in the road. If you're in the area in March, have a look at the yearly Kona Stampede Rodeo at the Honaunau Rodeo Grounds, located at the big bend in the road going down to Pu'uhonua O Honaunau, and watch the local cowboys rope steers.

Coffee Mills and Candy Factory

South of Captain Cook, you can't help noticing the trim coffee bushes planted along the hillside. On the highway almost to Honaunau, you find the **Royal Kona Coffee Mill and Museum,** 808/328-2511, www.royalkonacoffee.com, open daily for self-guided tours 8 A.M.–5 P.M. The tantalizing smell of roasting coffee and the lure of a "free cup" are more than enough stimulus to make you stop. Mark Twain did! The museum is small, of the non-touch variety. Mostly they're old black-and-white prints of the way Kona coffee country used to be. Some heavy machinery is displayed. The most interesting item is a homemade husker built from an old automobile. More or less integrated into the museum, is a small gift shop. You can pick up the usual souvenirs, but the real treats are gourmet honeys, jellies, jams, candies, and of course coffee. You can't beat the freshness of getting it right from the source. Refill anyone? Be sure to have a look at the mill while you are here, particularly during coffee processing season. You can witness the entire process from harvest to roast.

Two other coffee farms in the area that also offer tours of their mills are: **Bayview Farm,** a half mile north of St. Benedict's Church along Painted Church Road, 808/328-9658, www .bayviewfarmcoffees.com; and **Kona Pacific Farmers Cooperative,** on the way down to Napo'opo'o, 808/328-2411, www.kpfc.com. Bayview Farm also has an outlet for its coffee, gifts, and craft items up on the Hawaiian Belt Road highway. The Farmers Cooperative has a retail shop that sells local products and a Thursday farmers' market.

Is that sweet tooth of yours starting to crave a little attention? Stop for a visit to the **Kona Coast Macadamia Nut and Candy Factory,** 808/328-8141, near the intersection of the belt road and Middle Ke'ei Road, where you can slack the craving with roasted macadamia nuts, chocolate-covered nuts, and macadamia cookies and candy. For something not so sinful, go for the Kona coffee or other gift items.

Painted Church

Whether going to or coming from Pu'uhonua O Honaunau, make sure to take a short side trip off Rte. 160 to **St. Benedict's Painted Church.** This small house of worship is fronted by latticework, and with its gothic-style belfry looks like a little castle. Inside, a Belgian priest, John Berchman Velghe, took house paint and, with a fair measure of talent and religious fervor, painted biblical scenes on the walls and tropical skies and palm fronds on the ceiling. His masterpiece is a painted illusion behind the altar that gives you the impression of being in the famous Spanish cathedral in Burgos. Father John was pastor here 1899–1904, during which time he did these paintings, similar to others that he did in small churches throughout Polynesia. Before leaving, visit the cemetery to see its petroglyphs and homemade pipe crosses.

Napo'opo'o

In the town of Captain Cook, Napo'opo'o Road branches off Rte. 11 and begins a roller-coaster ride down to the sea, where it ends at Kealakekua Bay. Many counterculture types once took up residence in semi-abandoned "coffee shacks" throughout this hard-pressed economic area, but the cheap, idyllic, and convenience-free life isn't as easy to arrange as it once was. The area is being "rediscovered" and getting more popular. Near the bottom, you pass **Kahikolu Congregational Church** (1852), the burial site of Henry Opukaha'ia, a young native boy taken to New England, where he was educated and converted to Christianity. Through impassioned speeches begging for salvation for his pagan countrymen, he convinced the first Congregationalist missionaries to come to the islands in 1820.

Continue down Napo'opo'o Road to the once-thriving fishing village of Napo'opo'o (The Holes), now just a circle on the map with a few houses fronted by neat gardens. During much of the last century, Napo'opo'o was a thriving community and had an active port where commodities and animals were shipped. Now only remnants of the old pier remain. When Napo'opo'o Road nears the water, turn right for Kealakekua (Pathway of the God) Bay. At the end this short road is the rather ill-kept **Napo'opo'o Beach County Park,** with showers, picnic tables, and restrooms. The beach here is full of cobbles with a little sand strip along the water, but it draws locals and visitors alike who come to sunbathe. Fronting the beach is Hikiau Heiau. Taking a side road around the south side of the bay will bring you to the more secluded white-sand **Manini Beach.**

Just south of Napo'opo'o, down a narrow and very rugged road is the sleepy seaside village of **Ke'ei.** This side trip ends at a canoe launch area and a cozy white-sand beach good in spots for swimming. The wide reef here is a fine snorkeling spot and a favorite of surfers. A channel to an underwater grotto has been sliced through the coral. On the shore are the remains of Kamaiko Heiau, where humans were once sacrificed. In 1782, on the flats beyond this village, the **Battle of Moku'ohai** was fought, the first battle in King Kamehameha I's struggle to consolidate power not only over the island of Hawai'i but eventually all the islands.

Kealakekua Bay

Kealakekua Bay has been known as a safe anchorage since long before the arrival of Captain Cook and still draws boats of all descriptions. The entire bay is a 315-acre **Marine Life Conservation District,** and it lives up to its title by being an excellent scuba and snorkeling site. Organized tours from Kailua-Kona often flood the area with boats and divers in the area just off the Captain Cook monument, but the bay is vast and you can generally find your own secluded spot to enjoy the underwater show. The area between Napo'opo'o and Manini Beach, an area at the southern tip of the bay, is also excellent for coral formations, lava ledges, and fish. If you've just come for a quick dip or to enjoy the sunset, look for beautiful, yellow-tailed tropicbirds that frequent the bay.

Relax a minute and tune in all your sensors because you're in for a treat. The bay is not only a Marine Life Conservation District with top-notch snorkeling, but it drips with history. *Mauka,* at the county park parking lot, is the well-preserved **Hikiau Heiau,** dedicated to the god Lono, who had long been prophesied to return from the heavens to this very bay to usher in a "new order." Perhaps the soothsaying *kahuna* were a bit vague on the points of the new order, but it is undeniable that at this spot of initial contact between Europeans and Hawaiians, great changes occurred that radically altered the course of Hawaiian history.

The *heiau* lies at the base of a steep *pali* that form a well-engineered wall. From the temple priests had a panoramic view of the ocean to mark the approach of Lono's "floating island," heralded by tall white tapa banners. The *heiau* platform was meticulously backfilled with smooth, small stones; a series of stone footings, once the bases of grass and thatch houses used in the religious rites, is still very much intact. The *pali* above the bay is pocked with numerous burial caves that still hold the bones of the ancients.

Captain James Cook, leading his ships *Resolution* and *Discovery* under billowing white sails, entered the bay on the morning of January 17, 1778, during the height of the Makahiki Festival, and the awestruck natives were sure that Lono had returned. Immediately, traditional ways were challenged. Shortly after their arrival, an old crew member, William Watman, died, and Cook was

KONANE

Konane is a traditional board game played by Hawaiians that is similar to checkers. Old boards have been found at various locations around the islands, often close to the water. The "board" is a flat rock with small depressions ground into it. These depressions usually number around 100, but may be as many as 200. Each of the depressions is filed with an alternating white and black stone or shell. Although there are many variations to the game, one is as follows. Each of two players removes one of his stones, creating two blank spots. One of the two players starts by jumping an opponent's stone, capturing it and taking it off the board. Play then moves to the other person, who in turn jumps the opposite color stone, removing it. The game continues like this, each person alternately jumping the opponent's stones, until one player is no longer able to make a jump, which ends the game.

ROBERT NILSEN

konane **board**

invited to bury him and perform a Christian burial atop the *heiau*. This was, of course, the first Christian ceremony in the islands, and a plaque at the *heiau* entrance commemorates the event. On February 4, 1778, a few weeks after open-armed welcome, the goodwill camaraderie that had developed between the English voyagers and their island hosts turned sour, due to terrible cultural misunderstandings. The sad result was the death of Captain Cook. During a final conflict, this magnificent man, who had resolutely sailed and explored the greatest sea on earth, stood helplessly in knee-deep water, unable to swim to rescue boats sent from his waiting ships. Hawaiians, provoked to a furious frenzy because of an unintentional insult, beat, stabbed, and clubbed the great captain and four of his marines to death. A 27-foot obelisk of white marble erected to Cook's memory in 1874 "by some of his fellow countrymen" is at the far northern end of the bay.

The land immediately surrounding the monument is actually under British rule, somewhat like the grounds of a foreign consulate. Once a year, an Australian ship comes to tend it, and sometimes local people are hired to clear the weeds. The monument fence is fashioned from old cannons topped with cannon balls. Here too is a bronze plaque, often awash by the waves, that marks the exact spot where Cook fell. You can see the marble obelisk from the *heiau*, but actually getting to it is tough. Most people kayak across or take a tour boat from up the coast. Expert swimmers have braved the mile swim to the point, but be advised it's through open water. A rugged jeep/foot trail leads down the hill to the monument, but it's poorly marked and starts way back near the town of Captain Cook, almost immediately after Napo'opo'o Road branches off from Rte. 11. Behind the monument are the ruins of the Ka'awaloa village site, some of which can be seen in the trees. Ruins of a lighthouse and a boat launch are nearby.

Pu'uhonua O Honaunau National Historical Park

This historical park, the main attraction in the area, shouldn't be missed. Though it was once known as City of Refuge Park, the official name of Pu'uhonua O Honaunau is coming into more use in keeping with the emergence of Hawaiian heritage. One way to get there is to bounce along the narrow four miles of coastal road from Kealakekua Bay. The other more direct and much better road is Rte. 160, where it branches off Rte. 11 at Keokea around mile marker 104, a short distance south of Honaunau.

The setting of Pu'uhonua O Honaunau couldn't be more idyllic. It's a picture-perfect cove with many paths leading out onto the sea-washed lava flow. The tall royal palms surrounding this compound shimmer like neon against the black lava so prevalent in this part of Kona. Planted for this purpose, these beacons promised safety and salvation to the vanquished, weak, and war-tossed, as well as to the *kapu*-breakers of old Hawaii. If you made it to this "temple of refuge," scurrying frantically ahead of avenging warriors or leaping into the sea to swim the last desperate miles, the attendant *kahuna,* under pain of their own death, had to offer you sanctuary. *Kapu*-breakers were particularly pursued because their misdeeds could anger the always-moody gods, who might send a lava flow or tsunami to punish all. Only the *kahuna* could perform the rituals that would bathe you in the sacred mana and thus absolve you from all wrongdoing. This *pu'uhonua* (temple of refuge) was the largest in all Hawaii, and be it fact or fancy, you can feel its power to this day.

The temple complex sits on a 20-acre finger of lava bordered by the sea on all sides. A massive, 1,000-foot-long mortarless wall, measuring 10 feet high and 17 feet thick, borders the site on the landward side and marks it as a temple of refuge. Archaeological evidence dates use of the temple from the mid-16th century, and some scholars argue that it was a well-known sacred spot as much as 200 years earlier. Actually, three separate *heiau* are within the enclosure. In the mid-16th century, Keawe, a great chief of Kona and the great-grandfather of Kamehameha, ruled here. After his death, his bones were entombed in *Hale O Keawe Heiau* at the end of the great wall, and his mana re-infused the temple with cleansing powers. For 250 years the *ali'i* of Kona continued to be buried here, making the spot more and more powerful. Even the great Queen Ka'ahumanu came here seeking sanctuary. As a 17-year-old bride, she refused to submit to the will of her husband, Kamehameha, and defied him openly, often wantonly giving herself to lesser chiefs. To escape Kamehameha's rampage, she made for the temple. Ka'ahumanu chose a large rock to hide under, and she couldn't be found until her pet dog barked and gave her away. Ka'ahumanu was coaxed out only after a lengthy intercession by Capt. George Vancouver, who had become a friend of the king. The last royal personage buried here was a son of Kamehameha who died in 1818. Soon afterwards, the "old religion" of Hawaii died and the temple grounds were abandoned but not entirely destroyed. The foundations of this largest city of refuge in the Hawaiian Islands were left intact.

On the landward side of the refuge wall was the "palace grounds" where the *ali'i* of Kona lived. Set here and there around the sandy compound are numerous buildings that have been re-created to let you sense what it must have been like when *ali'i* walked here under the palms. The canoe shed, set directly back from the royal canoe landing site on the beach, was exceedingly important to the seagoing Hawaiians, and the temple helped sustain the mores and principles of the highly stratified and regimented society. Several fishponds lie in this compound that raised food for the chiefs, and a *konane* stone set next to the water—*konane* is a game similar to chess—is a modern version of one of the games that the old Hawaiians played. It is easy to envision this spot as one of power and prestige. Feel free to look around, but be respectful and acknowledge that Hawaiians still consider this a sacred spot.

In 1961, the National Park Service opened Pu'uhonua O Honaunau after a complete and faithful restoration was carried out. Careful consultation of old records and vintage sketches from early ships' artists gave the restoration a true sense of authenticity. Local artists used traditional tools and techniques to carve giant 'ohi'a logs into faithful renditions of the temple gods. They now stand again, protecting the *heiau* from evil. All the buildings are painstakingly lashed together in the Hawaiian fashion, but with nylon rope instead of traditional cordage, which would have added the perfect touch.

Stop at the visitor center to pick up a map and brochure for a self-guided tour. Exhibits line a wall, complete with murals done in heroic style. Push a button and the recorded messages give you a brief history of Hawaiian beliefs and the system governing daily life—educate yourself. For additional information, see www.nps.gov/puho. The visitor center, 808/328-2288, is open daily 8 A.M.–4:30 P.M. Entrance to the 180-acre park is $5 per person. The beach park section to the south of the compound is open 6 A.M. to mid-evening. Swimming, sunbathing, and picnicking are allowed there, while snorkeling and kayaking can be done in the bay right in front of the refuge. Kayaks and small boats can be launched from the boat ramp in the village just to the north and adjacent to the refuge.

Every year on the weekend closest to July 1 (the first was held in 1971), the free three-day Pu'uhonua O Honaunau Cultural Festival is held here, featuring traditional Hawaiian arts and crafts, music and dance, canoe rides, and food. Be sure to stop by for a peek into the past if you are in the area during this time.

Hotel

Manago Hotel, P.O. Box 145, Captain Cook, Kona, HI 96704, 808/323-2642, fax 808/323-3451, www.managohotel.com, has been in the Manago family since 1917, and anyone who puts his name on a place and keeps it there that long is doing something right. The Manago Hotel is clean and unpretentious with an old-Hawaii charm. There is nothing fancy going on here, just a decent room for a decent price. The old section of the hotel along the road is clean but a little worse for wear. The rooms are small with wooden floors, double beds, and utilitarian dressers, no fans, and shared bathrooms. Walk through to find a bridgeway into a garden area that's open, bright, and secluded away from the road. The new section features rooms with wall-to-wall carpeting, new furniture, private baths, louvered windows, ceiling fans, and private lanai. The rates are $25 single or $28 double for a room with a shared bath, $42–47 single and $45–50 double in the new section, plus $3 for an extra person. There is also one Japanese room that goes for $61 single or $64 double. Weekly and monthly discounts are available on all rooms. The views of the Kona Coast from the hotel grounds are terrific. Downstairs in the old building, the restaurant serves breakfast, lunch, and dinner every day except Monday.

Bed-and-Breakfasts

Areca Palms Estate Bed and Breakfast, P.O. Box 489, Captain Cook, HI 96704, 808/323-2276 or 800/545-4390, fax 808/323-3749, arecapalms@konabedandbreakfast.com, www.konabedandbreakfast.com, is considered, even by other B&B owners, to be one of the best on the island. Innkeepers Janice and Steve Glass are more than happy to share their home with you. The house itself is sprinkled with antiques and fine furniture. A smooth wood floor and area rugs cover the spacious living and dining rooms under a cathedral ceiling. The house is always perfumed by fresh cut flowers, and Hawaiian music plays in the background to set the mood. Bedspreads are thick, the quilts in floral designs, and carpets cover the bedroom floors. Set in a broad manicured lawn surrounded by tropical flowers and palms, the outdoor hot tub and deck is the premier spot on the property. Rates for the four rooms range $80–125, inclusive of the sumptuous breakfast feast, two nights minimum.

In the quiet of the hills above town along a narrow residential lane is **Cedar House** bed-and-breakfast and coffee farm. Guest rooms at this home of cedar and redwood overlook the farm's coffee trees with views of the ocean in the distance. Two rooms have queen beds and share a bath, two others downstairs are larger with king beds and separate baths. To the side is a detached, remodeled, and brightly painted cottage with two bedrooms and a full kitchen that serves the needs of a small family or for those who desire a bit more privacy. Rates are $70–95 for the rooms, breakfast included, and $110 for the cottage—no breakfast. Your hosts, Diana and Nik Von der Lühe, will gladly show you around the farm and tell you about raising coffee. For reservations, contact them at P.O. Box 823, Captain Cook, HI

96704, tel./fax 808/328-8829, cedrhse@aloha.net, www.cedarhouse-hawaii.com.

Just a few steps from the Royal Kona Coffee Mill is **Affordable Hawaii at Pomaika'i "Lucky" Farm B&B,** 83-5465 Mamalahoa Hwy., Captain Cook, HI 96704, 808/328-2112, 800/325-6427, fax 808/328-2255, nitabnb@kona.net, www.luckyfarm.com. This B&B is part of a working coffee and macadamia nut farm that has views of the coast from the back lanai of the main house. The one rental room in the farmhouse runs $55 a night, has its own bathroom, and lies off the sitting room with its TV and library. This room is a little close to the road and so may be a bit noisy during the day, but it all quiets down at night. The greenhouse, a newer addition down below, runs $65 a couple for each of its two rooms. Both have queen beds, futons for an extra two people, private entrances, and private baths. Then there's the coffee barn. Converted to a bedroom, it's been left with its roughsawn framing and bare walls, but a half-bath has been added inside and a shower set up just outside the door. Renting for $65, it's just right for a romantic honeymoon couple. All guests are served a farm-healthy, homemade breakfast each morning and you can pick fruit from the trees on the property. Pomaika'i Farm offers relaxation, affordability, and great food. For reservations, contact Nita Isherwood, innkeeper.

Also on a working coffee and macadamia nut farm is **Rainbow Plantation B&B,** P.O. Box 122, Captain Cook, HI 96704, 808/323-2393 or 800/494-2829, fax 808/323-9445, sunshine @aloha.net, www.aloha.net/~konabnb, a peaceful country place where chickens, potbellied pigs, and peacocks rule the yard. Each of the rooms in the main house and detached cottages has a private entrance and bathroom. Rooms in the main house run $75-85, while the cottages, one a converted fishing boat, are $85-95. The Kukui Cottage rents for $250 for five nights. Breakfast is served each morning on the lanai, and all may use the "gazebo" kitchen.

Lion's Gate, owned by Diane and Bill Shriner, P.O. Box 761, Honaunau, HI 96726, 808/328-2335 or 800/955-2332, fax 808/328-1123, innkeeper@coffeeofkona.com, www.coffeeofkona.com, offers bed-and-breakfast rooms on a working macadamia nut and Kona coffee farm. Follow the long row of tall palm trees down to the house. Minutes from the Pu'uhonua O Honaunau National Historical Park, Lion's Gate features a queen bed, refrigerator, TV, and microwave in each of the two rooms, great views of the coast from the wraparound deck, a gazebo for relaxing, a hot tub, and, of course, complimentary Kona coffee and macadamia nuts. Either of the rooms can be combined with a third room to create a suite. The rooms run $110, or $165 as a suite.

The Dragonfly Ranch, P.O. Box 675, Honaunau, HI 96762, 808/328-9570 or 800/487-2159, dfly@dragonflyranch.com, www.dragonflyranch.com, owned and operated by Barbara Moore, offers "tropical fantasy lodging" that's set amongst thick vegetation on the way down to Pu'unonua O Honaunau. Rooms are intriguing and range from the Honeymoon Suite featuring a king bed in a lattice room, the airy Lomi lomi and more private Writer's studios, to the smaller Pele and Dolphin rooms. All rooms include a small refrigerator and basic cooking apparatus, indoor bathroom, private outdoor shower, cable TV, stereo, and small library. Rates run $100-200 with substantial discounts for longer stays. This is an open, airy place, where the outside and inside boundaries begin to blur. To some, the touted tropical fantasy may be a "tropical nightmare." The hosts are very friendly and inviting, indeed, but definitely have an alternative, counter-culture, new-age leaning. Free-spirited adventurers will feel comfortable here; others may not. Dragonfly Ranch is one of those places people totally adore or else dash away from. Rainbow streamers and a Buddha in a butterfly banner greet you as you turn in the drive.

In Napo'opo'o there are several options. On the inland side of the road is a house with cottage. The house has three bedrooms and one bath and rents for $630 a week; with one bedroom, the smaller cottage goes for $525 a week. Call 808/328-2151 for information and reservations. Directly on the bay and much larger and newer are two other rental homes. The four-bedroom, three-bath home sleeps up to 10 and runs

$2,650–2,950 a week depending upon the season. A three-bedroom, three-bath house that sleeps up to 12 goes for $2,450–2,750. Not cheap, but the location can't be beat. For information, try 808/247-3637, fax 808/235-2644, hibeach@lava.net, www.hotspots.hawaii.com/beachrent1.html.

The least expensive place to stay in the area is **Pineapple Park,** tel./fax 808/323-2224 or 877/865-2266, ppark@aloha.net, www.pineapple-park.com. This clean and commodious hostel/B&B accommodation is in a converted plantation-era house along the main highway. Upstairs are the B&B rooms. Located around a common area, they run $40–65. Running $20 a bed, the dorm rooms are located in the converted walk-out basement which also has a TV lounge and inexpensive Internet access. All guests share baths, have use of laundry facilities and a large kitchen, and can rent kayaks and snorkel gear for minimal fees.

Food

Try the legendary pork chop dinner served at the **Manago Hotel Restaurant,** 808/323-2642, in downtown Captain Cook. This meal and other offerings on the menu are plain old American food with a strong Hawaiian overlay. Other items are New York steak, the most expensive at $11.50, beef teriyaki, teri chicken, and four or five fish selections. All come with three side dishes and rice. This food won't set your taste buds on fire, but you won't be complaining about being hungry or not having a wholesome meal. The restaurant is open for breakfast 7–9 A.M., lunch 11 A.M.–2 P.M., and dinner 5–7:30 P.M.; closed Monday.

On the highway just as you cruise into town is **Billy Bob's Park 'n Pork** barbecue restaurant, 808/323-3371, where you can order up barbecued ribs, chicken, hot biscuits, coleslaw, and salad. Also available, partner, are prime rib, veggie enchiladas, a mean Caesar salad, hog fries, and chili. Everything on the menu is less than $10, and you can order anything for takeout. Those in the know say it's the best barbecue on the Kona side. Lasso that little missus of yours and come on down any night except Wednesday.

A local stop for a quick meal like a plate lunch or bowl of saimin is **Cap's Drive-In.**

Perhaps the best view down onto the Napo'opo'o/Kealakakua Bay area is from the back lanai of **The Coffee Shack,** 808/328-9555, and aside from its superb view it has delicious treats at a fair price. Open 7 A.M.–5 P.M. daily, the Coffee Shack has a full list of coffee, simple breakfasts, soup, sandwiches, and pizza, but best of all, a wide variety of luscious cakes, pies, pastries, and a host of other sweet treats all made fresh daily here in the kitchen. Eat in or take out.

Looking for authentic Hawaiian food served by delightful people? Try **Super Js** takeout in Honaunau for *lomi lomi* salmon, *laulau,* macaroni salad, *poi,* and a variety of plate lunches that run about $6. Don't go too late, however, as it usually closes around sundown. Closed on Sundays.

People in the know give the **Ke'ei Cafe,** 808/328-8451, rave reviews. But, you'll ask yourself: What's a fine restaurant serving fusion foods doing way out here in the very ordinary and tiny community of Honaunau. Seemingly set on the edge of the world, this little eatery has a wonderful location as the mountainside drops off below it toward Kealakekua Bay and the National Historical Park. Small in size but big in stature, the Ke'ei Cafe has made a name for itself and is very popular. Open 5:15–8 P.M. for dinner only, you'll need to call for reservations. Start with a Greek salad or Brazilian seafood chowder, both $6.95. Entrées run $10–19 and include seafood pasta with heady herbs and spices, roast half chicken in white wine peppercorn gravy, pan-seared rib-eye steak, and fresh catch prepared with red Thai curry, pan seared in lemon caper butter, or sautéed, market price. Follow this with a coconut flan or tropical bread pudding dessert. Yum! While the menu is short, there is a sufficient but limited selection of domestic and imported beers and wines. This will be a memorable meal, and the drive will be worth it. No credit cards.

On the road down to Pu'umonua O Honaunau is **Wakefield Garden and Restaurant.** Open daily 11 A.M.–4 P.M., this is more or less a pie and coffee shop that also sells cold drinks, soups, and sandwiches. In the back is the garden. You can tour for free, however, it may be well-kept or not depending upon how much care has been put into it lately.

Shopping

The **Kealakekua Ranch Center,** in Captain Cook, is a two-story utilitarian mall with a few small shops, an Ace Hardware store, and a Choice Mart supermarket. Choice Mart is the last of the large markets along this road going south, so pick up supplies here. Open 7 A.M.–9 P.M. Mon.–Sat., until 8 P.M. on Sunday, this full-service grocery store also has a small deli section.

Along the highway as you enter town is **Antiques and Orchids** collectibles shop. With a wide selection of furniture and housewares (many small items too) and an amazing variety of potted orchids, this is a great shop for any discriminating shopper.

A few steps away is **The Rainbow Path,** 808/323-3828, an intriguing shop specializing in books on Hawaii, metaphysics, self-help, personal discovery, and books for children. You can also find tapes and CDs that include Hawaiian chants, Native American Indian music, Celtic music, and music especially composed to induce relaxation and relieve stress. Your body is taken care of with Ayurvedic medicine, incense, beeswax candles, bath and body products, and natural perfumes of island scents. The soul will stir with crystal pendants, pyramids, beaded necklaces, and dream catchers. Several evenings a week, metaphysical readings are given by appointment; see the monthly calendar of events. Check the bulletin board for information about alternative healing and new-age practitioners. All who are on the path will find this shop an oasis.

Virtually the only such shop in town, the **Art Farm** displays all sorts of arts and crafts in various mediums.

Bong Brothers, 84-5227 Mamalahoa Hwy., on the *makai* side of the road near mile marker 106, 808/328-9289, is open Mon.–Fri. 8:30 A.M.–6 P.M., Sunday 10 A.M.–6 P.M. It's housed in a coffee mill complex circa 1920, one of the oldest in Honaunau, and sells not only coffee but organic produce and health food deli items. The shelves hold dried mango, candied ginger, bulk coffee, chocolate-covered coffee beans, Puna honey, dried pineapple, apples, bananas, special sauces, and—no shop is complete without them—T-shirts. Also look for a stack of burlap coffee bags, some bearing the Bong Brothers logo, that make a nifty souvenir. Adjacent is **Gold Mountain Mill,** a functional roasting mill tended by Tom Bong and his dog Bear; if time permits they'll show you around the operation. Coffee from the surrounding area comes in to be roasted in the still functional, vintage 1930s roaster.

Also in Honaunau, **Scotty's** mini-mart has a Korean barbecue take-out window.

At the Rte. 160 turnoff, look for **Merv's** for basic supplies. A short way past is the **Higashi Store,** also for a limited supply of food and snack items. In Kealia, the **Fujihara Store** has a slightly wider selection and is the last chance for packaged food and drinks until you get to Ocean View.

Kayaking

In Captain Cook, **Adventures in Paradise,** 808/323-3005 or 866/824-2337, www.bigislandkayak.com, is the company to see for kayak rentals or tours.

FARTHER SOUTH

Ho'okena

If you want to see how the people of Kona still live, visit Ho'okena. A mile or two south of the Pu'uhonua O Honaunau turnoff, or 20 miles south of Kailua-Kona, take a well-marked spur road *makai* off Rte. 11 and follow it to the sea. The village is somewhat in a state of disrepair, but a number of homey cottages and some semi-permanent tents are used mostly on weekends by local fishermen. Ho'okena also boasts the **Ho'okena Beach County Park** with pavilions, restrooms, and picnic tables, but no potable water. Camping is allowed with a county permit. For drinking water, a tap is attached to the telephone pole near the beginning of your descent down the spur road. The gray-sand beach is broad, long, and probably *the* best in South Kona for both swimming and body surfing. If the sun gets too hot, some palms and other trees lining the beach provide not only shade but a picture-perfect setting. Until the road connecting Kona to Hilo was finally finished in the 1930s, Ho'okena shipped the produce of the surrounding area from its bustling wharf. At one time, Ho'okena was the main port in South Kona and even hosted Robert Louis Stevenson when he passed through the islands in 1889. Part of the wharf still remains, and nearby a fleet of outrigger fishing canoes is pulled up on shore. The surrounding cliffs are honeycombed with burial caves. If you walk a half mile north, you'll find the crumpled walls and steeple of **Maria Lanakila Church,** built in 1860 but leveled in an earthquake in 1950. The church was another "painted church" done by Father John Velghe in the same style as St. Benedict's.

Miloli'i

This active fishing village is approximately 15 miles south of Pu'uhonua O Honaunau. Again, look for signs to a spur road off Rte. 11 heading *makai.* The long and winding road, leading through bleak lava flows, is narrow but worth the detour. Miloli'i (Fine Twist) earned its name from times past when it was famous for producing *'aha,* a sennit made from coconut-husk fibers; and *olona,* a twine made from the *olona* plant and mostly used for fishnets. This is one of the last villages in Hawaii where traditional fishing is the major source of income and where old-timers are heard speaking Hawaiian. Fishermen still use small outrigger canoes, now powered by outboards, to catch *opelu,* a type of mackerel that schools in these waters. The method of catching the *opelu* has remained unchanged for centuries. Boats gather and drop packets of chum made primarily from poi, sweet potatoes, or rice. No meat is used so sharks won't be attracted.

The **Miloli'i Beach County Park** is a favorite

with local people on the weekends; camping is allowed by permit. Tents are pitched in and around the parking lot, just under the ironwoods at road's end. There are flushing toilets, a basketball court, and a brackish pond in which to rinse off, but no drinking water, so bring some. Swimming is safe inside the reef and the tidepools in the area are some of the best on the south coast. A 15-minute trail leads south to the coconut tree–fringed Honomalino Bay, where there's a secluded gray-sand and black-pebble beach great for swimming. But always check with the local people first about conditions! In the village, the small, understocked Miloli'i Grocery Store has little more than drinks and snacks but the price is right for being so far out.

For those looking for peace and quiet, try **Kaimana Guest House and Hostel,** P.O. Box 946, Captain Cook, HI 96704, 808/328-2207, kaimanavacations@msn.com, www.kaimanavacations.com, a two-story oceanside house in Miloli'i that has a kitchen, shared bath, and covered lanai. There's plenty of water equipment to borrow and great free stargazing. Hostel beds run $20, a private single room is $30, and a private double room is $40. A small detached cottage goes for $55 a night. No breakfast is served so if you're not cooking, the closest place for a meal is Ocean View. As remote as it is, you'll definitely need a rental car.

Macadamia Nut Farm

When back on the highway heading south, you'll notice a long stretch of macadamia nut trees on both sides of the road. Now a division of Blue Diamond Growers, Mac Nut Farms of Hawaii is the largest single-owner macadamia nut farm in the state. Unfortunately, the company offers no tours of its facility nor do they have an outlet to sell their products. You'll just have to satisfy yourself with the view of acre after acre of trees and wait until you get to town to make that nutty purchase.

South Kohala

The Kohala district is the peninsular thumb in the northwestern portion of the Big Island. At its tip is Upolu Point, only 40 miles from Maui across the 'Alenuihaha Channel. Kohala was the first section of the Big Island to rise from beneath the sea. The long-extinct volcanoes of the Kohala Mountains running down its spine have been reduced by time and the elements from lofty, ragged peaks to rounded domes of 5,000 feet or so. Kohala is divided into North and South Kohala. South Kohala boasts *the* most beautiful swimming beaches on the Big Island, along with world-class hotels and resorts. Inland is Waimea (Kamuela), the *paniolo* town and center of the massive Parker Ranch. Between the coast and Waimea lies the newer planned community of Waikoloa, with its clusters of condominiums, family homes, and a golf course. North Kohala, an area of dry coastal slopes, former sugar lands, a string of sleepy towns, and deeply incised lush valleys, forms the northernmost tip of the island.

South Kohala is a region of contrast. It's dry, hot, tortured by wind, and scored by countless old lava flows. The predominant land color here is black, and this is counterpointed by scrubby bushes and scraggly trees, a seemingly semi-arid wasteland. This was an area that the ancient Hawaiians seemed to have traveled through to get somewhere else, yet Hawaiians did live here—along the coast—and numerous archaeological sites dot the coastal plain. Still, South Kohala is stunning with its palm-fringed white-sand pockets of beach, luxury resorts, green landscaped golf courses, a proliferation of colorful planted flowers, and its deep blue inviting water. You don't generally travel here to appreciate the stunning landscape, although it too has its attraction, you come here to settle into a sedate resort community, to be pampered and pleased by the finer things that await at luxury resorts that are destinations in and of themselves.

ROBERT NILSEN

Old lava flows cover much of the South Kohala coastline. Kiholo Bay, one of the few exceptions, shows greenery and turquoise lagoons.

The Coast

The shoreline of South Kohala, from 'Anaeho'omalu Bay north to Kawaihae Bay, is rich with some of the finest super-deluxe resorts in the state. This coast's fabulous beaches are known not only for swimming and surfing, but for tidepooling and awe-inspiring sunsets as well. Also, two of the coast's main beaches offer camping and even rental cabins. There are little-disturbed and rarely visited archaeological sites, expressive petroglyph fields, the educational **Pu'ukohola Heiau,** and even a rodeo. No "towns" lie along the coast, in the sense of a laidout community with a main street and attendant businesses and services. The closest facsimile is Kawaihae, with a small cluster of restaurants, shops, a gas station, boat landing, and commercial harbor, but it's just an oversized village. Waikoloa Village, a planned community up above the coast, is a reasonably large town that's been carved from the dry uplands.

As you begin heading north from Kailua-Kona on coastal Rte. 19 (Queen Ka'ahumanu Hwy.), you leave civilization behind. There won't be a house or any structures at all, and you'll understand why they call it the "Big Island." Perhaps to soften the shock of what's ahead, magnificent bushes loaded with pink and purple flowers line the roadway for a while. Notice too that friends and lovers have gathered and placed white coral rocks on the black lava along the road, forming pleasant graffiti messages.

Suddenly you're in the midst of enormous flows of old 'a'a and pahoehoe as you pass through a huge and desolate lava desert. At first it appears ugly and uninviting, but the subtle beauty begins to grow. On clear days you can see Maui floating on the horizon, and *mauka* looms the formidable presence of Mauna Kea streaked by sunlight filtering through its crown of clouds. Along the roadside, wisps of grass have broken through the lava. Their color, a shade of pinkish gold, is quite extraordinary and made more striking juxtaposed with the inky-black lava. Caught by your headlights at night, or especially in the magical light of dusk, the grass wisps come alive, giving the illusion of wild-haired gnomes rising

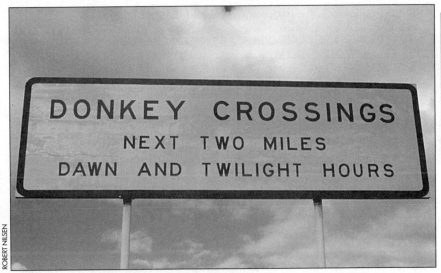

a gentle reminder to be aware of the Kona nightingales

from the earth. In actuality, it's fountain grass imported from Africa. This is also where you might catch a glimpse of the infamous "Kona nightingales," wild jackasses that roam throughout this area and can be road hazards, particularly at dawn and twilight. Watch for "Donkey Crossing" road signs.

Around mile marker 70, the land softens and changes. The lava is older, carpeted in rich green grass appearing as rolling hills of pastureland. These long, flat stretches of road can give you "lead foot." Be careful! The police patrol this strip heavily, using unmarked cars, looking for unsuspecting tourists who have been "road hypnotized." From Kailua-Kona to the Waikoloa Beach Resort is about 25 miles, with another five miles to the Mauna Kea Beach Resort near Kawaihae. If you're day-tripping to the beaches, expect to spend an hour traveling each way.

If you're approaching Kohala from Hilo or the east side of the island, you can take one of two routes. The Saddle Road (Rte. 200) comes directly west from Hilo and passes between Mauna Kea and Mauna Loa. This very scenic road has the alluring distinction of being the least favorite route of the car-rental agencies, which may forbid their cars to travel this route. The Saddle Road intersects Rte. 190, where you can turn north and drive for six miles to Waimea, south for 33 miles to Kailua-Kona, or take the 13-mile shortcut Waikoloa Road to the coast. Route 19, the main artery connecting Hilo with the west coast, changes its "locally known" name quite often, but it's always posted as Rte. 19. Directly north from Hilo as it hugs the Hamakua Coast, it's called the Hawaii Belt Road. When it turns west in Honoka'a, heading for Waimea, it's called the Mamalahoa Highway. From Waimea directly west to Kawaihae on the coast Rte. 19 becomes Kawaihae Road, and when it turns due south along the coast heading for Kailua-Kona, its moniker changes again to Queen Ka'ahumanu Highway.

SIGHTS

The following sights and beaches are listed from south to north. All lie along coastal Rte. 19.

Ka'upulehu Petroglyphs

Located just back from the ponds at the Kona Village Resort is a cluster of approximately 440 lava rock carvings, near where the ancient Kings Highway must have passed. This group of petroglyphs contains designs, many of them different from others along this coast. There are numerous human figures, some with paddles and fishing lines held in their hands, a turtle figure, and dozens that illustrate the lines of crab-claw sails of sailing canoes. While some of these carvings are speculated to be as much as 900 years old, others are obviously newer, as you can discern the date 1820 and some Western script—obviously done after contact with early white sailors. In 1998, the resort constructed a wooden boardwalk around the majority of these carved figures in order to protect the integrity of these fine works of art. Please stay on the wooden pathway during your self-guided tour. As this field lies on Kona Village property, you may need to contact the hotel in order to get permission to enter the property. Tours can be arranged through the concierge desk, 808/325-5555, where printed information and a map of the site are available.

Waikoloa Petroglyphs

Set along a reconstructed section of the King's Trail and surrounded by the Beach Course golf course is the Waikoloa Petroglyph field. Unlike others nearby, this grouping is done in an undulating area and also includes remains of temporary structures. While many and varied designs are seen here, a circular pattern is much in evidence. Cinder rock paths have been constructed throughout this petroglyph field. Stay on the paths; do not walk on the carvings. Approach this area from the King's Shops for a self-guided tour or take one of the free guided tours conducted by the shopping center, Tues.–Fri. at 10:30 A.M. or Saturday at 8:30 A.M. Wear sturdy shoes, a hat, and bring drinking water.

Puako Petroglyphs

These rock carvings, approximately 3,000 individual designs, are considered some of the finest and oldest in Hawaii, but carvings of horses and cattle signify ongoing art that happened long after Westerners appeared. Circles outlined by a series of small holes belonged to families who placed the umbilical cords of their infants into these indentations to tie them to the ʻaina and give them strength for a long and good life. State archaeologists and anthropologists have reported a deterioration of the site due to vandalism, so please look but don't deface, and stay on established paths. Access is by a well-marked, self-guiding trail starting from Holoholokai Beach Park, located on the north side of the Orchid at Mauna Lani Hotel.

Puako

Puako and its environs receive about 10 inches of rain a year, making it one of if not the driest areas of the state. This alluring area is located *makai* on a side road off Rte. 19 about four miles south of Kawaihae. Hawaiians lived here in times past, but a modern community has been building along the three-mile road past Puako Bay since the 1950s. This quiet, no-frills community is a mixture of working class homes, rental properties, and discreet vacation hideaways. Services amount to one reasonably well-stocked general store, a public telephone, and a vacation rental agency. A thin ribbon of white sand runs the length of the beach near the boat ramp that provides fair swimming. Sunsets here are magnificent, and you'll usually have the beach to yourself. The remainder of the shoreline through this community is mostly rock shelf with inlets and tidepools, for good fishing, snorkeling, and some surfing. Near-shore scuba diving is excellent, with huge caverns and caves to explore, and a colorful concentration of coral and marine life. There are half a dozen shoreline access routes along this strip road.

Along Puako Road is **Hokuloa Church,** built by Rev. Lorenzo Lyons in 1859. This musically talented reverend mastered the Hawaiian language and composed lovely ballads such as "Hawaii Aloha," which has become the unofficial anthem of the islands. The church is a thick-walled structure with a plain simple interior. Sunday service is held at 9 A.M.

Between here and Hapuna Beach State Recreation Area just up the coast is **Waialea Bay Ma-**

rine Life Conservation District, a 35-acre preserve. Turn off Puako Road onto Old Puako Road and then turn down a rough road near pole number 69 to reach the shore. The white sand beach here is best in summer. The reef is wonderful for snorkeling, better at its southern end. Although a bit hard to get to, it's a favorite for the local community.

Puʻukohola Heiau

Don't miss this restored Hawaiian temple, a National Historical Site located one mile south of Kawaihae where coastal Rte. 19 turns into Rte. 270 heading into North Kohala. This site, covering 77 acres, includes **Mailekini Heiau** and the **John Young's Homestead** site. Below the *heiau,* in the trees near the sea, Kamehameha I kept a royal household, and a short way offshore in the bay is an older *heiau* dedicated to the shark god. The shark god *heiau* silted over in the 1950s due, at least in part, to construction of the harbor facilities nearby, but to this day an inordinant number of black-tip reef sharks can be spotted near where this site was. Administered by the National Park Service, this sacred ground is open daily 7:30 A.M.–4 P.M.; free admission; website: www.nps.gov/puhe. As you enter, pick up a map highlighting the points of interest. It's worthwhile checking out the visitor center, 808/882-7218, where the rangers provide excellent information and pertinent informative books are available. The one trail through the park leads to its notable sites, and from it, a short section of a coastal trail runs to Spencer Beach County Park nearby. It's hot and dry at this site, so bring water and wear a hat. Puʻukohola (Whale Hill) received its name either because the hill itself resembles a whale, or because migrating whales pass very close offshore every year. It was fated to become a hill of destiny. For the best views of the *heiau,* enter the Kawaihaw Small Boat Harbor and take an immediate left down a crushed coral drive to the flats alongside the bay opposite the park land.

Kamehameha I built Puʻukohola Heiau in 1790–01 on the advice of Kapoukahi, a prophet from Kauaʻi who said that Kamehameha would unify all the islands only after he built a temple to his war-god Kukaʻilimoku. Kamehameha complied, building this last of the great Hawaiian *heiau* from mortarless stone that when finished measured 100 by 224 feet. The dedication ceremony of the *heiau* is fascinating history. Kamehameha's last rival was his cousin, Keoua Kuahuʻula. This warlike chief realized that his *mana* had deserted him and that it was Kamehameha who would rise to be sovereign of all the islands. Kamehameha invited him to the dedication ceremony, but en route Keoua, in preparation for the inevitable outcome, performed a death purification ceremony by circumcising his own penis. When the canoes reached the beach, they were met by a hail of spears and musket balls. Keoua was killed and his body laid on Kukaʻilimoku's altar as a noteworthy sacrifice. Kamehameha became the unopposed sovereign of the Big Island and, within a few years, of all Hawaii.

Every August on the weekend closest to Establishment Day, a free two-day Hawaiian Cultural Festival is held on the *heiau* grounds, including arts and crafts exhibitions, games, hula demonstrations, music and dance, and re-creation of ancient ceremonies in traditional dress.

Near the *heiau,* but on the upland side of the highway, is the house site of John Young, an English seaman who became a close adviser to Kamehameha. Young, dubbed ʻOlohana, "All Hands" by Kamehameha, taught the Hawaiians how to use cannons and muskets and fought alongside Kamehameha in many battles. He turned Mailekini Heiau into a fort, and over a century later the U.S. Army used it as an observation area during World War II. Young became a respected Hawaiian chief and grandfather of Queen Emma. Only he and one other white man have the honor of being buried at the Royal Mausoleum in Nuʻuanu Valley on Oʻahu. Little remains of the house itself, but it was certainly one of, if not the first, Western-style home and the first plastered structures in the islands. Apparently, John Young's wife didn't like the house too much; she had traditional-style structures built to the side for her use.

Puʻukohola Heiau from across the bay

ROBERT NILSEN

SOUTH KOHALA

ROBERT NILSEN

Kuki'o Bay and Beach

BEACHES AND PARKS

There are a number of excellent beaches along this coast, most with good to excellent facilities. In addition, all resorts offer access to their beaches with (limited) public parking.

Kahuwai Bay to Kua Bay

The picturesque Kahuwai Bay has a sandy bottom bounded by rocky shorelines on either side. It is a spot often chosen by green sea turtles to relax on the sand or to lay their eggs. Give them wide berth. Kona Village Resort fronts this bay and creates a fine Polynesian village background. Offshore is a fine reef for snorkeling and scuba. Next door, the Four Seasons Resort sits on a narrow strip of sandy beach and one swimming lagoon. Anchialine ponds here have been set aside as a fish management area. Beyond the Four Seasons is Kuki'o Beach, reachable by public access at the side of the Four Seasons Resort, and farther on is Kua Bay. Walking through hotel property, you can easily go between Kahuwai Beach and Kuki'o Beach.

Kuki'o Beach is bounded by rocky points, the aquamarine water pushes the steep and narrow brown sand beach up the dune, beyond which are more anchialine ponds. At the far end of this beach and tucked into the rocks is a much more protected and much smaller beach, just right for kids. Beyond this is a larger rocky cove. If you're adventurous, follow the very rough path across the a'a cobbles and around the point over broken coral. The path is not distinct and not easy, but once you get a ways around (it may take a half hour) you're rewarded with a fine view of the more isolated Kua Bay.

Kiholo Bay

Near mile marker 81 on the highway is a pull-off and overlook that offers a good glimpse of this stark lava-covered coast. Down on the coast just north of the pull-off you'll see Kiholo Bay and Luahinewai Pond. The pond was a favorite stop for Hawaiian sailors going up the coast, who would have a swim in its cool turquoise waters before continuing on. Look for a stand of royal palms marking the spot, and follow the rough but

ponds and lagoon at 'Anaeho'omalu Beach

passable 4WD road down to the beach, where you will find a large round wooden house that once belonged to Loretta Lynn. Close by, a path leads over the lava to a tiny cove made more dramatic by a black-sand beach.

'Anaeho'omalu Bay

After miles of the transfixing monochrome blackness of Kohala's lava flows, a green standout of palm trees beckons in the distance. Turn near mile marker 76 at the Waikoloa Beach Resort entrance, and follow the access road to historic 'Anaeho'omalu Bay, referred to locally as "A-Bay." Set back from the beach here is the Outrigger Waikoloa Beach. The bay area, with its freshwater springs, coconut trees, blue lagoon, and white-sand beach, is a picture-perfect seaside oasis. Between the large coconut grove and the beach are two well-preserved fishponds where mullet was raised for consumption only by the royalty who lived nearby or were happening by in seagoing canoes. Throughout the area along well-marked trails are petroglyphs, a segment of the

cobblestoned King's Highway, and numerous archaeological sites including house sites and some hard-to-find burial caves. The white-sand beach is open to the public, with access, parking, picnic tables, and beautiful lava stone showers/bathhouses. Although the sand is a bit grainy, the swimming, snorkeling, scuba diving, windsurfing, and just about any water sport are great. A walk north along the bay brings you to an area of excellent tidepools and waters heavily populated by marinelife.

Holoholokai Beach Park

Located adjacent to the Orchid at Mauna Lani Hotel on a well-marked access road, this picturesque beach park is open to the public daily 6:30 A.M.–7 P.M. and is improved with a bathroom, running water, picnic tables, and resort-quality landscaping. Unfortunately, the beach itself is mostly coral boulders with only tiny pockets offering very limited water access. However, the park is used very little and is perfect for relaxing under a palm tree or for a leisurely stroll to explore the many tidepools. A shoreline path leads to the sand beach fronting the Orchid at Mauna Lani and past that to the wider sand beach at the Mauna Lani Bay Hotel, which fronts Makaiwa Bay. From the back side of the parking lot at the public beach park, a trail heads into the *kiawe* and leads to Puako Petroglyphs.

Hapuna Beach State Recreation Area

Approximately seven miles north of 'Anaeho-'omalu is the *second*-best (some rate this the best), but most accessible, white-sand beach on the island. Hapuna Beach is wide and spacious, almost 700 yards long by 70 wide in summer, with a reduction by heavy surf in winter. A lava finger divides the beach into almost equal halves. During good weather the swimming is excellent and lifeguards are on duty. During heavy weather, usually in winter, the rips are fierce, and Hapuna has claimed more lives than any other beach park on all of Hawaii! At the north end is a small cove almost forming a pool that is usually safe, a favorite for snorkeling with families and children. Many classes in beginning scuba and snorkeling are held in this area, and shore fishing is good throughout. At the south end, good breaks make for tremendous body surfing (no boards allowed), and those familiar with the area make spectacular leaps from the seacliffs. Picnic tables, pavilions, restrooms, and plenty of parking are available in this nicely landscaped park.

Camping is available in six A-frame screened shelters that rent for $20 per night and accommodate up to four. Provided are sleeping platforms (you bring your own bedding), electric outlets, cold-water showers, and toilets in separate comfort stations, plus a shared range and refrigerator in a central pavilion. Although the spot is a little run-down, the A-frames are very popular, so reservations and a deposit are required. You can receive full information from the Division of State Parks, P.O. Box 936, Hilo, HI 96721, 808/974-6200; or visit the office at 75 Aupini St., Room 204, in Hilo.

SOUTH KOHALA

ROBERT NILSEN

Wide and long, Hapuna Beach is one of the finest strands of sand on the island.

Kauna'oa Beach

Better known as Mauna Kea Beach because of the nearby luxury hotel of the same name, Kauna'oa is less than a mile north of Hapuna Beach and is considered the best beach on the Big Island by not only the local population, but also by those who judge such things from a broader perspective. In times past, it was a nesting and mating ground for green sea turtles, and although these activities no longer occur because of human pressure on the habitat, turtles still visit the south end of the beach. Mauna Kea Beach is long and wide, and the sandy bottom makes for excellent swimming within the reef. It is more sheltered than Hapuna but can still be dangerous. Hotel beach boys, always in attendance, are unofficial lifeguards who have saved many unsuspecting tourists. During high surf, the shoreline is a favorite with surfers. Like all beaches in Hawaii, this one is public, but to keep the number of nonguests down, only 10 parking passes are handed out each day on a first-come, first-served basis. Pick up a pass at the guardhouse as you enter the hotel grounds. This entitles you to spend the day on the beach, but on weekends they're gone early. Alternately, park at Hapuna Beach and return via an easy mile-long trail connecting Hapuna and Mauna Kea Beaches.

Spencer Beach County Park

The entrance for this park is the same as that for Pu'ukohola Heiau on Rte. 19 just south of Kawaihae. A coastal trail leads from the beach park up to the *heiau,* so you can combine a day at the beach with a cultural education. The park is named after Samuel Mahuka Spencer, a longtime island resident who was born in Waimea, served as county mayor for 20 years, and died in 1960 at Honoka'a. The park provides pavilions, restrooms, cold-water showers, electricity, picnic facilities, and even tennis courts. Day use is free, but tent and trailer camping are by county permit only. Spencer Beach is protected from wind and heavy wave action by an offshore reef and by breakwaters built around Kawaihae Bay. These make it the safest swimming beach along South Kohala's shore and a favorite with local families with small children. The wide, shallow

reef is home to a wide spectrum of marinelife, making the snorkeling entertaining. The shoreline fishing is also excellent.

LUXURY RESORTS

The South Kohala Coast has four resort areas, all providing luxury accommodations, fine dining, golf courses, full-service resort amenities, the best beaches on the island, and a smattering of historical and cultural sites. They are, in effect, self-sufficient mini-villages. The first north of Kailua-Kona is not referred to by one name, but encompasses the adjacent properties of **Kona Village Resort** at Ka'upulehu and the **Four Seasons Resort** at Hualalai. A new time-share property with golf course is rising from the lava to the south and this development fronts Kuki'o Beach. These resorts are actually situated in the North Kona district but are discussed here as they are more similar to the South Kohala luxury resorts than to any hotel complex in Kailua or Keauhou to the south. Kona Village Resort, the oldest resort along this coast, is designed like a Polynesian village: low-slung, thatch roofs, palm trees, white-sand beach, and shoreline ponds. It's a welcome oasis in a land of stark black lava; it has kept up with the times and still offers one of the best get-away destinations in the state. The Four Seasons Resort is the island's newest, a modern complex of tasteful buildings, a counterpoint to Kona Village, where you will find golf, tennis, and water sport opportunities. It's new and fresh, a delight for the senses.

Next up the way is **Waikoloa Resort,** the largest, busiest, and most commercial of the resort complexes. Here you have the Outrigger Waikoloa Beach, a redesigned hotel that reflects the grandeur of Hawaii from the 1930s and '40s, the gargantuan Hilton Waikoloa Village, and three high-class condominiums. Here as well are the King's Shops, the only shopping center in the area, two superb golf courses, a multitude of tennis opportunities, a petroglyph field, remnants of the ancient King's Trail, anchialine ponds, and one of the best beaches on the coast. Just across the road is a commercial heliport. To ease getting around between shops, hotels, and condos, the Waikoloa Shuttle runs every 10 minutes between 10 A.M. and 9 P.M. at $1 per ride.

Mauna Lani Resort comes next, also big but not as commercial. Here too you find two magnificent hotels, five (and counting) condominiums, two golf courses, tennis, beaches, fishponds, two petroglyph fields, and a long history. There is no shopping complex here, but each hotel has a bevy of retail shops. This is a quality high-end resort, without glitz or hype.

Farthest to the north is the **Mauna Kea Resort.** Smaller and more intimate, it contains the grande dame of Kohala hotels, the Mauna Kea Beach Hotel, and its more recent addition, the Hapuna Beach Prince Hotel. Like bride and groom, these two hotels with their golf courses are sufficient unto themselves, and they sit on the two finest beaches on the island. While there are no major historical sites on the property, they lie a mile or two south of one of the most significant and well-kept *heiau* on this island.

Kona Village Resort

So you want to go "native," and you're dreaming of a "little grass shack" along a secluded beach? No problem! The Kona Village Resort, P.O. Box 1299, Kailua-Kona, HI 96745, 808/325-5555, 800/432-5450 in Hawaii, 800/367-5290 Mainland, kvr@aloha.net, www.konavillage.com, is a once-in-a-lifetime dream experience. Located on Kahuwai Bay, a picture-perfect cove of white sand dotted with coconut palms, the village lies seven miles north of the Kona Airport, surrounded by acres of seclusion. The accommodations are 125 distinctive "hales," individual renditions of thatch-roofed huts found throughout Polynesia and Hawaii. They are simple but luxurious, and in keeping with the idea of getting away from it all, have no TVs, radios, or telephones. All, however, do have ceiling fans and louvered windows to let the tropical breezes blow through. Beds are covered with distinctive quilts and pillows. Each hut features a wet bar, refrigerator, coffeemaker, and extra-large bathroom, and is either located along the water, around the lagoon, or back in a garden setting. At one time you had to fly into the hotel's private airstrip, but today you arrive by car. Almost exactly at

mile marker 87, turn in, make a right within 100 yards, and follow the access road that leads through coal-black lava fields. Don't despair! Down by the sea you can see the shimmering green palm trees as they beckon you to the resort. Kona Village gives you your money's worth, with a lei greeting, free valet service, a private tennis center, water sports, numerous cultural activities, and a lu'au. Guided tours are also offered to the petroglyph field on property, complete with history and legends of the area.

Meals are served in the Hale Moana, the main dining room, and at the Hale Moana Terrace, where a famous luncheon buffet is served daily. Hale Samoa is the fine dining restaurant, open daily except Wednesday and Friday for dinner only. Upon entering Hale Samoa, your spirits rise immediately with the sweep of cathedral ceiling. On the walls is an original painting by Herb Kane, Hawaii's foremost artist, that depicts *The Fair American,* a tiny ship commandeered by King Kamehameha that was instrumental in changing the history of old Hawaii. The walls also hold portraits of the hotel's original owner, Johnno Jackson, an oil geologist from Texas, who in 1960 sailed in with his wife Helen, their Labrador dog, a monkey, and a parrot—all in a 42-foot schooner—landed on these shores and declared, "This is the spot!" Also on the grounds are Hale Ho'okipa "House of Hospitality," where a lu'au is held on Friday nights as it has for over 30 years, and an international buffet dinner every Wednesday. Drinks and tropical libations are offered throughout the afternoon at the Shipwreck Bar next to the beachfront pool, and at the Bora Bora Bar in the evening next to Hale Moana, where soft musical entertainment soothes guests every evening.

Rates per night start at $505 per couple with full American plan (includes three meals), and go up to $895 for oceanfront huts. Two-room units for three adults run $825–1,500. Deduct $113 for single occupancy and add $38 for children 3–5, $143 for children 6–12, and $193 for an extra adult. There is a strict reservations and refund policy, so check. These rates also include transportation to and from the airport if you need it, all scheduled activities, use of the tennis and fitness centers, water sport equipment, and all activities except scuba, snuba, massage, and the Friday night lu'au. The hotel's Na Keiki in Paradise is a children's program included in the room price that will entertain and educate children ages six and up throughout the day. The beach shack is open every day for your pleasure, as are the jewelry store and gift shop. Hotel manager Fred Duerr has been at the facility since 1966, and most of his highly professional and seasoned staff tend to stay for years. They take pride in the hotel and do everything to help you have a rewarding, enjoyable, and relaxing stay at this premier resort. The Kona Village is a serene Hawaiian classic that deserves its well-earned reputation for excellence, and as a consequence gets 65 percent repeat visitors and 25 percent honeymooners.

Four Seasons Resort

The Four Seasons Resort, Hualalai, 100 Ka'upulehu Drive, Kailua-Kona, HI 96740, 808/325-8000 or 888/340-5662, fax 808/325-8100, www.fourseasons.com/hualalai, at historic Ka'upulehu, opened in late 1996. This 243-room AAA Five-Diamond resort is split into 36 low-rise bungalows in four crescent groups that front a half-mile beach and several natural lagoons just down from Kona Village Resort. Located in among old lava flows from the Hualalai volcano, 32 of these units have ocean access and four are located along the 18th green of the accompanying golf course. Contemporary Polynesian in style, the units are a mixture of dark mahogany wood, light wall colors and carpeting, pleasing medium brown rattan furniture, and gray slate flooring. Authentic Hawaiian art pieces from the late 1700s to the present are displayed throughout the hotel. There is no skimping on space, furnishings, or amenities in any of the rooms or suites. Large as well are the bathrooms, each of which looks out onto a private garden, lanai, or patio. The slate floors of the main rooms are covered with seagrass mats and the beds with material reminiscent of tapa cloth. An exceptional place, this all-inclusive destination resort is not cheap. Rooms run $500–725 per night, suites $850–6,450, $110 for a third adult in a

room. Numerous attractive packages are always offered, so inquire.

The resort's three restaurants will fill your every culinary need for all three meals of the day. Both the elegant AAA Four-Diamond **Pahu I'a Restaurant** and the casual **Beach Tree Bar and Grill** are set oceanside. With setting inside and out, Pahu I'a opens in the morning with local and international favorites, buffet or à la carte, and transforms in the evening into a more formal eatery with an emphasis on cuisines of the Pacific and the imaginative combinations of food and flavorings. Resort wear is required and reservations are necessary. Serving lunch and dinner, the Beach Tree offers grill items near the main pool. Several evenings a week, this restaurant offers theme nights with regional foods of the world. Nightly music is also a part of this venue, with a hula dancing performance several nights of the week. In addition, the **Hualalai Club Grille and Bar** at the golf clubhouse across the main entrance drive serves lunch and fine-dining dinners in a sophisticated but informal setting. For drinks and convivial late-night companionship there are several options. The Lava Lounge at the Pahu I'a is open evenings only and offers light music every night except Sunday. Set as close as you can get to the water without being in it, the Beach Tree bar dispenses libations throughout the day under its canopy roof and is an easygoing place to sit and watch the sun set.

On the ocean side of the meeting room building and the outdoor Hoku stage theater is Kids for all Seasons, the hotel's service of supervised care for five- to 12-year-olds that provides a wide variety of fun-filled and indoor and outdoor activities. For teens, Tsunami is the activity center for indoor games and it organizes outdoor excursions. Hualalai Tennis Club is open for hotel guests only. Located adjacent to the tennis courts is the Sports Club and Spa, a full-service facility that offers a variety of instructional classes, a 25-meter lap pool, exercise machines, massage and spa therapies, and sand volleyball and half-court basketball courts. For the duffer, the private Hualalai Golf Club offers 18 holes of challenging play along the ocean. A second course opened its front nine in 2002, with the back nine soon to come. Be sure to check out the Cultural Center with its 1,200-gallon reef aquarium just downstairs from the lobby, where you can learn about the surrounding waters, the Ka'upulehu area, and the life and lifestyle of ancient Hawaiians. In addition to the natural lagoons, the resort has both freshwater and saltwater swimming pools set just back from the beach. For those interested, a water sport kiosk on the beach can fix you up with needed gear or water activities.

Outrigger Waikoloa Beach Resort

Following a $25 million renovation and facelift, the former Royal Waikoloan re-emerged as the artful Outrigger Waikoloa Beach, 69-275 Waikoloa Beach Dr., Waikoloa, HI 96738, 808/886-6789 or 800/688-7444, www.outriggerwaikoloabeach.com. On a perfect spot fronting the palm-fringed 'Anaeho'omalu Bay, the hotel looks out over ponds that once stocked fish for passing *ali'i*. The hotel lobby is a spacious open-air affair that lets the trade winds blow through across its cool sandstone floor. Six floors of rooms extend out in wings on both sides, flanking the landscaped courtyard with swimming pool and water slide. Greeting you as you enter the lobby is a marvelous old koa outrigger canoe set in front of a three-part mural by renowned Hawaiian artist Herb Kane of a royal canoe and Western frigate meeting off the Kona coast. Walk farther and gaze down upon the landscaped courtyard, heavy with greenery and the pungent smell of tropical plants. The renovation has bequeathed a look and feel reminiscent of the '30s and '40s with its decorative artistic touches and imparts a sense of less hectic times. The Outrigger Waikoloa Beach Resort is a class act.

All 545 hotel rooms and suites are tastefully decorated in light soothing colors, with king-size beds, rattan furnishings, custom quilts, and island prints of a mid-20th century art deco style. Each room has a/c, color TV, *yakuta* robes, in-room safe, small refrigerator, marble vanities, and a private lanai. Rooms are reasonably priced at $315–485, while suites run $965–3,100 per night. Hotel services and amenities include an activities desk for all on-site and off-property

excursions and several retail shops and boutiques, and a Kahn Galleries shop for fine art. You can take part in daily Hawaiian cultural programs, use the business center, or have your kids properly cared for at the children's program. Enjoy the garden swimming pool, spa and fitness center, six tennis courts, and a grand beach with plenty of water activities. The hotel is just a few minutes' stroll past the royal fishponds to the beach or to the remains of a nearby ancient but now restored *heiau*.

The Outrigger Waikoloa Beach also has new dining facilities. Harking back to the days when Hawaiian music and news of the islands was transmitted to the world by radio, and when Pan Am Clipper Ships flew travelers to the islands, is **Hawaii Calls Restaurant,** the hotel's main dining room. Open for breakfast and dinner, the decor says yesteryear but the menu is thoroughly modern with a mix of Continental and Asian cuisine. As part of this open-air restaurant, the **Clipper Lounge** serves tropical drinks as smooth as a Clipper's landing on a mirror lagoon. This lounge serves up a late bistro menu and nightly entertainment 5–11:30 P.M., while the more casual poolside **Nalu Bar and Grill** is open 10 A.M.–sunset for snacks, fill-'er-ups, and drinks. Fit for the royalty who once called this bay their home, the twice weekly Royal Lu'au draws appreciative guests for food and entertainment.

The Shores at Waikoloa

The Shores at Waikoloa, 69-1035 Keana Place, Waikoloa, HI 96738, 808/885-5001—or contact Aston Hotel and Resorts, 800/321-2558 in Hawaii, 800/922-7866 Mainland and Canada—are secluded luxury condominiums nestled away in the planned community of Waikoloa. Enter through a security gate to see the peaceful and beautifully manicured grounds of these white-stucco and red-tile-roof condominiums. A few minutes away are the best beaches on Hawaii and all of the activities offered by the large luxury hotels, if you wish to participate. The condominium offers an activities desk where your outings can be arranged, a swimming pool and hot tub, two complimentary tennis courts, and outdoor barbecues. The condos are decorated by the individual owners so each room is unique, but there are guidelines and standards so every unit is tasteful and comfortable. All units are extremely spacious, with many boasting marble and terra cotta floors. All have huge bathrooms, full modern kitchens, laundry facilities, and light and airy sitting rooms complete with state-of-the-art entertainment centers. Rates range $275 for a one-bedroom to $700 for a three-bedroom golf villa. Low season brings a 10 percent reduction, and a number of packages are available. If you are after a luxury vacation within a vacation where you can get away from it all after you've gotten away from it all, The Shores at Waikoloa is a superb choice. The Shores is a AAA Three-Diamond award winner.

The Bay Club

Surrounded by golf links, The Bay Club, 69-450 Waikoloa Beach Drive, Kamuela, HI 96743, 808/886-7979 or 800/305-7979, has an ideal location. Like all other accommodations in this planned community of Waikoloa Beach Resort, The Bay Club is luxury living in a secure environment. On the property are tennis courts, a swimming pool with poolside cafe, a sauna and spa, fitness center, and activities center. You can partake in as much as you like or just lounge to your heart's content. The Bay Club is a timeshare property, however, units are rented based on availability but no more than 30 days in advance. One-bedroom units run $300 while those with two-bedrooms go for $400.

Hilton Waikoloa Village

At the Hilton Waikoloa Village, 425 Waikoloa Beach Dr., Waikoloa, HI 96738, 808/886-1234 or 800/445-8667, fax 808/886-2900, www .waikoloavillage.hilton.com, the idea was to create a reality so beautiful and naturally harmonious that anyone who came here, sinner or saint, would be guaranteed a glimpse of paradise. The architecture is "fantasy grand," and the grounds are grandly fantastic. The three main towers, each enclosing a miniature fern-filled botanical garden, are spread over the grounds almost a mile apart and are linked by pink flagstone walkways, canals navigated by hotel launches, and a quiet, space-age tram. Attention to the smallest detail is immediately apparent, and everywhere sculptures, art treasures, and brilliant flowers soothe the eyes. The museum promenade displays choice artworks from Hawaii, Oceania, and Asia—pick up a brochure from the sundries shops at the hotel explaining this $7 million collection—and here and there around the property are brilliant artistic flourishes. Nearly everywhere you look you delight in beauty. Songs of rare tropical birds and the wind whispering through a bamboo forest create the natural melody that surrounds you. The beach fronting the property offers excellent snorkeling, while two gigantic pools and a series of lagoons are perfect for water activities and sunbathing. You can swim in a private lagoon accompanied by dolphins, dine in first-rate restaurants, relax to a message at the spa, leave your kids for the day in the experienced hands of the Camp Menehune staff, pick up a memento at the retail shops, sweat over a game of tennis, or just let your cares slip away as you lounge in perfect tranquillity.

Like the hotel in general, its seven restaurants are culinary powerhouses, and every taste is provided for. **Donatoni's** features classic Northern Italian cuisine; **Palm Terrace** presents breakfast and dinner buffets, with a different theme nightly; **Imari** serves traditional Japanese fare; The Chinese **Kirin** restaurant offers dim sum lunches and seafood dinners; **Kamuela Provision Co.** specializes in steak and seafood; **Orchid Cafe** provides light breakfasts and lunches; and **Lagoon Grill** has casual lunches and tropical drinks. The hotel's bars, lounges, and casual poolside dining are other options, while twice weekly the **Legends of the Pacific** lu'au delights guests with fine food and an extravagant dinner show.

With all this splendor, the most talked-about feature at the hotel is still **Dolphin Quest.** A specially constructed saltwater pond is home to Atlantic bottlenose dolphins from Florida's Gulf Coast. Daily, on a lottery basis for adults, but with two months in advance reservations available to children up to 19 years of age, guests are allowed to interact with the dolphins. Dolphin Quest is an educational experience. Here you don't ride the dolphins and they don't do tricks for you. In the half-hour session, guests wade in chest-deep water with the dolphins gliding by while a staff member imparts information concerning not only dolphins, but all marinelife and human interdependence with it. The experience is voluntary on the dolphins' part—*they* choose to swim with *you* as a guest in their domain. Much of the proceeds from the program go toward marine research.

This resort is definitely a distinctive undertaking, a step apart from any other resort complex in the state. It has cut its own path and gone its own way. Yet with all the grandeur, it seems a bit like Disneyland on a lava flow; beautiful and expansive, yet incongruous and overblown. Forget intimacy. You don't come here to get away, you come here to participate. With 1,240 rooms on a 62-acre property, it's so big that entering the lobby can be like walking into Grand Central Station and navigating certain walkways like pushing through throngs at a fair. For all that, the Hilton still offers plenty for everyone and gives you unlimited options for a great vacation. You be the judge: is this paradise or something else?

This futuristic hotel complex has set a new standard; as you would expect, all this luxury comes at a price, but for the most part not unreasonable. Room rates are $189–450 for garden/mountain rooms, $229–540 for partial ocean views, $249–620 for deluxe ocean rooms, and $950–5,530 for suites!

The Orchid at Mauna Lani

In a tortured field of coal-black lava made more dramatic by pockets of jade-green lawn rises ivory-white The Orchid at Mauna Lani, One N. Kaniku Dr., Kohala Coast, HI 96743, 808/885-2000 or 800/845-9905, www.orchid-maunalani.com. A rolling drive lined with *haku lei* of flowering shrubs entwined with stately palms leads to the open-air porte cochère. Enter to find koa and marble reflecting the diffused and soothing light of the interior. Straight ahead, off the thrust-proscenium Sunset Terrace, a living blue-on-blue still-life of sea and sky is perfectly framed. Nature, powerful yet soothing, surrounds the hotel. Stroll the grounds, where gentle breezes always blow and where the

ever-present surf is the back beat of a melody created by trickling rivulets and falling waters as they meander past a magnificent free-form pool and trimmed tropical gardens of ferns and flowers. The hallways and lobbies open from the central area like the delicate ribs of a geisha's fan; walls are graced with Hawaiian quilts and excellent artwork on view everywhere; and every set of stairs boasts a velvety smooth koa banister carved with the pineapple motif, the Hawaiian symbol of hospitality. The Orchid is casually elegant, a place to relax in luxury and warm *aloha.*

Located in two six-story wings off the main reception hall, the 539 hotel rooms, each with private lanai and sensational view, are a mixture of kings, doubles, and suites. Done in neutral tones, the stylish and refined rooms feature hand-crafted quilts, twice-daily room attendance, an entertainment center, fully stocked honor bar, in-room safe, and spacious marble bathrooms. Room rates begin at $435 for a garden view to $705 for a deluxe oceanfront room. One-bedroom executive suites run $900 and the two magnificent Presidential Suites are … well, very expensive.

Dining at The Orchid can be everything from poolside casual to haute cuisine, prepared in various styles, using locally grown produce, herbs, meats, and seafood. The culinary results are not only mouth-watering but healthy and wonderfully nutritious. The Orchid's fine dining restaurant is **The Grill,** where crystal and dark koa wood set the scene and most dishes are either steak or fish. The Grill is open for dinner only; evening or alohawear requested. The **Orchid Court,** a casual restaurant featuring Pacific Rim and California cuisine, is the hotel's main dining room and is open for breakfast and dinner. Breakfasts are either à la carte or buffet, and a wide range of sandwiches, pizza, fish, meat, and pasta dishes are your choices for dinner. Poolside, **Brown's Beach House** is the most casual restaurant, where you dine alfresco in a garden setting for lunch and dinner, and where dinner entrées are inspirations of the islands and the Orient. Soft Hawaiian music accompanies a hula dancer in the evening. For a relaxing evening of drinks, a cigar, or billiards, and periodic live entertainment, lower yourself into an overstuffed leather chair at the Paniolo Lounge and Polo Bar.

The hotel offers first-rate guest services, amenities, and activities that include a small shopping mall with everything from sundries to designer boutiques, complimentary shuttle to and from Mauna Lani's famous championship golf courses, golf bag storage, 11 tennis courts (with seven lit for evening play), complimentary use of fitness center and snorkel equipment, a day spa with massage, body treatments, and exercise, an enormous swimming pool and sun deck, bicycles for short tours, double-hull canoe sailing, safe-deposit boxes, on-property car rental, baby-sitting, Keiki Aloha, a special instructional day-camp program for children ages 5–12, and much, much more.

Mauna Lani Bay Hotel and Bungalows

As soon as you turn off Rte. 19, the entrance road, trimmed in purple bougainvillea, sets the mood for Mauna Lani Bay Hotel and Bungalows, 68-1400 Mauna Lani Dr., Kohala Coast, HI 96743, 808/885-6622 or 800/367-2323, fax 808/885-1484, www.maunalani.com, a 350-room hotel that opened in 1983. Enter through a grand portico, whose blue tile floor, a mimic of the ever-present sea and sky, immediately creates a sense of sedate but beautiful grandeur. Below is a central courtyard, where full-size palms sway amidst a lava-rock water garden; cascading sheets of clear water splash through a series of koi ponds, making naturally soothing music. A short stroll leads you past the swimming pool and through a virtual botanical garden to a white-sand beach perfect for island relaxation. From here, any number of water sport activities can be arranged. Nearby are convoluted lagoons, and away from the shore you find the Sports Center with tennis courts, a lap pool, and weights, a full-service health spa, and exclusive shops. Surrounding the hotel is the marvelous Francis I'i Brown Golf Course, whose artistically laid-out fairways, greens, and sand traps make it a modern landscape sculpture.

The Mauna Lani offers superb dining options. The **Bay Terrace,** open daily for breakfast and dinner, offers the most casual dining, with a weekend seafood dinner buffet that shouldn't be missed and a Sunday brunch that draws visitors and locals alike. Set within the arms of a lagoon and overlooking the ocean is **CanoeHouse,** the hotel's signature restaurant. Open daily for dinner only, it delights you with Pacific Rim cuisine. Resort wear is required and reservations are highly recommended. Up at the golf clubhouse overlooking the fairways, **The Gallery Restaurant** serves lunch and dinner Tues.–Sat., while **Knickers Bar and Lounge** serves libations, sandwiches, and snacks. For lunch and cocktails, try the informal **Ocean Grill,** where you'll be comfortable in a bathing suit and cover-up. On the far side of Makaiwa Bay, the **Beach Club** also serves light lunches in an open-air environment until mid-afternoon. And for a perfect place to relax after a day of golf or tennis, seek out the **Honu Bar,** just off the atrium, where you will find a pool table and dance floor, an excellent selection of liqueurs, wine, and fine cigars, and be able to order light late-night meals and desserts.

Rooms at the AAA Five-Diamond award-winning Mauna Lani Bay Hotel run $375 mountain view to $725 for corner oceanfront, suites are $1,100. Rooms are oversized, the majority come with an ocean view, and each includes a private lanai, remote color TV and VCR, honor bar, in-room safe, and all the comforts of home. The very exclusive 4,000-square-foot, two-bedroom bungalows rent for $4,400–4,900 a night but each comes complete with a personal chef, butler, and swimming pool. In addition, one-, two-, and three-bedroom home-like villas go for $550–910, three-night minimum required. Weekly rates are available on the villas and bungalows. Guest privileges include complimentary use of snorkeling equipment, Hawaiian cultural classes, hula lessons, complimentary morning coffee, and resort and historic tours. For parents with young children who have come to the realization that "families who want to stay together don't always play together," the hotel offers a break from those little bundles of joy with Camp Mauna Lani for children ages 5–12. While you play, the kids are shepherded through games and activities. One of the favorite evening activities at the hotel takes place once a month at the Eva Parker Woods cottage. For this free event, Hawaiian musicians, dancers, and storytellers gather to share their cultural talents with community and resort guests. Ask the concierge for particulars and for information about the numerous daily activities.

Mauna Lani Condominiums

Sitting in the lap of luxury are two secure, private, modern, and very high-end condo properties. They are **Mauna Lani Point,** which is surrounded by golf fairways at oceanside, and **The Islands at Mauna Lani,** also surrounded by golf links but set away from the water. Each has superbly built, spacious units that leave nothing lacking. The Mauna Lani Point has one- and two-bedroom units that run $305–505 a night, while The Island rents two- and three-bedroom units for $495–695; three-night minimum. All guests can make use of the activities and amenities located within the Mauna Lani Resort complex. For reservations and information about either, contact Classic Resorts, 68-1050 Mauna Lani Point Dr., Kohala Coast, HI 96743, 808/885-5022 or 800/542-6284, fax 808/885-5015, info@classicresorts.com, www.classicresorts.com.

The Mauna Kea Beach Hotel

This hotel has set the standard of excellence along Kohala's coast ever since former Hawaii Governor William Quinn interested Laurance Rockefeller in the lucrative possibilities of building a luxury hideaway for the rich and famous. Beautiful coastal land was leased from the Parker Ranch, and the Mauna Kea Beach Hotel, 62-100 Mauna Kea Beach Drive, Kohala Coast, HI 96743, 808/882-7222 or 800/882-6060, www.maunakeabeachhotel.com, opened in 1965. The Mauna Kea was the only one of its kind for a few years, until others saw the possibilities, and more luxury hotels were built along this coast. Over the years, the Mauna Kea grew a bit aged and suffered stiff competition from newer resorts nearby. After an extensive restoration, the Mauna Kea reopened with youthful enthusiasm in December 1995 and shines again as the

princess it always was. Class is always class, and the Mauna Kea again receives very high accolades as a fine resort hotel.

The Mauna Kea fronts the beautiful Kauna'oa Beach, one of the best on the island. Million-dollar condos also grace the resort grounds, and hotel guests tend to come back year after year. The hotel itself is an eight-story terraced complex of simple, clean-cut design. The grounds and lobbies showcase more than 1,000 museum-quality art pieces from throughout the Pacific, and more than a half million plants add greenery and beauty to the surroundings. The landings and lobbies, open and large enough to hold full-grown palm trees, also display beautiful tapestries, bird cages with their singing captives, and huge copper pots on polished brick floors. The award-winning Mauna Kea Golf Course surrounds the grounds, and a multi-court tennis park overlooks the ocean. Swimmers can use the beach or the round courtyard swimming pool, set just off the small fitness center, and horseback riding is available at the Parker Ranch up in Waimea. A host of daily activities are scheduled, including a twice-weekly star gazing program, but perhaps the most unusual activity at the hotel is the evening manta ray viewing off Lookout Point.

Exceptional food is served in this exceptional environment. Serving classic Euro-Asian cuisine for dinner only is the **The Batik,** the hotel's finest restaurant. Dining here is truly a treat. For breakfast and dinner in an open-air setting with grand views of the coast, try the **Pavilion** restaurant. Near the beach, the **Hau Tree** does salads and sandwiches for lunch daily, and the **19th Hole** is a more casual spot at the golf course clubhouse that serves food from the East and West through midday. Three lounges also grace the grounds, each with its own entertainment. At the Saturday-evening clambake at the Hau Tree, you can feast buffet-style on Maine lobster, garlic shrimp, sumptuous steamed clams, and much, much more; Tuesday evenings are extra special as a lu'au is performed at the Lu'au Gardens at North Pointe; and Sunday Brunch is legendary for its selection and quality. For dining reservations, call 808/882-5810.

The 310 beautifully appointed rooms, starting at $360, feature an extra-large lanai and specially made wicker furniture. From there, rates rise to $530 for beachfront units, and suites run $950–1,400. Numerous packages are available. The rooms are, like the rest of the hotel, the epitome of understated elegance. A television-free resort at its inception, the hotel now has TVs in most of the rooms as part of the recent restoration. A resort shuttle operates between here and the Hapuna Beach Resort Hotel, where Mauna Kea guests have signing privileges.

Hapuna Beach Prince Hotel

Opened in 1994, the Hapuna Beach Prince Hotel, 62-100 Kaunaʻoa Dr., Kohala Coast, HI 96743, 808/880-1111 or 800/882-6060, www.hapunabeachprincehotel.com, fronts Hapuna Beach about one mile down the coast from the Mauna Kea Hotel. These two hotels are separate entities but function as one resort, joined as if in marriage. The princess, Mauna Kea, has finally found her prince. Long and lean, this hotel steps down the hillside toward the beach in eight levels. A formal portico fronts the main entryway, through which you have a splendid view of palm trees and the ocean. This entryway is simple in design yet welcoming in spirit. Chinese flagstone, stained reddish by iron oxide, paves the main entry floor. Walls are the color of sand, and the wood throughout is light brown or dark teak. Lines are simple and decoration subtle. An attempt has been made to simplify and let surrounding nature become part of the whole. As at the Mauna Kea, visitors are not overwhelmed with sensory overload. A shuttle connects the Hapuna Beach to the Mauna Kea and all services available at one are open to guests of the other.

Carpeted bedrooms are spacious, allowing for king-size beds, and the bathrooms have marble floors. Each of the 350 large and well-appointed rooms has an entertainment center, comfy chairs, live plants, prints on the walls, and a lanai. Although rooms are air-conditioned, they all have louvered doors, allowing you to keep out the sun while letting breezes flow through. Rates for the 350 guest rooms start at $360 and go up to $595 a night; suites run $1,200–7,000.

The Hapuna Beach Prince Hotel overlooks one of the finest beaches on the island.

Of the hotel's four restaurants, the ocean-front **Coast Grill** is its signature establishment. It specializes in fresh seafood, mixing flavors and preparations from the Pacific and Asia. The Oyster Bar here is renown and sushi is always top notch. Open only for dinner, reservations are recommended and resort attire is required. Serving buffet and à la carte breakfasts from its location overlooking the pool and ocean, the **Ocean Terrace** also does an evening Seafood feast buffet. Located in the clubhouse and catering mainly to the golfers, **Arnie's** serves standard American and health-conscious food with a few Oriental touches. Open for lunch only, with cocktails until late afternoon. In addition, you can get lunch items, afternoon snacks, and drinks at the **Beach Bar** down by the pool. Aside from the Beach Bar, the Reef Lounge serves up tropical drinks and nightly entertainment, and the Splash at Hapuna cocktail lounge and nightclub rounds out the evening with late night drinks, appetizers, music, and dancing. Splash is open Wednesday through Saturday 8:30 P.M.–12:30 A.M., music is a different style every evening, and there is a $5 cover. Every Friday is Paniolo Night, and this Western buffet and dinner show, served at the Kohala Gardens, is always a hit.

The Prince Keiki Club at the Hapuna offers a reprieve to parents who desire some time away from their energetic kids. Children 5–12 years old can fill their time with fun activities and educational projects. For Mom and Dad are the links-style Hapuna Golf Course and the hotel's physical fitness center. While the spa and fitness center has weights, its main focus is on dance, yoga, stretching, and alignment techniques, with various massage therapies and body treatments also available. Set in the garden below the lobby, the swimming pool is great recreation during the day and reflects the stars at night. Speaking of the stars, four nights a week, the hotel hosts a star gazing program for hotel guests, and numerous other activities are scheduled through the week. Shops include the Amaury St. Gilles contemporary fine art.

VACATION RENTAL AGENCIES

Along with a few high-end condos, luxury resorts are the mainstay of accommodations in coastal South Kohala. There are, however, a number of vacation rental homes and individual condo units available for those who want more privacy but still want the sun. Try the following agencies for options.

Hawaii Vacation Rentals, 7 Puako Beach Dr., Kamuela, HI 96743, 808/882-7000 or 800/332-7081, fax 808/882-7607, seaside@aloha.net, www.bigisland-vacation.com, handles properties almost exclusively in Puako, with a few others up and down the coast, that range from a studio cottage at $125 a night to a three-bedroom oceanfront mansion for $1,000 a night. A five- to seven-night minimum stay applies. This company also represents one or two units in Puako Beach Condominium, the only condo in this residential neighborhood and the only moderately priced, multiple-unit accommodation in this diamond-studded neck of the woods. The three-bedroom units run $135 a night, three nights minimum, with a kitchen, laundry, TV, and swimming pool.

For exclusive condo units and mansion-style homes at various resort complexes along the South Kohala Coast, try **South Kohala Management,** P.O. Box 384900 Waikoloa, HI 96738, 808/883-8500 or 800/822-4252, fax 808/883-9818, info@southkohala.com, www.southkohala.com. It handles premium properties only, with prices to match. Three nights minimum for condos and five nights minimum for homes.

MacArthur & Company, with an office in Waimea at the Historic Spencer House, 808/885-8885 or 877/885-8285, manages numerous rental homes mostly in the Kohala resort area, Puako, North Kohala, and Waimea with a few others south in Kona, that range mostly $500–1,000 a night, with several under $150 and a few over $3,500 a night. Write 65-1148 Mamalohoa Highway, Kamuela, HI 96743, info@letsgohawaii.com, www.letsgohawaii.com. **Kohala by the Sea Realty,** 808/882-1991, fax 808/882-1994, P.O. Box 44550 Kawaihae,

HI 96743, www.kohalacoast.com, has several condos from $100 a night to homes that mostly run $500–700. Many are booked months in advance so make your inquiry early.

FOOD

Except for a few community-oriented restaurants in Waikoloa Village, a handful of reasonably priced roadside restaurants in Kawaihae, and a gaggle of eating establishments in the King's Shops, all of the food in South Kohala is served in the elegant but expensive restaurants of the luxury resorts. The resort hotels also provide the lion's share of the entertainment along the coast, mostly in the form of quiet musical combos and dinner shows.

Restaurants at the King's Shops

Hama Yu Japanese Restaurant, 808/886-6333, is open daily 11:30 A.M.–3 P.M. and 5:30–9 P.M. With strikingly contemporary decor, Hama Yu serves authentic Japanese cuisine that's not cheap. Choose appetizers like soft-shell crab, yakitori, and a variety of sashimi and sushi. Dinners, mostly $25–38, include tempura, Japanese steak, and tonkatsu. Sit at western-style tables or choose the sushi bar. Lunches are simpler with less expensive soups, noodles, donburi, sushi, and other similar dishes.

The **Grand Palace Chinese Restaurant,** 808/886-6668, open daily 11 A.M.–9:30 P.M., serves appetizers ranging from deep fried won ton for $5 to a cold platter for $16. Soups run $9 for pork with mustard cabbage all the way up to $56 for shark's fin soup with shredded crabmeat. Chicken and duck dishes range from $9 for sweet and sour chicken to $48 for a whole Peking duck. Seafood includes sautéed shrimp with asparagus for $15 and squid with bean sprouts for $10. There are also your standard beef, pork, and vegetable dishes, as well as the unusual hot pot dishes and sizzling platters. With over 150 items on the menu and prices that are above average, this is not your ordinary Chinese restaurant but a dining experience.

The **Big Island Steakhouse,** 808/886-8805, featuring the Merry Wahine Bar, is open daily from 5 P.M., serving items like a *pu pu* platter with baby-back ribs and a variety of salads from simple onion and tomato to aloha salads with fish, chicken, or beef. Entrées, mostly $16–19, include New York strip steak, filet mignon, prime rib, teriyaki pork chops, coconut prawns, and fresh fish.

Roy's Waikoloa Bar and Grill, 808/886-4321, is well known throughout the islands for blending ingredients from East and West. Roy's produces imaginative cuisine that will titillate your taste buds. The menu changes daily and always features nightly specials, but some of what you might expect to find are cassoulet of escargot appetizers and ginger chicken and sesame shrimp salad. For main entrées, look for braised garlic parmesan lamb shank, lemongrass chicken breast, and blackened *'ahi*. Most dinner entrées are in the $21–28 range, with lunches somewhat less. Open 11:30 A.M.–2 P.M. and again from 5:30–9:30 P.M.; reservations are definitely recommended.

A separate area called **The Food Pavilion** will satisfy anyone on the run with everything from a Subway Sandwich to pizza and espresso coffee.

Beach Grill

More than just a clubhouse eatery, the Beach Grill restaurant at the Waikoloa Beach Course golf clubhouse, 808/886-6131, is a diverse dining establishment with a better than average wine list. Lunch items are mostly light sandwiches, *pu pu,* and salads, with few surprises, but dinner is a different story. Here you can order fresh catch done any number of ways at market price, Hawaiian *huli huli* chicken, teriyaki top sirloin, scampi Alfredo, or sautéed calamari, mostly in the $17–24 range. Each dinner comes with potatoes, rice, vegetables, and warm bread. The Beach Grill is conveniently located for all guests at Waikoloa Resort and is open for lunch 11 A.M.–4 P.M., dinner 5:30–9 P.M., and for appetizers and cocktails until midnight.

Lu'au

A sumptuous old-style feast is held at the **Kona Village Resort.** It's worth attending this lu'au just to visit and be pampered at this private hotel beach. Adults pay around $76, children 6–12 $46, children 3–5 $22. This lu'au is held every Friday by reservation only and as it's so popular you should call well in advance, perhaps even when you make your room reservation; 808/325-5555. The *imu* ceremony is at 6:30 P.M., followed by cocktails; the lu'au stars at 7 P.M. and the entertainment gets going at 8 P.M. The Kona Village Resort lu'au has been happening every Friday night for over 30 years, making it the longest-running lu'au on the island.

The **Royal Lu'au** at the Outrigger Waikoloa Beach, 808/886-6789, is offered on Sunday and Wednesday from 5:30 P.M., with the *imu* ceremony beginning at 6 P.M. followed by an open bar, dinner, and Polynesian entertainment of song and dance that ends about 8:30 P.M. Prices are adults $65, children 6–12 $33, free for children five and under.

Legends of the Pacific at the Hilton Waikoloa Village is performed by Tihati Productions each Friday evening 6–9 P.M. A full buffet dinner, one cocktail, and a rousing show of Tahitian music and dance is performed at the Kamehameha Court on the resort grounds. Tickets are $65 adults, $32 kids 5–12. Call 808/886-1234 for reservations.

The Mauna Kea **Old Hawaii 'Aha'aina Lu'au** is presented every Tuesday at the North Pointe Lu'au Grounds. While dinner and entertainment start at 6 P.M., you may watch the *imu* preparation at 9 A.M. and the *imu* opening ceremony at 5:30 P.M. Dinner is a veritable feast, followed by entertainment by Nani Lim and her award-winning *hula halau*. Adults pay $72, children 5–11 are half price. For reservations, call 808/882-5810.

SHOPPING

The King's Shops

The Waikoloa Beach Resort community has its own small but very adequate shopping center. The King's Shops, open daily 9:30 A.M.–9:30 P.M., feature more than 40 different shops and restaurants, along with entertainment, special events, a Hawaiian Visitors Bureau office, and a gas station. A number of Hawaiian artifacts and exhibits are displayed here and there around the center. Many shops carry clothing: Crazy Shirts has distinctive tops and tees; Kunahs has casual tropical wear, shorts, T-shirts, hats, and classic aloha shirts for men; Noa Noa has an excellent selection of imported fashions from throughout Southeast Asia and some *tapa* from the South Pacific; Malia carries fine women's wear; and Kane By Malia is for men. It's obvious what Zac's Photo and Copy Center handles; Whaler's General Store carries light groceries and sundries; Pacific Rim Collections is where you will find Hawaiian quilts, masks from throughout the South Pacific, and carved whales and dolphins; and the Endangered Species shop stocks items from T-shirts to sculptures, many with an animal or floral motif, where a portion of the proceeds goes to the World Wildlife Foundation. For artwork, try either Dolphin Galleries or Genesis Galleries, where you'll see pieces by Tabora, Lau Chun, and glass work by Chuhuly; Under the Koa Tree showcases Hawaiian artists who have turned their hands to koa woodwork and fine jewelry; Indochine has jewelry, gifts and art from the Orient; and at The UkuleleHouse you can find an amazing collection of these musical instruments in all styles and sizes plus an assortment of quilts made in the Philippines. If all this shopping hasn't worn you out, head for Macy's or the Galleria, where its many departments carry goods from around the world. The center wouldn't be complete without a place to eat, and you can find everything from fast food to a fine meal. There's something for everyone.

Although the schedule changes periodically, **free entertainment** is offered at the King's Shops every Tuesday 5:30–6:30 P.M. and Thursday 6–8 P.M. when a local *hula halau* comes to perform, and Sunday 4–6 P.M. when local musicians play traditional and contemporary Hawaiian music. These events are popular with both tourists and locals and are an excellent chance to have fun Hawaiian style.

Guided tours of native Hawaiian plants and the nearby petroglyph field start at 10:30 A.M. Tues.–Fri. from in front of the food pavilion. Additionally, a petroglyph tour also runs on Saturday from 8:30 A.M. These petroglyphs offer a link to the mythology and lore of ancient Hawaii. Wear comfortable clothing and bring water for this two-hour walk.

Puako

Basically the only other shopping option, aside from the stores in Kawaihae and Waikoloa, is at the **Puako General Store.** Open daily 8 A.M.– 7 P.M., this small shop carries a limited but sufficient assortment of groceries and sundries for those staying in this coastal community.

RECREATION
Golf

The resorts in South Kohala offer half a dozen of the best golf courses in the state, and they are all within a few miles of each other.

Surrounding the Mauna Lani Bay Hotel are the marvelous **Francis H. I'i Brown Golf Courses** (North and South courses), whose artistically laid-out fairways, greens, and sand traps make it a modern landscape sculpture. The courses are carved from lava, with striking ocean views in every direction. Call the Pro Shop at 808/885-6655 for information and tee times.

The Mauna Kea's classic, trend-setting **Mauna Kea Golf Course** was designed by the master, Robert Trent Jones, has been voted among America's 100 greatest courses and Hawaii's finest. It lies near the ocean and has recently been joined by the **Hapuna Golf Course,** designed by Arnold Palmer and Ed Seay, which has been cut into the lava up above the hotels. Both 18-hole courses give even the master players a challenge. For tee times at Mauna Kea, call 808/882-5400 and for Hapuna, call 808/880-3000.

Like rivers of green, the Waikoloa Beach **King's Golf Course** and **Beach Golf Course** wind their way around the hotels and condos of Waikoloa Beach Resort. Both have plenty of water and lava rock hazards. For the King's Course, call 808/886-7888 and for the Beach Course, call 808/886-6060.

The last minus one to be constructed along the coast is the Four Seasons' **Hualalai Golf Club.** This Jack Nicklaus course seems to be set in the starkest surroundings. Starting inland, you wind

over the tortured lava, finally returning to the water. The Pro Shop handles reservations at 808/325-8480. A second course at Hualalai opened its front nine in 2002 and this will be followed in due course by a back nine.

On the windy slope of Mauna Kea at Waikoloa Village is **Waikoloa Village Golf Club.** No slouch for difficulty, this Robert Trent Jones Jr. course is the most economical of the bunch. Call 808/883-9621 for a tee time.

If you are on vacation without your golf clubs and plan to play more than a round or two, consider renting clubs from **Island Discount Golf,** 75-5565 Luhia St., in Kailua-Kona, 808/334-1771, open daily. Rental rates start at $18 per day but go down for longer rental periods. These rental rates are cheaper than those at the golf courses.

Tennis

Virtually every hotel and condominium has at least a couple of tennis courts on its property. Most are for use by guests only, but a few tennis centers are open to the public, and these can always arrange lessons, round robins, and match play. All the following are non-lighted, day-use only courts. The Outrigger Waikoloa Beach tennis center has six courts with a $10 per hour court fee. Call 808/886-6666 for a court time. More expensive, at $30 an hour, are the eight courts at the Hilton Waikoloa Village Resort, 808/881-2222. Court time at the Mauna Lani Tennis Garden, 808/885-1485, is $20 an hour. With 13 courts, the largest court complex is at the Mauna Kea Beach Resort. Play for $12.50 per person a day; call 808/882-5420 to make arrangements. The Tennis Pavilion at the Orchid at Mauna Lani has 10 courts at $15 per person a day; call 808/887-7532.

Outrigger Canoe Ride

A 35-foot replica double-hull outrigger sailing canoe takes guests for rides along the Kohala Coast. Be part of the crew for a voyage. The *Halalua Lele* leaves from the beach in front of the Orchid at Mauna Lani; rides cost $95 per person. Call 808/885-2000 for reservations and departure times.

Water Sports

For general water sports activities including scuba dives, snorkel gear rental and tours, catamaran or mono-hull sailing cruises, kayak rental, hydro bikes, boogie boards, windsurfing, and more, check with either **Ocean Sports Waikoloa,** 808/886-6666 or 888/724-5234, or **Red Sail Sports,** 808/886-2876 or 877/733-7245. These companies operate from 'Anaeho'omalu Beach, and Red Sail also has a few activities happening at Hapuna Beach.

At the Four Seasons Resort, **Hualalai Water Sports,** 808/325-8222, can put you onto a snorkel cruise, into the water for scuba diving, or aboard a catamaran for a sunset sail. Snorkel gear rental is available as is scuba instruction and certification.

VISITORS INFORMATION

The **Big Island Visitors Bureau,** 808/886-1655, maintains their West Side office at the King's Shops. It's open regular hours for brochures and inquiries.

Towns

Kawaihae

This port town marks the northern end of the South Kohala Coast. Here, Rte. 19 turns eastward toward Waimea, or turns into Rte. 270 heading up the coast into North Kohala. Not really more than a village, Kawaihae town is basically utilitarian, with wharves, fuel tanks, and a boat ramp. A service cluster has numerous shops, restaurants, and a gas station. Unless you're stopping to eat, you'll probably pass right through.

The small **Kawaihae Shopping Center** can take care of your rudimentary shopping needs. There's a 7-Eleven convenience store, a couple clothing shops, Mountain Gold Jewelers, Black Pearl Gallery jewelers, and the Harbor Gallery art and gift shop. Restaurants are located on both levels. Across the highway, you can stop for fresh fish from local waters at Laau's Fish Market, open Mon.–Sat. 6 A.M.–6 P.M. Down the road a short way is Arts Pacifica, an art gallery and shop associated with the Amaury St. Gilles shop in the Hapuna Prince Hotel.

Pua Mau Place

Pua Mau Place botanical and sculpture garden has an unlikely location here in arid Kohala, but that's one of its drawing cards. Two decades in the making and still a work in progress, about 12 acres of Pua Mau (Ever Blooming) Place opened to the public in 2000. The focus here is on flowering plants, ones that thrive and flour-

ish in an arid environment. While many plants have established, some of the most showy are the hibiscus, plumeria, and date palm. With so much sunshine and so little rain, this is a harsh environment and only certain types of plants survive. A greater challenge for the plants is that no pesticides are sprayed and brackish water is used for irrigation. Only the hearty make it, and those that do seem to love it. Heavy mulch guides you along the well-signed paths and plant numbers correspond to a book you take on your self-guided tour. A bit of whimsy is added by a fair number of giant bronze sculptures of insects that dot the garden here and there. Payable at the gift shop, the entrance fee of $8 helps to support the nonprofit foundation that maintains the garden. Pua Mau is open Wed.–Sun. only 10 A.M.–5 P.M. For additional information, contact the gardens at 808/882-0888, P.O. Box 44555, Kawaihae, HI 96743, www.puamau.org.

Accommodation

Set high above the ocean a few miles north of Kawaihae (turn onto Ala Kahua street at mile marker 6) is **Hale Ho'onanea** bed-and-breakfast. Modern in design, with new amenities, all three detached suites on this property have private entrances and baths, a small kitchenette, and perhaps best of all, plenty of privacy. A continental breakfast will be waiting for you each morning when you get up. Just over 1.5 miles from the coast, there are great ocean views out over the surrounding ranch land, whale-watching in season, and unbeatable stargazing any time of the year. The Hale Suite, with its king bed and queen sofa sleeper, runs $120. Tranquillity Suite has a king bed and queen futon and goes for $100. The smallest, with a queen bed and queen futon, is the Garden Suite and it rents for $90. For information and reservations, contact Jeanne or Larry Roppolo at P.O. Box 6568, Kamuela, HI 96743, tel./fax 808/882-1653 or 877/882-1653, jroppolo@houseofrelaxation.com, www .houseofrelaxation.com.

Kawaihae Food

Who'd expect an upscale yuppie restaurant in the sleepy village of Kawaihae? **Café Pesto,** 808/882-1071, open Sun.–Thurs. 11 A.M.–9 P.M., Fri.–Sat. 11 A.M.–10 P.M., has a chic interior design with black-and-white checkerboard flooring and black tables trimmed with wood, similar to its sister café in Hilo. The bold gourmet menu tantalizes you with starters like crostini (French bread with a fresh, creamy herb garlic butter) and a host of freshly made salads from $3. Pasta dishes are scrumptious, including smoked-salmon pasta with mushrooms and sun-dried tomatoes, and fettuccine in saffron cream sauce. Lunch, served 11 A.M.–4 P.M., brings an assortment of calzones and hot sandwiches that includes everything from smoked ham to a chicken pita. Café Pesto also serves gourmet pizza with crust and sauces made fresh daily, all ranging in price up to about $18. Among its best pizzas are shiitake mushrooms and artichokes with rosemary Gorgonzola sauce. Dinner entrées are wild, with North Kohala fresh catch that can be grilled or sautéed for $19–22, and seafood risotto sumptuous with morsels of Keahole lobster, tiger prawns, and jumbo scallops for $19. Café Pesto is a perfect place to stop for a civilized meal as you explore the Kohala Coast.

Pancho Villa in aloha shirt and sombrero and riding a surfboard (!) would be instantly at home in **Tres Hombres Beach Grill,** 808/882-1031, located on the upper level of the Kawaihae Center and open Sun.–Thurs. 11:30 A.M.–9 P.M., until 10 P.M. on weekends. Besides being a south-of-the-border restaurant, Tres Hombres is an unofficial surfing museum filled with a fine collection of surfboards and surfing memorabilia donated by such legendary greats as Dewey Weber, Greg Knoll, and Jack Wise. The bamboo-appointed interior has a relaxed tropical effect. The extensive menu offers antojitos such as nachos, nachitos, calamari, and chimichangas for under $12. Substantial meals include all the Mexican favorites for $9–15, plus the grill also offers fish in tomato, pepper, and onion sauce, shrimp basted in lime butter, honey mustard chicken, and more unusual items like crab enchiladas, for up to $21. The full bar serves not only a range of beers and all the island favorites, but adds special concoctions like the Kawaihae Sunsets that will help you go down for the evening, and Mauna Kea Sunrises that, with a great deal of wishful thinking, will pop you back up. *Pu pu* are served 3–6 P.M. daily. Relax with an ice-cold margarita on the lanai of this casual restaurant, and experience an excellent change of pace from the luxury hotels just down the road.

A few steps away is the smaller **Akizuka's** which serves quick eats like *loco moco,* pot roast, fried saimin, plate lunches, sushi, coffee, and smoothies. While there are a few tables inside, most use this as a take-out place. Just down the way is the **Anuenue** pizza, ice cream, and shave ice window counter.

Kawaihae Harbor Grill serves lunch 11:30 A.M.–2:30 P.M. and dinner daily 5:30–9:30 P.M.; 808/882-1368. Climb the steps to the large veranda from where you have a bird's-eye view of Kawaihae and unfortunately an unobstructed view of the petrochemical tanks across the road. Dinners include fresh catch, steak and seafood combo, *huli*-style half chicken, and charbroiled rib eye steak, all $14–24. Lighter fare is also offered like a *pu pu* sampler, veggie platter, and crab cakes. Inside, the onetime village store is quite tasteful, with *lau hala* mats, lava lamps, and a glass partition that has been etched with an octopus and tropical fish. The Kawaihae Harbor Grill is tasteful and presented with pride.

Set at the edge of town along Rte. 270 is the **Blue Dolphin Restaurant,** 808/882-7771, open for dinner Wed.–Sat. 5–10 P.M., Friday until 11:30 P.M. Seating is all outdoors, but in the dry climate of Kawaihae that hardly matters. Dinner, mostly $13–22, begins with the soup of the day and appetizers like sautéed mushrooms and fresh ceviche. Entrées include crispy macadamia nut pork loin, *pulehu* (broiled) chicken breasts, nori-wrapped tempura ahi, and fresh catch. While the food is okay, the Blue Dolphin is perhaps best known for its music.

Kawaihae Activities

Kohala Divers, 808/882-7774, www.kohaladivers.com, open daily 8 A.M.–5 P.M., is a full-service dive shop that offers open-ocean certification for $550, two-tank boat dives for $99, an introductory dive for $145, scuba rentals for $15, and snorkeling gear rentals for $10. If there's room on the boat, Kohala Divers will take snorkelers along for $40. Kohala Divers is also a retail shop where you can buy boogie boards, fins, masks, snorkels, and scuba equipment. If you are a scuba enthusiast, you can come here to get your tanks refilled or overhaul your diving gear. It's a bit far to go from Kailua-Kona—much closer from the Kohala resorts—but rates are competitive. Divers are taken up the coast from Kawaihae. On the lower level of the Kawaihae Shopping Center.

Mauna Kea Divers, 808/882-1544, www.maunakeadivers.com, also rents scuba and snorkel gear in Kawaihae and offers comparable scuba tours. Two-tank dive run $90, certification is $600, and scuba gear rental $24. Mauna Kea Divers will work with you to give you the experience that you want. Mauna Kea Divers is located along the highway.

Also on the lower level of the shopping center is **Paniolo Adventures,** 808/889-5354, an outfit that offers a variety of outings, including open-range horseback rides, mountain biking through cattle country, and hikes into the upper part of their ranch.

Waikoloa Village

If you're interested in visiting Waimea as well as seeing the South Kohala coast, you might consider turning right off Rte. 19 near mile marker 75 onto Waikoloa Road. This route cuts inland for 13 miles, connecting coastal Rte. 19 with inland Rte. 190, which leads to Waimea. About halfway up, you pass the planned and quickly growing community of Waikoloa Village about six miles inland from Waikoloa Resort. Try to overlook the condo complexes along the road and head into the village itself, which is low-rise and quite tasteful. Waikoloa Village is a mixture of condominiums and single-family homes that is also home to Waikoloa Village Golf Club, whose course is open to the public, and Roussels restaurant at the clubhouse.

Waikoloa sits below the saddle that runs between Mauna Kea and the North Kohala Mountains. When the trade winds blow from the northeast, they funnel over this saddle and race down the slope, creating windy conditions that challenge golfers. For the dubious distinction of being a windy community, Waikoloa is sometimes jokingly called "Waiko-blow-a." The village is serviced by the **Waikoloa Highlands Shopping Center,** a small but adequate shopping mall with a gas station, full-service supermarket, First Hawaiian Bank, postal service store, small medical center, and a few restaurants and shops.

Fronting the ninth fairway of the golf course, you'll find **Waikoloa Villas,** 808/883-9144, or call Marc Resorts at 800/535-0085 for reservations. Rates for these condo units are one bedroom $169–189, two bedrooms $189–209, and three bedrooms $239–269, with a two-night minimum stay. Amenities include two swimming pools, spa, nearby golf, and weekly maid service. All units are fully furnished with complete kitchens, TV, and washers and dryers. The condo offers a money-saving condo/car package, as well as other discount packages. Check in at the Marc Resorts office in the Waikoloa Highlands Shopping Center, Suite 213.

Paniolo Greens, 808/883-0600 or 888/450-4646, a timeshare property nearby rents units when space is available. Starting at $230 a night, two-bedroom, two-bath condos come with a complete kitchen, washer and dryer, and entertainment center, and have tennis courts, exercise gym, and swimming pool on property.

Waikoloa has at least eight other condo/apartment properties that offer rental units, most in the economy and mid-range. For information about some of what is available, contact Triad Management at 808/329-6402 or Certified Management at 808/329-6063. **Aldridge Associates,** 808/883-8300, www.waikoloa.net, has vacation rentals in Waikoloa.

For those wanting to stay along the coast, **Roussels Waikoloa Village** is a bit out of the way, but for those willing to venture inland, the restaurant lies like a pot of gold at the end of the rainbow. In Waikoloa Village, turn onto Paniolo Avenue, then onto Lua Kula Street, and finally onto Malia Street and follow it to the golf course clubhouse where the Roussels sign will direct you to the restaurant. Roussels, 808/883-9644, is open seven days a week, for lunch 11 A.M.–2:30 P.M., appetizers 2–9:30 P.M., and dinner Tues.–Sat. 5–10 P.M. Reservations recommended. Roussels' niche is spicy Cajun food. It's the only restaurant on the island whose main emphasis is food from the Creole South. The shrimp, oyster, and okra gumbo at $6.95 a cup is outstanding and a specialty, as is the shrimp Creole for $17.95, or whet your appetite with crabmeat crepe, $8–9. A salad selection is the next course before you move to the Cajun entrées, which include chicken Pontalba, duck in hunter's sauce, trout meunière amandine, and blackened fresh catch, $17–25. All entrées are served with salad, vegetables, and fresh-baked bread. Complement the meal with a choice wine, choose from an assortment of cakes, pies, and mousses baked daily, and end with a wonderful liqueur. Lunches are a bit faster and geared toward the local golf clientele. Salads, burgers, and sandwiches are main menu items, but a few dinner selections also appear on the lunch menu in smaller, less expensive portions. This is upscale Cajun cooking in an upcountry island setting.

Waimea

Waimea (also called Kamuela) is in the South Kohala district, but because of its inland topography of high mountain pasture on the broad slope of Mauna Kea, it can be considered a district in its own right. It also has a unique culture inspired by the range-riding *paniolo* of the expansive **Parker Ranch.** This spread, founded early in the 19th century by John Palmer Parker, dominates the heart and soul of the region. Waimea revolves around ranch life and livestock. Herds of rodeos and "Wild West shows" are scheduled throughout the year. But a visit here isn't one-dimensional. In town are homey accommodations and inspired country dining, and the town supports arts and crafts in fine galleries, and a scientific community to staff a number of the observatories high on the mountain above. For fun and relaxation there's a visitor and ranch center; Pu'opelu, the Parker mansion and art collection; a wonderful museum operated by John

Parker's great-great-granddaughter and her sons; a litany of historic shrines and churches; and an abundance of fresh air and wide-open spaces, the latter not so easily found in the islands.

The town, at elevation 2,670 feet, is split almost directly down the center—the east side is the wet side, and the west is the dry side. Houses on the east side are easy to find and reasonable to rent; houses on the dry side are expensive and usually unavailable. You can literally walk from verdant green fields and tall trees to semi-arid landscape in a matter of minutes. This imaginary line also demarcates the local social order: upper-class ranch managers (dry), and working-class *paniolo* (wet). However, the air of Waimea, refreshed and cooled by *kipu'upu'u* (fine mists) and wind, combines with only 20 inches of rainfall a year

J.D. BISIGNANI

Waimea rangeland

WAIMEA

To Hilo

RD.

19

BELT

DON'S PAKE KITCHEN

DAN DE LUZ WOODS

KAMUELA LIQUOR

COOK'S DISCOVERIES

UILANI PLAZA

DAN PLAZA

HAWAII

Kuhio Village

C&S OUTFITTERS

POLICE

STATE OFFICES

FIRE STATION

'IMIOLA CHURCH

MEDICAL CENTER

PARKE RANCH STABLES

SEE DETAIL

WAIMEA SCHOOL

HOKUULA RD.

MAUNA KEA GARDENS

WAIMEA PARK

RD.

TAKO TACO

DANIEL THIEBAUT RESTAURANT

PANIOLO PARK

LINDSEY

KAMUELA INN

PARKER SQUARE MALL

KAWAI

RACE TRACK

OPELU RD.

MERRIMAN'S

EDELWEISS

WAIMEA VISITOR CENTER

QUILTED HORSE

KOHALA HWY

0.5 mi

0.5 km

0

0

OPELO PLAZA

WAIMEA COUNTRY STORE

WAIMEA-KOHALA AIRPORT

JACARANDA INN

RD.

PARKER RANCH HISTORIC HOMES

MAMALAHOA

190

LAE LAE RD

Stream

To Kona

Kohakohau

KAWAIHAE

Stream

Gulch

Haleaha

HAWAII PREP ACADEMY

POWER PLANT

KAMUELA MUSEUM

Keanuiomano

Waikoloa

To Hawi

250

AAAH, THE VIEWS

To Kawaihae

19

DETAIL

KECK OBSERVATORY OFFICE

KOA GRILL

SPENSER HOUSE

WAIMEA CENTER

UPCOUNTRY CONNECTION

PARKER RANCH CENTER

RANCH VISITOR CENTER AND MUSEUM

PARKER SCHOOL

WAIMEA COUNTRY LODGE

PANIOLO COUNTRY INN

BANK

KAHILU THEATER

KAPIOLANI RD.

LINDSEY RD.

WAIMEA PARK

LIBRARY

POST OFFICE

PARKER RANCH GRILL

HWY

MAMALAHOA

into the best mountain weather in Hawaii. Waimea is also known as Kamuela, the Hawaiianized version of Samuel, after one of John Parker's grandsons. Kamuela is used as the post office address, so as not to confuse Waimea with towns of the same name on the islands of Oʻahu and Kauaʻi.

For decades, Waimea was a sleepy insular ranch community. World War II brought an end to its isolation as thousands of GIs descended on the town when Camp Tarawa was built for training. To cater to all these eager young men, the town had to gear up to provide services, which it did in a rousing way. After the war, the town settled back to its quieter times. Recently, Waimea has experienced a growth spurt. In 1980 it had no traffic lights and was home to about 2,000 people. Now the population has grown threefold and there are traffic jams. Waimea is modernizing, and its cowboy backwoods character is rapidly changing.

Waimea is at the crossroads of the main east coast road (Rte. 19) from Hilo and Rte. 190 from Kailua-Kona. Route 19 continues west through town, reaching the coast at Kawaihae, where it turns south and cuts along the barren Kohala Coast to Kailua-Kona. The main artery connecting Waimea and Kailua-Kona is Rte. 190, also known as the Hawaii Belt Road. This stretch is locally called the Mamalahoa Highway. From Kailua-Kona, head out on Palani Road until it turns into Rte. 190. As you gain elevation heading into the interior, look left to see the broad and flat coastal lava flows. Seven miles before reaching Waimea, Saddle Road (Rte. 200) intersects this road from the right, and now the highlands, with grazing cattle amidst fields of cactus, look much more like Marlboro Country than the land of aloha.

HISTORY

John Palmer Parker was a seaman who left Newton, Massachusetts, on a trading vessel in 1809 and landed in Kealakekua, becoming a fast friend of Kamehameha the Great. Parker, then only 19, jumped ship and in 1816 married Kipikani, the granddaughter of King Kamehameha. Domesticated cattle, a present from Captain Vancouver to Kamehameha, had gone wild due to neglect and were becoming a dangerous nuisance all over the Big Island. Parker was hired to round up the best of them and to exterminate the rest. While doing so, he chose the finest head for his own herd. In 1847 King Kamehameha III divided the land by what was known as the Great Mahele, and John Parker was granted Royal Deed No. 7, for a two-acre parcel on the northeast slopes of Mauna Kea. His wife, being royal born, was entitled to 640 acres, and with these lands and tough determination, the mighty Parker Ranch began.

Unfortunately, many members of the Parker family died young. The first-born, John Palmer Parker II, married Hanai. His brother, Ebenezer, married Kilea, an *aliʻi* woman from Maui, who bore him four children. The oldest boy was Samuel Parker, known in Hawaiian as Kamuela, the co-name of Waimea town. Samuel married Napela, and together they had nine children. Samuel's father Ebenezer died at age 26. Kilea could never get over his death and visited his grave daily. Finally, she decided that she wanted to return to her family on Maui. She was advised by the people of the island not to go because of rough seas. Kilea did not heed the advice and along with her entourage was lost at sea.

John Palmer Parker II moved the family and ranch's central operation from the original homestead to Waimea in 1879. His wife, Hanai, gave birth to only one boy, who died within 12 months. Childless, they adopted one of their nephew Samuel's nine children as a *hanai* child, in a practice that continues to this day. He was the fifth child, John, who became John Palmer Parker III and who later married Elizabeth Dowsett, known as Aunt Tootsie. They had one girl, Thelma Parker, before John III died of pneumonia at age 19. Aunt Tootsie raised Thelma as a single parent and somehow managed to purchase Samuel Parker's and his eight children's half of the ranch. Thelma Parker married Gillian Smart. They had one boy, Richard Smart, before Thelma died at age 20 of tuberculosis. Aunt Tootsie literally took the bull by the horns to keep the ranch going, and when she passed away in 1943, she left everything to her grandson Richard. The ranch prospered under his ownership. After his death, the ranch became a charitable trust called the Parker Ranch Foundation Trust that benefits the people of Waimea and local communities long associated with its operation. Although the ranch at one time was a huge 500,000 acres, it is now down to 225,000 acres. When Richard Smart was alive, the Parker Ranch was the largest privately owned, single-owner ranch in the United States. Today, still at that size, it has 400 horses and 50,000 head of cattle that supply fully one-third of the beef in the Hawaiian Islands. The Parker Ranch Foundation Trust is the second largest landowner in the state, following the Bishop Estate. Find more information about the ranch and family at www.parkerranch.com.

Sights

Parker Ranch Historic Homes

Richard Smart, last heir to the gigantic Parker Ranch, opened **Pu'opelu,** a century-old family mansion, to the public just a few years before he passed away on November 12, 1992. On the grounds, the ranch's reconstructed original home is also open to visitors. Pu'opelu is located off Rte. 190 a few minutes southeast of town and is open daily 10 A.M.–5 P.M., admission $8.50 adults, $7.50 seniors, $6 children; 808/885-5433.

A formal drive lined with stately eucalyptus trees leads to the mansion. The home was begun in 1862 by an Englishman but bought by John Palmer Parker II in 1879. In 1910, Richard Smart's grandmother, Aunt Tootsie, added the living room, kitchen, and fireplace. In 1960, Richard Smart, who inherited the ranch lands and home from Aunt Tootsie, replaced the living room and raised its ceiling to 16 feet to accommodate his art collection, and he landscaped the grounds. He added elegant French doors and skylights, and the koa doorways were installed to match. Smart grew up in San Francisco and became enamored with the theater at a young age. He studied at the Pasadena Playhouse in the late '20s and later appeared on Broadway with such famous names as Carol Channing and Nanette Fabray. Smart performed in plays all over the United States, and recordings of his singing provide the background music as you tour the house.

Enter an elegant sitting room illuminated by a crystal chandelier to begin your tour. Inside this living museum, the works of prominent European artists are displayed, but since Smart's death, some artworks have been sold off and the collection diminished. The tour is self-guided, with all art pieces named. Besides paintings by famous artists, there are magnificent pieces of wooden furniture, tall cabinets holding yellow Chinese Peiping glass from the 19th century, silver tea sets, glassware, figurines, and magnificent chandeliers. Make sure to see the little side bedroom, called the Venetian Room, aptly decorated with paintings of gondolas and appointed with treasures from Venice. Lighting the room are two chandeliers, one pink and the other turquoise. Here, the filigreed art-deco mirrors are also fabulous. The feeling is of genteel elegance, but notice that the walls are rather rough board-and-batten covered with beautiful artwork. Recently opened is Richard Smart's bedroom, which is loaded with memorabilia from his stage performances and mementos given by the people he knew on Broadway. You get the feeling of class, but it's obvious that you are on a ranch. In the emerald-green kingdom that is the Parker Ranch, Pu'opelu is the crown jewel.

Just outside Pu'opelu is the reconstructed New England "saltbox" **Mana Hale,** the original Parker Ranch homestead. The home was built in 1847 by family patriarch John Palmer Parker from the durable native koa found at high elevations on the ranch lands. The sons, who were by then married, built two homes, and as children came, added more rooms in the sprawling New England tradition. They also built one large community kitchen, at which the entire family cooked and dined. A replica shows how the home grew over the years, and it is a good indicator of how the Parker fortunes grew along with it. As the children's children got older, they needed a schoolhouse, so they built one at the corner of the original site. It still stands and is maintained by a *paniolo* and his family who live there. The exterior of the original home, covered by a heavy slate roof, was too brittle to move from its original site 12 miles away, but the interior was removed, numbered, and put back together again like a giant jigsaw puzzle in the reconstructed home. A model in the living room shows you what the original site looked like back in the 1800s. To preserve the rich wood interior of the home, all that's required is to wipe it down once a year with lemon oil. At first the home seems like a small cabin, just what you'd expect from the 1850s, but in actuality it's a two-story home with one bedroom downstairs and three upstairs.

SIGHTS IN TOWN

Parker Ranch Visitor Center and Museum

This is the first place to stop while in town if you want an overview of the evolution of this upcountry domain. The visitor center, 808/885-7655, at the Parker Ranch Center, is open daily 9 A.M.–5 P.M. (last tickets sold at 4 P.M.); admission is adults $6, $5 seniors, children $4.50. Tickets for joint admission to the visitor center, museum, and historic homes are $12, $12, and $9.50, respectively; for the visitor center, museum, homes, and wagon ride, prices run $42, $40, and $35, respectively.

After spending an hour at the center's museum and taking in the slide presentation, you'll have a good overview of the history of the Parker Ranch and, by extension, Waimea. Exhibits at the John Palmer Parker Museum depict the history and genealogy of the six generations of Parkers who have owned the ranch. In the museum, old

ROBERT NILSEN

'Imiola Church

WAIMEA

family photos include one of Rev. Elias Bond, who presided over the Christian marriage of John Palmer Parker and his Hawaiian wife in 1820. Preserved also are old Bibles, clothing from the era, and an entire koa hut once occupied by wood-cutters and range riders. There are fine examples of quilting, stuffed animals, an arsenal of old weapons, and even a vintage printing press. The 15-minute video in the comfortable Thelma Parker Theater begins whenever enough people have assembled after going through the museum. The video presents a thorough and professional rendition of the Parker Ranch history, along with sensitive glimpses of ranch life of the still very active *paniolo*. To the rear of the shopping center is an old wood-and-stone corral.

'Imiola Church

Head east on Rte. 19 to "church row," a cluster of New England–style structures on the left, a few minutes past the Parker Ranch Visitor Center. Most famous among these old structures is 'Imiola (Seeking Life) Congregational Church. It was built from 1855 to 1857 by the Rev. Lorenzo Lyons, who mastered the Hawaiian language and translated some of the great old Christian hymns into Hawaiian, as well as melodic Hawaiian chants into English. Restored in 1976, the yellow clapboard church with white trim would be at home along any New England village green. When you enter, you'll notice an oddity: the pulpit is at the near side and you walk around it to face the rear of the church. Nearly all inside surfaces are of rich brown koa. The hymnals contain many of the songs translated by Father Lyons. Outside is a simple monument to Rev. Lyons, along with a number of his children's gravesites. Have a look inside or stop by for one of the two Sunday worship services.

Also along this row are the Ka Ola Mau Loa Hawaiian Church, the Kamuela Hongwanji Mission, the First Baptist Church, and the Waimea Chapel of the Church of Jesus Christ of Latter-day Saints.

Kamuela Museum

The Kamuela Museum, 808/885-4724, open every day of the year 8 A.M.–5 P.M., the largest pri-

vately owned museum in Hawaii, is a fantastic labor of love. For the founders and curators, Albert and Harriet Solomon (Albert died in 2001 while in his nineties), it was a vocation that started in 1968 and fulfilled a prophecy of Albert's grandmother, who was pure Hawaiian and a renowned *kahuna* from Pololu Valley. When Albert was only eight years old, his grandmother foretold that he would build "a great longhouse near three mountains and that he would become famous, visited by people from all over the world." This prediction struck him so much that he wrote it down and kept it throughout his life. When grown, he married Harriet, the great-great granddaughter of John Palmer Parker, and the two lived in Honolulu for most of their adult lives, where Albert was a policeman. For 50 years the Solomons collected, collected, and collected! Harriet, being a Parker, was given heirlooms by family members, which are also on exhibit. The museum is west of town center on Rte. 19, 50 yards west of the junction with Rte. 250 heading toward Hawi. Admission to the museum, dedicated to Mary Ann Parker, John Parker's only daughter, is adults $5, children under 12, $2. Plan on spending at least an hour.

As you enter, the screen door bangs like a shot to signal that another visitor has arrived. Inside it's easy to become overwhelmed as you're confronted with everything from sombreros to a stuffed albatross, moose head, and South American lizard. An extensive weapons collection includes Khyber rifles, Japanese machine guns, swords, and knives. If you enjoy Hawaiiana, check out the *kahili* and *konane* boards, poi pounders, stone sinkers and hooks, wooden surfboards, and a very unique "canoe buster." The museum has a few extremely rare stone idols and a good collection of furniture from Hawaiian nobility, including Prince Kuhio's council table. Antiques of every description include Japanese and Hawaiian feathered fans, carved Chinese furniture, a brass diving helmet, some of the first Hawaiian Bibles, and even buffalo robes used by the pioneers. Everywhere are old photos commemorating the lives of the Parkers down through the years. Before you leave, go into the front room, where the view through a huge picture window perfectly frames a pond and three round-topped mountains in *paniolo* country.

Practicalities

ACCOMMODATIONS

Inns

The **Kamuela Inn,** P.O. Box 1994, Kamuela, HI 96743, 808/885-4243 or 800/555-8968, fax 808/885-8857, kaminn@aloha.net, www.hawaii-bnb.com/kamuela.html, a onetime basic cinder-block motel, has been transformed into a bright and airy 31-unit boutique hotel. It is located down a short cul-de-sac off Rte. 19 just before Opelu Road. The owner takes personal pride in the hotel and offers each guest a complimentary continental breakfast each morning in the art gallery on premises. The pleasant grounds are appointed with flowers and manicured trees, and you'll find a swing to lull you into relaxation. The basic motel rooms are small, neat, and tidy with twin or double beds with wicker headboards, private bathrooms, and color TV, but no a/c (not needed) or phones. About one third of the units have kitchens. The deluxe Penthouse is upstairs and breaks into two joinable units that can accommodate up to five guests. The newer wing has tasteful larger rooms with hardwood floors, king-size or twin beds, and features deluxe Executive Suites with full kitchens. Prices range from $59 for a basic room and $72–85 for a deluxe, to $89–99 for suites with kitchenettes. The Penthouse suites, when sleeping five, and the Executive suites are $185. Smoking and non-smoking rooms are available. Reserve well in advance.

The **Waimea Country Lodge,** 65-1210 Lindsey Rd., Kamuela, HI 96743, 808/885-4100 or 800/367-5257, fax 808/885-6711, www.castleresorts.com, is located in "downtown" Waimea, but don't let "downtown" fool you because it's very quiet. Renovated in 1997, the rooms, many with kitchenettes and vaulted ceilings, have full baths and are well appointed with knotty pine furnishings, king- or queen-size beds with turned pine lamps, wicker easy chairs, fans and portable heaters, phones, and TVs. The barn-red board-and-batten inn sits off by itself and lives up to its place in *paniolo* country by giving the impres-

sion of a gentleman's bunkhouse. The view out the back toward the mountain is an added bonus. Rates are $95 standard, $100 superior, $110 with a kitchenette, $120 deluxe, and $10 for an additional person.

Built in 1897 as the Parker Ranch manager's house, this plantation estate has gone through several metamorphoses and most recently been renovated, expanded, and turned into **The Jacaranda Inn,** 65-1444 Kawaihae Rd., Kamuela, HI 96743, 808/885-8813, fax 808/885-6096, tji@ilhawaii.net, www.jacarandainn.com. This estate, with its raspberry-colored roof, dominates a broad lawn. A white ranch fence and bougainvillea hedge separate it from the road. Set amidst towering trees, the main house retains the original Hawaii Victorian flavor, with rich koa wood and numerous antiques. Enter the huge living room with its imposing fireplace, and from there you can move to the dining rooms, library, billiard room, bar, or terrace. Separate oversized suites have also been constructed to the rear as guest rooms. They are all decorated according to different themes and colors, and while each shows individual character and style, they all have a similar romantic feel. These are not ordinary rooms; they are designed to pamper guests in luxury. The eight guest rooms, with pretty flower names like White Lily, Iris, Orchid, and Passion Flower, rent for $95–225 or $189–300 a night depending upon the option. One option is daily hot breakfast and maid service, along with a bottle of wine on arrival and no minimum stay; the second option is a daily continental breakfast, maid service every three days, and a two night minimum. In addition, a three-bedroom, three-bath cottage that can sleep up to six goes for $550 or $650 a night with a five night minimum.

Bed-and-Breakfasts

No place could be more appropriately named than **aaah, The Views,** P.O. Box 6593, Kamuela, HI 96743, 808/885-3455 or 866/885-3455, fax 808/885-4031, tommare@aloha.net,

WAIMEA

www.beingsintouch.com. This bed-and-breakfast, located in a quiet residential neighborhood just downhill from central Waimea, has unimpeded views of Mauna Kea, Mauna Loa, and Mt. Hualalai to the south, and, of course, the ocean off the Kohala Coast to the west. Fine for the sunrise over the mountains, the sunsets on clear days are stupendous, and clear nights illuminate a star-studded sky. Aaah, The Views sits along a stream next to Parker Ranch land, so you may see cattle grazing nearby. Rooms in the two-bedroom suite of the detached house can be booked individually or together. Each has a sleeping room with a cozy loft and a small deck, and they share a good-sized bathroom with tub and shower. New and modern, these rooms are tastefully appointed and laid with berber carpet. Also in this detached building is a newer, tidy and compact garden studio, with its queen-bed room, loft, bath, and kitchen. While each room has a small refrigerator, microwave unit, and coffeemaker, a continental breakfast with plenty of fruits, pastries, cereals, and coffee is served each morning in the main house dining area or on a lanai that overlooks the stream. In the main house, the small Skylight Room is just big enough for one or a romantic couple. Room rates are $65–110, add $15 for an additional person.

Set along a pleasant stream a couple miles west of downtown Waimea is **Waimea Garden Cottage,** 808/885-8550. This lovely B&B is a quality professional place with plentiful modern amenities and a style that speaks of yesteryear with wainscoting, antique furniture, hardwood floors, and French doors. The two rooms run $145–155 double, $15 for one additional person in a room; three nights minimum.

Occupying the downstairs walkout apartment of a home in a quiet residential section east of the center of town is **Waimea Suite Bed and Breakfast,** 808/937-2833. This finely decorated apartment with its welcoming colors has two bedrooms, one with a king bed and the second with two twins, one pleasant bathroom, a full and modern kitchen stocked with necessities, and a koa-wood paneled living room with some antique furniture and a lava rock fireplace—wood provided. There is plenty of room inside and out on the lanai, where the lawn slopes away is a wooded expanse and beyond which is a good view of Mauna Loa. As the owner is a shopkeeper in town, there is no cooked breakfast, but all breakfast supplies and more are provided. No smoking is allowed indoors and no pets are accepted, but what this unit does offer in plenty is privacy, convenience, and comfort. Just right for one or two couples, or a small family, the rate is $125 a night for two, $25 for each additional adult or $15 for kids under age 12. Two nights minimum; weekly rates are available.

With great views over the long and broad Kohala Coast and up to Mauna Loa, Mauna Kea, and Hualalai, **Belle Vue** has a location that's just right. Spacious suites with living rooms, kitchenette, and fireplaces rent for $85–165 and this includes a fine breakfast. French and German spoken. Contact the owners at P.O. Box 1295, Kamuela, HI 96743, tel./fax 808/885-7732 or 808/772-5044, bellvue@aloha.net, www.hawaii-bellevue.com.

Vacation Rental Agency

With an office at the Historic Spencer House, **MacArthur & Company,** 808/885-8885 or 877/885-8285, fax 808/885-5538, handles several rental homes in Waimea, with prices from $75 to $250 a night. Contact the company at 65-1148 Mamalohoa Highway, Kamuela, HI 96743, info@letsgohawaii.com, www.letsgohawaii.com.

FOOD

Inexpensive

The cafeteria-style **Kamuela Deli** offers sirloin steak, grilled ham steak, and boneless spicy chicken, all priced around $7. They also have breakfasts like corned beef hash or hamburger patties with eggs and hash browns. Deli sandwiches, priced under $5, include teriyaki beef, shrimp burgers, and ham sandwiches. Plate lunches are also available. The good price and good food make this a favorite spot for locals.

Also in the Waimea Center is **Young's Kalbi,** a Korean restaurant open daily except Sunday, that serves dishes like kalbi chicken, shrimp tempura, oyster-sauce chicken, and spicy pork, all priced under $8. Young's is very basic but clean, and the food is tasty.

Don's Pake Kitchen, about one mile east of town on Rte. 19 and open daily 10 A.M.–8:30 P.M., Sunday from 3 P.M., is a Chinese family restaurant that has a good reputation for food at reasonable prices even though most of its selections are of the steam-table variety. Some items are ginger beef, oyster chicken, and shrimp-sauce pork, but many people come for the saimin. Don's also specializes in large pans of food that can feed entire families.

Waimea Coffee Company, in the Parker Square, is open Mon.–Fri. 7 A.M.–5 P.M., Saturday 8 A.M.–4 P.M. Order coffee beans in bulk and coffee by the cup. Lunch is served 11 A.M.–3 P.M., including turkey, ham, or tuna sandwiches, Caesar salad, quiches, and homemade soups.

The **Hawaiian Style Café,** in a modest building across from Parker Square, is open Mon.–Fri. 6 A.M.–12:45 P.M., Sunday 7:30–11 A.M., but closed the last Sat., Sun., and Mon. of the month. It offers local and American standard food at very reasonable prices. Inside the blue-painted interior, chairs line a low counter where the menu offers breakfasts of two eggs with Spam or bacon, a three-egg omelette with a side of pancakes, Hawaiian-style loco moco, and Belgian waffles with whipped butter, strawberries, and maple syrup, mostly under $6. Plate lunches, around $9, served with rice and potato or macaroni salad include curry stew, *lau lau,* chicken, pickled veggie, or a steak plate. A little short on Martha Stewart panache but long on pride, the Hawaiian Style Café will fill you up while being easy on your wallet.

Back up the highway a ways and across from the park is **Tako Taco,** 808/887-1717, a Mexican taqueria that's open Mon.–Sat. 11 A.M.–8 P.M. Here you can get regular tacos, burritos, tostadas, and the like, along with vegetarian items and those made with tofu. Sit inside or out. Tako Taco has gained a reputation for quick, fresh, and wholesome food.

Moderate

Paniolo Country Inn, on Lindsey Street, 808/885-4377, open daily for breakfast, lunch, and dinner, specializes in full country-style breakfasts, burgers, lunch platters, and flame-broiled steaks. Breakfast selections include omelettes, hotcakes, waffles, huevos rancheros, loco moco, and the *wiki wiki* breakfast of English muffin, banana bread or wheat toast, coffee, and small fruit juice. Breakfast selections generally run $3–7. Sandwiches and burgers cost around $7, with cowboy-size pizza for $7–27. More substantial Paniolo Platters like teriyaki short ribs, top sirloin, or porterhouse steak are mostly $10–18, and a selection of Mexican dishes is thrown in for good measure. Prime rib dinners are served Friday through Sunday evenings. The food is wholesome, the atmosphere American country, and the service prompt and friendly. Don't miss having a look at the cattle brands hanging on the walls.

Maha's Cafe, 808/885-0693, in the vintage Historic Spencer House at the Waimea Center, open Thurs.–Mon. 8 A.M.–4:30 P.M., offers coffee, tea, island-style food and desserts made fresh daily. The owner, "Maha," learned to cook for her large Hawaiian family but has worked professionally as a pastry chef and a sous chef at a number of resorts including the Mauna Lani Bay Resort. Maha's has window service but also sit-down service inside. From her diminutive kitchen comes breakfasts of poi pancakes with coconut syrup for $3.75 and an assortment of too-tempting pastries including homestyle banana bread, papaya coffee cake, croissants, or pan biscuits $2.75, and always-fresh Kona coffee. Lunch can be any number of sandwiches, or Waipi'o Ways, a plate of broiled fresh fish with sliced and steamed Waipi'o taro and sweet potato on a bed of Kahua greens with ginger vinaigrette dressing for $9.25, smoked 'ahi with *lilikoi* salsa at $10.75, or Kohala Harvest, a mounded delight of vegetables with feta cheese for $7.75. Aloha Ahi-ahi, a version of afternoon tea served 3–4:30 P.M., brings a sampler of Maha's pastries, including croissants, open-faced finger sandwiches, shortbreads, and cobblers. The classic and restored Spencer House was the first frame house ever built in Waimea, in 1852. Once the home of a Judge Bickerton, it was also put to use as a courthouse and as a hotel. The house was once surrounded by the lush green grasses of *paniolo* country but is now in the middle of the black asphalt of the Waimea Center's parking lot!

Perhaps slightly ignominiously located inside and at the back of the Waimea Country Store and gas station across from the Opelo Plaza is **Zappa's,** 808/885-1511. A glorified pizza joint, Zappa's also does hearty breakfasts, plate lunches, pasta, soups, salads, and sandwiches. Breakfast starts daily at 6:30 A.M. and runs through lunch until 1:30 P.M.; nightly except Tuesday, dinner hours are 4:30–8 P.M. Zappa's is a very local eatery that puts out tasty food in large portions at reasonable prices. Anything on the menu can be ordered for take-out.

Morelli's Pizza at the Waimea Center, 808/885-8557, is open daily from 11 A.M. Besides whole pizzas, the oven yields pizza by the slice ($2.25), garlic bread, and oven-baked sandwiches like turkey, pastrami, ham, or veggie, most for around $7. The pizzas range from a small cheese pizza for $6.75 to a three-topping monster tray at $18.50. Set items run $11.50–21.75. To round out your meal, you can also order garden and chef salads and homemade soup. A small dining room with picnic tables is provided if you choose to eat there.

Expensive

Located adjacent to Waimea Center is **Koa House Grill,** 808/885-2088, a well-liked casual place for Parker Ranch steak and ribs, lamb, chicken, and local greens. This is good standard American food at moderate prices, and has the only salad bar in town. While lunch meals are substantially cheaper, dinner entrées run mostly $14–25. The Koa House is open daily for lunch 11:30 A.M.–2 P.M. and 5:30–9 P.M. Lighter food is served all day at the bar, where happy hour is 5–6 P.M. Live music on Friday and karaoke on Saturday both run 9 P.M.–midnight.

Aioli's Restaurant, at Opelo Plaza, 808/885-6325, serves quick but tasty soups, salads, and sandwiches for lunch for under $10. The dinner menu changes every three weeks, and there is al-

ways a vegetarian entrée or two on the menu. The type of item that you might find on the menu includes herb crusted prime rib, seared scallops in a lime cream sauce, pan seared duck, and eggplant pasta. BYOB if you want—no corkage fee. Open at 11 A.M. except Sunday and Monday, the restaurant closes at 4 P.M. on Tuesday, 8 P.M. on Wednesday and Thursday, 9 P.M. on Friday and Saturday; on Sunday, hours are 8 A.M.–2 P.M. Definitely make dinner reservations as Aioli's is popular and there are only about a half dozen tables.

Fine Dining

The Edelweiss on Rte. 19 across from the Kamuela Inn, 808/885-6800, is Waimea's established gourmet restaurant, where chef Hans-Peter Hager, formerly of the super-exclusive Mauna Kea Beach Hotel, serves gourmet food in rustic but elegant surroundings. The Edelweiss is open Tues.–Sat. for lunch 11:30 A.M.–1:30 P.M. and for dinner 5–9 P.M. Inside, heavy posts and beams and dark wood plank paneling exude that "country feeling," but fine crystal and pure white tablecloths let you know you're in for some superb dining. The wine cellar is extensive, with selections of domestic, French, Italian, and German wines. Affordable lunches include offerings like soup, turkey sandwiches, and chicken salad in papaya. Dinner starts with appetizers such as melon with prosciutto, escargot, onion soup, and Caesar salad. Some Edelweiss specialties are sautéed veal, lamb, beef, and bacon with pfefferling; roast duck braised with a light orange sauce; half spring chicken diablo; and of course Swiss and German favorites like Wiener schnitzel and roast pork and sauerkraut, mostly $20–25. In addition to the short standard evening menu, there are often over a dozen specials. The cooking is rich and delicious, the proof a loyal clientele who return again and again.

Merriman's, in the Opelo Plaza, 808/885-6822, has received a great deal of well-deserved praise from travelers and residents alike for its excellent food. The restaurant, resembling a small house from the outside, is stylish with its tablecloths, table settings, and cushioned chairs of bent bamboo. Here, chefs create fusion cuisine from local organic ingredients when available.

WAIMEA

The menu changes every few months, but perennial appetizer and salad favorites that run $8–12 are sweet corn and shrimp fritters, vine-ripened Lokelani tomatoes with Maui onions, and spinach salad with balsamic vinaigrette dressing. Lunch fare, mostly $7–11, includes coconut curry grilled chicken with peanut dipping sauce and rice; grilled eggplant sandwich with Puna goat cheese, basil, and hot sauce; and grilled shrimp on Asian linguine. Entrées from $16 to $35 are superb and might be Peking duck and stir-fry noodles with lop chong sausage, vegetables, and spicy Hoisin sauce; wok-charred *ahi;* shrimp linguine, and prime New York steak. Vegetarians can graze on pan-fried Asian cake noodles and grilled tofu asparagus and mushroom donburi. Some of the most delicious offerings, however, are the fresh catch at market price, prepared in various gourmet styles including herb-grilled sesame-crusted and sautéed with *lilikoi* sauce, or sautéed with pineapple vinaigrette. Owned and operated by Peter Merriman, one of Pacific Rim Cuisine's originators, Merriman's is a Big Island classic. Open for lunch weekdays 11:30 A.M.–1:30 P.M. and dinner daily 5:30–9 P.M.; call for reservations.

The newest of the fine dining restaurants in town is the **Daniel Thiebaut Restaurant,** 808/887-2200, located along Rte. 19 near the Parker Square Mall in the renovated and rambling plantation-era Chock In Store building. Open Mon.–Fri. for lunch 11:30 A.M.–1:30 P.M. and dinner nightly 5:30–9:30 P.M., reservations are usually necessary. Chef Daniel and his attentive staff serve a fusion of French and Asian cuisine with excellent flavors and textures. While the lunch menu is much simpler, dinner entrées include such items as Hunan-style rack of lamb, Provençal crusted tenderloin of beef in balsamic vinegar–red wine sauce with wild mushrooms ragout and herb polenta, sautéed macadamia nut chicken breast with gingered dijon mustard sauce, pickled pineapple and pavà potatoes, and wok-fried sea scallops with Asian style risotto and warm coconut crab dressing. There is a long wine list to accompany each different entrée, but save room for one of the scrumptious desserts or an after-dinner liqueur.

RECREATION

Located behind the Parker Ranch Center is the Mauna Kea Ranch Stables, 808/885-4288, which has been offering horse rides over parts of the Parker Ranch for nearly three decades. Trail rides go several times a day Monday through Saturday and run $40 an hour or $70 for two hours. All rides are guided. Long pants and close-toe shoes are necessary.

You can pretend that you're a *paniolo* riding the range at the **Dahana Ranch,** 808/885-0057 or 888/399-0057. Spend a few hours tending cattle on this working ranch and learn about the history and culture of ranching the Big Island. Dahana Ranch will take just about anyone "three years to 300 pounds."

Kohala Carriages offers a tame 45-minute ranch wagon tour on Parker Ranch land, Tues.–Sat. every hour on the hour 10 A.M.–2 P.M., leaving from the Parker Ranch Visitor Center. Rides cost $15 adult, $12.50 seniors over 60, and $12 ages 4–11. Reserve a seat by calling 808/885-7655.

Every 4th of July, the Parker Ranch hosts a **rodeo** that is one of the best in the state.

Does a sunrise flight over the ranch sound like fun? It's a possibility with **Paradise Balloons, LLC,** 808/887-6455. Take off is from near Pu'opelu before the sun peaks over the mountains and the flight ends before lunch with a return celebration. Rides run $240 adult or $190 ages 5–12. All flights are weather permitting.

The best place in town to shop for good quality bikes and water gear is **C & S Outfitters,** 808/885-5005, located behind Cook's Discovery near the police station. This is a full-service shop that rents, sells, and repairs bicycles and rents kayaks. Stop here first if you're in need of such things.

Several miles east of town on the way to Honoka'a is the **Waimea Country Club** golf course, a pleasantly rolling Scottish links-style course carved from rangeland at over 2,000 feet in elevation. Enter between mile markers 51 and 52.

Periodically throughout the year, movies, plays, music, and a variety of other events are held at the

Kahilu Theater at the rear of the Parker Ranch Center. Call 808/885-6868 for what's currently on schedule.

Waipi'o Ridge Hike

It is possible once again to hike a portion of the Hamakua Ditch Trail, constructed a century ago when water was needed to irrigate the Hamakua sugar plantations. Drive along Hwy. 19 to the outskirts of Waimea and turn left onto White Road. Proceed to the end of the road and park as much off the roadway as possible. This is a narrow road and residents dislike cars parked on the roadway. If the way is not blocked, leave a donation at the trailhead and cross through the gate—you are crossing Hawaiian Homelands property. A gravel track leads around a water reservoir and on into the forest to the flume, which is in the forest reserve and open to the public. Follow the flume and hiking trail about an hour upstream, where it eventually skirts the edge of the upper reaches of the Waipi'o Valley and from where there are superb vistas (on a clear day) into the valley and a long thin waterfall. About a half hour farther along the trail, you can look back down the valley to the ocean and beach. This area often clouds in by late morning, so hit the trail early.

SHOPPING

Waimea's accelerated growth can be measured by the shopping centers springing up around town. These mostly small malls house boutiques that add to the shopping possibilities in Waimea's established centers.

Parker Ranch Center

This long-established mall was totally rebuilt in 2002, completely changing the face of the center of town. With more of a country look, the mall now has more store space than it originally held. A new Foodland grocery store occupies a spot along the highway on the Honoka'a end and nearby are KFC and Blockbuster Video. For an alternative food store, try Healthways II. The Parker Ranch Store has moved from its back location up to the front. Focused on its country cowboy heritage, the shop sells boots, cowboy hats, shirts, skirts, and buckles and bows, and many hand-crafted items are made on the premises. Also moved to the front is Reyn's for island fashions and alohawear. Reopening after a long hiatus and occupying a prominent location is the Parker Ranch Grill. For a mix of quicker foods, stop by the food court, or head to Starbucks or Dairy Queen for a cup of coffee or ice cream cone. As always, the Parker Ranch Visitor Center and Museum is open and available to give visitors a brief overview of this historic area.

Waimea Center

Well marked along the Mamalahoa Hwy. behind McDonald's, most Waimea Center stores are open weekdays 9 A.M.–5 P.M. and Saturday 10 A.M.–5 P.M. Among its shops you will find a KTA Super Store with everything from groceries to pharmaceuticals; Leilani Bakery has pastries and breads; head to Pack, Ship and Copy Depot, for copies, shipping, Internet access, and other business needs; the Men's Shop, whose name says it all; It's All Good, for women's fashions; Kamuela Kids for children's clothing; Big Island Surf has boards, swimsuits, and beachwear; and the intriguing Without Boundaries has an eclectic mix of gifts, travel items, and all around fun things. To keep you going through all this shopping are Morrelli's Pizza and some inexpensive restaurants.

For the photographer, Waimea Photo sells film and does photo developing. Just around the corner and along the highway, Positive Image also carries and develops film. Both shops are open Monday through Saturday only.

Parker Square

Located along Rte. 19, heading west from town center, this small mall has a collection of fine boutiques and shops. Here, like an old trunk filled with family heirlooms, the **Gallery of Great Things**, 808/885-7706, really is loaded with great things. Inside you'll find novelty items like a carousel horse, silk dresses, straw hats, koa paddles, Ni'ihau shellwork, vintage kimonos, an antique water jar from the Chiang Mai area of northern Thailand, Japanese woodblock prints, and less expensive items like shell earrings and koa hair sticks. The Gallery of Great Things represents about 200 local artists on a revolving basis, and the owner, Maria Brick, travels throughout the Pacific and Asia collecting art, some contemporary, some primitive. With its museum-quality items, the Gallery of Great Things is definitely worth a browse. But remember, most items are one of a kind—"now you see them, now you don't."

Sweet Wind, 808/885-0562, open daily, is packed with books, beads, and unique gifts. This "alternative thought and resource center" also sells incense, aromatherapy tinctures, and crystals. The beads come from the world over, and a display case holds Native American rattles, drums, and silver and amber jewelry. Visiting Sweet Wind is soothing for body and soul.

The **Silk Road Gallery,** 808/885-7474, open daily except Sunday, is resplendent with an exceptional collection of Asian antiques and craft items, specializing in creations from Japan and China. In this tasteful shop you will discover such treasures as carved ivory *netsuke,* a favorite of the well-dressed samurai; ornate silk kimonos; Sung Dynasty vases; and Satsumayaki painted pottery from Japan. As you look around you may spot lacquer tables and bowls, ornate *tansu* (chests), straw sandals, an actual water wheel, sacred scrolls that hang in a place of honor in Japanese homes, a Chinese jade bowl with elaborate dragon handles, and an 18th-century Chinese mogul lotus bowl. The owners make frequent trips to Asia, where they personally pick all the items in their shop, at which the artistic wonders of the ancient Silk Road are still on display.

Other stores in the center include **Bentley's Home and Garden Center,** with crockery, glassware, books, *lau hala* bags, and ceramics; **Imagination Toys,** hung with kites, Hawaiian dolls, stuffed gorillas, parrots, and puzzles; **Fine Jewelry by Jock,** where custom-made jewelry or stones can be procured; and **Waimea Coffee and Company,** for small estate Kona coffee and light food and drink. The **Waimea General Store** sells mostly high-end sundries with plenty of stationery, children's games, stuffed toys, books on Hawaiiana, and gadgets.

Other Shops

The word *kama'aina* was invented with Patti Cook in mind. The proprietor of **Cook's Discoveries,** 808/885-3633, open daily 10 A.M.– 6 P.M., Patti has filled her shop with personally chosen items displaying her impeccable taste and knowledge about all things relating to Hawaii. Everything inside Cook's Discoveries, fashioned by craftspeople from throughout the state, says "Hawaii." Shelves hold lustrous koa boxes, bracelets, cribbage boards, and pen sets, all easily transportable. Look for traditional pieces, including a carved ivory pendant (fossilized walrus tusk) representing a human tongue, the "voice of authority," traditionally worn only by the highest *ali'i,* hung from a necklace of woven black silk (substituting for human hair). Other traditional pieces are *lei o mano* (lei of sharks' teeth), a club-like war weapon yielded in battle or when absolute and immediate persuasion was necessary, *kukui* nut lei, distinctive warrior helmets with mushroomlike protuberances atop, poi bowls, and decorated gourds once used for food storage. Contemporary "made in Hawaii" articles include handmade coconut lotion and soap, plenty of jewelry, carved tiki walking sticks, and brush and mirror sets. You'll also find *mu'umu'u* and pareu in tropical designs and colors, T-shirts emblazoned with Nenewe the shark god, exquisite Hawaiian quilts, books on Hawaiian subjects, gourmet jars of jams, jellies, and sauces made from *lilikoi, ohelo* berries, and Waimea's famous strawberries, and the shop's own oatmeal, coconut, macadamia nut cookies. This is one-stop shopping for memorable Hawaiian gifts. Look for Cook's kitty-corner from the police station, just beyond 'Imiola Church.

Who would have thought that one of the best wine and liquor stores on the island would be in a country town like Waimea? Look for **Kamuela Liquor Store** east along the highway just past Cook's Discovery. It's been in business since 1946. Open 8 A.M.–7:30 P.M. Mon.–Sat. and 9 A.M.–5 P.M. on Sun., it has a great selection of bottled beers along with its wines and liqueurs.

Across from the liquor store is **Dan De Luz's Woods,** a fine shop and showroom selling large bowls and small boxes made from native woods.

These pieces are roughed out in Mountain View, where De Luz has another shop, and the blanks are finished in Waimea after a year of drying.

Perhaps the best place in town, and one of the best of the island, to see authentic Hawaiian antiques and collectibles is **Mauna Kea Galleries,** 808/887-2244 or 877/969-4852. Line drawings from the early years, prints from the 1930s, Aloha shirts from the 1950s, jewelry, books, artifacts, furniture, and more are all here, but don't expect to pinch pennies. These fine-quality items may cost a bundle.

A few doors away is **Waimea Antiques and Collectibles,** 808/887-0024, a varied collection with average prices.

Up the road is **Antiques by...,** 808/887-6466. One room here is filled with Hawaiiana, the rest of the house has more ordinary collectibles. Good pricing.

Near the main intersection in town is the **Upcountry Connection** art gallery, 808/885-0623. Open daily except Sunday, this gallery focuses on two basic themes, cultural Hawaiiana and cowboy art and crafts, and has a very decent collection of both. Well worth a stop.

Located directly to the front of the Waimea Visitors Center, **The Quilted Horse,** 808/887-0020, is a fun shop full of household items, gift, prepared food items, Christmas ornaments, knickknacks, and one of the best selections of quilts on the island. Reasonably priced, the quilts are made in the Philippines but designed in Hawaii.

Food Markets

For food shopping try the **KTA Super Store** at the Waimea Center, for everything from groceries to pharmaceuticals. Across the highway at the Parker Ranch Center, the newer **Foodland** also has a full range of options, plus **Kamuela Meat Market** features fine cuts of Parker Ranch beef.

The **Waimea Homestead Farmers' Market** is held every Saturday 7 A.M.–noon, when local farmers come to sell their produce, much of which is organic. Flowers, baked goods, and crafts are usually available. Look for the stalls in front of the Hawaiian Homelands office located along Rte. 19, about two miles east of town center heading toward Honoka'a.

Alternately, try the **Parker School Farmers' Market,** held Saturday 8 A.M.–noon at the Parker School.

SERVICES AND INFORMATION

The post office is located in the Parker Ranch Center. The U.S. Postal Service designates Waimea as Kamuela, so as not to confuse it with the Waimeas on O'ahu and Kaua'i.

The **Waimea Visitor Center,** 808/885-6707, is west of town along Rte. 19, next to Parker Square. Operated by the nonprofit Waimea Main Street organization, this office provides free maps and brochures of the area and public restrooms. This is a good stop to learn about the rich cultural history of the area and what's happening in town today.

The Police and Fire departments and district court are located in the civic center complex across the highway from Church Row.

Health

The full-service **North Hawaii Community Hospital,** 808/885-4444, is located across from the Keck Observatory Office along Rte. 19. Physicians are available at the **Lucy Henriques Medical Center,** 808/885-7921, also along the highway, and at the **Kaiser Permanente Waimea Clinic,** 808/881-4500, on Lindsey Road.

Airport

The **Waimea-Kohala Airport,** 808/887-8126, is along Rte. 190 just a mile or so before you enter town. This airport is used by private planes and a few daily flights by a small commuter airline. Facilities amount to a waiting lounge and basic restrooms. Unless a flight is scheduled, even these may be closed.

WAIMEA

North Kohala

In North Kohala, jungle trees with crocheted shawls of hanging vines stand in shadowed silence as tiny stores and humble homes abandoned by time melt slowly back into the muted earth. This secluded region changes very little, and very slowly. It also has an eastward list toward the wetter side of the island, so if you're suffering from "Kona shock" and want to see flowers, palms, banana trees, and Hawaiian jungle, head for the north coast. Here the island of Hawai'i lives up to its reputation of being not only big, but bold and beautiful as well.

North Kohala was the home of Kamehameha the Great. From this fiefdom he launched his conquest of all the islands. The shores and lands of North Kohala are rife with historical significance, and with beach parks where only a few local people ever go. Here cattle were introduced to the islands

in the 1790s by Captain Vancouver, an early explorer and friend of Kamehameha. Among North Kohala's cultural treasures is **Lapakahi State Historical Park,** a must-stop offering a walk-through village and "touchable" exhibits that allow you to become actively involved in Hawaii's traditional past. Northward is **Kamehameha's birthplace**—the very spot—and within walking distance is **Mo'okini Luakini,** one of the oldest *heiau* in Hawaii and still actively ministered by the current generation of a long line of *kahuna*.

Hawi was a sugar town whose economy turned sour when the last of the five sugar mills in the area stopped operations in the mid-1990s. Hawi is making a slow comeback, along with this entire northern shore, which has seen

North Kohala coastline near Pololu Valley

an influx of small, boutique businesses and art shops. In **Kapa'au,** a statue of Kamehameha I peering over the chief's ancestral dominions fulfills an old *kahuna* prophecy. On a nearby side road stands historic **Kalahikiola Church,** established in 1855 by Rev. Elias Bond. On the same side road is the old Bond Homestead, one of the most authentic missionary homes in all of Hawaii. The main coastal road ends at **Pololu Valley Lookout,** where you can overlook one of the premier taro-growing valleys of old Hawaii. A walk down the steep *pali* into this valley is a walk into timelessness, with civilization disappearing like an ebbing tide.

In Kawaihae, at the base of the North Kohala peninsula, Rte. 19 turns east and coastal Rte. 270, known as the Akoni Pule Hwy., heads north along the coast. It passes through both of North Kohala's two major towns, Hawi and Kapa'au, and ends at the *pali* overlooking Pololu Valley. All the historical sites, beach parks, and towns in the following sections are along this route.

Route 250, the back road to Hawi, is a delightful country lane that winds through gloriously green grazing lands for almost 20 miles along the leeward side of the Kohala Mountains. It begins in the western outskirts of Waimea and ends in Hawi. One of the most picturesque roads on the island, it's lined with ironwood trees, dotted with mood-setting cactus and small "line shacks," and herds of cattle graze in the pastures of the several ranches along the way. Vistas open to the west and far below are expansive panoramas of rolling hills tumbling to the sea. Just outside Hawi, Rte. 250 splits; going right takes you to Kapa'au, left to Hawi. If you're coming along coastal Rte. 270 from Kapa'au toward Hawi,

look for the H. Naito Store, and make a left there to go back over Rte. 250 to Waimea; you don't have to go all the way to Hawi to catch Rte. 250.

Upolu airstrip is a lonely runway at Upolu Point, the closest spot to Maui. A sign points the way at mile marker 20 along coastal Rte. 270. Here, you'll find only a bench and a public telephone. The strip is serviced only on request by small propeller planes.

Kawaihae Coast

Lapakahi State Historical Park

This 600-year-old reconstructed Hawaiian fishing village, combined with adjacent **Koai'e Cove Marine Conservation District,** is a standout hunk of coastline 12 miles north of Kawaihae. Gates are open daily except holidays 8 A.M.–4 P.M. for a self-guided tour, but the ranger's knowledgeable anecdotes make a guided tour much more educational, when offered. Arrive at least by 3 P.M. so you have enough time to fully appreciate this site before the gate is locked.

The small hut at the end of the entrance road stocks annotated brochures and water jugs with limited drinkable freshwater. As you walk clockwise around the numbered stations, you pass canoe sheds and a fish shrine dedicated to Ku'ula, to whom the fishermen always dedicated a portion of their catch. A salt-making area demonstrates how the Hawaiians evaporated seawater by moving it into progressively smaller "pans" carved in the rock. There are numerous homesites along the wood-chip trail. Particularly interesting to

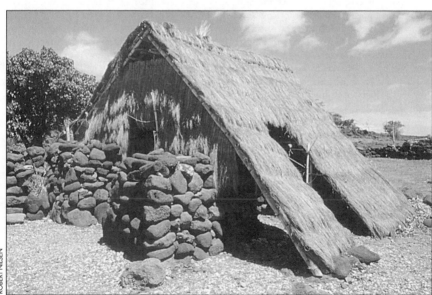

ROBERT NILSEN

re-created family house at Lapakahi

children are exhibits of games like *konane* (Hawaiian checkers) and *ulimika* (a form of bowling using stones) that the children are encouraged to try. Throughout the area, numerous trees, flowers, and shrubs are identified, and as an extra treat, migrating whales come close to shore Dec.–April. Don't leave without finding a shady spot and taking the time to look out to sea. In an otherwise forbidding coastal region, Lapakahi was home to generations of Hawaiians. A stop here is great for the opportunity to glimpse the remnants of this precontact fishing village and to imagine just what it took to sustain a community in this environment. For information write Lapakahi State Historical Park, P.O. Box 100, Kapa'au, HI 96755, 808/889-5566.

Mahukona and Kapa'a Beach County Parks

Mahukona Beach County Park is a few minutes north of Lapakahi down a well-marked side road. As you approach, notice a number of abandoned warehouses and a Hawaii Railroad Company office building from 1930. Mahukona was once an important port from which the Kohala Sugar Co. shipped its goods. Still there is a pier with a hoist used by local fishermen to launch their boats. The harbor is filled with industrial debris, which makes for some good underwater exploring, and snorkeling the offshore reef rewards you with an abundance of sealife. Only 150 yards offshore (follow the anchor chain from the landing) in only 20 feet of water lie the remains of a wrecked steamboat, the only wreck in Hawaii that's accessible from shore. The wooden boat has almost completely deteriorated, but you will find a huge boiler, engine, shaft, and propeller. Swimming off the pier is also good, but all water activities are dangerous during winter months and high surf. Picnic facilities include a large pavilion and tables. There are also cold-water showers and restrooms, and electricity is available in the pavilion. Both tent and trailer camping are allowed with a county permit near the parking lot.

Kapa'a Beach County Park is five minutes farther north. Turn *makai* on a side road and cross a cattle grate as you head toward the sea. This park

is even less visited than Mahukona. The rocky beach makes water entry difficult. It's primarily for day use and fishing, but there is a pavilion, some barbecue grills, and a restroom. Camping is allowed with a county permit. Neither of these two beaches is spectacular, but they are secluded and accessible. If you're interested in a very quiet spot to contemplate a lovely panorama of Maui in the distance, this is it.

Mo'okini Luakini Heiau

At mile marker 20, turn down a one-lane road to Upolu airstrip. Follow it until it reaches the dead end at the runway. Turn left here on a *very* rough dirt road to Mo'okini Luakini—this road may not be passable. This entire area is one of the most rugged and isolated on the Big Island, with wide windswept fields, steep seacliffs, and pounding surf. Pull off at any likely spot along the road and keep your eyes peeled for signs of cavorting humpback whales, which frequent this coast Nov.–May. After bumping down the road for about two miles, look for a tall transmission tower pointing its bony metal finger skyward, which marks the road to the *heiau*. Sometimes the road is closed with a locked gate and you'll have to walk five minutes uphill to gain access, but if the gate is open, you can drive in.

Only *ali'i nui* were allowed to came to the *heiau* to purify themselves and pray, sometimes offering human sacrifices. In 1963, Mo'okini Luakini was the first Hawaiian site to be listed in the National Historical Sites Registry. Legend says that the very first temple at Mo'okini was built as early as A.D. 480. This incredible date implies that Mo'okini must have been built immediately upon the arrival of the first Polynesian explorers, who many scholars maintain arrived in large numbers a full two centuries later. According to oral tradition, this original *heiau* was enlarged by the Tahitian high priest Pa'ao, who came with conquering warriors from the south in the 12th century, bringing the powerful *mana* of the fierce war-god Kuka'ilimoku. The oral tale relates that the stones for the temple were fitted in a single night, passed hand to hand by a human chain of 18,000 warriors for a distance of 14 miles from Pololu Valley. They created an ir-

According to oral tradition, Mo'okini Luakini Heiau was one of the first large *heiau* to be built on the island. It still stands strong and well-kept today, and overlooks the 'Alenuihaha Channel and Maui.

ROBERT NILSEN

regular rectangle measuring 125 by 250 feet, with 30-foot-high and 15-foot-thick walls in some sections. Regardless of its age, the integrity of the remaining structure is remarkable and shows great skill in construction.

When you visit the *heiau*, pick up a brochure from a box at the entrance (often empty); if none are available, a signboard nearby gives general information. The entire *heiau* is surrounded by a stone wall erected for its protection in 1981. In one corner of the enclosure is a traditional Hawaiian structure used in some of the temple ceremonies. On occasion, this building is blown down by the strong winds that lash this coast. Be aware of the integration of its stone platform and how perfectly suited this thatched structure is to provide comfort against the elements in Hawaii. Look through the door at a timeless panorama of the sea and surf. Notice that the leeward stones of the *heiau* wall are covered in lichens, giving them a greenish cast and testifying to their age. A large, flat stone outside the wall was used to prepare victims for the sacrificial altar. Next to it and embedded in the ground is

Kapakai, the guardian god in stone of the nearby King Kamehameha birthsite. This stone was removed here in the mid-1900s for protection, but will be returned to its original place when the time is right. The only entrance to the *heiau* itself is in the wall roughly facing southwest. Entering here, you pass the enclosure used by the *Mu*, the person responsible for finding and catching the human sacrifices that were offered at the temple. Once a closed temple, the *kapu* of restriction has been lifted so that all may now enter. However, please be respectful as you walk around, as this temple is still in use, and stay on the designated paths that are cordoned off by woven rope. Along the short wall closest to the sea is a "scalloped" altar, reputedly set up and used by Pa'ao, but where recent offerings are often seen. When you visit, bring a lei to place in respectful offering on the altar. Inside the *heiau* are remnants of enclosures used by the *ali'i* and space set aside for temple priests. The floor of the temple is carpeted with well-placed stones and tiny green plants that give a natural mosaic effect. By oral tradition, members of the Mo'okini family have been the priests and priestesses of the temple for at least 15 centuries, with the family line and duties of maintaining temples for the Polynesian rulers as they moved throughout the Pacific region that go back to the mists of time. Today, the inherited title of *kahuna nui* rests with Leimomi Moʻokini Lum, who has gone to great lengths to offer visitors information about the temple and particularly to instruct school children about its historical and religious significance.

Kamehameha's Birthplace

A few minutes' walk from the *heiau* along the dirt road, an HVB Warrior points to Kamehameha's birthplace, **Kamehameha ʻAkahi ʻAina Hanau.** The entrance to the area is at the back side, away from the sea. Inside the low stone wall, which always seems to radiate heat, are some large boulders believed to be the actual "birthing stones" where the high chieftess Kekuiapoiwa, wife of the warrior *aliʻi* Keoua Kupuapaikalananinui, gave birth to Kame-

hameha sometime around 1752. This male child, born as his father prepared a battle fleet to invade Maui, would grow to be the greatest of the Hawaiian chiefs—a brave, powerful, but lonely man, like the flat plateau upon which he drew his first breath. The temple's ritual drums and haunting chants dedicated to Ku were the infant's first lullabies. He would grow to accept Ku as his god, and together they would subjugate all of Hawaii. In this expansive North Kohala area, Kamehameha was confronted with unencumbered vistas and sweeping views of neighboring islands, unlike most Hawaiians, whose outlooks were held in check by the narrow, confining, but secure walls of steep-sided valleys. Only this man with this background could rise to become "The Lonely One," high chief of a unified kingdom.

Together, Moʻokini Heiau, King Kamehameha's birthplace, and several other nearby historical sites make up the seven-acre **Kohala Historical Sites State Monument.**

North Coast Towns

HAWI

As you come into Hawi along Rte. 270, you'll see a line of false-front buildings leaning shoulder-to-shoulder like patient old men knowing that something *will* happen, and it has! Introducing you to the town are Sacred Heart Church, Hawi Jodo Buddhist Mission, and the Kohala Seventh-Day Adventists Church, lovely temples of worship and symbols of Hawaii's diversified spirituality. In the middle of town at the gas station, Rte. 250, crossing the Kohala Mountains from Waimea, intersects the main road.

Hawi was once a bustling sugar town that boasted four movie theaters in its heyday. In the early 1970s, the Kohala Sugar Co. pulled up stakes, leaving the one-industry town high and dry. Still standing is the monumental stack of the sugarworks, a dormant reminder of what once was. The people of Hawi have always had grit, and instead of moving away they toughed it out and have revitalized their town. Spirit, elbow grease,

and paint were their chief allies. Hawi has risen from its slumber and is now making a comeback with new restaurants and galleries opening their doors. Here, too, are a handful of local shops selling food and fashions, some remarkable craft shops, an area information center, and the only functioning hotel in North Kohala.

A glowing example of Hawi's modern restoration and revitalization is the N. Takata building, now occupied by the Bamboo Restaurant and Gallery. This venerable old building was built by the Harada Family sometime before 1915 and served as a hotel for contract workers on their way to plantation work camps in the area. As the sugar trade took root, merchants came to town, and the hotel began catering to this more upscale clientele. These traveling salesmen were the epitome of the stereotype, and they desired evening entertainment. "Ladies of the night" took up residence in a few back rooms, and, with the proximity to the cane fields, might aptly have been known as "sugar babies." The fortunes of the

Harada family took a turn for the worse, and the building was bought in 1926 by the Takata family, who converted it to a grocery and dry goods store that served the community until 1991, when they moved shop, building a new store about one mile down the road. The old building fell into disrepair but was reopened as a restaurant after 16 months of restoration. New touches were added, like the old wicker chairs that once rocked wealthy vacationers into a light slumber at Waikiki's Moana Hotel, but they left the best alone, preserving the original feel of the building. Upon entering, notice the floor, heavily trodden over the decades, every nick marking a memory. The original wavy window glass is intact and still bears the original painted signs reading, "Fruits, Groceries, Cigars, Candy, Meats, and Coca Cola." The restaurant section, to the left as you enter, is perfect for an evening of dining; to the right is a gallery selling artworks. Browse before or after dinner and appreciate that this little community is finding a way to restore itself.

The Kohala Visitor Center dispenses maps, information, and *aloha*. It's open daily and located just west of the junction between Routes 270 and 250 in Hawi. The area post office is a large new facility on Rte. 270 between Hawi and Kapa'au near the H. Naito Store.

Accommodations

The 18-room **Kohala Village Inn,** 55-514 Hawi Rd., Hawi, HI 96755, 808/889-0419, has always catered to local working people or island families visiting the area, as well as passing tourists. Located just up from the intersection in Hawi, this old plantation-style building, white with blue trim and a blue roof, has a quiet central courtyard encircled by a wide and airy lanai. Most rooms have a television but none have phones; all have private baths. The standard room runs $52, or $47 with no television; connecting rooms that share a bath are $72 for both sides. Clean, adequate, and somewhat spartan, the hotel has a friendly, quiet atmosphere and evokes the spirit of the past.

Overlooking horse pastures and out across the channel toward Maui is **Cabin in the Treeline,** 808/884-5105, P.O. Box 190591, Hawi, HI

96719, cwej@vacationhi.com, www.vacationhi.com. Cabin in the Treeline has two buildings literally set at treeline at the edge of a pasture. These modern buildings with all modern amenities and conveniences have been designed in an old-style rustic *paniolo,* combination mainland mountain cabin, architectural style. The main house has a large living room, kitchen, two bathrooms, a master bedroom downstairs, and an upstairs bedroom. The barn-like Loft has one large bedroom upstairs with a queen bed and futon, television, and refrigerator. The bathroom with shower is downstairs with laundry facilities. Rates run $155–225 per night depending upon the number of guests.

If a larger, private home with space enough for a family is more what you need or if you just want more privacy, contact MacArthur and Company, 65-1148 Mamalahoa Highway, Kamuela, HI 96743, 808/885-8885 or 877/885-8285, info@letsgohawaii.com, www.letsgohawaii.com. This company offers a number of luxury properties in the Hawi area including several in a gated private ranch development that run $500–895 a night. Many of these homes have their own swimming pools and at least one has a private tennis court. Another option is the restored six-bedroom, six-bath plantation manager's house in Hawi, which runs $700 a night.

Food

Occupying the renovated N. Takata building is the **Bamboo Restaurant,** 808/889-5555, open Tues.–Sat. 11:30 A.M.–2:30 P.M. for lunch, 6–9 P.M. for dinner, and Sunday for brunch 11 A.M.–2 P.M., with live music on Friday and Saturday evenings. Lunch at the Bamboo can be a salad, sandwich, or one of the many entrées, like *kalua* pork and cabbage, herb-grilled fresh fish, or a Kohala quesadilla with your choice of main ingredient. Dinner begins with *pu pu* such as margaritaville prawns, calamari strips, or seared *poke,* but the restaurant is best known for its pot stickers, which are Thai seasoned chicken pieces with herbs and peanuts served with a sweet chili mint sauce. From the land comes flame-broiled rib-eye steak, pork tenderloin, or pineapple barbecued chicken. However, as you're so close to the sea, why not try the fish, which come in different preparations like herb-grilled in Thai flavors, crusted with macadamia nuts and pan fried, or sautéed and covered with margarita sauce and papaya relish. Sesame-nori crusted shrimp, shrimp alfredo, local-style stir-fry noodles, and teri chicken are also options. Sunday brunch is a crowd-pleaser, with the regular lunch menu plus platters like eggs Bamboo—poached egg on a toasted English muffin with a slice of smoked ham or vegetables and topped with *lilikoi* hollandaise sauce and served with fried potatoes or rice. While moderately expensive, the food at the Bamboo Restaurant is the finest and most sophisticated on the north coast. Reservations are often necessary, and while you wait try one of their famous passion fruit margaritas.

For a south-of-the-border taste treat, stop at **Hula La's Mexican Kitchen,** 808/889-5668, located at the back of the Kohala Trade Center building. Hula La's is known for its gut-filling burritos, tasty concoctions with beans, pork, chicken, or fish, fresh greens, other tasty morsels, and homemade salsa, $5.50–7.50. The Mexican-style plate lunches are also filling. If a burrito or plate lunch sounds like too much, choose a quesadilla or an order of nachitos, nachos, or tacos, or one of the menu specials. At this neat little eatery you can fill up for under $10 including a drink and be on your way in no time. Open weekdays 10 A.M.–9 P.M. and weekends from 8 A.M.

In tiny Hawi, you can find island-style food with an Asian touch and Mexican treats, so why not German food? On the *mauka* side is **Aunty's Place,** 808/889-0899, where you can enjoy wienerschnitzel, jagerschnitzel, schweinbraten, and bratwurst, along with a few selections from the rest of the continent, like chicken Cordon Bleu, lasagna, and pizza. For those with less of an appetite, Caesar, Greek, chef, and Chinese chicken salads are also on the menu. Most entrées run $9–13, so it goes easy on the wallet. Aunty's bar is at the front of this tiny restaurant. Happy hour is 4–6 P.M. and occasionally there will be live music in the evenings.

Sun, surf, and the trek to Hawi made you a bit droopy? Salvation is at hand at the **Kohala Cof-** fee Mill in downtown Hawi; open daily. Inside the remodeled vintage building, order Kona coffee, espresso, cappuccino, pastries, and soft drinks, or a Tropical Dreams ice cream cone. Shelves hold T-shirts, herbal teas, fruit jelly and jam, honey, and other packaged food and gifts. Whether you sit inside in the cool of the shade or out on the sidewalk, this is a perfect place to watch the slow life of Hawi amble by.

North Coast Recreation

There is little in the way of organized recreation along the north coast, but what there is can be exciting. Perhaps the most unusual activity is a kayak ride down a section of the Kohala Ditch. Completed in the early part of the 20th century and considered a feat of engineering, this 22-mile-long irrigation system supplied the Kohala Sugar mills with a steady supply of water until the plantation ceased business. Specially designed five-person inflatable kayaks put in above Makapala and drift down the flume, into and out of tunnels and over gullies for about three miles. Prepare to get wet. Tours go daily at 8:30 A.M. and 12:30 P.M. and run $85 for adults and $65 for children ages 5–18. Make reservations with **Flum'in da Ditch,** 808/889-6922 or 877/449-6922, www.flumindaditch.com, or stop into its office up from the banyan tree in the center of Hawi.

HMV Tour also takes you into the back mountain areas of the Kohala district but you ride in the relative luxury of a formidable 4WD Hummer. Morning and afternoon rides are offered weekdays, $95 for adults and $65 for children 5–15. Contact 808/889-6922 or 877/889-6944; http://hmvtours.com.

ATV Outfitters Hawaii will take you to out-of-the-way places along the coast and up into the rainforest on former Kohala sugar plantation land on its rugged four-wheel motorcycles. Several daily rides are offered, from a 1.5-hour ride for $90 to a five-hour ride for $250. Contact ATV Outfitters at 808/889-6000 or 888/288-7288, www.outfittershawaii.com.

Hawaii Forest and Trail offers a hiking experience along the Kohala Ditch trail to Kapoloa waterfall at the back of the Pololu Valley and a mule ride down the steep cliff face to the Pololu Valley floor and beach. Contact Hawaii Forest and Trail, 808/331-8505 or 800/464-1993, www.hawaii-forest.com.

Shopping

The **Nakahara Store** has been serving people of Hawi for decades, near the main intersection in town. One part of the store has groceries, while the other is a basic dry goods shop. **K. Takata** store is the best-stocked grocery store in Hawi. It's located along the highway about one mile east of the town center. At the intersection of highways 270 and 250 is **H. Naito Store,** another general grocery, dry goods, and fishing supplies store. **Kohala Health Food** in downtown Hawi, to the side of the Kohala Coffee Mill, is open Mon.–Fri. 10 A.M.–6 P.M. and Sat. 11 A.M.–4 P.M., closed Sundays. A small but vibrant establishment, its shelves hold herbs, vitamins, minerals, some packaged natural foods, and local organic produce and fruit when available. If you're looking for something not as healthy, **Kohala Spirits** stocks all sorts of beers, wines, and liquors. Across from the health food store, **Kohala Flowers** is alive with flowers and plants. Inside are small gift items and a cooler holding lei, perfect for brightening the day of that "special person," and perhaps for brightening the evening prospects for you.

Proof that two establishments can occupy the same place at the same time, the **Bamboo Gallery,** open when the restaurant is open, shares the vintage N. Takata Building with the Bamboo Restaurant. The gallery is lustrous with all types of artwork: koa furniture, covered photo albums, jewelry boxes, and sculptures, representing the work of many island artists. The furniture includes rocking chairs that beg to be sat in and fine koa dining room tables. Works of other well-known artists on display include lovely boxes, creamy white hand-thrown crystalline-glazed ceramics with flower or fish motifs, tapa-covered notebooks, replicas of sailing canoes, a smattering of aloha shirts, hand-painted silkwear, jewelry with an ocean motif, and bright prints.

Across the street and down a bit in the renovated Toyama Building is **As Hawi Turns,** a small but intriguing shop for fashions and distinctive gifts. Women will find dresses, skirts, wraps, sarongs, hats, slippers, jewelry, and accessories here and men have a selection of aloha shirts. Most everything is brightly colored with wild or distinctive designs. Other neat novelty items, gifts, crafts, and post cards are also carried.

The **L. Zeidman Gallery** shows an amazing collection of turned wooden bowls, some sculpted wooden pieces, and emotive paintings of Hawaiian subjects. If you haven't seen the work of Hawaiian woodturning craftsmen or a sampling of native and introduced Hawaiian woods, this is a good place to stop for a look.

Also worth a stop is **Hawi Gallery** for its fine furniture and boxes, and **Mother's Antiques and Fine Cigars** for collectibles and burnables. For more antiques and collectibles, head to **Kohala Fine Furniture and Collectibles** right at the main intersection.

Along the highway just east of the main intersection are several more galleries and gift shops. With hand-crafted works of art in clay, the small **Sugar Moon** gallery features the works of owners Tom and Julie Kostes. **Passion Flower** has art, antiques, and collectibles, while **Treaures of the Earth … and Beyond** will entice you with crystals, stones and other more metaphysical objects.

KAPA'AU

Kapa'au is a sleepy community, the last town for any amenities on Rte. 270 before you reach the end of the line at Pololu Overlook. In town are a library, bank, and police station, and the historic Nambu Building (1898) has recently been renovated. Some distance outside of town in either direction are the Union Market and the Arakawa Store. Most young people have moved away seeking economic opportunity, but the old folks remain, and macadamia nuts are bringing some vitality back into the area. Here too, but on a smaller scale than in Hawi, local artists and some new folks are starting shops and businesses catering to tourists.

The main attraction in town is **Kamehameha's statue,** in front of the Kapa'au Courthouse. The statue was commissioned by King Kalakaua in

1878, at which time an old *kahuna* said that the statue would feel at home only in the lands of Kamehameha's birth. Thomas Gould, an American sculptor living in Italy, was hired to do the statue, and he used John Baker, part Hawaiian and a close friend of Kalakaua, as the model. Gould was paid $10,000 to produce the remarkable and heroic sculpture, which was sent to Paris to be cast in bronze. It was freighted to Hawaii, but the ship carrying the original statue sank just off Port Stanley in the Falkland Islands, and the nine-ton statue was thought lost forever. With the insurance money, Gould was again commissioned and he produced another statue that arrived in Honolulu in 1883, where it still stands in front of the Judiciary Building. Within a few weeks, however, a British ship arrived in Honolulu, carrying the original statue, which had somehow been salvaged and unceremoniously dumped in a Port Stanley junkyard. The English captain bought it there and sold it to King Kalakaua for $850. There was only one place where the statue could be sent: to the then-thriving town of Kapa'au in the heart of Kamehameha's ancestral homelands. Every year, on the night before Kamehameha Day, the statue is painted with a fresh coat of house paint; the bronze underneath remains as strong as the great king's will.

Kamehameha County Park, down a marked side road, has a full recreation area, including an Olympic-size pool open to the public, basketball courts, and weight rooms in the main building along with outside tennis courts with night lighting and a driving range. There are restrooms, picnic tables, and a kiddie area, all free to use.

Kalahikiola Church

A few minutes east of town, a county lane leads to Kalahikiola Congregational Church. The road is delightfully lined with palm trees, pines, and macadamias like the formal driveway that it once was. Pass the weathering buildings of the Bond Estate and follow the road to the church on the hill. This church was built by Rev. Elias Bond and his wife Ellen, who arrived at Kohala in 1841 and dedicated the church in 1855. Rev. Bond and his parishioners were determined to over-

come many formidable obstacles in building Kalahikiola (Life from the Sun) Church, so that they could "sit in a dry and decent house in Jehovah's presence." They hauled timber for miles, quarried and carried stone from distant gulches, raised lime from the sea floor, and brought sand by the jarful all the way from Kawaihae to mix their mortar. After two years of backbreaking work and $8,000, the church finally stood in God's praise, 85 feet long by 45 feet wide. The attached bell tower, oddly out of place, looks like a shoebox standing on end topped by four meanlooking spikes. Note that the doors don't swing, but slide—some visitors leave because they think it's locked. Inside, the church is dark and cool and, inexplicably, the same type of spikes as on the bell tower flank both sides of the altar. There is also a remarkable koa table.

The Bond Estate

The *most* remarkable and undisturbed missionary estate still extant in Hawaii (and one of two undisturbed mission districts in the world—the other is in Nepal) is the old Bond Homestead and its attendant buildings, including the now defunct but partially renovated Kohala Girls' School up the road and the Kalahikiola Church. All three of these wonderful structures are on the National Historical Register. No tours are given, but you can have a look at the outside of the buildings on the homestead grounds and at the girls' school if the gate on the drive in is not locked.

Tong Wo Society Building

Behind the Rankin Gallery in Halawa is the lovely and historically significant Tong Wo Society building (1886) and cemetery—well worth a visit. As the third Chinese Triad hall in Hawaii, Tong Wo Kung Ssu, as it was called and as the placard over the door still reads, was one of the early formal meeting places for the Chinese immigrant workers, a place to push for the overthrow of the Manchu government in China, an organizational force for community action and mutual support, and a social center. Since 1970, work has been done to restore the building to its former splendor, and it now stands as a shin-

ROBERT NILSEN

Tong Wo Society Building

ing example, not only of the renovation of a structure, but also of the reinvigoration of a social organization, and the will of the community to remake one of its own.

Keokea Beach County Park

Two miles past Kapa'au toward Pololu you pass a small fruit stand and an access road heading *makai* to secluded Keokea Beach County Park. The park, on the side of the hill going down to the sea, is a favorite spot of North Kohala residents, especially on weekends, but it receives little use during the week. The rocky shoreline faces the open ocean, so swimming is not advised except during summer calm, yet there is a protected cove for the little ones. Amenities include a pavilion, restrooms, showers, and picnic tables. No camping is permitted.

Accommodations

Located a quarter-mile above Kapa'au is the **Kohala Country Adventures Guest House,** an island home with three units that could be your base for exploring North Kohala. The upstairs unit has a living area with king-size futon and double bed, a combination dining area and effi-

ciency kitchen, a bath with shower, and sun deck. It rents for $135 a night, multiple-night rentals preferred. Basically a room with a double bed and a bathroom, the economy room rents for $70 and can be adjoined to the suite for a larger family. The downstairs garden room, with its queen-size bed and single bed, kitchenette, full bath with spa tub, also has a deck off the bedroom and rents for $99. Each unit has its own private entrance and views of the garden. All guests receive a light continental breakfast in the morning to have at their leisure, or can elect not to have breakfast for a slightly reduced room rate. Two nights minimum requested. For reservations, call Bobi Moreno at 808/889-5663 or 866/892-2484, write P.O. Box 703, Kapa'au, HI 96755, or go to www.kcadventures.com.

Located near Kapa'au, *mauka* of the highway in a residential neighborhood, is **Cook's Cottage,** a studio with a full kitchen and bath, TV, laundry facilities, and separate entrance, available for $65 a night or $350 a week. Sleeps up to four. Contact Sue Cook at 808/889-0912.

In the village of Niuli'i, on the road down to Keokea Beach Park is **Kohala's Guest House,** P.O. Box 172 Hawi, HI 96719, 808/889-5606, fax 808/889-5572, http://home1.gte.net/svendsen, where you have a choice of studio or either half of a duplex. The studio comes with a queen-size bed and bath, kitchenette, color TV, and private entrance. Both halves of the duplex are fully contained houses with a full kitchen, living and dining areas, three bedrooms, two bathrooms, TV, and laundry facilities. The studio rents for $49 a night. The houses run up to $125 a night or $600 a week, depending upon the number of bedrooms that you need.

Food

Nambu Courtyard Café, 808/889-5546, is located in the historic Nambu Building. Open for breakfast and lunch Mon.–Fri. 6:30 A.M.–4 P.M., Sat. until 4 P.M., and Sun. until 1:30 P.M., this little café offers such items as bagels and English muffins with various toppings for breakfast. Grilled sandwiches like stuffed focaccia, spicy Italian, and Swiss beef, plus pastries and ice cream are best for lunch. Have these inside or with any number of coffees or other drinks in the back garden. The Nambu Courtyard Café is a great spot for a morning pick-me-up or a tasty bite during the day.

Jen's Kohala Cafe, 808/899-0099, open daily 10 A.M.–5 P.M. across the street from the Kamehameha Statue in Kapa'au, is the place to stop for wraps, sandwiches, burgers, soups, and smoothies. Some Saturdays and Sundays of the year, the cafe stays open 4:30–8:30 P.M. for Thai food nights.

J&R's Place offers local food, pizza, and coffee. You can't go wrong at this simple, clean, good, and inexpensive eatery.

Shopping

For food shopping in Kapa'au try **Union Market,** along Rte. 270 coming into Kapa'au, which sells not only general merchandise and meats, but also a hefty assortment of grains, nuts, fruits, and locally made pastries and breads. To the east of town is the **Arakawa Store,** also with a combination of groceries, general merchandise, and dry goods. The **Kamehameha Pharmacy** in downtown Kapa'au is a full-service pharmacy, 808/889-6161.

In Kapa'au, across from the Kamehameha statue, is **Ackerman Gallery,** 808/889-5971, open daily 9 A.M.–5:30 P.M., owned and operated by artist Gary Ackerman. Besides showcasing some of his own sensitive, island-inspired paintings, he displays local pottery, carvings, woven baskets and other natural fiber works, and one-of-a-kind jewelry. He also carries a smattering of artwork from throughout the Pacific. The artwork selections are tasteful and expensive. You can also choose a reasonably priced gift item, especially from the handmade jewelry section. Make sure to check out the display of beautiful hand-blown glass. The distinctive, iridescent glaze is achieved by using volcanic cinders—you can bring home a true island memento that includes a bit of Madame Pele herself. Gary has expanded by opening a second Ackerman Gallery just down the street. This lovely gallery, housed in a turn-of-the-century building, showcases only his paintings, known for their dramatic colors and textures, giclé and lithographs

of his work, and is a testament to the man and his enduring popularity.

Occupying another renovated old building along the highway is the **Sue Swerdlow Art Gallery,** 808/889-0002. Swerdlow, "a colorist," displays her own works of bold and bright colors, plus a selection of pieces by other artists.

In the renovated Nanbu Building is **Kohala Book Shop,** 808/889-6400, fax 808/889-6344, kohalabk@gte.net, reputedly the largest used bookstore in the state. It handles fiction and non-fiction, rare and unusual books, books on Hawaii and the Pacific, and even some cards and other gift items. Thousands of volumes line the shelves, and if you can't find what you're looking for, the owners will try to locate a copy by searching their sources for it. You can also search their listing of books by logging onto the www.abebooks.com website and finding the Kohala Book Shop link. If you want to visit the shop, stop by Tues.–Sat. 11 A.M.–5 P.M.

Also in the same building are the **Nambu Galleries,** the **Elements** jewelry and crafts shop, and **Victoria Fine Arts** gallery. Nambu Galleries shows landscapes by the owner and other paintings by artists from diverse places like California, China, and Colombia. Elements is more gift oriented with a diverse collection of pottery, wind chimes, jewelry, prints, painted scarves, Christmas ornaments, and much more.

The **Rankin Gallery,** 808/889-6849, occupies the historic Wo On (Harmony and Peace) general store in Halawa, which served the Chinese community during plantation days. This gallery displays a wide range of island-inspired paintings, turned wooden bowls, and some American Southwest art. Around the side and in the back is the Tong Wo Society building.

POLOLU VALLEY

Finally you come to Pololu Valley Overlook. It's about 12 miles from Pololu Valley to Waipi'o Valley, with five deep-cut valleys in between, including the majestic Waimanu, the largest. From the lookout it takes about 20 minutes to walk down to the floor of Pololu. The trail is well maintained as you pass

ROBERT NILSEN

Pololu Valley

through a heavy growth of *lau hala,* but it can be slippery when wet. **Kohala Ditch,** a monument to labor-intensive engineering, runs along the walls of this valley to its rear. It carried precious water to the sugar plantations, and today carries adventurous kayakers for a very unusual thrill ride. Pololu and the other valleys were once inhabited and were among the richest wet taro plantations of old Hawaii. Today, abandoned and neglected, they have been taken over by introduced vegetation. The black-sand beach fronting Pololu is lined with a thick forest of trees. The rip current here can be very dangerous, so enter the water only in summer months. The rip fortunately weakens not too far from shore; if you're caught, go with it and ride the waves back in. Many people hike into Pololu for seclusion and back-to-nature camping. Make sure to boil the stream water before drinking. Plenty of wild fruits can augment your food supply, and the shoreline fishing is excellent.

The Saddle Road

Slicing across the midriff of the island in a gentle arch from Mamalahoa Hwy. near Waimea to Hilo is Rte. 200, the Saddle Road. Everyone with a sense of adventure loves this bold cut across the Big Island through a broad high valley separating the two great mountains, Mauna Loa and Mauna Kea. Along this stretch of some 55 miles you pass rolling pastureland, broad swaths of lava flows, arid desert-like fields that look a bit like Nevada, a *nene* sanctuary, trailheads for several hiking trails, mist-shrouded rainforests, an explorable cave, and spur roads leading to the tops of Mauna Kea and Mauna Loa. Here as well is the largest military training reserve in the state, with its live firing range, and the Bradshaw Army Airfield. What you won't see is much traffic or many people. It's a great adventure for anyone traveling between Kona and Hilo. Keep your eyes peeled for convoys of tanks and armored personnel carriers as they sometimes sally forth from Pohakuloa Military Camp, and also watch out for those who want to make this a high-speed shortcut from one side of the island to the other.

Road Conditions

The Saddle Road was constructed in 1942 and left as gravel until about 25 years ago. While the road up both sides is at a good incline, the saddle itself is reasonably flat and at about 6,000–6,500 feet. Car-rental companies cringe when you mention the Saddle Road. Most still do not allow their cars on this road even though it is paved and well engineered. Check your rental agreement, as it'll be very specific on this point.

observatories atop Mauna Kea

ROBERT NILSEN

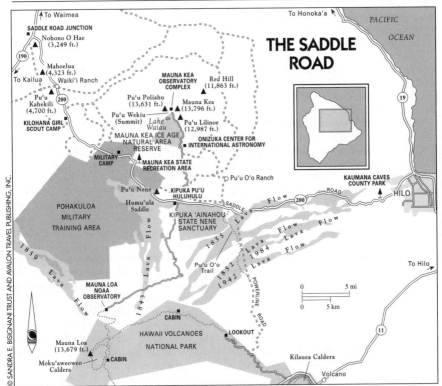

THE SADDLE ROAD

To Waimea
SADDLE ROAD JUNCTION
Nohono O Hae
(3,249 ft.)
190
To Kailua
Mahoelua
(4,323 ft.)
Waiki'i Ranch
200
Pu'u
Kahekili
(4,700 ft.)
KILOHANA GIRL
SCOUT CAMP

MAUNA KEA
OBSERVATORY
COMPLEX
Red Hill
(11,863 ft.)
Pu'u Poliahu
(13,631 ft.)
Mauna Kea
(13,796 ft.)
Pu'u Wekiu
(Summit)
Lake
Waiau
Pu'u Lilinoe
(12,987 ft.)
MAUNA KEA ICE AGE
NATURAL AREA
RESERVE
ONIZUKA CENTER FOR
INTERNATIONAL ASTRONOMY
MILITARY
CAMP
MAUNA KEA STATE
RECREATION AREA

To Honoka'a
PACIFIC
OCEAN

THE SADDLE
ROAD

19

Pu'u O'o Ranch
KAUMANA CAVES
COUNTY PARK
HILO

Pu'u Nene
KIPUKA PU'U
HULUHULU
Humu'ula
Saddle
KIPUKA 'AINAHOU
STATE NENE
SANCTUARY
SADDLE
ROAD
200

POHAKULOA
MILITARY
TRAINING AREA

1859
Lava
Flow

1855
Lava
Flow
1852
1942
1843

Pu'u O'o
Trail

1984
Lava
Flow

Lava
Flow
Lava
Flow

POWERLINE
ROAD

To Hilo

0   5 mi
0   5 km

MAUNA LOA
NOAA
OBSERVATORY

CABIN
LOOKOUT

HAWAII VOLCANOES
NATIONAL PARK

Mauna Loa
(13,679 ft.)
Moku'aweoweo
Caldera
CABIN

Kilauea Caldera

11

Volcano

© SANDRA E. BISIGNANI TRUST AND AVALON TRAVEL PUBLISHING, INC.

THE SADDLE ROAD

They're terrified you'll rattle their cars to death. For the most part, these fears are groundless, as there are only short sections that may be rough, due mostly to military use. By and large, it's a good road, no worse than many others around the island—the Hilo side is wider and has better shoulders than the Kona side. However, it *is* isolated, and there are no facilities whatsoever along its length. If you do have trouble, you'll need to go a long way for assistance, but if you bypass it, you'll miss some of the best scenery on the Big Island. On the Kona side, the Saddle Road turnoff is about six miles south of Waimea along Rte. 190, about halfway between Waimea and Waikoloa Road. From Hilo, follow Waianuenue Avenue inland. Saddle Road, Rte. 200, also signed as Kaumana Drive, splits left after about a mile and is clearly marked. Passing Kaumana Caves County Park, the road steadily gains ele-

vation as you pass into and then out of a layer of clouds. Expect fog or rain.

MAUNA KEA

There is old lava along both sides of the road as you approach the broad tableland of the saddle. Much of the lava here is from the mid-1800s, but some is from a more-recent 1935 flow. About 25 miles up from the Kona side, and 28 miles out of Hilo, a clearly marked access road to the north leads to the summit of 13,796-foot Mauna Kea (White Mountain). A sign warns you that this road is rough, unpaved, and narrow, with no water, food, fuel, restrooms, or shelters. Moreover, you can expect wind, rain, fog, hail, snow, and altitude sickness. Intrigued? Proceed—it's not as bad as it sounds. In fact, the road, while steep, is well paved for the first six miles to the **Onizuka Center for International Astronomy and Visitor Information Center** at 9,300 feet, where there are restrooms and drinking water. Beyond there, the road is gravel for several miles, but paved again at the very top. A 4WD vehicle is required beyond the visitor center, and if there's snow, the road may not be passable at all.

Just beyond the Onizuka Center is **Hale Pohaku** (House of Stone), which looks like a ski resort; many of the scientists from the observatory atop the mountain live here. From here, the road is graded, banked, and well maintained, with the upper four miles paved so that dust is kept to a minimum to protect the sensitive "eyes" of the telescopes. As you climb, you pass through the clouds to a barren world devoid of vegetation. The earth is a red, rolling series of volcanic cones. You get an incredible vista of Mauna Loa peeking through the clouds and what seems like the entire island lying at your feet. In the distance the lights of Maui flicker.

Off to your right is Pu'u Kahinahina, a small hill whose name means "hill of the silversword." It's one of the only places on the Big Island where you'll see this very rare plant. The mountaintop was at one time federal land, and funds were made available to eradicate feral goats, one of the worst destroyers of the silversword and many other native Hawaiian plants.

Lake Waiau, which translates as "Swirling Water," lies at 13,020 feet, making it the third-highest lake in the United States. For some reason, ladybugs love this area. This lake is less than two acres in size and quite shallow. Oddly, in an area that has very little precipitation and very dry air, this lake never dries up or drains away as it apparently is fed by a bed of melting permafrost four or more feet below the surface.

Here and there around the summit are small caves, remnants of ancient quarries where Hawaiians came to dig a special kind of fired rock that is the hardest in all Hawaii. They hauled roughed-out tools down to the lowlands, where they refined them into excellent implements that became coveted trade items. These adze quarries, Lake Waiau, and a large triangular section of the glaciated southern slope of the mountain

have been designated **Mauna Kea Ice Age Natural Area Reserve.**

A natural phenomenon is the strange thermal properties manifested by the cinder cones that dot the top of the mountain. Only 10 feet or so under their surface is permafrost that dates back 10,000 years to the Pleistocene Epoch. If you drill into the cones for 10–20 feet and put a pipe in, during daylight hours, air will be sucked into the pipe. At night, warm air comes out of the pipe with sufficient force to keep a hat levitating.

Mauna Kea is the only spot in the tropical Pacific that was thought to be glaciated until recent investigation provided evidence that suggests that Haleakala on Maui was also capped by a glacier when it was higher and much older. The entire summit of Mauna Kea was covered in 500 feet of ice. Toward the summit, you may notice piles of rock—these are terminal moraines of these ancient glaciers—or other flat surfaces that are grooved as if scratched by huge fingernails. The snows atop Mauna Kea are unpredictable. Some years it is merely a dusting, while in other years, such as 1982, there was enough snow to ski from late November to late July. Most skiers careen down what's known as the "poi bowl," northwest of the observatories, but they will ski wherever there is enough snow to run.

Evening brings an incredibly clean and cool breeze that flows down the mountain. The Hawaiians called it the Kehau Wind, whose source, according to ancient legend, is the burning heart of the mountain. To the Hawaiians, this inspiring heavenly summit was the home of Poliahu, The Goddess of Snow and Ice, who vied with the fiery Pele across the way on Mauna Loa for the love of a man. He could throw himself into the never-ending embrace of a mythical ice queen or a red-hot mama. Tough choice, poor fellow!

Hiking on the Mountain

Hiking on Mauna Kea means high altitude hiking. Although the height of the mountain is not the problem, the elevation gain in a short hour or two of getting to the top is. It takes time for the body to acclimatize, and when you drive up from the ocean you rob yourself of the chance to acclimatize easily. What you may expect to experience normally are slight dizziness, a shortness of breath due to reduced oxygen levels, and reduced ability to think clearly and react quickly. Some people are more prone to elevation problems, so if you experience more severe symptoms, get to a lower elevation immediately. These symptoms include prolonged or severe headache, loss of appetite, cramped muscles, prolonged malaise or weakness, dizziness, reduced muscle control and balance, and heart palpitations. Use your head, know your limits, and don't push yourself. Carry plenty of water (more than you would at a lower elevation) and food. Wear a brimmed hat, sunglasses, sunscreen, and lip balm, a long-sleeved shirt and long pants, and sturdy hiking boots or shoes. Carry a windbreaker, sweater, and gloves, as it can be cold and windy at and near the top. Don't alter the natural environment. Take out all that you take in.

The Hawaiians were the finest adze makers in Polynesia. One of the best stone quarries was atop Mauna Kea.

There are a few good day hike trails on the mountain. About six miles above the Visitor Center, a dirt track heads off the access road to the west and downhill to a parking lot. From the parking area, it's about one mile farther west, over the saddle between two small hills, to Lake Waiau and its placid waters. On the way, a trail from the top (about a 30-minute hike) crosses this path and heads down the mountain back to the Visitor Center. A couple of miles down this cross path is an adze quarry site. Perhaps the most convenient hike is that to the true summit of the mountain. Start from the roadway across from the University of Hawaii 2.2-meter Telescope, cross over the guardrail, and follow the rough path down into the saddle and steeply up the hill, a distance of less than half a mile.

MAUNA KEA OBSERVATORY COMPLEX

Atop the mountain is a mushroom grove of astronomical observatories, as incongruously striking as a futuristic earth colony on a remote planet of a distant galaxy. The crystal-clear air and lack of dust and light pollution make the Mauna Kea Observatory site *the* best in the world. At close to 14,000 feet, it is above 40 percent of the earth's atmosphere and 98 percent of its water vapor. Temperatures generally hover around 40–50 degrees during the day, and there's only 9–11 inches of precipitation annually, mostly in the form of snow. The astronomers have come to expect an average of 325 crystal-clear nights per year, perfect for observation. The state of Hawaii leases plots at the top of the mountain, upon which various institutions from all over the world have constructed telescopes. Those institutions in turn give the University of Hawaii up to 15 percent of their viewing time. The university sells the excess viewing time, which supports the entire astronomy program and makes a little money on the side. Those who work at the top must come down every four days because the thin air makes them forgetful and susceptible to making minor calculation errors. Scientists from around the world book months in advance for a squint through one of these phenomenal telescopes, and institutions from several countries maintain permanent outposts here.

The first telescope that you see on your left is the United Kingdom's **James Clerk Maxwell Telescope** (JCMT), a radio telescope with a primary reflecting surface more than 15 meters in diameter. This unit was operational in 1987. It was dedicated by Britain's Prince Philip, who rode all the way to the summit in a Rolls Royce. The 3.6-meter **Canada-France-Hawaii Telescope** (CFHT), finished in 1979 for $33 million, was the first to spot Halley's Comet in 1983.

A newer eye to the heavens atop Mauna Kea is the double **W. M. Keck Observatory.** Keck I was operational in 1992 and Keck II in 1996. The Keck Foundation, a philanthropic organization from Los Angeles, funded the telescopes to the tune of over $140 million, among the world's most high-tech, powerful, and expensive. Operated by the California Association for Research in Astronomy (CARA), a joint project of the University of California and Cal Tech, the telescopes have an aperture of 400 inches and employ entirely new and unique types of technology. The primary reflectors are fashioned from a mosaic of 36 hexagonal mirrors, each only three inches thick and six feet in diameter. These "small" mirrors have been very carefully joined together to form one incredibly huge, actively controlled light reflector surface. Each of the mirror segments is capable of being individually positioned to an accuracy of a millionth of an inch; each is computer-controlled to bring the heavenly objects into perfect focus. These titanic eyeballs have already spotted both the most distant known galaxy and the most distant known object in the universe, 12 and 13 billion light years from earth, respectively. The light received from these objects today was emitted not long after the "Big Bang" that created the universe theoretically occurred. In a very real sense, scientists are looking back toward the beginning of time! The Keck Observatory includes a gallery that's open to the public Mon.–Fri. 10 A.M.–4 P.M., a video presentation of the telescope, displays, a viewing area inside one of the domes, and restrooms. Alternately, one may visit the Keck Observatory office in Waimea for complete information about the telescope, without having to make the trek up to the top of the mountain.

In addition to these are the following: The **NASA Infrared Telescope Facility** (IRTF), on-line since 1979, does only infrared viewing with its three-meter mirror. Also with only infrared capabilities, the **United Kingdom Infrared Telescope** (UKIRT), in operation since 1979 as well, searches the sky with its 3.8-meter lens. Directly below it is the **University of Hawaii .6-meter Telescope.** Built in 1968, it was the first on the mountaintop and has the smallest reflective mirror. Completed in 1970, the **University of Hawaii 2.2-meter Telescope** was a huge improvement over its predecessor but is now the second smallest telescope at the top. The **Cal-**

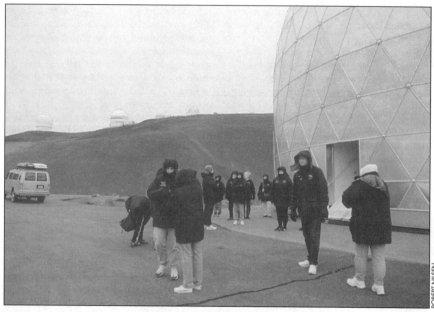

A tour group awaits sunset at the Mauna Kea Observatory complex.

ROBERT NILSEN

tech **Submillimeter Observatory** (CSO) has been looking into the sky since 1987 with its 10.4-meter radio telescope. **Subaru** (Japan National Large Telescope) is a monolithic 8.3-meter mirror capable of both optical and infrared viewing. It is the most recently completed telescope on the mountain, fully operational since 2000. The **Gemini Northern 8.1-meter Telescope,** also with both optical and infrared viewing, is run by a consortium from the United States, United Kingdom, Canada, Chile, Argentina, and Brazil. Its southern twin is located on a mountaintop in Chile, and together they have been viewing the heavens since 1999. Situated to the side and below the rest is the **Submillimeter Array,** a series of eight six-meter-wide antennae. About two miles distant from the top is the **Very Long Baseline Array,** a 25-meter-wide, centimeter wavelength radio dish that is one in a series of similar antennae that dot the 5,000-mile stretch between Hawaii and the Virgin Islands.

While the state is considering expansion of the complex to include additional telescopes and support facilities, a number of groups, including The Hawaiian-Environmental Alliance, are calling upon the state to proceed in a culturally and environmentally friendly manner or to not proceed at all.

The entire mountaintop complex, plus almost all of the land area above 12,000 feet, is managed by the University of Hawaii. Visitors are welcome to tour the complex and stop by the Visitor Center at the **Onizuka Center for International Astronomy,** www.ifa.hawaii.edu/info/vis, at the 9,300-foot level. Named in honor of astronaut Ellison Onizuka, born and raised on the Big Island, who died in the *Challenger* space shuttle tragedy in 1986, this center is a must-stop for stargazers. Inside are displays of astronomical and cultural subjects, informational handouts, and computer links to the observatories on the hill above, as well as evening videos and slide shows. Often, small 11- to 16-inch telescopes are set up outside during the day to view the sun and sunspots and in the evening to view the stars and other celestial objects. The Visitor Center is about one hour from Hilo and Waimea and about

two hours from Kailua-Kona. A stop here will allow visitors a chance to acclimatize to the thin, high-mountain air—another must. A stay of one hour here is recommended before you head up to the 13,796-foot summit. (Because of the high altitude and the remoteness of the mountaintop from emergency medical facilities, children under age 16 are prohibited from venturing to the summit. People with cardiopulmonary or respiratory problems or with physical infirmities or weakness, women who are pregnant, and those who are obese are also discouraged from attempting the trip. In addition, those who have been scuba diving should not attempt a trip to the top until at least 24 hours have elapsed.) The Visitor Center provides the last public restrooms before the summit and is a good place to stock up on water, also unavailable higher up. The Visitor Center is open Mon.–Fri. 9 A.M.–noon, 1–5 P.M., and 6–10 P.M., and Saturday and Sunday 9 A.M.–10 P.M. Free stargazing tours are offered daily 6–10 P.M. and a summit tour every Saturday and Sunday 1–5 P.M. (weather permitting). These programs are free of charge. For either activity, dress warmly. Evening temperatures will be 40–50 degrees in summer and might be below freezing in winter, and winds of 20 miles per hour are not atypical. For the summit tour, you must provide your own 4WD transportation from the Visitor Center to the summit. For more visitor and program information, call 808/961-2180; call 808/974-4203 for road conditions. For information on the Internet about the mountaintop observatories or the individual telescope installations, log onto the University of Hawaii Institute for Astronomy website (www.ifa.hawaii.edu/) and follow the links from there.

If you plan on continuing up to the summit, you must provide your own transportation and it must be a 4WD vehicle. As the observatories are used primarily at night, it is requested that visitors to the top come during daylight hours and leave by a half hour after sunset to minimize the use of headlights and reduce the dust from the road, both factors that might disrupt optimum viewing. For rental vehicles, contact **Harper Car and**

MAUNA KEA OBSERVATORIES' WEBSITES

University of Hawaii 2.2-meter Telescope:
www.ifa.hawaii.edu/88inch
NASA Infrared Telescope Facility:
http://irtfweb.ifa.hawaii.edu
Canada-France-Hawaii Telescope:
www.cfht.hawaii.edu
United Kingdom Infrared Telescope:
www.jach.hawaii.edu/UKIRT/home.html
James Clerk Maxwell Telescope:
www.jach.hawaii.edu/JACpublic/JCMT/home.
html

Caltech Submillimeter Observatory:
www.submm.caltech.edu/cso
Very Long Baseline Array:
www.nrao.edu/vlba/html/VLBA.html
W. M. Keck Observatory:
www2.keck.hawaii.edu
Subaru: www.naoj.org
Gemini Northern 8.1-meter Telescope:
www.gemini.edu
Submillimeter Array: sma2.harvard.edu

Truck Rentals in Hilo, 808/969-1478, which offers 4WD rentals certified for driving to the mountaintop. Alternately, make arrangements for a guided tour to the top. From the Kona side, try **Mauna Kea Summit Adventures,** 808/322-2366 or 888/322-2366, www.maunakea.com; **Hawaii Forest and Trail,** 808/331-5805 or 800/464-1993, www.hawaii-forest.com; or **Hawaiian Eyes Land Tours,** 808/326-2434. In Hilo, contact **Arnott's Hiking Adventures,** 808/969-7097, www.arnottslodge.com. Take extra layers of warm clothing and your camera. Photographers using fast film get some of the most dazzling shots *after* sunset. During the gloaming, the light show begins. Look down upon the clouds to see them filled with fire. This heavenly light is reflected off the mountain to the clouds and then back up like a celestial mirror in which you get a fleeting glimpse of the soul of the universe.

SIGHTS ALONG ROUTE 200
Pohakuloa
The broad, relatively flat saddle between Mauna Kea and Mauna Loa is an area known as Pohakuloa (Long Stone). At an elevation of roughly 6,500 feet, this plain alternates between lava flow, grassland, and semi-arid desert pockmarked with cinder cones. About seven miles west of the Mauna Kea Road, at a sharp bend in the road, you'll find a cluster of cabins that belong to the now-closed Mauna Kea State Recreation Area.

No overnight services are available here, but you can stop for a picnic and potty break. Nearby is a game management area, so expect hunting and shooting of wild pigs, sheep, and birds in season. A few minutes west is the **Pohakuloa Military Camp,** whose maneuvers can sometimes disturb the peace in this high mountain area.

Kipuka Pu'u Huluhulu
Bird-watchers or nature enthusiasts should turn into the Kipuka Pu'u Huluhulu parking lot across the road from the Mauna Kea Road turn-off. A *kipuka* is an area that has been surrounded by a lava flow, but never inundated, that preserves an older and established ecosystem. Here you will find a hunters' check-in station. From the parking lot, a hiking trail leads into this fenced, 38-acre nature preserve. Several loop trails run through the forest on the hill, and there are two exits on Mauna Loa Observatory Road, on its eastern edge. Pu'u Huluhulu means "Shaggy Hill," and this diminutive hill is covered in a wide variety of trees and bushes, which include *mamame, naio, 'iliahi* (sandalwood), koa, and 'ohi'a. Some of the birds most often seen are the greenish-yellow *'amakihi,* the red *'i'iwi* and *'apapane,* the dull brown and smoky-gray *'oma'o.* In addition, you may be lucky enough to spot a rare *'io,* Hawaiian hawk, or the more numerous *pueo,* short-eared owl. Even if you are not particularly drawn to the birds or the trees, this is a good place to get out of the car, stretch your legs, and get acclimatized to the elevation.

Pu'u O'o Trail

Just after mile marker 24 on the way up from Hilo is the trailhead for Pu'u O'o Trail. From the small parking lot along the road, this trail heads to the south about four miles where it meets Powerline Road, a rough 4WD track, and returns to the Saddle Road. This area is good for bird-watching, and you might have a chance to see the very rare *'akiapola'au* or *'apapane,* and even wild turkeys. This area is frequently shrouded in clouds or fog, and it could very well rain on you. You may want to walk only part way in and return on the same trail, rather than making the circle.

MAUNA LOA

The largest mass of mountain to make up the Big Island is Mauna Loa (Long Mountain). It lies to the south of Mauna Kea and dominates the southern half of the island. At 13,677 feet, it is about 100 feet shorter than Mauna Kea. The top of this mountain is the huge **Moku'aweoweo Caldera,** virtually as big as Kilauea Crater near Volcano. Connected to this caldera are the smaller but equally impressive North and South pits, each about as big as Halema'uma'u, which is within Kilauea Crater. Unlike Mauna Kea, Mauna Loa has had some

recent volcanic activity, spilling lava in 1949, 1950, 1975, and 1980. The top of this mountain is within the Hawaii Volcanoes National Park boundary. One of the longest and perhaps the most difficult hiking trail in the park runs up from the Volcano area to Red Hill cabin and from there on up to the top of the mountain. A 2.6-mile trail skirts the western edge of the caldera to the actual summit. Just over two miles long, another trail reaches the Mauna Loa cabin, perched on the eastern edge of the rim and directly across from the summit.

Mauna Loa Observatory Road, a rough gravel road maintained by the state, turns south off Rte. 200 and leads about 19 miles to the **Mauna Loa NOAA Observatory,** at 11,150 feet. This atmospheric observatory is not open to the public, but you can park near it. From the observatory, a rigorous 3.5-mile-long trail rises some 2,000 feet to the caldera rim. If you intend to hike the observatory trail, be aware that this is a very remote area. There are no services, restrooms, or water along the way. It can be cold and moist, snow and winter conditions can happen at any time of year, and there is virtually no protection from the weather until you get to the cabin on the eastern rim. Park officials estimate that about half of all hikers taking this trail get some degree of altitude sickness.

Hilo

Hilo is a blind date. Everyone tells you what a beautiful personality she has, but . . . But? . . . it rains—130 inches a year. Mostly the rains come in winter and spring and are limited to predictable afternoon showers, but they do scare some tourists away, keeping Hilo reasonably priced and low-key. In spite of, and because of, the rain, Hilo is gorgeous. It's one of the oldest permanently settled towns in Hawaii, and the largest on the windward coast of the island. Hilo's weather makes it a natural greenhouse.

Botanical gardens and flower farms surround Hilo like a giant lei, and shoulder-to-shoulder banyans canopy entire city blocks. To counterpoint this tropical explosion, Mauna Kea's winter snows backdrop the town. The crescent of Hilo Bay blazes gold at sunrise, while a sculpted lagoon, Asian pagodas, rock gardens, and even a tiny island connected by a footbridge line its shores. Downtown's waterfront has perfect historical buildings that always need a paint job. They lean on each other like "old salts" who've

Pe'epe'e Falls

ROBERT HOLMES

had one too many. Don't make the mistake of underestimating Hilo, or of counting it out because of its rainy reputation. For most, the blind date with this exotic beauty turns into a fun-filled love affair.

Hilo is a unique town in a unique state in America. You can walk down streets with names like Pu'u'eo and Keawe, and they could be streets in Anywhere, U.S.A., with neatly painted houses surrounded by white picket fences. Families live here. At just over 40,000, Hilo has the second-largest population in the state after Honolulu. It is the county seat, has a bustling commercial harbor, has a long tradition in agriculture and industry, boasts a branch of the University of Hawaii, and is home to the Hawai'i Community College. It was once the terminus of railway lines that stretched north along the Hamakua Coast, and south to Mt. View and Pahoa. There are roots and traditions, but the town is changing. Fishermen still come for the nightly ritual of soul-fishing and story-swapping from the bridge spanning the Wailuku River, while just down the street newly arrived chefs prepare Cajun blackened fish at a yuppie restaurant and mid-

night philosophers sip gourmet coffee and munch sweets elsewhere. Hilo is a classic tropical town. Some preserved buildings, proud again after new facelifts, are a few stories tall and date from the turn of the 20th century when Hilo was a major port of entry to Hawaii. Sidewalks in older sections are covered with awnings because of the rains, which adds a turn-of-the-20th-century gentility. Because Hilo is a town, most Americans can relate to it: it's big enough to have one-way streets and malls, but not so big that it's a metropolis like Honolulu, or so small that it's a village like Hana. You can walk the central area comfortably in an afternoon, but the town does sprawl. Teenagers in "boom box" cars cruise the main strip, which is lined with restaurants, antiques and collectibles shops, professional businesses, and mom-and-pop shops. This once vibrant town looks half dead in sections, with stores and shops falling silent due to the modern phenomena of new and large shopping malls in the outlying areas. Yet, there is a movement toward revival, and some old buildings are being enlivened with new uses and bold new shops are taking the places of the old and gone. There's

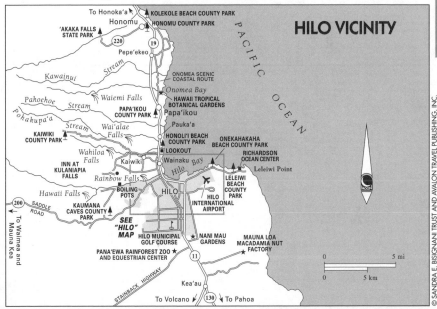

HILO

HILO

M

HILO

To Hamakua Coast and Waimea

SCENIC OVERLOOK

'Ale'ale'a Point

THE BAY HOUSE B&B

WILD GINGER INN

DOLPHIN BAY HOTEL

SHIPMAN HOUSE B&B

SCHOOL

Wailuku River

WAILUKU RIVER STATE PARK

Rainbow Falls

HILO MEDICAL CENTER

KAUMANA DR.

To Saddle Road, Kona, and Waimea

Keokea Point

SEE DETAIL

KEAUKAHA BEACH

KALANI'ANA'OLE AVE.

Hilo Breakwater

Hilo Bay

Hilo

Reeds Bay

Coconut Island

Banyan Dr.

HILO HARBOR

SHOOTER'S

REEDS BAY BEACH PARK

HARRINGTON'S

HILO SEASIDE HOTEL

KEN'S HOUSE OF PANCAKES

WAIAKEA KAI SHOPPING CENTER

HILO (137)

SILVA

UNCLE BILLY'S HILO BAY HOTEL

HAWAII NANILOA RESORT

HILO HAWAIIAN HOTEL

NANILOA COUNTRY CLUB

LILI'UOKALANI GARDENS

NIHON RESTAURANT

SUISAN FISH MARKET

BOAT SLIPS

HO'OLULU COUNTY PARK

FREDDIE'S

DON'S GRILL

BIG ISLAND CANDIES

KANOELEHUA AVE.

HUALANI ST.

KEKUANAO'A ST.

HILO BIKE HUB

MID PACIFIC IWHEELS

LEILANI ST.

HAWAII COMMUNITY COLLEGE

BORDERS BOOKS

HILO HATTIE

WAIAKEA CENTER

PRINCE KUHIO PLAZA

(11)

To Puna and Volcano

WAIAKEA VILLAS

SEE "DOWNTOWN HILO MAP"

KING KAMEHAMEHA STATUE

WAIOLI CENTER

WAIAKEA STATE BUILDING

WAIAKEA Pond

MEHANA BREWERY

HILO FORESTRY ARBORETUM

KILAUEA

KAWILI ST.

PU'AINAKO TOWN CENTER MALL

PU'AINAKO

ST.

(123)

KAMEHAMEHA HWY.

BAYFRONT HWY.

COUNTY BUILDING

KAIKO'O MALL

HILO SHOPPING CENTER

CAFE 100

KILAUEA KITCHEN

KINO'OLE ST.

ULULANI ST.

LANIKAULA ST.

UNIVERSITY OF HAWAII AT HILO

KOMOHANA RD.

KAMEHAMEHA AVE.

WAILOA RIVER STATE RECREATION AREA

POLICE STATION

KAPI'OLANI ST.

PONAHAWAI ST.

KUKUAU ST.

MONOHAU ST.

Wailoa River

0 2 mi

0 2 km

DETAIL

'UWA'U

RICHARDSON OCEAN CENTER

OEOE

KOLOA

FRIENDS OF FRIENDS

LEILEWI BEACH COUNTY PARK

KOLEA

MAUREEN'S BED & BREAKFAST

KIOEA

JAMES KEALOHA BEACH COUNTY PARK

SEASIDE RESTAURANT

LOKOAKA

NENE

HILO TROPICAL GARDENS

LOKO WAKA POND

ONEKAHAKAHA BEACH COUNTY PARK

ONEKAHAKAHA

ARNOTT'S LODGE

ANDREWS AVE.

KEOKEA

Keaukaha

KALANI'ANA'OLE AVE.

HILO INTERNATIONAL AIRPORT (GENERAL LYMAN FIELD)

TERMINAL

CAR RENTALS

COMMUTER TERMINAL

POST OFFICE

AIRPORT RD.

even a down-and-out section where guys hunker down in alleyways, smoking cigarettes and peering into the night. In the still night, there's the deep-throated sound of a ship's foghorn, a specter of times past when Hilo was a vibrant port. Hilo is the opposite of Kailua-Kona both spiritually and physically. There, everything runs fast; it's a clone of Honolulu. In Hilo the old beat, the old music, that feeling of a tropical place where rhythms are slow and sensual, still exist. Hilo nights are alive with sounds of the tropics and the heady smell of fruits and flowering trees wafting on the breeze. Slow down and relax; you'll start to feel at home. Hilo remains what it always was—a town, a place where people live.

Hilo is the eastern hub of the island. Choose a direction, and an hour's driving puts you in a time-lost valley deep in *paniolo* country, or on the blackness of a recent lava flow, or above the steaming fumaroles of Hawaii Volcanoes National Park. In and around town are museums, riverbank fishing, a cultural center, plenty of gardens, waterfalls, a potholed riverbed, and lava caves. Aside from the bay beach, which is generally not used for swimming, Hilo's beaches are small and rocky—perfect for keeping crowds away. Hilo is bite-size, but you'll need a rental car to visit most of the sights around town.

The main thoroughfares through the downtown area are Kamehameha Avenue, Kilauea Street, which merges into Keawe Street, and Kino'ole Street, all of which run parallel to the bay. The Bayfront Highway, Rte. 19, skirts the water and runs north up the Hamakua Coast and east past the Banyan Drive area to the beaches out in Keaukaha. Heading inland from the water from the river mouth to Rainbow Falls and Boiling Pots is Waianuenue Avenue, and off it branches Kaumana Drive, Rte. 200, which continues over the mountain as the Saddle Road. Kaneolehua Avenue starts at Banyan Drive and runs inland to Volcano. On both sides of this main thoroughfare are the town's newer commercial districts and the airport.

Sights

DOWNTOWN

Lyman Mission House and Museum

The preserved New England–style homestead of David and Sarah Lyman, Congregational missionaries who built it in 1839, is the oldest frame building still standing on the Big Island. In 1856, a second story was added, which provided more room and a perfect view of the harbor. In 1926, Haili Street was extended past the home, and at that time the Wilcox and Lyman families had the house turned parallel to the street so that it would front the entrance. The building is now on the National and State Registers of Historic Places.

The Lyman Mission House opened as a museum in 1932! The furniture is authentic "Sandwich Isles" circa 1850, the best pieces fashioned from koa. Much of it has come from other missionary homes, although many pieces belonged to the original occupants. The floors, mantels, and doors are deep, luxurious koa. The main door is a "Christian door," built by the Hilo Boys Boarding School. The top panels form a cross and the bottom depicts an open Bible. Many of the artifacts on the deep windowsills are tacked down because of earthquakes. One room was used as a schoolroom/dayroom where Mrs. Lyman taught arithmetic, mapmaking, and proper manners. The dining room holds an original family table that was set with the "Blue Willow" china seen in a nearby hutch. Some of the most interesting exhibits are of small personal items like a music box that still plays and a collection of New England autumn leaves that Mrs. Lyman had sent over to show her children what that season was like. Upstairs are bedrooms that were occupied by the parents and the seven children. Their portraits hang in a row. Mrs. Lyman kept a diary and faithfully recorded eruptions, earthquakes, and tsunami. Scientists still refer to it for some of the earliest recorded data on these natural disturbances. The master bedroom has a large bed with pineapples carved into the bedposts,

DOWNTOWN HILO

To Hamakua Coast and Waimea

To Airport

Hilo Bay

KAMEHAMEHA AVE.

WAILOA RIVER

STATE RECREATION AREA

Wailuku River

SINGING BRIDGE

MAUI'S CANOE

19

PUBLIC PARKING

CHAMBER OF COMMERCE

CRONIES BAR AND GRILL

PACIFIC TSUNAMI MUSEUM ★

BASICALLY BOOKS

KRESS THEATER

KRESS BUILDING

BUSTERMINAL

S. HATA BUILDING

REUBEN'S MEXICAN FOOD

MO'OHEAU BANDSTAND

ORCHIDLAND SURFBOARDS

HONU'S NEST

NAUTILUS DIVE CENTER

FARMERS MARKET

KEAWE

BEARS' COFFEE SHOP

SATSUKI'S

PALACE THEATER

PESCATORE

OCEAN SUSHI

DA KINE BIKE SHOP

CANOES CAFE

FURNEAUX

ABUNDANT LIFE NATURAL FOODS

KTA SUPER STORE

BYTES AND BITES

KEKAULIKE

FEDERAL BUILDING/ POST OFFICE

KALAKAUA PARK

HAWAIIAN JUNGLE RESTAURANT

KALAKAUA

HAWAIIAN TELEPHONE BUILDING

BIG ISLAND VISITORS BUREAU

HILO TSUNAMI GRILL

KILAUEA

ROYAL SIAM THAI RESTAURANT

NEW STAR CHINESE RESTAURANT

DRIVE

BEACH DOG RENTAL

WAILUKU

AVE.

EAST HAWAI'I CULTURAL CENTER

CENTRAL CHRISTIAN CHURCH

TAISHOJI SOTO MISSION

NAUNG MAI THAI KITCHEN

HILO SURPLUS

MAMO

LOW INTERNATIONAL FOOD

KINO'OLE

SACK'N SAVE

ULULANI

WAIANUENUE

HAILI CHURCH

HAILI

FIRE DEPARTMENT

PONAHAWAI

LIBRARY

ST. JOSEPH'S CATHOLIC CHURCH

KAPI'OLANI

KA'IULANI ST.

LYMAN MISSION HOUSE ★

LYMAN MUSEUM ★

100 yds

100 m

0

0

HILO

crafted by a ship's carpenter who lived with the family for about eight months. The bedroom mirror is an original, in which many Hawaiians received their first surprised look at themselves. A nursery holds a cradle used by all eight children. It's obvious that the Lymans did not live luxuriously, but they were comfortable in their island home.

The Lyman House is at 276 Haili St., 808/935-5021, www.lymanmuseum.org, and is open Mon.–Sat. 9 A.M.–4:30 P.M., admission $5 adults, $2.50 children 6–18. Guided tours are given six times a day by experienced and knowledgeable docents who relate many intriguing stories about the building and its occupants.

Next door to the Lyman House, in a modern two-story building, is the Lyman Museum. The 1st floor is designated the **Earth Heritage Gallery.** The mineral and rock collection here is rated one of the top 10 in the entire country, and by far the best in Polynesia. Marvel at thunder eggs, agates, jaspers, India blue mezolite, aquamarine lazurite from Afghanistan, and hunks of weirdly shaped lava. These displays are the lifelong collection of the great-grandson of the original Rev. Lyman. Anything coming from the earth can be exhibited here: shells named and categorized from around the world, petrified wood, glass paperweights, and crystals. Other exhibits explain the geology and volcanology of Kilauea and Mauna Kea, and a section is dedicated to the vanishing flora and fauna of Hawaii.

Upstairs is the **Island Heritage Gallery,** where a replica of a Hawaiian grass house, complete with thatched roof and floor mats, is proudly displayed. Nearby are Hawaiian tools: hammers of clinkstone, chisels of basalt, and state-of-the-art "stone age" polishing stones with varying textures used to rub bowls and canoes to a smooth finish. Hawaiian fiberwork, the best in Polynesia, is also displayed, as well as coconut, pandanus, and the pliable air root of the 'ie'ie. The material, dyed brown or black, was woven into intricate designs. You'll also see fishhooks, stone lamps, mortars and pestles, *lomi lomi* sticks, even a display on *kahuna,* with a fine text on the *kapu* system. Pre-contact displays give way to kimonos from Japan, a Chinese herbal medicine display, and displays dedicated to Filipino, Portuguese, and Korean heritage. In adjoining rooms are galleries dedicated to Chinese art, with a fine grouping of ceramic and jade pottery and statuary from the last three centuries with a few pieces as old as 2,000 years, and a collection of artwork by Hawaiian artists. Periodic exhibitions are shown in a third gallery. Saying good-bye is a bust of Mark Twain, carved from a piece of the very monkeypod tree he planted in Wai'ohinu in 1866. The museum is educational and worth some time, and the gift shop a good place to look for authentic Hawaiian products and books.

Pacific Tsunami Museum

Hilo suffered a devastating tsunami in 1946 and again in 1960. Both times, most of the waterfront area of the city was destroyed, but the 1930 Bishop National Bank building survived, owing to its structural integrity. Appropriately, the Pacific Tsunami Museum, 130 Kamehameha Ave., 808/935-0926, www.tsunami.org, is now housed in this fine art-deco structure and dedicated to those who lost their lives in the devastating waves that raked the city. The museum has numerous permanent displays, an audio-visual room, computer linkups to scientific sites, and periodic temporary exhibitions. While there is general scientific information, what's perhaps the most moving feature of this museum are the photographs of the last two terrible tsunamis that struck the city and the stories retold by the survivors of those events. Stop in Mon.–Sat. 9 A.M.–4 P.M. for a look, it's well worth the time. Admission is $5 adults, $4 seniors, and $2 students. Other permanent displays of photos relating to the tsunamis are hung in the Kress Building farther down Kamehameha Avenue and on the lower level of Wailoa Center.

Downtown Walking Tour

Start your tour of Hilo by picking up a pamphlet/map entitled *Walking Tour of Historic Downtown,* free at the HVB office and many restaurants, hotels, and shops. This self-guiding pamphlet takes you down the main streets and back lanes where you discover the unique architecture of Hilo's glory days. The majority of the

HILO

vintage buildings have been restored, and the architecture varies from the early 20th-century Kress and S. Hata Building to the continental style of the Hawaiian Telephone Building and the Zen Buddhist Taishoji Shoto Mission. Older is the Lyman House and nearby the New England–style Haili Congregational Church (1859; congregation founded in 1824) and St. Joseph's Catholic Church.

On the median strip between the Bayfront Highway and Kamehameha Ave. is a bandstand and main city bus stop. The **Mo'oheau Bandstand** is all that's left of the dozens of structures that lined the ocean side of Kamehameha Avenue before the 1946 tsunami. Miraculously, this structure survived. The bandstand is sometimes used by the Hawai'i County Band for concerts and for other community events. A **tourist information kiosk** near the bandstand and bus stop has brochures and maps to dispense about the city.

A remarkable building, the "Old Police Station" is located at 141 Kalakaua St., opposite Kalakaua Park. Built in 1932 and placed on the National and State Registers of Historic Places and Buildings in 1979, this old colonial structure is now the home of the **East Hawai'i Cultural Center,** 808/961-5711, a nonprofit organization that supports local arts and hosts varying festivals, performances, and workshops throughout the year, here and at other locations on the island. It also hosts Shakespeare in the Park performances by a local repertory group that stages, directs, designs, and enacts Shakespearean plays under the large banyan tree in Kalakaua Park, across the street, during the month of July. If you're in Hilo at this time, it shouldn't be missed. Monthly juried and non-juried art exhibits are shown on the main floor gallery; a venue for various performing artists is upstairs. The bulletin board is always filled with announcements of happenings in the local art scene. Stop in as there is always something of interest on the walls, and because this organization is worthy of support. The Big Island Dance Council, Hawai'i Concert Society, Hilo Community Players, and Bunka No Izumi

are all member groups. The center is open 10 A.M.–4 P.M. Mon.–Sat., donations acceped. For more information, seewww.lastplace.com/EXHIBITS/EHCC.index.htm.

Set aside for public use by King Kalakaua himself, **Kalakaua Park** is a grassy area overseen by a huge banyan tree, a midtown oasis. A seated statue of King David Kalakaua, the Merrie Monarch, takes center stage. Across Waianuenue Avenue is the solid and stately **Federal Building** with its offices and downtown post office. This stone structure dates from 1917.

A short walk up the street brings you to the **Hilo Public Library,** 300 Waianuenue Avenue. Sitting at the entrance are two large stones. The larger is called the **Naha Stone,** known for its ability to detect any offspring of the ruling Naha clan. The test was simple: Place a baby on the stone, and if the infant remained silent, he or she was Naha; if the baby cried, he or she wasn't. It is believed that this 7,000-pound monolith was brought from Kaua'i by canoe and placed near Pinao Temple in the immediate vicinity of what is now Wailuku Drive and Keawe Street. Kamehameha the Great supposedly fulfilled a prophecy of "moving a mountain" by budging this stone. The smaller stone is thought to be an entrance pillar of the Pinao Temple. Just behind the library is the Wailuku River. Pick any of its bridges for a panoramic view down to the sea. Often, local fishermen try their luck from the Wailuku's grassy banks. The massive boulder sitting near the river's mouth is known as **Maui's Canoe.** During the tsunami of 1946, the railroad bridge that crossed the river at bay's edge was torn from its base like a weak Tinker Toy construction. The metal bridge that crosses the river today is known as the "singing bridge" because the mesh that creates the roadway hums or "sings" as rubber tires spin across it.

Around Banyan Drive

If your Hilo hotel isn't situated along Banyan Drive, go there. This bucolic road skirts the edge of the Waiakea Peninsula that sticks out into Hilo Bay. Lining the drive is an almost uninterrupted series of banyan trees forming a giant canopy, while the fairways and greens of the

ROBERT NILSEN

Lili'uokalani Gardens

Naniloa Country Club golf course take up the center of the tiny peninsula. Skirting its edge are the Lili'uokalani Gardens, a concentration of hotels, and Reed's Bay. This peninsula was once a populated residential area, an offshoot of central Hilo. Like much of the city, it too was destroyed during the tsunami of 1960. Park your car at one end and take a stroll through this park-like atmosphere. The four dozen banyans that line this boulevard (the first planted in 1933, the last in 1972) were planted by notable Americans and foreigners, including Babe Ruth, President Franklin D. Roosevelt, King George V, Hawaiian volcanologist Dr. Jaggar, Hawaiian Princess Kawananakoa, pilot Amelia Earhart, and then-senator Richard Nixon. A placard in front of each tree gives particulars. Time has taken its toll here, however, and as grand as this drive once was, it is now a bit overgrown and unkempt in spots, with much of the area needing a little sprucing up.

Lili'uokalani Gardens are formal Japanese-style gardens located along the west end of Banyan Drive. Meditatively quiet, they offer a beautiful view of the bay. Along the footpaths are pagodas, torii gates, stone lanterns, and half-moon bridges spanning a series of ponds and streams. Along one side sits a formal Japanese Tea House where women come to be instructed in the art of the tea ceremony. Few people visit this 30-acre garden, and if it weren't for the striking fingers of black lava and the coconut trees, you could easily be in Japan.

Coconut Island (Moku Ola) is reached by footbridge from a spit of land just outside Lili'uokalani Gardens. It was at one time a *pu'uhonua* (place of refuge) opposite a human sacrificial *heiau* on the peninsula side. Coconut Island has restrooms, a pavilion, and picnic tables shaded by tall coconut trees and ironwoods. A favorite picnic spot for decades, kids often come to jump into the water from stone abutments here and older folks come for a leisurely dip in the cool water. The only decent place to swim in Hilo Bay, it also offers the best panorama of the city, bay, and Mauna Kea beyond.

Until 2001 when it closed, Suisan Fish Auction was at the corner of Banyan Drive and Lihiwai

Street, which crosses Kamehameha Avenue near the rivermouth. This fish auction drew island fishermen of every nationality and was great entertainment for visitors. Boats would tie up and fishermen would talk quietly about the prices; restaurateurs and housewives gathered before 6 A.M. to eyeball the catch of the day; and when the sale started, the auctioneer's staccato was pure pidgin. Later tourists would amble by, and it usually wound up a bit past 8 A.M. As colorful as it was, government regulations pressured its closure. While the auction no longer operates, the fish market next door is still open daily except Sunday to sell the fresh fish catch by the same local fisherman.

Cross Kamehameha Avenue heading south and you'll see **Ho'olulu County Park,** with the Civic Center Auditorium, numerous athletic stadiums, and a city nursery brimming with orchids. This is the town's center for organized athletic events, large cultural festivals, and the annual county fair. To the west is **Waiakea Pond,** a brackish lagoon where people often fish. The **Wailoa River State Recreation Area,** which en-

compasses the lagoon, is a 132-acre preserve set along both sides of this spring-fed pond in the center of Hilo. City residents use this big broad area for picnics, pleasure walks, informal get-togethers, fishing, and launching boats. On the eastern side are picnic pavilions and barbecue grills. Arching footbridges cross the river connecting the halves. Stop at the **Wailoa Center** on the western side for tourist information and cultural displays (open weekdays only). The walls in the upstairs gallery of this 10-sided building are used to display works of local artists and cultural/historic exhibits, changed on a regular basis. On the lower level hang astonishing pictures of the 1946 and 1960 tsunamis that washed through the city. The Wailoa Center sits in a broad swath of greenery, an open, idyllic park-like area that used to be a cramped bustling neighborhood known as Shinmachi. It, like much of the city, was almost totally destroyed during the tsunami of 1960. Nearby stands the **Tsunami Memorial** to the residents of this neighborhood who lost their lives in that natural disaster. Also close by is the county **Vietnam War Memorial,**

ROBERT NILSEN

Rainbow Falls

dedicated to those who died fighting that war, and a new **statue of King Kamehameha I,** a replica of that which graces the town of Kapaʻau at the northern tip of the island. Park at the Wailoa Center on Piopio Street, off Pauahi Street. Additional parking for this landscaped area is on the western side along Park Street at the end of Piʻilani Street.

Farther Afield

A few miles out of town, heading west on Waianuenue Avenue, are two natural spectacles definitely worth a look. Just past Hilo High School a sign directs you to Wailuku River State Park. Here is **Rainbow Falls,** a most spectacular yet easily visited natural wonder. You'll look down on a circular pool in the river below that's almost 100 feet in diameter; cascading into it is a lovely waterfall. The 80-foot falls deserve their name because as they hit the water below, their mists throw flocks of rainbows into the air. Underneath the falls is a huge cavern, held by legend to be the abode of Hina, mother of the god Maui. Most people are content to look from the vantage point near the parking lot, but if you walk to the left, you can take a stone stairway leading to a private viewing area directly over the falls. Here the river, strewn with volcanic boulders, pours over the edge. Follow the path for a minute or so along the bank to a gigantic banyan tree and a different vantage point. The falls may be best seen in the morning when the sunlight streams in from the front.

Follow Waianuenue Avenue for two more miles past Hilo Medical Center to the heights above town. A sign to turn right onto Peʻepeʻe Falls Street points to the **Boiling Pots,** another section of Wailuku River State Park. Few people visit here. Follow the path from the parking lot past the toilets to an overlook. Indented into the riverbed below is a series of irregularly shaped depressions that look as though a peg-legged giant left his peg prints in the hot lava. Seven or eight resemble naturally bubbling whirlpool tubs as river water cascades from one into the next. This phenomenon is best after a heavy rain. Turn your head upriver to see **Peʻepeʻe Falls,** a gorgeous, five-spouted waterfall. Although signs warn you not to descend to the river—risky during heavy rains—locals hike down to the river rocks below to sunbathe and swim in pools that do not have rushing water.

In 1881, Mauna Loa's tremendous eruption discharged a huge flow of lava. The river of lava crusted over, forming a tube through which molten lava continued to flow. Once the eruption ceased, the lava inside siphoned out, leaving the tube now called **Kaumana Caves.** The caves are only five miles out of downtown Hilo along Rte. 200, clearly marked next to the road. Oddly enough, they are posted as a fallout shelter. Follow a steep staircase down into a gray hole draped with green ferns and brightened by wildflowers. Smell the scent of the tropical vegetation. You can walk only a few yards into the cave before you'll need a strong flashlight. It's a thrill to turn around and look at the entrance, where blazing sunlight shoots through the ferns and wildflowers.

Not many travelers can visit a zoo in such a unique setting, where the animals virtually live in paradise. The 150 animals at this 12-acre zoo, where it rains about 130 inches a year, are endemic and introduced species that would naturally live in such an environment. While small and local, the zoo is a delight. The road to the **Panaʻewa Rainforest Zoo,** 808/959-7224, www.hilozoo.com, is a trip in itself, getting you back into the country. Follow Rte. 11 south past mile marker 4 until you see the sign pointing right up Stainback Hwy. to the zoo. Near the zoo is the **Panaʻewa Equestrian Center,** with a full-size horse racing track. On a typical weekday, you'll have the place much to yourself. The zoo, operated by the county Department of Parks and Recreation, is open daily 9 A.M.–4 P.M., closed Christmas and New Year's Day. Feedings are usually done around 9 A.M. and 3:15 P.M. and the petting zoo activities happen around 1:30 P.M., so you may want to be around for them. Admission is free, although donations to the nonprofit Friends of the Panaʻewa Zoo are appreciated. Here you have the feeling that the animals are not "fenced in" so much as you are "fenced out." The collection of about 75 species includes ordinary and exotic animals

M

HILO

from around the world. You'll see pygmy hippos from Africa, a rare white Bengal tiger named Namaste, a miniature horse and steer, Asian forest tortoises, water buffalo, monkeys, and a wide assortment of birds like pheasants and peacocks. The zoo hosts many endangered animals indigenous to Hawaii like the *nene,* Laysan duck, Hawaiian coot, *pueo,* Hawaiian gallinule, and even a feral pig in his own stone mini-condo. There are some great iguanas and mongooses, lemurs, and an aviary section with exotic birds like yellow-fronted parrots and blue and gold macaws. The back central area is a tigers' playground; a tall fence marks this rather large area where the tiger still rules his domain. It's got its own pond and tall grasses that make the tigers feel at home. The zoo makes a perfect side trip for families and will certainly delight the little ones.

Mauna Loa Macadamia Nut Factory, 808/966-8618, is located several miles south of Hilo off Rte. 11, nearly to Kea'au. Head down Macadamia Road for about three miles until you come to the Visitors Center. Inside is an informative free video explaining the development and processing of macadamia nuts in Hawaii. Walkways outside the windows of the processing center and chocolate shop let you view the process of turning these delicious nuts into tantalizing gift items, but this is best viewed from August through January when most of the processing is done. Then return to the snack shop for macadamia nut goodies like ice cream and cookies, and the gift shop for samples and an intriguing assortment of packaged macadamia nut items. While you're here, step out back and take a self-guided tour of the small garden where many introduced trees and plants

MACADAMIA NUT

Hawaii produces about 40 percent of the world's supply of macadamia nuts, and the majority of the state's crop is raised on the Big Island. About one million macadamia nut trees produce these tasty nuts at the Mauna Loa Macadamia Nut property outside Hilo, with a larger property producing nuts in South Kona. Smaller growers raise this crop at different locations on the Big Island, as well as on Moloka'i, O'ahu, and Kaua'i.

A native of Australia, macadamia nut trees were first brought to Hawaii and planted in Honoka'a in 1881 by the British agriculturist W. H. Purvis. One of these trees is still bearing! A number of these trees were again introduced to Hawaii in 1921 for study but failed to produce an acceptably significant and even-quality product. However, W. Pierre Naquin, then manager of the Honoka'a Sugar Co., thought that the nut might have some potential and started the first commercial nut farm in 1924. After years of grafting and experimentation on the island of O'ahu, over half a dozen varieties of the tree proved to yield acceptable nuts, and this led to large-scale commercial ventures in the '50s. Macadamia nut trees can grow to about 40 feet tall, branch out to about the same width, and have dark green leaves.

Trees require at least five years before they begin to produce nuts, and perhaps five to 10 additional years before they are in full production. Once mature, they can produce for years. Trees flower at different times over many months and produce nuts most of the year. This requires harvesting on a periodic basis. While some nuts are shaken from the trees, most fall naturally and are picked up from the ground. The nuts have a leathery skin that breaks open to reveal a very hard brown shell. This shell is cracked open to give forth the fruit itself, a light-colored, crisp and creamy orb about the size of a marble. In larger commercial ventures, the nuts are collected, dried, cracked, and sorted mechanically, while small-time growers may do some of this work by hand. Many of the nuts are roasted and salted, but some are set aside to be put into a brittle, glazed with various concoctions, or dipped in chocolate. Additionally, the nuts are often added to sauces, desserts, pastries, and confections. Some now are pressing the nut for its oil. Macadamia nuts contain mostly monounsaturated fat and traces of several minerals. Its high burn and smoke temperature makes it great for cooking and its smooth texture is appropriate for lighter foods.

are identified. The Visitors Center is open daily 8:30 A.M.–5 P.M.

GARDENS

Along Kilauea Avenue, between Lanikaula and Kawili Streets, the Department of Natural Resources, Division of Forestry maintains the **Hilo Forestry Arboretum,** open Mon.–Fri. 8 A.M.– 3 P.M., closed Saturday, Sunday, and holidays; no charge. This arboretum and tree nursery contains many of the trees present in Hawaii, including indigenous and imported specimens. Have a look at the diagram map of the grounds in the office before you head out back for a self-guided tour. The map attempts to name the trees by matching them with points on the map as you pass by, instead of referring to signs on each specimen. The trees are magnificent, and you will have this quiet area virtually to yourself. Originally the site was an animal quarantine station operated by the Territory of Hawaii; the 19.4 acres of the arboretum were established in 1920 by Brother Mathias Newell. Brother Newell was a nurseryman employed by the Catholic boys' school in Hilo. At that time the Division of Forestry was already actively introducing plant species from all over the world. For the 40 years between 1921 and 1961 the department was engaged in the development and maintenance of arboretums consisting primarily of plant species from Australia and Africa. Arboretum sites ranged from sea level to Mauna Kea. Plant materials were exchanged, and thousands of breadfruit cuttings were exported. Over 1,000 different tree species and 500 different fruit trees were field-tested. Here at the Hilo Arboretum over 1,000 trees were planted. A few trees such as the paper bark and some pines are more than 50 years old. Presently a small number of timber species are grown for reforestation purposes. Essentially the Hilo site is utilized for the propagation of rare and endangered plant species, for research, and for experimental pursuits.

ROBERT NILSEN

Nani Mau Gardens

Nani Mau Gardens is the largest in Hilo, and touring these spectacular displays is well worth an afternoon. Located at 421 Makalika St., Hilo, HI 96720, 808/959-3500, the gardens are open daily 8 A.M.–5 P.M. Admission is $10 adult, $5 children ages 4–10, and $5 per person for an optional tram tour. The gardens consist of 20 sculpted acres. More than a botanical garden, Nani Mau is a "floral theme park" designed as a tourist attraction. Walks throughout the garden are very tame but very beautiful; umbrellas are provided during rainy weather, which adds its own dripping, crystalline charm to the experience. Plants are labeled in English, Latin, and Japanese. The gardens are a huge but ordered display of flowers, flowering trees, and shrubbery. The wildly colored plumage of tropical birds here and there competes with the colors of the exotic blooms. The gardens are broken off into separate areas for hibiscus, anthurium, orchid, gardenia, and bromeliad, along with a Japanese garden, a fruit orchard, and stands of bamboo, palms, and other trees. It also features floral sculptures, a small reflective pond, and an assortment of flowers and shrubs laid out in geometric patterns, and even "aloha" and "Hilo Hawaii" spelled out. The Nani Mau Restaurant provides lunch only, 10:30 A.M.–1:30 P.M., and the tourist shop is exactly like a Japanese omiyagi (souvenir) shop. No wonder, since it's owned by ethnic Japanese, and the tour buses coming here are all filled with Japanese visitors. If you enjoy a clean outdoor experience surrounded by magnificent flowers, this is the place.

Established in 1948, apparently as the oldest botanical garden on the island, **Hilo Tropical Gardens,** 808/969-9873, has recently reopened at 1447 Kalaniana'ole Ave. and is slowly being brought back to life after a number of years of neglect; open daily except Thursday and Sunday. A thick profusion of tropical plants greet you as you enter this garden and a maze of walkways leads through its somewhat overgrown grounds. The garden is compact so not overwhelming and some of the plants are marked so you can know what you're looking at. Among the many are a host of anthuriums and orchids. Aside from the flowers, here and there along the walkways are

pools in lava sinks and a hidden lava tube or two. Entrance is $2 adult for a self-guided tour and free for children; enter through the gift shop, where you can find flowers, lei, gifts, and crafts, all of which can be shipped for you. When you're finished, stop next door for a scoop of Hilo Homemade Ice Cream.

Just a few minutes north of town, on the Onomea scenic coastal route, is the **Hawaii Tropical Botanical Gardens,** 808/964-5233, www.htbg.com, open daily 9 A.M.–5 P.M. for self-guided tours. Admission is adults $15, children 6–16 $5, and kids five and under are free. Remember that the entrance fee not only allows you to walk through the best-tamed tropical rainforest on the Big Island but helps preserve this wonderful area in perpetuity. The gardens were established in 1978 when Dan and Pauline Lutkenhouse purchased the property in order to educate the public to the beauty of tropical plants in their natural setting. The gardens have been open for viewing since 1984. Mr. Lutkenhouse, a retired San Francisco businessman, purchased the 25-acre valley and personally performed the work that transformed it into one of the most exotic spots in all of Hawaii. The locality was amazingly beautiful but inaccessible because it was so rugged. Through a personal investment of nearly $1 million and six painstaking years of toil aided by only two helpers, he hand-cleared the land, built trails and bridges, developed an irrigation system, acquired more than 2,000 different species of trees and plants, and established one mile of scenic trails and a water lily lake stocked with *koi* and tropical fish. Onomea was a favorite spot with the Hawaiians, who came to fish and camp for the night. The valley was a fishing village called Kahali'i in the early 1800s. Later on it became a rough-water seaport used for shipping sugarcane and other tropical products. A remake of *Lord of the Flies* was filmed here some years ago, and it's easy to see why the area made the perfect movie set.

Start at the visitors center along the road, where you'll find a gift shop, the tiny Onomea Museum, self-guided tour maps, drinking water, restrooms, umbrellas for your convenience, and jungle perfume—better known as mosquito repellent!

Cross the road to the garden entrance and descend into this lush valley. The steep trail into the valley is about 500 feet long; once into the heart of the garden, the trails are more level. Plants from the four corners of the globe, including Iran, Central China, Japan, tropical Africa, India, Borneo, Brazil, East Indies, South Pacific Islands, tropical America, and the Philippines, are named with a full botanical description. Native plants from Hawaii are included. As you walk, listen for the songs of the native birds that love this ancient spot. Choose one of the aptly named trails like Fern Circle, Heliconia Trail, or Waterfall Trail and lose yourself in the beauty of the surroundings. You are in the middle of a tamed jungle, walking along manicured paths. Stroll the Ocean Trail down to the sea, where the rugged coastline is dramatically pummeled by frothy waves, a sea arch provides dramatic sculpture, and turtles swim the bay. You can hear the waves entering submerged lava caves, where they blow in and out like a giant bellows. Away from the sea you'll encounter screened gazebos filled with exotic birds like cockatoos from Indonesia and blue-fronted Amazon parrots. Walk the inland trails past waterfalls, streams, ponds, a bamboo grove, palms, and innumerable flowers. For at least a brief time you get to feel the power and beauty of a living Garden of Eden.

BEACHES

If you define a beach as a long expanse of white sand covered by a thousand sunbathers and their beach umbrellas, then Hilo doesn't have any. If a beach, to you, can be a smaller, more intimate affair where a good number of tourists and families can spend the day on pockets of sand between fingers of black lava, then Hilo has plenty. Hilo's best beaches all lie to the east of the city along Kalaniana'ole Avenue, an area known as the Keaukaha Strip, which runs six miles from downtown Hilo to its dead end at Leleiwi Point. Not all beaches are clearly marked, but even those are easily spotted by cars parked along the road.

Hilo Bayfront Park is a thousand yards of gray-black sand that narrows considerably as it runs west from the Wailoa River toward downtown. At one time it went all the way to the Wailuku River and was renowned throughout the islands for its beauty, but commercialism of the waterfront ruined it. By 1960, so much sewage and industrial waste had been pumped into the bay that it was considered a public menace, and then the great tsunami came. Reclamation projects created the Wailoa River State Recreation Area at the east end, and shorefront land became a buffer zone against future inundation. Few swimmers come to the beach because the water is cloudy and chilly, but the sharks don't seem to mind! The bay is terrific for fishing and picnicking, and the sails of small craft and sailboards can always be seen. It's a perfect spot for canoe races, and many local teams come here to train. Notice the judging towers and canoe sheds. In the early 1800s, King Kamehameha I reputedly had 800 canoes made and launched from this beach for an assault on Kaua'i to bring that distant island under his control. The armada never made it, but eventually Kaua'i came under the great king's influence by diplomatic means. Toward the west end, near the mouth of the Wailuku River, surfers catch long rides during the winter months, entertaining spectators. There is public parking along the eastern half near the canoe clubs or at the Wailoa river mouth where the fishing boats dock.

Reeds Bay Beach Park is a largely undeveloped area on the east side of the Waiakea Peninsula. Technically part of Hilo Bay, the water is notoriously cold because of a constantly flowing freshwater spring, hence the name Ice Pond at its innermost end. Mostly frequented by fishermen, some sailors park their private boats here.

Keaukaha Beach at **Carlsmith Beach County Park,** located on Puhi Bay, is the first in a series of beaches as you head east on Kalaniana'ole Avenue. Look for Baker Avenue and pull off to the left into a rough parking area. This is a favorite spot with local people, who swim at "Cold Water Pond," a spring-fed inlet at the head of the bay. A sewage treatment plant fronts the western side of Puhi Bay. Much nicer areas await you just up Kalaniana'ole Avenue.

Onekahakaha Beach County Park has it all: safe swimming, white-sand beach, lifeguards, and all amenities. Turn left onto Onekahakaha

Road and park in the lot of Hilo's favorite "family" beach. Swim in the large, sandy-bottomed pool protected by a manmade breakwater. Outside the breakwater the currents can be fierce, and drownings have been recorded. Walk east along the shore to find an undeveloped area of the park with many small tidal pools. Beware of sea urchins.

James Kealoha Beach County Park, also known locally as "Four Mile Beach," is next; people swim, snorkel, and fish here, and during winter months it's a favorite surfing spot. A large grassy area is shaded by trees and a picnic pavilion. Just offshore is an island known as Scout Island because local Boy Scouts often camp there. This entire area was known for its fishponds, and inland, just across Kalaniana'ole Avenue, is the 60-acre Loko Waka Pond. This site of ancient Hawaiian aquaculture is now a commercial operation that raises mullet, trout, catfish, perch, tilapia, and others. The Seaside Restaurant operates here.

Leleiwi Beach County Park lies along a lovely residential area carved into the rugged coastline.

This park with its parking lot, life guard, three pavilions, trees, and rock wall is a favorite local spot for scuba divers. The shore here is open to the ocean, and currents may be strong. Plentiful sealife make this a good snorkeling spot. Almost adjacent is Richardson Ocean Park, known locally as **Richardson's Beach Park.** Richardson Ocean Center is located here. Use a shower that's coming out of the retaining wall surrounding the house to wash off. A seawall skirts the shore and a tiny cove with a black-sand beach is the first in a series. This is a terrific area for snorkeling, with plenty of marinelife, including *honu* (green sea turtles). Walk east to a natural lava breakwater. Behind it are pools filled and flushed by the surging tide. The water breaks over the top of the lava and rushes into the pools, making natural whirlpool tubs. This is one of the most picturesque swimming areas on the island.

Just beyond is the end of the road and undeveloped parkland. When the pavement stops, follow the dirt track. This unofficial camping area has no amenities whatsoever, and seems like a home-

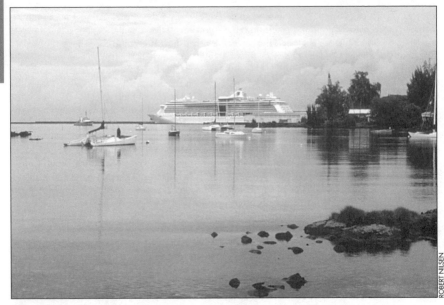

The frequent cruise ships that call at Hilo can easily be seen across Reeds Bay from Banyan Drive.

ROBERT NILSEN

less settlement. A series of pools like those at Richardson's are small, sandy-bottomed, and safe. Outside of the natural lava breakwater, currents are treacherous. Winter often sends tides surging inland here, making this area unusable.

Going north out of Hilo a few miles brings you to **Honoli'i Beach County Park.** Turn right onto Nahala Street, then left onto Kahoa, and follow it around until you see cars parked along the road. The water is down a steep series of steps, and while the black-sand beach is not much appreciated for swimming, it is known as one of the finest surfing spots on this side of the island.

Practicalities

ACCOMMODATIONS

Accommodations in Hilo are hardly ever booked up, and they're reasonably priced. Sounds great, but some hotels have "gone condo" to survive while others have simply shut their doors, so there aren't as many choices as there once were. During the Merrie Monarch Festival in April, the entire town is booked solid! The best hotels are clustered along Banyan Drive, with a few gems tucked away on the city streets.

Hostel

Arnott's Lodge, 98 Apapane Rd., Hilo, HI 96720, 808/969-7097, fax 808/961-9638, info@arnottslodge.com, www.arnottslodge.com, is a reasonably priced budget accommodation, safe, clean, and friendly, that offers most everything that a traveler might expect while on the road. Follow Kamehameha Avenue east until it turns into Kalaniana'ole Avenue; in about five minutes you'll see a lighted yellow sign pointing to Arnott's. Those without private transportation can be picked up by a free shuttle service operating 8 A.M.–8 P.M., with outbound departures set at 8 A.M., 12:30 P.M., and 5:30 P.M. A ride downtown or to the airport costs only $2, or $3 round-trip. Arnott's also offers inexpensive expeditions that are some of the best guided tours on the island. Other services are coin laundry, telephones, reasonable Internet access, safe storage of valuables and backpacks at no cost, and free use of bicycles and snorkel gear. Dormitory bunks—male, female, and coed—at $17 are spotlessly clean and cooled by cross ventilation and ceiling fans. Single rooms with bath, kitchen, and living room shared with one other

room are $37; a double room with the same setup is $47. With private baths, the singles and doubles run $57. A self-contained suite with two bedrooms, one with a double bed and the other with twins, includes a bathroom, kitchen, and living room for $120 for up to five people; each additional person is $15. Check-in is until 8 P.M.; late check-in is $5 extra, and no check-in after 10 P.M. Camping on the lawn with your own tent is now an option for $9 per person. Leisure time can be spent in a large entertainment area, where you can watch one of a huge selection of videos. A covered lanai with picnic tables has barbecue grills for your convenience, and to the side is a lanai platform built in a tree. Arnott's is an excellent hostel/lodge offering a quality, hassle-free stay with an international clientele.

Bed-and-Breakfasts

B&Bs are located here and there around town. Several are strung out along the highway north of town, a number are out toward Richardson's Beach, and a handful are scattered above town in residential pockets.

A short way past the "singing bridge," take the first right turn to get to **The Bay House B&B,** 42 Pukihae St., Hilo, HI 96720, 808/961-6311 or 888/235-8195, bigbayhouse@excite.com, www.bayhousehawaii.com. This new house with its three guest rooms sits on the cliff over Hilo Bay, as close as you can get to downtown Hilo. Rooms run $120 a night and each has a king or queen bed, private bath, television, telephone, and oceanside lanai, and from each you can watch the cruise ships come and go from port or the full moon shining on the bay. Decorations and accoutrements bring out the individual color

HILO

SHIPMAN HOUSE

A house can have presence, and, if it's brushed by magic like the Tin Man in *The Wizard of Oz*, it can even attain a heart. The home we're referring to was a purchase motivated by love and occupied by a large, dynamic family. The Shipman House, known locally as "the Castle," perched on five verdant acres high above Hilo, has such a heart.

After a quarter century on the Mainland, Barbara Ann Andersen, great-granddaughter of William H. "Willie" Shipman, the original owner, returned with her children and her husband Gary to restore to its former grandeur the residence where she spent her childhood summers, Easters, and Christmases. The house was figuratively stripped to its petticoats and outfitted in grand style.

To appreciate Shipman House B&B Inn fully, you must know its history, which goes back as far as the first tall ships that arrived from New England bearing the missionaries and their faith to the old kingdom. The first members of the family to reside in Hawaii were the Rev. William C. Shipman and his wife Jane, who arrived in the 1850s. The Rev. Shipman died young, leaving Jane alone and in need of a means to support herself and their three children; she accomplished this by opening a Hawaiian girls' boarding school in Hilo. Later she met and married Mr. Reed, a famous engineer responsible for most of Hilo's bridges and for whom, by strange coincidence, "Reed's Island," the section of Hilo where the mansion sits, was named.

One of the boys, William H. "Willie" Shipman, married Mary Melekahuia Johnson, one of the young Hawaiian ladies at his mother's school. Mary was descended from the ruling *ali'i*. Willie originally determined to study medicine, but one day his stepfather, Mr. Reed, made him an offer he couldn't refuse, saying, "Son, if you will give up medicine and take up the study of business, I'll give you a ranch to run." Willie knew a good opportunity when he saw it, and over the years he became one of the largest landholders on the Big Island, founding W. H. Shipman, Ltd.

Around the turn of the 20th century, Mary often implored Willie to take her for a drive, which would invariably pass by a lovely home being built on Ka'iulani Street. Holding his hand and looking into his eyes she would ask, "Willie, won't you buy me that house?" and he would reply, "I can't. The Wilsons own it." Finally, one day as they passed the house, Mary asked once again, but this time Willie smiled and said, "Yes, my dear. It's been ours for 30 days." They moved into the house in April 1901.

Mary was a dear friend of Hawaii's last queen, Lili'uokalani, who would visit at the Shipman house whenever she was in Hilo. While there the queen would preside over simple but elegant "poi luncheons," always seated at the place of honor at the huge round koa dining room table, where she could look out the bay windows at Hilo below. After lunch, Lili'uokalani would slip away to the "Library" to clandestinely savor a fine cigar.

To arrive at the Castle, ascend Waianuenue Avenue to Ka'iulani Street. There, turn right, cross the bridge, veer left, and you'll see the Shipman House on the rise. Climb the steps to the wraparound lanai, a necessity even for well-to-do families, who, like all Hawaii residents, spend a great deal of time outdoors. The broad landing provides a wonderful view of Hilo and the sea in the distance, with wild flowers and tangled greenery cascading into a tropical bowl at your feet. Two stained glass windows, encircled by a laurel wreath, the classic sign of a congenial home, greet you on entering. The Double Parlor, the 1st floor of the rounded three-story Tower that caps the home, is magnificent. Everywhere is glass—old-fashioned, handmade curved glass—its mottled and rippled texture giving a surrealistic twist to the panorama.

Pad along on the burnished fir flooring past koa-wainscoted walls to enter the Dining Room, where an enormous dining table and *pune'e* (movable couch) are still very functional. The back area of the home is called the Conservatory, really the center of the home for day-to-day life, where the family took their meals. Just off it is a Solarium and the Butler's Pantry, next to an "Otis in-home elevator," installed in the 1930s and probably

Hilo's first. Here, too, is a bedroom, formerly reserved for guests like Jack London and his wife Charmian. The peaceful Library, waiting to engulf an afternoon reader within its impressive 12-foot ceilings, is warmed by a brick fireplace with a koa mantel and is fringed by built-in koa bookcases.

Ascend the central staircase to the 2nd floor, where once upon a time a ballroom adorned in white wallpaper with twinkling stars swayed with dancing and music; nowadays part has been converted into a bedroom. At the back near the elevator, a window opening to a catwalk

led to a small room built over the water tank. That room served as great-grandfather Willie's "Office," his haven from the clamor of 10 children! In the back corner is a second bedroom. A spiral staircase ascends to the attic where a "canvas room" was the children's dormitory. A large, free-standing credenza holds hats and antique clothing. Also in the attic is the entrance to the Tower, a wine barrel of a room with wraparound windows.

Shipman House is once again one of *the* finest homes in all Hawaii in which to spend a quiet and elegant visit.

ROBERT NILSEN

and character of each room. Guests share a common entrance room with books, magazines, and refrigerator, and receive a breakfast of fruit, juice, pastries, coffee, and other goodies which you can have at your leisure when you wake up. Set even closer to the edge of the cliff is a hot tub, perfect for a starry-night soak. The Bay House is comfortable, plush, very clean, and quiet. No credit cards are accepted.

Accepting paying guests for 20 years and others for longer that that, Amy Gamble Lannan's **Lihi Kai** bed-and-breakfast, 30 Kahoa Road, Hilo, HI 96720, 808/935-7865, is a treasure and the longest running B&B in town. This sedate, contemporary-style house sits on the edge of a cliff just north of town and has a million-dollar view of Hilo Bay; it's less than two miles north of the "singing bridge." Guests of the two rooms share a bathroom and partake with Amy of a filling breakfast of fruit, pastries, and coffee to

start the day. A small swimming pool occupies part of the yard. While Lihi Kai is a treasure, Amy is the jewel. Full of life and love, with a witty sense of humor, she can offer you insight on where to eat, what to see, how to get around, and where to find adventure. Rooms are $55 a night plus $5 a night for less than three nights. Cash or personal check, please; no credit cards. Because the house is so close to the cliff edge, she's reluctant to take children under age eight. Make reservations well in advance, as her guests keep coming back again and again.

Set on a bluff overlooking the ocean just over two miles north of town is **Hale Kai,** 111 Honoli'i Pali, Hilo, HI 96720, 808/935-6330, fax 808/935-8439, bjornen@interpac.net, www.interpac.net/~halekai. This modern house has a small pool and hot tub. A sitting room for guests is shared, but each of the four rooms has its own bath and looks out over the ocean. Room rates run $90–100 a night with the suite at $110—no credit cards. The house is very comfortable, and the breakfast of fruits, pancakes, and sausages gives you a good start on the day.

Holmes' Sweet Home B&B, 107 Koʻula St., Hilo, HI 96720, 808/961-9089, fax 808/934-0711, homswhom@gte.net, www.stayhawaii .com/holmes.html, is the residence of John and Charlotte Holmes. On a quiet residential cul-de-sac high above town (more than 700 feet in elevation) with a view of Hilo Bay and the city lights, this B&B provides two comfy rooms priced $60–70 that feature a private entrance to a common room, guest refrigerator and microwave, and private bathrooms. A tropical continental breakfast is included.

The first place out along the Keaukaha strip is **Maureen's Bed and Breakfast,** 1896 Kalaniana'ole Ave., 808/935-9018 or 800/953-9018, fax 808/961-5596, maureen@maureenbnb.com, www.maureenbnb.com. Surrounded by landscaped lawns and koi ponds, this B&B was built in 1932 from redwood and cedar brought from the Mainland. With its high-ceilinged living room, arched windows and doors, balconies, and a Japanese tea room, it has plenty of charm in an East meets West kind of way. Comfortable and pleasingly decorated, the rooms rent for $50 single, $75 double with a shared bath, and $100 double with a private bath. A filling breakfast is always included. This is a bargain and an all around good place.

Friends of Friends, P.O. Box 5731, Hilo, HI 96720, 808/961-6556, bbell@aloha.net, http://vrbo.com/vrbo/1335.htm, is a basement studio that's been converted into a homey living area. While it has a low ceiling, everything else is standard. Two entrances open into the sitting and sleeping areas with its queen bed and single bed, and the full kitchen and bathroom are to the side. The unit comes with its own phone and cable TV, and opens onto a covered lanai. The rate is $275 a week, one week minimum. Sleeps two to three.

Located on 22 acres of macadamia nut and tropical fruit orchards north of the Boiling Pots, with views over Hilo and the ocean, and with the 120-foot Kulaniapia Waterfall on the property, is **The Inn at Kulaniapia Falls,** P.O. Box 11338, Hilo, HI 96721, 808/966-6373 or 888/838-6373, waterfall@hilo.net, www.waterfall.net. This contemporary-style B&B features four large second-story suites with private, granite-tiled baths and covered balconies: two face the ocean, two face inland. The room rate is $99 double, with $15 for an additional guest, and an expanded continental breakfast of tropical fruits, pastries, and coffee comes with an egg dish. Guests share the 1st-floor common room, a blend of island-style and Japanese motifs, and can use the kitchen and a barbecue grill. A good distance up from the highway, partially over an unpaved road, only the sound of the waterfall and the birds disturb the quiet.

Just four miles north of town is **Our Place Papaikou's B&B,** P.O. Box 469, Papaʻikou, HI 96781, tel./fax 808/964-5250, rplace@aloha.net, www.ourplacebandb.com. Set among thick vegetation in a little gulch, the three rooms of this cedar home open onto a large lanai that overlooks Kupua Stream, but if you can imagine it, the house would be just as much at home on a high Colorado mountainside. The Early American (double bed) and Oriental Room (queen bed) run $60 a night and share a bathroom, while the Master Bedroom with its king bed and day bed is $80 a night, two-night minimum. The lofty Great Room, open to all guests, has a cozy fireplace, TV, stereo, and a grand piano that loves to be tickled by someone who really knows how to play. When traveling up Hwy. 19, turn left at Pinky's convenience store, take the next two lefts, and turn down the driveway.

Shipman House B&B Inn, 131 Kaʻiulani St., Hilo, HI 96720, tel./fax 808/934-8002 or 800/627-8447, bighouse@bigisland.com, www .hilo-hawaii.com, is the grandest B&B in all Hawaii. The main house offers three guest rooms with antique beds, private bath, and stately views through enormous windows. Other guests will lodge in the Cottage, a separate building on the grounds, originally built for the express purpose of accommodating visitors. The Cottage contains two spacious bedrooms, each with queen bed, window seats, and private bath. Both rooms have private entrances, ceiling fans, and a small refrigerator. This is strictly a no smoking establishment and a "no TV zone," and children are not encouraged as there are so many antiques in the house and a steep ravine outside. Room rates are $154–184 single or double; $25 per extra person, add $25 for a single-night stay.

The Library is open to guests, along with use of the 1912 Steinway piano whose keys were once tickled by Lili'uokalani, and you can look around the house on your own in those areas where the doors are open. On Tuesday and Wednesday evenings, hula classes are held on the lanai and guests can participate. Breakfast, served 7:45–9 A.M. (earlier upon request, and special diets are accommodated), is an expanded continental with homemade cereals, hot cereals on request, assorted local fruits (there are 20 varieties of fruit trees on the property), fruit juices, Kona coffee, yogurt, fruit bread, muffins, popovers, or cinnamon rolls. Check in is 3–6 P.M., and checkout is at 10 A.M.

Banyan Drive Hotels

The following hotels lie along Banyan Drive. They range from moderate to a bit more than moderate. There are no luxury hotels in Hilo.

The **Hilo Seaside Hotel,** 126 Banyan Way, 808/935-0821 or 800/560-5557 in Hawaii, fax 808/969-9195, www.sand-seaside.com, is owned by the Kimi family. Like the others in this small island chain, it's clean and well kept and has Polynesian-inspired decor with a '60s or '70s feel. On the property is Luci's Grill, which serves basic Japanese and American breakfasts and dinners. Room prices are $88 standard, $100 superior pool view, $110 deluxe pool view, and $110 garden kitchenette; third person charge is $10 and breakfast is included for all but the standard rooms. Add approximately $25 for a room/car package. Ask about off-season, AAA, and AARP rates, and a better rate is sometimes offered depending on the amount of business at the time. Each room has a lanai, air conditioner and ceiling fan, television, and small refrigerator, and there is a coin laundry facility on premises. The grounds are laid out around a well-tended central courtyard garden, and the pool is secluded and away from the street; to the front, a large koi pond

lies in another garden. While flash and polish are not part of the routine, the place is very clean and well kept, and you will find two scoops of dignity and pride. At this family-style hotel with a motel atmosphere, the friendly staff goes out of its way to make you feel welcome. Located across from the Ice Pond, this is a good choice for a moderate price at a convenient location.

Uncle Billy's Hilo Bay Hotel is sandwiched between two larger hotels at 87 Banyan Dr., Hilo, HI 96720, 808/935-0861, 800/442-5841 in Hawaii, 800/367-5102 Mainland, resv@unclebilly.com, www.unclebilly.com,. The Hilo Bay's blue metal roof and white louvered shutters make it look a bit like "Long John Silver's Meets Polynesia." The lobby's rattan furniture and thatched longhouse theme are pure '50s-kitsch Hawaii. Definitely have a look. There is free parking and a guest pool. This is a no-frills establishment, but all rooms are clean and air-conditioned with a TV and phone. Rooms run $84–94 or studio kitchenettes $94–104, good value for the money, but don't expect anything too modern or too luxurious. Numerous discounts are available, so be sure to ask. The in-house Fish and Steakhouse restaurant serves reasonably priced food for breakfast and dinner only, and a free hula show is presented every evening at 6 P.M. in the lounge off the lobby. Uncle Billy's General Store, where you can buy everything from beer to sundries and ice cream to resort wear, is part of the complex.

The **Hilo Hawaiian Hotel,** 71 Banyan Dr., Hilo, HI 96720, 808/935-9361, 800/272-5275 in Hawaii, 800/367-5004 Mainland and Canada, occupies the most beautiful grounds of any hotel in Hilo. From the vantage of the hotel's colonnaded veranda, you overlook formal gardens, Coconut Island, and Hilo Bay. Designed as a huge arc, the hotel's architecture blends well with its surroundings and expresses the theme set by the bay, that of a long, sweeping crescent. While neat, clean, well maintained, and with all necessary amenities, the hotel still has somewhat of a '70s feel. If you want flash and glamour, try one of the new resorts on the Kona side. However, for down-home quality with a touch of class in Hilo, you can't do better than the Hilo

Hawaiian. Prices at this property run $119 for a standard room, $139 for a superior, $149 for an ocean-view room, and $183–360 for suites; all rooms have a/c, phone, and cable color TV, plus there's a swimming pool on the property. Guest services include a gift shop, Laundromat, free parking, and a front-desk safety deposit box. The Queen's Court restaurant, Wai'oli Lounge, and the Tranquil Waters day spa are all on the property for guests' convenience. Along Banyan Drive out front, the Banyan General Store for sundries and Bayview Farm Coffee shop are other options. This is the best accommodation Hilo has to offer.

Hawaii Naniloa Resort, 93 Banyan Dr., Hilo, HI 96720, 808/969-3333, 800/442-5845 in Hawaii, 800/367-5360 Mainland and Canada, hinani@aloha.net, www.naniloa.com, is a large, 325-room hotel. Rates start at $100 for garden view, $120 for partial ocean view, and $140 for oceanfront rooms; suites are available for $160–190. Numerous discounts are offered. The Naniloa offers air conditioning and a TV in all rooms, but only the higher end rooms have balconies. Other amenities include hotel parking, the Sandalwood and Ting Hao restaurants, a lounge, periodic entertainment in the Crown Room, a gift shop, Laundromat, and two pools. The original hotel dates back more than 60 years and over the years built a fine reputation for value and service. Unfortunately, the Naniloa has not kept up its facility as one might expect and has gotten a bit raggedy around the edges. It's become "very tired" and is much in need of a thorough overhaul to bring back the high standard that it once maintained.

Accommodations near Downtown

Dolphin Bay Hotel is a sparkling little gem— simply the best hotel bargain in Hilo, one of those places where you get more than you pay for. It sits on a side street in the Pu'u'eo section of town at the north end of Hilo Bay, at 333 'Iliahi St., Hilo, HI 96720, 808/935-1466, fax 808/935-1523, johnhili@gte.net, www.dolphinbayhilo.com. John Alexander, the owner/manager, is at the front desk nearly every day. He's a font of information about the Big Island and will happily dispense advice on how to make your day trips fulfilling. The hotel was built by his father, who spent years in Japan, and you'll be happy to discover this influence when you sink deep into the *ofuro*-type tubs in every room. All 18 units have small but sufficient modern kitchens. Rates are $66 single and $72 double for a standard room, $76 and $79 for a superior room, $89 for a one-bedroom, and $99 for a two-bedroom fully furnished unit; additional guests $10. Weekly rates can be arranged. The more deluxe units upstairs have open-beamed ceilings and lanai and, with three spacious rooms, feel like apartments. No swimming pool or a/c here, but there are color TVs and fans with excellent cross ventilation. The grounds and housekeeping are immaculate. Hotel guests can partake of free bananas, papayas, and other exotic fruits found in hanging baskets in the lobby, as well as free coffee. Make reservations, because everyone who has found the Dolphin Bay comes back again and again.

The Wild Ginger Inn, 100 Pu'u'eo St., Hilo, HI 96720, 808/935-5556 or 877/212-8276, fax 808/593-8183, wildgingerinn@usa.com, www.wildgingerinn.com, is a bubble-gum pink and vibrant green plantation-style hotel from the '40s, so don't expect the floors to be level or everything to be spotless. It's located a short two blocks from the north edge of downtown, a few steps from the Dolphin Bay Hotel. An open-air lobby leads to a corridor veranda overlooking the thick greenery of the side yard, with a small view of the bay in the distance. A double hammock and vintage rattan chairs in the lobby area are for your relaxation. Each of the more than 30 rooms, very basic but reasonably clean, has a ceiling fan, but no telephones; some also have TVs and microwaves, and most have small refrigerators and private baths. Room rates run $45–99 single or double, $64–94 triple, and $89–99 quad, depending upon the type of room: budget, standard, superior, lanai, deluxe, or suite. Discounts are available for longer stays. Every morning, fruit, juice, and pastries are put out for guests. The inn is completely non-smoking, with a special area provided for smokers in the garden. Internet access, laundry facilities, and front-desk security boxes are available to guests. New management promises to make long-needed repairs to the old building.

Near the Kaiko'o Mall is a funky, barebones place called **Off The Wall Mini Hotel,** 10 Wilson St., 808/934-8000. Rooms have been partitioned in this older house to make private and bunk rooms. One room has a bathroom, the others share, and the covered shower is in the garden out back. This is a no smoking place, and everyone shares a common TV lounge. Rooms run $25–35 a night; a bunk in the dorm goes for $15 with a three night minimum. There is no luxury here whatsoever and you get only the most basic of accommodations, but is a place to hang out for someone on a tight budget.

FOOD

Inexpensive

Named after the famous all-Japanese fighting battalion that predated even the famous "442," the **Cafe 100,** 969 Kilauea Ave., 808/935-8683, open Mon.–Thurs. 6:45 A.M.–8:30 P.M., Fri.–Sat. until 9:30 P.M., is a Hilo institution. The Miyashiro family has been serving food at its indoor-outdoor restaurant here since the late '50s. Although the loco moco, a cholesterol atom bomb containing a hamburger and egg atop rice smothered in gravy, was invented at Hilo's Lincoln Grill, the Cafe 100, serving it since 1961, has actually patented this belly-buster and turned it into an art form. There are the regular loco moco, teriyaki loco, spam loco, hot dog loco, oyako loco, and for the health conscious, the mahi loco. So, if your waistline, the surgeon general, and your arteries permit, this is *the* place to have one. With few exceptions, they cost $6 or less. Breakfast choices include everything from bacon and eggs to coffee and donuts, while lunches feature beef stew, salmon mixed plate, and fried chicken, or an assortment of sandwiches from teriyaki beef to good old BLT. Make your selection and sit at one of the picnic tables under the veranda to watch the people of Hilo go by.

All trips to Hilo must include a brief stop at **Low International Food,** 808/969-6652, long occupying the corner of Kilauea and Ponahawai Streets and open daily except Wednesday

9 A.M.–8 P.M., where *everyone* comes for the unique bread. Some of the more fanciful loaves are made from taro, breadfruit, guava, mango, passion fruit, coconut, banana, pumpkin, and cinnamon. The so-you-want-to-taste-it-all rainbow bread is a combination of taro, guava, and sweet bread. Loaves cost around $6, and arrangements can be made to ship them anywhere in the country. Breakfast, lunch, and dinner plates, most under $6, range from the shrimp black bean to grilled mahi mahi, *lau lau,* and Korean chicken. Choose a table under the pavilion and enjoy your picnic in downtown Hilo.

Open every day 7 A.M.–9 P.M. and a place that gets praise from local people is **Freddie's,** 454 Manono St., 808/935-1108. The decor might be called upscale Formica, but Freddie's serves down-home food, all for under $7. Lunch and all entrées are served with two scoops of rice, fries, or mashed potatoes. Among the items on the menu are saimin, teriyaki steak sandwich, chili dogs, and burgers.

Another favorite of locals and, at 485 Hinano St., not far away is **Don's Grill,** 808/935-9099, open daily except Monday 10:30 A.M.–9 P.M., until 10 P.M. on Friday. This American/Hawaiian family-style basic restaurant is known for a good square meals at reasonable prices. Inside find wood-trimmed blue Formica tables in a very modern yet functionally tasteful setting with additional seating is in the solarium. Here you find everything from *saimin* to sandwiches and fish to rotisserie chicken. Most entrées run $6.50–10.

If you want to eat anything but uninspired "American standard" in Hilo after 9 P.M., go to **Nori's Saimin and Snacks,** 688 Kino'ole St., 808/935-9133, stuck away and hard to spot (but worth it) in a little strip business across from the bowling alley. Here you can have a totally "island experience" in a humble, honest restaurant that specializes in authentic "local grinds." Inside, where the service is slow but friendly, are Formica tables and chairs, counter stools, and the "that's what you really look like" glow of fluorescent lighting. Boiling pots hold saimin of all sorts, which is generously ladled into steaming bowls and topped with fresh vegetables. Or order a plate lunch with a scoop of macaroni salad.

Two people can eat until they waddle at Nori's for about $15. There's no atmosphere, but the food is authentic and good.

New Star Chinese Restaurant 808/934-8874, is at 172 Kilauea Ave. and open daily 10 A.M.– 9 P.M. except Tuesday. If you want to eat with "the people," this is the spot. The servings are generous and for $8 you can fill up. This large restaurant is clean, the service is friendly, and the dining experience, while certainly not fancy, is definitely authentic. Takeout available.

When at the Prince Kuhio Plaza, stop at **Dotty's Family Restaurant,** 808/959-6477. Open for breakfast daily 7–11 A.M., for lunch Mon.–Sat. 10:30 A.M.–2 P.M., and for dinner Mon.–Thurs. 5–8 P.M., Friday 5–9 P.M., Dotty's is an institution where local people come for the hearty portions and the homestyle cooking. Breakfast favorites are corned beef hash and eggs or French toast made with thick slices of Punalu'u sweet bread. Lunch includes the grilled chicken supreme with mushrooms and Swiss cheese or Dotty's ultimate steak sandwich. Those in the know come for Dotty's famous oven-roasted turkey, fresh catch of the day, or barbecued pork ribs with house-made smoke-flavored sauce for dinner. Fresh vegetables, real mashed potatoes, and homemade soups (great chowder on Friday) come with all full meals, and there's plenty of homemade pie for dessert.

Bears' Coffee Shop, 106 Keawe, 808/935-0708, is an upscale coffee shop renowned for its breakfasts, served 7 A.M.–2:30 P.M. Mon.–Sat., 8 A.M.–noon on Sunday, but coffee is available 5:30 A.M.–5 P.M.. Bears' features Belgian waffles (made from malted flour), bagels, and an assortment of egg dishes. Lunch is hearty deli sandwiches of turkey, pastrami, chicken fillet, tuna, or ham, along with "designer" bagels and salads. You can get most anything for under $5. Beverages include Italian sodas, homemade lemonade, and a large selection of coffee, cappuccino, and café latte from the full espresso bar. All are perfect with desserts like carrot cake, Bear's brownies, cheesecake, and pies. A great place to relax, read the morning paper, check out the Teddy Bears on the wall, or watch Hilo life go by from the sidewalk bistro tables.

Satsuki's, 808/935-7880, at 180 Keawe St. receives the highest recommendation because when local people want a good meal at an inexpensive price they head here. It's open for lunch 11 A.M.–2 P.M., dinner 5–8:30 P.M., closed Tuesday. Specialties are oxtail soup and the Okinawa soba plate lunch. There are plenty of traditional favorites, and all meals come with miso soup, Japanese pickles and condiments, rice, and tea. Spotlessly clean and friendly. This is excellent food at excellent value.

Tsunami Grill and Tempura, 250 Keawe St., 808/961-6789, is open Mon.–Sat. 10:30 A.M.–2 P.M. and 4:30–8 P.M. On Sunday, it's only open for dinner, and then only for the buffet. Like many of the restaurants in town, the Tsunami Grill has its own loyal local clientele. The food is excellent and the prices are unbeatable. You'll walk away stuffed on traditional Japanese food like udon, soba, katsu, tempura, donburi, and saimin, or bento for about $10, or if you order the buffet, it is $24.95 on Sunday and $14.95 the rest of the week.

For food of the raw variety, head across the street to **Ocean Sushi,** Tsunami Grill's sister shop, 808/961-6625, where most sushi on the menu is $2.50–4 and the many kinds of rolls run about $4.50. There is a laundry list of possibilities, both traditional and contemporary. Also on the menu are the more expensive sushi boxes and sashimi platters, salads, miso soup, and the like. Open 10 A.M.–2:30 P.M. and 4:30–9 P.M. Mon.–Saturday.

Miyo's, 808/935-2273, overlooks Waiakea Pond from its second story location at Waiakea Villas. Here you find "homestyle Japanese cooking" done the way you might find in Japan, in simple surroundings, at a very reasonable price. Fresh fish daily, and vegetarian options are available. You can't go wrong here. Open for lunch 11 A.M.–2 P.M. and for dinner 5:30–8:30 P.M., closed Sunday.

The **Happy Valley Seafood Restaurant,** 808/933-1083, at the Hilo Shopping Center, has a typically Chinese long list of menu items and reasonably priced live lobster. Serves Mandarin and Szechwan, mixed plate, dim sum, and has take-out; open daily.

Ken's House of Pancakes is a place to get a good standard American meal for a good price. Open 24 hours every day of the year, it's conveniently located on the way to the airport at 1730 Kamehameha Ave., 808/935-8711.

Kitty-corner across the intersection is the local **Verna's,** 808/935-2776, for plate lunches, burgers, sandwiches, and a multitude of inexpensive fast local food with nothing much more than $5. Take-out or sit at the picnic table to the side. Located on Furneaux Ave., **Canoes Cafe,** 808/935-4070, has a large variety of inspired sandwiches, wraps, and salads available Mon.–Sat. 8 A.M.–3 P.M., 10 A.M.–2 P.M. on Sunday.

Ono Hawaiian serves plate lunches, burgers, and vegetarian entrées from its lunch wagon at the bayfront beach.

Pastries and Treats

Lanky's Pastries, Hilo Shopping Center, 808/935-6381, open 6:30 A.M.–9 P.M., deli side from 6 A.M., is a perfect place to head if you have a sweet tooth that *must* be satisfied. The deli/bakery is especially known for its "long johns,"—long, thin sugar donuts filled with custard—but it also has all kinds of baked goods from bread to apple turnovers.

Places for a refreshing scoop of ice cream are **Tropical Dreams Ice Cream** at the refurbished Kress Building downtown (you can get baked goods here too), **Hilo Homemade Ice Cream** either at 41 Waianuenue Ave. or at Hilo Tropical Gardens along Kalaiana'ole Ave. on the way to the beaches, and the **Big Island Candies** shop on Hinano Street. Both Tropical Dreams and Hilo Homemade ice creams are local brands made in town.

Hilo Seeds and Snacks at 15 Waianuenue Ave. and **Kilauea Preserve Center** at 187 Kilauea Ave. sell authentic crackseed. If you've never tried this unique island snack, here's your opportunity.

Moderate

Restaurant Miwa, at Hilo Shopping Center, 808/961-4454, is open 11 A.M.–2 P.M. and again 5–10 P.M., until 9 P.M. on Sunday. Very beautifully appointed, Miwa is a surprise, especially since it's stuck back in the corner of the shopping center. Enter to find traditional shoji screens and wooden tables adorned with fine linens, along with a classic sushi bar. The menu is excellent, with appetizers like sake-flavored steamed clams and crab sunomono (seaweed, cucumber slices, and crab meat). A specialty is nabemono, a hearty and zesty soup/stew prepared at your table for a minimum of two people. Traditional favorites popular with Westerners include beef sukiyaki and shabu shabu, and there's also a variety of combination dinners that give you a wider sampling of the menu at good value. Restaurant Miwa is an excellent choice for a traditional meal at a reasonable price in a congenial setting.

Near Hilo Shopping Center, at 1438 Kilauea Ave. is **Kilauea Kitchen,** 808/935-6664. Open for three meals a day, this simple eatery offers great food at very reasonable prices. Breakfast might be French toast, pancakes, *loco moco,* or a Japanese-style breakfast; the lunch menu includes sandwiches, burgers, and wraps. Dinners are a bit more sophisticated with entrées like pan seared mahi mahi, sweet chili chicken, and grilled New York steak, most under $8. In the same building is **Hilo-Shi-Bento-Ya and Bakery,** where noodles, udon, saimin, and sushi are available. Menu items here have been created with the help of the well-known Honolulu chef Russell Siu of 3660 On The Rise.

Very clean and down-home proud, the **Royal Siam Thai Restaurant,** 70 Mamo St., 808/961-6100, serves up tasty Thai treats daily 11 A.M.–2 P.M. and 5–8:30 P.M. Appetizers include a crispy Thai noodle dish for $6 and two of the several soups are coconut chicken soup for $6 and a seafood soup for $9. Entrées range from simple fried rice dishes through curries and meat dishes to seafood selections, mostly in the $7–10 range. There are specials nightly. Vegetarian selections are numerous and portions are large. This little restaurant gets good reviews and has a local following.

The tiny **Naung Mai Thai Kitchen,** 808/934-7540, at 86 Kilauea Ave. is open weekdays except Wednesdays for lunch and Monday–Saturday for dinner, and puts out some of the best Thai food in the state at very reasonable prices.

Although nicely decorated, people come for the flavors and fresh ingredients. Once you try, you'll want to go back, but go early as the half dozen tables and booths tend to fill up fast.

Fiasco's, at the Waiakea Kai Shopping Plaza, 200 Kanoelehua St., 808/935-7666, serves good square meals Sun.–Thurs. 11 A.M.–10 P.M., weekends to 11 P.M. Featuring a country inn flavor, Fiasco's has a cobblestoned entrance that leads you to the cozy, post-and-beam dining room appointed with stout wooden tables, with semiprivate booths lining the walls. The menu begins with appetizers, mostly $4–7, like fried mozzarella, escargot, or a big plate of onion rings. Lighter appetites might enjoy the huge and well-regarded soup and salad bar buffet at $9, or a grilled chicken Caesar salad for $8. Sandwiches and burgers also run about $8. Entrées include Mexican fare and American standards, with a few pasta dishes thrown in to round out the selection. Many are under $10, while the most expensive item on the menu is only $18; Friday night prime rib is $16. Families can save money with a special children's menu. The English-style pub has a full mahogany bar, a classic with polished lion's-head brass rails, offers comfortable stools with black leather booths, and serves up wine, mixed drinks, and perhaps the largest selection of beer on the island—island-made, domestic, and imports.

Along Kamehameha Avenue is a hole-in-the-wall eatery with a handful of tables called **Honu's Nest,** 808/935-9321, that's gained a good reputation and strong local clientele. Served are a variety of Japanese dishes like tempura, donburi, soba, curry, and full dinners with salad, miso, and rice. Nothing on the menu is over $10. Open Mon.–Sat. 11 A.M.–3 P.M., Honu's Nest is popular so you may have to wait for a table.

Nihon Restaurant, 808/969-1133 (reservations recommended), a second story establishment raised up on pilings at 123 Lihiwai St. and overlooking both Lili'uokalani Gardens and the bay, presents authentic Japanese meals, an excellent sushi bar, and combination dinners along with cultural and artistic displays. What you get here is like what you'd expect in Japan, with most everything under $17. Open daily except Sunday for lunch 11 A.M.–1:30 P.M. and dinner 5–9 P.M., sushi bar until 10 P.M.

Reuben's Mexican Food, 336 Kamehameha Ave., 808/961-2552, open Mon.–Fri. 11 A.M.–9 P.M., Saturday noon–9 P.M., will enliven your palate with its zesty dishes. The interior has the feel of Old Mexico with its bright murals and collection of sombreros and piñatas. Mariachi music wafts through the room, and you better like it because Pancho Villa is keeping an eye on you from the wall! The lengthy menu is reasonable, mostly $8–10, with selections like carne asada, steak tacos, chicken flautas, crab enchiladas, and a vegetarian bean chili verde burrito. All are served with beans and rice, and the portions are huge. The bar has a large selection of Mexican, American, and European *cerveza* for $2–3, but Reuben's is most famous for its margaritas—more than one will get you acting like a human chimichanga. *¡Olé!*

Near Kalakaua Park is **Hawaiian Jungle,** 808/934-0700, open daily 11 A.M.–9 P.M. for Mexican and Peruvian dishes. Many of the usual Mexican dishes are on the menu as are more substantial dinners. Unique here, however, are empanadas chillenas, a ham or spinach and cheese filled pastry, and lomo saltano, a Peruvian fajita, and there is a Peruvian special every night. Entrées run $9–17. Live music on the weekends.

Expensive

Queen's Court Restaurant at the Hilo Hawaiian Hotel on Banyan Drive, 808/935-9361, offers a nightly buffet that is *the* best in Hilo. Connoisseurs usually don't consider buffets to be gourmet quality, but the Queen's Court proves them wrong, and there's even nightly dinner music to match. Throughout the week, buffets include a prime rib and crab buffet Mon.–Thurs., a legendary seafood buffet on Friday, and a Hawaiian seafood buffet on Sunday. All are extraordinary and would give the finest restaurants anywhere a run for their money. The buffets run $24–27, with a 25 percent discount for seniors. The dining room is grand, with large archways and windows overlooking Hilo Bay. Sunday champagne brunch is more of the same quality at $24. Breakfast is served Mon.–Sat. 6:30–9:30 A.M., $10 for the buffet or à la carte with such items as eggs any style, a short stack of griddle cakes, an "Omelette by the Bay," or a local scramble. Lunch is also reasonably priced and served 11:15 A.M.–1:15 P.M. except Sunday, when the brunch runs 10:30 A.M.–1:30 P.M. Make reservations, especially on seafood night, because the Hilo Hawaiian attracts many Hilo residents who love great food.

Modern and chic with a black and white checkerboard floor, linen on the tables, an open-air kitchen, a high ceiling with ceiling fans, and the calming effect of ferns and flowers, is **Café Pesto**, at 308 Kamehameha Ave. in the historic S. Hata Bldg., 808/969-6640, open Sun.–Thurs. 11 A.M.–9 P.M., Fri.–Sat. until 10 P.M. One of Hilo's established restaurants, it offers affordable gourmet food in an open, airy, and unpretentious setting that looks out across the avenue to the bay. Pizzas from the 'ohi'a wood-fired oven can be anything from a simple cheese pie for $8 to a large Greek or chili-grilled shrimp pizza for $18; you can also create your own. Lunch calzones run about $11 but at dinner go for $15 with soup and salad. Lunchtime also features sandwiches and pasta. For dinner, try an appetizer like Asian Pacific crab cakes or sesame-crusted Hamakua goat cheese. Heartier appetites will be satisfied with the main dinner choices, which might be mango-glazed chicken, island seafood risotto, or a combination beef tenderloin and tiger prawns with garlic mashed potatoes for $15–29. Follow this with a warm coconut tart, liliko'i cheesecake, or creme brûlée and you'll be set for the evening. Café Pesto also has a brass-railed bar where you can order caffè latté or a fine glass of wine to top off your meal in one of the best island-cuisine restaurants in Hilo.

Sicilian fishermen would feel right at home at **Pescatore,** 235 Keawe St., 808/969-9090, open daily for breakfast 7:30–11 A.M., lunch 11 A.M.–2 P.M., dinner 5:30–9 P.M. for some of the finest Italian pasta and sandwiches in Hilo. The building has had multiple uses over the years and, as part of its colorful past, served as a house of ill repute. It is now a bright and cheery room with high-backed, red velvet armchairs and formally set tables with green linen tablecloths. Ital-

ian-style chandeliers, lace curtains, and koa trim add to the elegance. When the Italian in you desires antipasti, minestrone soup, cioppino classico alla pescatore, gamberetti Alfredo, or any number of other seafood dishes, head for Pescatore. Many dinner entrées run $16–25.

Harrington's, 135 Kalaniana'ole Ave., 808/961-4966, is open nightly for dinner 5:30–9:30 P.M., Sunday until 9 P.M., and lunch Mon.–Fri. 11 A.M.–3:30 P.M.; the lounge opens at 4 P.M. The restaurant overlooks the Ice Pond at Reed's Bay in a convivial setting. A sunset cocktail or dinner is enhanced with the melodic strains of live jazz, contemporary, or Hawaiian music playing softly in the background on the weekends. The continental cuisine of mostly steak and seafood features appetizers like seafood chowder, mushroom tempura, and escargot in casserole that run $4–9. Although the eggplant parmigiana at $15 is vegetarian, other mostly meat entrées include prawns scampi, scallops chardonnay, calamari meunière, Slavic steak, prime rib au jus, and chicken marsala for $16–20. Much appreciated by locals, the menu hasn't changed much since the '70s. While not inspired, Harrington's turns out eminently pleasing food in a pleasant atmosphere.

The Seaside Restaurant, 808/935-8825, appropriately named, is located out along the Keaukaha strip at 1790 Kalaniana'ole Ave. at a fish farm operation. If you want, have a look at the ponds before you head in for your meal. About a dozen varieties of freshwater and saltwater fish are available on the menu in a number of preparations, and for those who would rather, a few steak, chicken, and pasta selections are also available. For fish, come to the Seaside. Most fish dinners range from $17.95 to $25.95. All dinners come complete with salad, vegetables, rice, and apple pie. This is a popular place with locals, so make a reservation; open Tues.–Sun. 5–8:30 P.M.

Brewery
Hilo has its own microbrewery, **Mehana Brewing Company,** 275 E. Kawili St., 808/934-8211, www.mehana.com. A small operation—about 1,200 barrels a year—in business since 1996,

this microbrewery crafts five varieties of light beer with no preservatives, brewed especially for the tropical climate. Stop at the small tasting room for a sample any day except Sunday. If it's not too busy, someone may show you around. Open Mon.–Fri. 9 A.M.–5:30 P.M. and Sat. 10 A.M.–4 P.M.

ENTERTAINMENT

Hilo doesn't have a lot of nightlife, but neither is it a morgue.

One of the best places for weekend music and dancing, and quick easy food every night of the week except Sunday is the large and lively **Cronies Bar and Grill,** 808/935-5158, at the corner of Waianuenue and Kamehameha Avenues. Hamburgers, sandwiches, and *pu pu* in the $6–8 range, with a handful of more expensive entrées, are on the menu, and Cronies offers a full complement of drinks. On Friday and sometimes other nights of the week there's live music. Belly up to the bar, toss some darts at the electronic dartboard, or use the billiard table in the back while the music plays up front. Open at 11 A.M.

If you're looking for a night out in the Banyan Drive area, try **Shooter's,** 808/969-7069, at 121 Banyan Drive. Open 11 A.M.–2 A.M., Shooters is a bar and restaurant where you can dance seven nights a week. DJ music ranges from reggae to rock to rap depending upon the crowd and the night, with live music (cover charge) a couple times a month. The cavernous interior is like a giant rumpus room with cement floors, neon beer signs, a graffiti wall, and TVs at every angle; the decor is industrial chic. Don't be put off by the atmosphere, which can seem a bit stark and hard at first glance. Shooter's is friendly, has security, and boasts that "there hasn't been one confrontation since the day we opened." That's nice!

Wai'oli Lounge at the Hilo Hawaiian Hotel offers live contemporary Hawaiian music Fri.–Sat. nights, karaoke Sun.–Thurs, and complimentary *pu pu* daily 5–7 P.M. In the cocktail lounge at the Naniloa hotel, live music and dancing are an option on Friday and Saturday

evenings. **Uncle Billy's Fish and Steakhouse** at the Hilo Bay Hotel has a free hula show nightly 6–7:30 P.M. **Harrington's** offers live jazz, contemporary, or Hawaiian music Thurs.–Sat.; good for dinner or just for relaxing.

At Waiakea Villas, the **Karaoke Box,** 808/935-6269, is a place to sing to your heart's content. Open Mon.–Thurs. 5–10 P.M., Fri.–Sat. until 2 A.M., closed Sunday. Right next door is the **Hale Inu Sports Bar.** Stop in for a cold one and a game on the big screen.

Movie Theaters

To catch a flick, try the **Prince Kuhio Theaters,** at the Prince Kuhio Plaza, 808/951-3456, with eight screens and tickets for $7 adult or $5 student. Downtown in the refurbished Kress Building is the newer four-screen **Kress Cinemas,** 808/961-3456, where tickets cost $5.50. The renovated **Palace Theater** 38 Haili St., 808/934-7777, shows art films, is the venue of the yearly Hawaii International Film Festival, and hosts periodic live performances. Here you have stadium seating, a proscenium stage, and wonderful old murals. If you're into art-deco buildings and old cinemas, make this a stop. It's mostly open weekends at 7:30 P.M.; movie tickets are $6 adult and $5 student.

RECREATION

Bicycling

The **Hilo Bike Hub,** 318 E. Kawila, 808/961-4452, is perhaps the best shop in town for quality mountain bikes and accessories; sales, repair, and rentals. Stop here for information about island races and ideas for where to bike on-road or off-road on the island. Crossbreed mountain bikes rent for $25 a day, front suspension bikes are $20, and full suspension bikes run $45; rent for seven days at the price of four. Closed on Sunday, so if you rent a bike on Saturday, you must rent it for two days.

Mid Pacific Wheels, at 1133-C Manono St., 808/935-6211, sells and rents mid-range mountain bikes. Bikes rent for $15 a day; helmets, tubs, and bike rack are extra. Open daily.

Aquatic Perceptions, 808/933-1228, arranges bicycle tours to various locations on the island, including one through the tropical district of Puna and another around Kilauea Crater rim drive, for about $100 per person.

For recycled bicycles, sales, repair, or rentals, stop and talk with the owner of **Da Kine Bike Shop,** at 12 Furneaux Lane, 808/934-9861, just a few steps from Kamehameha Avenue in downtown Hilo. Nothing is new here, but you might find a bike to cruise the beach or one maybe to buy and sell back at the end of your trip. Open Tues.–Sat. only.

Scuba

The **Nautilus Dive Center,** 382 Kamehameha Ave., Hilo, 96720, 808/935-6939, derooy@gte .net, www.downtownhilo.com/nautilus, open Mon.–Sat. 9 A.M.–4 P.M., Sunday by appointment, owned and operated by certified instructor William DeRooy, is one of the longest established dive companies on the Hilo side. This full-service dive center offers three- to five-day PADI certification at a very reasonable $125 per person for a group of at least four or $300 for private lessons, and shore dives at $55 for one tank or $75 for two tanks for certified divers, including transportation. Boat dives can be arranged. New and used dive gear, scuba rental equipment, and snorkel gear rental at $5 for 24 hours are also available. DeRooy is willing to provide information over the phone for anyone coming to the Hilo side to dive or snorkel. He updates you on ocean conditions, suggests spots compatible with your ability, and even offers a free dive and snorkel map whether you're a customer or not. Bill is a font of information about the Big Island's water sports and shares it in the true *aloha* spirit. Definitely stop in!

With a wider range of water equipment for sale or rent can be found at **Planet Ocean Watersports,** 808/935-7277, at 100 Kamehameha Ave. Snorkel gear, scuba gear, and kayaks can be rented, and dive and kayak tours can be arranged.

Golf

The only county-maintained golf course on the island is located high above downtown Hilo.

Hilo Municipal Golf Course, 340 Haihai St., 808/959-7711, is a 6,325-yard, par-71 undulating course where non-residents can golf for $20 weekdays and $25 weekends. There are reduced rates for state and island residents. Cart rental is separate, and rental clubs are available. This is definitely a local course but does provide some challenge. Call ahead for tee times.

Occupying the center of the Waiakea Peninsula and surrounded by Banyan Drive is the **Naniloa Country Club** golf course, 808/935-3000. Maintained by the Naniloa hotel, this small nine-hole course is a par 35 over a flat 2,740 yards; $30 for two times around on weekends or $25 during the week. It's an easygoing place where lots of people come to learn and practice.

Arnott's Expeditions

Arnott's Lodge, 808/969-7097, www.arnottslodge .com/activity.html, offers a variety of hiking adventures to its guests and to those who do not stay at the lodge but want more of an adventure than organized tours usually offer. Although the schedule of offerings changes periodically, some of Arnott's mainstays are the hikes to the lava flow in Volcanoes National Park, a waterfall and valleys hike of Saturday, and the sunset and stargazing trek from the top of Mauna Kea. These van tours each run a full eight hours and take only as many as the van will hold. Rates run $48, higher for those not staying at the lodge. All trips are made weather permitting and only if there are enough takers to make a go of them. Some restrictions apply, so be sure to check with the staff at Arnott's Lodge, or check out its website for the current list of adventures.

SHOPPING

Shopping Malls

Hilo has the best general-purpose shopping on the island. **Prince Kuhio Plaza,** at 111 E. Pua'inako, open weekdays 10 A.M.–9 P.M., Saturday 9:30 A.M.–7 P.M., Sunday 10 A.M.–5 P.M., is the island's largest shopping mall with over 75 shops. It's basically an indoor covered mall with the addition of several large detached buildings. Jewelry shops, fashion and shoe stores, music and books, sporting goods, fast-food restaurants, and large department stores like Sears, JC Penney, and Macy's make this a one-stop shopping experience. Here too you'll find Longs Drugs, Safeway, and a Hilo Hattie's store in their own separate buildings. Across Maka'ala is the newer **Waiakea Center** with a Borders Books and Music, Island Naturals natural food store, Wal-Mart, and Office Max. These two malls together make the greatest concentration of Hilo shopping.

The strip mall **Pua'inako Town Center** is located a little farther up Kanoelehua Avenue (Rte. 11) and on the other side of the street, with lots of small shops, a Sack 'n Save Market, KTA Superstore, and one fast-food outlet after another.

The older shopping plazas are closer in toward the downtown area. **Kaiko'o Mall** is at 777 Kilauea Avenue near the state and county buildings. Once a thriving full-service mall, many of its shopping spaces are now vacant; however, one end has been remodeled and filled with several county offices, including the Department of Parks and Recreation. Still full of local shops and some excellent inexpensive restaurants, the **Hilo Shopping Center** sits along Kilauea Avenue at the corner of Kekuanao'a Street.

Downtown Shops

If you're looking for a simple yet authentic gift or souvenir try the **Lyman Museum gift shop,** which also has an excellent collection of books on Hawaiian subjects.

Ets'ko, 35 Waianuenue Ave., 808/961-3778, is Ginza and Paris in Hilo. This classy, eclectic little shop sells all sorts of expensive but very nice arts and craft items, gifts, furniture, jewelry, and a small selection of silk and natural fiber clothing. Perhaps a hand-painted silk tie for him or a Japanese *tansu* chest for her is just the piece you're looking for. Open Mon.–Sat. 9 A.M.–6 P.M. and until 4 P.M. on Sunday in a small and very compact shop.

Old Town Printers, 160 Kamehameha Ave., open Mon.–Sat., has been in business since 1962 selling stationery, office supplies, postcards, and a terrific selection of calendars. It is in the same

shop as Basically Books, the best book shop in town for Hawaiiana and maps.

Sig Zane Design, at 122 Kamehameha Ave., 808/935-7077, open Mon.–Sat. 9 A.M.–5 P.M., is one of the most unique and distinctive shops on the island. Here, owner and designer Sig Zane creates distinctive island wearables in 100 percent cotton. All designs are not only Hawaiian/tropical but also chronicle useful and medicinal Hawaiian plants and flowers. Sig's wife, Nalani, who helps in the shop, is a *kumu hula* who learned the intricate dance steps from her mother, Edith Kanakaole, a legendary dancer who has been memorialized with a local tennis stadium that bears her name. You can get shirts, dresses, and pareu, as well as affordable house slippers, sweatshirts, T-shirts, *hapi* coats, and even futon covers. The shelves also hold *lau hala* hats, hand-bound koa notebooks, and basketry made from natural fibers.

After having moved down to Kamehameha Avenue, business at **Fabric Impressions** has picked up. Stop here for bulk fabric, sewing accessories, quilt supplies, and quilts. Sewing classes and quilting workshops are also offered on a regular basis. Open except Sunday until 5 P.M.

If you're looking for surfboards ($20 a day), boogie boards, or surfwear, or just want to find out about surfing conditions in the area, stop by **Orchid Land Surfshop,** at 262 Kamehameha Ave., 808/935-1533, www.surfolhawaii.com. Established in 1972 and run by an avid surfer, this place will have what you need. Check its website for surf reports, conditions, and weather forecast.

Dreams of Paradise, 808/935-5670, is a gallery located in the restored S. Hata Building, erected in 1912. Some artists showcased in the gallery specialize in the flora and fauna of Hawaii, produce fine koa furniture, offer distinctive acrylic paintings, catch the sun in stained glass renditions of breadfruit, lotus blossoms, and various Hawaiian flowers, and produce lava sculptures and renditions of animal life. Shelves also hold gourmet food items, incidental bags, distinctive cooking aprons, and plenty of inexpensive but tasteful souvenirs. Also of interest in the S. Hata building are Kipuka Smoke Shop for cigars, Bugado's Fine Woods for turnings and furniture, and a Black Pearl jewelry shop. **Caravan Town** at 194 Kamehameha Ave. is open daily except Sunday. It is one of the most interesting junk stores in Hilo. The shelves hold an internationally eclectic mix of merchandise that includes pendulum clocks, plaster Greek goddesses, luggage, and paper lanterns. Also, the shop specializes in over-the-counter Chinese herbs and medicines purportedly effective for everything from constipation to impotence. Other antique and collectible shops along this street worth a look are **Pink Elephant, The Most Irresistible Shop in Hilo,** and the venerable old **Oshima's.**

Hilo Surplus Store, featuring raincoats, hats, military supplies, knives, backpacks, rubber rafts, plenty of old and new military uniforms, and some camping equipment can be found at 148 Mamo Street.

North of town several miles and just before the Hawaiian Tropical Botanical Gardens along the scenic coastal road is **Hawaiian Artifacts and Antiques,** 808/964-1729, open daily 9 A.M.–5 P.M., a shop owned and operated by Paul Gephart. Paul creates small wood boxes and ornaments, mainly from koa and 'ohi'a, and sculptures of whales, dolphins, birds, and poi bowls. He also has a small collection of tasteful jewelry and seashells, all at very decent prices. Most intriguing perhaps are the reproductions of old Hawaiian weapons.

Food Markets

For groceries and supplies try: **KTA Super Store,** downtown at 321 Keawe Ave. or in the Pu'ainako Town Center; **Safeway,** 111 E. Pu'ainako; or **Sack 'n Save** at Pu'ainako Town Center or 250 Kino'ole. **Suisan Fish Market,** at 85 Lihiwai St., is open 8 A.M.–5 P.M. daily except Sunday. Pick up a copy of the *Hawaii Fishing News* and *Fisherman's News* at the counter.

Since 1977, **Abundant Life Natural Foods** has been doing business in downtown Hilo at 292 Kamehameha Ave., 808/935-7411, open weekdays 8:30 A.M.–6:30 P.M., Wednesday and Saturday from 7 A.M., and Sunday 10 A.M.–4 P.M. The store's kitchen puts out daily specials of smoothies, soup, salads, sandwiches, and *bento,* most for under $6, while the shelves are stocked with an excellent selection of fresh fruits and veggies, bulk foods, cosmetics, vitamins, and herbs. The bookshelves cosmically vibrate with a selection of tomes on metaphysics and new-age literature.

In the Waiakea Center next to Borders Books is **Island Naturals** market and deli, 808/935-5533. This full-service shop is open Mon.–Sat. 8:30 A.M.–8 P.M. and Sunday 10 A.M.–7 P.M. Fresh fruit and produce line the shelves, as do packaged, refrigerated, and frozen natural foods, plus personal care items, supplements, vitamins, and minerals. The deli has ready to order foods and pre-made items. You'll get wholesome healthy foods here, with a good vibe from people who care about what they sell.

HILO

ROBERT NILSEN

A great place for organic farm-fresh fruits and vegetables is the twice-weekly farmers' market in Hilo.

All you folks with that affinity for chocolate will certainly be pleased by the **Big Island Candies** factory and gift shop at 585 Hinano St., 808/935-8890 or 800/935-5510, www.bigislandcandies .com. Stop by to look through the glass at the delicacies being produced and choose your favorite off the many shelves of possibilities. Hawaiian macadamia nut cookies, chocolate-dipped shortbread, and macadamia nut biscotti only start the selections. This store also sells Hilo Homemade ice cream and is open every day 8:30 A.M.–5 P.M. You can even peruse the offerings and order off the Web.

On Wednesday and Saturday mornings, stop by the corner of Kamehameha Avenue and Mamo Street for the **Hilo Farmers' Market.** This is a lively affair, great for local color, where you can get healthy locally grown produce and bouquets of colorful flowers at bargain prices. Across the street at The Market Place and also a few steps up the road under the big tents are more vendors selling flowers, arts and crafts, and other gift items.

Bookstores

Hilo has some excellent bookstores. **Basically Books,** downtown at 160 Kamehameha Ave., 808/961-0144, www.basicallybooks.com, open Mon.–Fri. 9 A.M.–5 P.M., Saturday until 3 P.M., has a good selection of Hawaiiana, out-of-print books, and an unbeatable selection of maps and charts. You can get anywhere you want to go with these nautical charts, road maps, and topographical maps, including sectionals for serious hikers. The store also features a very good selection of travel books, and flags from countries throughout the world. Owner and proprietress Christine Reed can help you with any of your literary needs.

The **Book Gallery,** at Prince Kuhio Plaza, 808/959-7744, is a full-selection bookstore featuring Hawaiiana, hardcovers, and paperbacks. Also at the Prince Kuhio Plaza is **Waldenbooks,** 808/959-6468, one of the city's largest and best-stocked bookstores.

The largest bookstore in Hilo is **Borders Books and Music,** 808/933-1410, open daily at the Waiakea Center, across Maka'ala Street from the Prince Kuhio Plaza. Borders has tens of thousands of hardcover and paperback books, full Hawaiiana and travel sections, plenty of road maps, and over a dozen newspapers from around the world. Readings, music performances, book and CD signings, and other special events are scheduled throughout the month. If browsing makes you thirsty, stop for a snack at the shop's Cafe Espresso.

SERVICES AND INFORMATION

Medical

Hilo Medical Center, 1190 Waianuenue Ave., 808/974-4700, has both outpatient services and a 24-hour emergency room. Just up the street at 1292 Waianuenue Avenue is a **Kaiser Permanente** clinic, 808/934-4000.

The **Hilo Pharmacy,** at 308 Kamehameha Ave. in the S. Hata Bldg., 808/961-9267, open Mon.–Fri. 8:30 A.M.–5:30 P.M., Saturday 8:30 A.M.–12:30 P.M., is a full-service pharmacy that also has a photo developing service. Others in town are **Shiigi Drug,** at the Kaiko'o Mall, 808/935-0001; **Windward Pharmacy,** 808/981-2055, at the Pua'inako Center, **Longs Drugs,** 555 Kilauea Ave., 808/935-3357; and the pharmacies at the **KTA Super Store** and **Wal-Mart.**

Information

Good sources of maps and helpful brochures are **Big Island Visitors Bureau,** at the corner of Keawe and Haili Streets, 808/961-5797, open Mon.–Fri. 8 A.M.–noon and 1–4:30 P.M.; the **Chamber of Commerce,** 106 Kamehameha Ave., 808/935-7178, and the **tourist information kiosk** next to the bus station.

Schools and Libraries

The **Hilo Public Library** is located at 300 Waianuenue St., 808/933-8888. The **University of Hawaii at Hilo,** 200 W. Kawili, 808/974-7311, is a branch of the state university system that has a strong Hawaiian language program. The **Hawaii Community College,** in a separate campus a short distance away, is a more skills-focused facility.

Banks and Post Office

All the state's big banks have branches in Hilo. Try **City Bank** at Kaiko'o Mall, 808/935-6844; **Central Pacific Bank,** 525 Kilauea Ave., 808/935-5251; **Bank of Hawaii,** 120 Pauahi St., 808/935-9701; **First Hawaiian Bank,** 1205 Kilauea Ave., 808/969-2211; or **American Savings Bank,** 100 Pauahi St., 808/935-0084.

The **Hilo Main Post Office,** open weekdays 9 A.M.–4:30 P.M., Saturday 9 A.M.–12:30 P.M., is an efficiently run, modern post office, clearly marked on the access road to the airport. It is extremely convenient for mailings prior to departure. A downtown postal station is located in the federal building on Waianuenue Avenue.

Internet Connection

Bytes and Bites is open daily 10 A.M.–10 P.M. for your Internet connection to the world at $2.50 for 15 minutes or $8 an hour, and for faxing, scanning, office programs, games, and computer instruction. Find it at 223-A Kilauea Ave., on the corner of Ponahawai across from Low International bakery and restaurant.

On the corner of Waianuenue and Kino'ole, across from the post office, **Beach Dog Rental** offers Internet access at $2 for 20 minutes or $6 an hour.

A number of accommodations around town also offer inexpensive Internet services. Try Arnott's Lodge or the Wild Ginger Inn.

Hamakua Coast

Along the shore, cobalt waves foam into razor-sharp valleys where cold mountain streams meet the sea at lonely pebbled beaches. Inland, the Hamakua Coast, once awash in a rolling green sea of sugarcane, is starting to be put to other uses. Along a 50-mile stretch of the Hawai'i Belt Road (Rte. 19) from Hilo to Waipi'o, the Big Island grew its cane for 100 years or more. Water was needed for sugar, a ton to produce a pound, and this coast has plenty. Huge flumes once carried the cut cane to the mills. In the 19th century so many Scots worked the plantations hereabouts that Hamakua was called the "Scotch Coast." Now most residents are a mixture of Scottish, Japanese, Filipino, and Portuguese ancestry. Side roads dip off Rte. 19 into one-family valleys where the modest, weather-beaten homes of plantation workers sit surrounded by garden plots on tiny, hand-hewn terraces. These valleys, as they march up the coast, are unromantically referred to as "gulches." From the Belt Road's many bridges, you can trace silvery-ribboned streams that mark the valley floors as they open to the sea. Each valley is jungle, lush with wildflowers and fruit trees transforming the steep sides to emerald-green velvet. This is a spectacular drive, and the coast shouldn't be missed.

This stretch of the island has recently been named the "Hilo-Hamakua Heritage Coast" in an effort to draw attention to its historic and cultural significance. When in Hilo, pick up a copy of *A Driver's Guide to the Hilo-Hamakua Heritage Coast* pamphlet and look for brown and white road signs indicating points of interest as you proceed along Route 19.

Waipi'o Valley

ROBERT NIELSEN

Onomea Scenic Drive

Route 19 heading north from Hilo toward Honoka'a is a must, with magnificent inland and coastal views one after another. Only five minutes from Hilo, you'll come to Papa'ikou town. Look for Pinky's convenience store on the right. Within a half mile, a road posted as a scenic drive dips down toward the coast. Take it. Almost immediately signs warn you to slow your speed because of the narrow winding road and one-lane bridges, letting you know what kind of area you're coming into. Start down this meandering lane past some very modest homes and into the jungle that covers the road like a living green tunnel. Prepare for tiny bridges crossing tiny valleys. Stop, and you can almost hear the jungle growing. This four-mile-long Onomea Scenic Drive is like a mini-version of Maui's Hana Road. Along this route are sections of an ancient coastal trail and the ruins of a former fishing village. Drive defensively, but take a look as you pass one fine view after another. This road runs past the Hawaii Tropical Botanical Gardens and rejoins Rte. 19 at Pepe'ekeo, a workers' village where you can get gas or supplies. For those requiring a stop along this route, try What's Shakin' for fresh smoothies, juices, and a few simple and quick eats.

Honomu to Honoka'a

The ride alone, as you head north on the Belt Road, is gorgeous enough to be considered a sight. But there's more! You can pull off the road into sleepy one-horse towns where dogs are safe snoozing in the middle of the road. You can visit plantation stores in Honomu on your way up to 'Akaka Falls, or take a cautious dip at one of the seaside beach parks. If you want solitude, you can go inland to a forest reserve and miles of trails. The largest town on the coast is Honoka'a, with supplies, handmade mementos, restaurants, accommodations, and even a golf course. You can veer west to Waimea from Honoka'a, but don't—yet. Take the spur road, Rte. 240, to Kukuihaele, and from there drop down into Waipi'o Valley, known as the "Valley of Kings," one of the most beautiful in all of Hawaii.

HAMAKUA COAST

HONOMU AND VICINITY

During its heyday, Honomu (Silent Bay) was a bustling center of the sugar industry boasting saloons, a hotel/bordello, and a church or two for repentance, and was even known as "Little Chicago." Now Honomu mainly serves as a stop as you head elsewhere, but definitely take the time to linger. Honomu is 10 miles north of Hilo and about a half mile or so inland on Rte. 220, which leads to 'Akaka Falls. On entering, you'll find a string of false-front buildings that are doing a great but unofficial rendition of a "living history museum." The town has recently awoken from a long nap and is now bustling—if that's possible in a two-block town—with wonderful art galleries, craft shops, and small cafés. At the south end of town, just at the turn to 'Akaka Falls, notice the **Odaishisan,** a beautifully preserved Buddhist Temple. Honomu is definitely worth a stop. It takes only minutes to walk the main street, but those minutes can give you a glimpse of history that will take you back 100 years.

Accommodation

Nestled into three oceanfront acres of fruit and nut trees, with the driveway lined in palms, is the luxuriant, neo-Victorian **The Palms Cliff House,** 808/963-6076, fax 808/963-6316, P.O. Box 189, Honomu, HI 96728, palms-cliffhouse@aol.com, www.palmscliffhouse .com. Overlooking a small bay where you can see whales in the winter and spinner dolphins all year round, this bed-and-breakfast caters to the discriminating crowd. The eight rooms, all done in individual themes (Orchid Suite, Bombay Nights, Bellisimo, Tropical Splendor...), are decorated with antique beds, custom-made Italian sheets, coordinated furniture, and artwork on the walls. Marble entryways and bathrooms, fireplaces in four rooms, whirlpool tubs in several, a wide lanai facing the ocean for each room that is blocked from the others for privacy, an entertainment center, and all plush amenities are what you might expect from such a high-end establishment. And to ensure a peaceful and uninterrupted getaway, there are

downtown Honomu

ROBERT NILSEN

no phones in the rooms and a separate hot tub sits in the garden. Gourmet breakfast specialties are cooked every morning in addition to fruits, juice, and other drinks. With all this luxury, room rates are not cheap. Set up for no more than two individuals in a room, they run $175–375 a night; six have king beds, one has a queen, and one has twins. With prior arrangement, special dinners, cooking classes or outings, weddings, massage, yoga, and other activities can be arranged.

Food

Before entering town proper you'll spot **Jan's,** a convenience store selling cold beer, groceries, and sundries. At the upper end of town is a small grocery store and bakery in the old Ishigo Building.

On the left as you drive along the main street are several shops for sit-down or take-out food. First up is **Akaka Cafe,** a little eatery serving such things as saimin, sandwiches, and plate lunches, all for easy-on-the-pocketbook prices. The interior of the old building holds a few tables with chairs salvaged from Honomu's defunct theater and a counter with little red stools. Akaka Cafe is clean, friendly, and caught in a time warp harkening back to the days when a burger was the treat of the week!

The **Woodshop Gallery/Café** has a more modern and artsy atmosphere as its part of the gallery. After perusing the fine artwork, sit down for a sandwich, burger, smoothie, or coffee. Choose a table inside, or head for the lanai where you can watch the "action" in the two-block downtown of Honomu.

Set out back behind the 'Ohana Gallery and surrounded by greenery is the **Bamboo Lanai Café.** Stop here to soothe your sweet tooth with a smoothie, cookie, ice cream, float, or a cup of coffee.

Open daily 11:30 A.M.–7:30 P.M., Friday and Saturday until 8 P.M., at the upper end of town, is **Pizza Hawaii.** Pick up a slice for $1.90 or a whole pie for $14–22, or satisfy your hunger with hot and cold sandwiches, hot dogs, or bagels with a variety of toppings.

Shopping

The **Woodshop Gallery/Café,** 808/963-6363 or 877/479-7995, www.woodshopgallery.com, open daily 10:30 A.M.–6 P.M., along Honomu's main street, offers a wonderful opportunity for browsing among fine tropical wood furniture and artworks. This is one of the island's finest collections of arts and crafts. Shelves shine with the lustrous patina of bowls, mirrors, and furniture fashioned from koa, mango, *milo,* and macadamia wood, as well as from Norfolk pine, which can be turned to a translucent thinness. All pieces can be shipped, as can wood planks if you desire to create your own furniture or art piece. Jeanette and Peter McLaren, the shop owners, create stained glass works and furniture, respectively. Other artists produce additional furniture, art glass, ceramics, pottery, prints, paintings, and a great selection of turned bowls. Less expensive items include chopsticks, wooden spoons made of coconut and wood, combs, barrettes, and lovely vanity mirrors that come in a velvet bag.

More craftsy than the Woodshop Gallery next door, **Honomu Plantation Gallery** has a whole host of arts and crafts that make perfect gifts from your trip. Open 9:30 A.M.–5:30 P.M. daily.

The **'Ohana Gallery,** 808/963-5467, operates with the philosophy that Hawaii's culture, history, and beauty are alive in the art of its people. Open daily except Sun. and Mon. 10 A.M.– 4 P.M., this is a combination fine arts cooperative gallery and gift shop that occupies part of the Ishigo Building, built in 1880 and the oldest building in Honomu. Gracing the shelves and walls of the two-story gallery are works of wood, clay, pottery, paint, paper, glass, stone, and other mediums, all by island artists.

The small **Hawaiian Creations** shop has a fine collection of boxes and other small wooden pieces that fall into the fine furniture category. Some jewelry is also displayed. Also showing jewelry and creations in wood is **Circle A Gifts,** where much of the work is done on premise.

Another establishment worth a visit is **Glass From the Past,** with vintage bottles, dug locally, and a variety of other collectibles.

One of the most unusual collections in town is at **Tribal Arts and Crafts of the South Pacific,** where clothing, crafts, carvings, woven goods, and numerous other objects are sold.

The **Flying Mermaid Gallery** sells clothing, gifts, post cards, and some packaged food items. It's located next to the **Honomu Emporium,** where you'll find almost anything connected to the Teddy Bear and dolls.

'Akaka Falls State Park

Follow Rte. 220 from Honomu past former sugarcane fields for three miles to the parking lot of 'Akaka Falls, at a little more than 1,000 feet in elevation. From here, walk counterclockwise along a paved "circle route" that takes you through everybody's idea of a pristine Hawaiian valley. For the 40-minute hike, you're surrounded by heliconia, *ti,* ginger, orchids, azaleas, ferns, and bamboo groves as you cross bubbling streams on wooden footbridges. Many varieties of plants that would be in window pots anywhere else are giants here, almost trees. An overlook provides views of Kahuna Falls spilling into a lush green valley below. The trail becomes an enchanted tunnel through hanging orchids and bougainvillea. In a few moments you arrive at 'Akaka Falls. The mountain cooperates with the perfect setting, forming a semicircle from which the falls tumble 442 feet in one sheer drop, the tallest single-tier waterfall in the state. After heavy rains, expect a mad torrent of power; during dry periods marvel at liquid-silver threads forming mist and rainbows. The area, maintained by the Division of State Parks, is one of the most easily accessible forays into Hawaii's beautiful interior.

Kolekole Beach Park

Look for the first tall bridge (100 feet high) a few minutes past Honomu, where a sign points to a small road that snakes its way down the valley to the beach park below. Slow down and keep a sharp eye out as the turnoff is right at the end of the bridge and easy to miss. Amenities include restrooms, grills, electricity, picnic tables, pavilions, and a camping area (county permit); no drinking water is available. Kolekole is very popular with local people, who use its pavilions for all manner of special occasions, usually on weekends. A black-sand beach fronts an extremely treacherous ocean. The entire valley was inundated with more than 30 feet of water during the great 1946 tsunami. The stream running through Kolekole comes from 'Akaka Falls, four miles inland. It forms a pool complete with waterfall that is safe for swimming but quite cold.

Wailea

Just a few miles beyond Kolekole Beach Park, above the highway on the old road, is the tiny community of Wailea. A former sugar town, it's now a sleepy village. Yet, despite this sleepiness there is much energy and direction. Occupying one of the old storefronts, The WaiOla Community Wellness Center has set its sights on community involvement, health and wellness issues, and the preservation of cultural crafts. Also in town is the easygoing and casual **Akiko's Buddhist Bed and Breakfast,** P.O. Box 272, Hakalau, HI 96710, tel./fax 808/963-6422,

'Akaka Falls

ROBERT NILSEN

HAMAKUA COAST

msakiko@aloha.net, www.alternative-hawaii
.com/akiko. You need not be a Buddhist to stay,
but you should come with an open mind and
open heart. The bright yellow main house clues
you in to the cheeriness and energy inside. Akiko's
offers four Japanese-style rooms in the main
building, a common kitchen, and bathroom with
shower. This building is called the Monastery
and is set aside for silence during the day. An
adjacent two-story plantation house also has four
rooms, plus a living room, kitchen, and a basic
bathroom with shower. A retreat studio is also
available in a third building, with basic cooking
appliances for longer stays. Breakfast is a group affair in the main house with fruits from the garden, fresh-baked bread, and other goodies created
by the talented Akiko. While it is not required,
you may want to attend one of the informal
meditations held every morning at 5 A.M. in the
main house meditation room, or tag along on
one of the morning walks. Yoga is done every
Sunday morning. The rooms in the main house
have futons on the floor; the plantation house
has both beds and futons. Rates are $40 single or
$55 double per night, and the plantation house
can be rented for $155 a night. Weekly and
monthly rates are $260 and $555 single or $355
and $750 double. The upstairs retreat studio has
a two-week minimum and goes for $420 single or
$585 double for that period. An easy place with
good vibes and always plenty going on, you can
rest and relax, participate or not, or head out to
explore the countryside yourself. Check the website for an activity calendar.

World Tropical Botanical Gardens
With such an impressive name, this garden
promises to be good. But wait, the gardens are
only in their infancy! Created on land that was
sugarcane just a few short years ago, the gardens,
which opened in 1995, are destined to be a wonderful sight. So far, however, and until the collection starts to mature and new plants are put in,
there are only small sections worth seeing near the
entrance of this 300-acre tract. By far, the most
impressive sight on the property is the three-tier
Umauma Waterfall—and it is sure to please. The
plan is to cultivate some 30,000 species—

arranged in evolutionary grouping—and every
year the gardens grow a little more in stature toward that goal. These gardens are open Mon.–Sat.
9 A.M.–5:30 P.M., and the entrance fee—which
helps to further the cause—is $7 adults or $3
for teens. For more information, call 808/963-
5427 or check out the website at www.wbgi.com.
Follow the signs up from the highway near mile
marker 16 to the visitor center.

LAUPAHOEHOE

This wave-lashed peninsula is a finger of smooth
pahoehoe lava that juts into the bay. Located
about halfway between Honomu and Honoka'a,
the valley at one time supported farmers and fishermen who specialized in catching turtles. Laupahoehoe was the best boat landing along the
coast, and for years canoes and, later, schooners
would stop here. A plaque commemorates the
tragic loss of 20 schoolchildren and their teacher
who were taken by the great tsunami of 1946.
Afterwards, the village was moved to the high
ground overlooking the point. **Laupahoehoe
Point County Park** now occupies the low peninsula; it has picnic tables, showers, electricity, and
a county camping area. The sea is too rough to
swim in but many fishermen come here, along
with some daring surfers. Laupahoehoe makes a
beautiful rest stop along the Belt Road. Turn near
mile marker 27, after the highway comes back
out of the valley. The road down to the park is
narrow and winding and runs past several rebuilt
homes and a restored Jodo Mission.

Near the Laupahoehoe scenic overlook, at 36-
2377 Mamalahoa Hwy., is the **Laupahoehoe
Train Museum,** 808/962-6300. Open weekdays 9 A.M.–4:30 P.M. and weekends 10 A.M.–
2 P.M., with an entrance fee of $3 adult or $2
children and seniors, this museum treats you to a
taste of the olden days when trains hauled sugarcane, commercial goods, and people up and
down this rugged coast. The museum once was
the home of the Superintendent of Maintenance
for this division, and is now filled with train
memorabilia, photographs, books, and furniture
that were either from the house or typical of the
era, and two videos give insight into the train

line and sugar era. The house itself has been lovingly restored as has the track "wye" on the grounds, and you can see remnants of a loading platform out front. Biding their time, several train cars wait to be rebuilt. This museum is a worthy enterprise that gives you a glimpse into late-19th-century and early-20th-century coastal culture and is a fine place to stop on your way up the road. This line was part of the railroad that ran down to Hilo and beyond to Pahoa and up to Mountain View, but this rail system came to an abrupt halt on the first day of April 1946 when a tsunami washed ashore and destroyed track, bridges, and other property. The railroad company never recovered.

Ten miles inland from Laupahoehoe Point along a very rugged jeep trail is **David Douglas Historical Monument.** This marks the spot where the naturalist, after whom the Douglas fir is named, lost his life under mysterious circumstances. Douglas, on a fact-gathering expedition on the rugged slopes of Mauna Kea, never returned. His body was found at the bottom of a deep pit that was used at the time to catch feral cattle. Douglas had spent the previous night at a cabin occupied by an Australian who had been a convict. Many suspected that the Australian had murdered Douglas in a robbery attempt and thrown his body into the pit to hide the deed. No hard evidence of murder could be found, and the death was officially termed accidental.

Practicalities

As you drive up the highway, you dip into and out of the **Maulua Gulch,** the biggest and one of the most impressive so far up this coast. Just before Laupahoehoe, look for a sign to **Papa'aloa.** Although now silent, you can almost imagine the hubbub of activity when this town, and others like it on the coast such as Niu and 'O'okala, were alive with sugar production. Turn here, and head down the road to the **Papaaloa Store,** where local people go to buy the area's *best* smoked meats and fish, and *laulau* made right at the store; macaroni salad and meals to go are also available.

In Laupahoehoe along Rte. 19, look for **M. Sakado Store,** open 7 A.M.–9 P.M., an old-fashioned convenience store. It sells basic items like milk, bread, and soft drinks, enough for a picnic. There's not too much else here but a post office, police station, and schools.

Maxi's Place, 808/972-0011, open 6 A.M.–6 P.M., in a white and turquoise, vintage gas station in Laupahoehoe Village, is a plate lunch restaurant. Plate lunches are the standard, from mahimahi to teriyaki beef, but burgers, loco moco, and snacks are also on the menu. Desserts are homemade cheesecake and ice cream, and drinks include shakes. The atmosphere is as local as you can get!

Pa'auilo

About 10 miles past Laupahoehoe is Pa'auilo, another ghost of a sugar town. Set close to the highway, the new town has a post office, several schools, and a former plantation manager's house. In business for about 100 years, **Paauilo Store** serves sundries, a few groceries, soda, sandwiches, and plate lunches. Down toward the sea were plantation workers' camps but are now just quiet forgotten neighborhoods, and on the coast are the old abandoned mill site and docks where raw sugar was loaded for transport.

Kalopa State Recreation Area

This spacious natural area is 12 miles north of Laupahoehoe, five miles southeast of Honoka'a, three miles inland on a well-marked secondary road, and 2,000 feet in elevation. Little used by tourists, it's a great place to get away from the coast and up into the hills. Hiking is terrific throughout the park and adjoining forest reserve on a series of nature trails where some of the flora has been identified. Most of the forest here is endemic, with few alien species. Some of what you will see are 'ohi'a, koa, the *hapu'u* tree fern, and *kopiko* and *pilo,* both species of the coffee tree family. Near the entrance and camping area is a young arboretum of Hawaiian and Polynesian plants. Beyond the arboretum is an easy three-quarter-mile nature loop trail through an 'ohi'a forest, and three-mile loop trail takes you along the gulch trail and back to camp via an old road. All trails are well marked and vary widely in difficulty. Birdlife here may not be as varied as high up the mountainside, but still you can catch sight of 'elipaio, auku'u (a night heron), the white-eye, cardinal, and the Hawaiian hoary bat. The park provides an excellent opportunity to explore some of the lush gulches of the Hamakua Coast, as well as day-use picnicking, tent camping, and furnished cabins (state permit required) that can house up to eight people. Camping and cabin use is limited to five consecutive days per party. The bunk-style cabins, each with a bathroom and shower, rent for $55 for one to eight campers. Linens and blankets are provided, and you may cook in the recreation hall. For reservations, contact the State Park office, 75 Aupuni St. #204, Hilo, HI 96721, 808/974-6200.

Honoka'a to Kukuihaele

HONOKA'A AND VICINITY

With a population of around 2,000, Honoka'a (Rolling Bay) is the major town on the Hamakua Coast. In the past, it was a center for cattle, sugar, and macadamia nut industries and a place where GIs stationed at Camp Tarawa in Waimea would come for R&R. Now it's mainly a tourist town and a center for controversy about land use issues now that sugar is no longer the economic behemoth of the region. One issue which has caused some uproar is the 18,000 acres of former cane land, now owned by the Bishop Estate after the Hamakua Sugar Mill went bankrupt in the mid-1990s, that's been turned into a huge eucalyptus tree farm. From here, you can continue on Rte. 19 for 16 miles to Waimea or take Rte. 240 north for nine miles to the edge of Waipi'o Valley, which you should not miss. First, however, stroll the main street of Honoka'a, Mamane Street, where there are a number of shops specializing in locally produced handicrafts, a gallery or two, restaurants, and general merchandise stores next to antiques shops. Also in town are a small health center, a post office, two banks, a movie theater, public library, a nine-hole golf course, and a small visitor information center. It's also the best place to stock up on supplies or gasoline—there are stations on both Routes 19 and 240. If you are proceeding north along Rte. 240, the coastal route heading to Waipi'o Valley, just past mile marker 6 on the left, keep an eye peeled for a lava-tube cave right along the roadway. This is just a tease of the amazing natural sights that follow.

Festivals

The **Hamakua Music Festival,** 808/775-3378, www.hamakuamusicfestival.com, held yearly in early October and lasting two weekends, attracts not only island musicians but musicians of national and international fame. While there is always jazz, classical, and Hawaiian music on the schedule, other genres of music are sometimes also performed. Major concerts are performed on the weekends at the Honoka'a People's Theater, with related events and local musical groups performing during the week. Tickets usually run about $20 per concert, very reasonable for big name performers, and excess profits from the festival are used to fund local music scholarships and the salary for a local music teacher.

The annual **Taro Festival** is held in November and it celebrates the most cherished of traditional Hawaiian foods. Events include Hawaiian music, hula, chanting, taro exhibits, food made from taro, and crafts and games. The whole town gets into the swing of things and this day-long event is a hit.

Western Days Weekend is scheduled for the end of May. Genuine cowboys as well as city slickers from the Mainland pretending to be paniolo will throw their Stetsons in the air and yell "yippie yi yo kai yea!" when this event rolls around. It's a time for all cowboys to gather for fun and games. Two rodeos are held during the weekend at the Honoka'a Arena for those who like that sort of rough and tumble affair—and for those who just like to watch. Aside from a lively parade that makes its way through town, there's horseshoe pitching, craft displays, a dinner and dance, and—everyone's favorite—the Saloon

Girl contest. For information about either the Western Days Weekend or the Taro Festival, contact the Honoka'a Business Association, P.O. Box 474, Honoka'a, HI 96727, www.alternative-hawaii.com/hba.

Accommodations

Centrally located along Rte. 240 in downtown Honoka'a is the **Hotel Honoka'a Club,** P.O. Box 247, Honoka'a, HI 96727, 808/775-0678 or 800/808-0678, honokaac@gte.net, http://home1 .gte.net/honokaac. Built in 1908 as the plantation manager's club, it's still infused with the grace and charm of the old days. Yet, what it lacks in elegance it makes up for in cleanliness and friendliness. The hotel, mostly used by local people, is old and well used but clean and comfortable, and the only accommodation right in town. Follow a wainscoted hallway from the front office to your room. All rooms are upgraded with carpeting and fluffy quilts; each features a view and TV. From the back rooms, you get a view over the tin roofs of residential Honoka'a and the ocean. There are more spartan but very clean rooms downstairs. Rooms run $80 for a two-room suite, $55–65 for an ocean view room with TV, private bath and, queen bed, and $45–50 for an economy room with a private bath. Rates include a simple continental breakfast. Hostel rooms, located in the basement, all with shared bath and kitchen facilities, are separated into three private rooms at $35 and two communal rooms (one sleeping three people and the other six people) that rent for $15, add $5 if you do not supply your own linens. The basement hostel rooms, although a bit dungeonesque, are clean, with windows to catch the breeze.

About four miles up above town in the pasture and forest land of Ahualoa is **Mountain Meadow Ranch B&B,** P.O. Box 1697, Honoka'a, HI 96727, tel./fax 808/775-9367, bill@mountainmeadowranch.com, www.mountainmeadowranch.com. Perfect for peace and quiet, the lower level of the ranch home has a living room with TV and VCR, sitting room with microwave and small refrigerator, two bedrooms, a dry sauna, tub, and shower, and its own entrance. A light continental breakfast left on the sideboard is included in the room price. This unit with one room runs $80 or $130 for the two bedrooms. A separate guest cottage with full kitchen, two bedrooms with queen beds, bath, wood stove, full entertainment center, and laundry room is also available, but no breakfast is included. There is a three-night minimum, and the rate is $125 a night or $800 a week. No smoking inside either unit.

The **Log Cabin** guesthouse in Ahualoa, P.O. Box 1994, Kamuela, HI 96743, 808/885-4243 or 800/555-8968, kaminn@aloha.net, www.hawaii-bnb.com/kamuela.html, is associated with Kamuela Inn in Waimea. It sits on a five-acre forested property in a cool mountain setting at about 2,500 feet. The log-style walls and framing and barn roof give this large house a welcoming country feel. This house has a large living room with fireplace, upstairs library, full kitchen, five guest bedrooms, and a hot tub stuck in a garden gazebo. Room rates are $59 with shared bath, $99 with private bath, or $375 a night for the whole house, continental breakfast included.

Surrounded by pastureland just outside Kalopa State Recreation Area, **Mauka Bed and Breakfast,** P.O. Box 767, Honoka'a, HI 96727, tel./fax 808/775-9983, maukabb@gte.net, www.stay-hawaii.com/mauka/mauka.html, is a quiet spot. At 1,700 feet in elevation, it is also cool and refreshing. There is one studio here with a private entrance, queen bed, bathroom, TV, and VCR. The room rate of $60 a night includes a simple continental breakfast. No credit cards. This is a basic, simple, inexpensive place with no frills, but it is near hiking and horse pastures.

Food

Local people thought that Jolene was such a good cook, they talked her into opening **Jolene's Kau Kau Corner** in downtown Honoka'a, 808/775-9498, open Mon.–Sat. 10:30 A.M.–3 P.M., closed Sunday. Most tried-and-true recipes were handed down by her extended family, who lends a hand in running the restaurant. The restaurant, located in a vintage storefront, is trim and neat, and the menu includes a variety of plate lunches like beef tips teriyaki and breaded shrimp, a steaming bowl of beef stew, saimin, and burgers and fries, all under $8. Jolene's is as down-home and local as you can get, with friendly service, hearty dishes, and reasonable prices. This is one of the best places to eat along the northern Hamakua Coast!

Follow the comforting aroma of fresh-baked bread to **Mamane Street Bakery & Café,** 808/775-9478, open Mon.–Sat. 6 A.M.–5 P.M., closed Sunday, owned and operated by Eliahu "Ely" Pessah. Ely bakes goodies including coconut turnovers, Danish pastries, and ensemada, a special type of cinnamon roll, but what the local people come in for are the honey-nut bran muffins, crunchy with chunks of macadamia nuts. Ely's oven also turns out ham and cheese croissants, mozzarella or marinara focaccia, or three-cheese focaccia. Eat in or take out while enjoying your purchase with a cup of steaming coffee or tea.

Almost across the street is **Cafe Il Mondo,** 808/775-7711, an Italian pizzeria and coffee bar that's open Mon.–Sat. 11 A.M.–8 P.M. This is a cheery place with Italian music on the sound system and Hawaiian prints on the walls. Here you feel the spirit of Italy. While pizzas, mostly $10–18, are the main focus, you can also get tasty calzones for $8, lasagna, sandwiches, salads, soup, ice cream, and gourmet coffee, of course! If you're on the road, ask for your pizza to go.

"On a Wing and a Prayer" is part of the logo welcoming you to **Simply Natural Ice Cream Parlor and Deli,** 808/775-0119, open Mon.–Sat. 9 A.M.–4 P.M.. Besides ice cream in tropical and standard flavors, a board offers a full sandwich menu with plenty of soups and vegetarian items, and breakfasts of omelettes and pancakes. Beverages include soft drinks, fresh-squeezed carrot juice, Kona coffee, espresso, and cappuccino.

Tex Drive In, 808/775-0598, open daily 5 A.M.–9 P.M. and a little later on weekends, is an institution in town. Everyone knows it and everyone's been there—many times. The long-established Hamakua restaurant is known for its fresh malasadas (sugared, holeless Portuguese donuts), production of which is showcased behind plate glass windows inside. Get some! They're a treat. But ask before 7 P.M. or they'll probably be sold out. Every month, 15,000 of these tasty treats are sold—sometimes many more. Tex has a fast-food look, a drive-up window, walk-up counter, and inside and outside tables, but the cavernous dining room in the back is still there and the food is still as filling and reasonable as ever. Serving "Ono Kine" food, it specializes in inexpensive local food like *kalua* pork, teriyaki chicken and beef, hamburgers, and fresh fish, and there are many ethnic items on the menu. Prices are very reasonable, with most dinners around $7 and sandwiches less. Local people and (an even better sign) the local police come here to chow down on good, easy-on-the-wallet food, and more than that, it's very clean. Tex Drive In is located along Route 19, at the corner of Pakalana Street.

Herb's Place, in downtown Honokaʻa, is open for breakfast, lunch, and dinner daily from 5:30 A.M. You get basic meals and cocktails in this little roadside joint.

C.C. Jon's, a local ethnic eatery open for breakfast and lunch, is right on the road as you enter town. Most of the plate lunch dishes are under $5.

Entertainment

The once run-down but classic "Last Picture Show" **Honokaʻa People's Theater,** along the main drag, has been renovated to its old 1930s splendor. It's a big-screen theater, seating about 500, that has a new surround sound system. First-run movies generally show Fri.–Sun. evenings, with art movies shown on Tuesday and Wednesday. Showtime is 7 P.M. and tickets run $6 for adults, $4 for seniors, and $3 for children. This theater is also used as a venue for the yearly Hawaii International Film Festival, for the autumn Hamakua Music Festival, and for other community events throughout the year. Call 808/775-0000 to hear what's showing.

Shopping

If you are at all interested in the history of Hawaii, make sure to stop by the **Hawaiian Artifacts and Antiques** shop along the main drag in downtown Honokaʻa. This amazing curio and art shop is owned and operated by

HAMAKUA COAST

Lokikamakahiki "Loki" Rice, who ran it for many years with her husband James, who passed away in the spring of 1996. Loki, elderly and in failing health, keeps no set hours, opening when she feels like it, usually for a few hours in the afternoon, but never before 2 P.M. At first glance the shop may look inauthentic, but once you're inside, that impression quickly melts away. Loki, a full-blooded Hawaiian, was born and raised in Waipi'o Valley, and James traveled the Pacific for years. The stories from the old days are almost endless. Notice a tiki that serves as a main beam, and two giant shields against the back wall. They belonged to Loki's father, a giant of a man just under seven feet tall and more than 450 pounds—he had to have a special coffin made when he was buried on the island of Ni'ihau. Local people bring in their carvings and handicrafts to sell, many of which are hula implements and instruments like drums and rattles. Some of the bric-a-brac is from the Philippines or other South Sea islands, but Loki will identify them for you. Mingled in with what seems to be junk are some real artifacts like poi pounders, adzes, and really good drums. Many have come from Loki's family, while others have been collected by the Rices over the years. But the real treasure is Loki, who will share her *aloha* as long as time and the call from above permits.

Toward the east end of the downtown row, **Seconds To Go,** open daily except Sunday 9:30 A.M.–5 P.M., is owned and operated by Elaine Carlsmith. The collectibles and antiques shop specializes in Hawaiian artifacts; it brims with classic Hawaiian ties and shirts from the '50s, dancing hula-doll lamps, antique hardware and building materials, clawfoot bathtubs, old books, Japanese bowls, a good collection of plates and saucers, and a ukulele. Elaine also sells used fishing gear in case you want to try your luck. If you like collectibles of any sort, you'll love it here.

The Honoka'a Trading Company, 808/775-0808, open daily 10 A.M.–5 P.M., is a discovery shop owned and operated by Denise Walker. Items come and go, but you can expect to find classic artwork from the Matson Steamship Lines, hula dolls, Japanese netsuke, poi bowls, costume jewelry, pots and pans, bottles, and old crockery. Denise has also filled this rambling building with a good selection of old books, Hawaiian instruments, Japanese fans, and vintage signs. Denise focuses not only on things *from* Hawaii, but on things brought *to* Hawaii. Much of the furniture and many of the antique items were brought to Hawaii by *kama'aina* and GI families.

If these shops haven't been enough for your antiques and collectibles needs, make your last stop at **Honoka'a Market Place,** 808/775-8255, where you can browse through furniture, clothing, and all sorts of old castoffs that now command a stiff price, and actually are, collectively, a window on the past. Here as well is a great selection of (imported) quilts and clothing.

Several shops that sell clothing, accessories, lotions, and gifts items are **Taro Patch Gifts, Maya's Clothing and Gifts** and **Mary Guava Designs.**

Kama'aina Woods, 808/775-7722, in Honoka'a a hundred yards down the hill from the post office, is usually open daily 9 A.M.–5 P.M. except Sunday but this depends on the weather, the owner's inclination, and how the spirits are moving on any particular day. The shop is owned and operated by Bill Keb, a talented woodworker who specializes in fabulous bowls turned from native woods like koa, *milo,* extremely rare *kou,* and a few introduced woods like mango and Norfolk Island pine. Boxes, platters, and other items are made by different island craftsmen. All of the wooden art pieces, priced from affordable to not-so-affordable, are one-of-a-kind and utilitarian. Less expensive items are koa or *milo* bracelets, letter openers, and rice paddles.

Farther down toward the ocean, in the old macadamia nuts factory, is **Hawaii's Only Live Arts Gallery.** Open 9 A.M.–5 P.M. daily, a large gallery shows works of local artists, some of whom do work here. On different days, you might see glass blowing, wood carving, oil painting, or pottery. A whole assortment of gifts are sold and coffee is roasted for the snack bar, where you have your choice of ice cream or other tasty treats.

The **Bamboo Gallery,** 808/775-0433, is a spacious showroom on the main drag where you will find an eclectic mix of wood, bamboo, fiber, canvas, multi-media, and glass art, all displayed in a sparse Oriental style. Nearby is **Hamakua Art Glass** with many more lovely examples of this art form. Toward the east end of town is **Starseed** for beads and gems.

S. Hasegawa has a few racks of local fashions and a few bolts of traditional Japanese cloth, as well as gifts and candies, cards, and cosmetics. This is an old-time general dry goods store. Next door is the very ethnic **Filipino Store;** stop in to soak up a cultural experience and to find an array of exotic spices and food ingredients.

For groceries and even a few health food items, stop at **T. Kaneshiro Store** and the much smaller **K.K. Super-Mart,** two well-stocked markets in town. A small selection of mostly local and organic produce, fruits, packaged and canned health foods, supplements and vitamins is available at the **Taro Junction** next to Hotel Honoka'a Club. Small but very healthy, it's open weekdays 10 A.M.–8:30 P.M. and 9 A.M.–5 P.M. on Saturdays.

KUKUIHAELE

For all of you looking for the "light at the end of the tunnel," Kukuihaele (Traveling Light) is it. A small plantation town, Kukuihaele now subsists on tourism. The new highway bypasses town. Take the old road down and in; it pops out again on the other side. At the far edge of town, on the cusp of the valley wall, is the **Waipi'o Valley Overlook,** an exceptional location for peering into this marvelous, mysterious, and legend-filled valley. For most tourists, this is as close as you'll get to the "Valley of Kings." But, oh, what a sight! Stand a while and soak in the surroundings: the valley and ocean, the black sand beach, the coastal cliffs, and the ever-changing clouds. During winter months you might be treated to a special sight when mama humpbacks bring their newborn babies to the bay below to teach them how to be whales.

On the old road just before town, the **Last Chance Store,** open daily except Wednesday and Sunday 9 A.M.–5 P.M., stocks basic grocery supplies plus a small assortment of handicrafts and gift items. The Last Chance has an excellent selection of domestic and imported beers, along with light snacks for a picnic lunch. The Last Chance Store is just that; there is no other shop beyond.

Waipi'o Valley Artworks, 808/775-0958 or 800/492-4746, open daily 9 A.M.–5:30 P.M., is an excellent shop in which to pick up an art object. There are plenty of offerings in wood by some of the island's best woodworkers that include carvings and bowls, but the shop also showcases various Hawaii-based artists working in different media. Definitely check out inspired prints, paintings, line drawings, pottery, and jewelry. You'll also find crafts, a smattering of souvenir items, a fairly extensive collection of books mostly on Hawaiiana, designer T-shirts, and other wearables. This is one of those wonderful finds, an out-of-the-way place that carries a good selection of excellent artwork—and they'll ship. The shop also features a counter serving ice cream, sandwiches, and soft drinks. Waipi'o Valley Artworks is the meeting place for Waipio Valley Shuttle, which will take you down to the valley, and for the biking, horseback, and van tours that explore the valley rim. All in all, Waipi'o Valley Artworks is the hub of activity in this not so bustling town.

Accommodations

A vintage home of a one-time plantation manager, **Waipio Wayside,** P.O. Box 840, Honoka'a, HI 96727, tel./fax 808/775-0275 or 800/833-8849, wayside@ilhawaii.net, www .waipiowayside.com, is owned and operated by Jackie Horne as a congenial B&B Inn. Look for the Waipio Wayside sign hung on a white picket fence exactly two miles toward Waipi'o from the Honoka'a post office. You enter through double French doors onto a rich wooden floor shining with a well-waxed patina. The walls are hand-laid vertical paneling, the prototype that modern paneling tries to emulate. Here is a formal dining area and an informal seating area with books, a television, videos, and music. The home contains five bedrooms, each with private bathroom, ranging in price $95–145, $25 extra for an additional person beyond two. The Birds Eye Room has a three-night minimum and the Library Room a two-night minimum, with a $10 surcharge for single-night stays. Spacious and airy, all rooms are individually decorated by theme and hung with beautiful Battenburg lace curtains. The back deck, where you will find hammocks in which to rock away your cares, overlooks manicured grounds that gently slope to a panoramic view of the coast. Jackie, whose meticulous and tastefully appointed home is straight from the pages of a designer magazine, is also a gourmet cook. Breakfast is sometimes waffles with strawberries and whipped cream, sometimes omelettes and biscuits, with fresh fruit from the property. Beverages are pure Hamakua coffee, juices, and gourmet teas from around the world, and there is always an assortment of snacks. A stay at Waipio Wayside is guaranteed to be civilized, relaxing, and totally enjoyable. As a benefit, Jackie will gladly arrange island activities for her guests.

Hale Kukui, 808/775-7130 or 800/444-7130, P.O. Box 5044, Honoka‘a, HI 96727, info@halekukui.com, www.halekukui.com, owned and operated by Bill and Sarah McCowatt. This is a secluded vacation rental on four acres that's perched high on the *pali,* from where you get a sweeping view down onto the Waipi‘o Valley beach, up the rugged coast, and out to the wide Pacific. Follow the main road *through* Kukuihaele and look for a sign pointing you down a private drive that leads about 200 yards to the finely landscaped yard and two comfortable cottages and a studio. The rental units are separate from the main house and each has a hot tub on the lanai. Inside, the units are tastefully decorated with comfy furniture and ceiling fans, and there are large windows on the lanai

side that provide the exceptional views. Full kitchens contains all that you'll need to cook a meal, and that's good as all meals are your responsibility. The studio has a queen-size bed and a queen-size pull-out sofa; the cottages have king beds with additional queen-size beds. Rates run $125 for the studio and $160 or $175 for the cottages; two nights minimum and the seventh night free. For the use of guests, a simple trail leads down to the semiprivate stream where you'll find a small but refreshing pool.

Enjoy the privacy of **Hamakua Hideaway,** P.O. Box 5104, Kukuihaele, HI 96727, 808/775-7425 or 808/775-0995 weekdays, jhunt@gte.net, http://home1.gte.net/jhunt. This rental is only a 15-minute walk from the Waipi‘o Valley overlook, tucked into trees with a lush garden surrounding. With living room, kitchenette, bath, television, and phone, the "treehouse" runs $95 a night or $85 a night for two nights or more, with reduced weekly and monthly rates available.

Surrounded by green acres of pasture on the edge of the sea cliff next to the Waipi‘o Valley Overlook is the **Cliff House,** 808/775-0005 or 800/492-4746, P.O. Box 5045, Kukuihaele, HI 96727. This two-story, two-bedroom house has a living room, full kitchen, laundry room, one bathroom, and lanai that looks over the ocean. This house runs $175 a night for a couple, two nights minimum, with an extra person charge of $20 for up to four. No credit cards. Check-in is at the Waipi‘o Valley Artworks shop.

With its ridgeside location, **Waipio Ridge Vacation Rental,** 808/775-0603, has an exceptional spot. From the front lawn, you can peer down onto the valley and out to the blue ocean with unobstructed views. This little studio has one bedroom, one bath, two queen beds and rents for $85 a night or $75 a night for two or more nights, with a $15 extra person charge.

Waipiʻo Valley

Waipiʻo is the way the Lord would have liked to fashion the Garden of Eden, if he hadn't been on such a tight schedule. You can read about this incredible valley, but you really can't believe it until you see it for yourself. Route 240 ends a minute outside of Kukuihaele at an overlook, and 900 feet below is Waipiʻo (Curving Water), the island's largest and most southerly valley of the many that slice the harsh Kohala Mountains. The valley is a mile across where it fronts the sea at a series of sand dunes, and six miles from the ocean to its back end. It's vibrantly green, always watered by Waipiʻo Stream and lesser streams that spout as waterfalls from the *pali* at the rear and to the side of the valley. The green is offset by a wide band of black-sand beach. The far side of the valley ends abruptly at a steep *pali* that is higher than the one on which you're standing. A six-mile trail leads over it to Waimanu Valley, smaller, more remote, and more luxuriant.

Travelers have long extolled the amazing abundance of Waipiʻo. From the overlook you can make out the overgrown outlines of garden terraces, taro patches, and fishponds in what was Hawaiʻi's largest cultivated valley. Every foodstuff known to the Hawaiians once flourished here; even Waipiʻo pigs were said to be bigger than pigs anywhere else. In times of famine, the produce from Waipiʻo could sustain the populace of the entire island (estimated at 100,000 people). On the valley floor and alongside the streams you'll still find avocados, bananas, coconuts, passion fruit, mountain apples, guavas, breadfruit, tapioca, lemons, limes, coffee, grapefruit, and pumpkins. The old fishponds and streams are alive with prawns, wild pigs roam the interior, as do wild horses, and there are abundant fish in the sea. Carrying on the traditions of farmers of old, some farmers in the valley still raise taro, and this has once again become one of the largest taro-producing regions on the island and one of the principal production centers in the state.

But the lovingly tended order, most homes, and the lifestyle were washed away in the tsunami of 1946. Now Waipiʻo is largely unkempt, a wild jungle of mutated abundance. The valley is a neglected maiden with a dirty face and disheveled, windblown hair. Only love and nurturing can refresh her lingering beauty.

HISTORY
Legend and Oral History
Waipiʻo is a mystical place. Inhabited for more than 1,000 years, it figures prominently in old Hawaiian lore. In the primordial past, Wakea, progenitor of all the islands, favored the valley, and oral tradition holds that the great gods Kane and Kanaloa dallied in Waipiʻo, intoxicating themselves on ʻawa. One oral chant relates that the demigod Maui, that wild prankster, met his untimely end here by trying to steal baked bananas from these two drunken heavyweights.

Waipiʻo Valley from up top

ROBERT NILSEN

One flung Maui against the rear valley wall, splattering blood everywhere, hence the distinctively red color of the earth at the far back reaches of the valley. Lono, god of the Makahiki, came to Waipi'o in search of a bride. He found Kaikilani, a beautiful maiden who lived in a breadfruit tree near **Hi'ilawe Waterfall,** which tumbles 1,000 feet in a cascade of three drops to the valley below and is the island's tallest waterfall.

Nenewe, a shark-man, lived near a pool at the bottom of another waterfall on the west side of Waipi'o. The pool was connected to the sea by an underwater tunnel. All went well for Nenewe until his grandfather disobeyed a warning never to feed his grandson meat. Once Nenewe tasted meat, he began eating Waipi'o residents after first warning them about sharks as they passed his sea-connected pool on their way to fish. His constant warnings aroused suspicions. Finally, the cape he always wore was ripped from his shoulders, and there on his back was a shark's mouth! He dove into his pool and left Waipi'o to hunt the waters of the other islands.

Pupualenalena, a *kupua* (nature spirit), takes the form of a yellow dog that can change its size from tiny to huge. He was sent by the chiefs of Waipi'o to steal a conch shell that mischievous water sprites were constantly blowing, just to irritate the people. The shell was inherited by Kamehameha and is now in the Bishop Museum. Another dog-spirit lives in a rock embedded in the hillside halfway down the road to Waipi'o. In times of danger, he comes out of his rock to stand in the middle of the road as a warning that bad things are about to happen.

Finally, a secret section of Waipi'o Beach is called **Lua o milu,** the legendary doorway to the land of the dead. At certain times, it is believed, ghosts of great *ali'i* come back to earth as "Marchers of the Night," and their strong chants and torch-lit processions fill the darkness in Waipi'o. Many great kings were buried in Waipi'o, and it's felt that because of their *mana,* no harm will come to the people who live here. Oddly enough, the horrible tsunami of 1946 and a raging flood in 1979 filled the valley with wild torrents of water. In both cases, the devastation to homes and the land was tremendous,

but not one life was lost. Everyone who still lives in Waipi'o will tell you they feel protected.

The remains of **Paka'alana Heiau** is in a grove of trees on the right-hand side of the beach as you face the sea. It dates from the 12th century and was a "temple of refuge" where *kapu* breakers, vanquished warriors, and the weak and infirm could find sanctuary. Paka'alana was a huge *heiau* with tremendous walls that were mostly intact until the tsunami of 1946. The tsunami sounded like an explosion when the waters hit the walls of Paka'alana, according to first-hand accounts. The rocks were scattered, and all was turned to ruins. Nearby, **Hanua'aloa** is another *heiau* in ruins. Archaeologists know even less about this *heiau,* but all agree that both were healing temples of body and spirit, and the local people feel that their positive *mana* is part of the protection in Waipi'o.

Recorded History

Great chiefs have dwelt in Waipi'o. King Umi planted taro just like a commoner and fished with his own hands. He went on to unite the island into one kingdom in the 15th century. Waipi'o was the traditional land of Kamehameha the Great and in many ways was the basis of his earthly and spiritual power. It was here that he was entrusted with the war god, Kuka'ilimoku, as King Kalani'opu'u was dying. Kamehameha came here to rest after heavy battles, and offshore was the scene of the first modern naval battle in Hawaii. Here, Kamehameha's war canoes faced those of his nemesis, Keoua. Both had recently acquired cannons bartered from passing sea captains. Kamehameha's artillery was manned by two white sailors, Davis and Young, who became trusted advisors. Kamehameha's forces won the engagement in what became known as the "Battle of the Red-Mouthed Gun."

When Captain Cook came to Hawaii, 4,000 natives lived in Waipi'o; a century later only 600 remained. At the turn of the 20th century many Chinese and Japanese moved to Waipi'o and began raising rice and taro. People moved in and out of the valley by horse and mule, and there were schools, stores, a post office, churches, and a strong community spirit. Waipi'o was painstakingly tended. The undergrowth was kept trimmed and you could see clearly from the back of the valley all the way to the sea. World War II arrived and many people were lured away from the remoteness of the valley by a changing lifestyle and a desire for modernity. The tsunami in 1946 swept away most of the homes, and the majority of the 200 people who lived there then pulled up stakes and moved away. For 25 years the valley lay virtually abandoned. The Peace Corps considered it a perfect place to build a compound in which to train volunteers headed for Southeast Asia. This too was later abandoned. Then in the late '60s and early '70s a few "back to nature" hippies started trickling in. Most only played "Tarzan and Jane" for a while and moved on, especially after Waipiʻo served them a "reality sandwich" in the form of the flood of 1979.

Waipiʻo is still very unpredictable. In a three-week period from late March to early April of 1989, 47 inches of rain drenched the valley. Roads were turned to quagmires, houses washed away, and more people left. Part of the problem is the imported trees in Waipiʻo. Until the 1940s, the valley was a manicured garden, but now it's very heavily forested. All of the trees you will see are new; the oldest are mangroves and coconuts. The trees are both a boon and a blight. They give shade and fruit, but when there are floods, they fall into the river, creating logjams that increase the flooding dramatically. Waipiʻo takes care of itself best when humans do not interfere. Taro farmers too have had problems because the irrigation system for their crops was washed away in the last flood. But, with hope and a prayer to Waipiʻoʻs spirits, they rebuild, knowing full well that there will be a next time. And so it goes.

Waipiʻo Now

Waipiʻo is at a crossroads. Many of the old people are dying or moving topside (above the valley) with relatives. Those who live here learned to accept life in Waipiʻo and genuinely love the valley, while others come only to exploit its beauty. Fortunately, the latter underestimate the raw power of Waipiʻo. Developers have eyed the area for years as a magnificent spot in which to build a luxury resort. But even they are wise enough to

realize that nature rules Waipiʻo, not humankind. For now the valley is secure. A few gutsy families with a real commitment have stayed on and continue to revitalize Waipiʻo. The valley now supports perhaps 40 residents. More people live topside but come down to Waipiʻo to tend their gardens. On entering the valley, you'll see a lotus-flower pond, and if you're lucky enough to be there in December, it will be in bloom. It's tended by an elderly Chinese gentleman, Nelson Chun, who wades into the chest-deep water to harvest the sausage-linked lotus roots by clipping them with his toes! Margaret Loo comes to harvest wild ferns. Seiko Kaneshiro is perhaps the most famous taro farmer because of his poi factory that produces Ono Ono Waipiʻo Brand Taro. Another old-timer is Charlie Kawashima, who still grows taro the old-fashioned way, an art form passed from father to son. He harvests the taro with an oʻo (digging stick) and after it's harvested cuts off the corm and sticks the *huli* (stalk) back into the ground, where it begins to sprout again in a week or so.

Aloha Distress

In the summer of 1992, the Bishop Museum requested an environmental impact survey on Waipiʻo Valley because the frequency of visitors to the valley had increased tremendously. Old-time residents were complaining not only about the overuse of the valley, but about the loss of their quiet and secluded lifestyle. Some tour operators cooperated fully and did their best to help in the preservation and reasonable use of one of Hawaii's grandest valleys; others did not. Because of the impact study, commercial tours are not allowed to go to the beach area on the far side of the stream, which is now open to foot traffic only, and the valley is closed on Sunday to commercial tours.

There also seems to be some kind of socio-ethnic battle evolving in the valley. Long-term residents, mostly but not exclusively of Hawaiian descent, are staking out the valley as their own and have largely withdrawn the spirit of *aloha* from the melanin-challenged visitors to their wonderful valley. Their dissatisfaction is not wholly without basis, as some who have come

nave been quite disrespectful, tres-
private property, threatening to sue
for injuries caused by themselves,
themselves stuck in a river that no
one in their right mind would try to cross in a
vehicle. Many wonderful, open, and loving people still live in the valley, but don't be too surprised to get the "stink face" treatment from
others. Be respectful and stay on public property. If the sign says *Kapu* or Keep Out, believe
it. It is everyone's right to walk along the beach,
the switchback that goes to Waimanu, and generally waterways. These are traditional free lands
in Hawaii open to all people, and they remain so.
It's really up to you. With proper behavior from
visitors, Waipi'o's mood can change, and *aloha*
will return.

Driving

The road leading down to Waipi'o is outra-
geously steep and narrow, averaging a 25 percent
gradient! If you attempt it in a regular car, it'll eat
you up and spit out your bones. More than 20
fatalities have occurred since people started driving it, and it has only been paved since the early
1970s. You'll definitely need 4WD, low range, to
make it; vehicles headed downhill yield to those
coming up. There is very little traffic on the
road except when surfing conditions are good.
Sometimes Waipi'o Beach has the first good
waves of the season, and this brings out the
surfers en masse.

Waipio Valley Shuttle, 808/775-7121, has its
office at Waipi'o Valley Artworks in Kukuihaele.
It's best to make a reservation. Comfortable air-
conditioned 4WD vans make the 90-minute descent and tour, Monday through Saturday at
9 A.M., 11 A.M., 1 P.M., and 3 P.M. Along the way,
you'll be regaled by legends and stories and shown
the most prominent sights in the valley by drivers
who live in the area. The tour costs $40 for adults,
$20 for children under 11. Buy your ticket at the
Artworks. This is the tamest, but safest, way to
enjoy the valley. These guys know what they're
doing—they've been in business since 1970. If
you decide to hike down or stay overnight, you
can make arrangements for the van to pick you up
or drop you off for an added cost.

RECREATION

Hiking

If you have the energy, the hike down the paved
section of the road is just over one mile, but it's a
tough mile coming back up! Once you're down in
the valley, make a hard right and follow the dirt
road to the beach or head straight ahead and
plunge into the heart of the valley. You should remember before you go too far that you will have
to cross one or more of the valley streams. There
are no bridges; you'll have to wade through.
None are deep or wide and are not usually a
problem, but when steady rains swell the streams,
stay out for your own sake, as you could easily be
swept downstream.

Waipi'o Beach

Stretching over a mile, this is the longest black-
sand beach on the island. A tall and somewhat
tangled stand of trees and bushes fronts this
beach. The surf here can be very dangerous, and
there are many riptides. If there is strong wave action, swimming is not advised. It is, however, a
good place for surfing and fishing. The road to
the beach leads along the east wall of the valley
and opens onto plenty of space to picnic under
the trees. In order to get to the long expanse of
beach across the mouth of the stream, you have
to wade across it, stepping carefully over the
boulders that lay on the bottom. To compound
matters, waves sometimes wash water up the
mouth of the stream. Be advised and be careful. Alternately, walk into the valley and find a
public path that leads to the beach on the far
side of the stream.

Horseback Riding in the Valley

For a fun-filled experience guaranteed to please,
try horseback riding with **Waipi'o Na'alapa Stables,** 808/775-0419. Sherri Hannum, a mother
of three who moved to Waipi'o from Missouri almost 30 years ago, and her husband Mark, own
and operate the trail rides. The adventure begins
at Waipi'o Valley Artworks in Kukuihaele, where
you begin a 4WD ride down to the ranch, which
gives you an excellent introduction to the valley. When you arrive, Sherri has the horses ready

to go. She puts you in the saddle of a sure-footed Waipi'o pony and spends two hours telling you legends and stories while leading you to waterfalls, swimming holes, gravesites, and finally a *heiau*. She knows the trails of Waipi'o intimately. The lineage of the horses of Waipi'o dates from the late 1700s. They were gifts to the *ali'i* from Capt. George Vancouver. Waipi'o was especially chosen because the horses were easy to corral and could not escape. Today, more than 150 semi-wild progeny of the original stock roam the valley floor. If the fruits of Waipi'o are happening, Sherri will point them out and you can munch to your heart's delight. Tours lasting 2.5 hours cost $75 and start at 9:30 A.M. and 1 P.M. Full-day tours can be arranged, but a minimum of two and a maximum of four riders is required. Sorry, no children under eight years old or riders weighing more than 230 pounds. Go prepared with long pants, shoes, and swimsuit.

Waipi'o On Horseback, 808/775-7291, also offers horseback riding through fabulous Waipi'o Valley. These sightseeing rides for all skill levels start at 9:30 A.M. and 1:30 P.M. and last about 2.5 hours. The cost of $75 for adult and $55 for kids under age 12 includes transportation from the Last Chance Store in Kukuihaele to the valley floor. Make reservations 24 hours in advance.

Wagon Tour

Waipio Valley Wagon Tours, P.O. Box 1340, Honoka'a, HI 96727, 808/775-9518, owned and operated by Peter Tolin, is one of the most fun-filled ways of exploring Waipi'o. This surrey-type wagon, which can hold about a dozen people, is drawn by two Tennessee mules. The fascinating 90-minute tours depart four times daily at 9:30 A.M., 11:30 A.M., 1:30 P.M., and 3:30 P.M. Cost is $40, children under 12 half price, children two and under free. To participate, make reservations 24 hours in advance, then check in 30 minutes before departure at the Last Chance Store, where a 4WD vehicle will come to fetch you. If you just drop by, you can ask at the store to see if there is space for you, but a last-minute opening is definitely not guaranteed. Lunch is not included, but if you bring your own, you can walk down to the beach

and have a great picnic. The original wagon was built by Peter himself from parts ordered from the Mainland. Unfortunately, every part he ordered broke down over a nine-month trial period. Peter had all new parts made at a local machine shop, three times thicker than the originals! Now that the wagon has been "Waipi'onized," the problems have ceased. The only high-tech aspect of the wagon ride is a set of small speakers through which Peter narrates the history, biology, and myths of Waipi'o as you roll along.

Upper Rim Adventures

The valley itself doesn't get all the attention. Recently, several other opportunities have opened for people to explore the east rim of the valley. You have your choice of hiking, horseback riding, mountain biking, and 4WD van exploration. Each adventure takes a different route, although some may overlap trails. All include a trip through former sugarcane land, and each brings you to wonderful vistas that overlook the broad expanse of the Waipi'o Valley from a height of over 1,000 feet. As you go, you'll be told stories and legends of the valley and vignettes of the culture and history of the area; some tours may even include a dip in a secluded pool under a tumbling waterfall.

Tours with **Hawaiian Walkways,** 808/775-0372 or 800/457-7759, hiwalk@aloha.net, www.hawaiianwalkways.com, led by Hugh Montgomery or one of his able staff, guide you through the rim-edge forest and over a long-abandoned former flume construction trail to the very edge of the valley. Here you can sneak up on and look down upon Hi'ilawe Waterfall and get to spots overlooking the valley that cannot be reached any other way. This is not just good physical exercise but also an education in the flora and fauna of the region, as Hugh is a proverbial fount of knowledge about the area. The Waipi'o Waterfall Adventure hike is moderate, takes about four hours, and goes daily for $90 per person. Lunch, drinks, and all necessary equipment are supplied. Meet at their office in Honoka'a.

Waipi'o Ridge Stables, 808/775-1007, offers a 2.5-hour rim ride for $75 and a six-hour valley rim and hidden waterfall ride for $145. Check-in is at 8:45 A.M. or 12:45 P.M. An **ATV Adventure** takes you over backroads and dirt trails to the edge of the valley. Tours leave at 9:30 A.M. and 1 P.M. The ride is about two hours long and includes a snack. No riders under 100 pounds or over 300 pounds please. Reserve your spot by calling 808/775-1701. Starting at 9:30 A.M., a three-hour 4WD tour is offered by **Waipi'o Rim Backroad Adventures,** 808/775-1122, that takes you in comfort to many of the same spots for exceptional vistas into the Waipi'o Valley. This catered ride runs $85 per adult or $40 for kids 12 and under and is less physical but just as rewarding as the other adventures. The ATV, horseback riding, and 4WD tours meet at Waipi'o Valley Artworks in Kukuihaele. Additional information and reservations for all three are available at 877/757-1414 or get information on the Web at www.topofwaipio.com.

Camping in Waipi'o

For camping in Waipi'o Valley you must get a permit from the Kamehameha Schools Bishop Estate, Kona Office, 78-6831 Ali'i Drive, Suite 232, Kailua-Kona, HI 96740, 808/322-5300. To get the permit, you must call at least two weeks in advance, giving the dates requested (four-day maximum) and number of people in your party. You will be mailed or faxed an application, and all adult members in your party must sign a "liability waiver" (parents or legal guardians must sign for any children) before the no-cost permit will be granted. Also, you must provide your own "Port-A-Potty" (yes, it's true) or "chemical toilet" and remove it when you leave. A small "camper style" potty, available in Hawaii at sporting goods stores, is sufficient. Camping is allowed in three designated areas only on the east side of Waipi'o Stream. A resident caretaker in the valley will check on campers. Many hikers and campers have stayed in Waipi'o overnight without a permit and usually have had no problem, but it is illegal! Remember, however, that most of the land, except for the beach, *is* privately owned.

The Waipi'o Overlook has a 24-hour parking limit. That's good for day use of the valley, but not sufficient for most campers or for those attempting the trek to Waimanu Valley beyond. Check with Waipi'o Valley Artworks for longer-stay parking arrangements.

WAIMANU VALLEY

The hike down to Waipi'o and over the *pali* to Waimanu Valley is considered by many to be one of the top three treks in Hawaii. You must be fully prepared for camping and in excellent condition to attempt this hike. Also, water from the streams and falls is not good for drinking due to irrigation and cattle grazing topside; bring purification tablets or boil or filter it to be safe. To get to Waimanu Valley, a switchback trail, locally called the Z trail, but otherwise known as the **Muliwai Trail,** leads up the 1,200-foot *pali,* starting about 100 yards inland from the west end of Waipi'o Beach. The beginning of the switchback trail has a post with a painting that reads "Caution Menehune." Waimanu was bought by the State of Hawaii some years ago, and it is responsible for trail maintenance. The trail ahead is rough, as you go in and out of more than a dozen gulches before reaching Waimanu. After the ninth gulch is a trail shelter. Finally, below is Waimanu Valley, half the size of Waipi'o but more verdant, and even wilder because it has been uninhabited for a longer time. Cross Waimanu Stream in the shallows where it meets the sea. The trail then continues along the beach and back into the valley about 1.5 miles, along the base of the far side, to Wai'ilikahi Falls, some 300 feet high. For drinking water (remember to treat it), walk along the west side of the *pali* until you find a likely waterfall. The Muliwai Trail to the Waimanu Valley floor is about 15 miles round-trip from the trailhead at the bottom of the *pali* in Waipi'o Valley, or 19 miles round-trip from Waipi'o Lookout. To stay overnight in Waimanu Valley you must have a (free) camping permit available through the Division of Forestry and Wildlife, P.O. Box 4849, Hilo, HI 96720, 808/974-4221, open Mon.–Fri. 8 A.M.–4 P.M. Apply not more than one month in advance. Your length of stay is limited to seven days and six nights. Each of the nine designated campsites along the beach has a fireplace, and there are three composting outhouses in the valley for use by campers. Carry out what you carry in!

Early in the 19th century, because of economic necessity brought on by the valley's remoteness, Waimanu was known for its 'okolehau (moonshine). Solomon, one of the elders of the community at the time, decided that Waimanu had to diversify for the good of its people. He decided to raise domesticated pigs introduced by the Chinese, who roasted them with spices in rock ovens as a great delicacy. Solomon began to raise and sell the pigs commercially, but when he died, out of respect, no one wanted to handle his pigs, so they let them run loose. The pigs began to interbreed with feral pigs, and after a while there

were so many pigs in Waimanu that they ate all the taro, bananas, and breadfruit. The porkers' voracious appetites caused a famine that forced the last remaining families of Waimanu to leave in the late 1940s. Most of the trails you will encounter are made by wild-pig hunters who still regularly go after Solomon's legacy.

According to oral tradition the first *kahuna lapa'au* (healing doctor) of Hawaii was from Waimanu Valley. His disciples crossed and recrossed Waipi'o Valley, greatly influencing the development of the area. Some of the *heiau* in Waipi'o are specifically dedicated to the healing of the human torso; their origins are traced to the healing *kahuna* of Waimanu.

Puna

The Puna district, south of Hilo on the southeast coast, was formed from rivers of lava spilling from Mauna Loa and Kilauea again and again over the last million years or so, and continues to be the most volcanically active part of the island today. The molten rivers stopped only when they hit the sea, where they fizzled and cooled, forming a chunk of semi-raw land that bulges into the Pacific—marking the state's easternmost point at **Cape Kumukahi.** These titanic lava flows have left phenomenal reminders of their power. The earth here is raw, rugged, and jagged. It has not yet had sufficient time to age and smooth. Black lava flows streak the land and grudgingly give over to green vegetation. On the coast, cliffs stand guard against the relentless sea,

and here and there lava tubes punctuate the coastline, leaving telltale signs of the mountains' might. Yet, the greatest of these features is the rift zone, where rupture lines dart out like streamers from a volcano's central crater. It is here along this zone that the unstable ground has slumped away and fallen into the ocean in great cataclysmic landslides and later settled to create benches of lowlands and the present coastline. It is along this rift zone that the mountain still shows its volatility, for the current active lava flow is disgorging from a vent along this line.

Pahoa is the major town in this region. It was at one time the terminus of a rail line that took commodities and people to Hilo. This was timber country and later sugarcane land, but since

The Red Road takes you along the steamy south coast of Puna.

ROBERT NIELSEN

PUNA

- OLA'A RAIN FOREST
- To Na'alehu and Kona
- STAINBACK HWY
- Kilauea Caldera
- Kilauea Iki Crater
- CRATER RIM DRIVE
- Volcano
- SEE "VOLCANO VILLAGE" MAP
- AKATSUKA ORCHID GARDENS
- Glenwood
- HAWAII BELT ROAD
- HAWAIIAN FLOWER GARDEN NURSERY
- PINEAPPLE PARK B&B HOSTEL
- Mountain View
- BED & BREAKFAST MOUNTAIN VIEW
- FUKU-BONSAI CULTURAL CENTER
- Kurtistown
- Kea'au
- To Hilo
- MAUNA LOA MACADAMIA NUT FACTORY
- KAHAUALE'A NATURAL AREA RESERVE
- WAO KELE O PUNA NATURAL AREA RESERVE
- PUNA FOREST RESERVE
- Pu'u O'o
- HAWAII VOLCANOES NATIONAL PARK
- CHAIN OF CRATERS ROAD
- AREA INUNDATED BY LAVA
- Kalapana
- Kaimu
- THE PAINTED CHURCH
- Kehena
- KEHENA BEACH
- KALANI OCEANSIDE RESORT
- 'Opihikao
- Kau'eleau
- YOGA OASIS
- MACKENZIE STATE RECREATION AREA
- ISAAC HALE BEACH COUNTY PARK
- PUALAA PARK AND THERMAL SPRING
- Pohoiki Bay
- RED ROAD
- POHOIKI ROAD
- STEAM VENTS
- Leilani Estates
- LAVA TREE STATE MONUMENT
- GREEN LAKE
- Pahoa
- HONOLULU LANDING
- Opihi Rock
- HAWAIIAN PARADISE COUNTY PARK
- PARADISE DR
- Paki Bay
- Cape Kumukahi
- KUMUKAHI LIGHTHOUSE
- KAPOHO TIDEPOOLS

SOME ROADS IN THIS AREA MAY BE CLOSED DUE TO VOLCANIC ACTIVITY; CHECK STATUS LOCALLY.

5 mi

5 km

0

the mills have closed, it's turned to producing acres of anthuriums and papayas. Down the hill from town, **Lava Tree State Monument** was once a rainforest whose giant trees were covered with lava, like hot dogs dipped in batter. The encased wood burned, leaving a hollow stone skeleton. You can stroll through this lichen-green rock forest before you head farther east into the brilliant sunshine of the coast. Roads take you past a multitude of anthurium and papaya farms, oases of color in a desert of solid black lava. A lighthouse sits atop Cape Kumukahi, and to the north an ancient paved trail passes beaches where almost no one ever goes.

Southward is a string of popular beaches. You can camp, swim, surf, or just play in the water to your heart's delight, but realize that there are few places to stop for food, gas, or supplies. Also along the coast you can visit natural areas where the sea tortured the hot lava into caves, tubes, arches, and even a natural hot bath. There are historical sites where petroglyphs tell vague stories from the past, where ancient villages lay, and where generations of families placed the umbilical cords of their newborns into manmade holes in the rock. Hawaii Volcanoes National Park's eastern end covers the southwestern corner of the Puna district. The park's Visitors Center that used to stand just before the beginning of Chain of Craters Road burned down in the summer of 1989 when lava surged across the road, severing this eastern gateway to the park and causing an old Catholic church to be moved to a new location. This road is still closed and will undoubtedly remain so until the current volcanic activity ceases, so there is no park access from this side. Yet, raw lava flows and new black-sand beaches are there to be explored.

The **Hawaii Belt Road** (Rte. 11) is a corridor cutting through the center of Puna, running uphill straight toward the town of Volcano. Cutting through well-established villages, this road passes some of the largest and best-known flower farms in the state, and on both sides of this highway are scattered housing developments. Back in these hills, new-wave gardeners grow "Puna Butter" *pakalolo,* a significant, though illegal, economic force in the region.

On the border of Puna and the Ka'u district to the south are the village of **Volcano,** where you will find accommodations, restaurants, and shopping, and Hawaii Volcanoes National Park. Here the goddess Pele resides at Kilauea Caldera, center of one of the world's most active volcanoes. The Hawaii Belt Road continues southwest through the park and into Ka'u, the southernmost district of the Big Island, and, rounding the bottom of the island, travels up into Kona.

Southeast Coast

The most enjoyable area in the Puna district is the southeast coast, with its beaches and points of natural and historical interest. It is an easygoing, steamy, tropical region, one of the most typically old Hawaiian on the island. If you take Rte. 130 south from Kea'au, in about 12 miles you reach Pahoa. Like Kea'au, Pahoa is primarily a crossroads. You can continue due south on Rte. 130, passing a series of steam vents, to the seaside village of Kaimu, beyond where Rte. 130 used to join coastal Rte. 137 at Kalapana and feed into Chain of Craters Road, before much of this area was buried by lava flows.

You might go directly east from Pahoa along Rte. 132. This lovely, tree-lined country road takes you past Lava Tree State Monument, which shouldn't be missed, and then continues to the coast, intersecting Rte. 137 and terminating at Cape Kumukahi. If this seems *too* far out of the way, head down Pohoiki Road where it branches just past the Lava Tree State Monument. Soon you bypass a controversial geothermal power station, pass through a section of huge mango trees that line both sides of the road (be careful when they drop fruit as this can cause the roadway to become slippery), then reach the coast at Isaac Hale Beach County Park. From there, Rte. 137 heads southwest down the coast to Kaimu, passing the best Puna beaches en route. Fortunately for you, this area of Puna is one of those places

ROBERT NILSEN

main street Pahoa

where no matter which way you decide to go, you really can't go wrong.

PAHOA AND VICINITY

You can breeze through this "one-street" town, but you won't regret stopping if even for a few minutes. A raised wooden sidewalk passing false-front shops is fun to walk along to get a feeling of the early 20th century. Yet, a revitalized '60s counterculture element thrives in town along with the workaday local population. The shops here are an eclectic mix of food vendors, restaurants, and antiques and crafts stores. The rest of town is a bit more utilitarian with a lumberyard, supermarkets, gas stations, more restaurants, clothing stores, a church, schools, police and fire departments, post office, Olympic-size swimming pool, and the island's oldest operating movie theater. At one time Pahoa boasted *the* largest sawmill in America. Its buzz saw ripped 'ohi'a railway ties for the Santa Fe and other railroads. It was into one of these ties that the golden spike uniting the East and West coasts of the Mainland was supposedly driven. Many local people earned their livelihood from 'ohi'a charcoal

that they made and sold all over the island until it was made obsolete by the widespread use of kerosene and gas introduced in the early 1950s. Pahoa's commercial heart went up in flames in 1955. Along the main street was a tofu factory that had a wood-fired furnace. The old fellow who owned the factory banked his fires as usual before he went home for the night. Somehow, they got out of control and burned all the way down to the main alley dividing the commercial district. The only reason the fire didn't jump the alley was because a papaya farmer happened to be around and had a load of water on the back of his truck, which he used to douse the buildings and save the town.

Pahoa is attempting to protect and revitalize its commercial center and bring new life to vintage buildings like the Akebono Theater, where classic movies are once again being shown. Pahoa has one of the highest concentrations of old buildings still standing in Hawaii that are easily accessible. Although the center of town has been bypassed by a new road, make sure to enter the town and stroll along the tiny backroads.

To replace timber and sugar, Pahoa is in the process of becoming the anthurium capital of

PUNA

the world. As you get close to Pahoa, coming from Kea'au, you'll see black shade cloth draping anthurium nurseries, sheltering magnificent specimens of the usually red flowers, plus plenty of white, green, and even black anthuriums. Papaya is also grown here in large quantities, and a number of farms are located below town toward the coast.

Lava Tree State Monument

In 1790, slick, fast-flowing pahoehoe lava surged through this 'ohi'a forest, covering the tree trunks from the ground to about a 12-foot level. The moisture inside the trees cooled the lava, forming a hardened shell. At the same time, tremors and huge fissures cracked the earth in the area. When the eruption ended, the still-hot lava drained away through the fissures, leaving the encased tree trunks standing like sentinels, only to burn away later. The floor of the forest is so smooth in some areas that the lava seems like asphalt. Each lava tree has its own personality; some resemble totem poles, and it doesn't take much imagination to see old, craggy faces staring back at you. Many still stand, while others have tumbled to the ground where you can look inside their pipe-like structure. The most spectacular part of the park is near the entrance. Immense trees loom over cavernous cracks *(puka)* in the earth and send their roots, like stilled waterfalls, tumbling down into them. A 20-minute walk around this park makes a pleasant stop on your journey. To get to Lava Tree, take Rte. 132 east from Pahoa and on about three miles through a tree tunnel of towering albizia trees to the well-marked entrance on the left. Drinking water is not available but toilets are.

Accommodations

Right downtown, occupying the upper floor of a building erected in 1910, is the **Pahoa Orchid Inn,** 808/965-9664. The stairway leads to a 2nd floor lobby above Luquin's Mexican Restaurant; as you ascend imagine how many others have grasped that rail over the decades. This small hotel has a handful of rooms, most with cable TV, lace curtains, and white wicker furniture like grandma used to have on her porch. Other furniture is reminiscent of the '30s and '40s, and ceiling fans help cool the rooms. While simple, everything is neat and clean, and it went through a renovation a few years ago. Rooms run $35–55 a night with a shared bath or $65 with a private bath.

There are a number of bed-and-breakfasts in the general Pahoa area. One in the Leilani Estates just south of town is **Pearl's Shell B&B,** 808/965-7015 or 877/202-4255, at 13-3432 Kupono St., pearlsh@aloha.net, www.pearl-shellbb.com. Pearl's Shell has three rooms, two larger rooms with queen beds, and private entrances and baths, and a smaller room off the common room with a double bed and private bath. A full breakfast on the lanai is included in the room prices, which run $55 for the small room and $70 for the two larger rooms. An ordinary place in an extraordinary location, this bed-and-breakfast has a finely landscaped yard where flowers will delight your eyes and birds will call out in melodies from the surrounding thick forest.

Food

Luquin's Mexican Restaurant, 808/965-9990, open daily until 9 P.M., is a reasonably priced Mexican restaurant that offers the usual enchiladas, burritos, tacos, combination platters, and Mexican and American breakfasts, most in the $6–8 range but with some up to $15. Some say it's the best on the island. Margaritas are a house specialty at the cantina. A local favorite, you'll be hard pressed to find a seat on Friday or Saturday evenings.

Paolo's Bistro Tuscan Italian restaurant, 808/965-7033, open Tues.–Sun. 5:30–9 P.M., is the place for fine dining in town. Dine inside at tables topped with fine tablecloths or have a seat in the patio outside. Start with an appetizer, $7–8, like a bowl of minestrone soup or fresh mozzarella antipasto, and follow that with ravioli with spinach and ricotta or pasta with prawns. Other entrées might be chicken Marcella, cioppino, raviolli gorgonzola, or pasta al pesto, mostly in the $13–18 range, and there are always desserts like tiramisu or strawberries marinated in chardonnay. To round out the meal, have a cup of espresso or a caffé latté. A bit pricier than other places in town, Paolo's serves wonderfully tasty food that's worth the extra cost.

Almost next door is **Sawasdee Thai Cuisine,** 808/965-8186. Open daily except Sunday 5–8:30 P.M., this intimate eatery serves memorable Thai food with a fine blend of herbs and spices. Your mouth will not be disappointed. Using local organic ingredients, menu choices include appetizers like po pia spring rolls, soups such as po tak hot and sour seafood soup, and a variety of salads. Rice, noodle, and curry dishes make up the main entrée choices, most in the $7–12 range, and any can be made vegetarian if you wish.

Across the street is **Papa's,** a café with nearly everything under $6 and all choices are organic, healthy, and nutritious. Open every day except Sunday.

Other eateries in town include **Ludi's** for Filipino and local grinds and **Big Jake's Island BBQ. Jo Mama** is a bar that occasionally has music but features a local-style breakfast all day long. For the late night drinkers and revelers, try the very local **Punatix Lounge.**

Shopping

When you pull into Pahoa you are greeted by the **Pahoa Village Center,** a small shopping center where you'll find a Laundromat, a video store, pharmacy, and the Black Rock Restaurant. Across the street is a 7-Eleven, and just down the road is the full-service **Pahoa Cash and Carry** grocery store, which has enough for any supplies or incidentals that you may need.

Pahoa Natural Groceries, 808/965-8322, now in a new building on a side street just off the main drag, is open weekdays 7:30 A.M.–8 P.M., Sunday until 6 P.M. The store specializes in organic food items and is one of the finest health food stores on the Big Island. It has an excellent selection of fresh veggies, organic bulk grains, herbs and minerals, deli items, a hot food table, and a very good bakery selection. There's a kitchen on the premises, so the food is not only healthful but very fresh.

At the corner is **Pahoa Natural Emporium,** 808/965-6634, open daily 10 A.M.–6 P.M., with a small but excellent selection of jewelry, Guatemalan clothing, Balinese batik, Yucatan hammocks, gifts, magazines, and cards. The Emporium also displays artwork, some by local artists, and a colorful selection of rugs. The shirts and dresses are all cotton and rayon. Some of the clothing is designed or handmade here in Puna. The back room displays a profusion of these vibrant rainbow-colored clothes.

You'll find two **farmers' markets** in town. On Saturday 7:30 A.M.–noon at the Sacred Heart Catholic Church is the more typical of these markets, with a variety of food and flowers. More a combination farmers' market and flea market, the other is held Sunday 9 A.M.–1 P.M., down the highway near mile marker 8. Very popular, look for the signs and the crowds.

ALONG THE COAST

All of Puna's beaches, parks, and campgrounds lie along coastal Rte. 137 stretching for 20 miles from Kumukahi to Kaimu. Route 137 is also called Kapoho-Kalapana Beach Road or simply the "Red Road" because of its distinctive crushed red lava rock color. Surfers, families, transients, even nude-sunbathing "buffs" have their favorite spots along this southeast coast. For the most part, swimming is possible, but be cautious during high tide. There is plenty of sun, snorkeling sites, and good fishing, and the campgrounds are almost always available.

Cape Kumukahi

It's fitting that Kumukahi means "First Beginning" since it is the easternmost point of Hawaii and was recognized as such by the original Polynesian settlers. Follow Rte. 132 past Lava Tree for about 10 miles to the coast, where a lighthouse sits like an exclamation point on clinker lava. Along the way, get an instant course in volcanology: You can easily chart the destructive and regenerative forces at work on Hawaii. At the five-mile marker you have a glimpse of the lava flow of 1955. Tiny plants give the lava a greenish cast, and shrubs are already eating into it, turning it to soil. Papaya orchards grow in the raw lava of an extensive flat basin. The contrast between the black, lifeless earth and the vibrant green trees is startling. In the center of the flatland rises a cinder cone, a caldera of a much older mini-volcano unscathed by the modern flows; it is gorgeous with lush vegetation. Farther on is the lava flow of 1960, and you can see at a glance how different it was from the flow of five years earlier. When Rte. 132 intersects Rte. 137, continue straight ahead down the unpaved road for about two miles to the Cape Kumukahi Lighthouse. People in these parts swear that on the fateful night in 1960 when the nearby village of Kapoho was consumed by the lava flow, an old woman (a favorite guise of Madame Pele) came to town begging for food and was turned away by everyone. She next went to the lighthouse asking for help and was cordially treated by the lighthouse keeper. When the flow was at its strongest, it came within yards of the lighthouse and then miraculously split, completely encircling the structure but leaving it unharmed as the flow continued out to sea for a considerable distance.

Route 137 continues north and in short order plunges into a forest of trees; the road turns into

a rugged and rutted dirt lane that is often full of potholes and pools of water. Proceed with caution, this stretch is not kind to low-slung rental cars. If you continue, you will pass secluded private property and as-yet-undeveloped county park land and pop out on the other side at the bottom of the Hawaiian Shores Estates subdivision, which cascades down the hill from Pahoa. You're better off to turn south and enjoy other sights of the coast.

Kapoho Tidepools

Although the old village of Kapoho was covered by lava a few short decades ago, a new community has been rebuilt to take its place. This new village has a mixture of retirees, working-class families, and vacation rentals. The section closest to the lighthouse is a gated community; the next one south is open. You can snorkel in the tidepools along the coast fronting this village. They can be enjoyed by anyone who takes the time to seek them out. Remember that this is a quiet rural community with pride in its natural resources, so be respectful when you visit. Turn onto Kapoho Kai Drive and head down into this small development. Park off the roadway along the road farthest down toward the water. It's a short way across the lava field toward the ocean before these pools become apparent. Wear shoes, as the lava is sharp. Best at high tide or when the tide is coming in, the pools provide good snorkeling in a safe environment.

Across the highway from the entrance road to the gated community is Kapoho Crater, sometimes called Green Mountain. This is a low volcanic cone that is thickly covered in trees and that has a small natural lake in its caldera known as Green Lake.

Puala'a Park and Thermal Spring

Back on Rte. 137, continue south under the dense tree cover. Between mile markers 10 and 11, just after the road narrows, you come upon **Puala'a Park,** also known as Ahalanui. Quietly opened by the County of Hawai'i on July 4, 1993, this lovely, 1.3-acre park was an ancient fishing village where a few families still maintain homes. The park features a sand-bottom

ROBERT NILSEN

Pohoiki Road leads through Puna's tropical rainforest to the coast.

PUNA

pond that's been formed into a pool, thermally heated to a perfect temperature. Step in and relax in its soothing warmness. Some people use the pond to do watsu, a type of in-water massage. The swimming is safe except during periods of very high surf, when ocean water washes in over the outer cement wall. The park is perfect for families with young children. The pond is now watched over by a lifeguard, and toilets have been set up for your convenience. The new parking area is open 7 A.M.–7 P.M.; otherwise park across the street in the old lot.

Isaac Hale Beach County Park

You can't miss this beach park (often referred to as Pohoiki) located on Pohoiki Bay at the junction of Rte. 137 and Pohoiki Road. Just look for a jumble of boats and trailers parked under the palms. At one time Pohoiki Bay served the Hawaiians as a canoe landing, then later became the site of a commercial wharf for the Puna Sugar Company. It remains the only boat launching area for the entire Puna Coast, used by pleasure boaters and commercial fishermen. Due to this dual role, it's often very crowded. Amenities include a pavilion, restrooms, and a picnic area; potable water is not available. Camping is permitted with a county permit. Experienced surfers dodge the rip-current in the center of the bay. Pohoiki Bay is also one of the best scuba and snorkel sites on the island. Within walking distance of the salt-and-pepper beach is another thermal spring in a lava sink surrounded by lush vegetation. It's popular with tourists and residents alike and provides a unique and relaxing way to wash away sand and salt. To find it, face away from the sea and go to the left along a small but well-worn path that leads between the water and a beach house. Be sure to ask permission if someone is around. The pools are warm, small, and tranquil. Harmless, tiny brine shrimp nibble at your toes while you soak.

MacKenzie State Recreation Area

This state park was named for forest ranger A. J. MacKenzie, highly regarded throughout the Puna district. He was killed in the area in 1938. The park's 13 acres sit among a cool grove of iron-woods originally planted by MacKenzie. A portion of the old King's Hwy., scratched out by prisoners in the 19th century as a form of community service, bisects the area. In the past, many people who first arrived on the Big Island hung out at MacKenzie until they could get their start. Consequently, the park received its share of hardcore types, which has earned it a reputation for rip-offs. Mostly it's safe, rather deserted, and not particularly well looked after now, but if you're camping, take precautions with your valuables. The entire coastline along MacKenzie is bordered by low but rugged black-lava seacliffs. Swimming is dangerous, but the fishing is excellent. Be extremely careful when walking along the water's edge, especially out on the fingers of lava; over the years, people have been swept away by freak waves. Within the park is a skylight of a collapsed lava tube, one end of which exits at the seacliff and the other a stone's throw inland and across the road. Take a flashlight and be careful if you venture inside. MacKenzie Park is located along Rte. 137, two miles south of Pohoiki. Picnic facilities are available, but there is no drinking water. A state permit is required for overnight camping.

Kehena Beach

Pass the tiny village of 'Opihikao, where Kama'ili Road drops down from Rte. 130 to the Red Road. 'Opihikao was a major town along this coast in the 1800s but has faded away into quaint quietude. Just beyond this community the close canopy of trees opens, the road becomes wider, and the vistas broaden. Here are picture postcard coastal scenes as good as any on the island. Cross over two sections of the 1955 lava flow and soon you come upon Kehena Beach. Kehena is actually two pockets of black-sand beach below a low seacliff. Entrance to the beach is marked only by a scenic pulloff, about four miles south of 'Opihikao; usually a half dozen cars are parked there. At one time Kehena was very popular, and a stone staircase led down to the beach. In 1975 a strong earthquake jolted the area, breaking up the stairway and lowering the beach by three feet. Now access is via a well-worn path, but make sure to wear sneakers because the lava is rough. The ocean here is dangerous, and often pebbles and rocks whisked along by the surf can injure your legs. Once down on the beach, head north for the smaller patch of sand, because the larger patch is open to the sea and can often be awash in waves. The black sand is hot, but a row of coconut palms provides shade. The inaccessibility of Kehena makes it a favorite "no-hassle" nude beach with many "full" sunbathers congregating here.

End of the Road

Just near the lava-inundated village of Kalapana, Routes 130 and 137 come to an abrupt halt where Madame Pele has repaved the road with lava. At the end of the line near the village of Kaimu you come to a barricaded area. Volcanic activity has continued virtually unabated beyond here since January 1983, when lava fountains soared 1,500 feet into the sky and produced a cone more than 800 feet tall. The initial lava flow was localized at Puʻu Oʻo vent, but after dozens of eruptive episodes it shifted eastward to Kupaʻianaha, which continuously produced about half a million cubic yards of lava per day. Today, it is mostly erupting once again from flank vents on Puʻu Oʻo. The lava flows eight miles to the sea, mostly through lava tubes. It has inundated almost 40 square miles, caused $61 million worth of property damage, and added more than 500 acres of new land to the Puna Coast—and it's still growing. Unfortunately, these lava flows have also completely covered the very popular Kaimu Beach Park (also known as Black Sand Beach), Harry K. Brown Beach Park, the national park's visitors center, and 13th-century **Wahaʻulu Heiau.** For a full description of **Chain of Craters Road** and recent volcanic activity, see the following chapter on Hawaii Volcanoes National Park. Parts of the road are still open, but only *within* the park and from the other end.

Volcanic activity has pretty much ceased in the Kaimu area and the lava solidified. You can walk out over the new lava directly toward the sea to a new black-sand beach but you are prohibited from going west where you can experience

difficulty if you walk too far toward where the lava still flows. Some hazards you may encounter are brushfires, smoke, ash, and methane gas, which is extremely explosive. You can also fall through the thin-crusted lava into a tube, which will immediately reduce you to a burnt offering to Pele and unceremoniously deposit your ashes into the sea! New lava can cut like broken glass, and molten lava can be flung through the air by steam explosions, especially near the coastline. Seacliffs collapse frequently, and huge boulders can be tossed several hundred feet into the air. The steam clouds contain minerals that can cause burning eyes, throat and skin irritations, and difficulty breathing.

If you are still intrigued, realize that you are on the most unstable piece of real estate on the face of the earth. For those maniacs, fools, adventurers, and thrill-seekers who just can't stay away, give yourself up for dead, and proceed. Follow the old roadbed, up and down, over the lava. When you can no longer discern the road, pick your way across the undulating lava field, but don't get too close to the sea or the active flows. Observers say that every day, huge chunks fall off into the sea. As you look back at the mountain you can see heat waves rising from the land upon which you are standing. A camera with a zoom lens or a pair of binoculars accentuates this phenomenon. The whole mountain waves in front of you. As you walk closer to the sea, the lava cools and you can see every type there is: rope lava, lava toes, lava fingers. The tortured flow, which may crinkle as you walk over it, has created many imaginative shapes: gargoyles, medieval faces, dolphins, and mythical creatures. At the coast, when lava pours into the sea, it may create a white spume of steam lifting 200–300 feet into the air. No other place in the world gives you the opportunity to be the first person to tread upon the earth's newest land.

In Kaimu, you can safely walk the short distance over the lava to the ocean. At the end of the road, head straight toward the water and in 15 minutes you are there. The new beach is seaward about a quarter mile from where Kaimu Beach Park used to be. Now, raw and rugged lava meets the sea and is slowly being turned into black sand once again.

In August 2001, the mayor allowed a road to be plowed from the end of Route 130 toward the lava flow for a better view of the activity. Many island people applauded this effort to open access to the inundated area of Kalapana, but the road was closed in March 2002 when part of the new access route was destroyed by additional lava flow. Time will tell if and when this area will again be opened to traffic.

The Painted Church

Star of the Sea Catholic Church is a small but famous structure better known as "The Painted Church." Originally located near Kalapana, this church was in grave danger of being overrun by a lava flow. An effort to save the historic church from the lava was mounted, and it has been moved to a location along Rte. 130, just above Kaimu. A brief history of the area asserts that the now-inundated Kalapana was a spiritual magnet for Roman Catholic priests. Old Spanish documents support evidence that a Spanish priest, crossing the Pacific from Mexico, actually landed very near here in 1555. Father Damien, famous priest of the Molokai Leper Colony, established a grass church about two miles north and conducted a school when he first arrived in the islands in 1864. The present church dates from 1928, when Father Everest Gielen began its construction. Like an inspired but much less talented Michelangelo, this priest painted the ceiling of the church, working mostly at night by oil lamp. Father Everest was transferred to Lanai in 1941, and the work wasn't completed until 1964, when George Heidler, an artist from Atlanta, Georgia, came to Kalapana and decided to paint the unfinished altar section. The artwork itself can only be described as gaudy but sincere. The colors are wild blues, purples, and oranges. The ceiling is adorned with symbols, portraits of Christ, the angel Gabriel, and scenes from the Nativity. Behind the altar, a painted perspective gives the impression that you're looking down a long hallway at an altar that hangs suspended in air. The church is definitely worth a few minutes.

Steam Vents

Along Rte. 130, about halfway between Pahoa and Kaimu, look for a small, unobtrusive sign that reads Scenic Overlook. Pull off and walk about 75 yards toward the sea until you find four non-toxic steam vents. Low mounds of lava with warm steam issuing from cracks in the earth, they are used by many local people as natural saunas. People come here to climb into the openings and relax in the warmth. On occasion, these vents will be overused, garbage is left around, or the surrounding area soiled as a toilet, but by and large they provide a wonderful natural experience.

Accommodations

For vacation rental homes at Kapoho, contact **A Piece of Paradise,** P.O. Box 1314, Pahoa, HI 96778, 808/965-1224, www.apoParadise.com. Located in the oceanfront gated community, a one-bedroom cottage here rents for $99 a night while several two- and three-bedroom homes run $120–195 a night; three nights minimum. Each is completely furnished with full kitchen and living areas and located a few short steps from the ocean and tidepools.

The embracing arms of the Puna rainforest surround you as you make your way down the driveway to the quiet and secluded **Yoga Oasis** retreat center. Set on 26 acres of forest, with plenty of fruit and nut trees and numerous stands of bamboo, this yoga center and alternative accommodation offers yoga workshops and, on occasion, other health related retreats. While you can come for the accommodation only, the optional morning yoga classes are a treat and the seclusion is perfect for those who just want a little time to themselves, but the location offers easy access to coastal Puna sights, restaurants in Pahoa, and is close enough to both Hilo and Hawaii Volcanoes National Park for easy day trips. Private rooms with shared bath in the main building or a tentalow run $60 single or $80 double, a little higher with a yoga package (morning yoga class and a vegetarian breakfast). The secluded Coconut Grove tentalow with its outdoor shower runs $125 single or $145 double, and this includes breakfast and yoga class. Two nights

PUNA

minimum for these. Sleeping up to four, the redwood and cedar "treehouse" runs $225 a night for a couple, breakfast and morning yoga included; each additional person $25, three nights minimum. Healthy, home-made vegetarian meals are created three times a day and run $10–15, while massage and other activities are added features at additional cost. Workshops and classes are held in the large screened exercise rooms on the 2nd floor of the main building. For information about yoga classes and reservations for staying, call 800/965-8460 or 800/274-4446, info@yogaoasis .org, www.yogaoasis.org.

Kalani Oceanside Resort, RR 2 Box 4500, Pahoa Beach Rd., HI 96778, 808/965-7828 or 800/800-6886, kalani@kalani.com, www.kalani .com, is a nonprofit, international conference and holistic retreat center, a haven where people come when they truly want to step aside for a time. The entrance is located a few miles east of Kaimu on Rte. 137 between mile markers 17 and 18, on the mountain side of the road. Look for a large Visitors Welcome sign and proceed uphill until you see the office and sundries shop. Depending upon the yearly schedule, a variety of activities include massage, hula, meditation, yoga, lei-making, *lau hala*-weaving, and hikes, for men, women, couples, and families, gay and straight. The grounds have a botanical atmosphere, with a rain-fed swimming pool (clothing optional after 7:30 P.M.), a watsu pool, hot tub, whirlpool tub, assembly studios, classrooms, cottages, and cedar lodges with kitchen facilities. Kalani is not an oceanfront property and only some rooms have an ocean view over the trees. Rates are $60 single for a dorm room with shared bath, $105 single and $110 double for a private room with shared bath, $125 single and $135 double for a private room with private bath, $135 single and $150 double for a guest cottage, and $210 single and $240 double for the tree house. Rates are $10 higher from November through the end of April. You can also camp for $20 a night, or cheaper than that per person as a family. A blown conch shell calls you to breakfast at 8 A.M., lunch at noon, and dinner at 6 P.M. (nonguests welcome). The meals cost $8, $10, and $16 respectively, with a meal ticket pre-purchased at the office. Food is served from the buffet line in the open-air dining hall, and fruits and vegetables from the property are used when possible. Entertainment by resident or local musicians is performed in a very casual setting at the Olelo Cafe next to the office some evenings until 11 P.M. The generator (and hence the lights) goes off at 11 P.M., but candles are provided for night owls. Kalani is not for everyone, but if you are looking for unpretentious peace and quiet, healthful food, and inner development, this is one place you may find it.

During a recent eruption of the volcano, lava stopped about 20 feet from the front of **Hale Kipa O Kiana,** 808/965-8661 or 800/682-3592, RR 2 Box 4874 Kalapana Shores, Pahoa, HI 96778, haleokiana@aol.com, www.halekipaokiana .com. Open again, the one downstairs room with a private entrance and bath goes for $335 a week with a modified continental breakfast each morning; one week minimum, monthly rates available. No credit cards. The room has a small refrigerator and microwave, television, phone, and laundry facilities. Located on a cul de sac, this house is quiet, fairly secluded, and perfect for naturists, although anyone is welcome.

For a larger house to rent, contact **Kaimu Bay Vacation Rentals,** 808/878-6682, fax 808/878-3204, kaufman@maui.net. Located at the end of the road, across from new lava and near the new black-sand beach, this basic contemporary style house has a kitchen, living area, with two bedrooms and a bath upstairs and an additional bedroom and bath down, television, phone, and laundry facilities. Rent runs $83 a night for the two bedroom or $105 for the entire house; weekly rates are available.

Set next to the steam vents is **Steam Vent Inn,** a large home with rental rooms that also has a couple of steam vents on its property. Each of the four rooms has two queen beds and runs $75–120, including a continental breakfast. Four hostel rooms with private or shared baths run $17–35. For information, contact 808/965-8800 or look at www.steamventinn.com.

Food

Right where the roads ends you'll find **Verna's V Drive In** for quick and easy local eats. Have yourself a plate lunch, loco moco, or burger, fries, and a drink, before you head out for the short jaunt over the lava to the water. Usually open until 5 P.M., this is a favorite lunch spot for tour buses that bring guests to view the new lava and beach.

Along the Hawai'i Belt Road

KEA'AU

Kea'au is the first town south of Hilo on Rte. 11, and although pleasant enough, it's little more than a Y in the road. Before the sugar mill closed in the mid-1990s, this was a bustling town with great swaths of the surrounding land in cane. Kea'au and the numerous subdivisions that have mushroomed on both sides of the highway running to Pahoa and up to Volcano have become bedroom communities to Hilo. At the junction of Rte. 11 (Hawai'i Belt Road) and Rte. 130 is **Kea'au Shopping Center,** a small shopping mall with a handful of variety stores, a Laundromat, a post office, restaurants, a Bank of America, and gas station. Here, the Sure Save Supermarket has not only groceries but plenty of sundries and a decent camera department. Route 130 heads southeast from here to the steamy south coast, while Route 11 (Hawai'i Belt Road) heads southwest and passes through the mountain villages of Kurtistown, Mountain View, Glenwood, and Volcano at approximately 10-mile intervals, then enters Hawaii Volcanoes National Park. The Belt Road, although only two lanes, is straight, well surfaced, and scrupulously maintained. When heading to the Puna coast, it's easiest now to take the Kea'au Bypass Road around the east side of town, right past the old sugar mill, so you don't get bogged down in town traffic.

Food

The local Dairy Queen, in the Kea'au Town Center, not only makes malts and sundaes but serves breakfast, lunch, and dinner. Also in the shopping center is **Kea'au Natural Foods,** 808/966-8877, with a large stock of organic food items, herbs, and grains but no juice or snack bar. However, pre-made sandwiches from the deli case are always available. Have a look at the bulletin board for information on alternative happenings in the community. Open Mon.–Fri. 8:30 A.M.–8 P.M., Saturday until 7 P.M., and Sunday 9:30 A.M.–5 P.M. Have a beer while you wait for your laundry to wash at the Suds 'n Duds Laundromat.

For a more congenial environment, try **Charley's Bar and Grill,** 808/966-7589, for a cool one or a light meal. Serving sandwiches, burgers, pasta, and a few other entrées, Charley's is open Wed.–Sat. until 2 A.M. and other nights until midnight. Several nights a week there are live bands and dancing (cover), and on other evenings you can still sing along to the karaoke music, shoot pool, or throw darts. This is perhaps the nicest place in town for a relaxing evening out.

Lemongrass, a simple unadorned Vietnamese and Thai restaurant, serves ethnic foods in filling portions with hardly anything more than $8. Just as basic, just as cheap, but even smaller, the **Kea'au Chop Suey House** next door has a good variety in its menu, including several vegetarian dishes.

On the far side of the shopping center, **Verna's Drive-In** serves plate lunches and drinks.

MOUNTAIN TOWNS

Kurtistown

Near the highway in what might be considered the center of town are the post office, B. J.'s 76 Service Station, and the **J. Hara Store,** the best-stocked store on the highway for sundries and groceries.

Just south of there, down 'Ola'a Road is the **Fuku-Bonsai Cultural Center.** This institution is a combination nursery, mail-order shop, bonsai display garden, and bonsai exhibition center. It is also the nonprofit Mid-Pacific Bonsai Foundation's Hawaii State Bonsai Repository. Have a walk through the garden and marvel at the miniature trees and plants demonstrating Japanese,

PUNA

ANTHURIUM

Originally a native of Central America, the anthurium was introduced into Hawaii in 1889 by Samuel M. Damon, an English missionary. Damon discovered that Hawaii's climate and volcanic soil made an ideal environment for this exotic flower. Over the years since then, anthurium production has turned into a million-dollar export industry with all the major growers located on the Big Island. Anthurium grow on a tall stock as a glossy and heart-shaped flower bract, with a yellowish flower spike arising from the stock at the bract's base, and accompanied by large shiny green leaves. The most common anthurium has dark red bracts about the size of the palm of a hand, but they have been bred in a variety of colors, from lily white to green, purple, and black, and from silver dollar size to as big as a plate.

anthurium, obake variety

small wood boxes, and other small objects made of tropical island woods. With such a variety, one look here gives you a good sense of the types of wood that are grown on the island.

Look for a vintage plantation house painted blue a short ways beyond and on the opposite side of the highway. This is **Tinny Fisher's Antique Shop,** owned and operated by Charles and Dorothy Wittig. What started as "yard sale treasures" turned into a unique curio, antiques, and collectibles shop. Open daily except Monday noon–6 P.M., the shop has all kinds of antiques and collectibles from Asia and Hawaii, including glass balls, Asian furniture, jewelry, and glassware galore. Tinny's also features a good Hawaiiana collection, with artifacts from the ancient days like *kukui* nut lamps, poi pounders, and stone knives.

Mountain View

Mountain View is a village of nurseries specializing in anthuriums. Many of them sport signs and some invite you to look around. **Hawaiian Flower Gardens Nursery,** 808/968-8255 or 877/434-0555, open daily except Sunday, is one. There you can learn a little about the history of these fancy exotic flowers and see all sizes and colors. This is the home of the Toyama Red Anthurium, but they come in all shades from stark white to green and deep purple, and sizes from delicate tiny petals and those as big as a spade. Several other nurseries that not only grow but ship these lovely flowers are **Albert Isa Nursery,** P.O. Box 17, Mt. View, HI 96771, 808/968-6125; and **Hale Ohia Gardens,** P.O. Box 1042, Mt. View, HI 96771, 800/273-3848, fax 808/968-6892. For mail-order flowers, prices generally range $35–75 plus shipping costs, depending upon the mix.

Along the highway is a mini-mart, a post office, gas station, and **Verna's Too Drive In** serving plate lunches, sandwiches, burgers, and shakes. As you pass through, take a minute to

Chinese, and Hawaiian styles, and note the similarities and differences. There are some 200 specimens in formal exhibition. Inside are educational displays of tools, techniques, and more plants. Diminutive plants can be purchased in the shop to carry away, or they can be shipped anywhere in the country. Fuku-Bonsai is open Mon.–Sat. 8 A.M.–4 P.M. For anyone interested in raising bonsai or simply looking at these wonderfully sculpted plants, this is a worthy stop. For a mail-order catalog, contact P.O. Box 6000, Kurtistown, HI 96760, 808/982-9880, sales@fukubonsai.com, www.fukubonsai.com.

Just over two miles up the road is the **Dan De Luz's Woods** showroom, 808/968-6607, which displays all sorts of turned wooden bowls, explore the short side road into the village itself. It seems that every house has a garden of ferns, flowers, and native trees. On this old road through the village is **Mt. View Bakery,** open 8 A.M.–3:30 P.M. except Sunday, home of the famous stone cookies—have them with milk!

Accommodations

Bed & Breakfast Mountain View, P.O. Box 963, Kurtistown, HI 96760, 808/968-6868 or 888/698-9896, fax 808/968-7017, info@ bbmtview.com, www.bbmtview.com, is owned and operated by Jane and Linus Chao, both internationally known artists. The couple's inspired artwork graces the home. A residence and artist studio, this B&B lies just outside the village of Mountain View along S. Kulani Road, on a landscaped four-acre parcel with a marvelous view north to Mauna Kea. Enter through an iron gate under a canopy of trees. The spacious guest rooms are modern in all amenities and equipped with king, queen, or twin beds; two have private bathrooms, two others share. Everyone has use of the common room for reading, TV, or simply appreciating the fine view. A full breakfast is served each morning in the dining room, and each day the offering is different. Room rates run $55–95 daily. For peace and serenity and inspiration of the artistic soul, there is no better place than Bed & Breakfast Mountain View.

Farther into this labyrinth of roads south of Mt. View, down along Pikake Street, is **Pineapple Park B&B Hostel,** P.O. Box 639, Kurtistown, HI 96760, 808/968-8170 or 877/865-2266, park@aloha.net, www.pineapple-park.com. This is country living in modern style. A bed in the bunkroom runs $20 a night and a double room runs $55; these rooms share kitchen and bath facilities and have use of the common room

where there's Internet access. No breakfast is provided. A private room for $85 is available with breakfast, and a detached bungalow large enough for six people can be rented for $175 a night. Tenting runs $12 and old buses converted into sleeping rooms with shared detached toilets run $35. Check-out is before 10 A.M., check-in until 9 P.M., and quiet time after 11 P.M. This is a smoke-free environment.

Glenwood

Located between mile markers 19 and 20, this town offers a gas station and **Hirano's General Store** for a few basic provisions. Tours of the Kazumura Lava Tube, reputedly the longest lava tube system in the world, are offered three times daily except Sunday. Call 808/969-9622 for reservations; pick up is across the street from Hirano's store. Alternately, call Harry Shick, 808/967-7208, for a guided tour of a portion of the cave. Volcano Cave Adventures, 808/968-0763 or 808/968-8606, also offers unpretentious personalized tours into a rainforest cave. These underground adventures travel several hundred feet through undeveloped lava tubes for a raw glimpse of the bowels of Mother Nature. Each trip runs about 1.5–2 hours.

A few minutes beyond town you pass **Akatsuka Orchid Gardens,** 808/967-8234, open daily 8:30 A.M.–5 P.M., except major holidays. If tour buses don't overflow the parking lot, stop in for a look at how orchids are grown. In the covered showroom, an incredible variety of orchids are on display and for sale, and neat little souvenirs are sold in the gift shop. Akatsuka ships cut flowers and potted orchids anywhere in the country. For a mail-order catalog, contact P.O. Box 220, Volcano, HI 96785, 888/967-6669, fax 808/967-7140.

PUNA

Volcano Village

You shouldn't miss taking a ride through the village of Volcano, a beautiful old settlement with truly charming houses and cottages outlined in ferns. Follow the signs off the main highway near mile marker 26 to the Old Volcano Highway, which is the main drag through the village. Tiny one-lane roads lace this community, which sits virtually atop one of the world's undeniable "power spots." This is a heavily forested area with no sidewalks or street lights. Lighting is generally subdued, so it can be very dark at night. At about 4,000 feet, it gets surprisingly cool and, of course, it often rains—over 150 inches a year. Summer daytime temperatures average 75°F, around 65°F in winter. At night it drops to 55°F in summer and into the 40s or less in winter. The fog rolls in most late afternoons, obscuring distant views but bestowing on the village an otherworldly charm. The area is so green and so vibrant that it appears surrealistic. With flowers, ferns, and trees everywhere, it is hard to imagine a more picturesque village in all of America. But even in this little parcel of paradise, things are changing, if slowly. The town of about 1,500 people boasts two general stores, a hardware store, two small gift shops/galleries, a post office, a farmers' market, a winery, several restaurants, an abundance of accommodations, several artists' studios, and newer and larger subdivisions south of the highway.

Volcano Golf and Country Club

What's most amazing about this course is where it is. Imagine! You're teeing off atop an active volcano surrounded by one of the last pristine forests in the state. At the right time of year, the surrounding 'ohi'a turn scarlet when they are in bloom. The fairways are carved from lava, while in the distance Mauna Loa looms. Hit a poor shot and you can watch your ball disappear down a steam vent. Just kidding—you're not that close! The course began about 80 years ago when a group of local golfers hand-cleared three "greens," placing stakes that served as holes. Later this was improved to sand greens with tin cans for holes, and after an eruption in 1924 blanketed the area with volcanic

ash that served as excellent fertilizer, the grass grew and the course became a lush green. After World War II the course was extended to 18 holes, and a clubhouse was added. Finally, Jack Snyder, a well-known course architect, redesigned the course to its present par-72 layout. Rates are $62.50 with shared cart; reduced rates for Big Island residents. The course is located just north of the Belt Road, about two miles west of the park entrance. Turn on Pi'i Mauna Drive, sometimes called Golf Course Road. Phone 808/967-7331 for more information and tee times. After a round of golf, stop for lunch at the clubhouse restaurant.

Volcano Winery

About one mile beyond the golf course at the end of Pi'i Mauna Road and off to your left are the buildings of the Volcano Winery, 808/967-7479, www.volcanowinery.com. This is the only winery on the Big Island and the southernmost in the United States. It's a hands-on operation where everything is done manually. Because the land is at an elevation of about 4,000 feet, the patented Symphony grape (a combination of grenache gris and muscat of Alexandria grapes) is grown to take best advantage of the climatic conditions, which are similar to those in Oregon and Washington. About 14 acres of this rough countryside are currently being cultivated with grapes, producing about three tons of grapes per acre, and another four acres have been planted in half a dozen other varieties to see if they too will produce acceptable wine. Bottled are dry and semi-dry wines, and three wine and fruit blends including guava/chablis, jaboticaba/chablis, and a macadamia honey wine. A local favorite, the jaboticaba blend is made with a Brazilian fruit of that name; the honey "wines" are made without any grapes. All bottles cost $13–16 apiece. Although no tours of the winery are available, a tasting room is open daily 10 A.M.–5:30 P.M. Have a sip at the glass-covered koa bar and maybe you'll want to purchase a bottle for later in the evening or a six-bottle case to share with friends when you get home. There also is a small boutique on

To Hilo

VOLCANO VILLAGE

0   0.5 mi

0   0.5 km

To National Park,
Kailua-Kona

© SANDRA E. BISIGNANI TRUST AND AVALON TRAVEL PUBLISHING, INC.

the premises selling T-shirts, jewelry, *kukui* nut leis, postcards, and other gift items.

ACCOMMODATIONS

There are a great number of accommodations in and around Volcano Village. While most are near the heart of the village, several are located in the fern forests south of the highway and a few are located around the golf course about two miles west of town. Most are bed-and-breakfasts, some are vacation homes where you take care of your own meals, and there is one hostel. These places run from budget and homey to luxurious and elegant, but most are moderate in price and amenities. Some of these establishments also act as agents for other rental homes in the area, so your choices are many. See also the Volcano House listing in the National Park chapter below.

Hostel

Volcano has a hostel, and a fine one it is! Al-though a modern structure, this all-wood forest house is an old-style place with a comforting, traditional hostel feel. **Holo Holo In,** P.O. Box 784, Volcano Village, HI 96785, 808/967-7950, fax 808/967-8025, holoholo@interpac.net, www.enable.org/holoholo, snuggles under the towering trees in a residential area of the village, next to the old Japanese schoolhouse at 19-4036 Kalani Honua Road. Owned, operated, and built by Satoshi Yabuki, a world traveler himself when he was younger, this is a one-man operation; his office hours are 6:30–9 A.M. and 4:30–9 P.M. Having taken guests for over a dozen years, this hostel has been an AYH member for about half that time. On the downstairs level is a huge kitchen with all needed appliances and utensils and a library of books and information. You are more than welcome to cook, but please clean up after yourself. Here too are a laundry facility and a sauna ($4 per person per use). Upstairs are the men's and women's dorms and the TV room, and there are bathrooms up and down. Rates are $17 per person for the dorm ($15 for AYH members), or $40 per couple for the one private room (can sleep four, so good for a small family). Please bring your own sheets or there will be a nominal extra charge. This is a great little accommodation at a bargain price—a real find.

$50–100

Down the lane behind the post office is **Aloha Junction,** a renovated bed-and-breakfast surrounded by green lawns and *hapu'u* ferns. A converted plantation manager's home, this house has three bedrooms upstairs, one down, and a suite in a separate building to the rear. Each bedroom has comfortable queen or twin beds with quilts and old-style lace curtains on the windows. All three main floor bedrooms share one bathroom. In the common room, the fireplace is warm and welcoming, and the huge television and entertainment center or quick Internet access computer will keep you occupied in the evening if you don't care to venture out. Out back, under a patio cover in case of rain, is the hot tub. All guests receive a filling home-cooked breakfast—different every morning—that's served family style with friendly conversation that makes a pleasant way to start the day. Room rates are $75 a night. For information and reservations, contact Robert or Susan Hughes at 808/967-7289 or 888/967-7286, relax@bbvolcano.com, http://bbvolcano.com.

A B&B with an excellent reputation is **My Island Bed and Breakfast Inn,** P.O. Box 100, Volcano, HI 96785, 808/967-7216, fax 808/967-7719, myisland@ilhawaii.net, www.myislandinnhawaii.com. The main house, the oldest in the village, is a New England–style three-level house from 1886 that was the Lyman summer home for many years. Rooms in this building rent for a reasonable $45–55 single to $60–70 double; some share a bathroom. A few steps away, the two garden units go for $70–95. A fully furnished vacation house on the property, plus four other vacation homes in the village and up near the golf course, go for $125 double with an extra charge for additional guests. No credit cards are accepted. All guests are served a "world-class" breakfast each morning in the main house. Spend some time in the exquisite seven-acre flower garden here as it is a wonderful extra benefit to this property.

Located at the end of Old Volcano Highway on the lower end of town, **Volcano Inn,** 808/967-7293 or 800/997-2292, fax 808/985-7349, volcano@volcanoinn.com, www.volcanoinn.com, has four rooms and several cottages at separate locations. The main three-story house is of modern design, with a common room and huge dining room where complimentary breakfasts are served to all guests. Rooms run $65–85 a night single, $85–105 a couple. Each has a private entrance and bath, TV and VCR, refrigerator, and coffeemaker. The cottages, at locations on the south side of the highway in a fern forest, go for $80–155, and two are big enough for a small family. A 10 percent discount is given for AAA members. The inn also operates horseback riding tours. Inquire about what's currently offered.

Located on the downhill side of the highway, the **Country Goose Bed and Breakfast,** P.O. Box 597, Volcano, HI 06785, 808/967-7759 or 800/238-7101 Mainland, fax 808/985-8673, cgoose@interpac.net, www.countrygoose.com, is a very pleasant place with lots of knickknacks on the walls. The knotty pine on the walls, open-beamed ceiling, and decor all say easy country living. Comfortable and homey, rooms include private baths and entrances, and the common room is open to all guests. Everyone is served a hearty country-style breakfast each morning in the dining room. Nestled under 'ohi'a trees and ferns, half a mile from the highway, this little place is quiet. The gracious owner, Joan Early, has built herself a fine retreat here and loves to share it with others who love the area. Rooms rent for $75 a night for two, with an extra $10 for a third person. Joan also represents several one-, two-, and three-bedroom homes in the village and out near the golf course that are available for nightly, weekly, or longer stays.

Owned and operated by Bonnie Goodell, **The Guest House at Volcano,** P.O. Box 6, Volcano, HI 96785, 808/967-7775 or 866/886-5226, fax 808/967-8295, innkeeper@volcanguesthouse.com, www.volcanoguesthouse.com, is a very friendly hideaway on the farthest back road of Mauna Loa Estates subdivision, south of the highway from Volcano Village. The fully furnished cottage is designed as a self-sufficient unit where guests are guaranteed peace and quiet on a lovely six-acre homesite. Bring your own food. Bonnie grew up in Hawaii and was for many years the education director for the Honolulu Botanical Gardens. She *knows* her plants and is willing to chat with her guests. The two-story guest home is bright and airy. Enter into a combo living room, kitchen, and dining area, with twin beds in a bedroom. Upstairs is a sleeping area with two twin beds and a queen bed. Futons can sleep even more. In the main house, a one-bedroom apartment called Claudia's Place has its own entrance and bathroom. It's completely handicapped-accessible and will sleep up to three. Two newer units have been built down the drive. They are mirror footprints of each other and face one another across a covered patio. The Twins are also fully accessible, each has a living room, kitchen, queen and twin beds, and sleeps up to four. The rate for Claudia's Place is $75, $85 for either of the Twins, and $95 for the cottage, $15 for each additional adult over two, $10 for kids. Two nights minimum, with the seventh night at no charge. Sometimes Bonnie will allow an emergency one-night stay, but then there is a $15 surcharge.

$100–150

Kilauea Lodge, P.O. Box 116, Volcano Village, HI 96785, 808/967-7366, fax 967-7367, stay@kilauealodge.com, www.kilauealodge.com, owned and operated by Lorna and Albert Jeyte, is the premier restaurant and lodge atop Volcano, as well as one of the very best on the island. The solid stone and timber structure was built in 1938 as a YMCA camp and functioned as such until 1962, when it became a "mom and pop operation," often failing and changing ownership. It faded into the ferns until Lorna and Albert revitalized it in 1987, opening in 1988. The lodge is a classic, with a vaulted, open-beamed ceiling. A warm and cozy "international fireplace" dating from the days of the YMCA camp is embedded with stones and plaques from all over the world. This building houses the restaurant and the office. An assortment of rooms, ranging $125–145 and including a complete breakfast for all guests in the restaurant, are located in three adjacent buildings on the property, and there is a hot tub for guests in the rear garden. The brooding rooms of the original guesthouse section were transformed into bright, cozy, and romantic suites. The rooms, all differently appointed, range in decor from Hawaiian-European to Asian with a motif of Japanese fans. Each

Kilauea Lodge

room has a bathroom with vaulted 18-foot ceilings and a skylight, a working fireplace, queen or twin beds, and swivel rocking chair. A separate one-bedroom cottage, set in the ferns to the side, features a wood-burning stove (central heat too), wet bar, a queen-size bed, private bath, and small living room with queen-size pull-out sofa. In 1991, Kilauea Lodge opened the Hale Aloha building with its seven new units centered around a commodious common room where you can read and snooze by a crackling fire. All rooms in the new section are very spacious, with vaulted ceilings (upstairs) and tastefully furnished with wicker furniture, white curtains, and fluffy quilts to keep off the evening chill. Many are hung with original artwork by Gwendolyn O'Connor. Check-in is 3–5 P.M. at the office; after that, check in at the restaurant. The Kilauea Lodge provides one of the most *civilized* atmospheres in Hawaii in one of its most powerful natural areas. The combination is hard to beat.

Just up the road from the Kilauea Lodge is the cute little two-bedroom cottage, **Tutu's Place.** Built in 1929 by the Uncle Billy of hotel chain fame for "tutu" (grandma), it was bought several decades later by the Warner family. Mr. Warner was a minister and was involved in Hawaiian politics. His wife, Ruth Warner, lived in the cottage for 30 years until it was bought in 1995 by Lorna Larson-Jeyte, the owner of the Kilauea Lodge, who used to visit as a child. Although it's been completely refurbished, people in the know say that the cottage is still imbued with the spirit of Ruth Warner. It's done in a theme of rattan and koa, with a fireplace in the living room, a full kitchen, and a wonderful little bathroom. For a small place, it has a surprisingly roomy feel. The rate is $155 for two people, including breakfast at the Kilauea Lodge, plus $15 for each additional person. To make reservations, call the Kilauea Lodge, and ask for Tutu's Place.

Next door to Tutu's Place, and conveniently located near stores and restaurants, is **Oma's Hapu'u Hideaway,** a modern semi-A-frame mountain house of cedar that's great for a family. Here you have all you need: a full kitchen, living room, bathroom, two bedrooms downstairs, one with bunks that's great for kids, and a master

bedroom loft upstairs. The house comes with TV and VCR and phone. It's a cozy place that goes for $105 a night. The owners live across the street in a plantation house, and in the rear is **The Maid's Quarters,** a self-contained cottage with full kitchen, living room tiled with marble, fireplace, spacious bedroom, completely updated bathroom, and a hot tub. This is a lovely place, just right for a romantic couple. This cottage runs $95 a night. Next door is the refurbished **Haunani House**. Also good for a family, it has three bedrooms, two baths, a full kitchen, living room with gas fireplace, washer and dryer, and television, and rents for $115 a night. All three are good value for the money. Each has a two night minimum with a fifth night free; $15 for each additional person over two. No breakfast is served. For information, write P.O. Box 611, Volcano, HI 96785; 808/985-8959, todd@volcanovillage.net, www .volcanovillage.net.

Kate's Volcano Places is a winner! A pleasant, homey, and cozy place, the cottage is a modern reconstruction with full attention to detail that combines Western cabin and Scandinavian styles with a touch of the Orient. One large room, this cottage has a king bed, separate bathroom, and full kitchen equipped with all conveniences and stocked with supplies. The sitting area sports a built-in entertainment center and opens onto the back deck. Up front, the reconditioned island-style Kahi Malu house has two bedrooms, one bathroom, and a full kitchen; the living room, amazingly, is solid koa. Like the cottage, it too has been brought up to snuff with all modern conveniences. This house and cottage are set toward the back of the village and are very quiet and private. At a separate location, the three-bedroom Hiiaka house from 1939 is surrounded by a large yard. This house is perfect for a family of up to eight with its huge living room and fireplace, full kitchen, and three bedrooms. Rental rates are $95 for the cottage, $125 for Kahi Mahi, and $135 for Hiiaka, and this includes breakfast goodies stocked in the refrigerator for each morning that you'll be there. For information and reservations, contact Kathryn Grout, P.O. Box 159 Volcano, HI 96785, 808/967-7990 or 877/967-

7990, kathryn@volcanoplaces.com, www.volcanoplaces.com.

Volcano Country Cottages, P.O. Box 545, Volcano, HI 96785, 808/967-7960 or 800/967-7960, aloha@volcanocottages.com, www.volcanocottages.com, are conveniently located in the heart of the village at one of its oldest homes. Available are the Ohelo Berry Cottage for $95 for one night and the two-bedroom Artist's House for $120; $15 for each additional person beyond two. The studio cottage is a cozy one-room affair with kitchenette, bathroom, and room heater that snuggles into the back vegetation. It's perfect for a couple but can also sleep two kids on futons. A covered lanai outside the front door is a wonderful spot to sit during a light rain. Each morning, a filling and tasty breakfast of fruits and baked goods is left for you to have at your leisure. Set closer to the front of the property under towering tsugi trees, the Artist's House contains a full kitchen, also stocked with morning treats, a woodstove, and washer and dryer. It sleeps four comfortably and up to four more on pull-out futons. For use by all guests, the hot tub sits behind the main house in the fern forest. This is a gracious place, one of peace and tranquillity, with the added gift of artwork hung on the walls. Check-in is 3–5 P.M. The Wellspring Center for yoga and stress reduction operates on property.

Follow a private mountain lane for a few minutes into an enchanted clearing where the artwork of a meticulous Japanese garden surrounds a New England gabled and turreted home and its attendant cottages of red-on-brown rough-cut shingles. Once the hideaway of the Dillinghams, an old and influential *kama'aina* family, **Hale Ohia,** P.O. Box 758, Volcano Village, HI 96785, 808/967-7986 or 800/455-3803, fax 808/967-8610, haleohia@bigisland.com, www.haleohia.com, is now owned and operated by Michael D. Tuttle, who purchased the property after falling hopelessly in love at first sight. The main house holds the Dillingham Suite, $110 per night, with its own sitting room, bath, and glass-covered lanai. Simple and clean, with hardwood floors and wainscoted walls, the home is the epitome of country elegance, Hawaiian style. Adjacent in the main house, occupying one bedroom, a big bath, and the main living room, is the Master Suite for $140. Hale Ohia Cottage, once the gardener's residence, has two stories, with the bottom floor front occupied by the Iiwi and Camellia suites, $95, which are wheelchair-accessible and can be combined for larger groups. Stained-glass windows with a calla lily-and-poppy motif add a special touch, while the low ceilings are reminiscent of the captain's quarters on a sailing ship. The 1st floor rear has a full kitchen and a covered lanai complete with barbecue grill that makes it perfect for evening relaxation. Narrow stairs lead to a full bath located on the first landing, and the upstairs opens into a bright and airy parlor and adjacent bedrooms that can sleep five comfortably, $130. Hale Lehua, once a private study, is secluded down its own lava footpath and rents for $110. The interior is cozy with its own fireplace, bamboo and wicker furniture, self-contained bathroom, covered lanai, partial kitchen, and leaded glass windows through which the surrounding fern forest will emit its emerald radiance. Similar but more luxurious is the Ihilani Cottage, at $125. Newest of the units is Cottage #44—created from a water tank! The round redwood tank has been turned into the bedroom, and attached to it in a newly built structure are the living room, efficiency kitchen, bathroom with shower and whirlpool tub, and covered lanai. No expense was spared for this cute little unit and it rents for $150. To make your stay even more delightful, room rates include an "extended" continental breakfast, and guests are welcome to immerse themselves in the bubbling whirlpool tub that awaits under a canopy of Japanese cedars and glimmering stars. No TV and no smoking, but there is an on-site phone in the wisteria-covered gazebo.

Embraced within the arms of ferns and 'ohi'a are the three cottages of **Volcano Rainforest Retreat,** 808/985-8696 or 800/550-8696, volrain@bigisland.net, www.volcanoretreat.com, a luxury accommodation for discriminating guests wanting privacy for their stay in the rainforest. Constructed in an open style of cedar and redwood, these buildings are warm and welcoming and rich in color and detail. Hale Kipa has a living room with kitchen and sleeping loft. The octagonal Hale Nahele is one large room with a bed,

PUNA

seating area, and a kitchenette. The six-sided Hale Ho'ano, smallest and with the most obvious Japanese influence, has the benefit of an outdoor ofuro tub and shower. Rates are $170, $140, and $95, respectively; discounts for three nights or longer.

Ka Hale Iki Kilauea is a very romantic home away from home, canopied by the forest trees, screened from the road by tall ferns, and 50 feet through the jungle from the driveway. Much like a cabin with a porch all around, the inside opens to a high open-beamed ceiling, living room with a woodstove, and full kitchen. Sliding doors and picture windows all around frame the living green tapestry outside. In the bath is a huge tub fit for two; bathe by candlelight and open the full-length windows to let in the night air. Up the ladder-like narrow stairway is the bedroom and queen bed, where you can drift away with the moon and starlight gently filtering through the skylight windows. The rental rate is $135 a night for a couple and $15 more for an extra person, or $700 a week, breakfast included. For reservations, contact Joan Early at the Country Goose, 808/967-7759 or 800/238-7101, www.vrbo.com/vrbo/1438.htm.

Deep in the fern forest, **Carson's Volcano Cottages,** P.O. Box 503, Volcano, HI 96785, 808/967-7683 or 800/845-LAVA, fax 808/967-8094, carsons@aloha.net, www.carsonscottage.com, owned and operated by Tom and Brenda Carson, offers two B&B rooms in the main house, but by far the nicer accommodations are in the detached cottages. The suites in the main house are located upstairs and run $125–155 a night. The cottage accommodations all have private baths, entrances, and decks, and in the garden is a hot tub for everyone to use. The one-acre property is naturally landscaped with 'ohi'a and fern, and moss-covered sculptures of Balinese gods peek through the foliage. Nick's Cabin #19, $125 double, a miniature plantation house with corrugated roof and woodstove, has a mini-kitchen and a bath with a skylight—rustic country charm. The three-room cottage, $105–110 per room, has vaulted ceilings and queen beds, and rooms decorated in Hawaiian Monarchy, Oriental, and tropical floral styles. Leaded glass windows open

to a private porch. Tom and Brenda provide an extended continental breakfast for all guests in their dining room that might include banana bread, French toast, passion fruit juice, bagels and lox, or strawberry crepes. You'll be comfortable in front of the living room fireplace or enjoying the evening sky from the hot tub. The Carsons also rent out four other one- and two-bedroom, fully furnished cottages in the village that run $125–165 and a seaside retreat down in Kapoho if you are going that direction.

$150 and up

Peeking from the *hapu'u* fern forest in a manicured glen is **Chalet Kilauea,** 998 Wright Road, Volcano Village, HI 96785, 808/967-7786 or 800/937-7786, fax 808/967-8660 or 800/577-1849, reservations@volcano-hawaii.com, www.volcano-hawaii.com, where you will be cordially accommodated by owners Lisha and Brian Crawford and their staff. Downstairs there's an outdoor lounge area, and a black-and-white checkerboard dining room where wrought-iron tables sit before a huge picture window. A three-course candlelight breakfast is served here every morning. Enter the second level of the main house to find a guest living room where you can while away the hours playing chess, listening to a large collection of CDs, or gazing from the wraparound windows at a treetop view of the surrounding forest, ferns, and impeccable grounds. Beyond the koi pond in the garden, a free-standing gazebo houses an eight-person hot tub available 24 hours a day.

The main house, called The Inn at Volcano, is known for elegance and luxury. It holds four suites and two theme rooms, $139–399. The Oriental Jade Room is richly appointed with Chinese folding screens, samurai murals, Oriental carpet, and jade-green bedspread. The green marble bathroom adds to the green theme of the surrounding vegetation. The lanai outside is shared with the Out of Africa Room, which has a strong color theme of burgundy and brass, and appointed with bold wood carvings and some basketwork. The Continental Lace Suite is fluff and lace, the bridal suite. Here the colors are white, gold, and pink; a wedding dress hangs in the corner to accentuate the theme. Located on the 1st floor, the Owners' Suite is designed for up to three people. Pink carpet covers the floor and a green floral spread covers the bed. With two shower heads in the shower stall, a couple can be happy showering together. Connected by a deck to the main house is the Treehouse Suite, a two-story unit with bath, sitting room, wet bar, and kitchenette downstairs, and a large bedroom on the upper floor. The surrounding glass makes the living forest part of the decor. A private lanai overlooks the garden, and a hand-crafted wooden circular staircase connects the two floors. An adjacent "cabin" is the Hapu'u Suite. It has a fireplace in the cozy living room but perhaps its best feature is the master bathroom which looks out onto the back garden.

Chalet Kilauea also has many other accommodations in Volcano Village including Castle Suites at Mauna Loa, a modern Victorian home set on the golf course, where three suites range $189–249. Lokahi Lodge has four rooms that run $99–149, or $590 for a group of up to 14 people. For those on a tighter budget, the Volcano Bed and Breakfast rents rooms for $49–69 and still has plenty of common space. The entire house can be rented for $293 a night and can sleep 13. In addition, five vacation homes dotted here and there about town in the secluded privacy of the forest are available for $139–379. Whatever your price range and whatever your needs, Chalet Kilauea will have something for you, and breakfast is an option at most accommodations.

FOOD

The **Kilauea Lodge Restaurant,** open for dinner 5:30–9 P.M. nightly (reservations a must), is an extraordinary restaurant serving gourmet continental cuisine—the premier restaurant in Volcano Village. A large fireplace dominates one side of the room with an inviting couch at its front. The hardwood floor reflects light from the two chandeliers that hang from the open-beamed wooden ceiling. Prints of Hawaiian scenes hang from the walls, and beer mugs line the stone mantle. A warm, welcoming, and homey place, the Kilauea Lodge Restaurant has fine dining in an unpretentious setting. A very friendly and professional staff

serves the excellent food prepared by Albert, the owner, and his kitchen help. Although the menu changes a bit every night, you'll start off with fresh bread—studded like the fireplace, but with sunflower and sesame seeds. Appetizers such as mushroom caps stuffed with crab and cheese will titillate your palate, or try the baked brie cheese, a specialty. Entrées, ranging $17–28, include soup, salad, and vegetables. The menu is strong on the meats, with its heavy German influence, but vegetarians will be delighted with their options too. Dinner features seafood Mauna Kea (succulent pieces of seafood served atop a bed of fettuccine) and paupiettes of beef (prime rib slices rolled around herbs and mushrooms in a special sauce). Always a great choice, the catch of the day is blackened, broiled, or sautéed with a savory sauce. There is always a nightly special, and each dish is infused with herbs and pungent seasonings. To match any meal, you can select from the extensive wine list, which includes a special reserve section. Desserts are wonderful, and the meal can be topped off with a cup of Irish or Italian coffee.

Situated behind the Kilauea General Store is **Lava Rock Cafe,** 808/967-8526, the most local of the eateries in the village. The Lava Rock is open 7:30–10:30 A.M. for breakfast, until 5 P.M. for lunch (4 P.M. on Sunday), and dinner is served Tues.–Sat. until 9 P.M. Start your day with eggs, griddle items, or loco moco. For lunch you can get a plate lunch, burger, or sandwich, along with sides, fountain drinks, and coffee. Dinners are a bit heartier with the likes of teriyaki chicken and New York steak, and almost everything is under $12, except for a few of the meat dishes that run up to $17.50. While not gourmet, this is good food. You get plentiful portions at a good price in pleasant surroundings—and there's even Internet access.

A fine addition to the restaurant scene in Volcano is **Thai Thai Restaurant,** 808/967-7969, open for dinner 5–9 P.M. every day except Wednesday. This restaurant puts out food that will transport you to the Orient. It has established a good reputation in town for tasty food and large portions. Start with an appetizer (some as big as entrées), like deep-fried tofu or chicken satay. Traditional soups and salads come next, followed by curries or stir-fried selections, most of which can be made with your choice of shrimp, chicken, beef, or pork. Almost everything on the menu is in the $9–13 range, so it's not exorbitant. Take-out available.

Around the side and behind the Volcano Store is **JP's Volcano Cafe.** This quick-serve café has eggs and local favorites for breakfast and sandwiches, salads, and soup for lunch, plus lots of coffee all day long. Open 6 A.M.–4 P.M. Seating is outside under the awning.

You can get away from the crowds and have a satisfying breakfast or lunch at **Volcano Country Club Restaurant,** 808/967-8228, at the golf course clubhouse. No dinner meals are served. The green and white interior complements the fairways, which can be seen through the surrounding plate glass windows. A fireplace fills the center of this country kitchen style room. Complete breakfast is served daily 8–10 A.M. (6:30 A.M. on weekends), a full lunch menu daily 10:30 A.M.–2 P.M. For breakfast choose omelettes, hotcakes, or other standard American fare. Lunch selections include hearty sandwiches, salads, and burgers, as well as local favorites like teriyaki beef, saimin, or loco moco. Many stop by just for the Portuguese bean soup. Most everything on the menu is under $9. The bar is well stocked, so enjoy an exotic drink, beer, or glass of wine after your round of golf. Good choice for lunch.

Wouldn't it be fun to have a full multi-course gourmet dinner prepared and delivered to your door by a trained chef and served on linen and fine china, with the dishes whisked away after you're finished so you can turn your attention to more romantic matters? Well, you can do just that here in the tiny village of Volcano for $30 per person plus gratuity and wine. Call the **Culinary Crusaders,** 808/985-7167, 24-hour advance notice requested. It is not inexpensive, but an experience to be remembered.

If you're looking for something faster and not so gourmet, try **Big O's Pizza,** 808/985-9995. The basic 12-inch pie runs $12.50 with each extra at 50 cents. Open 5–10 P.M. Tues.–Sat. and 4–6:30 P.M. Sunday and Monday. Call in your order and pick it up at the Kilauea General Store.

See also Volcano House Restaurant in the National Park chapter below.

SHOPPING

A **farmers' market** open every Sunday 8:30–11 A.M. sells local produce, fruit, flowers, baked goods, soups and other prepared foods, used books, and other items. It's located along Wright Road at the Cooper Center. Come early for the food. This is a wonderful community event. Don't miss it.

Volcano Store, 808/967-7210, also called the "upper store," is open daily 5 A.M.–7 P.M. and sells gasoline, film, a few camping supplies, tropical flowers, a good selection of basic foods, and general dry goods items. For events happening around the village, see the community bulletin board on the wall outside. There are public telephone booths out front, and a few steps away is the full-service post office.

Just down the road, **Kilauea General Store,** 808/967-7555, also called the "lower store," is open daily 7 A.M.–7:30 P.M. (until 7 P.M. on Sundays). This store also sells gas, and although it is not as well stocked as a grocery, it does have a deli case, a good selection of beer and liquor, postcards, videos, an ATM machine, and an excellent community bulletin board. It's here that you can order and pick up your Big O's pizza.

Set between these two is **True Value Hardware** for all your home and yard needs. Open daily 7 A.M.–5:30 P.M., 5 P.M. on weekends.

In a separate building behind the Kilauea General Store is **Kilauea Kreations,** a shop that carries gifts, crafts, and art by local artists. Perhaps best of what they have is quilts, quilting supplies, and materials. For other arts and crafts by local artists, souvenirs (much imported), as well as information about the area, have a look at the **Village Art Store** above the hardware store.

Volcano Wash and Dry sits behind the hardware store and is open 8 A.M.–7 P.M. Buy soap up front at the hardware store.

Many artists have found a home at Volcano, and a few studios dot the backroads. Ask at one of the stores for a map of those studios open to guests.

For Internet access, check at the Lava Rock Cafe.

Hawaii Volcanoes National Park

Introduction

Hawaii Volcanoes National Park (HVNP) is an unparalleled experience in geological grandeur. The upper end of the park is the summit of stupendous Mauna Loa, the most massive mountain on earth. Mauna Loa Road branches off Hwy. 11 and ends at a foot trail for the hale and hearty who trek to the 13,679-foot summit. The park's heart is **Kilauea Caldera,** almost three miles across, 400 feet deep, and encircled by 11 miles of **Crater Rim Drive.** At the park **Visitors Center** you can give yourself a crash course in geology while picking up park maps, information, and backcountry camping permits. Nearby is **Volcano House,** Hawaii's oldest hotel, which has hosted a steady stream of adventurers, luminaries, royalty, and heads of state ever since it opened its doors in the 1860s. Just a short drive away is a pocket of indigenous forest, providing the perfect setting for a bird sanctuary. In

Halema'uma'u Crater appears small in the immense expanse of Kilauea Caldera.

HAWAII VOLCANOES NAT'L PARK

To Hilo

ROAD

BELT

Mountain View

HAWAI'I

Glenwood

11

Volcano

OLA'A
RAIN
FOREST

To Saddle Road

HAWAII VOLCANOES
NATIONAL PARK

MAUNA LOA ROAD

MAUNA LOA
LOOKOUT

RED HILL
CABIN

HAWAII
VOLCANOES
NATIONAL PARK

Mauna
Loa
Trail

Cabin Trail

MAUNA LOA
NOAA
OBSERVATORY

MAUNA LOA
CABIN

Summit Trail

Mauna Loa
(13,679 ft.)

Moku'aweoweo
Caldera

East Rift Zone

Kupa'ianaha

lava inundation
since 1983

Pu'u O'o

WAHA'ULA
HEIAU
SITE

Holei
Sea Arch

PU'U LOA
PETROGLYPH
FIELD

Napau
Crater

Napau Trail

Pu'u
Huluhulu

Makaopuhi
Crater

Mauna
Ulu

CHAIN OF CRATERS RD.

KEALAKOMO

APUA
CAMPSITE

Pauahi
Crater

KEAUHOU
SHELTER

HALAPA
SHELTER

HAWAII
VOLCANOES

NATIONAL

PARK

Ko'oko'olau
Crater

Kīlauea
Caldera

SEE
DETAIL

Mauna Iki
Trail

HILINA PALI RD.

Hilina Pali Trail

HILINA PALI
OVERLOOK

KA'AHA
SHELTER

KA'U
DESERT
FOOTPRINTS

Ka'u Desert

Ka'u Desert Trail

KULANAOKUAIKI
CAMPGROUND

PEPEIAO
CABIN

Ka'aha Trail

Ka'u Trail

Southwest Rift Zone

HAWAII BELT RD.

PACIFIC

OCEAN

Puna Coast Trail

Hilina Pali

5 mi

5 km

0

DETAIL

KIPUKA
PUAULU

TREE MOLDS

VOLCANO
WINERY

KILAUEA
MILITARY
CAMP

Sandalwood
Trail

VOLCANO COUNTRY CLUB/
GOLF COURSE

PARK HEADQUARTERS,
MUSEUM,
AND VISITOR
AND ART
CENTERS

Volcano

KILAUEA IKI
OVERLOOK

THURSTON
LAVA TUBE

TREE FERN AND
OHIA FOREST

VOLCANO HOUSE

SULFUR
BANKS

STEAM
VENTS

Steaming
Bluff

Kilauea Iki
Tr.

Waldron
Ledge

Halema'uma'u Trail

BIRD PARK
PICNIC AREA

NAMAKANI PAIO
CAMPGROUND

VOLCANO
OBSERVATORY

JAGGAR
MUSEUM

KILAUEA
OVERLOOK

Kilauea
Caldera

Halema'uma'u
Crater

Byron Ledge

OVERLOOK

CRATER RIM DRIVE

Ka'u Desert Tr.

Crater Rim Trail

Keanakako'i
Crater

Byron
Ledge
Trail

Lua Manu
Crater

Devastation
Trail

Puhimau
Crater

To Kailua-Kona

Pahala

a separate detached section of the park is **'Ola'a Forest,** a pristine wilderness area of unspoiled flora and fauna.

Crater Rim Drive circles Kilauea Caldera past steam vents, sulfur springs, and tortured fault lines that always seem on the verge of gaping wide and swallowing. On the way you can peer into the maw of **Halema'uma'u Crater,** home of the fire goddess, Pele, and you'll pass **Hawaiian Volcano Observatory** (not open to public), which has been monitoring geologic activity since the turn of the 20th century. Adjacent to the observatory is the **Thomas A. Jaggar Museum,** an excellent facility where you can educate yourself on the past and present volcanology of the park. A fantastic walk is **Devastation Trail,** a paved path across a desolate cinder field where gray, lifeless trunks of a suffocated forest lean like old gravestones. Within minutes is **Thurston Lava Tube,** a magnificent natural tunnel *"leid"* by amazingly vibrant fern grottoes at the entrance and exit.

The southwestern section of the park is dominated by the **Ka'u Desert,** not a plain of sand but a semi-arid slope of lava flow, cinder, scrub bush, and heat that's been defiled by the wind-blown debris and gasses of Kilauea Volcano and fractured by the sinking coastline. It is a desolate region, an area crossed by a few trails that are a challenge even to the sturdy and experienced hiker. Most visitors, however, head down the **Chain of Craters Road,** first through the 'ohi'a and fern forests, then past numerous secondary craters and down the *pali* to the coast where the road ends abruptly at a hardened flow of lava and from where visitors can glean information about current volcanic activities from the small ranger station and try to glimpse the current volcanic activity in the distance.

The indomitable power of Volcanoes National Park is apparent to all who come here. Mark Twain, enchanted by his sojourn through Volcanoes in the 1860s, quipped, "The smell of sulfur is strong, but not unpleasant to a sinner." Amen, brother! Wherever you stop to gaze, realize that you are standing on a thin skin of cooled lava in an unstable earthquake zone atop one of the world's most active volcanoes.

Established in 1916 as the 13th U.S. national park, HVNP now covers 377 square miles. Based on its scientific and scenic value, the park was named an International Biosphere Reserve by UNESCO in 1980 and given World Heritage Site status in 1982 by the same organization, giving it greater national and international prestige. With about 2.5 million visitors a year, this is one of the top visitor attractions in the state.

Admission to the park is $10 per vehicle (good for multiple entries over a seven-day period), $20 for an annual permit, $5 for bicycle and motorcycle traffic and hikers, and free to those 62 and over with a Golden Age, Golden Eagle, or Golden Access passport. These "passports" are available at the park headquarters and are good at any national park in the United States. For information about the park, write to Hawaii Volcanoes National Park, P.O. Box 52, Hawaii National Park, HI 96718-0052; call 808/985-6000 for a recorded message; or visit www.nps.gov/havo.

Geologic History: Science Versus Madame Pele

The goddess Pele is an irascible old dame. Perhaps it's because she had such a bad childhood. All she wanted was a home of her own where she could house her family and entertain her lover, a handsome chief from Kaua'i. But her sea goddess sister, Namakaokaha'i, flooded her out wherever she went after Pele seduced her husband, and the pig god, Kamapua'a, ravished Pele for good measure. So Pele finally built her love nest at Halema'uma'u Crater at the south end of Kilauea Caldera. Being a goddess obviously isn't as heavenly as one would think, and whenever the pressures of life get too much for Pele, she blows her stack. These tempestuous outbursts made Pele one of the most revered gods in the Hawaiian pantheon because her presence and might were so easily felt.

For a thousand years Pele was appeased by offerings of pigs, dogs, sacred *'ohelo* berries (her favorite), and now and again an outcast man or two (never women) who would hopefully turn her energy from destruction to more comfortable pursuits. Also, if Pele was your family's personal goddess, your remains were sometimes allowed to be thrown into the fire pit as a sign of great respect. In the early 1820s, the chieftess Kapiʻolani, an ardent convert to Christianity, officially challenged Pele in an attempt to topple her like the other gods of old. Kapiʻolani climbed down into Pele's crater and ate the sacred *ʻohelo* berries, flagrantly violating the ageless *kapu*. She then took large stones and defiantly hurled them into the fire pit below while bellowing, "Jehovah is my God. It is He, not Pele, that kindled these flames."

Yet today, most residents, regardless of background, have an inexplicable reverence for Pele. The Volcano Post Office receives an average of three packages a week containing lava rocks taken by tourists as souvenirs. Some hold that Pele looks upon these rocks as her children and taking them from her is kidnapping. The accompanying letters implore the officials to return the rocks because ever since the offender brought them home, luck has been bad. The officials take the requests very seriously, returning the rocks with the customary peace offering. Many follow-up "thank you" letters have been written to express relief that the bad luck has been lifted. There is no reference in Hawaiian folklore to this phenomenon, although Hawaiians did hold certain rocks sacred. Park rangers will tell you that the idea of "the bad-luck rocks" was initiated a few decades back by a tour bus driver who became sick and tired of tourists getting his bus dirty by piling aboard their souvenirs. *Voilà!* Another ancient Hawaiian myth! Know, however, that the rocks in Hawaii Volcanoes National Park are protected by federal law, much meaner and more vindictive than Pele.

Pele is believed to take human form. She customarily appears before an eruption as a ravishing beauty or a withered old hag, often accompanied by a little white dog. She expects to be treated cordially, and it's said that she will stand by the roadside at night hitching a ride. After a brief encounter, she departs and seems to mysteriously evaporate into the ether. Kindness on your part is the key; if you come across a strange woman at night, treat her well—it might not help, but it definitely won't hurt.

VOLCANO ACTIVITY

For current information on volcano activity in the area, check the Hawaiian Volcano Observatory "Volcano Watch" website at http://hvo.wr.usgs.gov/volcanowatch. Related volcano and earthquake information for the Big Island is also available at http://hvo.wr.usgs.gov and from the Hawaii Center for Volcanology website at www.soest.hawaii.edu/GG/HCV/kilauea; or by calling 808/985-6000 for the Park Service's recorded message. Should there be any major increase in activity, local radio stations give up-to-the-minute news.

Eruptions

The first white man atop Kilauea was Rev. William Ellis, who scaled it in 1823. Until the 1920s, the floor of the caldera was exactly what people thought a volcano would be: a molten lake of lava. Then the forces of nature changed, and the fiery lava subsided and hardened over. Today, Kilauea is called the only "drive-in" volcano in the world, and in recent years it has been one of the most active, erupting almost continuously since 1983 at vents along its eastern fault. When it begins gushing, the result is not a nightmare scene of people scrambling away for their lives, but just the opposite; people flock *to* the volcano. Most thrill-seekers are in much greater danger of being run over by a tour bus hustling to see the fireworks than of being entombed in lava. The volcanic action, while soul-shakingly powerful and not really predictable, is almost totally safe. The Hawaiian Volcano Observatory has been keeping watch since 1912, making Kilauea one of the best-understood volcanoes in the world. The vast volcanic field is creased by rift zones, or natural pressure valves. When the underground magma builds up, instead of *kaboom!* as in Mt. St. Helens, it bubbles to the surface like a spring and gushes out as a river of lava. Naturally, anyone or anything in its path would be burned to a cinder, but scientists routinely walk within a few feet of the still-flowing lava to take samples and readings. In much the way canaries detected mine gas, longtime lava observers pay attention to their ears. When the skin on top begins to blister, they know they are too close. The lava establishes a course that it follows much like an impromptu mountain stream caused by heavy rains.

This does not mean that the lava flows are entirely benign, or that anyone should visit the area during an eruption without prior approval by the park service. When anything is happening, the local radio stations give up-to-the-minute news, and the park service provides a recorded message at 808/985-6000. In 1790 a puff of noxious gases was emitted from Kilauea and descended on the Ka'u Desert, asphyxiating a rival army of Kamehameha's that just happened to be in the area. Eighty people died in their tracks. In 1881 a flow of lava spilled toward undeveloped Hilo and engulfed an area within today's city limits. In 1942, a heavy flow came within 12 miles of the city. Still, this was child's play in comparison with the unbelievable flow of 1950. Luckily, this went down the western rift zone where only scattered homes were in its path. It took no lives as it disgorged well over 600 million cubic yards of magma that covered 35 square miles! The flow continued for 23 days and produced seven huge torrents of lava that sliced across the Belt Road in three different areas. At its height, the lava front traveled six miles per hour and put out enough material to pave an eight-lane freeway twice around the world. In 1960, a flow swallowed the town of Kapoho on the east coast. In 1975, an earthquake caused a tsunami to hit the southeast coast, killing two campers and sinking a section of the coast by three feet.

The most recent—and very dramatic—series of eruptions that spectacularly began on January 3, 1983, has continued virtually unabated ever since, producing more than one cubic kilometer of lava. Magma bubbled to the surface about two miles away from Pu'u O'o. The gigantic fissure fountained lava and formed Pu'u O'o Cinder Cone, now 800 feet high and almost 1,000 feet across. Over a 3.5-year period, there were 47 episodic eruptions from this vent. On July 20, 1986, a new fissure broke upon the surface at Kupa'ianaha just outside the park in a nature reserve and formed a lava lake about one acre in surface size and 180 feet deep. At the end of April 1987 all activity suddenly stopped and the lava drained from the lake and tube system, allowing scientists to accurately gauge the depth. About three weeks later, it started up again when lava poured back into the lake, went through the tube system, and flowed back down to the ocean.

More episodic eruptions followed and from that point the flow turned destructive and started taking homes. It flowed about seven miles to the coast through tubes and on the surface, wiping out Kapa'ahu, parts of Kalapana, and most of the Royal Gardens Subdivision, with more than 180 homes incinerated. In May 1989 it moved into the national park proper, and on June 22, it swallowed the park Visitors Center at Waha'ula. Since 1992, lava has been flowing into the ocean within the park. Unexpectedly, in January 1997 the dramatic activity shifted two miles westward to the Napau Crater, where lava erupted in spouts of fire and flows, and Pu'u O'o ceased spewing. Since February 1997, the majority of activity moved back to Pu'u O'o Cinder Cone, where there has been a continual shift of vent locations on the west and southwestern flanks and constant renewed activity inside the crater. Until 1997, remote Waha'ula Heiau was spared, but in August of that year lava inundated and buried the sacred spot. The destruction has caused more than $61 million worth of damage. Many of the homesteaders in the worst areas of the flow were rugged individualists and back-to-nature alternative types who lived in homes that generally had no electricity, running water, or telephones. The homes were wiped out. Some disreputable insurance companies with legitimate policyholders tried to wiggle out of paying premiums for lost homes, although the policies specifically stipulated loss by lava flow. The insurance companies whined that the 2,200°F lava never really touched some of the homes, and therefore they were exonerated from covering the losses. Their claims were resoundingly repudiated in the courts, and people were paid for their losses.

At its height, the output of lava was estimated at 650,000 cubic yards per day, which is equal to 55,000 truckloads of cement, enough to cover a football field 38 miles high. Since this activity started in 1983, it has averaged 300,000–600,000 cubic yards a day (that's over two billion cubic yards!!), added 560 acres of new land to the park and greater acreage to the areas outside the park, and buried about 13 miles of the Chain of Craters Road. For a history of the park's volcanic activity plus up-to-the-minute reports on current activity, see http://hvo.wr.usgs.gov. Related information is also available at www.soest .hawaii.edu/GG/HCV.

Mauna Loa

At 13,679 feet, this magnificent mountain is a mere 117 feet shorter than its neighbor Mauna Kea, which is the tallest peak in the Pacific, and by some accounts, tallest in the world. Measured from its base, 18,000 feet beneath the sea, it would top even Mt. Everest. Mauna Loa is the most massive mountain on earth, containing 19,000 cubic miles of solid, iron-hard lava, and it's estimated that this titan weighs more than California's entire Sierra Nevada mountain range! In fact, Mauna Loa (Long Mountain), at 60 miles long and 30 miles wide, occupies the entire southern half of the Big Island, with Hawaii Volcanoes National Park merely a section of its great expanse.

The summit of Mauna Loa with its mighty **Maku'aweoweo Caldera** and a broad swath of wilderness on the flank of the mountain rising up to it from Kilauea Caldera are all within park boundaries. This is the least visited part of the park, and in a sense the most separate. In order to visit here you have to hike.

The 17-mile hike to the summit of Mauna Loa is the most grueling in the park. The trailhead (6,662 feet) is at the lookout at the end of the pavement of Mauna Loa Road. Hikers in excellent condition can make the summit in three days round-trip, but four would be more comfortable. There is a considerable elevation gain, so expect freezing weather even in summer and snow in winter. Altitude sickness can also be a problem. En route you pass through *nene* country, with a good chance to spot these lava-adapted geese. Fences keep out feral goats, so remember to close gates after you. The first cabin is at Red

Hill (10,035 feet) and the second is on the rim of Moku'aweoweo Caldera (13,250 feet) at the mountaintop. Water is from roof catchments and should be boiled. Mauna Loa's oval-shape Moku'aweoweo Caldera is more than three miles long and 1.5 miles wide and has vertical walls towering 600 feet. At each end is a smaller round pit crater. From November to May, if there is snow, steam rises from the caldera. The two-mile-long **Cabin Trail** runs along the south rim of the summit caldera, while the 2.5-mile-long **Summit Trail** slips along the north rim to the highest point. The 3.5-mile **Observatory Trail** will also get you to the summit from the Mauna Loa NOAA Weather Observatory on the north slope, but you must ascend via the Saddle Road. The summit treats you to a sweeping panorama that includes the great majority of the Big Island and Haleakala on Maui.

Special Notes

Everything in the park—flora and fauna, rocks, buildings, trails, etc.—is protected by federal law. Be respectful and do not carry anything away with you! Do not climb on any ancient rock structures and do not deface any petroglyph carvings. The ***nene,*** Hawaii's state bird, is endangered. By feeding these birds, visitors have taught them to stand in parking lots and by the roadside. What appears to be a humane and harmless practice actually helps kill these rare birds. Being run over by automobiles has become the leading cause of death of adult birds in the park. Please look, but do not try to approach, feed, or harass the *nene* in any way.

Bicycles are permitted in the park on paved roads only and paved sections of the Crater Rim Trail.

Hiking

There are over 150 miles of hiking trails within the park. One long trail heads up the flank of Mauna Loa to its top; a spiderweb of trails loops around and across Kilauea Caldera and into the adjoining craters; and from a point along the Chain of Craters Road, another trail heads east toward the source of the most recent volcanic activity. But by far the greatest number of trails, and those with the greatest total distance, are those that cut through the Ka'u Desert and along the barren and isolated coast. Many have shelters, and trails that require overnight stays provide cabins or primitive campsites.

Because of the possibility of an eruption or earthquake, it is *imperative* to check in at park headquarters, where you can also pick up current trail information and excellent maps. In fact, a hiking permit is required for most trails outside the Crater Rim Drive area and the stretch along the coast beyond the end of Chain of Craters Drive. Pick up your free permit no more than one day in advance. When hiking, wear long pants and closed-toe shoes or boots. Much of the park is hot and dry, so carry plenty of drinking water. Wear a hat, sunscreen, and sunglasses, but don't forget raingear because it often rains in the green areas of the park. Stay on trails and stay away from steep edges, cracks, new lava flows and any area where lava is flowing into the sea.

If you will be hiking along the trails in the Kilauea Caldera, the free park maps are sufficient to navigate your way. To aid with hikes elsewhere, it's best to purchase and use larger and more detailed topographical maps. Two that are readily available and of high quality are the *Hawaii Volcanoes National Park* by Trails Illustrated and the Earthwalk Press's *Hawaii Volcanoes National Park Recreation Map.*

Kilauea Caldera

Many sights of Hawaii Volcanoes National Park are arranged one after another along **Crater Rim Drive.** Most of these sights are the "drive-up" variety, but plenty of major and minor trails lead off here and there.

Expect to spend a long full day atop Kilauea to take in all the sights, and never forget that you're on a rumbling volcano where a misstep or loss of concentration at the wrong moment can lead to severe injury or even death. Try to arrive by 9 A.M. with a picnic lunch to save time and hassles. Kilauea Caldera, at 4,000 feet, is about 10°F cooler than the coast. It's often overcast, and there can be showers. Wear walking shoes and bring a sweater and/or windbreaker. Binoculars, sunglasses, and a hat will also come in handy.

Small children, pregnant women, and people with respiratory ailments should note that the fumes from the volcano can cause problems. Stay away from sulfur vents and don't overdo it, and you should be fine.

A very dramatic way to experience the awesome power of the volcano is to take a helicopter tour. The choppers are perfectly suited for the maneuverability necessary to get an intimate bird's-eye view. The pilots will fly you over the areas offering the most activity, often dipping low over lava pools, skimming still-glowing flows, and circling the towering steam clouds rising from where lava meets the sea. When activity is really happening, tours are jammed, and prices, like lava fountains, go sky-high. Remember, however, that these tours are increasingly resented by hikers and anyone else trying to have a quiet experience, and that new regulations might limit flights over the lava area.

VISITORS CENTER AREA

The best place to start is at the Visitors Center and Park Headquarters. The turn-off is clearly marked along Hwy. 11 at mile marker 30. By midmorning it's jammed, so try to be an early bird. The center is well run by the National Park Service, which offers a free film about geology and volcanism, with tremendous highlights of past eruptions and plenty of detail on Hawaiian culture and natural history. It runs every hour on the hour starting at 9 A.M. Free ranger-led tours of the nearby area are also given on a regular basis, and their start times and meeting places are posted near the center's front doors. Also posted are After Dark in the Park educational interpretive program activities. A self-guided natural history museum gives more information about the geology of the area, with plenty of exhibits on flora and fauna. You will greatly enrich your visit if you take a half-hour tour of the museum, even though more volcano-specific information is available at the state-of-the-art Thomas A. Jaggar Museum a few minutes up the road.

For safety's sake, anyone trekking to the backcountry *must* register with the rangers at the Visitors Center, especially during times of eruption. Do not be foolhardy! There is no charge for camping, and rangers can give you up-to-the-minute information on trails, backcountry shelters, and cabins. Trails routinely close due to lava flows, tremors, and rock slides. The rangers cannot help you if they don't know where you are. Many day trails leading into the caldera from the rim road are easy walks that need no special preparation. The backcountry trails can be very challenging, and detailed maps (highly recommended) are sold at the center along with special-interest geology and natural history publications prepared by the Hawaii Natural History Association. The Visitors Center is open daily 7:45 A.M.–5 P.M.; call 808/985-6000 for trail, camping, or volcanic activity information.

For those who are not traveling by rental car, the public Hele-On Bus stops once a day in front of the Visitors Center Monday–Friday. There are no scheduled stops on weekends. Pick-up for the bus going to Hilo is at 8 A.M. and the cost is $2.25 for a ticket and $1 for a backpack. Coming from Hilo, the bus leaves at 2:40 P.M. from the Mo'oheau Bus Terminal downtown and arrives at Volcano about 3:45 P.M.

Volcano House

Have you ever dreamed of sleeping with a goddess? Well, you can cuddle up with Pele by staying at Volcano House. If your plans don't include an overnight stop, go in for a look. Sometimes this is impossible, because not only do tour buses from the Big Island disgorge here, but tour groups are flown in from Honolulu as well. A stop at the bar provides refreshments and a tremendous view of the crater. Volcano House still has the feel of a country inn. This particular building dates from the 1940s, but the site has remained the same since a grass hut was perched on the rim of the crater by a sugar planter in 1846. He charged $1 a night for lodging. A steady stream of

notable visitors has come ever since: almost all of Hawaii's kings and queens dating from the middle of the 19th century, as well as royalty from Europe. Mark Twain was a guest, followed by Franklin Roosevelt. Most recently, a contingent of astronauts lodged here and used the crater floor to prepare for walking on the moon. In 1866 a larger grass hut replaced the first, and in 1877 a wooden hotel was built. It is now the Volcano Art Center and has been moved just across the road. In 1885, an expansion added 14 rooms and the dining room, and 35 more rooms were constructed in the mid-1920s. An accident caused the hotel to burn down in 1940, but it was rebuilt the next year.

The person who owned/operated Volcano House the longest was George Lycurgus, who took over management of the hotel in the 1890s. His son, Nick, followed him and managed the hotel until 1969. Since 1986, the hotel has once again been under local management as a concessionaire to the park service.

Volcano Art Center

Art and history buffs should walk across the street to the Volcano Art Center, 808/967-7565, which is the original 1877 Volcano House, Hawaii's oldest hotel. You not only get to see some fine arts and crafts, but you can take a self-guided tour of this mini-museum, open daily 9 A.M.–5 P.M. except Christmas. A new show featuring one of the many superlative island artists on display is presented monthly, and there are always ongoing demonstrations and special events. Artworks on display are in a variety of media, including canvas, paper, wood, glass, metal, ceramic, fiber, and photographs. There is also a profusion of less expensive but distinctive items like posters, cards, and earthy basketry made from natural fibers collected locally. One of the functions of the art center is to provide interpretation for the national park. All of the 350 or so artists who exhibit here do works that in some way relate to Hawaii's environment and culture. Volcano Art Center is one of the finest art galleries in the entire state, boasting works from the best the islands have to offer. Definitely make this a stop.

As a community-oriented organization, the Volcano Art Center sponsors classes and workshops in arts, crafts, and language; an Elderhostel program; and a season of performing arts, which includes musical concerts, dance performances, and stage plays. Some involve local performers, while others headline visiting artists. Performances, classes, and workshops take place at the Kilauea Theater at the military camp or in town at the Old Japanese Schoolhouse. Tickets for performances are sold individually at local outlets or you can buy a season ticket. For current information and pricing, call the center office at 808/967-8222 or check out the art center website at www.volcanoartcenter.org for what's happening.

CRATER RIM DRIVE

There are so many intriguing nooks and crannies to stop at along Crater Rim Drive that you'll have to force yourself to be picky if you intend to cover the park in one day. Crater Rim Drive is a circular route; it matters little which way you proceed. Take your choice, but the following sights are listed counterclockwise beginning from Kilauea Visitors Center. Along this road you will travel from a tropical zone into desert, then through a volcanic zone before returning to lush rainforest. The change is often immediate and differences dramatic. Keep this in mind as you travel around the caldera. Your biggest problem on this route will be timing your arrival at the "drive-in" sights to avoid the steady stream of tour buses. Also remember that the Jaggar Museum closes at 5 P.M., so be sure to get around to that point with time enough to allow yourself to appreciate what it has to offer.

Sulfur Banks

You can easily walk to Sulfur Banks from the Visitors Center along a 10-minute trail. If you're driving, signs along Crater Rim Drive direct you, and your nose will tell you when you're close. As you approach these fumaroles, the earth surrounding them turns a deep reddish-brown, covered over in yellowish-green sulfur. The rising steam is caused by surface water leaking into the

cracks where it becomes heated and rises as vapor. Kilauea releases hundreds of tons of sulfur gases every day, with Sulfur Banks being an example. This gaseous activity stunts the growth of vegetation. And when atmospheric conditions create a low ceiling, the gases sometimes cause the eyes and nose to water. The area is best avoided by those with heart and lung conditions.

Steam Vents

Within a half mile you'll come to Steam Vents, which are also fumaroles, but without sulfur. The entire field behind the partitioned area steams. The feeling is like being in a sauna. There are no strong fumes to contend with here, just the tour buses. A short hike from here leads to the Crater Rim Trail, where you can view the Steaming Bluff, which is more pronounced when the temperature is cooler, such as early in the morning. **Kilauea Military Camp** is located beyond the vents and is not open to the public except for community events at the theater, the bowling alley, and the cafeteria. The camp serves as an R&R facility for active duty and retired military personnel, and certain other government employees.

Observatory and Museum

Some distance farther is **Kilauea Overlook,** as good a spot as any to get a look into the caldera, and there are picnic tables near the parking lot. Here too is **Uwekahuna (Wailing Priest) Bluff,** where the *kahuna* made offerings of appeasement to Pele. A Hawaiian prayer commemorates their religious rites. Unless you're stopping for lunch or making your own (appropriate) offering, it's perhaps better to continue on to the observatory and museum, where you not only have the view outside but get a scientific explanation of what's happening around you.

The **Hawaiian Volcano Observatory,** http://hvo.wr.usgs.gov, has been keeping tabs on the volcanic activity in the area since the turn of the 20th century. The actual observatory is filled with delicate seismic equipment and is closed to the public, but a lookout nearby gives you a dentist's view into the mouth of Halema'uma'u

Crater (House of Ferns), Pele's home. Steam rises and you can feel the power, but until 1924 the view was even more phenomenally spectacular: a lake of molten lava. The lava has since crusted over and the floor is again black. Scientists do not predict a recurrence in the near future, but no one knows Pele's mind. This is a major stop for the tour buses. Information plaques in the immediate area tell of the history and volcanology of the park. One points out a spot from which to observe the perfect shield volcano form of Mauna Loa—most times too cloudy to see. Another reminds you that you're in the middle of the Pacific, an incredible detail you tend to forget when atop these mountains.

The newest addition to the national park is located next door to the observatory, and offers a fantastic multi-media display of the amazing geology and volcanology of the area. The state-of-the-art **Thomas A. Jaggar Museum,** complete with a miniseries of spectacular photos on movable walls, topographical maps, inspired paintings, and video presentations, is open daily 8:30 A.M.–5 P.M., admission free. The expert staff constantly upgrades the displays to keep the public informed on the newest eruptions. The 30–45 minutes it takes to explore the teaching museum will enhance your understanding of the volcanic area immeasurably. Do yourself a favor and visit this museum before setting out on any explorations, and stop at the book/gift shop for something to take home.

Halema'uma'u Crater

A string of interesting stops follows the observatory. One points out the Ka'u Desert, an inhospitable lava plain studded with a few scraggly plants. Next comes the **Southwest Rift,** a series of cracks running from Kilauea's summit to the sea. You can observe at a glance that you are standing directly over a major earthquake fault. Dated lava flows follow in rapid succession until you arrive at **Halema'uma'u Overlook** parking lot. A well-maintained cinder trail to the overlook is only one-quarter mile long and gives an up-close view of the crater. The area is rife with fumaroles leaking sulfur dioxide and should be avoided by those with respiratory problems. At the end you're treated to a full explanation of Halema'uma'u. Until this crater crusted over after an explosion in 1942, Halema'uma'u could be seen as a red glow and sometimes as a fabulous display of spouting lava from the Volcano House Hotel. From here, two trails make tracks across the caldera floor to the far side and back to park headquarters. Farther along the road is a spot that was once an observation point that caved in. You won't take the ground under your feet for granted!

Keanakako'i Crater

Keanakako'i Overlook is set on the rim of the diminutive crater of the same name. This was a prehistoric adze quarry from which superior stone was gathered to make tools. It was destroyed by a flow in 1877. If that seems in the remote past, realize that you just crossed a section of road that was naturally paved over with lava from a "quickie" eruption in 1982!

Devastation Trail

Most visitors hike along the half-mile Devastation Trail, which could aptly be renamed "Regeneration Trail." The half mile it covers is fascinating, one of the most-photographed areas in the park. It leads across a field devastated by a tremendous eruption from **Kilauea Iki** (Little Kilauea) in 1959, when fountains of lava shot 1,900 feet into the air. The area was once an 'ohi'a forest that was denuded of limbs and leaves, then choked by black pumice and ash. The vegetation has regenerated since then, and the recuperative power of the flora is part of an ongoing study. Blackberries, not indigenous to Hawaii, are slowly taking over. The good news is that you'll be able to pick and eat blackberries as you hike along the paved trail, but the rangers are waging a mighty war against them. Notice that many of the trees have sprouted aerial roots trailing down from the branches: this is total adaptation to the situation, as these roots don't normally appear. As you move farther along the trail, tufts of grass and bushes peek out of the pumice. Then the surroundings become totally barren and look like the nightmare of a nuclear holocaust.

ROBERT NILSEN

'ohi'a and fern forest

Thurston Lava Tube

If the Devastation Trail produced a sense of melancholy, the Thurston Lava Tube, otherwise called Nahuku, makes you feel like Alice walking through the looking glass. Inside is a fairy kingdom. As you approach, the expected signboard gives you the lowdown on the geology and flora and fauna of the area. Take the five minutes to educate yourself. The paved trail starts as a steep incline, which quickly enters a fern forest. All about you are fern trees, vibrantly green, with native birds flitting here and there. As you approach the lava tube, it seems almost manmade, like a perfectly formed tunnel leading into a mine. Ferns and moss hang from the entrance, and if you stand just inside the entrance looking out, it's as if the very air is tinged with green. If there were such things as elves and gnomes, they would surely live here. The walk through takes about 10 minutes, undulating through the narrow passage. At the other end, the fantasy world of ferns and moss reappears.

Hikes

The **Crater Rim Loop Trail** begins at Volcano House and parallels Crater Rim Drive. Hiking the entire 11.5 miles takes a full day, but you can take it in sections as time and energy permit. It's a well-marked and well-maintained trail, mostly paved or cinder; all you need are proper clothing, water, and determination. For your efforts, you'll get an up-close view of all of the sights outlined along Crater Rim Drive plus other views and vistas.

Halema'uma'u Trail provides some of the best scenery for the effort. It begins at park headquarters and descends into Kilauea Caldera, running about 2.5 miles to the Halema'uma'u Crater pit and crossing lava fields that are only 20–25 years old. Circle back via the Byron Ledge Trail, about three miles long, or arrange to be picked up at the Halema'uma'u parking area on the south side of the Crater Rim Drive.

Kilauea Iki Trail begins at the Thurston Lava Tube parking lot or at the Kilauea Iki Overlook. One of the most popular, easiest, and picturesque hikes in the park, this four-mile trail generally takes two hours round-trip and passes over the floor of Kilauea Iki Crater, which was a sea of lava in 1959 when an exceedingly tall spume of lava spouted from the crater rim, creating the most spectacular show the volcano has performed in memory. Start by taking the section of the Crater Rim Trail that follows the rim of the Kilauea Iki Crater, then branch west and descend the western edge of the crater wall. From there it's back across the crater floor, where you pass the spouting site and adjacent ash hill, and a zigzag up the eastern side. Or do it in the reverse. If conditions are right, the cracked and buckled floor of the pit might steam as you walk across. It's easy to link up with the Byron Ledge Trail near the west end of this loop, from where you can walk into Halemaʻumaʻu Caldera or back to park headquarters.

On the south side of Kilauea Iki Crater, the one-mile-long **Devastation Trail** links Puʻu Puaʻi Overlook and the Devastation Trail parking area, from where there is a link trail to the Byron Ledge Trail on the Kilauea Caldera rim.

A shorter hike that takes you along the north edge of the rim and back via the Sulfur Banks is the **ʻIliahi (Sandalwood) Trail,** a hike of just over one mile round-trip. Along this hike, you're not only treated to the sights and sounds of trees and birds, but also to the mysteries of steam vents, faults, and cracks.

Alternately, go left out of Volcano House and follow the **Earthquake Trail,** a section of the Crater Rim Loop Trail, along **Waldron Ledge.** The easy trail takes you along a paved section of the old Chain of Craters Road that was damaged by a 6.6 magnitude quake in 1983. Sections of the road are buckled, and parts have slid down the edge of the rim.

Kilauea Iki Crater with Kilauea Caldera and Halemaʻumaʻu Crater in the background. A hike across the floor of Kilauea Iki Crater is one of the easiest in the park.

Chain of Craters Road

The Chain of Craters Road that once linked the park with Kalapana village on the coast was severed by an enormous lava flow in 1995 and can now only be driven to where the flow crosses the road beyond the Holei Sea Arch. Remember that the volcanic activity in this area is unpredictable, and that the road can be closed at a moment's notice. As you head down the road, every bend—and they are uncountable—offers a panoramic vista. There are numerous pull-offs; plaques provide geological information about past eruptions and lava flows. The grandeur, power, and immensity of the forces that have been creating the earth from the beginning of time are right before your eyes. Although the road starts off in the 'ohi'a forest, it opens to broader views and soon cuts diagonally across the *pali* to reach the littoral plain. Much of this section of the road was buried under lava flows from 1969 to 1974. When the road almost reaches the coast, look for a roadside marker that indicates the Puna Coast Trail. Just across the road is the Pu'u Loa Petroglyph Field trailhead. The lower part of the road is spectacular. Here, blacker-than-black seacliffs, covered by a thin layer of green, abruptly stop at the sea. The surf rolls in, sending up spumes of sea water. In the distance, steam billows into the air where the lava flows into the sea. At road's end you will find a barricade and an information hut that's staffed by park rangers throughout the afternoon and into the evening. Read the information and heed the warnings. The 20-mile drive from atop the volcano to the barricade takes about 30 minutes and drops 3,700 feet in elevation.

While hiking to the lava flow is not encouraged, park staff do not stop you from venturing out. They warn you of the dangers and the reality ahead. Many visitors do make the hike (more than three miles one-way), but there is no trail. The way is over new and rough lava that tears at the bottom of your shoes. If you go in the evening when the spectacle is more apparent, a flashlight with several extra batteries is absolutely necessary. To hike there and back could take three to four hours. If you decide to hike, bring plenty of water. There is no shade or water along the way, and the wind often blows along this coast. Do not hike to or near the edge of the water, as sections of lava could break off without warning. Depending upon how the lava is flowing, it may or not be worth the effort. When the lava is flowing, it is often possible to see the reddish glow at night from the end of the road, but you probably won't see much that's distinguishable unless you use high-power binoculars.

Craters

As you head down Chain of Craters Road you immediately pass a number of depressions for

the old road covered by lava

ROBERT NILSEN

which the road is named. First on the right side is **Lua Manu Crater,** a deep depression now lined with green vegetation. Farther is **Puhimau Crater.** Walk the few steps to the viewing stand at the crater edge for a look. Many people come here to hear the echo of their voices as they talk or sing into this pit. Next comes **Ko'oko'olau Crater,** then **Hi'iaka Crater** and **Pauahi Crater.** Just beyond is a turn-off to the east, which follows a short section of the old road. This road ends at the lava flow, and from here a trail runs as far as **Napau Crater.**

The first mile or more of the Napau Trail takes you over lava from 1974, through forest *kipuka,* past lava tree molds, and up the treed slopes of **Pu'u Huluhulu.** From this cone you have a view down on Mauna Ulu, from which the 1969–74 lava flow disgorged, and east toward **Pu'u O'o** and the currently active volcanic vents, some seven miles distant. Due to the current volcanic activity farther along the rift zone, you will need a permit to day hike beyond Pu'u Huluhulu; the

ROBERT NILSEN

Holei Sea Arch

trail itself may be closed depending upon where the volcanic activity is taking place. However, the trail does continue over the shoulder of Makaopuhi Crater to the primitive campsite at Napau Crater, passing more cones and pit craters, lava flows, and sections of rainforest. A four-hour ranger-led hike out this way runs on Wednesday afternoon only. It's popular and limited to a dozen people, so call to reserve a place at 808/985-6017.

Roadside Sights

For several miles, Chain of Craters Road traverses lava that was laid down about 40 years ago; remnants of the old road can still be seen in spots. There are long stretches of smooth pahoehoe lava interspersed with flows of clinker 'a'a. Here and there, a bit of green pokes through a crack in the rock, bringing new life to this stark landscape. Everywhere you look, you can see the wild "action" of these lava flows, stopped in all their magnificent forms. At one vantage point on the way is **Kealakomo,** a picnic overlook where you have unobstructed views of the coast. Stop and enjoy the sight before proceeding. Several other lookouts and pull-offs have been created along the road to call attention to one sight or another.

The last section of road runs very close the edge of the sea, where cliffs rise up from the pounding surf. Near the end of the road is the **Holei Sea Arch,** a spot where the wave action has undercut the rock to leave a bridge of stone. This is small but a dramatic sight. Enjoy the scene, but don't lean too far out trying to get that perfect picture!

Pu'u Loa Petroglyphs

The walk out to Pu'u Loa Petroglyphs is delightful, highly educational, and takes less than one hour. The trail, although it traverses solid lava, is discernible. The tread of feet over the centuries has smoothed and discolored the rock. As you walk along, note the *ahu,* traditional trail markers that are piles of stone shaped like little Christmas trees. Most of the lava field leading to the petroglyphs is undulating pahoehoe and looks like a frozen sea. You can

ROBERT NILSEN

end of Chain of Craters Road

climb bumps of lava, from eight to 10 feet high, to scout the immediate territory. Mountainside, the *pali* is quite visible and you can pick out the most recent lava flows—the blackest and least vegetated. As you approach the site, the lava changes dramatically and looks like long strands of braided rope.

The petroglyphs are in an area about the size of a soccer field. A wooden walkway encircles most of them and helps to ensure their protection. A common motif of the petroglyphs is a circle with a hole in the middle, like a donut; you'll also see designs of men with triangular-shaped heads. Some rocks are entirely covered with designs, while others have only a symbolic scratch or two. These carvings are impressive more for their sheer numbers than the multiplicity of design. If you stand on the walkway and trek off at the two o'clock position, you'll see a small hill. Go over and down it, and you will discover even better petroglyphs that include a sailing canoe about two feet high. At the back end of the walkway a sign proclaims that Pu'u Loa meant "Long Hill,"

which the Hawaiians turned into the metaphor "Long Life." For countless generations, fathers would come here to place pieces of their infants' umbilical cords into small holes as offerings to the gods to grant long life to their children. Concentric circles surrounded the holes that held the umbilical cords. The entire area, an obvious power spot, screams in utter silence, and the still-strong *mana* is easily felt.

The Big Island has the largest concentration of petroglyphs in the state, and this site holds its greatest number. One estimate puts the number at 28,000!

Waha'ula Heiau

Waha'ula Heiau (Temple of the Red Mouth) radically changed the rituals and practices of the relatively benign Hawaiian religion by introducing the idea of human sacrifice. The 13th century marked the end of the frequent comings and goings between Hawaii and the "Lands to the South" (Tahiti), and began the isolation that would last 500 years until Captain Cook arrived.

Unfortunately, this last influx of Polynesians brought a rash of conquering warriors carrying ferocious gods who lusted for human blood before they would be appeased. Pa'ao, a powerful Tahitian priest, supervised the building of Waha'ula and brought in a new chief, Pili, to strengthen the diminished *mana* of the Hawaiian chiefs due to their practice of intermarriage with commoners. Waha'ula became the foremost *luakini* (human sacrifice) temple in the island kingdom and held this position until the demise of the old ways in 1819. Not at all grandiose, the *heiau* was merely an elevated rock platform smoothed over with pebbles.

Waha'ula lay along the coast road near the eastern end of the park. This entire area is now completely inundated by recent lava flows. Until 1997, the *heiau* itself was a small island in a sea of black lava that miraculously escaped destruction, but in August of that year lava oozed over these 700-year-old walls and filled the compound. Madame Pele has taken back her own.

Other Park Areas

KA'U DESERT

Hilina Pali Road

About two miles down the Chain of Craters Road, the Hilina Pali Road shoots off to the southwest over a narrow roughly paved road all the way to the end at **Hilina Pali Lookout**—about nine miles. Soon after you leave the Chain of Craters Road the vegetation turns drier and you enter the semi-arid Ka'u Desert. The road picks its way around and over old volcanic flows, and you can see the vegetation struggling to maintain a foothold. On the way you pass the Mauna Iki trailhead, Kulanaokuaiki Campground, and former Kipuka Nene Campground—closed to help the *nene* recover their threatened population. You should see geese here, but please leave them alone and definitely don't feed them. The road ends right on the edge of the rift, with expansive views over the benched coastline, from the area of current volcanic flow all the way to South Point. From here, one trail heads down the hill to the coast while another pushes on along the top of the cliff and farther into the dry landscape. At the pali lookout is a pavilion and restrooms, but no drinking water. This is not a pleasure ride as the road is rough, but it is passable. For most it probably isn't worth the time, but for those looking for isolation and a special vantage point, this could be it.

ROBERT NILSEN

Nene inhabit several areas of the park, including sections along the Hilina Pali Road. Please do not disturb these birds.

Ka'u Desert Trails

Ka'u Desert Trail starts along Crater Rim Drive past the Jaggar Museum and heads southwest into the desolation. It runs for about six miles before it meets the Mauna Iki Trail. A second entry to the desert trail starts about eight miles south of the park entrance along Rte. 11, between mile markers 37 and 38. It's a short 20-minute hike from this trailhead to the **Ka'u Desert Footprints.** The trek across the small section of desert is fascinating, and the history of the footprints makes the experience more evocative. The trail is only 1.6 miles round-trip, but allow at least an hour, mostly for observation. The predominant foliage is *'ohi'a* that contrasts with the bleak surroundings—the feeling throughout the area is one of foreboding. You pass a wasteland of 'a'a and pahoehoe lava flows to arrive at the footprints. A metal fence in a sturdy pavilion surrounds the prints, which look as though they're cast in cement. Actually they're formed from pisolites: particles of ash stuck together with moisture, which formed mud that hardened like plaster. Eroded and not very visible, the story of these footprints is far more exciting than the prints themselves.

In 1790 Kamehameha was waging war with Keoua over control of the Big Island. One of Keoua's warrior parties of approximately 80 people attempted to cross the desert while Kilauea was erupting. Toxic gases descended upon them, and the warriors and their families were enveloped and suffocated. They literally died in their tracks, but the preserved footprints, although romanticism would have it otherwise, were probably made by a party of people who came well after the eruption. This unfortunate occurrence was regarded by the Hawaiians as a direct message from the gods proclaiming their support for Kamehameha. Keoua, who could not deny the sacred signs, felt abandoned and shortly thereafter became a human sacrifice at Pu'ukohola Heiau, built by Kamehameha to honor his war god, Kuka'ilimoku.

From the footprints, **Mauna Iki Trail** heads east, crossing a 1974 flow to connect with the Hilina Pali Road at Kulanaokuaiki Campground. You'll have to follow rock cairns some of the way. The Ka'u Desert Trail continues south and swings around to the east, passing Pepeiao Cabin on the way to the Hilina Pali Overlook. From the cabin, **Ka'aha Trail** heads down to and along the coast to Ka'aha Shelter, where it meets a trail coming down from the overlook. From here, the **Puna Coast Trail** mostly parallels the coast, passing Halape and Keauhou shelters and 'Apua Point campsite before it meets the Chain of Craters Road near

the petroglyph site. At the shelters, rain catchment tanks provide drinking water. In 1975, an earthquake rocked this area, generating a tsunami that killed two campers; more than 30 others had to be helicoptered to safety. All campers must register at the Kilauea Visitors Center. Registering will alert authorities to your whereabouts in case of a disaster. Hiking in the Ka'u Desert requires full hiking and camping gear. Bring plenty of water.

SMALL DETOURS
Mauna Loa Road

About 2.5 miles west of the park entrance on the Belt Road, Mauna Loa Road turns off to the north. This road will lead you to the Tree Molds and a bird sanctuary, as well as to the trailhead for the Mauna Loa summit trail. As an added incentive, a minute down this road leaves 99 percent of the tourists behind.

Tree Molds is an ordinary name for an extraordinary place. Turn right off Mauna Loa Road soon after leaving the Belt Road and follow the signs for five minutes. This road runs in to the tree molds area and loops back onto itself. At the loop, a signboard explains what occurred here. In a moment, you realize that you're standing atop a lava flow, and that the scattered potholes were entombed tree trunks, most likely the remains of a once-giant koa forest. Unlike at Lava Tree State Monument, where the magma encased the tree and flowed away, the opposite action happened here. The lava stayed put while the tree trunk burned away, leaving the 15- to 18-foot-deep holes. While the "sights" of this site may not excite some visitors, realizing what happened here and how it happened is an eye-opener.

Kipuka Puaulu is a sanctuary for birds and nature lovers who want to leave the crowds behind, just under three miles from Rte. 11 up Mauna Loa Road. The sanctuary is an island atop an island. A *kipuka* is a piece of land that is surrounded by lava but has not been inundated by it, leaving the original vegetation and land contour intact. A few hundred yards away, small scrub vegetation struggles, but in the sanctuary the trees form a towering canopy a hundred feet tall. The first sign takes you to an ideal picnic area called Bird Park with cooking grills; the second, 100 yards beyond, takes you to Kipuka Puaulu Loop Trail. As you enter the trail, a bulletin board describes the birds and plants, some of the last remaining indigenous fauna and flora in Hawaii. Please follow all rules. The dirt trail is self-guided, and pamphlets describing the stations along the way may be dispensed from a box near the start of the path. The loop is only one mile long, but to really assimilate the area, especially if you plan to do any bird-watching, expect to spend an hour minimum. It doesn't take long to realize that you are privileged to see some of the world's rarest plants, such as a small, nondescript bush called *'a'ali'i*. In the branches of the towering 'ohi'a trees you might see an *'elepaio* or an *'apapane,* two birds native to Hawaii. Common finches and Japanese white eyes are imported birds that are here to stay. There's an example of a lava tube, a huge koa tree, and an explanation of how ash from eruptions provided soil and nutrients for the forest. Blue morning glories have taken over entire hillsides. Once considered a pest and aggressively eradicated, they have recently been given a reprieve and are now considered good ground cover—perhaps even indigenous. When you do come across a native Hawaiian plant, it seems somehow older, almost prehistoric. If a precontact Hawaiian could come back today, he or she would recognize only a few plants and trees seen here in this preserve. As you leave, listen for the melodies coming from the treetops, and hope the day never comes when no birds sing. To hear the birds at their best, come in early morning or late afternoon.

Mauna Loa Road continues westward and gains elevation for approximately 10 miles. It passes through thick forests of lichen-covered koa trees, cuts across **Kipuka Ki,** and traverses the narrow **Ke'amoku Flow.** At the end of the pavement, at 6,662 feet, you find a parking area and lookout. If the weather is cooperating, you'll be able to see much of the mountainside; if not, your field of vision will be much restricted. A trail leads from here to the summit of Mauna Loa. It takes two long and difficult days to hike. Under no circumstances should it be attempted by novice hikers or those unprepared for cold alpine conditions. At times, this road may be closed due to extreme fire conditions.

'Ola'a Forest

Off Rte. 11 close to Volcano village, turn on Wright Road (or County Rd. 148) heading toward Mauna Loa. On a clear morning you can see the mountain dead ahead. Continue for approximately three miles until you see a barbed-wire fence. The fence is distinctive because along it you'll see a profusion of *hapu'u* ferns that are in sharp contrast to the adjacent ranch property. Here is an *'ola'a* rainforest, part of the national park and open to the public, although park biologists like to keep it quiet. Be aware that the area is laced with cracks and lava tubes. Most are small ankle twisters, but others can open up under you like a glacial crevasse. Here is a true example of a quickly disappearing native forest. What's beautiful about an endemic forest is that virtually all species coexist wonderfully. The ground cover is a rich mulch of decomposing ferns and leaves, fragrant and amazingly soft.

Although open to the public, entrance to this area is *not* encouraged. There are no maintained trails, no well-recognized and marked trailheads, and no services whatsoever. It's a thick, dense forest that provides no easy visible clues to direction or location, and the park has no maps of the forest that it gives out to visitors. While there are some hunting trails that lace the area, it is not user-friendly and it's very easy to get lost. If you get lost and if no one knows you're in there, it could be life threatening. If you do venture in, bring a compass, a cell phone, plenty of water, warm clothing, and rain gear. Leave your name and telephone number with someone on the outside and set aside a time to contact that person. Also, be aware that you may be trampling native species or inadvertently introducing alien species. The park service is trying to bring the area back to its native Hawaiian rainforest condition through eradication of alien plants and elimination of feral pigs.

Practicalities

ACCOMMODATIONS

If you intend to spend the night atop Kilauea, your choices of accommodations are few and simple. Volcano House provides the only hotel, but cabins are available at the campgrounds, and there are a handful of tent campsites along the hiking trails. For military personnel, lodging is offered at the Kilauea Military Camp.

Cabins and Camping

The main campground in Volcanoes, **Namakani Paio,** clearly marked off Rte. 11, is situated in a stately eucalyptus grove. There is no charge for tent camping and no reservations are required. It's first-come, first-served. There are cooking grills by each campsite, but no wood or drinking water is provided. While there are toilets, there are no shower facilities for those camping and hiking

within the park, so make sure you're with people who like you a whole bunch. Ten small **cabins** are available here through Volcano House. Each accommodates four people and costs $40 single or double, and $8 each for a third or fourth person. A $12 refundable key deposit gives access to the shower and toilet, and a $20 refundable deposit gets you linens, soap, towels, and a blanket (extra sleeping bag recommended). Each cabin contains one double bed and two single bunk beds and an electric light, but no electrical outlets. Outside are a picnic table and barbecue grill, but you must provide your own charcoal and cooking utensils. Check in at Volcano House after 3 P.M. and check out by noon.

There are also camping spaces and restrooms at **Kulanaokuaiki,** located halfway down Hilina Pali Road. As at Namakani Paio, these are on a first-come, first-served basis. No reservations are

cabins at Namakani Paio Campground

ROBERT NILSEN

required and no fee is charged. As it sits in the middle of this arid desert, it's hot, dry, and has little shade. No drinking water is provided.

For backcountry overnight camping, apply at the Kilauea Visitors Center (7:45 A.M.–4:45 P.M.) for a free permit no earlier than the day before you plan to hike. Camping is permitted only in established sites and at trail shelters. No open fires are permitted. Carry all the drinking water you will need, and carry out all that you take in.

Volcano House

If you decide to lodge at Volcano House, P.O. Box 53, Hawaii Volcanoes National Park, HI 96718, 808/967-7321 or 800/325-3535, don't be frightened away by the daytime crowds. They disappear with the sun. Since the mid-1980s, Volcano House has gone through a slow renovation and once again shines as what it always has been: a quiet country inn. The 42 rooms are comfy but old-fashioned. Who needs a pool or TV when you can look out your window into a volcano caldera? To the left of the reception area indoors, a crackling fireplace warms you from the chill in the mountain air, and this fire has burned virtually nonstop since the early days of the hotel. In front of the fireplace are stuffed leather chairs and a wonderful wooden rocker. Paintings and vintage photographs of the Hawaiian kings and queens of the Kamehameha line and magnificent photos of eruptions of the mountain hang on the walls. The hotel, owned and operated by a *kama'aina* family, is an authorized concession of the park. Room rates are main building with crater view $165–185, non-crater view $135; Ohia Wing standard room $85, garden view $95; $15 extra for each additional person. No charge for children 12 and under occupying the same room as their parents. Rooms include koa wood furniture, Hawaiian quilted comforters, a telephone, and room heater, and each has a private bath or shower. Efficiently run, the hotel has a restaurant, lounge, two gift shops, 24-hour front desk service, maid service, and safe-deposit boxes. Besides that, you could hardly get closer to the crater if you tried.

Kilauea Military Camp

One mile west of the park entrance, within the park boundary, is the Kilauea Military Camp. Offering rooms and meals, this facility is open to active duty and retired military personnel, civilian employees of the Department of Defense, and their families. Available are dormitory rooms, one-, two-, and three-bedroom cottages, and apartments. Services include a lounge bar, recreation facility, tennis courts, athletic fields, a general store, post office, Laundromat, and gas station—all for guests only. Open to the public are the cafeteria, which serves three meals a day; the theater, which hosts community events; a bowling alley with state-of-the-art equipment and its snack bar, open daily 3–10 P.M. Tours of the island can be arranged by the front office staff, and shuttle pick-up from the Hilo airport can also be arranged with advance notice. For additional information, availability, and fees, write KMC Lodging, A Joint Services Recreation Center, Attn.: Reservations, Hawaii Volcanoes National Park, HI 96718; 808/967-8333, fax 808/967-8343, reservations@kmc-volcano.com, www.kmc-volcano.com.

FOOD AND SHOPPING

Food

Volcano House Restaurant offers a breakfast buffet daily 7–10:30 A.M. for $9.50 or $5.50 for children ages 2–11, that includes cereals, milk, and juices, an assortment of pastries, pancakes topped with fruit and macadamia nuts, sweet bread French toast, scrambled eggs, and Portuguese sausage. A lighter continental breakfast is $5.50. The lunch buffet, $12.50 adult or $7.50 per child, is served daily 11 A.M.–2 P.M. Often terribly crowded because of tour buses, the lunch buffet offers tossed greens and assorted vegetables, fresh fruit platters, stuffed mahimahi, pot roast, honey-dipped chicken, and drinks. If there are too many tour buses parked outside during the lunch hour, give it a miss and try later. Dinner, nightly 5:30–9 P.M., starts with appetizers like sautéed mushrooms and a fruit platter. It moves on to entrées like seafood linguine, scampi, New York steak, catch of the day, and roast prime rib, the specialty. Most entrées run $15–22. A child's menu is also available with dishes under $8. The quality is good, portions large, and the prices reasonable; reservations are recommended. More than the food, however, the view out the big picture window over the caldera is worth the price.

For a nightcap, Uncle George's Lounge, just off the main entry, is a perfect spot to relax and watch the crater disappear into the dark. It closes when the restaurant stops serving.

The **KMC cafeteria** is open to the public for buffet-style dining three meals a day: 7–9:30 A.M., 11 A.M.–1 P.M., and 5:30–8 P.M. Fairly nondescript, this cafeteria is pleasant enough and scrupulously clean. Warmers on the buffet line keep the food trays steaming like the steam vents

down the road. While not exceptional in any way, the food is hearty, filling, military fare that's very easy on the pocketbook.

Shopping

If you are after an exquisite piece of art, a unique memento, or an inexpensive but distinctive souvenir, be sure to visit the **Volcano Art Center.** It's a treat.

When your little tummy starts grumbling, head for the snack shop at the hotel to appease it; it's open 9 A.M.–5 P.M. The hotel also has two gift shops that carry a wide assortment of tourist gifts, crafts, postcards, film, souvenirs, and a selection of logo wear. They are open 7 A.M.–7:15 P.M. Along the road, the Jaggar Museum has a small gift shop that carries a fine selection of books and gifts relating to Hawaii's natural environment.

Ka'u

The Ka'u district is as simple and straightforward as the broad, open face of a country gentleman. It's not boring, and it does hold pleasant surprises for those willing to look. Formed entirely from the massive slopes of Mauna Loa, the district presents some of the most ecologically diverse land in the islands. The bulk of it stretches 50 miles from north to south and almost 30 miles from east to west, tumbling from the snow-capped mountains through the cool green canopy of highland forests. The domain of sugar until 1995, its middle elevations now support stands of macadamia nut trees, eucalyptus, koa, and coffee. At lower elevations it becomes pastureland of belly-deep grass ending in blistering-hot black sands along the coast that are encircled by a necklace of foamy white sea. Much has been scored by recent lava flows and shaken by powerful earthquakes—the worst in 1868. At the bottom of Ka'u is **Ka Lae** (South Point), the southernmost tip of Hawaii and the southernmost point in the United States. It lies at a latitude 500 miles farther south than Miami and twice that below Los Angeles. Ka Lae was probably the first landfall made by the Polynesian explorers on the islands, and the entire area, particularly the more watered coastal spots, seems to have been heavily populated by early immigrants. A variety of archaeological remains support this belief.

Punalu'u's black-sand beach

ROBERT NILSEN

Most people dash through Ka'u on the Hawaii Belt Road, heading to or from Volcanoes National Park. Its main towns, **Pahala** and **Na'alehu,** are little more than pit stops. The Belt Road follows the old Mamalahoa Trail where, for centuries, nothing moved faster than a contented man's stroll. Ka'u's beauties, mostly tucked away down secondary roads, are hardly given a look by most unknowing visitors. If you take the time and get off the beaten track, you'll discover black- and green-sand beaches, turtles basking on the shore, Wild West rodeos, a Tibetan Buddhist temple, and an electricity farm sprouting windmill generators. The upper slopes and broad pasturelands are the domain of hunters, hikers, and *paniolo,* who still ride the range on sure-footed horses. In Ka'u are sleepy plantation towns that don't even know how quaint they are, and beach parks where you can count on finding a secluded spot to pitch a tent. Time in Ka'u moves slowly, and *aloha* still forms the basis of day-to-day life.

The majority of Ka'u's pleasures are accessible by standard rental car, but many secluded coastal spots can be reached only by 4WD. For example, **Ka'iliki'i,** just west of Ka Lae, was an important fishing village in times past. A few archaeological remains are found here, and the beach has a green cast due to the lava's high olivine content. Few tourists ever visit, although hardy souls come to angle the coastal waters. Spots of this type abound, especially in Ka'u's remote sections. But civilization has found Ka'u as well: When you pass mile marker 63, look down to the coast and notice a stand of royal palms and a large brackish pond. This is Luahinivai Beach, one of the finest on the island, where country and western star Loretta Lynn built a fabulous home. Those willing to abandon their cars and hike the sparsely populated coast or interior of Ka'u are rewarded with areas unchanged and untouched for generations.

Towns and Sights

PAHALA

Some 22 miles southwest of Volcano is Pahala, clearly marked off Rte. 11. The Hawaii Belt Road flashes past this town, but if you drive into it, you'll find one of the best-preserved examples of a classic sugar town in the islands. Not long ago, the hillsides around Pahala were blanketed by fields of cane and dotted with camps of plantation workers. It was once gospel that sugar would be "king" in these parts forever, but the huge mill is gone, and the background whir of a modern macadamia nut-processing plant now breaks the stillness.

With 1,500 people, Pahala has the largest population in the district, even though some people left with the closing of the mill. In town you'll find the basics—a gas station, district hospital, small shopping center, post office, several churches and temples, a Bank of Hawaii office, Mizuno's Superette, and a plate lunch restaurant. Recently, Tex Drive-In of Honoka'a has

opened a branch in Pahala, so now you're able to get excellent quality local food and hot *malasadas* at a reasonable price. On the outskirts of town, just beyond where the mill used to stand, is Pahala Plantation Store. This shop is open daily, selling gifts, souvenirs, some artwork, coffee, snacks, T-shirts, books, and more.

Pahala Plantation Cottages

When the sugar mill closed, many people left Pahala and the surrounding area. The town slumped but never disappeared. It has hung on and has slowly managed to infuse life back into itself. Recently, travelers have started to discover what a peaceful area of the island this is and what a fine example Pahala is of a former plantation community. To cater to the traveling public, Pahala Plantation Cottages offers a number of vacation rental accommodations in town, including the renovated seven-bedroom, four-bath plantation manager's house, which rents for $500 a night or $85 a room. Other nearby renovated

To Kailua-Kona

Pu'u O Ka'oka'o
(6,875 ft.)

KA'U

WOOD VALLEY TEMPLE

MANUKA STATE WAYSIDE

MANUKA NATURAL AREA RESERVE

Hawaiian Ocean View Estates

MACADAMIA NUT ORCHARDS

RUINS

Kauna Point

Kaupua'a Bay

KULA KAI CAVERNS

BOUGAINVILLEA BED AND BREAKFAST

SOUTH POINT B&B

Pahala

SCENIC OVERLOOK

Kahuku Ranch

KAUAHA'AO CHURCH

SEA MOUNTAIN RESORT

MARK TWAIN MONKEYPOD TREE

SEA MOUNTAIN AT PUNALU'U GOLF COURSE

Punalu'u

PETROGLYPHS

Wai'ohinu

HOKULOA CHURCH

KAMAO'A RD.

LOOKOUT

WHITTINGTON BEACH COUNTY PARK

MARGO'S CORNER

Na'alehu

PUNALU'U BEACH COUNTY PARK

MACADAMIA MEADOWS FARM B&B.

Honu'apo Bay

Waipouli Bay

KAMOA WIND FARM

Kimo Point

KA'ILIKI'I SITE

Manaka'a Point

Waikapuna Bay

SOUTH POINT RD.

HAWAI'I BELT RD.

0   4 mi
0   4 km

Ka Lae (South Point)

Ka'alu'alu Bay

Onikinalu Cove

Green Sand Beach

Mahana Bay

Kaulana Bay

PACIFIC

© SANDRA E. BISIGNANI TRUST AND AVALON TRAVEL PUBLISHING, INC.

KA'U

and spacious one- to four-bedroom plantation cottages run $85–185 a night and are sizable enough for a family. As each has a full kitchen, no meals are provided. For information, contact Julie Neal at P.O. Box 940, Pahala, HI 96777, 808/928-9811, mahalo@aloha.net, www.pahala-hawaii.com.

Wood Valley Temple

Also known as Nechung Dorje Drayang Ling, or Immutable Island of Melodious Sound, the Wood Valley Temple, P.O. Box 250, Pahala, HI 96777, 808/928-8539, fax 808/928-6271, nechung@aloha.net, www.planet-hawaii.com/nechung, is true to its name. This simple vermilion and yellow Tibetan Buddhist temple sits like a sparkling jewel surrounded by the emerald-green velvet of its manicured grounds, which are scented by an aromatic stand of majestic eucalyptus trees. The grounds, like a botanical garden, vibrate with life and energy.

The Buddha gave the world essentially 84,000 different teachings to pacify, purify, and develop the

mind. In Tibetan Buddhism there are four major lineages, and this temple, founded by Tibetan master Nechung Rinpoche, is a classic synthesis of all four. Monks, lama, and scholars from different schools of Buddhism are periodically invited to come and lecture as resident teachers. The Dalai Lama came in 1980 to dedicate the temple and graced the temple once again in 1994 when he addressed an audience here of more than 3,500 people. Programs vary, but people genuinely interested in Buddhism come here for meditation and soul-searching as well as for peace, quiet, relaxation, and direction. Morning and evening services at 7 A.M. and 6:30 P.M. are led by the Tibetan monk in residence. Formal classes depend upon which guest teacher is in residence.

Buddhists strive to become wise and compassionate people. The focus of the temple is to bring together all meditation and church groups in the community. Plenty of local Christian and Buddhist groups use the nonsectarian facilities. Any group that is spiritually, socially, and community oriented and that has a positive outlook

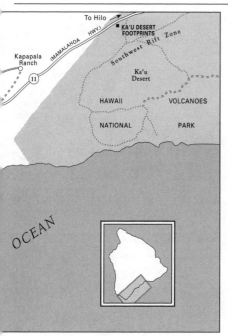

only one night. Weekly discounts and group rates are available. Definitely call or write to make reservations and get directions.

Kapapala Ranch

Even though sugar is gone, ranching is not. The 24,000-acre Kapapala Ranch still manages a working enterprise between the town of Pahala and the national park and offers excursions onto the property. A two-hour trail ride runs $75 per person, a 4WD day-long work adventure with the owner is $100 per person, limit two, while a 4WD tour runs $150 an hour with a two-hour minimum for up to five passengers. Also offered is an overnight camping experience on ranch land that can be done by horse, hiking with pack mules, or vehicle. Arrange cost with the ranch. Near the ranch home, several of the ranch hand cabins have been refurbished and turned into cozy and homey guest cottages. Able to sleep up to six, each has a full kitchen, bathroom, and bedrooms. For reservations, rates, and other inquiries, call 808/968-6585, fax 808/968-6059, pre@bigisland.net, www.kapapala.com.

is welcome. Wood Valley Temple can't promise nirvana, but they can point you to the path.

The retreat facility is called the Tara Temple and at one time housed a Japanese Shingon Mission in Pahala. When the Shingon sect moved to a new facility in Kona, this building was abandoned and given to Wood Valley Temple. A local contractor moved it to its present location in 1978, cranked it up one story, and built dormitories underneath. The grounds, hallowed and consecrated for decades, already held a Nichiren temple, the main temple here today, that was dismantled in 1919 at its original location and rebuilt on its present site to protect it from lowland flooding.

If you wish to visit, please do so on weekends and be respectful, as this is a retreat center. For those staying, either as guests or as part of a program, rates at the retreat facility are private room single $50, double room $70; bunk in the dorm $35, with use of a large communal kitchen and shared bath. Meals are not provided. All require a two-night minimum stay or a $10 surcharge for

PUNALU'U

Along the coast just south of Pahala are the small communities of Punalu'u and Ninole. Punalu'u was an important port during the sugar boom of the 1880s and even had a railroad. Notice the tall coconut palms in the vicinity, unusual for Ka'u. Punalu'u means "Diving Spring," so named because freshwater springs can be found on the floor of the bay. Native divers once paddled out to sea, then dove with calabashes that they filled with fresh water from the underwater springs. This was the main source of drinking water for the region.

What was Ninole is now home to the **Sea Mountain Resort and Golf Course,** built in the early 1970s by a branch of the C. Brewer Company. The string of flat-topped hills in the background is the remains of volcano cones that became dormant about 100,000 years ago. In sharp contrast with them is **Lo'ihi Seamount,** 20 miles offshore and about 3,000 feet below the surface of the sea. This very active submarine

Wood Valley Temple

volcano is steadily building and should reach the surface in just a few tens of thousands of years. Near Ninole is **Hokuloa Church,** which houses a memorial to Henry Opukaha'ia, the Hawaiian most responsible for encouraging the first missionaries to go to Hawaii to save his people from damnation.

Punalu'u Beach County Park

Punalu'u Beach Park (near mile marker 56) is a county park with full amenities and famous for its black-sand beach. Here you'll find a pavilion, bathrooms, showers, drinking water, telephone, and open camping area (permit required). During the day there are plenty of tourists around, but at night the beach park empties, and you virtually have it to yourself. Punalu'u boasts some of the only safe swimming on the south coast, but that doesn't mean that it can't have its treacherous moments. Head for the northeast section of the black-sand beach near the boat ramp. Stay close to shore because a

prevailing rip current lurks just outside the bay. Hawaiian green sea turtles and hawksbill turtles use this beach for building their nests and they're often seen swimming in the bay. When they're around, please give them plenty of room and don't harass them—it's the law.

A *kaukau* wagon often parks at Punalu'u Beach, offering island sandwiches, shave ice, cold drinks, and snacks.

Sea Mountain Resort

Sea Mountain Resort, P.O. Box 70, Pahala, HI 96777, 808/928-8301 or 800/488-8301, fax 808/928-8008, is a time-share condominium that also rents available units to the general public—but only up to 60 days in advance. Options include a studio at $80 garden view or $100 ocean view, one bedroom $100–125, and two bedrooms $125–155. Because of its rural location, Sea Mountain can offer secluded accommodations for reasonable prices. Your condo unit will be a low-rise, Polynesian-inspired bungalow with a shake roof. The standard units, all tastefully furnished, offer remote color TVs, full kitchens, full baths, ceiling fans, and a lanai. The resort itself has a swimming pool and spa pool, laundry facilities, four unlit tennis courts, and a golf course. Although the units vary, all are furnished in island theme, typically with rattan couches and easy chairs. The feeling throughout the resort is a friendly, home-away-from-home atmosphere. Outside your door are the resort's fairways and greens, backdropped by the spectacular coast. If you're after peace and quiet, Sea Mountain is hard to beat.

Ninole Cove Park, part of the Sea Mountain Resort, is within walking distance and open to the public. For day use, you might consider parking near the pro shop. As you walk to the beach from here you pass a freshwater pond, quite cold but good for swimming.

The **Sea Mountain at Punalu'u Golf Course,** 808/928-6222, is a 6,416-yard, 18-hole, par-72 course. As it's set right on the coast, the winds can be strong and usually blow across the fairways, creating challenging play. Greens fees are $32 weekdays and $35 weekends for guests, $42 and 45, respectively, for visitors; clubs are available to rent. Range balls are $5 a bucket and golf lessons $25 an hour. The clubhouse offers morning coffee at 7 A.M., serves a limited menu of sandwiches and *pu pu* from 10 A.M.–2 P.M., and has a full bar that's open later.

NA'ALEHU AND VICINITY

Between Punalu'u and Na'alehu, the coastal area is majestic; stretching into the aqua-blue sea is a tableland of black lava with waves crashing against it in a surrealistic seascape that seems to go on forever.

Whittington Beach County Park

Three miles north of Na'alehu is a county park with full amenities and camping, but no drinking water. To its side are ponds and palm trees, a

ROBERT NILSEN

Punalu'u Beach County Park

spot sometimes used by fishermen. This park is tough to spot from the road because it's not clearly marked. Before the hill going up to Na'alehu you'll see a bridge at the bottom. Turn right and proceed down the access road. The park is never crowded. Here you'll encounter some old ruins from the turn of the 20th century when Honu'apo Bay was an important sugar port. Before that, this was a sizable Hawaiian settlement. On the way up the hill, pause at the lookout, enjoy the seascape, and consider that only the tiny specks of the South Pacific islands are between here and Antarctica! If that starts a chill on your shoulders, also know that Ka'u is the warmest region of the island, and Na'alehu hit 100 degrees in 1931, the highest temperature recorded in the state.

Open daily across from Whittington Beach is a souvenir and neat tourist junk shop. Inside, find hula skirts, wooden boxes, *kukui* nut lei, wooden platters, straw hats, and tiki carvings.

Na'alehu

Na'alehu, the largest town in the area and the most southern town in the United States, is lush. Check out the overhanging monkeypod trees. They form a magnificent living tunnel as you go down Rte. 11 through the center of town. Every Fourth of July, a down-home rodeo is held in town for all the amateur riders of the district. Come and enjoy. Na'alehu is a former sugar town, but it still maintains a small downtown business area, has a post office, and supports a gas station.

Na'alehu Practicalities

Becky's Bed & Breakfast, P.O. Box 673, Na'alehu, HI 96772, tel./fax 808/929-9690 or 866/422-3259, beckys@hi-inns.com, http://1bb.com/Beckys, is about 100 yards east of the theater, *mauka* of the road. Available in this modest but cheery plantation home, built originally for the company doctor in 1937, are two spacious rooms with queen beds and one room with two double beds. Each room has a private bath, and two have private entrances. They run $70 single or $75 double. To help you relax, the B&B features a backyard deck. To get you started, a full

breakfast of juice, fruit, and a griddle entrée is served every morning except Sunday.

On the west side of town, at the intersection with the Na'alehu Theater, grocery and hardware stores, a large, easily spotted sign marks the **Punalu'u Bake Shop and Visitor Center,** 808/929-7343, open daily 9 A.M.–5 P.M. The bake shop, tempting with all kinds of pastries, is especially known for its *pao dolce,* sweet bread. Park and follow daily busloads of tourists down a cement pathway to the retail shop for baked goods, sandwiches, ice cream, coffee, cold drinks, and a smattering of souvenirs. Punalu'u sweet bread is well known throughout the island. Have a look at the operation through the viewing windows. The cool and pleasing gardens here make a fine rest stop for the long stretches through this part of the island.

For a quick sandwich or full meal try the **Na'alehu Coffee Shop,** 808/929-7238, open until 8 P.M. except Wednesdays and Sundays. Many of the local people call this restaurant "Roy's," after the owner's first name. The menu is typical island cuisine with a Japanese flavor; the best item is the fresh fish from local waters. The restaurant is basic and clean, with most meals on the menu around $9. In the attached Menehune Treasure Chest shop there's a wide assortment of souvenirs and tourist junk. Look for the big yellow building near the shopping center as you enter town.

With more diversity in its menu, **Shaka Restaurant,** 808/929-7404, is the second local eatery in town and located just up from the theater. Open daily except Monday 10 A.M.–9 P.M., this eatery is clean and well run, with tapa patterns on the tablecloths and chair cushions. Friday brings live evening entertainment and a prime rib special. Extensive breakfast and lunch menus feed hungry folks during the day and in the evening your choices include grilled chicken fillet, baby back ribs, fresh catch, New York steak, and veggie stir-fry. Meals come with soup and a dinner salad, and a kid's menu helps keep the prices down for families. Not gourmet by any means, you won't go away hungry or disappointed.

Na'alehu Fruit Stand, 808/929-9009, open Mon.–Thurs. 9 A.M.–6 P.M., Friday and Saturday until 7 P.M., Sunday until 5 P.M., is a favorite with local people, always a tip-off that the food is great. Along with fresh fruit, it sells submarines, hot dogs, pizza, quiche, salads, soda, tea, coffee, fresh baked goods, and a good selection of grains, minerals, vitamins, and health foods. If you're staying in the area, check out the rental video collection. Outside is a bulletin board for local events. This is the best place on the south coast for a light meal or picnic lunch.

About 100 yards from the Na'alehu Fruit Stand, notice the baseball park. Here **Kalaiki Plate Lunch,** open daily 6:30 A.M.–3 P.M., run by the Hanoa family, serves hearty sandwiches and island favorites ready to go. This place is especially known for its full breakfasts, only $5.

If you are in town on Saturday morning, stop by the **farmers market** at the theater.

Na'alehu Shopping Center is along the road at the west end of town. In the small complex you'll find the small but full-service, open daily **Island Market** grocery store and Ed's Laundromat. Across the street is an Ace Hardware store.

The **Na'alehu Theater,** 808/929-9133, is a large building along the highway in front of the shopping center. It's a classic old-time theater usually open on weekends, and a venue of the Hawaii International Film Festival. Call for what's showing.

Wai'ohinu

A tall church steeple welcomes you to the small town of Wai'ohinu. There's nothing remarkable about this village, except that as you pass through you'll be seeing an example of the real Hawaiian country lifestyle as it exists today. Wai'ohinu was an important agricultural region in centuries past, and King Kamehameha even had personal land here. Just before the well-marked Shirakawa Motel on the *mauka* side of the road is the **Mark Twain Monkeypod Tree.** Unfortunately, Wai'ohinu's only claim to fame—except for its undisturbed peace and quiet—blew down in a heavy windstorm in 1957. Part of the original trunk, carved into a bust of Twain, is on display at the Lyman House Museum in Hilo. A shoot from the original trunk has grown to become a sizable descendant of the town's original attraction.

Wai'ohinu Practicalities

The **Shirakawa Motel,** P.O. Box 467, Na'alehu, HI 96772, 808/929-7462, is a small, clean, comfortable, "hang loose bruddah" motel where your peace and quiet are guaranteed. The Shirakawa has been open since 1928. The original two-story hotel has now been converted to the home of the retired second-generation owners. Their son now runs the dozen-room, dark green, red roof motel, which consists of clean and utilitarian single-story detached buildings to the side. Prices are a reasonable $30 single, $35 double, $42 kitchenette, $8 for "rollaway children" and $10 for "rollaway adult" (if only it were that easy!). There's a 10 percent discount for a one-week stay, 15 percent for longer.

A short hop west of town is **Macadamia Meadows Farm B&B,** P.O. Box 756, Na'alehu, HI 96772, tel./fax 808/929-8097 or 888/929-8118, kaleena@aloha.net, www.macadamia-meadows.com, set as you might expect, in the middle of an eight-acre working macadamia nut farm. But this is more than just a B&B. With the full-size tennis court, swimming pool, and basketball court, it seems like a mini-resort, and when you get restless, you can stroll through the orchard. The huge main house, with open kitchen, dining and living areas, and wraparound lanai, looks out on the back lawn and nut trees. In the main house are the spacious Mukupuni Room for $75, Volcano Room for $75, and smaller Hawaiian Room at $65. Downstairs is the Honeymoon Suite with its canopy queen bed and clawfoot tub for $125. In the newer detached building, the Pauli room with its queen and king beds runs $85, but when combined with an adjacent room and its full bed goes for $120 for up to four people. All rooms have private entrances and television, and only the Hawaiian and Volcano rooms share a bathroom. A hearty and taste-tempting breakfast is served to all guests, and the owners will gladly show you around the farm and introduce you to the world of nut farming.

Margo Hobbs and Philip Shaw of **Margo's Corner,** P.O. Box 447, Na'alehu, HI 96772, 808/929-9614, margos@bigisland.com, can accommodate you in their strikingly original pentagonal guesthouse for $60 single or $75 double. The guesthouse, with a private bath and shower, has a queen-size bed. Brightly painted outside, it's also a rainbow of cheery colors on the inside. Two nights minimum is preferred. Down below, the Adobe Suite, with its private bath and sauna, sleeps four to six people. A bit like a cave, with its curved walls and earthen feel, it's not dark and confining but bright and intriguing with all its detail. This suite has a queen-size futon in the living area and two raised beds in the bedroom. It rents for $100 a night single and $15 for each additional person; two nights minimum. The rate for indoor guests includes full gourmet vegetarian dinners and breakfast every day. Touring bicyclists and backpackers can camp for $25 per person in the yard among Norfolk pines; a shower is available. An organic vegetable garden is out back—food for your meals. No smoking and no excessive drinking, please. For your extra food needs, Margo's maintains a small but well-stocked health food store that's open in the afternoon. Margo's is about halfway between Na'alehu and the South Point Road, just south of Kama'oa Road in the Discovery Harbor subdivision. Call for exact directions and reservations.

You can pick up supplies and buy gas at **Wong Yuen Store** and gas station, 808/929-7223, open Mon.–Sat. 8 A.M.–7 P.M., Sunday to 5 P.M.

SOUTH POINT

The Hawaiians simply called this Ka Lae (The Point). Some scholars believe Polynesian sailors made landfall here as early as A.D. 150, and that their amazing exploits became navigating legend long before colonization began. A paved, narrow, but passable road branches off from Rte. 11 approximately six miles west of Na'alehu, and it drops directly south for 12 miles to land's end. Luckily the shoulders are firm, so you can pull over to let another car go by. Car-rental agencies may warn against using this road, but their fears are unfounded. You proceed through a flat,

treeless area of rangeland for cattle and horses. Suddenly, incongruously, huge mechanical windmills appear, beating their arms against the sky. This is the **Kamoa Wind Farm.** Notice that this futuristic experiment at America's most southern point uses windmills made in Japan by Mitsubishi! The trees here are bent over by the prevailing wind, demonstrating the obviously excellent wind-power potential of the area. However strong the potential, the wind can also be a liability. You will notice that some of the windmills have been damaged by winds that were too strong. Farther along, you enter countryside controlled by the Hawaiian Homelands agency, some of which you are forbidden to enter. That means that you are not welcome on the land, but you do have the right to remain on the road.

Here the road splits left and right. Go right until road's end, where you'll find a parking area usually filled with the pickup trucks of local fishermen. Walk to the cliff and notice attached ladders that plummet straight down to where fishing

fishing at South Point

boats can anchor. Local skippers moor their boats here and bring supplies and their catch up and down the ladders, or transfer loads via rope. Nearby is a tall white structure with a big square sign turned sideways like a diamond and a navigational light on its top. It marks the true **South Point,** the southernmost tip of the United States. Directly below this marker is an ancient *heiau* and at water's edge are holes curiously carved into some rocks. These are reputed to be **anchor points** used by early Hawaiians to secure their canoes to shore by long ropes while the current carried them a short way offshore. In this manner, they could fish without being swept away. Usually, a few people are line-fishing from the point, and today fishermen use floats or tiny boats to carry only their lines out to sea. The *ulua*, tuna, and *ahi* fishing is renowned throughout this area. The fishing grounds here have always been extremely fertile, and thousands of shell and bone fishhooks have been found throughout the area. Scuba divers say that the rocks off South Point are covered with broken fishing line that the currents have woven into wild macramé. The rocks are covered with Hawaiian dental floss—monofilament fishing line that has been snapped. Survey the mighty Pacific and realize that the closest continental landfall is Antarctica, 7,500 miles to the south.

Back where the road Ys, follow the road left and pass a series of WWII barracks being reclaimed by nature. This road, too, leads to a parking area and small Hawaiian Homelands office and information center where you pay a few bucks to park. Out front stands a short statue of a native Hawaiian wrapped in chains, symbolic of their situation as a disenfranchised people in their own land. Beyond is Kaulana boat ramp (*kaulana* means "boat landing") where a few seaworthy craft are bobbing away at their moorings and still farther is the trail to Green Sand Beach.

When the Kona winds blow out of the South Pacific, South Point takes it on the chin. The weather should always be a consideration when you visit. In times past, any canoe caught in the wicked currents was considered lost. Even today, only experienced boaters brave South Point, and only during fine weather.

There is no official camping or facilities of any kind at South Point, but plenty of boat owners bivouac for a night to get an early start in the morning. The lava flow in this area is quite old and grass-covered, and the constant winds act like a natural lawn mower.

Green Sand Beach

The trail to Green Sand Beach starts near the boat ramp at Kaulana Bay. Head east from there past the gate. All along are remnants of precontact habitation, including the remains of a *heiau* foundation. If you walk for three miles, you'll come to Papakolea, better known as Green Sand Beach, at Mahana Bay. The lava in this area contains olivine, a green semiprecious stone that weathered into sand-like particles distributed along the beach. You're walking into the wind going there, but it's not a rough go—there's no elevation gain to speak of. The lava in the area is 'a'a, weathered and overlaid by thick ground cover. An ancient eruption deposited 15–18 feet of ash right here, and the grasses grew.

About three miles on, you see what is obviously an eroded cinder cone at the edge of the sea. Peer over the edge to have a peek at the beach with its definite green tinge. This is the only beach along the way, so it's hard to mistake. Green Sand Beach definitely lives up to its name, but don't expect emerald green. It's more like a dull army olive green. Getting down to it can be treacherous. Around the side of the cove, you'll be scrambling over tough lava rock, and you'll have to make drops of four to five feet in certain spots—or you could slide down the sand at the back end. Once you get over the lip of heavy-duty rock, the trail down is not so bad. When you begin your descent, notice overhangs, almost like caves, where rocks have been piled up to extend them. These rocked-in areas make great shelters, and you can see remnants of recent campfires in spots perfect for a night's bivouac. Down at the beach, be very aware of the wave action. The currents can be wicked here, and you should only enter the water on very calm days. No one is around to save you, and you don't want to wind up as flotsam in Antarctica.

OCEAN VIEW

Before you get to Ocean View, you have a sense of what the area is like when you stop at the highway scenic lookout spot near mile marker 75 and view the strong black lava flows that fill the horizon. Ocean View is often referred to as the largest subdivision in the state. In fact, it is a conglomeration of five subdivisions that is several miles wide and that pushes up the mountain about six miles and down toward the ocean another three. The highest lots are at about 5,000 feet. This unincorporated town of self-sufficient individuals who don't want to be bothered by anyone has been carved out of rough volcanic rubble with an overlay of trees and bush. While not the most scenic, it is attractive in its own untamed way. If you're curious, have a drive through.

Services are located in two small shopping centers that flank the highway. Above the highway, you'll find an Ace Hardware, Ocean View Pizzaria, and the Kahuku Market. Below the highway is a second gas station, the post office, the full-service Ocean View Market, Desert Rose Cafe, and a laundromat. Down the road a piece is Mister Bell's Restaurant and bar. Aside from house lots and a community center, there's not much else here. This area was hit hard by the downturn in the state economy during the 1990s, and often people had to drive long distances to get work—if they could find it at all. Now the area seems to be growing in a slow and steady manner, but people still have a long distance to commute.

There frankly is little to do in Ocean View itself if you are a visitor, but as there are few lights and little air pollution, this is one of the greatest locations for stargazing in the islands without going up to the top of the mountain.

Kula Kai Caverns

The newest and perhaps most curious offering of this region is the Kula Kai Caverns, P.O. Box 6313, Ocean View, HI 96737, 808/929-7539, www.kulakaicaverns.com. In contrast to the Ka'eleku Caverns on Maui, which are about 30,000 years old, the Kula Kai Cavern system—

13 miles of tunnel have been surveyed—is a mere baby at about 1,000 years old. A tour underground here gives you a look at the bowels of the largest mountain in the world, once used for shelter and as a place to collect water in this region of low rainfall. Like other lava tubes in the world, the Kula Kai Caverns shows fine examples of lava shelves, pillars, lava balls, and other customary lava formations. As these interconnected tubes are so close to the surface in some spots, roots of 'ohi'a trees have penetrated the ceiling of the cave and hang like hairy tendrils. The inside cave temperature averages 68°F year round. An easy 30-minute interpretive walking tour ($12 for adults and $8 for kids) leads through the lighted section of the caverns. The more rigorous two-hour spelunking tour ($45, age eight and above) takes you deeper into the maze. On either, the intent is to be an educational and cultural experience. More than to just have a look, it's preferable to learn of the island's volcanic history, how lava tubes form, and how they have been used by man. Other cave tours can be arranged, depending upon your interest and skill level, and all tours are given be prior arrangement only. Long pants and closed-toe shoes are required; gloves, knee pads, hard hats, and lights are provided.

Accommodations

Bougainvillea Bed and Breakfast, P.O. Box 6045, Ocean View, HI 96737, tel./fax 808/929-7089 or 800/688-1763, peaceful@interpac.net, www.hi-inns.com/bouga, has views of the ocean and South Point. The inn is quiet and romantic, with fine landscaping all around, and each room has a private entrance and bath. Guests share the swimming pool, hot tub, barbecue area, TV, and the game and video library. There is nothing out here to block your view, so at night there is unbeatable stargazing! As your sightseeing options are limited in Ocean View, owners Martie and Don Nitsche gladly offer suggestions for activities and can make arrangements for you. A full nutritious homemade breakfast—different each day—is served every morning. Rooms are $65 single or $69 double; $15 for an extra person; two night minimum.

Set just above the highway, **South Point Bed and Breakfast,** 808/939-9049, fax 808/939-7557, P.O. Box 6589, Ocean View, HI 96737, southpointbandb@aol.com, also has views of South Point. As it's reasonably close to the road, there is some traffic noise, but this is somewhat muffled by the tall trees and thick vegetation on property. The bed-and-breakfast rooms run $55–65 double, while one room with a mini-kitchen and no served breakfast has the same rate. A discount of 10 percent is offered for two nights and 15 percent for five nights or longer; no credit cards. For the starry nights you find here, there's no better place to be in the evening than soaking in the hot tub contemplating the universe.

Food

Ocean View Pizzaria, 808/929-9677, is open Sun.–Thurs. 11 A.M.–7 P.M. and weekends until 8 P.M. While the focus is pizza, smalls run $8 and large pies go for $10, with extra cost for the toppings of your choice, you can also get a salad, hot and cold sandwiches, and even a few baked goods.

The Desert Rose Cafe, 808/939-7673, is down below the highway. Advertised as "the southernmost cafe in the USA," the Desert Rose is open for three meals a day. Expect eggs and scrambles for breakfast, sandwiches and burgers for lunch, and a variety of fish and red meat entrées in the $12–15 range for dinner. Basic and clean, this eatery puts out fine nutritious food.

Manuka State Wayside

The Manuka State Wayside is 12 miles west of South Point Road and just inside the Ka'u district. This civilized scene has restrooms, a pavilion, and a two-mile trail through a native and introduced forest, all of which lies within the Manuka Natural Area Reserve. The forested slopes above Manuka provide ample habitat for introduced, and now totally successful, colonies of wild pigs, pheasants, and turkeys. Shelter camping (no tents) is allowed on the grounds. This is an excellent rest or picnic stop, but bring your own drinking water. Within a couple of miles, you're in South Kona, heading up the coast past the world's largest single-owner macadamia nut farm, toward Captain Cook and Kailua.

Resources

Hawaiian Glossary

The list on the following pages gives you a "taste" of Hawaiian and provides a basic vocabulary of words in common usage that you are likely to hear. Becoming familiar with them is not a strict necessity, but they will definitely enhance your experience and make talking with local people more congenial. Many islanders spice their speech with certain words, especially when they're speaking "pidgin," and you too can use them just as soon as you feel comfortable. You might even discover some Hawaiian words that are so perfectly expressive they'll become regular parts of your vocabulary. Many Hawaiian words have been absorbed into the English dictionary. The definitions given are not exhaustive, but are generally considered the most common.

Words marked with an asterisk (*) are used commonly throughout the islands.

'a'a*—rough clinker lava. 'A'a has become the correct geological term to describe this type of lava found anywhere in the world.

'ae—yes

ahupua'a—pie-shaped land divisions running from mountain to sea that were governed by *konohiki,* local *ali'i* who owed their allegiance to a reigning chief

aikane—friend; pal; buddy

'aina—land; the binding spirit to all Hawaiians. Love of the land is paramount in traditional Hawaiian beliefs.

akamai—smart; clever; wise

akua—a god, or simply "divine"

ali'i*—a Hawaiian chief or noble

aloha*—the most common greeting in the islands; can mean both hello and good-bye, welcome and farewell. It can also mean romantic love, affection, or best wishes.

'a'ole—no

'aumakua—a personal or family god, often an ancestral spirit

auwe—alas; ouch! When a great chief or loved one died, it was a traditional wail of mourning.

'awa—also known as *kava,* a mildly intoxicating traditional drink made from the juice of chewed *'awa* root, spat into a bowl, and used in religious ceremonies

halakahiki—pineapple

hale*—house or building; often combined with other words to name a specific place, such as Haleakala (House of the Sun), or Hale Pa'i at Lahainaluna, meaning Printing House

hana*—work; combined with *pau* means end of work or quitting time

hanai—literally "to feed." Part of the true *aloha* spirit. A *hanai* is a permanent guest, or an adopted family member, usually an old person or a child. This is an enduring cultural phenomenon in Hawaii, in which a child from one family (perhaps that of a brother or sister, and quite often one's grandchild) is raised as one's own without formal adoption.

haole*—a word that at one time meant foreigner, but which now means a white person or Caucasian

hapa*—half, as in a mixed-blooded person being referred to as *hapa haole*

hapai*—pregnant; used by all ethnic groups when a *keiki* is on the way

haupia*—a coconut custard dessert often served at a lu'au

heiau*—A platform made of skillfully fitted rocks, upon which temporary structures were built as temples and offerings made to the gods.

holomu*—an ankle-length dress that is much more fitted than a mu'umu'u, and which is often worn on formal occasions

hono—bay, as in Honolulu (Sheltered Bay)

honu—green sea turtle; endangered

ho'oilo—traditional Hawaiian winter that began in November

ho'olaulea—any happy event, but especially a family outing or picnic

ho'omalimali*—sweet talk; flattery

huhu*—angry; irritated

hui*—a group; meeting; society. Often used to refer to Chinese businesspeople or family members who pool their money to get businesses started.

hukilau—traditional shoreline fish-gathering in which everyone lends a hand to *huki* (pull) the huge net. Anyone taking part shares in the *lau* (food). It is much more like a party than hard work, and if you're lucky you'll be able to take part in one.

hula*—a native Hawaiian dance in which the rhythm of the islands is captured by swaying hips and stories told by lyrically moving hands. A *halau* is a group or school of hula.

huli huli—barbecue, as in *huli huli* chicken

i'a—fish in general. *I'a maka* is raw fish.

imu*—underground oven filled with hot rocks and used for baking. The main cooking method featured at a lu'au, used to steam-bake pork and other succulent dishes. The tending of the *imu* was traditionally for men only.

ipo—sweetheart; lover; girl- or boyfriend

kahili—a tall pole topped with feathers, resembling a huge feather duster. It was used by an *ali'i* to announce his or her presence.

kahuna*—priest; sorcerer; doctor; skillful person. In old Hawaii *kahuna* had tremendous power, which they used for both good and evil. The *kahuna ana'ana* was a feared individual who practiced "black magic" and could pray a person to death, while the *kahuna lapa'au* was a medical practitioner bringing aid and comfort to the people.

kai—the sea. Many businesses and hotels employ *kai* as part of their name.

kalua—means roasted underground in an *imu*. A favorite island food is *kalua* pork.

kama'aina*—a child of the land; an old-timer; a longtime island resident of any ethnic background; a resident of Hawaii or native son or daughter. Hotels and airlines often offer discounts called *"kama'aina* rates" to anyone who can prove island residency.

kanaka—man or commoner; later used to distinguish a Hawaiian from other races. Tone of voice can make it a derisive expression.

kane*—means man, but actually used to signify a relationship such as husband or boyfriend. Written on a lavatory door it means "men's room."

kapu*—forbidden; taboo; keep out; do not touch

kaukau*—slang word meaning food or chow; grub. Some of the best food in Hawaii comes from the *kaukau* wagons, trucks that sell plate lunches and other morsels.

kauwa—a landless, untouchable caste once confined to living on reservations. Members of this caste were often used as human sacrifices at *heiau*. Calling someone *kauwa* is still a grave insult.

kava—see *'awa*

keiki*—child or children; used by all ethnic groups. "Have you hugged your *keiki* today?"

kiawe—an algaroba tree from South America commonly found in Hawaii along the shore. It grows a nasty long thorn that can easily puncture a tire. Legend has it that the trees were introduced to the islands by a misguided missionary who hoped the thorns would coerce natives into wearing shoes. Actually, they are good for fuel, as fodder for hogs and cattle, and for reforestation, none of which you'll appreciate if you step on one of the thorns or flatten a tire on your rental car!

ko'ala*—any food that has been broiled or barbecued

kokua—help. As in "Your *kokua* is needed to keep Hawaii free from litter."

kona wind*—a muggy subtropical wind that blows from the south and hits the leeward side of the islands. It usually brings sticky hot weather and one of the few times when air-conditioning will be appreciated.

konane—a traditional Hawaiian game, similar to checkers, played with pebbles on a large flat stone used as a board

ko'olau—windward side of the island

kukui—a candlenut tree whose pods are polished and then strung together to make a beautiful lei. Traditionally the oil-rich nuts were strung on the rib of a coconut leaf and used as a candle.

kuleana—homesite; the old homestead; small farms. Especially used to describe the small spreads on Hawaiian Homelands on Moloka'i.

*Kumulipo**—ancient Hawaiian genealogical chant that records the pantheon of gods, creation, and the beginning of humankind

kupuna—a grandparent or old-timer; usually means someone who has gained wisdom. The statewide school system now invites *kupuna* to talk to the children about the old ways and methods.

la—the sun. Often combined with other words to be more descriptive, such as *La*haina (Merciless Sun) or Haleakala (House of the Sun).

lanai*—veranda or porch. You'll pay more for a hotel room if it has a lanai with an ocean view.

lani—sky or the heavens

*lau hala**—traditional Hawaiian weaving of mats, hats, etc., from the prepared fronds of the pandanus (screw pine)

lei*—a traditional garland of flowers or vines. One of Hawaii's most beautiful customs. Given at any auspicious occasion, but especially when arriving or leaving Hawaii.

lele—the stone altar at a *heiau*

limu—edible seaweed of various types. Gathered from the shoreline, it makes an excellent salad. It's used to garnish many island dishes and is a favorite at lu'au.

lomi lomi—traditional Hawaiian massage; also, raw salmon made into a vinegared salad with chopped onion and spices

*lua**—the toilet; the head; the bathroom

luakini—a human-sacrifice temple. Introduced to Hawaii in the 13th century at Waha'ula Heiau on the Big Island.

*lu'au**—a Hawaiian feast featuring poi, *imu*-baked pork, and other traditional foods. Good ones provide some of the best gastronomic delights in the world.

luna—foreman or overseer in the plantation fields. They were often mounted on horseback and were renowned for either their fairness or their cruelty. Representing the middle class, they served as a buffer between plantation workers and white plantation owners.

*mahalo**—thank you. *Mahalo nui* means "big thanks" or "thank you very much."

mahele—division. The "Great Mahele" of 1848 changed Hawaii forever when the traditional common lands were broken up into privately owned plots.

mahimahi*—a favorite eating fish. Often called a dolphin, but a mahimahi is a true fish, not a cetacean.

mahu—a homosexual; often used derisively like "fag" or "queer"

maile—a fragrant vine used in traditional lei. It looks ordinary but smells delightful.

maka'ainana—a commoner; a person "belonging" to the *'aina* (land), who supported the *ali'i* by fishing and farming and as a warrior

*makai**—toward the sea; used by most islanders when giving directions

make—dead; deceased

*malihini**—what you are if you have just arrived: a newcomer; a tenderfoot; a recent arrival

malo—the native Hawaiian loincloth. Never worn anymore except at festivals or pageants.

mana*—power from the spirit world; innate energy of all things animate or inanimate; the grace of god. Mana could be passed on from one person to another, or even stolen. Great care was taken to protect the *ali'i* from having their *mana* defiled. Commoners were required to lie flat on the ground and cover their faces whenever a great *ali'i* approached. *Kahuna* were often employed in the regaining or transference of *mana*.

manini—stingy; tight; a Hawaiianized word taken from the name of Don Francisco *Marin*, who was instrumental in bringing many fruits and plants to Hawaii. He was known for never sharing any of the bounty from his substantial gardens on Vineyard Street in Honolulu; therefore, his name came to mean "stingy."

manuahi—free; gratis; extra

*mauka**—toward the mountains; used by most islanders when giving directions

mauna—mountain. Often combined with other words to be more descriptive, such as Mauna Kea (White Mountain) *mele*—a song or chant in the Hawaiian oral tradition that records the history and genealogies of the *ali'i*

Menehune—the legendary "little people" of Hawaii. Like leprechauns, they are said to shun humans and possess magical powers.

moa—chicken; fowl

moana*—the ocean; the sea. Many businesses and hotels as well as places have *moana* as part of their name.

moe—sleep

mo'olelo—ancient tales kept alive by the oral tradition and recited only by day

mu'umu'u*—a "Mother Hubbard," an ankle-length dress with a high neckline introduced by the missionaries to cover the nakedness of the Hawaiians. It has become fashionable attire for almost any occasion in Hawaii.

nani—beautiful

nui—big; great; large; as in *mahalo nui* (thank you very much)

'ohana—a family; the fundamental social division; extended family. Now often used to denote a social organization with grassroots overtones.

'okolehau—literally "iron bottom"; a traditional booze made from *ti* root. *'Okole* means "rear end" and *hau* means "iron," which was descriptive of the huge blubber pots in which *'okolehau* was made. Also, if you drink too much it'll surely knock you on your *'okole*.

oli—chant not done to a musical accompaniment

ono*—delicious; delightful; the best. *Ono ono* means "extra or absolutely delicious."

'opihi—a shellfish or limpet that clings to rocks and is gathered as one of the islands' favorite *pu pu*. Custom dictates that you never remove all of the *'opihi* from a rock; some are always left to grow for future generations.

'opu—belly; stomach

pahoehoe*—smooth, ropy lava that looks like burnt pancake batter. It is now the correct geological term used to describe this type of lava found anywhere in the world.

pakalolo—"crazy smoke"; grass; smoke; dope; marijuana

pake—a Chinese person. Can be derisive, depending on the tone in which it is used. It is a bastardization of the Chinese word meaning "uncle."

pali*—a cliff; precipice. Hawaii's geology makes them quite common. The most famous are the *pali* of Oahu where a major battle was fought.

paniolo*—a Hawaiian cowboy. Derived from the Spanish *espa-ol*. The first cowboys brought to Hawaii during the early 19th century were Mexicans from California.

papale—hat. Except for the feathered helmets of the *ali'i* warriors of old Hawaii, hats were generally not worn. However, once the islanders saw their practical uses and how fashionable they were, they began weaving them from various materials and quickly became experts at manufacture and design.

pa'u—long split skirt often worn by women when horseback riding. In the 1800s, an island treat was watching *pa'u* riders in their beautiful dresses at Kapi'olani Park in Honolulu. The tradition is carried on today at many of Hawaii's rodeos.

pau*—finished; done; completed. Often combined into *pau hana,* which means end of work or quitting time.

pilau—stink; bad smell; stench

pilikia—trouble of any kind, big or small; bad times

poi*—a glutinous paste made from the pounded corm of taro, which ferments slightly and has a light sour taste. Purplish in color, it's a staple at lu'au, where it is called "one-, two-, or three-finger" poi, depending upon its thickness.

pono—righteous or excellent

pua—flower

puka*—a hole of any size. *Puka* is used by all island residents, whether talking about a pinhole in a rubber boat or a tunnel through a mountain.

punalua—a traditional practice, before the missionaries arrived, of sharing mates. Western seamen took advantage of it, leading to the spread of contagious diseases and eventual rapid decline of the Hawaiian people.

pune'e*—bed; narrow couch. Used by all ethnic groups. To recline on a *pune'e* on a breezy lanai is a true island treat.

pu pu*—an appetizer; a snack; hors d'oeuvres; can be anything from cheese and crackers to sushi. Oftentimes, bars or nightclubs offer them free.

pupule—crazy; nuts; out of your mind

pu'u—hill, as in Pu'u 'Ula'ula (Red Hill)

tapa*—a traditional paper cloth made from beaten bark. Intricate designs were stamped in using beaters, and natural dyes added color. The tradition was lost for many years but is now making a comeback, and provides some of the most beautiful folk art in the islands. Also called Kapa.

taro*—the staple of old Hawaii. A plant with a distinctive broad leaf that produces a starchy root. It was brought by the first Polynesians and was grown on magnificently irrigated plantations. According to the oral tradition, the life-giving properties of taro hold mystical significance for Hawaiians, since it was created by the gods at about the same time as humans.

ti—a broad-leafed plant that was used for many purposes, from plates to hula skirts. Especially used to wrap religious offerings presented at the *heiau*.

tutu*—grandmother; granny; older woman. Used by all as a term of respect and endearment.

ukulele*—*uku* means "flea" and *lele* means "jumping," so literally "jumping flea"—the way the Hawaiians perceived the quick finger movements used on the banjo-like Portuguese folk instrument called a *cavaquinho*. The ukulele quickly became synonymous with the islands.

wahine*—young woman; female; girl; wife. Used by all ethnic groups. When written on a lavatory door it means "women's room."

wai—fresh water; drinking water

wela—hot. *Wela kahao* is a "hot time" or "making whoopee."

wiki*—quickly; fast; in a hurry. Often seen as *wiki wiki* (very fast), as in "Wiki Wiki Messenger Service."

Useful Phrases

Aloha ahiahi—Good evening

Aloha au ia 'oe—I love you

Aloha kakahiaka—Good morning

Aloha nui loa—much love; fondest regards

Hau'oli la hanau—Happy birthday

Hau'oli makahiki hou—Happy New Year

Komo mai—please come in; enter; welcome

Mele kalikimaka—Merry Christmas

'Okole maluna—bottoms up; salute; cheers; kampai

Suggested Reading

Many publishers print books on Hawaii. Following are a few that focus on Hawaiian topics. **University of Hawai'i Press,** www.uhpress .hawaii.edu, has the best overall general list of titles on Hawaii. The **Bishop Museum Press,** www.bishopmuseum.org/bishop/press, puts out many scholarly works on Hawaiiana, as does **Kamehameha Schools Press,** www.ksbe.edu/ newsroom/kspress. Also good, with a more general-interest list, are **Bess Press,** www.besspress .com; **Mutual Publishing,** www.mutualpublishing .com; and **Petrogylph Press,** www.basically-books.com. A website specifically oriented toward books on Hawaii, Hawaiian music, and other things Hawaiian is **Hawaii Books** at hawaiibooks.com.

Astronomy

Bryan, E.H. *Stars over Hawaii.* Hilo, HI: Petroglyph Press, 1977. An introduction to astronomy, with information about the constellations and charts featuring the stars filling the night sky in Hawaii, by month. A excellent primer.

Rhoads, Samuel. *The Sky Tonight—A Guided Tour of the Stars over Hawaii.* Honolulu: Bishop Museum, 1993. Four pages per month of star charts—one each for the horizon in every cardinal direction. Exceptional!

Cooking

Alexander, Agnes. *How to Use Hawaiian Fruit.* Hilo, HI: Petroglyph Press, 1984. A slim volume of recipes using delicious and different Hawaiian fruits.

Beeman, Judy, and Martin Beeman. *Joys of Hawaiian Cooking.* Hilo, HI: Petroglyph Press, 1977. A collection of favorite recipes from Big Island chefs.

Choy, Sam. *Cooking from the Heart with Sam Choy.* Honolulu: Mutual Publishing, 1995. This beautiful, hand-bound cookbook contains many color photos by Douglas Peebles.

Fukuda, Sachi. *Pupus, An Island Tradition.* Honolulu: Bess Press, 1995.

Margah, Irish, and Elvira Monroe. *Hawaii, Cooking with Aloha.* San Carlos, CA: Wide World, 1984. Island recipes, as well as hints on decor.

Rizzuto, Shirley. *Fish Dishes of the Pacific—from the Fishwife.* Honolulu: Hawaii Fishing News, 1986. Features recipes using all the fish commonly caught in Hawaiian waters (husband Jim Rizzuto is the author of *Fishing, Hawaiian Style*).

Culture

Dudley, Michael Kioni. *Man, Gods, and Nature.* Honolulu: Na Kane O Ka Malo Press, 1990. An examination of the philosophical underpinnings of Hawaiian beliefs and their interconnected reality.

Hartwell, Jay. *Na Mamo: Hawaiian People Today.* Honolulu: Ai Pohaku Press, 1996. Profiles 12 people practicing Hawaiian traditions in the modern world.

Heyerdahl, Thor. *American Indians in the Pacific.* London: Allen and Unwin Ltd., 1952. Theoretical and anthropological accounts of the influence on Polynesia of the Indians along the Pacific coast of North and South America. Though no longer in print, this book is fascinating reading, presenting unsubstantiated yet intriguing theories.

Kamehameha Schools Press. *Life in Early Hawai'i: The Ahupua'a.* 3rd ed. Honolulu: Kamehameha Schools Press, 1994. Written for schoolchildren to better understand the basic organization of old Hawaiian land use and its function, this slim volume is a good primer for people of any age who wish to understand this fundamental societal fixture.

Kirch, Patrick V. *Feathered Gods and Fishhooks: An Introduction to Hawaiian Archaeology and Prehistory.* Honolulu: University of Hawai'i Press, 1997. This scholarly, lavishly illustrated, yet very readable book gives new insight into the development of precontact Hawaiian civilization. It focuses on the sites and major settlements of old Hawai'i and chronicles the main cultural developments while weaving in the social climate that contributed to change. A very worthwhile read.

Fauna

Boom, Robert. *Hawaiian Seashells.* Honolulu: Waikiki Aquarium, 1972. Photos by Jerry Kringle. A collection of 137 seashells found in Hawaiian waters, featuring many found nowhere else on earth. Broken into categories with accompanying text including common and scientific names, physical descriptions, and likely habitats. A must for shell collectors.

Carpenter, Blyth, and Russell Carpenter. *Fish Watching in Hawaii.* San Mateo, CA: Natural World Press, 1981. A color guide to many of the reef fish found in Hawaii and often spotted by snorkelers. If you're interested in the fish that you'll be looking at, this guide will be very helpful.

Fielding, Ann, and Ed Robinson. *An Underwater Guide to Hawai'i.* Honolulu: University of Hawai'i Press, 1987. If you've ever had a desire to snorkel/scuba the living reef waters of Hawaii and to be familiar with what you're seeing, get this small but fact-packed book.

The amazing array of marine life found throughout the archipelago is captured in glossy photos with accompanying informative text. Both the scientific and common names of specimens are given. This book will enrich your underwater experience and serve as an easily understood reference guide for many years.

Goodson, Gar. *The Many-Splendored Fishes of Hawaii.* Stanford, CA: Stanford University Press, 1985. This small but thorough "fishwatchers" book includes entries on some deepsea fish.

Hawaiian Audubon Society. *Hawaii's Birds.* 5th ed. Honolulu: Hawaii Audubon Society, 1997. Excellent bird book, giving description, range, voice, and habits of the over 100 species. Slim volume; good for carrying while hiking.

Hobson, Edmund, and E.H. Chave. *Hawaiian Reef Animals.* Honolulu: University of Hawai'i Press, 1987. Colorful photos and descriptions of the fish, invertebrates, turtles, and seals that call Hawaiian reefs their home.

Kay, Alison, and Olive Schoenberg-Dole. *Shells of Hawai'i.* Honolulu: University of Hawai'i Press, 1991. Color photos and tips on where to look.

Mahaney, Casey. *Hawaiian Reef Fish, The Identification Book.* Thailand: Planet Ocean Publishing, 1993. A spiral-bound reference work featuring many color photos and descriptions of common reef fish found in Hawaiian waters.

Nickerson, Roy. *Brother Whale, A Pacific Whalewatcher's Log.* San Francisco: Chronicle Books, 1977. Introduces the average person to the life of earth's greatest mammals. Provides historical accounts, photos, and tips on whalewatching. Well-written, descriptive, and the best "first time" book on whales.

Pratt, Douglas. *A Field Guide to the Birds of Hawaii and the Tropical Pacific.* Princeton, N.J.: Princeton University Press, 1987. Useful field guide for novice and expert birdwatchers, covering Hawaii as well as other Pacific Island groups.

Pratt, Douglas. *A Pocket Guide to Hawaii's Birds.* Honolulu: Mutual Publishing, 1996. A condensed version of Pratt's larger work with a focus on bird's of the state.

Tomich, P. Quentin. *Mammals in Hawai'i.* Honolulu: Bishop Museum Press, 1986. Quintessential scholarly text on all mammal species in Hawaii, with description of distribution and historical references. Lengthy bibliography.

van Riper, Charles, and Sandra van Riper. *A Field Guide to the Mammals of Hawaii.* Honolulu: Oriental Publishing. A guide to the surprising number of mammals introduced into Hawaii. Full-color pages document description, uses, tendencies, and habitat. Small and thin, this book makes a worthwhile addition to any serious hiker's backpack.

Flora

Kepler, Angela. *Hawaiian Heritage Plants.* Honolulu: University of Hawai'i Press, 1998. A treatise on 32 utilitarian plants used by the early Hawaiians.

Kepler, Angela. *Hawai'i's Floral Splendor.* Honolulu: Mutual Publishing, 1997. A general reference to flowers of Hawaii.

Kepler, Angela. *Tropicals of Hawaii.* Honolulu: Mutual Publishing, 1989. This small-format book features many color photos of nonnative flowers.

Kuck, Lorraine, and Richard Togg. *Hawaiian Flowers and Flowering Trees.* Rutland, VT: Tuttle, 1960. A classic, though no longer in print,

field guide to tropical and subtropical flora illustrated in watercolor. A "to the point" description of Hawaiian plants and flowers with a brief history of their places of origin and their introduction to Hawaii.

Merrill, Elmer. *Plant Life of the Pacific World.* Rutland, VT: Tuttle, 1983. This is the definitive book for anyone planning a botanical tour to the entire Pacific Basin. Originally published in the 1930s, it remains a tremendous work, worth tracking down through out-of-print book services.

Miyano, Leland. *Hawai'i, A Floral Paradise.* Honolulu: Mutual Publishing, 1995. Photographed by Douglas Peebles, this large-format book is filled with informative text and beautiful color shots of tropical flowers commonly seen in Hawaii.

Miyano, Leland. *A Pocket Guide to Hawai'i's Flowers.* Honolulu: Mutual Publishing, 2001. A small guide to readily seen flowers in the state. Good for the backpack or back pocket.

Sohmer, S.H., and R. Gustafson. *Plants and Flowers of Hawai'i.* Honolulu: University of Hawai'i Press, 1987. Sohmer and Gustafson cover the vegetation zones of Hawaii, from mountains to coast, introducing you to the wide and varied floral biology of the islands. They give a good introduction to the history and unique evolution of Hawaiian plantlife. Beautiful color plates are accompanied by clear and concise plant descriptions, with the scientific and common Hawaiian names listed.

Teho, Fortunato. *Plants of Hawaii—How to Grow Them.* Hilo, HI: Petroglyph Press, 1992. A small but useful book for those who want their backyards to bloom into tropical paradises.

Wagner, Warren L., Derral R. Herbst, and H. S. Sohner. *Manual of the Flowering Plants of*

Suggested Reading

Hawai'i, revised edition, vol. 2. Honolulu: University of Hawai'i Press in association with Bishop Museum Press, 1999. Considered the Bible for Hawaii's botanical world. Scholarly.

Valier, Kathy. *Ferns of Hawaii*. Honolulu: University of Hawai'i Press, 1995. One of the few books that treat the state's ferns as a single subject.

Health

Gutmanis, June. *Kahuna La'au Lapa'au*. Honolulu: Island Heritage, rev. ed. 2001. Text on Hawaiian herbal medicines: diseases, treatments, and medicinal plants, with illustrations.

McBride, L.R. *Practical Folk Medicine of Hawaii*. Hilo, HI: Petroglyph Press, 1975. An illustrated guide to Hawaii's medicinal plants as used by the *kahuna lapa'au* (medical healers). Includes a thorough section on ailments, diagnosis, and the proper folk remedy. Illustrated by the author, a renowned botanical researcher and former ranger at Hawaii Volcanoes National Park.

Wilkerson, James A., M.D., ed. *Medicine for Mountaineering and Other Wilderness*. 4th ed. Seattle: The Mountaineers, 1992. Don't let the title fool you. Although the book focuses on specific health problems that may be encountered while mountaineering, it is the best first-aid and general health guide available today. Written by doctors for the layperson to use until help arrives, it is jam-packed with easily understandable techniques and procedures. For those planning extended hikes, it is a must.

History

Apple, Russell A. *Trails: From Steppingstones to Kerbstones*. Honolulu: Bishop Museum Press, 1965. This "Special Publication #53" is a special-interest archaeological survey focusing on trails, roadways, footpaths, and highways and how they were designed and maintained throughout the years. Many "royal highways" from precontact Hawaii are cited.

Ashdown, Inez MacPhee. *Kaho'olawe*. Honolulu: Topgallant Publishing, 1979. The tortured story of the lonely island of Kaho'olawe by one of the family who owned the island until it was turned into a military bombing target during World War II. It's also a first-person account of life on the island.

Ashdown, Inez MacPhee. *Ke Alaloa o Maui*. Wailuku, HI: Kama'aina Historians Inc., 1971. A compilation of the history and legends connected to sites on the island of Maui. Ashdown was at one time a "lady in waiting" for Queen Lili'uokalani and was later proclaimed Maui's "Historian Emeritus."

Barnes, Phil. *A Concise History of the Hawaiian Islands*. Hilo, HI; Petroglyph Press, 1999. An examination of the main currents of Hawaiian history and its major players, focusing on the important factors in shaping the social, economic, and political trends of the islands. An easy read.

Cameron, Roderick. *The Golden Haze*. New York: World Publishing, 1964. An account of Captain James Cook's voyages of discovery throughout the South Seas. Uses original diaries and journals for an "on the spot" reconstruction of this great seafaring adventure.

Cox, J. Halley, and Edward Stasack. *Hawaiian Petroglyphs*. Honolulu: Bishop Museum Press, 1970. The most thorough examination of petroglyph sites throughout the islands.

Daws, Gavan. *Shoal of Time, A History of the Hawaiian Islands*. Honolulu: University of Hawai'i Press, 1974. A highly readable history of Hawaii dating from its "discovery" by the Western world down to its acceptance as the 50th state. Good insight into the psychological makeup of influential characters who helped form Hawaii's past.

Donohugh, Douglas. *The Story of Koloa: A Kauai Plantation Town.* Honolulu: Mutual Publishing, 2001.

Dorrance, William H. and Francis S. Morgan. *Sugar Islands: The 165-Year Story of Sugar in Hawai'i.* Honolulu: Mutual Publishing, 2000. An overall sketch of the sugar industry in Hawaii from inception to decline, with data on many individual plantations and mills around the islands. Definitely a story from the industry's point of view.

Finney, Ben, and James D. Houston. *Surfing, A History of the Ancient Hawaiian Sport.* Los Angeles: Pomegranate, 1996. Features many early etchings and old photos of Hawaiian surfers practicing their native sport.

Fornander, Abraham. *An Account of the Polynesian Race; Its Origins and Migrations, and the Ancient History of the Hawaiian People to the Times of Kamehameha I.* Rutland, VT: C.E. Tuttle Co., 1969. This is a reprint of a three-volume opus originally published 1878–85. It is still one of the best sources of information on Hawaiian myth and legend.

Free, David. *Vignettes of Old Hawaii.* Honolulu: Crossroads Press, 1994. A collection of short essays on a variety of subjects.

Fuchs, Lawrence. *Hawaii Pono.* Honolulu: Bess Press, 1961. A detailed, scholarly work presenting an overview of Hawaii's history, based upon ethnic and sociological interpretations. Encompasses most socio-ethnological groups from native Hawaiians to modern entrepreneurs. This book is a must for obtaining some social historical background.

Handy, E.S., and Elizabeth Handy. *Native Planters in Old Hawaii.* Honolulu: Bishop Museum Press, 1972. A superbly written, easily understood scholarly work on the intimate relationship of precontact Hawaiians and the
aina (land). Much more than its title implies, this book should be read by anyone seriously interested in Polynesian Hawaii.

Ii, John Papa. *Fragments of Hawaiian History.* Honolulu: Bishop Museum, 1959. Hawaii's history under Kamehameha I as told by a Hawaiian who actually experienced it.

Joesting, Edward. *Hawaii: An Uncommon History.* New York: W.W. Norton Co., 1978. A truly uncommon history told in a series of vignettes relating to the lives and personalities of the first Caucasians in Hawaii, Hawaiian nobility, sea captains, writers, and adventurers. Brings history to life. Absolutely excellent!

Joesting, Edward. *Kauai: The Separate Kingdom.* Honolulu: University of Hawai'i Press, 1984. The history of Kaua'i through the end of the Hawaiian monarchy. Joesting brings the story of the island to life through the people who shaped it.

Kamakau, S. M. *Ruling Chiefs of Hawaii,* revised edition. Honolulu: Kamehameha Schools Press, 1992.

Krauss, Robert. *Grove Farm Plantation: The Biography of a Hawaiian Sugar Plantation.* Palo Alto, CA: Pacific Books, 1984. A history of the Grove Farm, the Wilcox family, and the economy of sugar on Kaua'i.

Kurisu, Yasushi. *Sugar Town, Hawaiian Plantation Days Remembered.* Honolulu: Watermark Publishing, 1995. Reminiscences of life growing up on sugar plantations on the Hamakua Coast of the Big Island. Features many old photos.

Lili'uokalani. *Hawaii's Story by Hawaii's Queen.* Reprint, Honolulu: Mutual Publishing, 1990. Originally written in 1898, this moving personal account recounts Hawaii's inevitable move from monarchy to U.S. Territory by its last queen, Lili'uokalani. The facts can be found in other histories, but none provides the emotion or point of view expressed by Hawaii's deposed monarch. This is a must-read to get the whole picture.

McBride, Likeke. *Petroglyphs of Hawaii.* Hilo, HI: Petroglyph Press, 1997. A revised and updated guide to petroglyphs found in the Hawaiian Islands. A basic introduction to these old Hawaiian picture stories.

Nickerson, Roy. *Lahaina, Royal Capital of Hawaii.* Honolulu: Hawaiian Service, 1978. The story of Lahaina from whaling days to present, spiced with ample photographs.

Tabrah, Ruth M. *Ni'ihau: The Last Hawaiian Island.* Kailua, Hawaii: Press Pacifica, 1987. Sympathetic history of the privately owned island of Ni'ihau.

Takaki, Ronald. *Pau Hana: Plantation Life and Labor in Hawaii.* Honolulu: University of Hawai'i Press, 1983. The story of immigrant labor and the sugar industry in Hawaii until the 1920s from the worker's perspective.

Introductory

Carroll, Rick, and Marcie Carroll, ed. *Hawai'i: True Stories of the Island Spirit.* San Francisco: Travelers' Tales, Inc., 1999. A collection of stories by a variety of authors that were chosen to elicit the essence of Hawaii and Hawaiian experiences. A great read.

Cohen, David, and Rick Smolan. *A Day in the Life of Hawaii.* New York: Workman, 1984. On December 2, 1983, 50 of the world's top photojournalists were invited to Hawaii to photograph the variety of daily life on the islands. The photos are excellently reproduced, and accompanied by a minimum of text.

Day, A.G., and C. Stroven. *A Hawaiian Reader.* 1959. Reprint, Honolulu: Mutual Publishing, 1984. A poignant compilation of essays, diary entries, and fictitious writings that takes you from the death of Captain Cook through the "statehood services."

Department of Geography, University of Hawai'i, Hilo. *Atlas of Hawai'i.* 3rd ed. Honolulu: University of Hawai'i Press, 1998. Much more than an atlas filled with reference maps, this also contains commentary on the natural environment, culture, and sociology; a gazetteer; and statistical tables. Actually a mini-encyclopedia on Hawai'i.

Michener, James A. *Hawaii.* New York: Random House, 1959. Michener's fictionalized historical novel has done more to inform *and* misinform readers about Hawaii than any other book ever written. A great tale with plenty of local color and information, but read it for pleasure, not facts.

Piercy, LaRue. *Hawaii This and That.* Honolulu: Mutual Publishing, 1994. Illustrated by Scot Ebanez. A 60-page book filled with one-sentence facts and oddities about all manner of things Hawaiian. Informative, amazing, and fun to read.

Steele, R. Thomas: *The Hawaiian Shirt: Its Art and History.* New York: Abbeville Press, 1984.

Language

Elbert, Samuel. *Spoken Hawaiian.* Honolulu: University of Hawai'i Press, 1970. Progressive conversational lessons.

Elbert, Samuel, and Mary Pukui. *Hawaiian Dictionary.* Honolulu: University of Hawai'i Press, 1986. The best dictionary available on the Hawaiian language. The *Pocket Hawaiian Dictionary* is a less expensive, condensed version of this dictionary, and adequate for most travelers with a general interest in the language.

Pukui, Mary Kawena, Samuel Elbert, and Esther T. Mookini. *Place Names of Hawaii*. Honolulu: University of Hawai'i Press, 1974. The most current and comprehensive listing of Hawaiian and foreign place-names in the state, giving pronunciation, spelling, meaning, and location.

Schutz, Albert J. *All About Hawaiian*. Honolulu: University of Hawai'i Press, 1995. A brief primer on Hawaiian pronunciation, grammar, and vocabulary. A solid introduction.

Mythology and Legends

Beckwith, Martha. *Hawaiian Mythology.* Reprint, Honolulu: University of Hawai'i Press, 1976. Over 60 years after its original printing in 1940, this work remains the definitive text on Hawaiian mythology. Beckwith compiled this book from many sources, giving exhaustive cross-references to genealogies and legends expressed in the oral tradition. If you are going to read one book on Hawaii's folklore, this should be it.

Beckwith, Martha. *The Kumulipo.* 1951. Reprint, Honolulu: University of Hawai'i Press, 1972. Translation of the Hawaiian creation chant.

Colum, Padraic. *Legends of Hawaii.* New Haven: Yale University Press, 1937. Selected legends of old Hawaii, reinterpreted but closely based upon the originals.

Elbert, S.H., ed. *Hawaiian Antiquities and Folklore.* Honolulu: University of Hawai'i Press, 1959. Illustrated by Jean Charlot. A selection of the main legends from Abraham Fornander's great work, *An Account of the Polynesian Race.*

Kalakaua, His Hawaiian Majesty, King David. *The Legends and Myths of Hawaii.* Edited by R.M. Daggett, with a foreword by Glen Grant. Honolulu: Mutual Publishing, 1990. Originally published in 1888, Hawaii's own King Kalakaua draws upon his scholarly and formidable knowledge of the classic oral tradition to bring alive ancient tales from pre-contact Hawaii. A powerful yet somewhat Victorian voice from Hawaii's past speaks clearly and boldly, especially about the intimate role of pre-Christian religion in the lives of the Hawaiian people.

Melville, Leinanai. *Children of the Rainbow.* Wheaton, IL: Theosophical Publishing, 1969. A book on higher spiritual consciousness attuned to nature, which was the basic belief of pre-Christian Hawaii. The appendix contains illustrations of mystical symbols used by the *kahuna.* An enlightening book in many ways.

Pukui, Mary Kawena, and Caroline Curtis. *Hawaii Island Legends.* Honolulu: The Kamehameha Schools Press, 1996. Hawaiian tales and legends for youngsters.

Pukui, Mary Kawena, and Caroline Curtis. *Tales of the Menehune.* Honolulu: The Kamehameha Schools Press, 1960. Compilation of legends relating to Hawaii's "little people."

Pukui, Mary Kawena, and Caroline Curtis. *The Waters of Kane and other Hawaiian Legends.* Honolulu: The Kamehameha Schools Press, 1994. Tales and legends for adolescents.

Thrum, Thomas. *Hawaiian Folk Tales.* 1907. Reprint, Chicago: McClurg and Co., 1950. A collection of Hawaiian tales from the oral tradition as told to the author from various sources.

Westervelt, W.D. *Hawaiian Legends of Volcanoes.* 1916. Reprint, Boston: Ellis Press, 1991. A small book concerning the volcanic legends of Hawaii and how they related to the fledgling field of volcanism in the early 1900s. The vintage photos alone are worth a look.

Suggested Reading

Natural Sciences and Geography

Carlquist, Sherwin. *Hawaii: A Natural History.* National Tropical Botanical Garden, 1984. Definitive account of Hawaii's natural history.

Clark, John. *Beaches of the Big Island.* Honolulu: University of Hawai'i Press, 1997. Definitive guide to beaches, including many off the beaten path. Features maps and black-and-white photos. Also *Beaches of O'ahu, Beaches of Kaua'i and Ni'ihau,* and *Beaches of Maui County.*

Hazlett, Richard, and Donald Hyndman. *Roadside Geology of Hawai'i.* Missoula, MT: Mountain Press Publishing, 1996. Begins with a general discussion of the geology of the Hawaiian Islands, followed by a road guide to the individual islands offering descriptions of easily seen features. A great book to have in the car as you tour the islands.

Hubbard, Douglass, and Gordon Macdonald. *Volcanoes of the National Parks of Hawaii.* 1982. Reprint, Volcanoes, HI: Hawaii Natural History Association, 1989. The volcanology of Hawaii, documenting the major lava flows and their geological effect on the state.

Kay, E. Alison, comp. *A Natural History of the Hawaiian Islands.* Honolulu: University of Hawai'i Press, 1994. A selection of concise articles by experts in the fields of volcanism, oceanography, meteorology, and biology. An excellent reference source.

Macdonald, Gorden, Agatin Abbott, and Frank Peterson. *Volcanoes in the Sea.* Honolulu: University of Hawai'i Press, 1983. The best reference to Hawaiian geology. Well-explained for easy understanding. Illustrated.

Periodicals

Hawaii Magazine. 3 Burroughs, Irvine, CA 92618. This magazine covers the Hawaiian islands like a tropical breeze. Feature articles on all aspects of life in the islands, with special departments on travel, events, exhibits, and restaurant reviews. Up-to-the-minute information, and a fine read.

Naturist Society Magazine. P.O. Box 132, Oshkosh, WI 54920. This excellent magazine not only *uncovers* bathing-suit-optional beaches throughout the islands, giving tips for naturalists visiting Hawaii, but also reports on local politics, environment, and conservation measures from the health-conscious nudist point of view. A fine publication.

Pictorials

La Brucherie, Roger. *Hawaiian World, Hawaiian Heart.* Pine Valley, CA: Imagenes Press, 1989.

Political Science

Albertini, Jim, et al. *The Dark Side of Paradise, Hawaii in a Nuclear War.* Honolulu: cAtholic Action of Hawaii. Well-documented research outlining Hawaii's role and vulnerability in a nuclear world. This book presents the antinuclear and antimilitary side of the political issue in Hawaii.

Bell, Roger. *Last Among Equals: Hawaiian Statehood and American Politics.* Honolulu: University of Hawai'i Press, 1984. Documents Hawaii's long and rocky road to statehood, tracing political partisanship, racism, and social change.

Sports and Recreation

Alford, John, D. *Mountain Biking the Hawaiian Islands.* Ohana Publishing, 1997. Good off-road biking guide to the main Hawaiian islands.

Ambrose, Greg. *Surfer's Guide to Hawai'i.* Honolulu: Bess Press, 1991. Island-by-island guide to surfing spots.

Ball, Stuart. *The Hiker's Guide to the Hawaiian Islands*. Honolulu: University of Hawai'i Press, 2000. This excellent guide includes 44 hikes on each of the four main islands. Ball has also written *The Hikers Guide to O'ahu*.

Cagala, George. *Hawaii: A Camping Guide*. Boston: Hunter Publishing, 1994. Useful.

Chisholm, Craig. *Hawaiian Hiking Trails*. Lake Oswego, OR: Fernglen Press, 1989. Also *Kauai Hiking Trails*.

Cisco, Dan. *Hawai'i Sports*. Honolulu: University of Hawai'i Press, 1999. A compendium of popular and little-known sporting events and figures, with facts, tidbits, and statistical information. Go here first for a general overview.

Lueras, Leonard. *Surfing, the Ultimate Pleasure*. Honolulu: Emphasis International, 1984. One of the most brilliant books ever written on surfing.

McMahon, Richard. *Camping Hawai'i: A Complete Guide*. Honolulu: University of Hawai'i Press, 1997. This book has all you need to know about camping in Hawaii, with descriptions of different campsites.

Morey, Kathy. *Hawaii Trails*. Berkeley, CA: Wilderness Press, 1997. Morey's books are specialized, detailed hiker's guides to Hawaii's outdoors. Complete with useful maps, historical references, official procedures, and plants and animals encountered along the way. If you're focused on hiking, these are the best to take along. *Maui Trails, Oahu Trails,* and *Kauai Trails* are also available.

Rosenberg, Steve. *Diving Hawaii*. Locust Valley, NY: Aqua Quest, 1990. Describes diving locations on the major islands as well as the marine life divers are likely to see. Includes many color photos.

Smith, Robert. *Hawaii's Best Hiking Trails*. Kula, Maui, HI: Hawaiian Outdoor Adventures, 1991. Other guides by this author include *Hiking Oahu, Hiking Maui, Hiking Hawaii,* and *Hiking Kauai*.

Sutherland, Audrey. *Paddling Hawai'i,* revised edition. Honolulu: University of Hawai'i Press, 1998. All you need to know about sea kayaking in Hawaiian waters.

Wallin, Doug. *Diving & Snorkeling Guide to the Hawaiian Islands,* 2nd ed. Pisces Books, 1991. A guide offering brief descriptions of diving locations on the four major islands.

Internet Resources

The following websites have information about the Big Island of Hawai'i and the state of Hawaii that may be useful in preparation for a trip to the islands and for general interest.

www.hawaii-county.com

The official website of Hawai'i County. Includes, among other items, a county data book, information about parks and camping, and island bus schedules.

www.gohawaii.com

This official site of the Hawaii Visitors Bureau, the state-run tourism organization, has information about all the major Hawaiian islands: transportation, accommodations, eating, activities, shopping, Hawaiian products, an events calendar, a travel planner, and a resource guide for a host of topics, as well as information about meetings, conventions, and the organization itself.

www.bigisland.org

The official site of the Big Island Visitors Bureau, a branch of the Hawaii Visitors Bureau, has much the same information as the above website but specific to the island of Hawai'i. A very useful resource.

www.bestplaceshawaii.com

Produced and maintained by H&S Publishing, this first-rate commercial site has general and specific information about all major Hawaiian islands, a vacation planner, and suggestions for things to do and places to see. This is a great place to start a search for tourist information about the state or any of its major islands. One of dozens of sites on the Internet with a focus on Hawaii tourism-related information.

www.konaweb.com

This site offers a multiplicity of tourist information for those wishing to visit or move to the island, information on island living, and an events calendar.

www.alternative-hawaii.com

Alternative source for eco-friendly general information and links to specific businesses, with some cultural, historical, and events information.

www.hawaiiecotourism.org

Official Hawaii Ecotourism Association website. Lists goals, members, and activities and provides links to member organizations and related ecotourism groups.

http://calendar.gohawaii.com

For events of all sorts happening throughout the state, visit the calendar of events listing on the Hawaii Visitors Bureau website. Information can be accessed by island, date, or type.

www.state.hi.us/sfca/culturecalendar.html

This site of the State Foundation of Culture and the Arts features a calendar of arts and cultural events, activities, and programs held throughout the state. Information is available by island and type.

www.hawaiianair.com
www.alohaairlines.com
www.pacificwings.com

These websites for Hawaiian Airlines, Aloha Airlines, and Pacific Wings list virtually all regularly scheduled commercial air links throughout the state.

www.mele.com

Check out the Hawaiian music scene at Hawaiian Music Island, one of the largest music websites that focuses on Hawaiian music, books and videos related to Hawaiian music and culture, concert schedules, Hawaiian music awards, and links to music companies and musicians. Others with broad listings and general interest information are: Nahenahenet, **www.nahenahe.net,** and Hawaiian Music Guide, **www.hawaii-music.com.**

www.uhpress.hawaii.edu

The University of Hawai'i Press website has the best overall list of titles for books published on Hawaiian themes and topics. Other publishers to check for substantial lists of books on Hawaiiana are the Bishop Museum Press, **www.bishopmuseum.org/bishop/press;** Kamehameha Schools Press, **www.ksbe.edu/newsroom/kspress;** Bess Press, **www.besspress.com;** Mutual Publishing, **www.mutualpublishing.com;** and Petroglyph Press, **www.basicallybooks.com.**

www.hawaiimuseums.org

This site is dedicated to the promotion of museums and cultural attractions in the state of Hawaii with links to member sites on each of the islands. A member organization.

www.bishopmuseum.org

Site of the premier ethnological and cultural museum dedicated to Hawaiian people, their culture, and cultural artifacts.

www.nps.gov/havo

This official site of Hawaii Volcanoes National Park is a wealth of general information about the park. Related sites are **www.nps.gov/puho,** for Pu'uhonua O Honaunau, a restored Hawaiian temple of refuge, and **www.nps.gov/puhe,** for Pu'ukohola Heiau, a restored Hawaiian temple, both national historical sites administered by the National Park Service.

www.ifa.hawaii.edu

For information about the astronomical observatories and individual telescope installations on the top of Mauna Kea on the Big Island as well as the Onizuka Center for International Astronomy on the mountain's flank, log onto this University of Hawaii Institute for Astronomy website and follow the links from there.

http://hvo.wr.usgs.gov

For a history of the Kilauea Volcano volcanic activity, plus up-to-the-minute reports on current activity, see this Hawaii Volcano Observatory website. Related volcanic information is also available at **www.soest.hawaii.edu/GG/HCV.**

www.stayhawaii.com

Website for the Hawaii Island Bed and Breakfast Association, Inc., the only island-wide B&B member organization. Lists a majority of the island's registered B&Bs. Some registered B&Bs are not members of this organization.

www.gohilo.com

Hawaii Island Chamber of Commerce site strong on business and economic issues, particularly relating to the eastern side of the island. Much additional general information.

www.kona-kohala.com

Chamber of Commerce website for west Hawai'i.

www.westhawaiitoday.com
www.hilohawaiitribune.com

Web presence for the newspapers *West Hawaii Today,* published in Kona, and *Hawaii Tribune-Herald,* published in Hilo. Good for local and statewide news. Both have the same parent company.

www.kau-landing.com

Providing an alternative and progressive view on island issues is the *Ka'u Landing,* a monthly newspaper out of Ocean View.

www.starbulletin.com
www.honoluluadvertiser.com

Websites for Hawaii's two main English-language dailies, the *Honolulu Star Bulletin* and the *Honolulu Advertiser,* both published in Honolulu. Both have a concentration of news coverage about O'ahu but also cover major news from the neighbor islands.

www.oha.org
Official site for the state-mandated organization that deals with native Hawaii-related affairs.

www.kalahui.org
Site for the oldest and largest organization of native Hawaiians who are advocating for sovereignty. There are several dozen independent native Hawaiian rights organizations that are pushing for various degrees of sovereignty or independence for native Hawaiian people; some of the major groups are listed below: Nation of Hawai'i, **www.hawaii-nation.org;** Reinstated Hawaiian Government, **www.reinstated.org;** Kingdom of Hawaii, **www.freehawaii.org;** (another) Kingdom of Hawaii, **www.pixi.com/~kingdom;** the Hawaiian Kingdom, **www.hawaiiankingdom.org.**

Index

A

'a'a lava: 7

'a'ali'i: 368

'a'ama: 121

accommodations: 109–116; Captain Cook: 210–212; Hawaii Volcanoes National Park: 369–370; Hawi: 261; Hilo: 291–297; Holualoa: 199–200; Honoka'a: 316; Honomu: 310–311; Kailua-Kona: 174–179; Kapa'au: 265; Kawaihae: 237–238; Kukuihaele: 319–320; Kurtistown: 341; Miloli'i: 214; Na'alehu: 378; Ocean View: 382–383; Pahala: 373–374; Pahoa: 332; Puna: 337–338; Punalu'u: 376–377; South Kohala: 224–234; Volcano Village: 343–349; Wailea: 312–313; Waimea: 247–248; Wai'ohinu: 379–380

African violets: 15

agricultural inspections: 130

agriculture: 42–43

'ahi: 121

Ahu'ena Heiau: 159, 163

AJAs: see Americans of Japanese Ancestry (AJAs)

Air Canada: 134

airfares: 128

Air New Zealand: 134

Air Pacific: 134

airports: 130–132

air tours: 98–100

air travel: 125–138

'Akaka Falls State Park: 312

'akepa: 18–19

'akiapola'au: 17–18

'alae ke'oke'o: 18

alala: 17

Ali'i Drive: 167–169

Aloha Airlines: 133, 137

alohawear: 107

'amakihi: 18, 274

American Airlines: 133

Americans of Japanese Ancestry (AJAs): 48–49

Amy B. H. Greenwell Ethnobotanical Garden: 15, 204–205

'Anaeho'omalu Bay: 222

animals: see fauna

anthurium: 340

antique shops: 254, 263, 305, 317–318, 340

'a'o: 18

'apapane: 18, 274, 368

arboretums: see gardens

art galleries: 105; Hawi: 263; Hilo: 304–305; Holualoa: 196–197; Honoka'a: 318–319; Honomu: 311; Kailua-Kona: 192; Kainaliu: 202; Kapa'au: 266; Waimea: 254

arts and artwork: 59–63, 106–109

assault: 151–152

ATV tours: 98, 326

a'u: 121

avocados: 122

B

baggage tips: 129–130

ballooning: 100, 251

bananas: 122

banks: 157, 194, 307

Banyan Drive, Hilo: 282–285

bats, Hawaiian hoary: 19–20

Battle of Moku'ohai: 207

bed-and-breakfasts: 114–115; Captain Cook: 210–212; Hilo: 291–295; Holualoa: 199–200; Honoka'a: 316; Kawaihae: 237–238; Kurtistown: 341; Na'alehu: 378; Ocean View: 382–383; Pahoa: 332; Volcano Village: 344–345; Wailea: 312–313; Waimea: 247–248; Wai'ohinu: 379

bento: 119

bicycling: 95–97, 188–189, 251, 302–303

billfish: 21, 101

birds: 16–19, 274, 367–368

Boiling Pots: 285

Bond Estate, The: 264

bookstores: 106, 193, 203, 266, 306

botanical gardens: 14–15, 204–205, 287–289; see also gardens

breadfruit: 123

breweries: 186, 301–302

buffets: 119

bugs: see insects

bus tours: 97

bus travel: 144

Beaches

general discussion: 8, 76–77
'Anaeho'omalu Bay: 222
Carlsmith Beach County Park: 289
Four Mile Beach: 290
Green Sand Beach: 381
Hapuna Beach State Recreation Area: 223
Hilo: 289–291
Hilo Bayfront Park: 289
Holoholokai Beach Park: 222–223
Honokohau Beach: 172–173
Honoli'i Beach County Park: 291
Isaac Hale Beach County Park: 335
James Kealoha Beach County Park: 290
Kahalu'u Beach Park: 172
Kahuwai Beach: 221
Kailua-Kona: 171–174
Kaloko Beach: 173
Kamakahonu Beach: 171
Kapa'a Beach County Park: 258
Kauna'oa Beach: 224
Keaukaha Beach: 289
Kehena Beach: 335–336
Keokea Beach County Park: 265
Kiholo Bay: 221–222
Kolekole Beach Park: 312
Kua Bay: 174, 221
Kuki'o Beach: 221
Leleiwi Beach County Park: 290
Mahai'ula Beach: 173
Mahukona Beach County Park: 258
Makalawena Beach: 173–174
Manini Beach: 207
Mauna Kea Beach: 224
Napo'opo'o Beach County Park: 207
Old Kona Airport State Recreation Area: 172
Onekahakaha Beach County Park: 289–290
Pahoehoe Beach County Park: 172
Pine Trees: 173
Puna: 333–336
Punalu'u Beach County Park: 376
Reeds Bay Beach Park: 289
Richardson's Beach Park: 290–291
Spencer Beach County Park: 224
Waipi'o Beach: 324
Wawaloli Beach: 173
White Sands Beach County Park: 171–172
Whittington Beach County Park: 377–378

C

cactus, prickly pear: 14–15
Caltech Submillimeter Observatory (CSO): 272–273
camera shops: 106, 193–194
camping: 69–72, 223, 326, 335, 369–370, 375, 383
Canada-France-Hawaii Telescope: 271
canoe makers: 59–60
Cape Kumukahi: 5, 328, 333–334
Captain Cook (town): 206–213
Carlsmith Beach County Park: 289
car rentals: 139–143, 273–274
car travel: 138–143
carving: 60–61, 108
caste system: 45
cattle, feral: 20
Caucasian population: 49–50
Chain of Craters Road: 336, 363–366
charters: air travel: 128–129; fishing: 101–102; sailing: 86; snorkeling: 81, 84
children, travel with: 129
China Airlines: 134
Chinese population: 47
Christ Church Episcopal: 203
cinemas: 192, 302, 317
climate: 8–11, 241
clothing recommendations: 152–153
coastal fish: 102
cockroaches: 146
Coconut Island: 283
coconuts: 122–123
coffee: 42–43, 125, 198, 203–204, 206
coffee plantations: 3, 197–199
condominiums: 112–113, 177–178, 227–228, 231, 376–377; see also resorts
consumer protection: 155
Continental Airlines: 133
Cook, James: 25–28, 207–208
coral: 21–22, 147

crackseed: 122
Crater Rim Drive: 359–362
Crater Rim Loop Trail: 361
credit cards: 157
creeper, Hawaiian: 19
crime: 150–152
crow, Hawaiian: 17
cruises: 81, 84, 85–88, 138, 189
currency: 157
cycling: *see* bicycling

D
Dai Fukuji Soto Buddhist Mission: 200
David Douglas Historical Monument: 314
death marchers: 57
deep-sea fishing: 101
Delta Air Lines: 133
Devastation Trail: 360, 362
dinner cruises: 87
disabilities, travel with: 143, 149–150
diving: 239; *see also* scuba diving
dogs, feral: 20
Dolphin Quest: 228–229
domestic airlines: 132–133
donkeys, feral: 20
drinks: 124–125
drosophila, Hawaiian: 20
drugs, illegal: 150
D. Uchida Coffee Farm: 204

E
early-bird special meals: 119
Earth Heritage Gallery: 281
earthquakes: 8
Earthquake Trail: 362
easternmost point of Hawaii: 5, 328, 333–334
East Hawai'i Cultural Center: 282
East Hawai'i Cultural Council: 65
economy: 41–43
ecotours: 136, 192
eels, moray: 147
Elderhostel Hawaii: 136
electricity: 157
'elepaio: 18, 368
emergency services: 155, 194
eruptions: 354–356
ethnic groups: 44–51

F
fauna: 16–22; evolution of: 12; *see also specific animal; specific bird*
feather work: 61
Federal Building, Hilo: 282
ferns: 14
festivals and events: 66–68, 315–316
Filipino population: 51–52
film development: 106, 194
fishing: 100–103, 381
fitness centers: 226, 233
fixed-wing air tours: 100
flora: 13–16; evolution of: 12; Kipuka Pu'u Hu-luhulu: 274; 'Ola'a Forest: 368; *see also specific plant*
folk medicine: 148–149
food: 116–125; Captain Cook: 212–213; gift items: 109; Hawaii Volcanoes National Park: 370–371; Hawi: 261–262; Hilo: 297–302; Holualoa: 200; Honalo: 200–201; Honoka'a: 316–317; Honomu: 311; Kailua-Kona: 179–186; Kainaliu: 200–201; Kapa'au: 265–266; Kawaihae: 238–239; Kea'au: 339; Kealakekua: 204–205; Na'alehu: 378–379; Ocean View: 383; Pahoa: 332–333; Puna: 338–339; South Kohala: 234–235; Volcano Village: 349–350; Waimea: 248–251
food stores and markets: 119–120, 192–193, 202–203, 254, 305–306, 333, 379
foreign airlines: 133–134
Four Mile Beach: 290
freshwater fish: 102
fruits, tropical: 122–123
Fuku-Bonsai Cultural Center: 339–340

G
game animals: 104
game birds: 104
game fish: 101
gardens: 14–15, 204–205, 283, 287–289, 339–340
Gemini Northern 8.1-meter Telescope: 273
geology: 5–8, 353–356
gesneriads: 15
ghosts: 56–57
gift shops: 105–106, 166, 192, 202, 263, 304
glass-bottom boat tours: 87

Glenwood: 341
goats, feral: 104
gods: 55–56, 353–354
golf: 88–92; Hilo: 283, 303; Kona: 189;
    Punalu'u: 375, 377; South Kohala: 231, 233,
    236; Volcano Village: 342; Waimea: 251
government: 41
green flash: 10
Green Sand Beach: 381
guavas: 123

H

Hakalau Forest National Wildlife Refuge: 19
Hale Halawai O Holualoa Congregational
    Church: 167
Halema'uma'u Crater: 360
Halema'uma'u Trail: 361
Hale Pohaku: 270
Hamakua Coast: 4, 308–327
Hamakua Ditch Trail: 252
Hamakua Music Festival: 315
Hanua'aloa: 322
haole rot: 146
Hapai Ali'i Heiau: 168
Hapuna Beach State Recreation Area: 223
hassles: 151–152
Hawaiian Airlines: 132–133, 137
Hawaiian foods: 116–125
Hawaiian language: 54–55
Hawaiian Volcano Observatory: 359–360
Hawaii Belt Road: 330
Hawaii Tropical Botanical Gardens: 14, 288–289
Hawaii Visitors Bureau: 154–155
Hawaii Volcanoes National Park: 71, 351–371
Hawi: 260–263
hawk, Hawaiian: 17
health: 145–150, 194, 254
heiau: 56; Ahu'ena Heiau: 159, 163; Hanua'aloa:
    322; Hapai Ali'i Heiau: 168; Hikiau Heiau:
    207–208; Kapuanoni Heiau: 168;
    Kealakowa'a Heiau: 167; Ke'eku Heiau: 168;
    Ku'emanu Heiau: 168; Mailekini Heiau: 219;
    Mo'okini Luakini Heiau: 258–260; Paka'alana
    Heiau: 322; Pu'ukohola Heiau: 219–220;
    Waha'ulu Heiau: 336, 365–366
helicopter tours: 98–99
Hi'iaka Crater: 364
Hi'ilawe Waterfall: 322, 325
Hikiau Heiau: 207–208
hiking: 72–76; Arnott's Expeditions: 303;

Cabin Trail: 356; Crater Rim Loop Trail:
361; Devastation Trail: 360, 362; Earthquake
Trail: 362; Halema'uma'u Trail: 360, 361;
Hawaii Volcanoes National Park: 356–357;
high altitude effects: 270–271; 'Iliahi (San-
dalwood) Trail: 362; Ka'aha Trail: 367; Ka'u
Desert Trail: 366–367; Kilauea Iki Trail:
361–362; Kipuka Puaulu Loop Trail: 368;
Kipuka Pu'u Huluhulu: 274; Kohala Ditch
trail: 262–263, 266–267; Manuka State
Wayside: 383; Mauna Iki Trail: 367; Mauna
Kea: 270–271; Mauna Loa: 356; Muliwai
Trail: 326; Napau Trail: 364; Observatory
Trail: 356; Pololu Valley: 266–267; Puna
Coast Trail: 367; Pu'u O'o Trail: 275; Sum-
mit Trail: 356; Waipi'o Ridge Hike: 252;
Waipi'o Valley: 324
Hilina Pali Road: 366
Hilo: 4, 276–307
Hilo Bayfront Park: 289
Hilo Forestry Arboretum: 14, 287
Hilo International Airport: 130–131
Hilo Public Library: 282
Hilo Tropical Gardens: 14, 288
history: 22–40, 243–244, 321–324
hitchhiking: 145
Hokuloa Church: 219, 376
Holei Sea Arch: 364
Holoholokai Beach Park: 222–223
holua: 170
Holualoa: 195–200
home exchanges: 116
Honalo: 200–203
Honoka'a: 315–320
Honokohau Beach: 172–173
Honokohau Harbor: 169
Honoli'i Beach County Park: 291
Honomu: 310–313
honu 'ea: 20–21
Ho'okena: 213–214
Ho'okena Beach County Park: 213–214
Ho'olulu County Park: 284
horseback riding: 93–95, 205, 251, 324–325
hostels: 115–116, 174, 214, 291, 343–344
hotels: 109–112, 174–175, 199, 210, 295–297;
    see also resorts
Hualalai, Mount: 3, 6, 159
Hualalai Road: 195
hula: 62
Hulihe'e Palace: 60, 165–166

humpback whale: 20
hunting: 103–104
hurricanes: 10–11

I
idols: 56
'i'iwi: 18, 274
'Iliahi (Sandalwood) Trail: 362
'ilio: 20
illegal drugs: 150
'Imiola Church: 246
information services: 154–156, 194, 254,
   306–307
inhabitants: 44–51
inns: 247
insects: 20, 146
interisland airlines: 136–138
Internet services: 194, 307, 350
'io: 17, 274
Isaac Hale Beach County Park: 335
Island Air: 137
island drinks: 124–125
island facts: 157
Island Heritage Gallery: 281
island treats: 121–122

J
James Clerk Maxwell Telescope: 271
James Kealoha Beach County Park: 290
Japan Air Lines: 134
Japanese population: 48–49
jellyfish: 147
jetskiing: 85
jewelry: 108–109, 192
John Young Homestead site: 220

K
Ka'aha Trail: 367
Ka'ahumanu, Queen: 33–34, 209
Kahalu'u Beach Park: 172
Kahikolu Congregational Church: 207
Kahuwai Beach: 221
Kailua-Kona: 159–195
Kailua Pier: 163
Kaimu: 336
Kainaliu: 200–203
Ka Lae: 5, 372, 380–381
Kalahikiola Congregational Church: 264
Kalakaua Park: 282
Kaloko Beach: 173

Kaloko-Honokohau National Historical Park:
   172–173
Kalopa State Recreation Area: 314–315
Kamakahonu Beach: 171
Kamehameha: 29–32, 219–220, 260, 263–264,
   322, 367
Kamehameha 'Akahi 'Aina Hanau: 260
Kamehameha County Park: 264
Kamehameha III (Kauikeaouli): 35–36
Kamehameha II (Liholiho): 33–34
Kamehameha IV (Alexander Liholiho): 38
Kamehameha V (Lot Kamehameha): 38
Kamoa Wind Farm: 380
Kamuela: see Waimea
Kamuela Museum: 61, 246
Kapa'a Beach County Park: 258
Kapa'au: 263–266
Kapapala Ranch: 375
Kapoho Tidepools: 334
Kapoloa waterfall: 262
Kapuanoni Heiau: 168
Ka'u: 5, 372–383
Ka'u Desert: 366–367
Ka'u Desert Footprints: 366–367
Ka'u Desert Trail: 366–367
kaukau wagons: 119
Kaumana Caves: 285
Kauna'oa Beach: 224
Ka'upulehu Petroglyphs: 218
Kawaihae: 237
Kawaihae Coast: 257–260
kayaking: 85, 187–188, 205–206, 213, 237, 251
Kazumura Lava Tube: 341
Kea'au: 339
Kealakekua: 203–206
Kealakekua Bay: 159, 207–208
Kealakomo: 364
Kealakowa'a Heiau: 167
Ke'amoku Flow: 368
Keanakako'i Crater: 360
Keauhou Bay: 168
Keaukaha Beach: 289
Ke'ei: 207
Ke'eku Heiau: 168
Kekaha Kai State Park: 173–174
Keokea Beach County Park: 265
Kiholo Bay: 221–222
Kilauea Caldera: 6, 351, 353–362
Kilauea Iki: 360
Kilauea Iki Trail: 361–362

Index

Kilauea Military Camp: 359, 370
Kilauea Overlook: 359
Kimura Lauhala Shop: 195–196
Kipuka Ki: 368
Kipuka Puaulu: 367–368
Kipuka Puaulu Loop Trail: 368
Kipuka Pu'u Huluhulu: 274
koa: 13, 274
Koai'e Cove Marine Conservation District: 257
Kohala: 3–4
Kohala Historical Sites State Monument: 260
Kohala Mountains: 6
kohola: 20
Kolekole Beach Park: 312
koloa maoli: 18
Kona: 3, 158–214
Kona Arts Center: 196
Kona Historical Society Museum: 61, 203–204
Kona International Airport: 131–132
konane: 208
Kona nightingales: 20, 218
kona winds: 10
Ko'oko'olau Crater: 364
Korean Air: 134
Koyasan Daishiji Shingon: 197
Kua Bay: 174, 221
Ku'emanu Heiau: 168
Kuki'o Beach: 221
kukui: 148
Kukuihaele: 319–320
Kula Kai Caverns: 382
Kulanaokuaiki: 369–370
Kumulipo, The: 22–23
Kurtistown: 339–340

L

Lake Waiau: 6, 270
Lanakila Congregational Church: 200
land: 5–8
land ownership: 42, 43
land tours: 97–98
language: 51–55
Lapakahi State Historical Park: 257–258
laundromats: 155, 194, 350
Laupahoehoe: 313–314
Laupahoehoe Point County Park: 313
Laupahoehoe Train Museum: 61, 313–314
Lava Tree State Monument: 330, 332
lei: 62–63
Leke Leke Burial Grounds: 168

Lava Flows

Cape Kumukahi: 328, 330, 333–334
Chain of Craters Road: 336, 363–366
geologic history: 6–7, 353–356
Hawaii Volcanoes National Park: 71, 351–371
Hilo: 285
Kaimu: 336–337
Ka'u: 372–383
Ka'u Desert: 366–367
Kaumana Caves: 285
Kazumura Lava Tube: 341
Ke'amoku Flow: 368
Kehena Beach: 335–336
Kilauea Caldera: 6, 351, 357–362
Kilauea Iki: 360
Lava Tree State Monument: 330, 332
South Kohala: 217–218
Thurston Lava Tube: 361
Tree Molds: 367
Waha'ula Heiau: 365–366

Leleiwi Beach County Park: 290
Leptospirosis: 148
libraries: 155–156, 194, 282, 306
Lili'uokalani Gardens: 283
Lili'uokalani, Queen: 38–39
limu: 121
litchis: 124
lobelia: 15
Lo'ihi Seamount: 375–376
lomi lomi salmon: 122
Lua Manu Crater: 364
Lua o milu: 322
lu'au: 118, 187, 234–235
Lyman Mission House and Museum: 60, 279, 281

M

macadamia nuts: 123, 214, 286
MacKenzie State Recreation Area: 335
Mahai'ula Beach: 173
mahimahi: 120–121
Mahukona Beach County Park: 258
mail: see post offices
Mailekini Heiau: 219
Makalawena Beach: 173–174

Maku'aweoweo Caldera: 356
malasadas: 122
Mana Hale: 244–245
mangoes: 123
manini: 121
Manini Beach: 207
Manuka State Wayside: 383
map sources: 76
marchers of the night: 57
Maria Lanakila Church: 214
Marine Life Conservation District: 207
marine reports: 155
Mark Twain Monkeypod Tree: 379
marlin: 21, 101
Marquesas: 24, 45
Masters and Servants Act of 1850: 37
Maui (hero): 57–58
Maui's Canoe: 282
Maulua Gulch: 314
Mauna Iki Trail: 367
Mauna Kea: 5–6, 269–271
Mauna Kea Beach: 224
Mauna Kea Ice Age Natural Area Reserve: 270
Mauna Kea Observatory Complex: 271–274
Mauna Loa: 6, 275, 356
Mauna Loa Macadamia Nut Factory: 286–287
Mauna Loa NOAA Observatory: 275
Mauna Loa Road: 367–368
measurement systems: 157
medical services: 149, 194, 254, 306
military history: 39–40
military personnel: 43
Miloli'i: 214
Miloli'i Beach County Park: 214
missionaries: 34–36, 58
moi: 121
Moku'aikaua Church: 163–164
Moku'aweoweo Caldera: 275
money: 157
monk seal: 19
Mo'oheau Bandstand: 282
Mo'okini Luakini Heiau: 258–260
moray eels: 147
mosquitoes: 16, 146
motorcycles: 143
mountains: Kilauea Caldera: 6, 351, 353–362; Kohala Mountains: 6; Mauna Kea: 5–6, 269–271; Mauna Loa: 6, 275, 356; Mount Hualalai: 6, 159

Museums

Hulihe'e Palace: 60, 165–166
Kamuela Museum: 61, 246
Kona Historical Society Museum: 61, 203–204
Laupahoehoe Train Museum: 61, 313–314
Lyman Mission House and Museum: 60, 279, 281
Onizuka Space Center: 61, 170–171
Pacific Tsunami Museum: 60, 281
Parker Ranch Historic Homes: 60, 241, 244–246
Parker Ranch Visitor Center and Museum: 61, 245–246
Royal Kona Coffee Mill and Museum: 206
Thomas A. Jaggar Museum: 61, 360

Mountain View: 340–341
movies: *see* cinemas; theaters
Muliwai Trail: 326
munchies: 121–122
music: 63–66

N
Na'alehu: 378–379
Naha Stone: 282
Namakani Paio: 369
Nani Mau Gardens: 14, 288
Napau Crater: 364
Napau Trail: 364
Napo'opo'o Beach County Park: 207
Napo'opo'o Road: 206–207
NASA Infrared Telescope Facility (IRTF): 272
native Hawaiians: 44–47
native trees: 13–14
Natural Energy Laboratory of Hawaii Authority (NELHA): 169–170
nautical charts: 76
nene: 16–17, 356
Newell's shearwater: 18
newspapers: 156
nicknames: 157
nightlife: 186–187, 201–202, 302
North Kohala: 255–267
Northwest Airlines: 133
nuts: 123, 214, 286

O

observatories: Caltech Submillimeter Observatory (CSO): 272–273; Canada-France-Hawaii Telescope: 271; Gemini Northern 8.1-meter Telescope: 273; Hawaiian Volcano Observatory: 359–360; James Clerk Maxwell Telescope: 271; Mauna Kea Observatory Complex: 271–274; Mauna Loa NOAA Observatory: 275; NASA Infrared Telescope Facility (IRTF): 272; observatories' websites: 274; Subaru (Japanese National Large Telescope): 273; Submillimeter Array: 273; United Kingdom Infrared Telescope (UKIRT): 272; University of Hawaii 2.2-meter Telescope: 272; University of Hawaii .6-meter Telescope: 272; Very Long Baseline Array: 273; W. M. Keck Observatory: 271–272

ocean tours: 85–88

Ocean View: 382–383

Odaishisan: 310

'ohi'a: 13–14, 274, 367

'Ola'a Forest: 368

Old Kona Airport State Recreation Area: 172

Olowalu Massacre, The: 30

'oma'o: 18, 274

Onekahakaha Beach County Park: 289–290

Onizuka Center for International Astronomy and Visitor Information Center: 270, 273

Onizuka Space Center: 61, 170–171

ono: 121

Onomea Scenic Drive: 309

'ope'ape'a: 19–20

orchids: 341

outrigger canoe rides: 236

P

Pa'auilo: 314

Pacific Tsunami Museum: 60, 281

Pacific Wings: 137–138

package tours: 128, 134–136

Pahala: 373–375

Pahala Plantation Cottages: 373–374

Pahoa: 328, 331–333

Pahoehoe Beach County Park: 172

pahoehoe lava: 7

Painted Church, The: 337

Paka'alana Heiau: 322

pakalolo: 150

palila: 19

Pana'ewa Rainforest Zoo: 285–286

pao dolce: 122

Papa'aloa: 314

papayas: 123

parasailing: 84–85

Parker, John Palmer: 241, 243–244

Parker Ranch Historic Homes: 60, 241, 244–246

Parker Ranch Visitor Center and Museum: 61, 245–246

parks: 70–71; 'Akaka Falls State Park: 312; Carlsmith Beach County Park: 289; Harry K. Brown Beach Park: 336; Hawaii Volcanoes National Park: 71; Hilo Bayfront Park: 289; Holoholokai Beach Park: 222–223; Honoli'i Beach County Park: 291; Ho'okena Beach County Park: 213–214; Ho'olulu County Park: 284; Isaac Hale Beach County Park: 335; James Kealoha Beach County Park: 290; Kahalu'u Beach Park: 172; Kailua-Kona: 171–174; Kaimu Beach Park: 336; Kalakaua Park: 282; Kaloko-Honokohau National Historical Park: 172–173; Kamehameha County Park: 264; Kapa'a Beach County Park: 258; Kekaha Kai State Park: 173–174; Keokea Beach County Park: 265; Kolekole Beach Park: 312; Lapakahi State Historical Park: 257–258; Laupahoehoe Point County Park: 313; Leleiwi Beach County Park: 290; Mahukona Beach County Park: 258; Miloli'i Beach County Park: 214; Napo'opo'o Beach County Park: 207; Onekahakaha Beach County Park: 289–290; Pahoehoe Beach County Park: 172; Puala'a Park: 334–335; Punalu'u Beach County Park: 376; Pu'uhonua O Honaunau National Historical Park: 208–210; Reeds Bay Beach Park: 289; Richardson's Beach Park: 290–291; Spencer Beach County Park: 224; Wailuku River State Park: 285; White Sands Beach County Park: 171–172; Whittington Beach County Park: 377–378

passion fruit: 123

Pauahi Crater: 364

Pele, Madame: 7, 353–354

petrel, Hawaiian dark-rumped: 18

petroglyphs: Ka'upulehu Petroglyphs: 218; Puako Petroglyphs: 218–219; Pu'u Loa Petroglyphs: 364–365; Waikoloa Petroglyphs: 218

pets: 130

pharmacies: 149, 194, 266, 306

Phillippine Airlines: 134

photographic supplies: 106, 193–194

pidgin: 52–53

pigs, feral: 16, 104
Pine Trees: 173
plants: *see* flora
plate lunches: 119
Pohakuloa: 274
Pohakuloa Military Camp: 274
poi: 117
Pololu Valley: 266–267
Polynesia: 22–24, 44–45
Polynesian Airlines: 134
ponds: 8
population: 44–51
Portuguese man-of-war: 147
post offices: 155, 194, 307
precipitation: 9
pu'ahanui: 15
Puako: 219
Puako Petroglyphs: 218–219
Puala'a Park: 334–335
Pua Mau Place: 15, 237
pueo: 274
Puhimau Crater: 364
Puna: 4–5, 328–350
Puna Coast Trail: 367
Punalu'u: 375–377
Punalu'u Beach County Park: 376
Pu'opelu: 244
pu pu: 121–122
Pu'uhonua O Honaunau National Historical
    Park: 208–210
Pu'u Huluhulu: 364
Pu'ukohola Heiau: 219–220
Pu'u Loa Petroglyphs: 364–365
Pu'u O'o Cinder Cone: 336–337, 355, 364
Pu'u O'o Trail: 275

QR
Qantas: 134
quarantine: 130
quilts: 108, 254, 304
radio stations: 156
rainfall: *see* precipitation
rainforests: 15–16, 285
Reciprocity Act (1875): 37
recreation: 69–104; Hawi: 262–263; Hilo:
    302–303; Kailua-Kona: 187–189; Kawaihae:
    239; Mauna Kea: 274; South Kohala: 236–237;
    Waimea: 251–252; Waipi'o Valley: 324–326
Reeds Bay Beach Park: 289
reef fish: 82–83

religion: 55–59
rental cars: 139–143
resorts: 175–176, 224–233, 338
Richardson's Beach Park: 290–291
road conditions, The Saddle Road: 268–269
Royal Kona Coffee Mill and Museum: 206
RV rentals: 143

S
Saddle Road, The: 4, 218, 268–275
Sadie Seymour Botanical Gardens: 15, 166–167
safety: 147–148, 150–152
sailing tours: 86
saimin: 119
schools: 306
scrimshaw: 107–108
scuba diving: 77–80; Hilo: 303; Kealakekua Bay:
    207; Kona: 188; Puna: 335; South Kohala:
    222, 223, 237, 239
seafood: 120–121
seasickness: 87
sea urchins: 147
sharks: 147
shave ice: 122
sheep, feral: 20, 104
sheep, mouflon: 20, 104
Shipman House: 292–293
shopping: 104–109; Captain Cook: 213;
    Hawaii Volcanoes National Park: 371; Hawi:
    263; Hilo: 303–306; Holualoa: 195–197;
    Honoka'a: 317–319; Honomu: 311–312;
    Kailua-Kona: 189–194; Kainaliu: 202–203;
    Kapa'au: 266; Kealakekua: 205; Pahoa: 333;
    South Kohala: 235–236; Volcano Village:
    350; Waimea: 252–254
shuttle tours: 97
shuttle travel: 144–145, 194–195, 324
sightseeing: Hilo: 279–291; Kona: 159–171; The
    Saddle Road: 274–275; South Kohala:
    218–220; Waimea: 244–246
skiing: 88
Slipper Dog: 146–147
Smart, Richard: 243–244
snuba: 84
southernmost point of United States: 5, 372,
    380–381
South Kohala: 215–240
South Point: 380–381
Southwest Rift: 360
Spencer Beach County Park: 224

Snorkeling

general discussion: 80–81, 84
'Anaeho'omalu Bay: 222
Hapuna Beach State Recreation Area: 223
Hilo: 303
Isaac Hale Beach County Park: 335
James Kealoha Beach County Park: 290
Kailua-Kona: 187–188
Kaloko Beach: 173
Kapoho Tidepools: 334
Kawaihae: 239
Kealakekua Bay: 207
Ke'ei: 207
Richardson's Beach Park: 290–291
South Kohala: 228, 237
Spencer Beach County Park: 224
Waialea Bay Marine Life Conservation District: 219

statehood: 40
St. Benedict's Painted Church: 206
steam vents: 337, 359
St. Paul's Catholic Church: 200
St. Peter's Catholic Church: 168
Subaru (Japanese National Large Telescope): 273
submarine tours: 88, 189
Submillimeter Array: 273
sugar industry: 37–38, 43
Sulfur Banks: 359
sunburn: 145–146
surfing: 84, 207, 223, 291, 335
sushi: 121

T
tapa cloth: 61–62
taro chips: 122
Taro Festival: 315
taxis: 145
telephone system: 156
temperature: 8–9
tennis: 92–93, 189, 225, 226, 236
theaters: 251–252, 302, 317, 379
theft: 150–151
thermal springs: 334–335
Thomas A. Jaggar Museum: 61, 360
thrush, Hawaiian: 18
Thurston Lava Tube: 361

time of day: 155
time zones: 156–157
Tong Wo Society Building: 264–265
tourism: 41–42
tourist information: 154–156, 237, 254, 261, 282, 306
trade winds: 9–10
transportation: 125–145; Kailua-Kona: 194–195
travel agents: 127–128
traveler's checks: 157
travelers with disabilities: 143, 149–150
travel necessities: 152–153
tree molds: 364, 367
tropical fruits: 122–123
tropical rainforests: 15–16
tsunami: 7–8
Tsunami Memorial: 284
turtles, green sea: 21, 221
turtles, hawksbill: 20–21

U
'ua'u: 18
uku: 121
ulua: 121
Umauma Waterfall: 15, 313
United Airlines: 133
United Kingdom Infrared Telescope (UKIRT): 272
universities: 306
University of Hawaii 2.2-meter Telescope: 272
University of Hawaii .6-meter Telescope: 272
Uwekahuna (Wailing Priest) Bluff: 359

Volcanoes

Chain of Craters Road: 336, 363–366
eruptions: 354–356
geologic history: 5–7, 353–354
Hawaii Volcanoes National Park: 71, 351–371
Hualalai, Mt.: 3, 6, 159
Kilauea Caldera: 6, 351, 353–362
Lo'ihi Seamount: 375–376
Mauna Kea: 5–6, 269–271
Mauna Loa: 6, 275, 356
Pu'u O'o Cinder Cone: 336–337, 355, 364
volcano activity reports: 155

V

vacation rentals: 113–114, 178–179, 233–234, 248, 320, 337–338
Very Long Baseline Array: 273
Vietnam War Memorial: 284
visas: 130
visitor information: *see* information services; tourist information
volcano activity reports: 155
Volcano Art Center: 65, 358–359
Volcano House: 358, 370
Volcano Village: 330, 342–350
Volcano Winery: 342–343
voltage: 157

WXYZ

wagon rides: 95, 251, 325
Waha'ulu Heiau: 336, 365–366
Waiakea Pond: 284
Waialea Bay Marine Life Conservation District: 219
Waikoloa Petroglyphs: 218
Waikoloa Village: 239–240
Wailea: 312–313
Wailoa Center: 284
Wailoa River State Recreation Area: 284
Wailuku River State Park: 285
Waimanu Valley: 326–327
Waimea: 241–254
Waimea-Kohala Airport: 132, 254
Wai'ohinu: 379–380
Waipi'o Beach: 324
Waipi'o Ridge Hike: 252
Waipi'o Valley: 321–327
Waipi'o Valley Overlook: 319
Waldron Ledge: 362

M

Index

Waterfalls

'Akaka Falls: 4
'Akaka Falls State Park: 312
Hi'ilawe Waterfall: 322, 325
Kahuna Falls: 312
Kapoloa waterfall: 262
Kolekole Beach Park: 312
Pe'epe'e Falls: 285
Rainbow Falls: 285
Umauma Waterfall: 15, 313
Wai'ilikahi Falls: 326

walking tours: 166, 204, 235–236, 281–282, 325
water safety: 77, 147–148
Wawaloli Beach: 173
weather: *see* climate
weather reports: 155
weaving: 60–61, 108
Western Days Weekend: 315–316
whalers: 35–36
whale-watching cruises: 87–88
White Sands Beach County Park: 171–172
Whittington Beach County Park: 377–378
wildlife: *see* fauna
windmills: 380
windsurfing: 84, 222, 237
wineries: 342–343
W. M. Keck Observatory: 271–272
Wood Valley Temple: 374–375
World Tropical Botanical Gardens: 15, 313
Young, John: 220
zodiac tours: 86
zoos: 285–286

Acknowledgments

Since the passing of J. D. Bisignani, the original author of *Moon Handbooks Big Island of Hawai'i,* I have taken on the great task of revising this book and others in his series of guides to Hawaii. Joe, you have been an inspiration to me and have laid a solid foundation for the present revision. Even though you are gone, you've been with me with each word. To you, my good friend, a big thank you.

As always, the staff at Avalon Travel Publishing has been professional in every way. A sincere thank you to everyone.

The following individuals require special thanks for their assistance in the revision of this book: Patti Kimi Woodd, Nancy Daniels, Nita Isherwood, Don and Martie Nitsche, Charlene Cowan, Susan and Robert Hughes, Brian Crawford, Kathryn Grout, Star Townsend, Diana Allegra, Christine Jimenez, Barbara Anderson, John and Michele Gamble, Jackie Horne, Carolyn Cascavilla, Chris O'Connor, Joan Palmtag, Susan Bredo, Danny Breatchel, Laurence Montcastle, Doug Arnott, Haunani Vieira, Lorene Suzuki-Nowicki, Stu Globerman, Geoff Hand, Kathy Lane, and my wife, Linda Nilsen. A sincere *"mahalo"* to you all.

U.S. ~ Metric Conversion

1 inch	=	2.54 centimeters (cm)
1 foot	=	.304 meters (m)
1 yard	=	0.914 meters
1 mile	=	1.6093 kilometers (km)
1 km	=	.6214 miles
1 fathom	=	1.8288 m
1 chain	=	20.1168 m
1 furlong	=	201.168 m
1 acre	=	.4047 hectares
1 sq km	=	100 hectares
1 sq mile	=	2.59 square km
1 ounce	=	28.35 grams
1 pound	=	.4536 kilograms
1 short ton	=	.90718 metric ton
1 short ton	=	2000 pounds
1 long ton	=	1.016 metric tons
1 long ton	=	2240 pounds
1 metric ton	=	1000 kilograms
1 quart	=	.94635 liters
1 US gallon	=	3.7854 liters
1 Imperial gallon	=	4.5459 liters
1 nautical mile	=	1.852 km

To compute Celsius temperatures, subtract 32 from Fahrenheit and divide by 1.8. To go the other way, multiply Celsius by 1.8 and add 32.